BORLAND DELPHI HOW-TO

The Definitive Delphi Problem Solver

GARY FRERKING, NATHAN WALLACE, WAYNE NIDDERY

WAITE GROUP PRESS™
CORTE MADERA, CA

Publisher **Mitchell Waite**
Editor-in-Chief **Charles Drucker**
Editorial Director **John Crudo**
Aquisitions Editor **Jill Pisoni**
Managing Editor **Joe Ferrie**
Content Editor **Judith Brown**
Copy Editor **Judith Brown**
Technical Reviewer **Pat Richie, et al.**
Production Director **Julianne Ososke**
Production Manager **Cecile Kaufman**
Design and Production **Karen Johnston, Tom Debolski, Jude Levinson**
Illustrations **Pat Rogondino**
Cover Design **Karen Johnston**
Cover Illustration **Joe Fleming**

Published by Waite Group Press™, 200 Tamal Plaza, Corte Madera, CA 94925.

Waite Group Press™ is distributed to bookstores and book wholesalers by Publishers Group West, Box 8843, Emeryville, CA 94662, 1-800-788-3123 (in California 1-510-658-3453).

Printed in the United States of America
95 96 97 • 10 9 8 7 6 5 4 3 2 1

Frerking, Gary.
Borland Delphi how-to / Gary Frerking. Nathan Wallace. Wayne Niddery.
p. cm.
Includes index.
ISBN: 1-57169-019-0
1. Electronic digital computers--Programming. 2. Delphi (Computer file)
I. Niddery, Wayne. II. Wallace, Nathan. III. Title.
QA76.6.F735 1995
005.265--dc20

95-3195
CIP

Dedication

To my wife Leslie, for understanding; to my daughter Elizabeth, for helping me as much as a two-year-old could; and to my daughter Lindsey, whom I never really had a chance to know.

Gary Frerking

To Laura, for all the years, and to Alex, for everything.

Nathan Wallace

To those who think programming should be serious fun.

Wayne Niddery

Message from the **Publisher**

Welcome to Our Nervous System

Some people say that the World Wide Web is a graphical extension of the information superhighway, just a network of humans and machines sending each other long lists of the equivalent of digital junk mail.

I think it is much more than that. To me the Web is nothing less than the nervous system of the entire planet—not just a collection of computer brains connected together, but more like a billion silicon neurons entangled and recirculating electro-chemical signals of information and data, each contributing to the birth of another CPU and another Web site.

Think of each person's hard disk connected at once to every other hard disk on earth, driven by human navigators searching like Columbus for the New World. Seen this way the Web is more of a super entity, a growing, living thing, controlled by the universal human will to expand, to be more. Yet unlike a purposeful business plan with rigid rules, the Web expands in a nonlinear, unpredictable, creative way that echoes natural evolution.

We created our Web site not just to extend the reach of our computer book products but to be part of this synaptic neural network, to experience, like a nerve in the body, the flow of ideas and then to pass those ideas up the food chain of the mind. Your mind. Even more, we wanted to pump some of our own creative juices into this rich wine of technology.

Taste our Digital Wine

And so we ask you to taste our wine by visiting the body of our business. Begin by understanding the metaphor we have created for our Web site—a universal learning center, situated in outer space in the form of a space station. A place where you can journey to study any topic from the convenience of your own screen. Right now we are focusing on computer topics, but the stars are the limit on the Web.

If you are interested in discussing this Web site, or finding out more about the Waite Group, please send me email with your comments and I will be happy to respond. Being a programmer myself, I love to talk about technology and find out what our readers are looking for.

Sincerely,

Mitchell Waite

Mitchell Waite, C.E.O. and Publisher

200 Tamal Plaza
Corte Madera CA 94925
415 924 2575
415 924 2576 fax

Internet email:
mwaite@waite.com

CompuServe email:
75146,3515

Website:
http://www.waite.com/waite

Creating the Highest Quality Computer Books in the Industry

Waite Group Press
Waite Group New Media

About the Authors

Gary Frerking

started programming on a Radio Shack TRS-80 that came fully equipped with a cassette tape drive. Shortly after high school, he joined the Navy and served as a Reactor Operator aboard nuclear powered submarines. Writing utility programs for the engineering departments of his various duty stations honed his programming skills. Eventually growing tired of the up and down lifestyle of a submariner, Gary decided to strike out on his own as a computer consultant. While writing this book, he was given the opportunity to work at TurboPower Software Company, so he pulled up stakes and moved from Keyport, WA to Colorado Springs, CO, where he hopes to live happily ever after.

Wayne Niddery

has been programming professionally for more than twelve years, developing online bank, pharmacy, and library systems, as well as various other applications. He has used numerous languages, including Cobol, Assembler, C, Basic, and a few proprietary languages; Pascal has been his personal favorite for several years. This is Wayne's first writing venture. He lives in the Toronto area with his wife, Sonoe, and their dog, Patch.

Nathan Wallace

began programming on an IBM 360 in the mid 1970's using (shudder) punched cards in FORTRAN. He soon progressed to programming in Applesoft Basic on an Apple IIe, and to Borland's Turbo Basic on a NEC 8080, where he developed several text-based windowing and database applications for government and industry. He then served as a project leader for a group using Turbo Pascal 4.0 and later 5.5 on IBM PS/2 platforms to develop hypermedia applications. He has recently been working in the Unix environment to create artificial neural-network simulations of the behavior of living nerve cells. His current projects include completion of HyperSpace, an HTML-based hypermedia information browser, and *Conquest of the Milky Way*, the first "infinite adventure online role-playing computer game."

Table of Contents

Contents

Acknowledgments

Writing a book is an incredible undertaking. It seems the closer you get to something that's "really good," the harder life reaches out and tries to make you stumble. Without the incredible team at Waite Group Press, this book might never have made it to the bookstores.

We would first like to express appreciation to Mitch Waite, for giving us the opportunity to participate in the magical, terrible, but always rewarding process of book creation and development. Mitch's unique approach to acquiring authors and nurturing them gives the industry a breath of fresh air!

Special thanks to Joe Ferrie, John Crudo, Judith Brown, and Jill Pisoni from Waite Group Press. These folks helped us keep our wits through an incredible amount of adversity. They went through hundreds of pages of cryptic manuscript that was written in the wee hours of the morning, and made it actually resemble something understandable. Whether we were in another country or moving from state to state, they managed to keep in touch with us and gently prod us along when we thought it would be impossible to finish the book.

Nathan Wallace wishes to thank all those people on CompuServe and the Internet who were willing to spend a few minutes discussing Delphi with the rest of us. Delphi will be the first major programming environment born since the Internet explosion, and the information superhighway will undoubtedly play a major role in its life cycle.

Gary Frerking wishes to thank Danny Thorpe, Allen Bauer, Nan Borreson, and many other folks at Borland who patiently answered our many questions. Also, thanks to the members of Borland's "TeamB" volunteer group for giving answers to our questions when we wanted to give the Borland engineers a break. Thanks to Scott Samet and many others in the various areas of CompuServe and the Internet for providing ideas for our projects.

Wayne Niddery wishes to thank his wife, Sonoe, for her encouragement, and his co-authors for their hard work and dedication.

Introduction

What This Book Is About

If you are someone who has a working knowledge of Delphi, but wants to stretch the capabilities that come "out of the box," who wants to create programs in Delphi that equal commercial applications written in C or assembly language in power and scope, then this is the book for you. If, on the other hand, you are still learning the Pascal language, or are uncertain how to connect components and code, then an introductory book on Delphi is a better choice. Once you're up to speed on basic use of Delphi, though, this book will give it warp engines!

Delphi At Warp Speed

Delphi is without question the most powerful development environment currently available for the PC platform. It combines visual development with a complete OOP language and full access to the underlying Windows API system in a user-friendly and intuitive way never before seen in any environment. Rather than rehash the manuals and help files that come with the Delphi system, this book shows how to take a basic understanding of the program and do things in tiny amounts of code which previously required hundreds or even thousands of lines of C and assembly language programming. Included here is complete source code and visual information for an HTML browser with multimedia capabilities, an Installation program that creates Program Manager groups, and a Windows hardware analysis utility. Also included are applications with detailed source code that utilize the Delphi environment's extendability, adding a new Visual Component and Property Editor to the system.

Windows API Calls Unlock Delphi's Power

The use of Object Pascal allows complete access to the Windows 3.x (and soon, Windows 95) Application Programming Interface (API). Delphi comes with complete documention online for this interface, and this gives the environment capabilities equal to the C or C++ languages. By calling the Windows API, the How-To's in this book can play sound files and video clips, access the serial port to create a terminal program using Windows rather than DOS communications functions, and display sprite animation with transparent backgrounds. Complete source code is provided for all these examples, as well as detailed comments both in the text and in the code to explain how the calls work.

OOP Puts Delphi On The Cutting Edge

Object-Oriented Programming (OOP) is considered by most computer scientists and industry analysts to be the next major breakthrough in computer software development.

Delphi uses Object Pascal as its underlying language, and all Delphi capabilities are accessed as objects. While this book is not a primer on the use of OOP, it does contain many examples of using the objects which encapsulate Delphi functionality, and of expanding their capabilities with the power of the Object Pascal language. By the end of this book, readers will have a solid grasp of the practical techniques used in OOP and how to apply them in their own work.

Question And Answer Format

This book is arranged in a problem/solution format that allows readers to either focus on solving a particular problem they have encountered or to experience a total workout of Delphi's capabilities with a front-to-back reading. Starting with simple techniques for manipulating Delphi Forms, the book progresses into more sophisticated capabilities for the Standard Components that come with Delphi. Tips for using Edit and Memo controls are then outlined as are ways to manipulate the display of data on forms, followed by How-To's that concentrate on mouse control and menu customization. The real power of Delphi starts to appear in the Graphics chapter, which showcases the amazing TCanvas component, followed by an API-rich chapter on Multimedia, including the HTML browser. Tips to maximize the application's interactions with Windows follow, and another advanced chapter on the Printer, Speaker, and Serial Port covers peripherals. A comprehensive overview of Delphi's Database support is next, and then some very nice applications for OLE and DDE. The last chapters cover polishing up one's applications, and then how to use the advanced capabilities of Delphi, such as adding new VCL components and using VBX controls.

Shareware, Demos, and Goodies

Delphi is an environment which makes creation of programs quick and easy. As a result, a number of shareware authors are already taking advantage of the new environment to produce new versions of existing software and create entirely new utilities. A number of these programs are included on the CD which comes with this book. Also, several commercial companies have contributed demonstration programs; these are likewise found on the CD, including items from Turbo Power Software and CIUPKC software. Finally, several projects were slated for inclusion with the book but were dropped for space or time constraints; they've been added in a Goodies section. These include an HTML editor, a sprite Animation editor, and a Windows resource analyst.

Expected Level of Reader

This is not a "dummies" book! Readers are expected to understand the basics of creating forms, adding new components, and linking components with code. Beyond that, however, this book is for anyone who wants to unleash the powerhouse hidden inside Delphi. Beginners will learn basic techniques of customizing forms and controls and making API calls. Intermediate level programmers can study the use of OOP to extend the functionality of VCL components as well as learn the exciting new features of Delphi such as Exception handling and API encapsulation. Advanced developers can use the book to learn how to port their favored techniques into the Delphi environment, as well as discovering how to utilize features unique to Delphi, such as Property Editors and DLL-based forms.

What You Need To Use This Book

In order to use this book you need either the Desktop or Client/Server version of Delphi for Windows, running on a PC capable of reading a CD-ROM (i.e. either with a CD-ROM drive installed or access to one over a network). Although the How-To's are sized for a VGA display and are set up to work with standard VGA colors, the graphics and multimedia demos are really only useful at 256 color resolutions and above. A mouse is not required, but certainly makes things easier!

How This Book Is Organized

This book is organized into twelve chapters and one appendix, as follows:

Chapter 1: Forms

Forms are the core of any visual programming environment, and Delphi forms have more than the usual functionality. This chapter will demonstrate ways to automatically center a form, resize controls on a form automatically, and remember form sizes and locations when the program is run again. Also included are How-To's that flash the title bar, check for changes in a form's data prior to closing, create forms at run time, and drag a form with no caption bar. More advanced topics are also covered including MDI background painting, creating system modal forms, and setting size limits for forms.

Chapter 2: Standard Components

Delphi comes with a very solid set of standard components called the Visual Component Library or VCL. The How-To's in this chapter demonstrate ways to expand VCL functionality by creating custom check boxes, creating and positioning controls at run time, and displaying "streaming" text on a button. More advanced topics covered include assigning unique ID's to each instance of a program running under Windows, creating API-based dynamic listboxes which "best match" user input, and use drag-and-drop between separate listboxes. Professional techniques discussed include putting graphics in the title bar of a window, using an XOR splitter bar to resize controls at run time, and adding full text editing capabilities to listbox controls.

Chapter 3: Documents and Text

The single task most often performed by computer applications is reading user input, either as a single line of text or in a group. The second most common task is manipulating a display of data in response to user requests. This chapter has detailed coverage of Delphi's builtin form scrolling capabilities, as well as those of the TPaintBox and TScrollBox components. More complex topics covered include using TScrollBar components to manipulate color information, and the scrolling capabilities of the TStringGrid component. Text input is covered thoroughly with How-To's on the TEdit and TMemo components, demonstrating how to create a README file viewer, adding search capabilties to a TMemo field, setting edit masks in a TEdit control, and controlling the appearance of the input caret in the input fields. String manipulation, an essential part of user input, is outlined with examples that remove trailing blanks and accept input from TStringGrid components.

Chapter 4: Mouse and Menu

The mouse is Windows' primary input device; this chapter demonstrates creation of sophisticated applications using "rubber banding" to select rectangles with the mouse onscreen; also shown is the clever technique to distinguish between single and double mouse clicks. Menus are an integral part of most Windows applications; these How-To's show the behind-the-scenes tricks to modify the system menu of a window, put bitmaps in a menu, change default menu characteristics like check marks, and customize menus at run time. Advanced topics cover putting custom typefaces into menus and having more than one shortcut per menu item.

Chapter 5: Graphics

Although Windows is a graphical environment, using graphics is still a difficult process. Delphi has considerably eased these restrictions, and this chapter exploits this with powerful examples that control iconic desktop application layout, autosize forms around pictures and vice versa, and animate icons. Programming concerns are covered with demonstrations of the Pen amd Copy mode settings and creation of hot spots on pictures. The professional end of graphics gets unlocked with detailed instructions for animating sprite bitmaps and fading text and graphics into other images.

Chapter 6: Multimedia

The modern PC is more and more a showcase for video and sound as well as text and images. This chapter breaks barriers with explicit How-To's covering playing sound files, CD audio, and AVI video under Delphi. The crowning jewel of the book is then laid out with five separate examples that create a complete HTML browser that is hypertext linked and displays sound, graphics, sprite animations, and CD audio and video in user-created documents. (With the shareware Winsock component, this browser can become a mini-Webscape Internet application!)

Chapter 7: Environment and System

Windows is an operating system, and thus has a lot of functionality available to applications. This chapter demonstrates using Delphi to access this power, with How-To's covering running other applications from within a Delphi program, controling program shutdown, preventing multiple copies of an application from running, and determining which application is currently being used. Deeper topics covered include determining available system resources, finding out hardware configurations such as the number of function keys available, and calculating various levels of memory available. File interactions are covered with examples of determining whether Share is running, finding out a drive letter's type, and locating the directory containing Windows itself.

Chapter 8: Peripherals

Even with the power of modern computers, many elements remain from the smaller and less sophisticated era which preceded them, such as difficulties interacting with peripheral devices like printers or modems. This chapter unleashes Delphi's capabilities to demystify access to serial communications with a phone dialer and full terminal application. Sound functions are covered as well, showing how to access the speaker from Windows. The very effective Delphi Printer unit is also showcased with How-To's that illustrate controlling page size, the appearance of printer settings dialogs, and maintaining similarity between screen and hard copy displays. A utility is also created that completely outlines all the hardware capabilities of the screen and printer on a system.

Chapter 9: Database

Delphi is in many ways a database-oriented environment, and it has extensive support for database interactions in the standard VCL. This chapter showcases Delphi's off-the-shelf database powers, with How-To's on viewing the contents of record-based and SQL databases, using data-aware VCL controls to display and navigate databases, and search and edit database files. Advanced topics are also covered with examples of controlling table display at design and run time, and using data-aware components to automate display of database tables.

Chapter 10: OLE and DDE

OLE (Object Linking and Embedding) and DDE (Dynamic Data Exchange) are two cutting edge technologies which are becoming increasingly important in the Windows environment. This chapter demonstrates the powerful components included in the VCL for handling DDE with examples of an installation program and several versions of a NetDDE Chat client (similar to the Unix Talk utility). OLE is also showcased with How-To's using the OLE container component to display OLE files and create an OLE compound document.

Chapter 11: The Polished Application

Delphi makes it easier than ever to add little touches to an application that really give it a professional, "polished" appearance. This chapter goes into methods for customizing program error responses, creating professional About Box displays, and adding unique fonts to an application. Advanced areas are covered also, including creating a "drag-and-drop" toolbar with bitmap cursors and adding context-sensitive help onscreen.

Chapter 12: Tips and Tricks

Delphi is a programming environment unlike any other. This chapter goes into detailed examples of how to use the OOP capabilities of Object Pascal to create new VCL components, add custom Property Editors, and override default behavior at run time. Visual Basic controls (VBX) are examined in context with the Delphi environment, as are ways to emulate VB "control arrays" in Delphi. Using DLL's in Delphi is demonstrated, and ways to customize the Exception mechanism are outlined.

Appendix A: About the CD

The CD distributed with the book is outlined here, and comments are briefly included about the shareware distributed with the disk.

Installation

What's On The CD

The CD bundled with Delphi How-To contains complete files needed to both run and to re-create every application in the book. The standalone EXE files do not need a runtime module (like VBRUNXXX) and so may be used as is. The Delphi files, including .PAS, .DFM, .RES, and so on, need to be kept together so that the Delphi environment can re-create the programs. Also included are a number of shareware programs and additional applications to further showcase the power of the Delphi environment.

How to Install the CD Files

Note: Before installing the files, be sure to read the README.1ST file on the CD. It contains any last minute instructions and warnings. Also, check the README.1ST files in each project directory for last minute information about changes to the project files and differences from the book versions of the programs. (Much of the book was written using the last beta version of Delphi and some minor changes were needed once the commercial version was released.)

Using File Manager, or a similar program, move to the CD-ROM drive in your computer, navigate to the Install Directory and select the INSTALL.EXE program. Double-click to run the program, or use the File|Run command. You will see a screen similar to Figure 0-1 below.

You may use the Install program at any time to copy files from the CD to your hard drive. Next to each Chapter's check box is an edit field where you may enter the desired directory for the hard drive installation. If you leave the "Install All Files"

Figure 0-1 Delphi CD Installation Program Startup Form

checked in a particular chapter, all the How-To's for a given chapter will be installed. If you uncheck it, a second form appears as shown in Figure 0-2 below.

Each Chapter has a different form, depending on how many How-To's are in the chapter. Check each How-To's box to install it. Next to each How-To is a set of radio buttons, which give the options below:

- Install All Files This option puts all the files from the How-To onto your hard drive.
- Install EXE Only This option only installs the EXE files and any optional data files required by the application onto the hard drive.
- Install Delphi Only This option only installs the Delphi files needed to re-create the application. This takes up considerably less space on the drive.

After the chapter listings are three extra boxes, for the Shareware, Demo programs, and Goodies. Each of them has identical options to the How-To files except the Demo files don't have extended options since they are executable files only.

Running And Compiling The How-To Files

The executable files from the CD can be run directly; no runtime module is needed. The Delphi code must be loaded into the environment and the Compile option selected.

The DSM, DSK, and OPT files have been omitted as these are environment specific and might not be appropriate for all users. These files are not required to load and compile the How-To source files.

Note: If an "Error in Symbol" file dialog appears when you load a project file, select the OK button and then choose Compile | Build All. This will re-create the symbol file and allow normal program manipulation in the IDE.

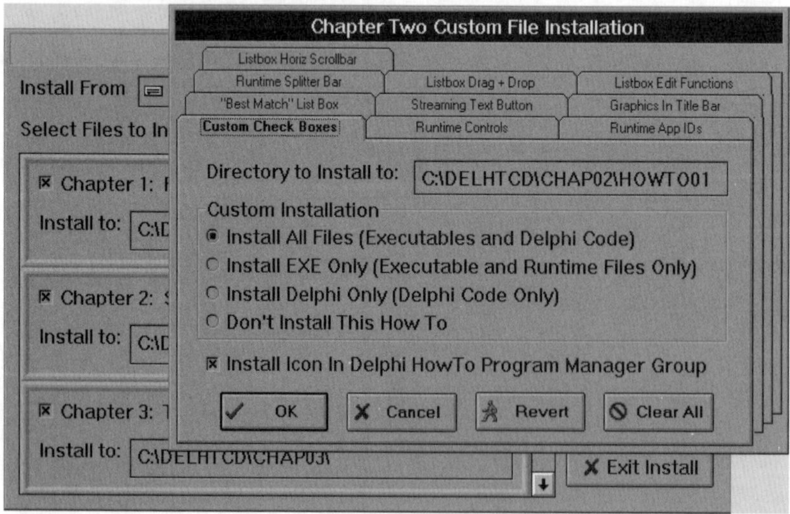

Figure 0-2 Delphi CD Installation Program Custom File Installation Form

1

1

FORMS

How do I...

Delphi applications are form based. While it is possible to write a Delphi application without using forms, it's unlikely that you will need to do so—besides, you would lose the visual interface that makes Delphi so easy to use. Forms act as containers to organize controls in a logical manner—for the benefit of both programmer and user. The tricks and techniques in this chapter focus on showing you how to maximize the benefits of the form paradigm in your applications. You'll learn how to add professional touches to your forms, such as allowing the user the choice of using the ENTER key to navigate between fields on your form instead of the CUA standard TAB key. You'll learn how to get the user's attention by flashing the title bar of the form. You'll also learn to make your applications user friendly by remembering where users like to position their forms.

1.1 Automatically center a form in my application

Delphi has a property that determines the initial position of a form when it opens. One of the available options is to open the form in the center of the screen. This does not guarantee that the form is opened in the center of the application, because the application's main form itself may not be centered in the screen when the child form is opened. This How-To shows you how to center a form in your application no matter where it is on the screen.

1.2 Size a form's controls automatically

In certain situations it is handy to have child controls automatically size and position themselves as their form is being resized. This technique is popular in Visual Basic programs. This How-To shows that Delphi programs can do it also!

1.3 Remember the sizes and locations of my forms

It can be frustrating to users if the default positions of your forms are not to their liking. If their screen size and/or resolution is different from the one you used when designing the program, they must reposition all of the forms every time they start your program. Why not help them out by saving the position of the forms?

1.4 Flash the title bar of my forms

There are times when you need to get the user's attention, such as at the end of a long process or if an error occurs. One way to catch the user's eye is to flash the title bar of the application. This How-To demonstrates a way of doing this that works even if the application is minimized.

1.5 Find out if a child component's data has been changed

When a user closes your application, you can query the open forms to find out whether they can safely be closed or some changes need to be made. Each form must in turn query its controls to find out if data has been modified. This is fairly easy to accomplish, and this How-To leads the way.

1.6 Create a form on the fly at run time

Occasionally you may need to create and design a form at run time. This may support a database application that morphs itself according to the database it is connected to. It takes a little work, but it is well worth the effort if you want to create a generic application that is adaptable in this way.

1.7 Drag a captionless window

Sometimes you have a small form that you don't want to make any larger by adding a caption to it. You might still want to allow the user to move the form around using the mouse. The floating clock that comes with Windows does it, and so can you!

1.8 Create a system modal form

Delphi lets you create modal forms in relation to your application, but not in relation to the rest of the system. There are times when you need this functionality, such as when you have a password dialog up and want to prevent the user from switching to another application and snooping on your application's files. This How-To shows how to make a dialog *system modal.*

1.9 Set minimum and maximum sizes for my forms

Users appreciate the ability to resize forms. It allows them to customize your application to their computer setup and operating habits. With certain types of forms, however, excessive sizing can make things pretty darn ugly. To keep things under control, you can limit the sizing to a certain amount. This How-To walks you through the steps of setting minimum and maximum sizes for forms.

1.10 Make the ENTER key act like the TAB key in my forms

Users who are moving from DOS programs to Windows programs sometimes find it difficult to adjust to the Windows CUA standard of using the TAB key to move from field to field on a data entry form. This How-To shows you how to give these users the option of using the more familiar ENTER key to move from field to field.

1.11 Paint an interesting background on an MDI parent form

Delphi allows you to change the background color of all forms, including forms that have the FormStyle property set to fsMDIForm. However, going beyond simply setting the background color with an MDI form is more complex, because there is an additional window called the MDI client that can cover up your efforts. This How-To shows how to overcome this limitation.

1.1 How do I...
Automatically center a form in my application?

COMPLEXITY: INTERMEDIATE

Problem

Delphi offers an option to initially position my forms at the center of the screen, but this doesn't look professional when the application itself is not centered on the screen. Can I center my form in the application's main form instead of the screen?

Technique

Centering the form in the application's main window only takes a few lines of code to calculate where the form belongs and place it there prior to showing it.

Steps

Run CENTER.EXE. Size and position the main form anywhere on the screen. Select Form|Show and notice that the child form is always centered within the application's main window, as shown in Figure 1-1. Close the centered form and experiment a few more times with the main form in various positions and sizes.

1. Create a new project with a blank form and name it CENTER.DPR. Name the unit CENTMAIN.PAS. Add a second form to the project and name its unit CENTFORM.PAS.

2. Set Form1's properties as shown in Table 1-1.

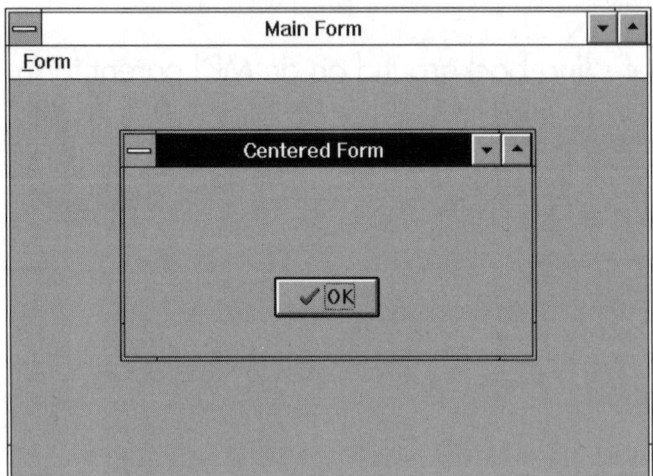

Figure 1-1 CENTER at run time

Table 1-1 Properties and settings for Form1 in the CENTER project

COMPONENT	PROPERTY	SETTING
Form1	Left	239
	Top	118
	Width	435
	Height	300
	Caption	Main Form

3. Add a main menu component to Form1 and double-click on the component to show the Menu Designer. Create a Form menu item and add two subitems — Show and Exit. Close the Menu Designer.
4. Create an OnClick event handler for the Form|Exit item of Form1's main menu. Add the following code to your event handler.

Note: Delphi has already written most of the code for you; you just add Close.

```
procedure TForm1.Exit1Click(Sender: TObject);
begin
  Close;
end;
```

5. Create an OnClick event handler for the Form|Show item of Form1's main menu. Again, Delphi writes some code in the Code Editor and places the cursor within the resulting event handler. Type the following code:

```
procedure TForm1.Show1Click(Sender: TObject);
var
  R: TRect;
begin
  R := Application.MainForm.BoundsRect;
  with Form2 do
  { Calculate size/position of Form2, then show it }
  begin
    Top := (((R.Bottom-R.Top)-Height)div 2) + R.Top;
    Left := (((R.Right-R.Left)-Width)div 2) + R.Left;
    Show;
  end;
end;
```

6. Before you leave the Code Editor, there's one more thing you need to do. You have to tell Delphi where to look for Form2. Move up through the code until you find a line that reads *implementation*. Right after that line, type **uses CentForm;**, so the resulting code looks like this:

```
implementation

uses CentForm;

{$R *.DFM}
```

7. Click on Form2 to give it focus. Add a BitBtn to Form2 and set properties as shown in Table 1-2.

Table 1-2 Components, properties, and settings for Form2 in the CENTER project

COMPONENT	PROPERTY	SETTING
Form2	Width	349
	Height	187
	Caption	Centered Form
BitBtn1	Left	126
	Top	88
	Width	89
	Height	33
	Kind	bkOk

8. Create an OnClick event handler for BitBtn1 and add the following code.

```
procedure TForm2.BitBtn1Click(Sender: TObject);
begin
  Close;
end;
```

9. Compile and test the project.

How It Works

The code that centers the form is in Form1's Show1Click event handler. This handler is activated when you click on Form|Show in Form1's main menu. The size and position of the main form are determined by calling Application.MainForm.BoundsRect. In this example program, simply calling BoundsRect would be equivalent since Form1 is the main form. The former method, used here, demonstrates how to ensure that you are getting the BoundsRect property of the application's main form.

After finding the size and position of the main form, it's simply a matter of calculating the required values for the Top and Left properties, setting them, and showing the form.

Comments

This How-To relies on the fact that Delphi applications create all of their forms at program startup. If you do not go with this default, you will have to add code to create the form before centering it.

1.2 How do I...
Size a form's controls automatically?

COMPLEXITY: INTERMEDIATE

Problem

I want users to be able to size my forms, but when they make the form smaller, controls are sometimes cut off. How can I automatically size and position the form's controls so they remain visible?

Technique

When you change RESIZEIT's size, it calculates how much it was changed, iterates through all of its child components, and sizes them appropriately. It does this automatically to all of the components that you have placed on the form—you do not have to add code for each component you add.

Steps

Run RESIZEIT.EXE. The form is shown in Figure 1-2. Size the form and notice that all of the components, with the exception of the panel at the top, size in proportion to the changes you made to the form. If you wish, you can add more components to the form, and they will automatically resize as well.

Note: If you want to exclude a control from resizing, you can set its Tag property to something other than zero.

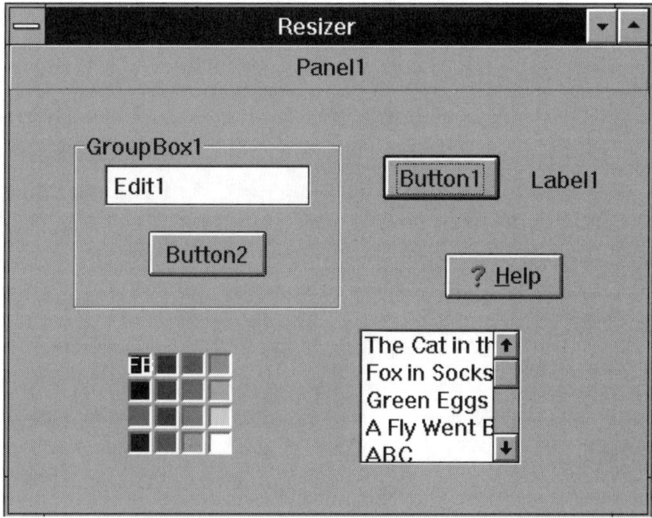

Figure 1-2 RESIZEIT at run time

1. Create a new project with a blank form and save it as RESIZEIT.DPR. Name the unit RESIZE.PAS.
2. Add components to Form1 and set their properties as shown in Table 1-3.

Table 1-3 Components, properties, and settings for Form1 in the RESIZEIT project

COMPONENT	PROPERTY	SETTING
Form1	Name	Resizer
	Left	289
	Top	118
	Width	491
	Height	377
	+HScrollBar	
	-Visible	False
	+VScrollbar	
	-Visible	False
	Caption	Resizer
Label1	Left	392
	Top	88
Button1	Left	280
	Top	80
ListBox1	Left	264
	Top	208
	Width	121
	Height	97
	Items.Strings	The Cat in the Hat
		Fox in Socks
		Green Eggs and Ham
		A Fly Went By
		ABC
		The Foot Book
		One Fish, Two Fish, Red Fish, Blue Fish
		Marvin K. Mooney Will You Please Go Now
		Hand, Hand, Fingers, Thumb
ColorGrid1	Left	88
	Top	224
	Width	81
	Height	76

COMPONENT	PROPERTY	SETTING
BitBtn1	Left	328
	Top	152
	Width	89
	Height	33
	Kind	bkHelp
GroupBox1	Left	48
	Top	64
	Width	201
	Height	129
Panel1	Align	alTop
	Height	33
	Tag	1

3. For GroupBox1, add the components and set their properties as shown in Table 1-4.

Table 1-4 Components, properties, and settings for GroupBox1 in the RESIZEIT project

COMPONENT	PROPERTY	SETTING
Edit1	Left	24
	Top	24
Button2	Left	56
	Top	72

4. Create an OnCreate event handler for Form1. Type the following code in the FormCreate event handler. This saves the values for the height and width of the form when it is first created, so a point of reference is available when the user sizes the form.

```
{ Save Height/Width, so we can compare later }
procedure TResizer.FormCreate(Sender: TObject);
begin
  BH := Height;
  BW := Width;
end;
```

5. While still in the Code Editor, move up to the type definition for TResizer and add the BH and BW variables to the *private* section of the object, as shown in the following code. These variables are used by more than one method so they have to be declared in the object itself, rather than locally in the individual methods.

```
TResizer = class(TForm)
    Button1: TButton;
    ListBox1: TListBox;
    ColorGrid1: TColorGrid;
    Label1: TLabel;
    BitBtn1: TBitBtn;
    GroupBox1: TGroupBox;
    Edit1: TEdit;
    Button2: TButton;
    Panel1: TPanel;
    procedure FormCreate(Sender: TObject);
  private
    { Private declarations }
    BH: Word;                        { Beginning Height }
    BW: Word;                        { Beginning Width }
  public
    { Public declarations }
  end;
```

6. Create an OnResize event handler for Form1. Add the following code to the FormResize event handler. This is the code that actually resizes the individual components on the form based on how much the form was resized.

```
procedure TResizer.FormResize(Sender: TObject);
var
  AH, AW: Word;
  R: TRect;
  I: Integer;
begin
  AH := Height;
  AW := Width;
  { Iterate through all components on form }
  for I := 0 to ComponentCount - 1 do
  { Skip sizing if component is not a TControl descendant }
  if Components[I] is TControl then
  { Skip sizing if component's Tag <> 0 (sizing not desired) }
  if Components[I].Tag = 0 then
  begin
    { Resize component }
    R := TControl(Components[I]).BoundsRect;
    R.Left := MulDiv(R.Left, AW, BW);
    R.Top := MulDiv(R.Top, AH, BH);
    R.Right := MulDiv(R.Right, AW, BW);
    R.Bottom := MulDiv(R.Bottom, AH, BH);
    TControl(Components[I]).BoundsRect := R;
  end;
  { Update Height/Width for next time }
  BH := Height;
  BW := Width;
end;
```

7. Compile and test the project.

How It Works

When the form is created, the code in the OnCreate handler sets the form's BH and BW variables to record the initial height and width of the form. Each time the form is resized, the OnResize event is fired. By the time the OnResize event handler is called, the form itself has changed to its new size, so the form's Height and Width properties can be used to set the AH and AW variables (After Height and After Width). Since you are only interested in sizing descendants of TControl, you use runtime type information to discriminate against any other types of components. The Tag property is a convenient means to identify whether a component should be sized or not. You then iterate through the form's components array, changing the size of each component by the same proportions that the form was changed.

Comments

This is a surprisingly easy solution that would be very difficult to accomplish in languages such as C or C++. There are other considerations that you may take into account, such as changing the font size of the form and/or components. This is fairly convenient to do if the ParentFont property is set to True for the child components. If you change the size of the font, be aware that some video drivers will cause a General Protection Fault (GPF) if the requested font size is too small. You can avoid this by limiting the size of the font. Also, take care when you are resizing some controls and not others. If the components are not placed carefully, they may overlap in some cases. Be sure to test this kind of thing thoroughly. You might also avoid potential problems by setting the form's maximum and/or minimum sizes, as described in How-To 1.9.

1.3 How do I...
Remember the sizes and locations of my forms?

COMPLEXITY: INTERMEDIATE

Problem

I've used programs that can remember the location of their forms. With this convenient feature I could set the location of the forms once, then have the program set the forms properly for subsequent runs. Is there a way I can add this functionality to my Delphi programs?

Technique

The key to remembering things is writing them down, right? Windows programs typically use a standardized text file format called an INI file to "write things down" that they want to remember. There are Windows API functions that aid in maintaining these files, but Delphi helps even more. The TIniFile object is dedicated to maintaining INI files. This object is nonvisual, but it's not too tough to work with.

Steps

Run POSSAVE.EXE. The main form is shown in Figure 1-3. Move the form around the screen, then close it by double-clicking on the system menu. Run the program again, and notice that the form opens in the same position and size as when you closed it. Click on the button to show the other form and note that its position gets saved also.

1. Create a new project with a blank form and name the project POSSAVE.DPR. Name the unit POSFORM1.PAS.

2. Add components and set their properties as shown in Table 1-5.

Table 1-5 Components, properties, and settings for Form1 in the POSSAVE project

COMPONENT	PROPERTY	SETTING
Form1	Left	248
	Top	202
	Width	435
	Height	300
	Caption	Joe's Form
Button1	Left	133
	Top	192
	Width	161
	Height	33
	Caption	Show Bob's Form

3. Add a new blank form to the project and name the unit POSFORM2.PAS. Set the form's properties as shown in Table 1-6.

Table 1-6 Components, properties, and settings for Form2 in the POSSAVE project

COMPONENT	PROPERTY	SETTING
Form2	Left	226
	Top	260
	Width	435
	Height	300
	Caption	Bob's Form

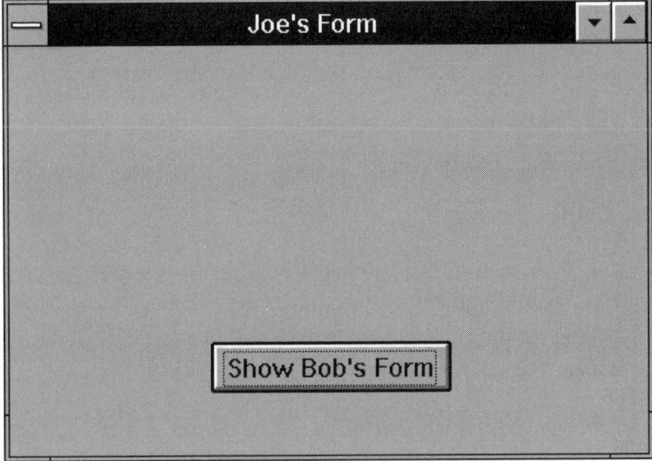

Figure 1-3 POSSAVE at run time

4. Create an OnClick event handler for Button1 on Form1. Add the following code to the event handler.

```
procedure TForm1.Button1Click(Sender: TObject);
begin
  Form2.Show;
end;
```

5. Create an OnCreate event handler for Form1. Add the following code to the event handler. This code calls the procedure that gets the desired size and position of the form.

```
{ Get form's last size/state/position and set form's properties }
procedure TForm1.FormCreate(Sender: TObject);
begin
  SetFormPos(Self, 'Form1');
end;
```

6. Create an OnDestroy event handler for Form1. Add the following code to the event handler. This code calls the procedure that will save the form's size and position prior to destroying the form.

```
{ Save form's size/state/position }
procedure TForm1.FormDestroy(Sender: TObject);
begin
  SaveFormPos(Self,'Form1');
end;
```

7. While still in the Code Editor, move up to the *implementation* keyword and add a *uses* clause as shown in the following code. This tells Delphi's compiler where to look for information that is not in the current unit.

```
implementation

uses PosForm2, HowUtils;

{$R *.DFM}
```

8. Create an OnCreate event handler for Form2. Add the following code to the event handler.

```
{ Get form's last size/state/position and set form's properties }
procedure TForm2.FormCreate(Sender: TObject);
begin
  SetFormPos(Self, 'Form2');
end;
```

9. Create an OnDestroy event handler for Form2. Add the following code to the event handler.

```
{ Save form's size/state/position }
procedure TForm2.FormDestroy(Sender: TObject);
begin
  SaveFormPos(Self, 'Form2');
end;
```

10. While still in the Code Editor, move up to the *implementation* keyword and add a *uses* clause as shown here:

```
implementation

uses HowUtils;

{$R *.DFM}
```

11. Add a new unit to the project by selecting File|New Unit in Delphi's main menu. Save the unit as HOWUTILS.PAS. Add a *uses* clause and two procedure declarations following the *interface* keyword as shown in the following code.

```
unit HowUtils;

interface

uses
  SysUtils, WinTypes, WinProcs, Messages, Classes, Controls,
  Forms, IniFiles;

procedure SaveFormPos(AForm: TForm; Name: String);
procedure SetFormPos(AForm: TForm; Name: String);

implementation
```

12. Add a type declaration for a record you will be using after the *implementation* keyword as follows:

```
implementation

type

  TPosRec = record
    Top,
    Left,
    Height,
    Width,
    State : integer;
  end;

end.
```

13. Following the record type declaration and before the final *end.* statement of the unit, add two helper functions as shown next. Since these functions were not declared in the *interface* section of the unit, only procedures and functions within the unit can use them.

```
  TPosRec = record
  ...
  end;

{ Convert enumerated type to word }
function WinStateToInt(AState: TWindowState): Word;
begin
  Result := Ord(AState);
end;

{ Convert word to enumerated type }
function IntToWinState(Int: Word): TWindowState;
begin
  case Int of
    0 : Result := wsNormal;
    1 : Result := wsMinimized;
    2 : Result := wsMaximized
  else Result := wsNormal;
  end;
end;

end.
```

14. Add two more helper functions, again, between the functions you just added and the final *end.* statement of the unit.

```
function IntToWinState(Int: Word): TWindowState;
begin
...
end;

{ Convert to string for INI file }
```

continued on next page

continued from previous page

```
function PosRecToStr(Pos:TPosRec): String;
begin
  with Pos do
  if State <> 2 then
    Result := IntToStr(State)+' '+IntToStr(Top)+' '+
      IntToStr(Left)+' '+IntToStr(Height)+' '+IntToStr(Width)
  else Result := IntToStr(State);
end;

{ Parse numbers out of string }
function StrToPosRec(AString: String): TPosRec;
var
  Temp: String;
  I,J: Integer;
  Blanks: array[1..4] of integer;
begin
  { Initialize variables }
  I := 1;
  J := 1;
  FillChar(Result, SizeOf(Result), #0);
  FillChar(Blanks, SizeOf(Blanks), #0);
  { Check window state Ñ if it's wsMaximized, we're done }
  Temp := Copy(AString, 1, 1);
  Result.State := StrToInt(Temp);
  if Result.State = 2 then exit;
  { Find out where all the spaces are in the string }
  repeat
    if AString[I] = ' ' then
    begin
      Blanks[J] := I;
      Inc(J);
    end;
    Inc(I);
  until (I = Length(AString)) or (J = 5);
  { Extract numbers from string }
  Temp := Copy(AString, Blanks[1]+1, Blanks[2]-Blanks[1]-1);
  Result.Top := StrToInt(Temp);
  Temp := Copy(AString, Blanks[2]+1, Blanks[3]-Blanks[2]-1);
  Result.Left := StrToInt(Temp);
  Temp := Copy(AString, Blanks[3]+1, Blanks[4]-Blanks[3]-1);
  Result.Height := StrToInt(Temp);
  Temp := Copy(AString, Blanks[4]+1, Length(AString)-Blanks[4]);
  Result.Width := StrToInt(Temp);
end;

end.
```

15. Add the final two procedures of the unit. These are the ones that you actually call from your form's OnCreate and OnDestroy event handlers. Again, they go between the code you just added and the final *end.* statement of the unit.

```
function StrToPosRec(AString: String): TPosRec;
...
end;
```

```
{ Write form size/state/position to INI file }
procedure SaveFormPos(AForm: TForm; Name: String);
var
  IniFile: TIniFile;
  PosRec: TPosRec;
begin
  { Initialize }
  FillChar(PosRec, SizeOf(PosRec), #0);
  IniFile := TIniFile.Create
    (ChangeFileExt(ExtractFileName(ParamStr(0)), '.INI'));
  { Get form's properties }
  with PosRec do
  begin
    State := WinStateToInt(AForm.WindowState);
    Top := AForm.Top;
    Left := AForm.Left;
    Width := AForm.Width;
    Height := AForm.Height;
  end;
  { Write entry to INI file }
  IniFile.WriteString('Positions', Name, PosRecToStr(PosRec));
  IniFile.Free;
end;

{ Read form size/state/position from INI file }
procedure SetFormPos(AForm: TForm; Name: String);
var
  IniFile: TIniFile;
  PosString: String;
  PosRec: TPosRec;
begin
  { Initialize }
  FillChar(PosRec, SizeOf(PosRec), #0);
  IniFile := TIniFile.Create
    (ChangeFileExt(ExtractFileName(ParamStr(0)), '.INI'));
  { Read info from INI file }
  PosString := IniFile.ReadString('Positions', Name, 'Default');
  IniFile.Free;
  { If there wasn't any info, we're done }
  if PosString = 'Default' then exit;
  PosRec := StrToPosRec(PosString);
  { Set form's properties }
  with AForm do
  begin
    WindowState := IntToWinState(PosRec.State);
    if PosRec.State = 2 then exit;
    Top := PosRec.Top;
    Left := PosRec.Left;
    Width := PosRec.Width;
    Height := PosRec.Height;
  end;
end;

end.
```

16. Compile and test the project.

How It Works

The code in the form units is pretty trivial. Calls are made to the SetFormPos and SaveFormPos procedures, supplying a pointer to the form object (Self) and the name of the form. The bulk of the code and functionality is found in the HOWUTILS.PAS unit, which contains the two procedures called and a few more helper routines.

The first two helper functions simply convert the value you get from the form's WindowState property to a format that can easily be stored to an INI file and back. TWindowState is known as an *enumerated* type. The Delphi Ord function is handy for converting enumerated types to integers. The integer is converted back to an enumerated type using a *case* statement in the IntToWinState function.

The next two functions support putting the form's window state, position, and size information in a single line of the INI file.

Note: Technically, these functions are not required to make the program functional—but they give the INI file a more professional and clean-looking appearance by giving each form just one line of data instead of five.

The PosRecToStr function simply converts each integer to a string using Delphi's IntToStr function and then concatenates the strings, adding a space between each integer's section. The StrToPosRec function is a little more complicated. Its job is to get an input string and separate or *parse* it into individual integers. The first few lines of the procedure initialize the data structures—note that the Delphi FillChar procedure is a very efficient way to initialize structures such as records and arrays. The beginning of the string (the window state) is then analyzed to see if it is a 2. If so, the saved window state was maximized. No more information is required, so you call Exit to bail out of the procedure. If the window state was not a 2, the rest of the line is parsed into individual integers by first scanning the string to find all of the blanks (these were used to separate the integers), then using the position of the blanks to convert the integers and copy them into the TPosRec record structure.

The SaveFormPos and SetFormPos procedures are the ones that are actually called from the OnCreate and OnDestroy event handlers of each form. The SaveFormPos procedure first creates an instance of the TIniFile object (the EXE's file name is extracted from the full path returned by our call to ParamStr(0) and converted to an INI file name in the constructor). It then gets the necessary properties from the form and loads them in the PosRec, and makes an INI file entry by calling the TIniFile.WriteString method. The IniFile object is freed at the end of the procedure. SetFormPos does the reverse: it creates an instance of TIniFile, reads the appropriate string from the INI file, converts it, and sets the appropriate form properties. If no matching string is present in the INI file, the procedure is exited and the form's properties are left as they are.

Comments

As noted, the bulk of the code is placed in a separate unit—HOWUTILS.PAS. This keeps these handy procedures a *uses* clause away. More procedures and functions will be added to HOWUTILS in other sections of this book.

Keep a few things in mind when using these procedures. First of all, you'll have to be very careful using them with MDI child windows, since you can have multiple instances of an MDI child. Also, the procedures are meant mainly for demonstration; we haven't considered the possibility of a user tampering with the INI file, for example. Also the main form's Window State property does not get properly saved if the form is minimized, due to the way the VCL handles minimizing an application's main form.

1.4 How do I...
Flash the title bar of my forms?

COMPLEXITY: EASY

Problem

There are times when I need to get the user's attention, such as at the end of a long process or following an error condition. Is there a way to do this even if my application is minimized or the user doesn't have a speaker?

Technique

A Windows API called FlashWindow is designed especially for this purpose. The ease of making API calls in Delphi becomes apparent here, and there's a lesson to be learned along the way.

Steps

Run FLASH.EXE. The form is simple, as shown in Figure 1-4. Click the button and notice that the caption flashes. If you minimize the application, the icon blinks on and off.

1. Create a new project with a blank form. Name the project FLASH.DPR and name the unit FLASHFRM.PAS.

2. Add components and properties as shown in Table 1-7.

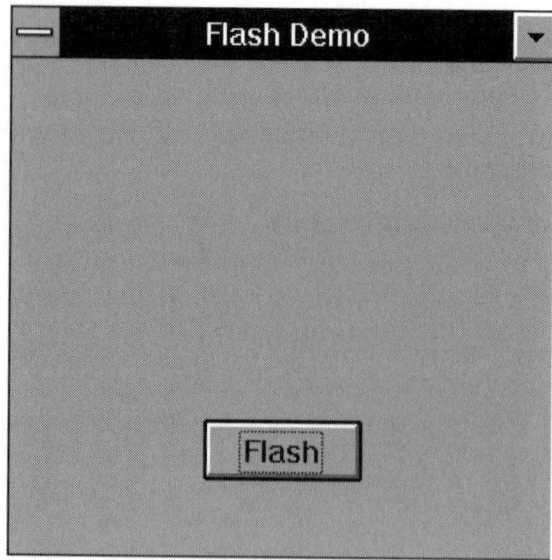

Figure 1-4 FLASH at run time

Table 1-7 Components, properties, and settings for Form1 in the FLASH project

COMPONENT	PROPERTY	SETTING
Form1	Left	260
	Top	141
	Width	305
	Height	294
	+BorderIcons	
	-biMaximize	False
	BorderStyle	bsSingle
	Caption	Flash Demo
Button1	Left	107
	Top	192
	Width	89
	Height	33
	Caption	Flash

3. Place a Timer component on the form. Set the Enabled property to False and the Interval property to 500. Create an OnTimer event handler for the Timer component. Add the following code to the event handler.

```
{ Flash the application's icon and form's caption bar }
procedure TForm1.Timer1Timer(Sender: TObject);
begin
  FlashWindow(Handle, True);
  FlashWindow(Application.Handle, True);
end;
```

4. Create an OnClick event handler for Button1. Add the following code to the event handler. This toggles the Enabled property of the timer, which in turn starts or stops the flashing of the form.

```
{ Start/stop timer and set button's caption appropriately }
procedure TForm1.Button1Click(Sender: TObject);
begin
  Timer1.Enabled := not(Timer1.Enabled);
  if Timer1.Enabled then
    Button1.Caption := 'Stop'
  else Button1.Caption := 'Flash';
end;
```

5. Compile and test the project.

How It Works

When the timer is enabled by clicking on the Show button, the OnTimer event fires every half second. When the event fires, FlashWindow inverts the color of the form's caption. There are two calls to the FlashWindow API function because there are two windows that must flash. The first window, represented simply by Handle, is the form itself. The second window is the *application window.* Every Delphi application has an application window that is usually hidden (actually it is sized with zero height and width, rather than officially hidden). This application window manages the icon, so if you need to do something with the icon, you use the handle of the application window or Application.Handle.

Button1's OnClick event handler inverts the status of Timer.Enabled and sets the correct caption for the button.

Comments

Admittedly this is a fairly simple How-To, but was some learning accomplished? The application window is an important concept to keep in the back of your mind. We will revisit it in other sections of this book.

1.5 How do I...
Find out if a child component's data has been changed?

COMPLEXITY: INTERMEDIATE

Problem

Delphi forms have an event called OnCloseQuery that is called prior to closing a form. This event can be used to "ask" the form if it is ready to be closed. The form itself doesn't automatically know if any of the data in its child components has been changed and should be saved. How do I check whether the user has changed data in the child components on my form?

Technique

All descendants of TCustomEdit have a Boolean Modified property that returns True if the data in the edit has been modified. The trick is finding a way to efficiently iterate through all of the form's components, checking whether they have been modified. The form's component array is handy for this purpose.

Steps

Run SAVEQRY.EXE. The main form will display, as shown in Figure 1-5. Try modifying data in any of the edit fields, then close the form by using the system menu or clicking on the Cancel button. If data has been modified, you will be prompted to save. If data has not been modified, the form will close.

Note: Clicking on the OK button simulates saving the data, so the form closes regardless of whether you've modified data or not.

1. Create a new project and blank form. Save the project as SAVEQRY.DPR and save the unit as SAVEQRY1.PAS.

2. Add components and set their properties as shown in Table 1-8.

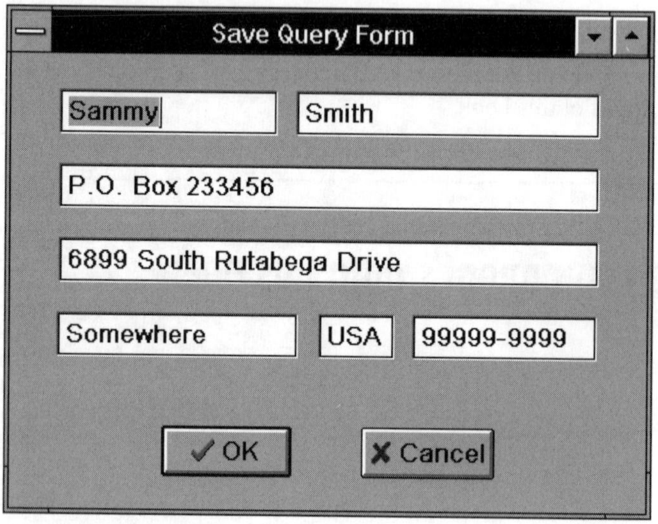

Figure 1-5 SAVEQRY at run time

Table 1-8 Components, properties, and settings for Form1 in the SAVEQRY project

COMPONENT	PROPERTY	SETTING
Form1	Left	240
	Top	119
	Width	435
	Height	329
	Caption	Save Query Form
	+Font	
	-Name	Arial
	-Style	[fsBold]
	-Size	10
Edit1	Left	33
	Top	24
	Width	145
	Height	27
	Text	Sammy
Edit2	Left	193
	Top	24
	Width	201
	Height	27
	Text	Smith
Edit3	Left	33
	Top	72
	Width	361
	Height	27
	Text	P.O. Box 233456
Edit4	Left	33
	Top	120
	Width	361
	Height	27
	Text	6899 South Rutabega Drive
Edit5	Left	32
	Top	168
	Width	161
	Height	27
	Text	Somewhere
Edit6	Left	209

continued on next page

continued from previous page

COMPONENT	PROPERTY	SETTING
	Top	168
	Width	49
	Height	27
	Text	USA
MaskEdit1	Left	272
	Top	168
	Width	121
	Height	27
	EditMask	00000\-9999;1;_ (Long Zip Code)
	Text	99999-9999
BitBtn1	Left	101
	Top	240
	Width	89
	Height	33
	Kind	bkOk
BitBtn2	Left	237
	Top	240
	Width	89
	Height	33
	Kind	bkCancel

3. Create an OnCloseQuery event handler for Form1. Add the following code to the event handler. This code determines whether any of the edit controls on the form have been modified.

```
procedure TForm1.FormCloseQuery(Sender: TObject; var CanClose: Boolean);
var
  I : Integer;
  Dirty : Boolean;
  ButtonSelected : Word;
begin
  { Initialize }
  I := 0;
  Dirty := False;
  { Iterate through form's components checking if modified }
  Repeat
    if Components[I] is TCustomEdit then
      Dirty := TCustomEdit(Components[I]).Modified;
    Inc(I);
  { Stop looping if we find a modified component, or reach end }
  until (Dirty or (I = ComponentCount));
  if Dirty then
  begin
```

```
    ButtonSelected := MessageDlg('Data has changed, do you wish to save?',
      mtInformation, mbYesNoCancel, 0);
    { Simulates saving/exiting if yes, exiting without saving if no }
    { A real application would require more code here }
    if ButtonSelected in [mrYes, mrNo] then
      CanClose := True
    else
      { If Cancel is picked, return to form }
      CanClose := False;
  end
  { No components were modified, so close without message }
  else CanClose := True;
end;
```

4. Create an OnClick event handler for BitBtn1 (the OK button). Add the following code to the event handler. This code simulates saving and exiting the application.

```
{ Simulates saving/exiting }
procedure TForm1.BitBtn1Click(Sender: TObject);
begin
  Application.Terminate;
end;
```

5. Create an OnClick event handler for BitBtn2 (the Cancel button). Add the following code to the resulting OnClick event handler.

```
{ Tries to close form, which triggers OnCloseQuery }
procedure TForm1.BitBtn2Click(Sender: TObject);
begin
  Close;
end;
```

6. Compile and test the project.

How It Works

When the OnCloseQuery event is fired, the form's Components array is used to iterate through all of the components owned by the form. The runtime type information *is* operator is used to determine whether a component is a descendant of TCustomEdit (therefore having a Modified property). If it is, the Modified property is tested. When a modified TCustomEdit descendant is found or the end of the components array is reached, the loop terminates. The Dirty variable is then tested to determine whether a modified component was found. If so, the user is queried to find out whether the data should be saved, and appropriate action for the answer is taken.

Comments

This How-To demonstrates iterating through a form's components using the Components array, a technique that is very useful. You may have noticed that it was also used in the RESIZEIT project of How-To 1.2. Note that forms also have a Controls array, which technically could have been used for this project. The Controls array holds only controls instead of all components. In addition, the Controls array only holds controls that are *parented* by the form. This means that if you had any TCustomEdits contained in TPanels, TGroupboxes, or other container components, they would not be in the Controls array and therefore would be skipped by the iteration loop. Since there are no TCustomEdits parented by anything other than the form in this demo, the Controls array would work fine.

Another important point demonstrated here is that Application.Terminate (used in the OK button's OnClick event handler) does *not* fire the OnCloseQuery event. This is important to remember! If you have data that might need to be saved in a program, you should not shut the program down by calling Application.Terminate. A better choice would be Application.MainForm.Close, which can also be called anywhere in the application and will fire the OnCloseQuery event for the main form.

1.6 How do I...
Create a form on the fly at run time?

COMPLEXITY: ADVANCED

Problem

I would like to write an application that can create its own data entry forms based on the schema of the database table that I connect it to. This might be useful for a generic database application that could be used with different database tables. Can I do this with Delphi?

Technique

This technique is a sleeping giant. It has the potential to allow you to create applications that are fully customizable by the user or that adapt to whatever database they are connected to. Basically, all you need to do is create an instance of a form at run time, populate it with various components, and set properties.

Steps

Run RUNTIME.EXE. Press the New Form button as shown in Figure 1-6; a new form is created. This new form was defined and created at run time. Click on the Change Edit button on the new form, and the edit component will be updated.

Note: You can create as many forms as your system will allow.

1. Create a new project with a blank form. Name the project RUNTIME.DPR and the unit RUNTIME1.PAS.
2. Add components and set properties as shown in Table 1-9.

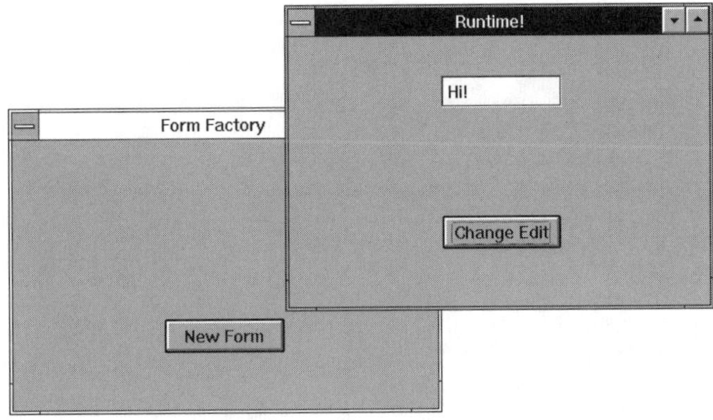

Figure 1-6 RUNTIME's main form and the new form created on the fly

Table 1-9 Components, properties, and settings for Form1 in the RUNTIME project

COMPONENT	PROPERTY	SETTING
Form1	Left	200
	Top	118
	Width	435
	Height	300
	Caption	Form Factory
Button1	Left	153
	Top	176
	Width	121
	Height	33
	Caption	New Form

3. Create an OnClick event handler for Button1 and add the following code to the event handler.

```
{ Generates and shows form from scratch }
procedure TForm1.Button1Click(Sender: TObject);
var
  NewForm: TNewForm;
begin
  { Create new form }
  NewForm := TNewForm.CreateNew(Application);
  { Set its properties }
  with NewForm do
  begin
```

continued on next page

continued from previous page

```
    Top := 140;
    Left := 220;
    Width := 435;
    Height := 300;
    Caption := 'Runtime!';
    { Create new edit component }
    NewEdit := TEdit.Create(NewForm);
    { Set its properties }
    with NewEdit do
    begin
      Parent := NewForm;
      Left := 153;
      Top := 40;
      Width := 121;
      Height := 29;
      TabOrder := 1;
      Text := 'Edit1';
    end;
    { Create new button component }
    NewButton := TButton.Create(NewForm);
    { Set its properties }
    with NewButton do
    begin
      Parent := NewForm;
      Left := 153;
      Top := 176;
      Width := 121;
      Height := 33;
      TabOrder := 0;
      Caption := 'Change Edit';
      { Wire the component to OnClick handler }
      OnClick := NewButtonClick;
    end;
    Show;
  end;
end;
```

4. While still in the Code Editor, move up to the type declaration area where Form1 has been declared. Add a declaration for your new form class above the Form1 declaration:

```
type

  TNewForm = class(TForm)
    NewEdit: TEdit;
    NewButton: TButton;
    procedure NewButtonClick(Sender: TObject);
  end;

  TForm1 = class(TForm)
    Button1: TButton;
    procedure Button1Click(Sender: TObject);
  private
    { Private declarations }
```

```
  public
    { Public declarations }
  end;
```

5. While still in the Code Editor, move down to Form1's Button1Click event handler and add the TNewForm.NewButtonClick event handler prior to Form1's Button1Click event handler, as shown here:

```
implementation

{$R *.DFM}

{ OnClick handler for generated forms }
procedure TNewForm.NewButtonClick(Sender: TObject);
begin
  NewEdit.Text := 'Hi!';
end;

{ Generates and shows form from scratch }
procedure TForm1.Button1Click(Sender: TObject);
var
  NewForm: TNewForm;
begin
...
```

6. Compile and test the project.

How It Works

The OnClick handler for Form1 creates a new form using the TForm.CreateNew constructor. This constructor is designed to create forms without a corresponding DFM file. Properties for the form are then set the same way you set them at run time. The edit component and button component are created and added to the form. When you create components in this way, be sure to set the component's Parent—otherwise, the component will not be visible. In most cases the Parent will be the form, but if you are putting the component in a container such as a TPanel or TGroupbox (for example) the Parent will be the TPanel or TGroupbox. In all cases, the form will be the owner.

Note: To assist in setting properties, you can build a dummy form visually, then cut the components from the form and paste them in the code where you want them. You'll have to make some modifications to what is pasted there, but it's still a big help.

Comments

As stated in the "Technique" section, there are a lot of possibilities for creating forms and components at run time. In this How-To, all of the values used to set the properties for the form and its components are constant values—but there's nothing that says they have to stay that way. They could be variables—allowing the data to be read from a text file, entered by the user, or read from a database.

1.7 How do I...

Drag a captionless window?

COMPLEXITY: EASY

Problem

I'd like to make a small application such as a clock or resource monitor take up as little space as possible. I want the user to be able to move the application's window, but I don't want to increase the window's size by adding a caption bar. The clock application that comes with Windows doesn't have a caption and can still be dragged. How can I do this with my Delphi applications?

Technique

There are a couple of ways to accomplish this. The basic technique is to make Windows think that the entire form (or at least the area you designate) is the form's caption. When the user drags your form with the mouse, the form moves exactly as if the user was dragging the caption of a normal form.

Steps

Run NOCAPDRG.EXE. A clock form will display, as shown in Figure 1-7. Try moving the form around the screen using the mouse. You can put the mouse anywhere in the form to move it. If you right-click on the form, a pop-up menu shows. It gives you two options: make the form stay on top of all windows or exit the program.

1. Create a new project with a blank form and name it NOCAPDRG.DPR. Name the unit NOCAP.PAS.
2. Add components and set their properties as shown in Table 1-10.

7:58:53 PM

4/27/95

Figure 1-7 NOCAPDRG at run time

Table 1-10 Components, properties, and settings for Form1 in the NOCAPDRG project

COMPONENT	PROPERTY	SETTING
Form1	Name	NoCapForm
	Left	441
	Top	251
	Width	136
	AutoScroll	False
	BorderStyle	bsSingle
	Color	clAqua
	+Font	
	-Color	clBlack
	-Name	System
	-Style	[fsBold]
	-Size	10
Label1	Left	14
	Top	5
	Width	100
	Height	20
	Alignment	taCenter
	AutoSize	False
Label2	Left	14
	Top	30
	Width	100
	Height	20
	Alignment	taCenter
	AutoSize	False
Form1	PopupMenu	PopupMenu1
	Height	90

3. Add a PopupMenu component to the form and double-click on it to bring up the Menu Designer. Add two items to the pop-up menu: E&xit and &Stay On Top.

Note: You may have to adjust the size of the form temporarily to position and work with some of the components; just return the height to 90 when you're done.

4. Create an OnClick event handler for the Exit menu item and add the following code to the event handler.

```
procedure TNoCapForm.ExitClick(Sender: TObject);
begin
  Close;
end;
```

5. Create an OnClick event handler for the Stay On Top menu item and add the following code to the event handler.

```
{ Set FormStyle, update menu check as appropriate }
procedure TNoCapForm.StayOnTopClick(Sender: TObject);
begin
  StayOnTop.Checked := not(StayOnTop.Checked);
  if StayOnTop.Checked then
    FormStyle := fsStayOnTop
  else FormStyle := fsNormal;
end;
```

6. Close the Menu Designer. You need a somewhat different type of form for this project than you can make using Delphi's standard form properties, so you have to set the form's style by overriding the form's CreateParams method. In the Code Editor, declare the CreateParams method in the form's object declaration as shown.

```
type
  TNoCapForm = class(TForm)
    Label1: TLabel;
    Label2: TLabel;
    PopupMenu1: TPopupMenu;
    Exit: TMenuItem;
    StayOnTop: TMenuItem;
    procedure Timer1Timer(Sender: TObject);
    procedure ExitClick(Sender: TObject);
    procedure StayOnTopClick(Sender: TObject);
  private
    { Private declarations }
    procedure CreateParams(var Params: TCreateParams); override;
  public
    { Public declarations }
end;
```

7. In the Code Editor, add the CreateParams method to the *implemetation* section of the unit as shown.

```
implementation

{$R *.DFM}

{ Override form's style because what we want is not a normal form type }
procedure TNoCapForm.CreateParams(var Params: TCreateParams);
begin
  inherited CreateParams (Params);
  Params.Style := ws_Popup or ws_ClipChildren or ws_ClipSiblings or ws_Border;
end;
```

8. You can make Windows treat the entire form as if it is the caption by responding to the wm_NCHitTest message. In the Code Editor, declare a message handler for this purpose as follows:

```
type
  TNoCapForm = class(TForm)
    Label1: TLabel;
    Label2: TLabel;
    Timer1: TTimer;
    PopupMenu1: TPopupMenu;
    Exit: TMenuItem;
    StayOnTop: TMenuItem;
    procedure Timer1Timer(Sender: TObject);
    procedure ExitClick(Sender: TObject);
    procedure StayOnTopClick(Sender: TObject);
  private
    { Private declarations }
    procedure CreateParams(var Params: TCreateParams); override;
    procedure WMNCHitTest(var Msg: TMessage);  message WM_NCHITTEST;
  public
    { Public declarations }
  end;
```

9. Add the code for the WMNCHitTest message handler to the *implementation* section of the unit as follows:

```
implementation

{$R *.DFM}

procedure TNoCapForm.WMNCHitTest(var Msg: TMessage);
begin
  if GetAsyncKeyState(VK_LBUTTON) < 0 then
    Msg.Result := HTCAPTION
  else
    Msg.Result := HTCLIENT;
end;
```

10. Add a Timer component to the form and create an OnTimer event handler for it. Add the following code to the event handler.

```
procedure TNoCapForm.Timer1Timer(Sender: TObject);
begin
  Label1.Caption := TimeToStr(Time);
  Label2.Caption := DateToStr(Date);
end;
```

11. Select the form in the Object Inspector. On the Events page, click in the right-hand column of the OnCreate event, drop down the list of handlers, and select the Timer1Timer event handler.

12. Compile and test the project.

How It Works

To understand how this works, let's take an abbreviated look at some of the things that are going on between a typical form and Windows. Whenever you move the mouse cursor over a form, Windows sends the form wm_NCHitTest (Non-Client Hit Test) messages. The form responds to Windows by returning whether the mouse is over a client or non-client (such as the caption or sizing border) area of the form. Windows uses this information to determine what kind of message to send the form if an event (such as the user pressing a mouse button) occurs. When a MouseDown event occurs in a non-client region of the form, Windows sends a special type of message called a *system command* to the form. This message tells the form to perform special actions such as moving or sizing, depending on the type of non-client area that the mouse cursor is on.

If the left mouse button is down during the wm_NCHitTest message, the message returned tells Windows that the mouse is in the caption area of the form. Windows responds to this by sending a system command message to the form, indicating that the user wants to move the form.

The remaining code is pretty straightforward. The timer is used to update the labels each second so that they display the current date and time. The form's OnCreate handler is "wired" to the OnTimer event so that the correct time and date are in the labels when the form is first created. The StayOnTopClick event allows the user to specify whether the form will stay on top of all other windows even when it doesn't have focus.

Comments

The implementation of this How-To is fairly easy, but the results are powerful and used by some of the top Windows programmers. Only one application of this technique out of the many possibilities was demonstrated here.

1.8 How do I...
Create a system modal form?

COMPLEXITY: EASY

Problem

I have an application that uses a modal dialog box for password entry. The modal property keeps the user out of my application until the password is entered, but I've found that it's possible to switch to a different application and snoop around in the files. Is there a way to prevent the user from doing this?

Technique

Delphi allows you to make a form modal by calling the ShowModal method of the form when showing it. This creates an *application modal* form, which prevents users from doing anything in your application until the modal form is closed; but users can switch to other applications and do anything they want outside of your application. In most cases, an application modal form will fit your needs. If you require more control over the user for a particular action, you may need a *system modal* form, which prevents users from doing anything in Windows short of rebooting the machine.

Steps

Run SYSMODAL.EXE. There is a check box on the main form that controls whether the child form is opened as a system modal form, as shown in Figure 1-8. Try opening the form in both modes and switching between applications, or moving icons on the desktop, and so on. Notice that the child form can switch itself between application modal and system modal modes.

1. Create a new project with a blank form and name it SYSMODAL.DPR. Name the unit SYSMODE.PAS.

2. Add components and properties as shown in Table 1-11.

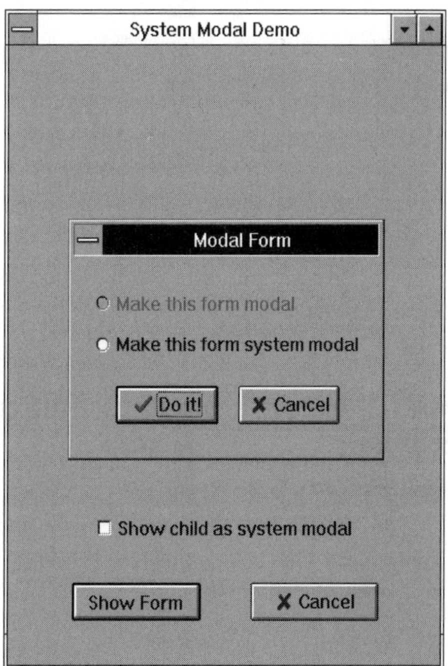

Figure 1-8 SYSMODAL at run time

Table 1-11 Components, properties, and settings for MainForm in the SYSMODAL project

COMPONENT	PROPERTY	SETTING
Form1	Name	MainForm
	Left	236
	Top	119
	Width	417
	Height	570
	Caption	System Modal Demo
	Position	poScreenCenter
Button1	Left	60
	Top	464
	Width	121
	Height	33
	Caption	Show Form
BitBtn1	Left	228
	Top	464
	Width	121
	Height	33
	Kind	bkCancel
Checkbox1	Left	84
	Top	408
	Width	241
	Height	17
	Caption	Show child as system modal

3. Add a blank form to the project and save its unit as SYSDLG.PAS. Add the components and set the properties as shown in Table 1-12.

Table 1-12 Components, properties, and settings for Form1 in the SYSMODAL project

COMPONENT	PROPERTY	SETTING
Form1	Left	297
	Top	206
	Width	298
	Height	208
	BorderStyle	bsDialog
	Caption	Modal Form

COMPONENT	PROPERTY	SETTING
	Position	poScreenCenter
BitBtn1	Left	155
	Top	112
	Width	96
	Height	33
	Kind	bkCancel
BitBtn2	Left	40
	Top	112
	Width	96
	Height	33
	Kind	bkOK
	Default	False
	Caption	Do It!
	ModalResult	mrNone
RadioButton1	Left	21
	Top	32
	Width	193
	Height	17
	Caption	Make this form modal
RadioButton2	Left	21
	Top	64
	Width	249
	Height	25
	Caption	Make this form system modal

4. Select Options|Project on Delphi's main menu. On the Forms page of the Project Options dialog, move Form1 to the right-hand list box, titled Available Forms.

5. Create an OnClick event handler for Button1 (the Show Form button) and add the following code to the event handler.

```
{ Create and free modal dialog }
procedure TMainForm.Button1Click(Sender: TObject);
begin
  with TForm1.Create(Application) do
  try
    if Checkbox1.Checked then
    begin
      SetSysModalWindow(Handle);
      Caption := 'System Modal Form';
      RadioButton2.Enabled := False;
```

continued on next page

continued from previous page

```
    end
    else RadioButton1.Enabled := False;
    ShowModal;
  finally
    Free;
  end;
end;
```

6. Create an OnClick event handler for BitBtn1 (the Cancel button) and add the following code to the event handler.

```
procedure TMainForm.BitBtn1Click(Sender: TObject);
begin
  Close;
end;
```

7. While still in the Code Editor, move up and add a *uses* clause with SysDlg after *implementation*, as shown in the following code.

```
implementation

uses SysDlg;

{$R *.DFM}
```

8. Create an OnClick event handler BitBtn2 (the Do It! button) on Form1 and add the following code to the event handler.

```
{ Set modal type and manage radio buttons }
procedure TForm1.BitBtn2Click(Sender: TObject);
begin
  if RadioButton1.Checked then
  begin
    SetSysModalWindow(0);
    Caption := 'Modal Form';
    RadioButton1.Checked := False;
    RadioButton1.Enabled := False;
    RadioButton2.Enabled := True;
  end;
  if RadioButton2.Checked then
  begin
    SetSysModalWindow(Handle);
    Caption := 'System Modal Form';
    RadioButton2.Checked := False;
    RadioButton2.Enabled := False;
    RadioButton1.Enabled := True;
  end;
end;
```

9. Compile and test the project.

How It Works

Making a form system modal is a fairly trivial task—a single call to the Windows API function SetSysModalWindow with the form's handle will do it. There are some other things demonstrated here, though. You'll notice that the OnClick event handler for the Show Form button is a little different from what we've used before. It actually creates the form instead of simply showing it. This goes along with the fact that the modal form was removed from the autocreate list in the Project Options dialog. Normally, a Delphi application creates all of its forms, whether they are visible or not, when the application starts. This is usually a very convenient way to handle things, and the method we recommend the majority of the time.

The OnClick event handler for the Show Form button also demonstrates the use of a *try...finally* resource protection block. This code ensures that the modal form gets properly freed when you are done with it and also frees it if there are any errors while creating or running the form. Notice in step 5 that *try...finally...end* can effectively replace the usual *begin...end* that you would use when working with statements such as *with Something do*.

Note: There will be other examples in this book that demonstrate Delphi's exception handling ability, and you can get more information on exceptions in the "Writing Robust Applications" chapter in the Delphi User's Manual.

The remaining code simply manages the state of the radio buttons and the modal form's caption.

Comments

Use system modal forms with caution, and only when you really need them. Users could mistakenly think that their computer is locked up if they try to switch to another application while your system modal dialog is showing. It is also possible to make a hidden system modal form (which would be impossible for users to close), which is one of the reasons that we elected not to use Delphi's autocreate feature for this form.

1.9 How do I... Set minimum and maximum sizes for my forms?

COMPLEXITY: INTERMEDIATE

Problem

Users are asking that I make my forms sizable so they can make better use of larger screens. I've experimented with this, but when I make the forms very large or very small, they start to look pretty darn ugly. I'm proud of my work, and I want to maintain control over how it looks while allowing some flexibility for users. How can I deal with this?

Technique

You can deal with this by limiting the maximum and/or minimum sizes of your form. This isn't too difficult, but you will have to wander beyond the confines of Delphi to find a solution. The answer is found with the wm_GetMinMaxInfo message of the

Windows API. Once you set values in response to this message, everything is handled by Windows.

Steps

Run MINMAX.EXE. This simple form is shown in Figure 1-9. Try making it both larger and smaller. Notice that it will only size to a certain point. Try to maximize it. Notice that there is a limit to that, also—and that it always goes to a certain position on the screen when maximized.

1. Create a new project with a blank form and name it MINMAX.DPR. Name the unit MINMAX1.PAS.

Figure 1-9 MINMAX at run time

2. Set the properties of the form as shown in Table 1-13.

Table 1-13 Components, properties, and settings for Form1 in the MINMAX project

COMPONENT	PROPERTY	SETTING
Form1	Caption	Min/Max Form
	Height	131
	Left	285
	Top	192
	Width	250

3. Add the message handler for wm_GetMinMaxInfo in the form's object declaration, as shown in the following code.

```
type
  TForm1 = class(TForm)
  private
    { Private declarations }
    procedure WMGetMinMaxInfo(var Message: TWMGetMinMaxInfo);
      message WM_GETMINMAXINFO;
  public
    { Public declarations }
  end;
```

4. Add the code for the message handler to the *implementation* section of your form's code unit.

Note: The *inherit* keyword is especially important with MDI child forms to ensure that the TMinMaxInfo structure is properly initialized.

```
implementation

{$R *.DFM}

{ Respond to message, setting values as needed... }
{ If you don't want to set a particular value, delete its line. }
procedure TForm1.WMGetMinMaxInfo(var Message: TWMGetMinMaxInfo);
var
  MinMax: PMinMaxInfo;
begin
  inherited;
  MinMax := Message.MinMaxInfo;

  MinMax^.ptMaxSize.X := 500;
  MinMax^.ptMaxSize.Y := 500;

  MinMax^.ptMaxPosition.X := 200;
  MinMax^.ptMaxPosition.Y := 200;

  MinMax^.ptMaxTrackSize.X := 300;
  MinMax^.ptMaxTrackSize.Y := 300;

  MinMax^.ptMinTrackSize.X := 200;
  MinMax^.ptMinTrackSize.Y := 200;
end;

end.
```

5. Compile and test the project.

How It Works

As you can see, there isn't much to this example—but it accomplishes exactly what you set out to do. It's a matter of having the right tool for the job. Basically any time a user sizes your form, Windows sends a wm_GetMinMaxInfo message to the form to find out if there are any limits that should be imposed on the sizing. Contained within that message is a pointer to the TMinMaxInfo structure. The form responds by using that pointer to fill the structure with the data that you specified in the WMGetMinMaxInfo procedure.

Fill in only the data fields that you want to restrict. If there are any fields you don't want to fill in, delete the entire line from the procedure. Fill in ptMaxSize to specify a size when the user maximizes the form; fill in ptMaxPosition to set the position of the form when the user maximizes it. Fill in ptMaxTrackSize to prevent the user from sizing the form beyond a certain point, and set ptMinTrackSize to prevent the user from making a form too small.

Note: Each of these fields has an X and Y value, which correspond to a width and height value for the size fields or a left and top value for the position fields.

Comments

Experiment to get a feel for what's going on here. Try changing some of the values for the various fields of the TMinMaxInfo structure. This How-To is a good example of how easy it is to get to the Windows API if you need to.

1.10 How do I...

Make the ENTER key act like the TAB key in my forms?

COMPLEXITY: INTERMEDIATE

Problem

I am using Delphi to write a Windows version of an existing DOS program. In the DOS version, users press the ENTER key to move to the next field in the data entry forms. This is different from the standard Windows behavior of pressing the TAB key to go to the next field. Is it possible to give users the option of using the more familiar ENTER key?

Technique

There is more than one way to accomplish this behavior. It can be done by subclassing the individual edit controls, or by intercepting the keystrokes before they get to the controls. Delphi allows you to preview the user's keystrokes at the form level, providing a fairly easy way to accomplish the task at hand.

Steps

Run ENTR2TAB.EXE. The form is shown in Figure 1-10. If you press ENTER with the check box focused, nothing will happen—but if you enable the Enter to Tab

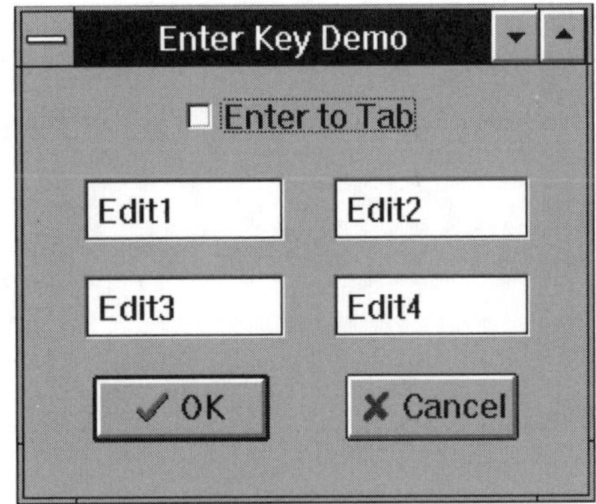

Figure 1-10 ENTR2TAB at run time

option by clicking on the check box, pressing ENTER will advance the focus to the next control on the form. Pressing ENTER while a button has focus will fire the OnClick event for the focused button.

1. Create a new project with a blank form. Save the project as ENTR2TAB.DPR and save the unit as ENTR2TAB.PAS.
2. Add components and set properties as shown in Table 1-14.

Table 1-14 Components, properties, and settings for the ENTR2TAB project

COMPONENT	PROPERTY	SETTING
Form1	Left	305
	Top	139
	Width	296
	Height	247
	Caption	Enter Key Demo
	KeyPreview	True
CheckBox1	Left	83
	Top	16
	Width	121
	Height	17
	Caption	Enter to Tab
Edit1	Left	32

continued on next page

continued from previous page

COMPONENT	PROPERTY	SETTING
	Top	56
	Width	99
	Height	29
Edit2	Left	158
	Top	56
	Width	99
	Height	29
Edit3	Left	32
	Top	104
	Width	99
	Height	29
Edit4	Left	158
	Top	104
	Width	99
	Height	29
BitBtn1	Left	35
	Top	152
	Width	89
	Height	33
	Kind	bkOk
	Default	False
BitBtn2	Left	163
	Top	152
	Width	89
	Height	33
	Kind	bkCancel

3. Create an OnClick event handler for the Cancel button and add the following:

```
procedure TForm1.BitBtn2Click(Sender: TObject);
begin
  Close;
end;
```

4. Create an OnClick event handler for the OK button and add the following:

```
procedure TForm1.BitBtn1Click(Sender: TObject);
begin
  Close;
end;
```

5. Create an OnKeyPress event handler for Form1 and add the following code. This is where the ENTER key is intercepted.

```
procedure TForm1.FormKeyPress(Sender: TObject; var Key: Char);
begin
  { If Enter2Tab action is desired }
  if CheckBox1.Checked then
    if Key = #13 then
    begin
      Key := #0;
      { move focus to next control in tab order. }
      Perform(wm_NextDlgCtl,0,0);
    end;
end;
```

6. Compile and test the project.

How It Works

When you press the ENTER key in a form, Windows normally sends a wm_Command message to the control that has the focus. If the form's KeyPreview property is set to True, the form's OnKeyPress event gets called before the event is passed to the control.

The form's OnKeyPress event handler determines whether the "Enter to Tab" behavior is desired by the user by testing the state of the check box. The check box is used in this How-To mainly for demonstration purposes. In an actual application, this option would most likely be set in an options dialog and stored in an INI file. If the check box returns True, the character associated with the ENTER key is changed to a null character—preventing the focused edit control from responding to the key stroke. The TForm.Perform method is then used to simulate sending a wm_NextDlgCtrl to the form to shift the focus to the next control in the form's tab order. Using the TForm.Perform method is essentially equivalent to sending a message to the form; but the message in this case is sent directly to the form through the VCL, bypassing Windows' normal message handling.

Note: If you press ENTER while a button is focused, the button's OnClick event handler is fired, as expected.

Comments

In most cases, this technique serves the purpose very well. The behavior is normally as the user would expect. If you have memos in your forms, you'll have to work with it a little more, depending on how you want the memos to behave. Keep in mind that you are deviating from standard Windows behavior here, so take extra care to ensure that it will not be confusing to the user. You should make this modified behavior available as an option only, not as the default behavior of your application.

1.11 How do I... Paint an interesting background on an MDI parent form?

COMPLEXITY: ADVANCED

Problem

Normally I can change the background color of my Delphi forms, but I can't seem to put a design or bitmap on forms that have the FormStyle property set to fsMDIForm. Why is this? How can I do this with Delphi?

Technique

These problems arise from the fact that MDI forms have an extra window layered over them called the *MDI client window.* This window is responsible for the management of MDI child windows and is common to all MDI programs—not just Delphi programs. Unfortunately, Delphi does not provide easy access to the client window, so you must gain access through a technique called *subclassing*. In effect, you set up a detour for the flow of messages to the client window.

Steps

Run MDIAPP.EXE. This application is based on the MDI template included with Delphi. You'll notice some differences right away, however, as shown in Figure 1-11. From the Options menu, try selecting different backgrounds.

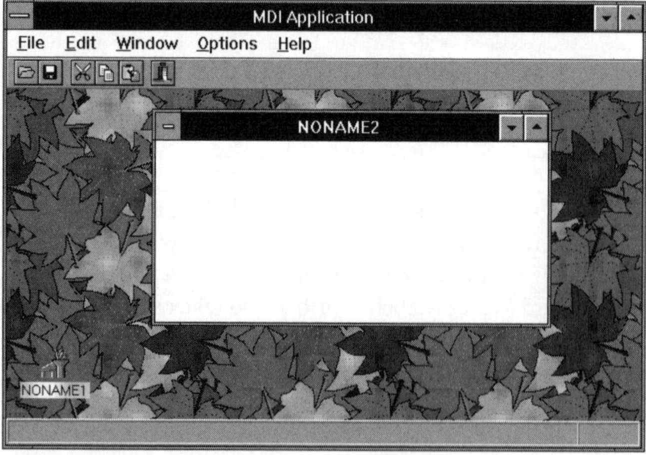

Figure 1-11 MDIAPP at run time

1. Create a new project based on the MDI template, specifying your desired directory.

2. Switch to the Code Editor and view the Main unit. In the form's type declaration, override the TForm.CreateWnd method by adding the declaration to the end of the *private* section of the TMainForm object, as shown in the following example.

```
type
  TMainForm = class(TForm)
...
private
    { Private declarations }
    procedure CreateMDIChild(const Name: string);
    procedure ShowHint(Sender: TObject);
    procedure CreateWnd; override;
  public
    { Public declarations }
  end;
```

3. Add the TMainForm.CreateWnd method in the *implementation* section of the unit, as shown in the following example. This is where you actually do the subclassing using the SetWindowLong API function.

```
implementation

{$R *.DFM}

uses ChildWin;

{ Subclass the MDI Client window }
procedure TMainForm.CreateWnd;
begin
  inherited CreateWnd;
  FClientInstance := MakeObjectInstance(ClientWndProc);
  FDefClientProc := Pointer(SetWindowLong(ClientHandle, GWL_WNDPROC,
    LongInt(FClientInstance)));
end;
```

4. In the CreateWnd method references are made to variables called FDefClientProc and FClientInstance, which haven't been defined yet. Another method in the object will need to have access to these variables, so they must be defined in the object itself. Add them as shown in the following example. You also need to define the ClientWndProc method as shown.

```
type
  TMainForm = class(TForm)
...
private
    { Private declarations }
    FDefClientProc: Pointer;
    FClientInstance: TFarProc;
    procedure CreateMDIChild(const Name: string);
    procedure ClientWndProc(var Message: TMessage);
```

continued on next page

continued from previous page

```
    procedure ShowHint(Sender: TObject);
    procedure CreateWnd; override;
  public
    { Public declarations }
  end;
```

5. The SetWindowLong API call told Windows that you replaced the client window's WndProc with a function of your own called ClientWndProc. The WndProc of a window is a special function that handles the messages sent to the window. Add this function prior to the CreateWnd method, as shown in the following example.

```
implementation

{$R *.DFM}

uses ChildWin;

{ This is our access to the client window }
procedure TMainForm.ClientWndProc(var Message: TMessage);

  procedure Default;
  begin
    with Message do
      Result := CallWindowProc(FDefClientProc, ClientHandle, Msg, wParam, lParam);
  end;

begin
  with Message do
  if Msg = wm_EraseBkGnd then
  begin
    case MainForm.Tag of
      1 : begin
            PaintGradient(WParam);
            Result := 1;
          end;
      2 : begin
            TilePicture(WParam);
            Result := 1;
          end
     else
       Default;
    end;
  end
  else Default;
end;

{ Subclass the MDI Client window }
procedure TMainForm.CreateWnd;
begin
  inherited CreateWnd;
  FDefClientProc := Pointer(SetWindowLong(ClientHandle, GWL_WNDPROC,
    LongInt(@ClientWndProc)));
end;
```

6. Now you add some procedures to paint the various designs on the MDI client window. First add the TilePicture procedure prior to the ClientWndProc procedure, as shown in the following example.

```
implementation

{$R *.DFM}

uses ChildWin;

{ Tile client with whatever bitmap is stored in Image1 }
procedure TilePicture(DC: hDC);
var
  CRect, IRect: TRect;
  I, J, Rows, Cols, CRow, CCol: Integer;
begin
  { Get size of client and image }
  GetClientRect(MainForm.ClientHandle, CRect);
  IRect := MainForm.Image1.ClientRect;
  { Calculate required # of rows and columns }
  Cols := CRect.Right div IRect.Right;
  Rows := CRect.Bottom div IRect.Bottom;
  { Blast the bitmaps on the client }
  for I := 0 to Rows do
  begin
    CRow := I * IRect.Bottom;
    for J := 0 to Cols do
    begin
      CCol := J * IRect.Right;
      BitBlt(DC, CCol, CRow, IRect.Right, IRect.Bottom,
        MainForm.Image1.Canvas.Handle, 0, 0, SRCCOPY);
    end;
  end;
end;

{ This is our access to the client window }
procedure TMainForm.ClientWndProc(var Message: TMessage);
```

7. Add the PaintGradient procedure prior to the TilePicture procedure, as shown in the following example.

```
implementation

{$R *.DFM}

uses ChildWin;

var
  FDefClientProc: Pointer;

{ Paint a blue to black gradient like Windows Setup does }
procedure PaintGradient(DC: hDC);
const
  Shades = 64;
var
```

continued on next page

continued from previous page

```
  CRect: TRect;
  NewBrush, OldBrush: hBrush;
  I, FillBoxHeight: Integer;
  RectArray: array[1..Shades] of TRect;
begin
  GetClientRect(MainForm.ClientHandle, CRect);
  FillBoxHeight := CRect.Bottom div Shades;
  { Set up Rects in array... }
  for I := 1 to Shades do
  with RectArray[I] do
  begin
    Left := CRect.Left;
    Right := CRect.Right;
    Top := (I - 1) * FillBoxHeight;
    Bottom := Top + FillBoxHeight;
  end;
  { Make up for any slop at bottom }
  RectArray[Shades].Bottom := CRect.Bottom;
  { Fill 'em up! }
  for I := (Shades - 1) downto 0 do
  begin
    NewBrush := CreateSolidBrush(RGB(0,0,((I + 1) * 4 - 1)));
    OldBrush := SelectObject(DC, NewBrush);
    FillRect(DC, RectArray[Shades-I], NewBrush);
    SelectObject(DC, OldBrush);
    DeleteObject(NewBrush);
  end;
end;

{ Tile client with bitmap stored in Image1 }
procedure TilePicture(DC: hDC);
var
  CRect, IRect: TRect;
  I, J, Rows, Cols, CRow, CCol: Integer;
begin
...
end;
```

8. Add the components to the main form and set properties as shown in Table 1-15.

Table 1-15 Components, properties, and settings for MainForm in the MDIAPP project

COMPONENT	PROPERTY	SETTING
Image1	Left	8
	Top	40
	Autosize	True
ColorDialog1	Ctl3D	True
	Color	clBlack
OpenDialog1	DefaultExt	BMP
	Filter	Windows Bitmap|*.BMP

COMPONENT	PROPERTY	SETTING
	+Options	
	-ofFileMustExist	True
	Title	Load Bitmap

9. Double-click on the main form's MainMenu component to bring up the Menu Designer. Click the Help item on the menu bar and press INS This will allow you to add a menu item on the menu bar prior to the Help item. Type **&Options** and press ENTER. Add a menu item below the Options item with a caption of **&Desktop**. With the Desktop menu item highlighted, press CONTROL-→ to add a submenu to the Desktop item. Add the menu items shown in Table 1-16 to the submenu.

Table 1-16 Menu items and captions for the Desktop submenu

MENU ITEM	CAPTION
SolidColor1	&Solid Color
Gradient1	&Gradient
TileBitmap1	&Tile Bitmap

10. Close the Menu Designer. Create an OnClick event handler for the SolidColor menu item in MainForm's main menu and add the following code to the event handler.

```
{ Allow user to pick color, then force client repaint }
procedure TMainForm.SolidColor1Click(Sender: TObject);
var
  I : integer;
begin
  Tag := 0;
  if ColorDialog1.Execute then
  begin
    Color := ColorDialog1.Color;
    InvalidateRect(MainForm.ClientHandle, Nil, True);
    for I := 0 to MDIChildCount - 1 do
      InvalidateRect(MDIChildren[I].Handle, nil, True);
  end;
end;
```

11. Create an OnClick event handler for the Gradient menu item in MainForm's main menu and add the following code to the event handler.

```
{ Switch to gradient, force client repaint }
procedure TMainForm.Gradient1Click(Sender: TObject);
var
  I : integer;
```

continued on next page

continued from previous page

```
begin
  Tag := 1;
  Color := clBlack;
  InvalidateRect(MainForm.ClientHandle, Nil, True);
    for I := 0 to MDIChildCount - 1 do
      InvalidateRect(MDIChildren[I].Handle, nil, True);
end;
```

12. Create an OnClick event handler for the Tile Bitmap menu item in MainForm's main menu and add the following code to the event handler.

```
{ Allow user to pick bitmap, force repaint }
procedure TMainForm.TiledBitmap1Click(Sender: TObject);
var
  I : integer;
begin
  if OpenDialog1.Execute then
  begin
    Tag := 2;
    Color := clGray;
    Image1.Picture.LoadFromFile(OpenDialog1.FileName);
    InvalidateRect(MainForm.ClientHandle, Nil, True);
    for I := 0 to MDIChildCount - 1 do
      InvalidateRect(MDIChildren[I].Handle, nil, True);
  end;
end;
```

13. Compile and test the project.

How It Works

The biggest part of this How-To is the actual subclassing of the MDI client window. This is done with a call to the SetWindowLong API function in the TMainForm.CreateWnd method. You tell Windows that the messages should be sent to the ClientWndProc procedure instead of the client window's normal WndProc procedure. In the ClientWndProc procedure, you sort through the messages and respond to the ones you want to, then pass the remaining messages to the client window's normal WndProc. Incidentally, if you have a need to respond to other client window messages, you could add them to ClientWndProc.

When a wm_EraseBkgnd message is received in ClientWndProc, the appropriate procedure is called to paint the client window. In this case MainForm's Tag property is used to identify the desired type of wallpaper so it could be chosen at design time using the Object Inspector. If you have another need for Tag, you can certainly find another way of keeping track of the wallpaper type. Setting Msg.Result to 1 tells Windows that we have handled the message. If a message other than wm_EraseBkgnd is received, it is passed on to the client window's normal WndProc using the CallWindowProc API function in the Default procedure.

The paint procedures included use normal GDI calls instead of the VCL. This is because the client window does not have an associated VCL object and therefore does not have a Canvas property.

Note: The paint procedures are good examples that you can build upon if you want to.

Comments

This How-To demonstrates the power of Delphi. Even though the designers of Delphi did not give us direct access to the client window, you can work around this limitation with relative ease using object-oriented techniques and Windows API calls. Accomplishing the same thing in a language such as Visual Basic would be impossible without using a control written in another language such as C/C++ (or Delphi!). By the way, this project was designed to be used as a template. You can replace the existing MDI template in the Gallery, or add it in addition to the existing MDI template (you'll probably have to change the file names to prevent overwriting the other MDI template in this case).

You may want to enhance the painting of the MDI child icons to make the transparent truly invisible. In order to do this, you will have to respond to the wm_IconEraseBkgnd message in the TMDIChild class. This How-To simply allows the MDI child's inherited WMIconEraseBkGnd method to paint a solid color in the transparent area of the icon.

2

2

STANDARD COMPONENTS

How do I...

2.1 Make custom check boxes that use both mouse buttons

2.2 Add automatically sized and placed controls at run time

2.3 Run multiple copies of the same program with unique captions

2.4 Create a dynamic list box that "best matches" user input

2.5 Make a text button with a streaming banner

2.6 Customize a window's title bar with graphics

2.7 Implement a splitter bar to resize controls dynamically

2.8 Use drag-and-drop to move items from one list box to another

2.9 Add copy/cut/paste/undo support to list boxes

2.10 Add a horizontal scroll bar to a list box

Delphi comes with a tremendous feature set right out of the box, but there are a number of capabilities that are not standard features of Delphi's off-the-shelf components. This chapter shows you how to enhance the power of several classes of Delphi objects, ranging from text buttons to list boxes. It also covers special features for dynamically creating controls, accessing the Windows task list, and putting a graphic image in the non-client area of a form.

2.1 Make custom check boxes that use both mouse buttons

Commercial Windows applications often enhance the visual appearance of the standard check boxes and radio buttons. This How-To demonstrates a check box that uses 3D bitmaps combined with left and right mouse button functionality.

2.2 Add automatically sized and placed controls at run time

It can be useful for your application to create its controls at run time, rather than design time, and user input may play a role. This How-To shows the method to create unlimited text buttons at run time based on user input, and assign their event handlers to preset methods.

2.3 Run multiple copies of the same program with unique captions

While many applications can have only one instance running at a time, some (like Notepad) allow multiple copies to be in use simultaneously. It can be helpful for users to know which window is running which copy of the application. This How-To details a way to use information from the Windows task list to place a unique identifier for each copy of a program in its caption bar.

2.4 Create a dynamic list box that "best matches" user input

Sophisticated applications have linked edit controls that allow list boxes to skip their current selection and choose a "best match" to users' input as they type. This How-To shows how to use the Windows API to achieve this effect in your applications.

2.5 Make a text button with a streaming banner

Controls available from third-party developers feature windows with text that "crawls" across like a bulletin on a television screen. This How-To uses Delphi's ProcessMessages method in combination with simple string manipulation to duplicate the text banner effect.

2.6 Customize a window's title bar with graphics

Normally your application cannot have graphics on its non-client areas, such as the title bar. This How-To shows the trick to overcome this limitation, putting a real-time clock display in the title bar of a Delphi form without altering the caption text.

2.7 Implement a splitter bar to resize controls dynamically

File Manager allows users to dynamically resize the two list boxes in its display, and even has a nice cursor that appears over the line used to drag the resize control. This

How-To reproduces this effect using a Delphi panel control and the PatBlt Windows API function.

2.8 Use drag-and-drop to move items from one list box to another

In many commercial applications users can drag-and-drop information with the mouse. This How-To will implement this functionality using two list boxes to demonstrate the issues involved in maintaining data consistency.

2.9 Add copy/cut/paste/undo support to list boxes

Delphi's Textedit form implements the useful editing functions, cut, copy, paste, and undo for text controls. This How-To expands these capabilities into list boxes, demonstrating the use of the StringList object's built-in methods.

2.10 Add a horizontal scroll bar to a list box

Delphi's list box components do not have a property that supports a horizontal scroll bar. This How-To shows a workaround using a Windows API list box control message to provide this functionality.

2.1 How do I... Make custom check boxes that use both mouse buttons?

COMPLEXITY: EASY

Problem

Professional programs often change the default appearance of check boxes to something more sophisticated. Can I do this in Delphi?

Technique

You can easily create your own check box controls in Delphi using panels and image controls. In this How-To you will create a futuristic "light button" set of check boxes, which also respond to right as well as left mouse button clicks.

Steps

Run CUSTCHEK.EXE. You will see a display similar to Figure 2-1. Click on any green light with the left mouse button and it will turn gray; click again and it will turn green like a normal check box. But click on either color with the right button

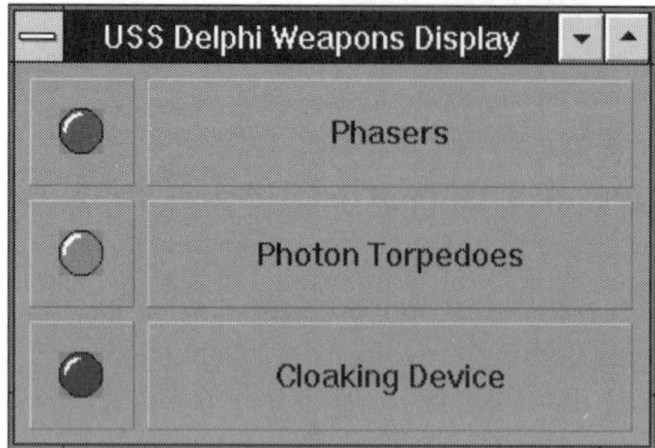

Figure 2-1 CUSTCHEK at run time with custom bitmaps for check boxes

and it will turn red. Click again and gray will reappear. (Note that a red button will not respond to left button clicks.)

1. Create a new blank project and name it CUSTCHEK.DPR. Name the unit BULBCHEK.PAS.
2. Add components to Form1 and set their properties as shown in Table 2-1.

Note: The three TImage components go inside the first three TPanel components; this is important so that they display correctly.

Table 2-1 Components, properties, and settings for Form1 in CUSTCHEK

COMPONENT	PROPERTY	SETTING
Form1	Type	Application Main Form
	Width	354
	Height	235
	Left	40
	Top	29
	Caption	USS Delphi Weapons Display
Panel1	Type	TPanel
	Left	8
	Top	8
	Width	57
	Height	57
	Caption	(blank)

COMPONENT	PROPERTY	SETTING
Panel2	Type	TPanel
	Left	8
	Top	72
	Width	57
	Height	57
	Caption	(blank)
Panel3	Type	TPanel
	Left	8
	Top	136
	Width	57
	Height	57
	Caption	(blank)
Panel4	Type	TPanel
	Left	72
	Top	8
	Width	265
	Height	57
	Caption	Phasers
Panel5	Type	TPanel
	Left	72
	Top	72
	Width	265
	Height	57
	Caption	Photon Torpedoes
Panel6	Type	TPanel
	Left	72
	Top	136
	Width	265
	Height	57
	Caption	Cloaking Device
Image1	Type	TImage
	Left	16
	Top	16
	Width	25
	Height	25
	Picture	'GrnChek.Bmp'

continued on next page

continued from previous page

COMPONENT	PROPERTY	SETTING
Image2	Type	TImage
	Left	16
	Top	16
	Width	25
	Height	25
	Picture	'NonChek.Bmp'
Image3	Type	TImage
	Left	16
	Top	16
	Width	25
	Height	25
	Picture	'RedChek.Bmp'

3. Select the OnCreate event of Form1 and enter the following code to initialize the application.

```
procedure TForm1.FormCreate(Sender: TObject);
begin
{ Create the three bitmaps to hold button images }
  RedBmp := TBitmap.Create;
  GreenBmp := TBitmap.Create;
  GrayBmp := TBitmap.Create;
  { Load the three images }
  RedBmp.LoadFromFile( 'RedChek.Bmp' );
  GreenBmp.LoadFromFile( 'GrnChek.Bmp' );
  GrayBmp.LoadFromFile( 'NonChek.Bmp' );
  { Set a spread of states for the demo }
  CB1State := 1;
  CB2State := 0;
  CB3State := -1;
end;
```

4. While still in the Code Editor, move up to the *var* keyword and type in the following helper variables to hold the custom bitmaps and check box state data.

```
var
  Form1: TForm1;
{ These variable hold bitmap information for the buttons }
  RedBmp ,
  GreenBmp ,
  GrayBmp     : TBitmap;
  { These variables hold state information for the buttons }
  CB1State ,
  CB2State ,
  CB3State    : Integer;
```

5. Select the OnMouseDown event handler of Panel1. Enter the function shown in the following listing. Do the same for Panel2 and Panel3. These event handlers create the pressed-in appearance of a selected check box while the mouse button is down.

```
procedure TForm1.Panel1MouseDown(Sender: TObject; Button: TMouseButton;
  Shift: TShiftState; X, Y: Integer);
begin
  { Set the outer bevel of the two panels to lowered to }
  { simulate being depressed by the mouse click        }
  Panel1.BevelOuter := bvLowered;
  Panel4.BevelOuter := bvLowered;
end;
procedure TForm1.Panel2MouseDown(Sender: TObject; Button: TMouseButton;
  Shift: TShiftState; X, Y: Integer);
begin
  { Set the outer bevel of the two panels to lowered to }
  { simulate being depressed by the mouse click        }
  Panel2.BevelOuter := bvLowered;
  Panel5.BevelOuter := bvLowered;
end;

procedure TForm1.Panel3MouseDown(Sender: TObject; Button: TMouseButton;
  Shift: TShiftState; X, Y: Integer);
begin
  { Set the outer bevel of the two panels to lowered to }
  { simulate being depressed by the mouse click        }
  Panel3.BevelOuter := bvLowered;
  Panel6.BevelOuter := bvLowered;
end;
```

6. Back in the Object Inspector, select the three TImage components and set their OnMouseDown properties to those of their respective panels. Then select the OnMouseUp event handlers for each of the three panels and enter the following code. Finally, select the TImage OnMouseUp event handlers and make them the same as their panels' again.

```
procedure TForm1.Panel1MouseUp(Sender: TObject; Button: TMouseButton;
  Shift: TShiftState; X, Y: Integer);
begin
  { Set the outer bevel of the two panels to raised to }
  { simulate being raised by the mouse release        }
  Panel1.BevelOuter := bvRaised;
  Panel4.BevelOuter := bvRaised;
  { If the button is the left button }
  if Button = mbLeft then
  begin
    case CB1State of
      { If previously grayed return to green }
      0 : begin
            Image1.Picture.Bitmap := GreenBmp;
            CB1State := 1;
          end;
      { Otherwise set to gray }
```

continued on next page

continued from previous page

```
      1 : begin
            Image1.Picture.Bitmap := GrayBmp;
            CB1State := 0;
          end;
    end;
  end
  else
  begin
    { the button is the right button }
    case CB1State of
      { If the button was previously red set to gray }
      -1 : begin
            Image1.Picture.Bitmap := GrayBmp;
            CB1State := 0;
          end;
      { If the button was previously green or gray set to red }
      0 : begin
            Image1.Picture.Bitmap := RedBmp;
            CB1State := -1;
          end;
      1 : begin
            Image1.Picture.Bitmap := RedBmp;
            CB1State := -1;
          end;
    end;
  end;
end;
procedure TForm1.Panel2MouseUp(Sender: TObject; Button: TMouseButton;
  Shift: TShiftState; X, Y: Integer);
begin
  { Set the outer bevel of the two panels to raised to }
  { simulate being raised by the mouse release        }
  Panel2.BevelOuter := bvRaised;
  Panel5.BevelOuter := bvRaised;
  { If the button is the left button }
  if Button = mbLeft then
  begin
    case CB2State of
      { If previously grayed return to green }
      0 : begin
            Image2.Picture.Bitmap := GreenBmp;
            CB2State := 1;
          end;
      { Otherwise set to gray }
      1 : begin
            Image2.Picture.Bitmap := GrayBmp;
            CB2State := 0;
          end;
    end;
  end
  else
  begin
    { the button is the right button }
    case CB2State of
      { If the button was previously red set to gray }
```

```
      -1 : begin
             Image2.Picture.Bitmap := GrayBmp;
             CB2State := 0;
           end;
      { If the button was previously green or gray set to red }
      0 : begin
             Image2.Picture.Bitmap := RedBmp;
             CB2State := -1;
           end;
      1 : begin
             Image2.Picture.Bitmap := RedBmp;
             CB2State := -1;
           end;
    end;
  end;
end;

procedure TForm1.Panel3MouseUp(Sender: TObject; Button: TMouseButton;
  Shift: TShiftState; X, Y: Integer);
begin
  { Set the outer bevel of the two panels to raised to }
  { simulate being raised by the mouse release         }
  Panel3.BevelOuter := bvRaised;
  Panel6.BevelOuter := bvRaised;
  { If the button is the left button }
  if Button = mbLeft then
  begin
    case CB3State of
      { If previously grayed return to green }
      0 : begin
             Image3.Picture.Bitmap := GreenBmp;
             CB3State := 1;
           end;
      { Otherwise set to gray }
      1 : begin
             Image3.Picture.Bitmap := GrayBmp;
             CB3State := 0;
           end;
    end;
  end
  else
  begin
    { the button is the right button }
    case CB3State of
      { If the button was previously red set to gray }
      -1 : begin
             Image3.Picture.Bitmap := GrayBmp;
             CB3State := 0;
           end;
      { If the button was previously green or gray set to red }
      0 : begin
             Image3.Picture.Bitmap := RedBmp;
             CB3State := -1;
           end;
      1 : begin
```

continued on next page

continued from previous page

```
            Image3.Picture.Bitmap := RedBmp;
            CB3State := -1;
          end;
    end;
  end;
end;
```

7. Compile and test the project.

How It Works

This How-To makes use of the ability to easily change the picture element displayed by a Delphi TImage control. All three images needed for the state changes are stored in TBitmap controls for later use. The panels' BevelOuter property is inverted whenever the mouse is down (regardless of which button is pressed). This inverts the bevel colors to simulate pushing in the check box. When the mouse is released, the BevelOuter property is reset, and the check box appears to push back out.

The response of these custom check boxes is determined by both the state of the check box and which mouse button is clicked. Left clicks flip a check box state to green or gray, but never red. Right clicks switch between gray and red. As a final chrome element, a left click on a red check box is ignored.

This system is possible because the TImage component can accept any TBitmap object as its Picture property's Bitmap property setting. Together with the mouse message control Delphi offers, this allows you to create custom controls of any desired complexity.

Another point worth commenting on is the way in which Delphi automatically dereferences pointers. Almost all Delphi components and their properties and methods exist as pointers; in standard Pascal, this would require using the ^ operator. As an example, the following line of code would read:

```
Image3^.Picture^.Bitmap^ := RedBmp;
```

under standard Pascal (although in fact there is more complexity involving components and properties going on behind the scenes, so that pure Pascal code isn't exactly equivalent.) Instead it reads:

```
Image3.Picture.Bitmap := RedBmp;
```

To avoid unnecessary complexity, the compiler allows using pointers directly; handling the conversion from pointers to actual objects or other data types behind the scenes. This makes Delphi code much more readable.

Comments

For simplicity, this How-To used separate panels to demonstrate the custom control concepts. You can design a more sophisticated version that has all the built-in properties of the standard check box control, as well as considerable added functionality.

This is demonstrated in the file CUCBDEMO.EXE in the shareware section of the CD which you'll find it in the DEMOS\CIUPKC\CUCHEKBX directory. There are numerous other component demos in the CIUPKE directory.

2.2 How do I... Add automatically sized and placed controls at run time?

COMPLEXITY: INTERMEDIATE

Problem

Sometimes I need to create controls in response to changing runtime conditions. Is there a way in Delphi to add controls at run time and set their properties dynamically?

Technique

Perhaps the single most powerful feature of Delphi is its ability to create all of its visual elements as coded components at run time, complete with properties (including methods). In this How-To you will create a simple text button generator to illustrate this capability.

Steps

Run RUNTIMCT.EXE. Type some text in the edit control and then press the button. Do this several times, and you will see a display similar to Figure 2-2. Pressing any of the new buttons will close the form.

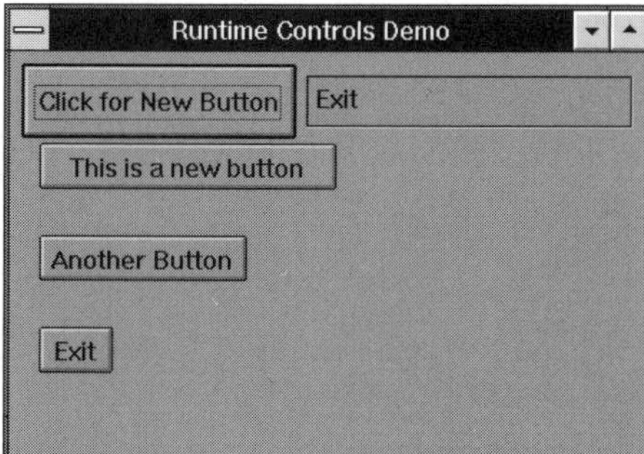

Figure 2-2 RUNTIMCT at run time showing user-created text buttons

1. Create a new blank project and name it RUNTIMCT.DPR. Name the unit RTCONTS.PAS.
2. Add components to Form1 and set their properties as shown in Table 2-2.

Table 2-2 Components, properties, and settings for Form1 in RUNTIMCT

COMPONENT	PROPERTY	SETTING
Form1	Type	Application Main Form
	Width	435
	Height	300
	Left	37
	Top	31
	Caption	Run-Time Controls Demo
Button1	Type	TButton
	Left	8
	Top	8
	Width	185
	Height	49
	Caption	Click For New Button
Edit1	Type	TEdit
	Left	200
	Top	16
	Width	217
	Height	33
	Text	(blank)

3. Select the OnClick event of Button1 and enter the following code to create a new text button.

```
procedure TForm1.Button1Click(Sender: TObject);
var TheNewButton :TButton;
begin
  { Create the new button using the object type as source }
  { and the current form as the owner                     }
  TheNewButton := TButton.Create( Self );
  { Set up the left and top parameters }
  TheNewButton.Left := 20;
  TheNewButton.Top := Counter_Top;
Counter_Top := Counter_Top + 60;
  { Set the caption with the text from the edit control }
  TheNewButton.Caption := Edit1.Text;
TheNewButton.Height := 30;
  { Set the width parameter based on length of the edit string }
  TheNewButton.Width := ( Length(TheNewButton.Caption) * 10 );
  { If the string is too short or empty, set a minimum width }
  if TheNewButton.Width < 50 then TheNewButton.Width := 50;
  { Set the parent value for the new control to the current form }
  TheNewButton.Parent := Self;
  { Add the default handler procedure to the OnClick method }
  TheNewButton.OnClick := AssignedClick;
end;
```

4. While in the Code Editor, move up to the *public* keyword and enter the following assistant procedure declaration. Then go down to the *var* keyword and add a helper variable.

```
public
    { Public declarations }
procedure AssignedClick(Sender: TObject );
  end;

var
  Form1: TForm1;
Counter_Top : Integer;
```

5. Move down under the *implementation* keyword and type in this helper procedure code:

```
procedure TForm1.AssignedClick(Sender: TObject);
begin
  Close;
end;
```

6. Finally, select the OnCreate event in the Object Inspector and add the following code to initialize the helper variable.

```
procedure TForm1.FormCreate(Sender: TObject);
begin
  { Set the default value for the new windows vertical position }
  Counter_Top := 60;
end;
```

7. Compile and test the project.

How It Works

A detailed look at the button creation procedure illustrates the tremendous power that Delphi gives programmers by allowing all of its components to be created and manipulated at run time. Let's start with the following line:

```
TheNewButton := TButton.Create( Self );
```

An important consideration for this line of code is that the new button is created with the method introduced in Borland Pascal 7.0 of making a call to the type name of the object rather than calling the New function. Thus a line of code like this,

```
TheNewButton.Create( Self );
```

would result in a runtime GPF because TheNewButton has not been allocated a memory location and would thus be an invalid address.

Use of the Self variable is also important. Every object in Delphi created from Tobject has a variable Self, which contains a pointer to the object for internal use.

Here, it tells the system to mark TheNewButton as being owned by the object whose procedure was active when the Create method was called, in this case the Form1 object of the application. This is vital to make sure Delphi handles cleanup of the new object — such as deallocating memory and releasing Windows resources—when the program closes. If an application that continually causes resource leakage is written in Delphi, it should be checked to make sure a valid owner variable is passed to every runtime Create call.

The following program lines show the manner in which any available property in the Object Inspector can be initialized at run time, either with an explicit value or through a type-compatible variable.

```
TheNewButton.Left := 20;
TheNewButton.Top := Counter_Top;
TheNewButton.Height := 30;
```

In this next line, the new button's Caption property is assigned to the Text property of the edit control. This illustrates how any two accessible properties of objects that are base-type compatible can be assigned directly to one another — a powerful capability.

```
TheNewButton.Caption := Edit1.Text;
```

The following code shows that properties can also be given values based on attributes of other properties, and manipulated in normal logical expressions, such as *if . . . then . . . else.*

```
TheNewButton.Width := ( Length(TheNewButton.Caption) * 10 );
if TheNewButton.Width < 50 then TheNewButton.Width := 50;
```

This line is of critical importance:

```
TheNewButton.Parent := Self;
```

Again the Self variable is used, but this time to assign to the Parent property. This assignment places the new button in the Controls array of the parent object, in this case the main form of the application. This placement makes sure it is redrawn whenever the main form needs to repaint itself, and also puts the button in the control hierarchy for message passing and focus shifting. This is particularly important because if a component's Parent property is not set to a valid object name, the component will never be visible on the screen!

Here is perhaps the single most important section of the code:

```
TheNewButton.OnClick := AssignedClick;
```

In it a method that serves as an event handler, namely OnClick, is assigned another method name, AssignedClick. AssignedClick is a method created by the programmer at design time, but OnClick is a built-in part of the button object. Delphi has performed, behind the scenes, the necessary conversion of pointer information to reassign the procedure address of OnClick for the new button to that of the user-entered AssignedClick procedure. The net effect is that functions and procedures that are methods of a TObject object can be assigned to one another, within compatibility limits, just like variables.

Comments

According to Pat Richie, a member of Borland's TeamB development group, the Delphi compiler was written in pure assembly code while all the rest was developed in Object Pascal. Delphi's object-oriented underpinnings are evidenced by the Object Inspector's ability to display user-written property editors, such as the one developed in Chapter 12 of this book. Examination of the VCL source code confirms that except for a few assembly language procedures, almost all of the standard components are also written in Object Pascal. And as noted in the documentation, Delphi has fully implemented facilities to display and use components developed by end users. Eventually, if Borland makes the appropriate specifications available, third-party developers could add modules directly to Delphi itself, further extending its already considerable functionality.

2.3 How do I...
Run multiple copies of the same program with unique captions?

COMPLEXITY: EASY

Problem

When users run multiple copies of my application, is there some way to help them keep track of which copy a given window is displaying?

Technique

Windows keeps track of how many copies of a given program are running at once. You can obtain this information via the Windows API and modify each copy of a program at run time accordingly.

Steps

Run TASKADD.EXE. Type some text in the edit control and then press the button. Then start another copy of TASKADD.EXE and perform a similar action; you'll see a display something like Figure 2-3. Notice the different numbers in the caption bars of the two instances.

1. Create a new blank project and name it TASKADD.DPR. Name the unit TASKLIST.PAS.

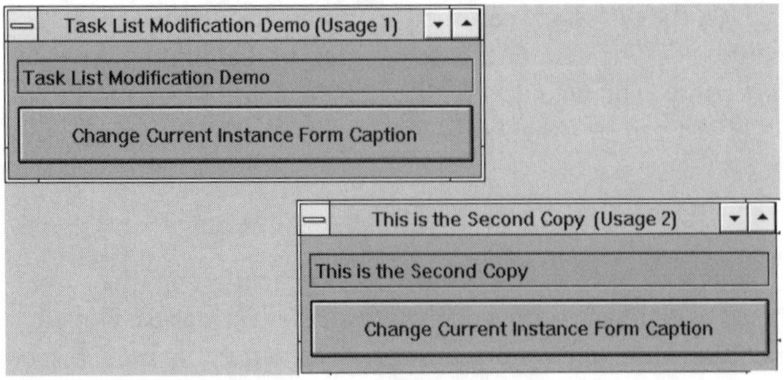

Figure 2-3 TASKADD at run time displaying two unique caption bars with identifying instance numbers

2. Add components to Form1 and set their properties as shown in Table 2-3.

Table 2-3 Components, properties, and settings for Form1 in TASKADD

COMPONENT	PROPERTY	SETTING
Form1	Type	Application Main Form
	Width	431
	Height	153
	Left	43
	Top	15
	Caption	Form1
Button1	Type	TButton
	Left	8
	Top	56
	Width	409
	Height	49
	Caption	Change Current Instance Form Caption
Edit1	Type	TEdit
	Left	8
	Top	16
	Width	409
	Height	29
	Text	Task List Modification Demo

3. This program has a single procedure. Select the OnClick event handler for the Button1 component and add the following code, which will create a unique caption for each copy of the running application.

```
procedure TForm1.Button1Click(Sender: TObject);
var TheHandle : THandle;
TheString ,
    OtherString : String;
TheUsage   : Integer;
TheWindowHandle : hWnd;
ThePChar : array[ 0 .. 79 ] of char;
begin
  { TheHandle is used to hold the windows internal variable }
  { for the current instance of the program                 }
  TheHandle := GetModuleHandle( 'TaskAdd.Exe' );
  { TheUsage is used to hold the total copies of the program }
  { currently running                                         }
  TheUsage := GetModuleUsage( TheHandle );
TheString := Edit1.Text;
Str( TheUsage , OtherString );
TheString := TheString + ' (Usage ' +
   OtherString + ')';
  { TheWindowHandle is used to hold the internal id of the }
  { parent window for the application's main form. This is }
  { not needed in Delphi but would be in Visual Basic       }
  TheWindowHandle := GetWindow(Handle , GW_OWNER );
StrPCopy( ThePChar , TheString );
  { And put it into the window caption bar }
  SetWindowText( TheWindowHandle , ThePChar );
  Caption := TheString;
end;
```

4. Compile and test the project.

How It Works

To understand how this application works, you must understand two important Windows concepts: the window and the handle.

Windows got its name from the element it uses to display information on the screen and keep track of its internal bookkeeping. As far as Windows is concerned, any visual object that can receive the input focus is a window, to which Windows devotes a substantial amount of system resources and information. Nonwindowed items such as timers cannot receive input focus, and so do not have the underlying complexity needed to send and receive Windows messages. (In Delphi, such items can receive Windows messages via the Delphi message-passing facilities, but Windows itself is completely ignorant of this.)

Handles are numbers representing nonwindowed items and other elements to programs that want to interact with them via the Windows operating system. There are many flavors of handles, all representing a class of data that Windows knows how to manipulate. Delphi's Object Pascal has created types for most of the Windows handles, all based on the generic Thandle type, and all coercible from it. The most common handle used by programmers is the hWnd type, or window handle; the Handle property of most Delphi windowed controls is of this type.

The application in this How-To calls two API functions that require handles to do their work. The first is:

```
TheHandle := GetModuleHandle( 'TaskAdd.Exe' );
```

The GetModuleHandle function returns a Thandle type that internally identifies the current instance of the named executable file. Notice that no directory information is needed to make this function call. The returned Thandle item does not need to be coerced to anything, because the second function called accepts this data type as its parameter:

```
TheUsage := GetModuleUsage( TheHandle );
```

The returned Thandle is sent to the GetModuleUsage function. This is the API function that returns the total number of copies of a given module, or executable program, which are in use at a given time.

Note: It is possible to prevent having multiple copies of a given program running at the same time; see the "Comments" section.

Having obtained the information needed to uniquely identify a given copy of a running program, the application next needs to access the specific window element that contains the currently displayed form. To do this, another API function is called:

```
TheWindowHandle := GetWindow( Form1.Handle , GW_OWNER );
```

TheWindowHandle is of type hWnd; it receives the handle to the owner window of the current form, as indicated by the style parameter GW_OWNER. You might wonder why this is necessary, since normally the handle to a given window is present directly in the VCL. The reason is that, similar to Visual Basic, the Delphi Application object creates an invisible window (its size set to 0) and creates all other windows from this. Thus there is need to obtain the real owner of the window in question, namely the Application one.

With the hWnd to the form's application main window available, the next API call sets its internal caption data:

```
SetWindowText( TheWindowHandle , ThePChar );
```

ThePChar is the caption text in a Windows ASCIIZ format. A final call is then made to the Delphi Caption property with an Object Pascal string containing the same information.

Comments

At first this may seem a trivial exercise, given that the application doesn't do anything but identify multiple copies of the program. But consider the value of having an exact user ID for each copy of a running program on a networked system. You could flag changes to a data file, for example, and thus attribute them to a specific user or machine. A password program could keep track of exactly which copy in the calling sequence entered which password to detect break-in attempts.

An interesting exercise for Delphi programmers is to duplicate the ability of Borland Pascal 7.0 Object Windows Library (OWL) program to prevent multiple copies of itself from running. The key in OWL lies in the difference between InitApplication, which is called only once for a given program in a Windows session as long as the program runs, and InitMainWindow, which is called each time the program is run, even if multiple copies are running. By placing a control variable in an overridden version of the InitApplication method and then calling the inherited InitApplication method, a program could check this variable in the InitMainWindow method and call Halt if another copy was already in use.

Delphi has equivalent functionality; Chapter 7 includes a How-To that describes how to use it.

Finally, let's examine a couple of points about Delphi's automation of Windows API functionality. The call to GetModuleHandle isn't technically necessary, since all Delphi applications have a variable called hInstance which holds this value automatically. Also, by entering this line of code:

```
Application.Title := Caption;
```

you avoid having to manually call SetWindowText with the new caption, because changing the Title property of the Application object does this automatically.

2.4 How do I...
Create a dynamic list box that "best matches" user input?

COMPLEXITY: EASY

Problem

Commercial applications often have an edit control paired with a list box; when the user types in the edit control, the list box selection moves to the closest match in its list. Does Delphi have a way to duplicate this functionality?

Technique

On the surface this seems a trivial problem, but in fact it is rather subtle. You can use the SendMessage function to link an edit control with a list box while avoiding a potentially fatal "infinite loop" problem.

Steps

Run LISTSRCH.EXE. You'll see a set of files from the directory where Delphi starts the program. Start typing in the edit control, and the list box selects the closest matching file to what you've typed, even if you backspace. An example is shown in Figure 2-4.

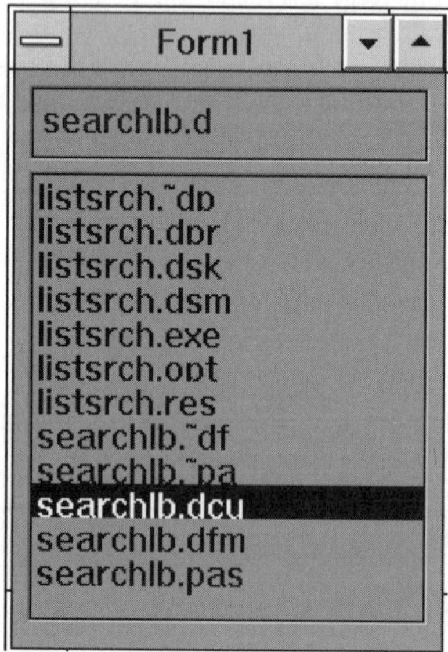

Figure 2-4 LISTSRCH at run time showing a best-match selection to the user input

1. Create a new blank project and name it LISTSRCH.DPR. Name the unit SEARCHLB.PAS.

2. Add components to Form1 and set their properties as shown in Table 2-4.

Table 2-4 Components, properties, and settings for Form1 of LISTSRCH

COMPONENT	PROPERTY	SETTING
Form1	Type	Application Main Form
	Width	217
	Height	305
	Left	54
	Top	25
	Caption	Form1
FileListBox1	Type	TFileListBox
	Left	8
	Top	48
	Width	193
	Height	209
Edit1	Type	TEdit
	Left	8
	Top	8
	Width	193
	Height	33
	Text	(blank)

3. Select the OnClick event handler of the FileListBox1 component and type the following code into the Code Editor. This places the current selection from the list box into the edit control.

```
procedure TForm1.FileListBox1Click(Sender: TObject);
begin
{ When a file is selected in the filelist put it in }
  { the edit control                                  }
  Edit1.Text := FileListBox1.Items[ FileListBox1.ItemIndex ];
end;
```

4. Choose the OnChange event handler and add these program lines, which allow updating the list box selection without causing an endless loop.

```
procedure TForm1.Edit1Change(Sender: TObject);
var ThePChar : array[0..79] of char;
TheString : String;
TheIndex ,
TheError : Integer;
begin
TheString := Edit1.Text;
If TheString  '' then
  begin
    { Turn the string into a windows text format }
```

continued on next page

continued from previous page

```
    StrPCopy( ThePChar , TheString );
    { Put the closest matching index of the listbox into TheIndex }
    { via the LB_SELECTSTRING message                             }
    TheIndex := SendMessage( FileListBox1.Handle ,
                LB_SELECTSTRING , 65535 , Longint( @ThePChar ));
    { Tell the listbox to reset itself to the matching item }
    TheError := SendMessage( FileListBox1.Handle ,
                LB_SETTOPINDEX , TheIndex , 0 );
  end
  else
  begin
    { Otherwise tell the listbox to reset itself to no item }
    TheError := SendMessage( FileListBox1.Handle ,
                LB_SETCURSEL , 65535 , 0 );
    TheError := SendMessage( FileListBox1.Handle ,
                LB_SETTOPINDEX , 0 , 0 );
  end;
end;
```

5. Compile and test the project.

How It Works

The most intuitive way to solve the problem in this How-To would be to use a simple search loop against the contents of the list box and set its selection manually. But since you also want to have the edit control show the name of a user-selected file in the list box, this presents a subtle problem. Setting the selection of a list box in Delphi produces a message equivalent to making a selection with the mouse. In the intuitive scheme, this would trigger a call to reset the edit control's text. Since changing the edit control's text would then cause a new search to be made, the entire application would lock up in an "infinite loop"!

Instead, this How-To uses some built-in Windows functionality of list boxes to set their selection internally. The first call,

```
TheIndex := SendMessage( FileListBox1.Handle , LB_SELECTSTRING ,
65535 , Longint( @ThePChar ));
```

uses the Handle property of the list box to send it a Windows message:

```
LB_SELECTSTRING
```

Along with this message, the next parameter is set to the value 65535. What you really want here is to send a -1 to the list box, but the parameter type is Word, which in the strongly typed Pascal language won't accept a negative number. The number 65535 works because, in the binary representation used by the computer for signed integers, a highest bit set to 1 indicates a negative value. The number 65535 is just high enough to set the highest order bit to 1, and thus becomes -1 to the Windows system.

The last parameter is even more unusual. It requires obtaining the memory address of the variable ThePChar (which is a pointer to a small array of characters ending in a null character) and then making a typecast to send it as a Longint. This is necessary because of the general nature of the Windows messaging system and the fact that it is written in C, which is much less strongly typed than Pascal, and allows passing parameters much more freely. What Windows really wants in the last parameter space is a four-byte number that can represent anything. It is up to the recipient of the message to determine what information was actually sent to it.

The LB_SELECTSTRING message is the key to this entire How-To. A check of the Windows API references shows that this message causes a list box to search its entries starting just after the value sent in the word parameter *wparam*, unless the entry is -1, in which case all entries in the list box are searched. Depending on the style of the list box, the search is made against either an ASCIIZ string in the *lparam* value, as in this example, or against an absolute 32-bit value for nontext list boxes with unique identifiers for each entry. The message returns either the 0-based index of the first entry in the list box, which contains all of the search text, or an error message. Since C is case sensitive, the search is case sensitive.

The second SendMessage call,

```
TheError := SendMessage( FileListBox1.Handle , LB_SETTOPINDEX , TheIndex , 0 );
```

again uses the Handle of the list box. But this time it sends the LB_SETTOPINDEX message, along with the value TheIndex returned from the first SendMessage call, and an empty parameter in the *lparam* position. This message causes the list box to make the entry specified in the *wparam* position the first visible entry in its window, and selects it as well, but without sending a selection message that would cause an endless loop.

The How-To also deals with the possibility that no text is entered in the edit control, due to user deletion of previous text. In this case, a previous selection in the list box must be removed. This call to the API,

```
TheError := SendMessage( FileListBox1.Handle,LB_SETCURSEL ,65535 ,       0 );
```

calls SendMessage with the LB_SETCURSEL message along with a faked -1 and 0 parameters. This tells the list box to reset its current selection to none, due to the -1 entry in the *wparam* field. The next call,

```
TheError := SendMessage( FileListBox1.Handle , LB_SETTOPINDEX , 0 ,      0 );
```

tells the list box to move its top visible entry back to the first one, which is useful for list boxes with numerous entries.

Note: In several cases, the SendMessage calls returned error values. This How-To did not use the error codes, but a more robust application could produce dialog boxes to inform users of invalid actions. List box error codes are either *lb_err*, which is a generic error code, or *lb_errspace*, which indicates the list box is out of memory and cannot perform the requested operation.

Comments

The SendMessage Windows API function is one of the most powerful available to Delphi programmers. It has several advantages, and some drawbacks.

The advantages of SendMessage are that it can target a specific Windows element, identified by its Handle property, and can then use a wide range of message-based commands to send or receive data, change the appearance or state of the target object, and produce other messages either to the sender or other Windows objects. Also, SendMessage can be called with user-defined messages, allowing virtually unlimited control over program behavior. Due to the generic nature of the *wparam* and *lparam* fields, pointers can be coerced into these fields and sent, allowing the recipient to obtain a pointer to any VCL object desired.

The drawbacks to SendMessage are that it effectively suspends processing by the calling procedure, until the called object returns a value at the end of its response method. In addition, if either the calling or sending object becomes invalid before the SendMessage call returns (such as in a Destroy call), Windows will signal a GPF. This behavior is not well documented in either Borland Pascal or Delphi, and can be the cause of considerable frustration.

Another Windows API function, PostMessage, gets around both of these drawbacks. It puts the message on the global Windows message queue, and if the sender or target handle has become invalid, merely disposes of the message without fuss. There are two caveats to using PostMessage: The message must be in the WM_XXX range, which is not clearly spelled out in the Delphi documentation; and due to the cyclical nature of message processing in Windows, it is difficult to predict, much less guarantee a time of execution for the posted message. If the response method must act at a given point in the program, SendMessage is a better choice.

Note: If you need more information on Windows messaging, or on the Windows API generally, *Windows API Bible* (Waite Group Press) is an excellent reference.

2.5 How do I... Make a text button with a streaming banner?

COMPLEXITY: INTERMEDIATE

Problem

Third-party control libraries offer text displays that crawl across the screen, similar to the bulletins you see on television. Is there a way to do this in Delphi?

Technique

There are two issues involved in creating a streaming text banner. First, you need to manipulate strings to loop the desired text back on itself. Then you create a loop that does not lock all other Windows applications out of the system while it is running. Delphi provides excellent string handling routines, and the ProcessMessages function permits a loop to run continuously in the background.

Steps

Run STREAMER.EXE. You'll see a display similar to Figure 2-5. Press the button and the text will start streaming to the left; press it again and the text will freeze. With the button running, activate another program (Notepad, for example). Notice that you can continue to type text into Notepad while the banner moves across the button.

1. Create a new blank project and name it STREAMER.DPR. Name the unit STRM-BUTN.PAS.

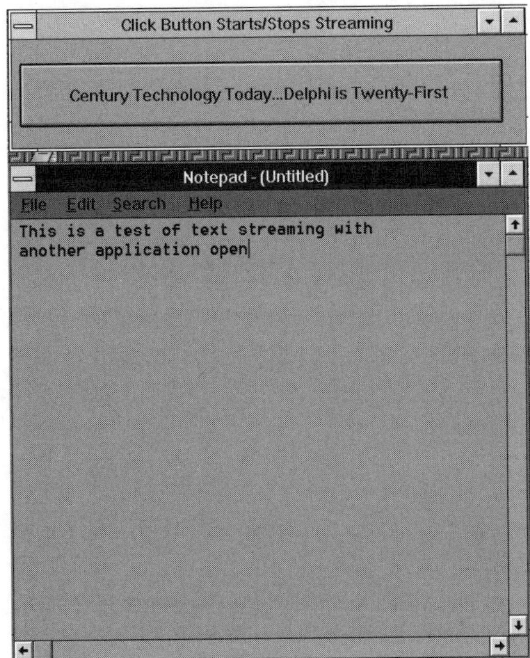

Figure 2-5 STREAMER at run time showing Notepad open while text streams across the button

2. Add components to Form1 and set their properties as shown in Table 2-5.

Table 2-5 Components, properties, and settings for Form1 in STREAMER

COMPONENT	PROPERTY	SETTING
Form1	Type	Application Main Form
	Width	544
	Height	145
	Left	44
	Top	14
	Caption	Click Button Starts/Stops Streaming
Button1	Type	TButton
	Left	8
	Top	24
	Width	505
	Height	65
	Caption	(blank)

3. Select the OnClick event handler of Button1 and type in the following code to toggle the banner effect on the text button.

```
procedure TForm1.Button1Click(Sender: TObject);
begin
{ Flip the state of the NowStreaming variable }
  NowStreaming := not NowStreaming;
  { If now streaming call DoTheStream to lock in endless loop }
  if NowStreaming then DoTheStream;
end;
```

4. While still in the Code Editor, move up to the *private* keyword and add the following code. This allows Delphi to recognize the assistant procedure and function that you will enter in a moment.

```
private
    { Private declarations }
function GetWrappedString( TheIndex : Integer ) : String;
procedure DoTheStream;
```

5. Move down to the *var* keyword and add these helper variables to hold the text string, its current wrap position, and the streaming control flag.

```
var
  Form1: TForm1;
StorageString : String;
StringCounter : Integer;
NowStreaming  : Boolean;
```

6. Move down below the *implementation* keyword and enter the following asssistant function, which handles looping the display string back on itself for the banner effect.

```
function TForm1.GetWrappedString( TheIndex : Integer ) : String;
var HoldString : String;
begin
  { Get the remainder of the display string into HoldString }
  HoldString := Copy( StorageString , TheIndex ,
  ( Length(StorageString) - TheIndex ) + 1 );
  { Put it first, then add the front end to its back end }
  { This creates the illusion of moving text in a loop    }
  HoldString := HoldString + Copy( StorageString , 1 , TheIndex - 1 );
  { Return the manipulated string as result }
  GetWrappedString := HoldString;
end;
```

7. Below the previous code, enter the next helper function to take care of running continuously in the background and streaming text across the button.

```
procedure TForm1.DoTheStream;
var Counter_1 : Longint;
    Dummy : Integer;
TheString : String;
begin
  { Run forever until the user clicks the button again }
  while NowStreaming do
  begin
    { Increaste the global string position counter }
    StringCounter := StringCounter + 1;
    { If it runs off the end of the display string reset it to 1 }
    if StringCounter > Length(StorageString) then
     StringCounter := 1;
    { Get the new moved string from the wrapper function }
    TheString := GetWrappedString( StringCounter );
    { Set it to be the button caption }
    Button1.Caption := TheString;
    { Yield control to anybody that wants to run now }
    Application.ProcessMessages;
    { Run this loop on a 66 mzh 486 to get readable streaming;  }
    { reduce or increase the value as needed by experimentation }
    for Counter_1 := 1 to 100000 do
    begin
      dummy := 1;
    end;
  end;
end;
```

8. Select the Form1 OnCreate handler and enter these program lines to set up the application.

```
procedure TForm1.FormCreate(Sender: TObject);
begin
{ Set the button text string for wrapping }
  StorageString := 'Delphi is Twenty-First Century Technology Today...';
```

continued on next page

continued from previous page

```
  { Set the position counter at 1 }
  StringCounter := 1;
  { Put the display string in the button }
  Button1.Caption := StorageString;
  { And wait till the user clicks to start streaming text }
  NowStreaming := false;
end;
```

9. Compile and test the project.

How It Works

This How-To illustrates several important issues in Delphi. First, it shows how to let a procedure yield control to other Windows applications. Second, it demonstrates how to manipulate text strings in a fairly sophisticated way. Third, it shows a method to use looping to control the time behavior of events.

Yielding Control to Other Applications

The following procedure call takes care of allowing other Windows applications to run inside the DoTheStream loop:

```
Application.ProcessMessages;
```

This line of code shows two important features, starting with the use of the Application object. All Delphi programs have a TApplication object to handle running the program's code at execution. It is created automatically and stored in the Application variable. TApplication offers a number of methods to allow programmers considerable runtime control, one of which is ProcessMessages. In order to understand the importance of ProcessMessages, a bit of territory about Windows messages, multitasking, and event handling must be covered.

Windows is an event-driven operating system, which means that rather than having one large program running at once and internally yielding control to its subroutines, a program is broken down into smaller procedures, each of which is called by the operating system in response to messages being sent from other procedures and functions, both user-written and system-level. When a procedure is called with a message, it can either ignore the message, (in which case Windows moves on to the next candidate procedure to handle the message), process the message but leave it in the message queue, or process the message and remove it from the list. When all messages have been removed from the queue, Windows enters idle mode until new events (mouse clicks, keypresses, timer events, interrupt calls, and so forth) generate new messages.

DOS is a single-tasking environment; this means that only one program can run at a time. Even TSR programs (Terminate and Stay Resident) don't violate this rule, since when they run they fully take over the machine. In Windows' multitasking environment multiple programs can be executing at once. There are two flavors of multitasking environments: preemptive and cooperative. *Preemptive multitasking systems* arbitrarily take control from one program and give it to another, usually very quickly, and handle all the resulting complexity at the operating system level. UNIX and Windows NT are preemptive multitasking environments. Windows 3.1 is a *cooperative multitasking environment*. It requires a given program to use built-in API calls to yield control to other applications when desired. There are several API calls that do this, including PeekMessages and Yield.

Because Delphi has added several extra layers of insulation around the Windows messaging environment, it is not advisable to use either PeekMessages or Yield from within a Delphi program. Instead, TApplication's ProcessMessages method takes care of cooperative multitasking by interfacing with the Windows message queue and yielding control to other applications until the queue is empty. At that point it returns to the calling Delphi procedure, which can then resume execution. The major drawback to using this approach is that it makes the procedure a "CPU hog," grabbing all available machine time that Windows hasn't given to someone else. A TTimer component could avoid this by making calls every second to the string manipulation function instead; but in some cases timers aren't appropriate, and for these cases it's important to understand how to use the ProcessMessages method.

String Manipulation

String manipulation is one of the most common tasks any programmer faces. Delphi provides a rich feature set of both Pascal-style String functions and Windows ASCIIZ Pchar procedures. The following call illustrates one of the most powerful:

```
HoldString := Copy(StorageString , TheIndex , (Length(StorageString) - TheIndex ) + 1 );
```

Copy is the Delphi equivalent of BASIC's SUBSTR$ function. It takes a target string (in this case StorageString) and starts at the string character given in the second parameter and copies the number of characters in the third parameter (in this example, all the remaining characters in the target string) to the destination (HoldString). Notice that StorageString is not affected by this operation. In combination with the Pos function, any arbitrary substring can be obtained from a given string using Copy.

Looping

Finally, the following code illustrates how to use an internal loop to control execution speed of a program.

```
for Counter_1 := 1 to 100000 do dummy := 1;
```

This type of loop simply eats up CPU cycles doing a useless assignment to an otherwise unused variable. By varying the number of iterations in the loop the speed of the delay can be finely controlled.

The C language offers a Sleep function that permits entering a similar loop at the compiler level. Delphi could use similar functionality.

Comments

You can use OnIdle, another TApplication method, to yield control to other applications, by setting its Done property to True. The difference between the two methods is that the ProcessMessages call can be made at specific points in program execution. OnIdle is called by Delphi's message handling system when no internal messages are waiting for processing and cannot be called directly at run time.

2.6 How do I...
Customize a window's title bar with graphics?

COMPLEXITY: ADVANCED

Problem

I want to draw on the parts of my application's window outside its client area, such as the title bar. Does Delphi offer a way around this limitation?

Technique

Windows normally supplies a display context only for a window's client area. However, the GetWindowDC API call returns a DC to the entire window, which can then be used to place graphics on the title bar. Display contexts and client areas will be discussed in more detail in the How It Works section of this chapter.

Steps

Run TIMECAPT.EXE. You'll see a display similar to Figure 2-6, with the continually updated time shown in the left side of the caption bar. Minimize the window and restore it, and you will notice that the time remains correct.

1. Create a new blank project and name it TIMECAPT.DPR. Name the unit TIMRCAPT.PAS.

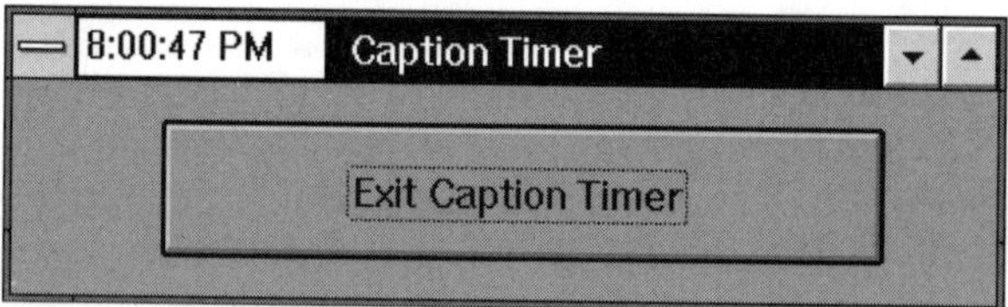

Figure 2-6 TIMECAPT at run time showing a digital clock graphic in the caption bar

2. Add components to Form1 and set their properties as shown in Table 2-6.

Table 2-6 Components, properties, and settings for Form1 in TIMECAPT

COMPONENT	PROPERTY	SETTING
Form1	Type	Application Main Form
	Width	433
	Height	124
	Left	41
	Top	13
	Caption	Caption Timer
Button1	Type	TButton
	Left	64
	Top	16
	Width	313
	Height	57
	Caption	Exit Caption Timer
Timer1	Type	TTimer
	Interval	1000
	Enabled	True

3. Select the OnClick event handler of Button1 and type in the following code to close the application.

```
procedure TForm1.Button1Click(Sender: TObject);
begin
Close;
end;
```

4. While still in the Code Editor, move up to the *var* keyword and enter these assistant variables.

```
var
  Form1: TForm1;
The_PChar : array[ 0 .. 79 ] of char;
The_Time_String : String;
```

5. Select the OnPaint event handler of Form1 and add these program lines to redraw the form when Windows needs it.

```
procedure TForm1.FormPaint(Sender: Tobject);
var hDc_Window : hDC;
begin
   { Obtain the DC for the entire window including nc area }
   hDC_Window := GetWindowDC( Handle );
   { Draw a white filled black outline rectangle just inside }
   { the title bar                                         }
   Rectangle( hDC_Window , 31 , 4 , 140 , 30 );
```

continued on next page

continued from previous page

```
    { Obtain the time via the TimeToStr function and Time call }
    The_Time_String := TimeToStr( Time );
    { Put the Delphi string into windows format }
    StrPCopy( The_PChar , The_Time_String );
    { Draw it in the rectangle on the caption bar }
    TextOut( hDC_Window , 35 , 6 , The_PChar , StrLen( The_PChar ));
    { be sure to release the DC so windows won't lock up! }
    ReleaseDC( Handle , hDC_Window );
end;
```

6. Select the OnTimer event handler of Timer1 and add the following program code to continually update the clock display.

```
procedure TForm1.Timer1Timer(Sender: TObject);
var hDc_Window : hDC;
begin
  { Obtain the DC for the entire window including nc area }
  hDC_Window := GetWindowDC( Handle );
  { Draw a white filled black outline rectangle just inside }
  { the title bar                                            }
  Rectangle( hDC_Window , 31 , 4 , 140 , 30 );
  { Obtain the time via the TimeToStr function and Time call }
  The_Time_String := TimeToStr( Time );
  { Put the Delphi string into windows format }
  StrPCopy( The_PChar , The_Time_String );
  { Draw it in the rectangle on the caption bar }
  TextOut( hDC_Window , 35 , 6 , The_PChar , StrLen( The_PChar ));
  { be sure to release the DC so windows won't lock up! }
  ReleaseDC( Handle , hDC_Window );
end;
```

7. Compile and test the project.

How It Works

At the heart of this How-To are the concepts of device contexts and client areas. *Device contexts* (also sometimes called display contexts) are internal data structures in Windows that are used to allow device-independent graphical operations. Windows 3.1 has a very small number of these powerful objects, which is why whenever one is obtained it must be quickly released or the system will freeze, unable to draw on the screen.

Client areas are mathematical models of the areas of a given window object that the window itself is responsible for drawing (such as in response to an OnPaint message). Non-client areas of a window are those portions which Windows itself takes care of, such as the title bar, minimize button, system menu, and so on. Normally when Windows sends a DC to a window to allow it to paint its client area, the internal structure is set up so that drawing elsewhere is impossible.

The GetWindowDC API function is the way around this limitation. Unlike GetDC, it returns a display context based on the entire window, rather than just its client portion. This allows you to place graphics anywhere within the window area, including its non-client portions. However, since your application may have drawn over normal Windows screen objects, you are responsible for any confusion a user may experience. For example if the program were to draw over the system menu, you would either want to provide an alternate way to access the system menu, or at least warn the user that the menu is still there, just not visible.

Another important point about this technique is that you cannot use it to place or manipulate Delphi windows controls (such as buttons, list boxes, and so forth). Windows requires that you place these types of controls within the client area of a window unless they are independent popup windows. However, all normal Windows GDI functions work with the DC obtained from GetWindowDC; so if you wish to handle the overhead of drawing them within the application, you can use this approach to set complex images in the non-client areas.

The TimeToStr and Time functions are both part of the Delphi API. Time returns a complex packed string with considerable date and time information. TimeToStr and DateToStr unpack the data that Time returns into times and dates. The FormatDateTime function allows considerable user control over how the date and time information are reported. There are also a number of typed constants in the SysUtils unit that control standard date/time formatting.

Notice that the application handles both an OnTimer and OnPaint event. This ensures that if the form is repainted between time clicks the correct value is still in the clock rectangle.

Comments

There is another, more complicated way to obtain a device context to non-client areas of a window. In this How-To, you called GetWindowDc with the handle to the current window. The alternative is to make this call:

```
GetDC( 0 );
```

which, because of the zero parameter, returns a device context to the entire screen.

Having obtained a DC to the entire screen, you can draw anywhere you please. However, unlike the GetWindowDC method, the coordinates for drawing on a screen DC start at the upper-left corner of the display, rather than the upper-left corner of the client area or target window. In some cases this may require converting coordinates before drawing to achieve the desired results.

It is also useful to remember that you can access the TIcon and TBitmap components via the Windows API using their Handle properties, provided that an appropriate device context can be obtained. This way you can use them to draw complex images anywhere, not just within a Delphi form's client area.

One clear use of the technique of drawing on the entire display is to create a Windows wallpaper display program independent of the simple built-in system. The principal difficulty with such a program is intercepting the required painting messages when the background image needs refreshing. This involves trapping a window's non-client messages, all of which have the WM_NC_XXX format.

Note: For more information on all these topics select the Help topic in Delphi and then select API, which activates the Windows API programming help system.

2.7 How do I...
Implement a splitter bar to resize controls dynamically?

COMPLEXITY: INTERMEDIATE

Problem

File Manager implements a "splitter" bar, which allows users to resize the directory and file list box areas. Can I reproduce this functionality in Delphi?

Technique

Although it is possible to dynamically resize Delphi components at run time, in practice another approach works more effectively. You can use the PatBlt Windows API function call along with a built-in Cursor property to duplicate File Manager's capability.

Steps

Run SPLITSIZ.EXE. Move the mouse cursor over the center panel, and you will see the cursor change into the HScrollBar cursor. Press the left button and drag either way, and the two list boxes will resize automatically. An example is shown in Figure 2-7.

1. Create a new blank project and name it SPLITSIZ.DPR. Name the unit SPLITTER.PAS.

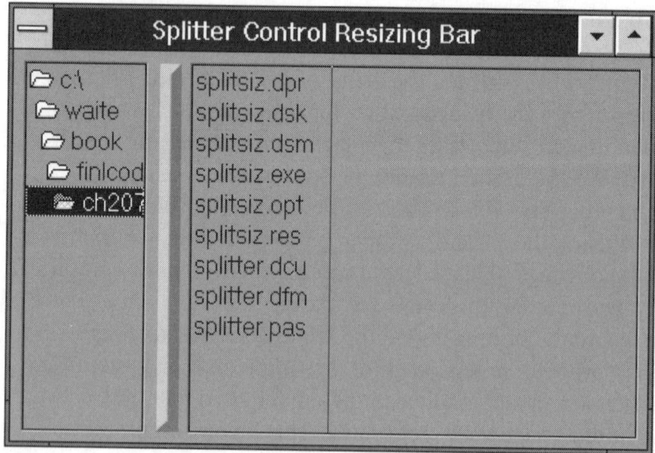

Figure 2-7 SPLITSIZ at run time showing resizing in progress

2. Add components to Form1 and set their properties as shown in Table 2-7.

Table 2-7 Components, properties, and settings for Form1 in SPLITSIZ

COMPONENT	PROPERTY	SETTING
Form1	Type	Application Main Form
	Width	432
	Height	292
	Left	42
	Top	13
	Caption	Splitter Control Resizing Bar
DirectoryListBox1	Type	TDirectoryListBox
	Left	8
	Top	8
	Width	161
	Height	241
	FileList	241
FileListBox1	Type	FileListBox1
	Left	200
	Top	8
	Width	217
	Height	241
Panel1	Type	TPanel
	Left	176
	Top	8
	Width	17
	Height	241
	BevelOuter	bvRaised
	BevelWidth	8
	Cursor	crHSplit

3. Select the OnMouseDown event handler for the Panel1 component and enter the following code, which starts the resize operation.

```
procedure TForm1.Panel1MouseDown(Sender: TObject; Button: TMouseButton;
begin
  { Set Sizesplitting to indicate start of a resize operation }
  SizeSplitting := True;
  { Set Start_X to the current mouse position }
  Start_X := X;
```

continued on next page

continued from previous page

```
  { Set LeftWidth to the current width of the left listbox }
  LeftWidth := DirectoryListBox1.Width;
  { Set RightWidth to the current width of the right listbox }
  RightWidth := FileListBox1.Width;
  { Set RightLeft to the current left edge of the right listbox }
  RightLeft := FileListBox1.Left;
  { Set Panleft to the current left edge of the panel component }
  PanLeft := Panel1.Left;
  { Put a dummy value in OldX }
  OldX := -1;
  { Set no current need to re-patblt }
  NeedReDraw := false;
end;
```

4. While still in the Code Editor, move up under the *var* keyword and enter these assistant variables to keep track of interim position information and program state.

```
var
  Form1: TForm1;
SizeSplitting : Boolean;
Start_X ,
  { PanLeft is used to hold the starting left of the panel}
  PanLeft ,
LeftWidth,
RightWidth,
RightLeft ,
OldX            : Integer;
NeedReDraw   : boolean;
```

5. Activate the OnMouseMove event handler. Add the following code to produce the moving line effect for the resize operation in progress.

```
procedure TForm1.Panel1MouseMove(Sender: TObject; Shift: TShiftState; X,
  Y: Integer);
var TheDC : HDC;
begin
  { If currently resizing then handle latest change }
  if SizeSplitting then
  begin
    { Don't go past left edge }
    if Panel1.Left + X < 0 then Exit;
    { Don't go past right edge }
    if Form1.Left + Panel1.Left + x > Form1.Left + Form1.Width then Exit;
    { If need to clear a previous patblt do so }
    if NeedReDraw then
    begin
      { Get the dc for the entire screen }
      TheDc := GetDC( 0 );
      { Use PatBlt to put a line on the screen in XOR mode at previous position}
      PatBlt( TheDC , OldX , Form1.Top + DirectoryListBox1.Top + 30 ,
       1 , DirectoryListBox1.Height , DstInvert );
      { give up the dc }
      ReleaseDC( 0 , TheDC );
```

```
      { And indicate no need to redraw again }
      NeedReDraw := false;
    end;
    { Now get the dc again }
    TheDc := GetDC( 0 );
    { Draw another line on the screen at the new mouse position}
    PatBlt( TheDC , Form1.Left + Panel1.Left + X ,
      Form1.Top + DirectoryListBox1.Top + 30 , 1 , DirectoryListBox1.Height ,
       DstInvert );
    { Free the DC again }
    ReleaseDC( 0 , TheDC );
    { Set need to redraw again  }
    NeedReDraw := true;
    { Set OldX to the new drawing position }
    OldX := Form1.Left + Panel1.Left + X;
  end;
end;
```

6. Select the OnMouseUp event handler and add this code to do the actual resizing of the controls.

```
procedure TForm1.Panel1MouseUp(Sender: TObject; Button: TMouseButton;
  Shift: TShiftState; X, Y: Integer);
var TheDC : HDC;
TheDiff : Integer;
begin
  { if a resize operation was in progress then handle moving stuff }
  if SizeSplitting then
  begin
    { If need to clear the final xor draw then do so }
    if NeedReDraw then
    begin
      { Get the DC for the entire screen }
      TheDc := GetDC( 0 );
      { XOR another line to erase the previous one }
      PatBlt( TheDC , OldX , Form1.Top + DirectoryListBox1.Top + 30,
       1 , DirectoryListBox1.Height , DstInvert );
      { Release the DC to keep windows from locking up! }
      ReleaseDC( 0 , TheDC );
      { And clear redraw flag for next move }
      NeedReDraw := false;
    end;
    { handle a move to the left }
    if X < Start_X then
    begin
      { Determine the amount of movement }
      TheDiff := Start_X - X;
      { Reset the width of the left listbox to be less }
      DirectoryListBox1.Width := LeftWidth - TheDiff;
      { Move the left hand side of the right list box left }
      FileListBox1.Left := RightLeft - TheDiff;
      { Increase the right listbox's width }
      FileListBox1.Width := RightWidth + TheDiff;
      { And move the panel left }
      Panel1.Left := PanLeft - TheDiff;
```

continued on next page

continued from previous page

```
    end
    else
    begin
      { Handle a move right by the amount of movement }
      TheDiff := X - Start_X;
      { Increase the width of the left hand listbox }
      DirectoryListBox1.Width := LeftWidth + TheDiff;
      { Move the right hand listbox right }
      FileListBox1.Left := RightLeft + TheDiff;
      { Decrease the width of the righthand listbox }
      FileListBox1.Width := RightWidth - TheDiff;
      { Move the panel to the right }
      Panel1.Left := PanLeft + TheDiff;
    end;
  end;
  { Redraw the window (not really needed) }
  Invalidate;
  { And turn off the move operation flag }
  SizeSplitting := False;
end;
```

7. Finally, select the OnCreate event handler for Form1 and add this code to initialize the application.

```
procedure TForm1.FormCreate(Sender: TObject);
begin
  { Set the SizeSplitting flag to false }
  SizeSplitting := false;
end;
```

8. Compile and test the project.

How It Works

This application demonstrates several useful techniques: how to set component cursors, how to draw an "erasable" line on the screen, and how to dynamically resize Delphi controls at run time.

Each Delphi component has a Cursor property, which holds the cursor that Windows will display whenever the mouse is within the window's extents. Figure 2-8 shows the standard cursors available as enumerated types in Delphi from the Object Inspector. You can also use the Image Editor tool to create additional cursors, which can then be added to the Delphi application as a RES file and loaded at run time.

Many commercial programs use "erasable" lines that clean up after themselves, even on areas of the screen outside their own window. As noted in the previous How-To, the GetDC function will return a display context to the entire screen if called with a 0 parameter rather than a valid window handle. What allows the erasability, however, is this line of code:

```
PatBlt( TheDC , OldX , Form1.Top + DirectoryListBox1.Top + 30 , 1 , DirectoryListBox1.Height , DstInvert );
```

The PatBlt Windows API function is a bitmap manipulation function that takes a DC, coordinates for location, height, and width, and an operation code. It then

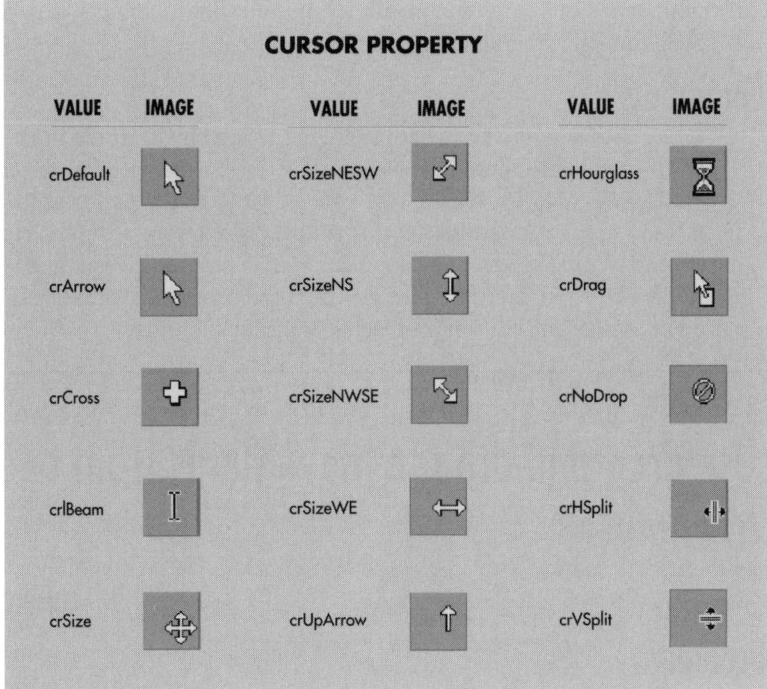

Figure 2-8 Stock Delphi cursors available in the Object Inspector

changes the bits in the DC's memory according to the logical operation contained in the code.

The key to erasable lines is using DstInvert as the code; this code simply inverts a bit from 0 to 1 or 1 to 0, producing the ghost (or XOR) effect common to erasable lines. The ability to restore what was under the line comes from the mathematical fact that a bit can have only two states, 1 or 0. A second inversion operation restores the bits to their original state and erases the line.

Note: The Windows API help contains complete listings of all the possible operation codes, and their effects, for the Blt API calls.

Delphi hides considerable power under its hood, thanks to object-oriented programming. A call to reset the Top or Left properties, for example, involves not only changing the internal position value, but also calling the object's Paint method so that it can redraw itself, as well as calling other objects' Paint methods so they can redraw themselves in response to a changed window display.

It is also worth noting the considerable *heuristics*, or artificial intelligence, hidden in Delphi. Not all methods call the Paint method; and if more than one property that needs redrawing changes in the same procedure, Delphi only does one redraw, apparently detecting the changes during compilation and caching them until the end of the operation. This compiler-level optimization is another reason Delphi is a breakthrough programming environment.

Comments

One criticism often leveled at Delphi is that it's implemented in Pascal rather than C or C++, which supposedly makes it slow. To test the speed of the code produced by the Delphi compiler, change this application so that it performs its resizing calculations in the OnMouseMove event handler, rather than using the erasable line approach. This produces an application that is not as elegant as the one developed for this How-To, but the speed at which the components redraw themselves clearly demonstrates the efficiency of Delphi's executable code.

2.8 How do I...
Use drag-and-drop to move items from one list box to another?

COMPLEXITY: INTERMEDIATE

Problem

My application requires a substantial amount of user input via selections from list boxes. Is there a way in Delphi to use drag-and-drop between list boxes?

Technique

List boxes, like all Delphi components, have built-in drag-and-drop functionality. The key issue is maintaining data integrity when items are moved. The standard list box components have all the functions needed to handle this problem.

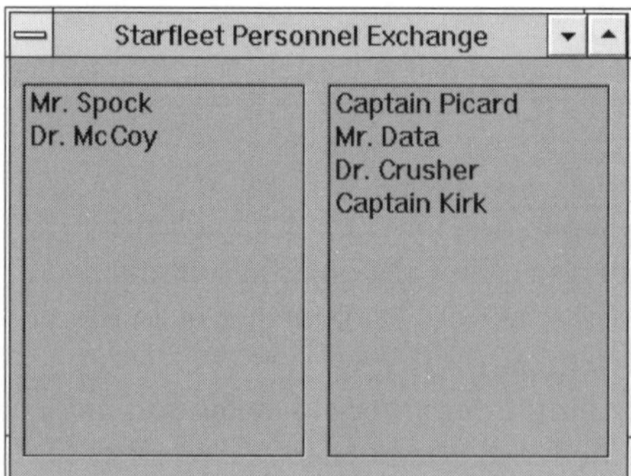

Figure 2-9 LBDRAGDP at run time showing a drag-and-drop data exchange

Steps

Run LBDRAGDP.EXE. Select a member of either crew you would prefer to see in the other crew and "drag" them over. Voilà! The list changes automatically, as shown in Figure 2-9.

1. Create a new blank project and name it LBDRAGDP.DPR. Name the unit LBDR-DROP.PAS.

2. Add components to Form1 and set their properties as shown in Table 2-8.

Table 2-8 Components, properties, and settings for Form1 in LBDRAGDP

COMPONENT	PROPERTY	SETTING
Form1	Type	Application Main Form
	Width	396
	Height	290
	Left	41
	Top	51
	Caption	Starfleet Personnel Exchange
ListBox1	Type	TListBox
	Left	8
	Top	16
	Width	177
	Height	255
	Items	Captain Kirk
		Mr Spock
		Dr McCoy
ListBox2	Type	TListBox
	Left	200
	Top	16
	Width	177
	Height	225
	Items	Captain Picard
		Mr Data
		Dr Crusher

3. Select the OnMouseDown event handler for ListBox1 from the Object Inspector and enter the following code. Connect it to the event handler for OnMouseDown

for Listbox2. The handler checks to make sure there is something selected before beginning a drag-and-drop operation.

```
procedure TForm1.ListBox1MouseDown(Sender: TObject; Button: TMouseButton;
  Shift: TShiftState; X, Y: Integer);
begin
  { If using the left button }
  if Button = mbLeft then
    { make sure to accept only from a listbox }
    with Sender as TListBox do
    begin
      { If there is something in the lb at mouse pos start drag }
      if ItemAtPos( Point( X , Y ), True ) >= 0 then
        BeginDrag( False );
    end;
end;
```

4. In the Object Inspector, activate the OnDragOver event handler for Listbox1 and type in the following code. Connect the handler to the method for Listbox2. These handlers deal with allowing the drag-and-drop to proceed if the source is a list box component.

```
procedure TForm1.ListBox1DragOver(Sender, Source: TObject; X, Y: Integer;
  State: TDragState; var Accept: Boolean);
begin
  { If the source of a drag is a listbox then accept it }
  if Source is TListBox then
    Accept := True;
end;
```

5. Select the OnDragDrop event handler for both list boxes and type in these lines of code, which handle adding the dropped items to the target list box. (Type in the code only for the first listbox; use the event handler duplication procedure described in the *User's Guide* to connect the second Listbox's handler to the first one.)

```
procedure TForm1.ListBox1DragDrop(Sender, Source: TObject; X, Y: Integer);
var Holder, Counter_1 : Integer;
begin
  { If the source is listbox then do drop action }
  with Source as TListBox do
  begin
    { Get total items in the listbox }
    Holder := Items.Count;
    { Loop through and if one is selected move it }
    for Counter_1 := 0 to Holder - 1 do
    begin
      if Selected[ Counter_1 ] then
       TListBox( Sender ).Items.Add( Items[ Counter_1 ] );
    end;
  end;
end;
```

6. Finally, activate the OnEndDrag event handlers for both list boxes and type in the following lines to take care of deleting the dragged items from their source list box. (Again enter only one procedure, using the handler connection feature for the second listbox entry.)

```
procedure TForm1.ListBox1EndDrag(Sender, Target: TObject; X, Y: Integer);
var Counter_1 : Integer;
done : Boolean;
begin
  { If a successful drag was accomplished }
  if Target  nil then
  begin
    { Set the loop control to start processing }
    done := false;
    { Begin at the top listbox item }
    Counter_1 := 0;
    { run through the list box items }
    while not done do
    begin
      { Delete a selected item which was moved }
      if TListBox( Sender ).selected[ Counter_1 ] then
       TListBox( Sender ).Items.Delete( Counter_1 );
      { Increment the counter }
      if ( Counter_1 + 1 ) <= TListbox( Sender ).Items.Count then
       if not TListBox( Sender ).Selected[ Counter_1 ] then
        Counter_1 := Counter_1 + 1;
      { If at the new end of the lb then exit loop }
      if Counter_1 >= TListBox( Sender ).Items.Count then
       done := True;
    end;
  end;
end;
```

7. Compile and test the project.

How It Works

Drag-and-drop is covered in more detail in Chapter 10, but there are several points to notice here. First, note the keywords *as* and *is* in the following lines of code:

```
with Sender as TListBox do
if Source is TListBox then
```

These are new operators in Delphi, which perform implicit type checking on the specified data type against the preceding object reference. In the case of the *is* operator, the result is a Boolean logical test like *if . . . then . . . else*. The keyword *as*, however, does more. Working in combination with the *with* keyword, it creates a typecast version of the referenced object inside the *with* statement so that appropriate fields, properties, and methods can be accessed just as if the object has been explicitly passed by value. If the typecast fails, however, the entire *with* loop is ignored, and execution moves to the next statement below it.

Next, notice the reference to Items in this code statement:

```
Holder := Items.Count;
```

Items is a property called Strings of the list box component. Strings are groups of Pascal strings in an array, managed by a number of very powerful methods. The remainder of the application uses these methods, which will be covered in greater detail in the next How-To. However, what is important for this How-To is the ability to dynamically alter the contents of the Items property at run time, using Add and Delete methods.

Another key item of list box functionality is used in this line of code:

```
if ListBox2.selected[ Counter_1 ] then
```

Each list box component maintains a selected property, which is an array of Boolean values with entries equal to its Items.Count property. Using this property, an application can check through all entries in the list box and determine whether the user has selected them. This is only necessary if the MultiSelect property is set to True; otherwise only a single entry may be selected at one time, and its value can be obtained via the ItemIndex property. (There is an additional property, ExtendedSelect, which allows using the SHIFT key with the mouse to select a range of items. It also only applies if MultiSelect is True.)

As mentioned under "Technique," a key issue in using drag-and-drop for list boxes is maintaining data consistency. The reason lies in the way the Delete method works. Study the following code fragment:

```
while not done do
    begin
      { Delete a selected item which was moved }
      if ListBox2.selected[ Counter_1 ] then
       ListBox2.Items.Delete( Counter_1 );
      { Increment the counter }
      if ( Counter_1 + 1 ) <= Listbox2.Items.Count then
       if not ListBox2.Selected[ Counter_1 ] then
        Counter_1 := Counter_1 + 1;
      { If at the new end of the lb then exit loop }
      if Counter_1 >= ListBox2.Items.Count then
       done := True;
    end;
```

Notice two important points: First, instead of using a *for . . . do* loop, the code implements a *while . . . do* construct. Now study the code that determines whether to increment the counter for checking the next item; notice that two different tests are required.

The reason for both these elements is this: when Delphi deletes an item from a list box using its Delete method, the indexes of all the remaining elements under that item immediately decrease by one, and the total available items also decreases by one at once.

Thus if you used a *for* loop, you would invariably encounter two problems. First, a *for* loop would always attempt to read past the end of the list box, since the list box would, by definition, delete one item. Second, the *for* loop would miss any item directly below a deleted item, because that item would be moved up to the spot just deleted, and the counter would be incremented past the spot just deleted.

Finally, you need the double test for incrementing the counter due to the fact that if all elements of the list are to be deleted, the counter will always stay in position zero. Eventually all items will be deleted, leaving a Count of zero. Unless a test is made using the *incremented* counter against the total items remaining before an attempt is made to access the Items property, an exception will occur.

Comments

List boxes are a major element of both the Delphi and Windows environment. However, there are some critical elements missing from their off-the-shelf functionality, particularly involving editing operations. The next How-To will add several very useful capabilities to standard Delphi list box components.

2.9 How do I... Add copy/cut/paste/undo support to list boxes?

COMPLEXITY: ADVANCED

Problem

Data-centric applications often focus user input through list boxes. It would be very helpful to use mouse-based editing on the data in list boxes, as in Delphi's Textedit sample application. Is there a way to implement list box editing in Delphi?

Technique

You can use Delphi's sophisticated and powerful list box engine to implement a word processor-style set of cut, paste, copy, and undo functions for a list box.

Steps

Run LISTEDIT.EXE. The list box shows the primary colors (known to far too many generations of schoolkids by the mnemonic "Roy G. Biv"). Selecting any item enables cutting or copying. Once a cut or copy has been done, paste is enabled. Once a cut or paste occurs, undo becomes available. Undo returns the list box to the state it was in before the last cut or paste and then becomes inactive. An example cut and paste is shown in Figure 2-10.

1. Create a new blank project and name it LISTEDIT.DPR. Name the unit LBEDIT.PAS.

2. Add components to Form1 and set their properties as shown in Table 2-9.

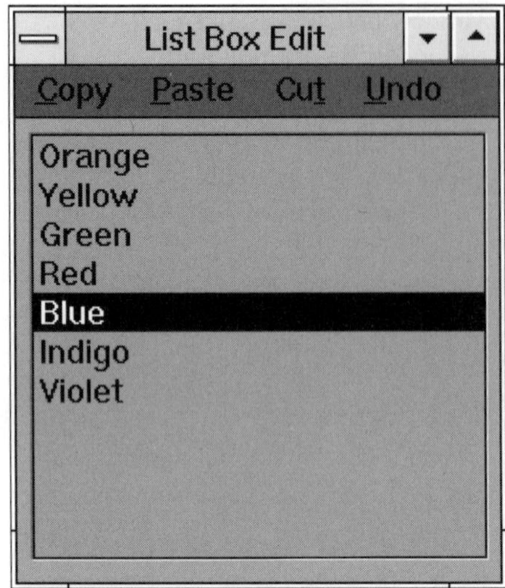

Figure 2-10 LISTEDIT at run time showing a cut and paste operation

Table 2-9 Components, properties, and settings for Form1 in LISTEDIT

COMPONENT	PROPERTY	SETTING
Form1	Type	Application Main Form
	Width	264
	Height	299
	Left	39
	Top	85
	Caption	List Box Edit
ListBox1	Type	TListBox
	Left	8
	Top	8
	Width	241
	Height	217
	Items	Red
		Orange
		Yellow
		Green
		Blue
		Indigo

COMPONENT	PROPERTY	SETTING
		Violet
MainMenu1	Type	TMainMenu
Copy1	Type	TMenuItem (top level)
	Caption	&Copy
	Enabled	False
Paste1	Type	TMenuItem (top level)
	Caption	&Paste
	Enabled	False
Cut1	Type	TMenuItem (top level)
	Caption	Cu&t
	Enabled	False
Undo1	Type	TMenuItem (top level)
	Caption	&Undo
	Enabled	False

3. Activate the OnCreate event for Form1 and type in this code to initialize the StringList data holder variables.

```
procedure TForm1.FormCreate(Sender: TObject);
begin
{ Create the clipboard list }
  TheStringList := TStringList.Create;
  { Create the undo list }
  TheUndoStringList := TStringList.Create;
end;
```

4. While still in the Code Editor, move up to the *var* keyword and add these helper variables for the editing data.

```
var
  Form1: Tform1;
TheStringList,
  TheUndoStringList : TStringList;
```

5. Back in the Object Inspector, select the Copy1 OnClick event handler and enter the following code to take care of copying items from the list box into the holding variable.

```
procedure TForm1.Copy1Click(Sender: TObject);
var Counter_1 ,
Holder       : Integer;
begin
  { Clear the cut/copy/paste stringlist }
  TheStringList.Clear;
  { Store total items to check }
```

continued on next page

continued from previous page

```
  Holder := ListBox1.Items.Count;
  { run through all lb items }
  for Counter_1 := 0 to Holder - 1 do
  begin
    { If an item is selected copy it to the holding array }
    if ListBox1.Selected[ Counter_1 ] then
     TheStringList.Add( ListBox1.Items[ Counter_1 ] );
  end;
  { Allow pasting since something is on the "clipboard" }
  MainMenu1.Items[ 1 ].Enabled := True;
end;
```

6. Next activate the Paste1 OnClick event handler and type the following lines into the Code Editor. They will handle pasting items in from the *clipboard* variable.

```
procedure TForm1.Paste1Click(Sender: TObject);
var StartPos ,
Holder    ,
Counter_1   : Integer;
begin
  { Clear previous undo }
  TheUndoStringList.Clear;
  { Get total items in lb}
  Holder := ListBox1.Items.Count;
  { Copy entire lb to undo list }
  for Counter_1 := 0 to Holder - 1 do
  begin
    TheUndoStringList.Add( ListBox1.Items[ Counter_1 ] );
  end;
  { Enable undo }
  MainMenu1.Items[ 3 ].Enabled := True;
  { Get the position to start pasting }
  StartPos := ListBox1.ItemIndex;
  { Get total items in clipboard }
  Holder := TheStringList.Count;
  { Run through the clipboard }
  for Counter_1 := 0 to Holder - 1 do
  begin
    { Paste the next clipboard item into the primary lb }
    ListBox1.Items.Insert( StartPos , TheStringList.Strings[ Counter_1 ] );
    { Increment the insert position }
    StartPos := StartPos + 1;
  end;
end;
```

7. Choose the Cut1 OnClick event handler and put in this program information to enable cutting items from the list box to the *clipboard* variable.

```
procedure TForm1.Cut1Click(Sender: TObject);
var Counter_1 ,
Holder        : Integer;
done : boolean;
begin
  { Clear the previous undo }
  TheUndoStringList.Clear;
```

```
  { Get total items in the lb }
  Holder := ListBox1.Items.Count;
  { if there are no items to cut then leave }
  if Holder <= 0 then exit;
  { Otherwise loop through the items and put the entire lb into the undo list }
  for Counter_1 := 0 to Holder - 1 do
  begin
    TheUndoStringList.Add( ListBox1.Items[ Counter_1 ] );
  end;
  { Enable the Undo item }
  MainMenu1.Items[ 3 ].Enabled := True;
  { Clear the previous clipboard }
  TheStringList.Clear;
  { Get total items in the lb }
  Holder := ListBox1.Items.Count;
  { Run through all the items and put the selections in the clipboard }
  for Counter_1 := 0 to Holder - 1 do
  begin
    if ListBox1.Selected[ Counter_1 ] then
     TheStringList.Add( ListBox1.Items[ Counter_1 ] );
  end;
  { Clear the loop control flag }
  done := false;
  { Start at the top }
  Counter_1 := 0;
  { Run until finished }
  while not done do
  begin
    { Delete selected items }
    if ListBox1.Selected[ Counter_1 ] then
    begin
      ListBox1.Items.Delete( Counter_1 );
    end;
    { Increment the position counter only if current item     }
    { is no longer selected and at least 1 more item remains }
    if ( Counter_1 + 1 ) <= ListBox1.Items.Count then
     if not Listbox1.Selected[ Counter_1 ] then
      Counter_1 := Counter_1 + 1;
    { Get the remaining total items }
    Holder := ListBox1.Items.Count;
    { if at the end then exit }
    if Counter_1 >= Holder then done := true;
  end;
  { Turn off copying }
  MainMenu1.Items[ 0 ].Enabled := False;
  { Turn on pasting }
  MainMenu1.Items[ 1 ].Enabled := True;
  { Turn off cutting }
  MainMenu1.Items[ 2 ].Enabled := False;
end;
```

8. Finally, select the Undo1 OnClick handler and enter this program data to permit undoing a previous operation.

```
procedure TForm1.Undo1Click(Sender: TObject);
var Counter_1 ,
Holder      : Integer;
begin
  { Clear primary lb }
  ListBox1.Items.Clear
  { Get total items in undo lb };
  Holder := TheUndoStringList.Count;
  { Loop through the list }
  for Counter_1 := 0 to Holder - 1 do
  begin
    { Add next item in undo lb to cleared primary lb }
    ListBox1.Items.Add( TheUndoStringList.Strings[ Counter_1 ] );
  end;
  { Clear the undo list to avoid duplicate undos }
  TheUndoStringList.Clear;
  { Clear all the menu items since nothing should be selected yet }
  MainMenu1.Items[ 0 ].Enabled := False;
  MainMenu1.Items[ 1 ].Enabled := False;
  MainMenu1.Items[ 2 ].Enabled := False;
  MainMenu1.Items[ 3 ].Enabled := False;
end;
```

9. Compile and test the project.

How It Works

There are two different components involved in the application, each with three major methods used heavily in the program.

List boxes have an Items property, which is of type Tstrings. Tstrings are arrays of Pascal-type strings with a number of properties, including a selected property to allow multiple selections. TStringLists are identical to Tstrings with one major exception: Tstrings have no internal storage for their Strings property, counting instead on their owning object to provide storage. TStringLists, on the other hand, have storage allocation built in through their Add property.

The three most powerful methods used by both types are Add, Insert, and Delete. Add is called as follows:

```
ListBox1.Items.Add(TheUndoStringList.Strings[ Counter_1 ] );
```

The Add method takes a Pascal-type string and puts it on the end of the current list. If there are no current entries it becomes entry 0; otherwise it becomes entry Count.

The Insert method has the following syntax:

```
ListBox1.Items.Insert(StartPos,TheStringList.Strings[ Counter_1 ]);
```

Unlike Add, Insert takes the string in its second parameter and inserts it before the item at the first parameter. If the starting position is invalid, an exception occurs.

The Delete method is called as follows:

```
ListBox1.Items.Delete( Counter_1 );
```

The integer parameter taken by the Delete method is an index into the Strings list, starting at zero. When the deletion occurs, all remaining items below the input number are moved up by one, and the Count property is reduced by one. This happens immediately, so loop-based deletion is not practical.

Comments

An example of how the functionality demonstrated here might be useful is in a phone and address book application. Entries will be coming and going continually, and the user might prefer to display them in a different order at different times.

2.10 How do I...
Add a horizontal scroll bar to a list box?

COMPLEXITY: EASY

Problem

I have a list box with very long strings, but I can't seem to find a way to scroll my text horizontally. Does Delphi have a way to do this?

Technique

There are actually several ways to implement this functionality. This How-To uses a Windows API message to trick the list box into creating its own scroll bar.

Steps

Run LBHORSC.EXE. Use the scroll bar to move the text around, as shown in Figure 2-11.

1. Create a new blank project and name it LBHORSC.DPR. Name the unit LBHSCROL.PAS.

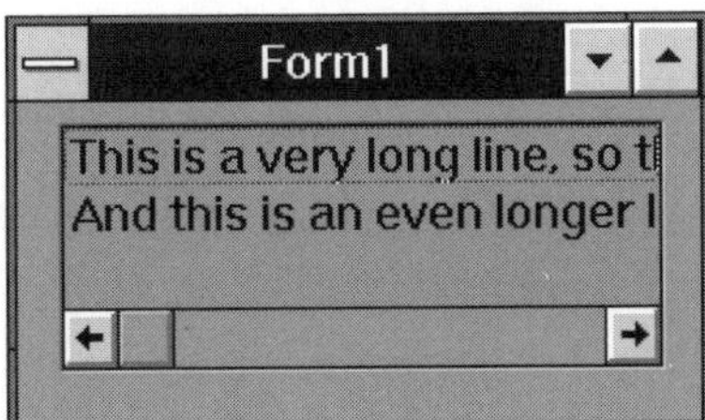

Figure 2-11 LBHORSC at run time

2. Add components to Form1 and set their properties as shown in Table 2-10.

Table 2-10 Components, properties, and settings for Form1 in LBHORSC

COMPONENT	PROPERTY	SETTING
Form1	Type	Application Main Form
	Width	255
	Height	148
	Left	56
	Top	51
	Caption	Form1
ListBox1	Type	TListBox
	Left	16
	Top	8
	Width	217
	Height	65
	Items	This is a very long line, so there!
		And this is an even longer line, too!

3. Select the OnActivate event handler of Form1 and add the following code to tell the list box to add its internal scroll bar.

```
procedure TForm1.FormActivate(Sender: TObject);
begin
  { The entire functionality is handled by sending    }
  { a resize message to the listbox bigger than its   }
  { current instance size; this triggers the creation }
  { of an internal horizontal scrollbar.               }
  sendmessage( Listbox1.Handle ,
           LB_SetHorizontalExtent ,
           1000 ,
           longint( 0 ) );
end;
```

4. Compile and test the project.

How It Works

To force the list box to display a scroll bar, the application sends it the LB_SETHORIZONTALEXTENT message, which is used when a list box needs to change its display area. Since the corresponding visible display is less than the values sent (1000), Windows automatically adds the scroll bar.

Comments

There is another method, deeply hidden in the Help system, called ScrollBy. Unfortunately, it is not intended to work with list boxes or similar components.

Delphi is rich with features, and not all are available from the Object Inspector. A detailed reading of help topics for the various components can yield surprising and rewarding discoveries.

3

DOCUMENTS AND TEXT

How do I...

3.1 Scroll portions of a dialog

3.2 Scroll text and graphics under program control

3.3 Create a README file viewer

3.4 Build a simple editor that remembers the last file opened

3.5 Add search and replace to my editor

3.6 Determine and modify the blink rate of the caret

3.7 Use scroll bars to select colors

3.8 Limit text entry to certain characters

3.9 Print simple text documents

3.10 Justify text within a specified frame

Text display and manipulation is an essential ingredient in most applications. How you use text affects both the functionality of your application and the way it looks and feels to the user. It can also affect how well information is stored and retrieved. This chapter deals with various aspects of displaying, inputting, processing, and printing text data. Along the way, you will create a complete, full-function text editor.

Windows and many Windows-based applications use scrolling extensively. The most common use of it is in various text or graphics editing windows that contain scroll bars to allow viewing areas larger than the physical screen or the active window. However, scrolling is not limited to text and graphics; you can scroll just about anything that can be displayed. You can also scroll under program control rather than only when the user requests it, and you can scroll areas even if there are no scroll bars. TScrollBar components are also often used as stand-alone controls for such things as adjusting color or volume. Delphi has built scrolling into many of its components and has made it easier than ever to wield complete control over it.

3.1 Scroll portions of a dialog

This How-To shows a practical use for TScrollBox. There will be times when you want to create a dialog-style form that has a large group of related controls, such as a list of check boxes or radio buttons, but you'd like to keep the overall size of the dialog fairly small or preserve space for other controls such as edit or memo controls. You could make the entire dialog scrollable, but this usually ends up looking rather unprofessional. You can use a TScrollBox component to make a specific portion of a form scrollable.

3.2 Scroll text and graphics under program control

This How-To features another TScrollBox, but this time the contents can be scrolled in any direction using buttons instead of scroll bars. It shows how to control scrolling from within your application.

3.3 Create a README file viewer

It's easy to build a useful read-only text viewer, and no toolbox should be without one. Build it into any application you create to give users up-to-the minute information about your product.

3.4 Build a simple editor that remembers the last file opened

Create a functional text editor complete with standard Clipboard functions. With just a few additional lines of code, you'll make this editor remember the last directory and file name that was opened.

3.5 Add search and replace to my editor

You'll build upon the simple editor created in How-To 3.4 by adding search and replace abilities. The search code is presented clearly, and it is ideal for saving in your personal toolbox, ready to be used whenever you need it.

3.6 Determine and modify the blink rate of the caret

Create a little utility to update the rate at which the caret blinks. This utility allows a larger range of settings than does the Windows Control Panel applet. It uses the TIniFile object to easily update the infamous WIN.INI file.

3.7 Use scroll bars to select colors

This How-To presents another useful utility that lets you see the effects of different primary (RGB) color combinations. When you are trying to choose colors for various uses, this will make it easier to determine the values you want .

3.8 Limit text entry to certain characters

Delphi offers a Masked Edit control, which is excellent if you want to specify a special mask such as a phone number or zip code, but what if you simply want to limit the user to a particular range, such as only alphabetic characters? This How-To shows the technique required.

3.9 Print simple text documents

Just about all applications that deal with documents must be able to print those documents. This How-To introduces the Printers unit and common print dialogs and shows how easy it is to print text documents from a TMemo component. It also incorporates the standard Font dialog to allow display and printing of the document in the user's chosen font.

3.10 Justify text within a specified frame

There are many instances when you will want to display text within a specified rectangular region. This region may be on a form or other component, or it may be a region of a printed page. This How-To shows you how to use word wrap and justification to fit text of any length within a specified width.

3.1 How do I...
Scroll portions of a dialog?

COMPLEXITY: EASY

Problem

I want to create a dialog that has a large number of options for the user to set. It also needs to contain a few other controls, including a TMemo component. In order to keep the dialog compact, I want the user to be able to scroll the area containing the options without scrolling the entire dialog. How do I do this with Delphi?

Technique

Delphi's TScrollBox component lets you make any specific portion of a form scrollable without requiring the rest of the form to scroll with it. This is ideal for setting up an array of controls such as check boxes or radio buttons. It allows you to create a compact form while still providing easy access to any number of controls. The TScrollBox component can take up any portion of the form, even the entire client area of the form.

Steps

Run SCROLBOX.EXE. You will see a scroll bar on the right side of the form (Figure 3-1 shows the form as displayed in the Form Designer). Clicking the scrollbar scrolls the radio buttons and check boxes up and down in the form. You can check any of the buttons on and off, and they retain their settings even when scrolled out of sight. By making only a portion of the form scrollable, other controls on the left side of the form remain available at all times.

1. Create a new project with a blank form. Save UNIT1.PAS as SCROBOX1.PAS and save PROJECT1.DPR as SCROLBOX.DPR.

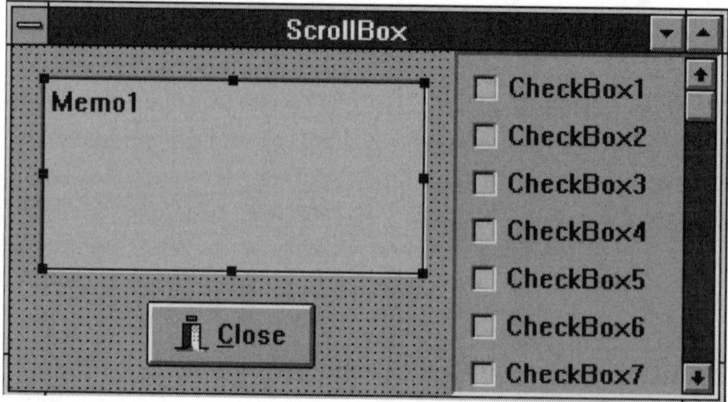

Figure 3-1 The SCROLBOX form design

2. Add the components with the properties as shown in Table 3-1.

Note: To make it easier to add multiple components and settings, use the following Delphi shortcuts:

- When you are ready to place the check boxes, hold the SHIFT key down as you click on the CheckBox tool button. This invokes repeat mode, allowing you to place any number of controls with repeated clicks of the mouse. Do the same for the radio buttons.

- With the check boxes and radio buttons placed, hold the CTRL key down and click on a spot within the scroll box but above and left of the top check box, drag the mouse until you see a bounding box that surrounds all check boxes and radio buttons, and release the mouse. The Object Inspector will now display all properties common to all selected components. Set the Left value once, as specified in Table 3-1, and it will be set for all selected controls.

Table 3-1 Components, properties, and settings for the SCROLBOX form

COMPONENT	PROPERTY	SETTING
Form	BorderStyle	bsDialog
	Caption	ScrollBox
	Height	201
	Position	poScreenCenter
	Scaled	False
	Width	379
Memo	Height	97
	Left	16
	Top	16
	Width	201
BitBtn	Caption	&Close
	Kind	bkClose
	Left	72
	Top	128
Panel	Align	alRight
	BevelInner	bvLowered
	BevelOuter	bvLowered
	Caption	
	Left	232

3. On the TPanel component specified in Table 3-1, add a TScrollBox component as specified in Table 3-2. Then add the check boxes and radio buttons to the scroll box, also as shown in Table 3-2.

Table 3-2 Components, properties, and settings of the Panel component in SCROLBOX

COMPONENT	PROPERTY	SETTING
ScrollBox	Align	alClient
	BorderStyle	bsNone
CheckBox	Top	8

continued on next page

continued from previous page

COMPONENT	PROPERTY	SETTING
	Left	8
CheckBox	Top	32
	Left	8
CheckBox	Top	56
	Left	8
CheckBox	Top	80
	Left	8
CheckBox	Top	104
	Left	8
CheckBox	Top	128
	Left	8
CheckBox	Top	152
	Left	8
RadioButton	Top	176
	Left	8
RadioButton	Top	200
	Left	8
RadioButton	Top	224
	Left	8
RadioButton	Top	248
	Left	8
RadioButton	Top	272
	Left	8
RadioButton	Top	296
	Left	8
RadioButton	Top	320
	Left	8

4. Compile and run the application.

How It Works

The TScrollBox component, like TPanel, is a *container*; meaning you can place other components inside it. When you place controls into it whose positions exceed the visible dimensions of the TScrollBox component, TScrollBox automatically enables the appropriate scroll bar to allow scrolling of all contained components. Note that this works in design mode as well as at run time. As with TPanel, all contained controls are still directly owned by the form, so there is nothing special or different you need to do to access them in your code.

Comments

In this How-To, the scroll box is positioned to take up only the right portion of the form. You can, of course, place it anywhere you like. You can also place it directly on the form rather than on a TPanel as is done here. The TPanel contributes to a better 3D effect. If you like, the scroll box can take up the entire client area of the form, making all controls on the form scrollable. However, you will probably want to keep at least some controls (an OK or Close button, for example) visible at all times. This way users can access such controls quickly, making the application more user-friendly and professional.

3.2 How do I... Scroll text and graphics under program control?

COMPLEXITY: EASY

Problem

I'd like to set up a scrolling region in my form that can scroll smoothly up the screen under program control. Many programs use this to display credits in an About box. Is there a way to do this in Delphi?

Technique

With Delphi's flexible TScrollBox component you can place objects inside a scroll box that exceed its visible bounds but without displaying any scroll bars. It's extremely easy to control the TScrollBox from within the program at run time. This How-To requires the user to initiate scrolling, but then, depending on the condition of a check box, scrolling will either continue until another button is pressed or stop upon release of a button.

Steps

Run SCROLL.EXE. Try out the four different directional buttons, as shown in Figure 3-2. If you hold down a button, the picture will continue to scroll. It will stop when you release the button. Now click on the Continuous check box and click one of the directional buttons. The picture continues to scroll even when you release the mouse button! Clicking another button changes direction without stopping the movement. Click on the check box again; scrolling stops.

1. Create a new project. Save UNIT1.PAS as SCROLL1.PAS and save PROJECT1.DPR as SCROLL.DPR.
2. Add the components with the properties as shown in Table 3-3.

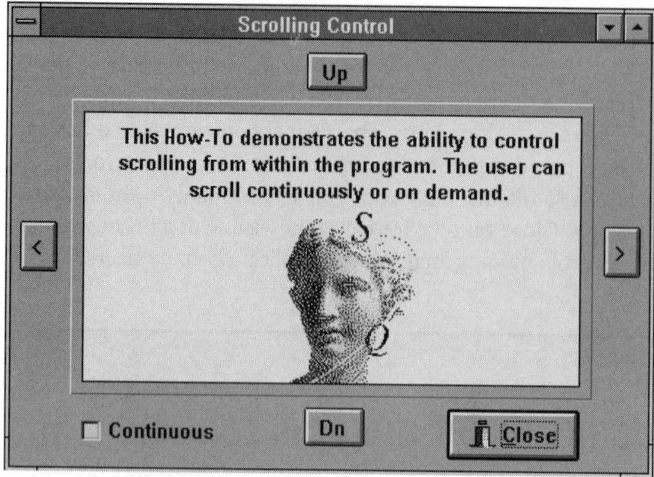

Figure 3-2 The SCROLL program

Table 3-3 Components, properties, and settings for the SCROLL project

COMPONENT	PROPERTY	SETTING
Form	Caption	Scrolling Control
	Height	307
	Position	poScreenCenter
	Width	423
Bevel	Height	193
	Left	40
	Shape	bsBox
	Style	bsRaised
	Top	40
	Width	353
ScrollBox	Height	177
	+HorzScrollBar	
	-Visible	False
	Left	48
	Top	48
	+VertScrollBar	
	-Visible	False
	Width	337

COMPONENT	PROPERTY	SETTING
TImage	AutoSize	True
	Left	0
	Picture	\CHAP03\SCROLL.BMP
	Stretch	False
	Top	0
Timer	Interval	10
Button	Caption	Up
	Height	25
	Left	200
	Name	BtnUp
	Top	8
	Width	41
Button	Caption	Dn
	Height	25
	Left	200
	Name	BtnDn
	Top	240
	Width	41
Button	Caption	<
	Height	33
	Left	6
	Name	BtnLeft
	Top	120
	Width	25
Button	Caption	>
	Height	33
	Left	400
	Name	BtnRight
	Top	120
	Width	25
BitBtn	Kind	bkClose
	Left	296
	Top	240
CheckBox	Caption	Continuous
	Left	48
	Top	248

3. Just below the *implementation* statement, enter the following typed-constant declarations. These will keep track of the current scrolling direction.

```
implementation
const
  XDir: integer = 0;
  YDir: integer = 0;
```

4. Select the Events page of Timer1 in the Object Inspector and double-click the OnTimer event. Enter the following line to scroll the TScrollBox component in the current direction on each timer tick.

```
procedure Form1.Timer1Timer(Sender: TObject);
begin
  Scrollbox1.Scrollby(XDir, YDir);
end;
```

5. Holding the SHIFT key down, click on each of the four direction buttons; then, on the Events page, enter **BtnMouseDown** as the name for the OnMouseDown event handler. Double-click the OnMouseDown event and enter the following code. This updates the current direction values according to the direction button pressed by the user.

```
procedure TForm1.BtnMouseDown(Sender: TObject; Button: TMouseButton;
  Shift: TShiftState; X, Y: Integer);
  if Sender = BtnUp then begin
    YDir := 1; XDir := 0;
  end
  else if Sender = BtnDown then begin
    YDir := -1; XDir := 0;
  end
  else if Sender = BtnLeft then begin
    XDir := 1; YDir := 0;
  end
  else if Sender = BtnRight then begin
    XDir := -1; YDir := 0;
  end;
  Timer1.Enabled := True;
end;
```

6. Again, holding the SHIFT key down, click on each of the four direction buttons, and also click on the check box. On the Events page, enter **BtnMouseUp** as the name for the OnMouseUp event handler. Double-click the OnMouseUp event and enter the following code. This determines whether the check box is currently checked and sets Timer1 accordingly.

```
procedure TForm1.BtnMouseUp(Sender: TObject; Button: TMouseButton;
  Shift: TShiftState; X, Y: Integer);
```

```
begin
  if not CheckBox1.Checked then begin
    Xdir := 0; YDir := 0;
    Timer1.Enabled := False;
  end;
```

7. Compile and test the project

How It Works

The ScrollBy method of the TScrollBox component performs all the work of scrolling. All you need to supply is the amount to scroll in pixels, one value for horizontal and one for vertical. Deciding what value to supply to get the desired direction of scroll can be confusing at first. Positive values cause the region to move down or to the right; negative values move the region up or left. This matches the standard coordinate system of all forms and components in Delphi (and for the most part, Windows itself). The confusion arises from the perspective of the user. For instance, when moving the region down (using a positive value), the user perceives this as scrolling *up* because it uncovers a region that was *above* the previously visible region. This is why the setting of a positive value is triggered by pressing the Up and Left buttons.

For most applications, it is typical to respond simply to the OnClick event alone for a button because buttons are normally used to trigger *discrete* events. In this case, you are interested in *continuous* events. The OnClick event does not take place until the user has both pressed and released the mouse button. In order to make something happen as soon as the user presses the mouse button, you need to respond to the OnMouseDown event. At that point there is a choice: you can allow some action to continue until some other button or control is pressed, or you can stop the action when the button is released by responding to the OnMouseUp event.

Both choices are demonstrated here. If the Continuous check box is checked, the code for the OnMouseUp event does nothing, which allows the scrolling action to continue; pressing another button simply changes the direction of the scroll. If the check box is not checked, the code resets the direction values and turns off the timer as soon as the mouse button is released.

Note: It isn't really necessary to set the direction values to zero since turning off the timer will stop all scrolling action; but if some other portion of a program needs to know if scrolling is currently taking place, or is sensitive to the current scroll direction, this will make it easy to check.

This How-To presents a very important feature of Delphi: it is not necessary to generate a separate procedure for each component for the same event. Delphi encourages the reuse of the same event handlers for any number of components whenever this makes sense within the logic of the program. In this case you see that there is only a single event handler for all of the OnMouseDown events and another for the OnMouseUp events. All four direction buttons share the handler for OnMouseDown; the same four along with the check box share the handler for OnMouseUp. In a shared event handler, it's easy to determine which component the event came from simply by comparing the Sender parameter to each of the controls that shares that handler. If the action to be taken for a control is very different from other controls, it's usually better to give it its own event handler. This makes your program much more understandable, and it is easier to find the particular code. In this example, however, the purpose is the same for all four direction buttons: to set the direction of scroll. Keeping the code together in one procedure makes sense here. Note that in the handler for OnMouseUp, it isn't necessary to know where the message came from; you always want to stop any current scrolling on this event.

Comments

Although this example requires the user to press a button in order to start the scrolling action, you could start the scrolling as soon as the form is displayed. Simply initialize one of the direction values (YDir or XDir) to 1 or -1 instead of 0 and start the timer in the FormCreate event handler (or enable it in design mode).

You could easily expand this program to allow diagonal scrolling as well. Since the ScrollBy method takes two parameters, one for each axis, you can set them both to nonzero values. As an exercise, try adding more buttons to the form to allow diagonal choices and figure out the required values for these directions. You can also easily adjust the speed of scrolling by changing the values of the VertScrollBar and HorzScrollBar properties within the TScrollBox component. Again, you can make these take effect at design time or run time.

3.3 How do I...
Create a README file viewer?

COMPLEXITY: EASY

Problem

When users install one of my applications, I'd like them to be able to display a README-type text file containing late-breaking information not yet in the manual or online help. It should be read-only so they can't change the contents, and it should automatically display a file I specify at design time. How can I do this in Delphi?

Technique

Building a basic ReadMe Viewer is a snap with Delphi's TMemo component. To load a text file into TMemo, you simply pass the name of the file to the LoadFromFile method in TMemo's Lines property. To specify the file that should be opened, you'll take advantage of a TMemo property that is not otherwise needed for this application.

Steps

Run README.EXE. It immediately displays your computer's AUTOEXEC.BAT file, as shown in Figure 3-3. Since this program doesn't allow any options for the user other than to read the displayed document, there is no need for a menu. A Close button is provided for convenience, but the user can also use the Close item in the system menu. Since there is enough unused space on the TPanel that contains the Close button, you can use it to display the file name. Notice when you resize the form, the Close button always stays aligned with the right side.

1. Create a new project. Save the default unit as README1.PAS and the default project as README.DPR.

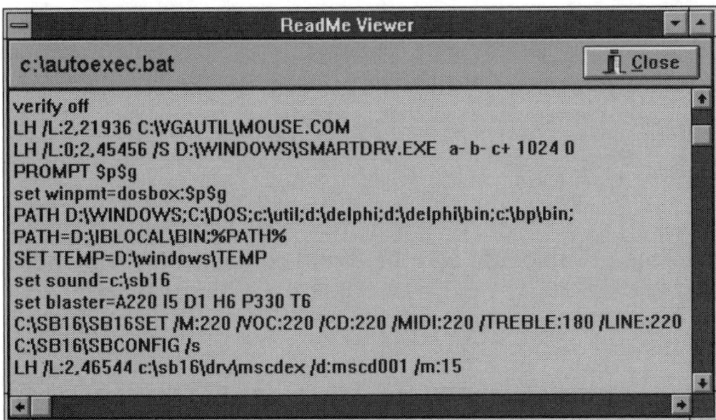

Figure 3-3 The ReadMe Viewer displaying a file

2. Add the components with the properties as shown in Table 3-4.

Table 3-4 Components, properties, and settings for the README project

COMPONENT	PROPERTY	SETTING
Form	Caption	ReadMe Viewer
	Name	VReadMe
Panel	Align	alTop
	BorderStyle	bsSingle
	Caption	
Memo	Align	alClient
	Hint	C:\AUTOEXEC.BAT
	ReadOnly	True
	ScrollBars	ssVertical

3. On the Panel specified in Table 3-4, add the components and properties as shown in Table 3-5.

Table 3-5 Components, properties, and settings for the Panel specified in Table 3-4

COMPONENT	PROPERTY	SETTING
Label	Font.Color	clBlue
	Font.Name	Arial
	Font.Size	12
	Font.Style	fsBold
	Left	8
	Top	8
Panel	Align	alRight
	BevelOuter	bvNone
	Caption	
	Width	97

4. On the Panel specified in Table 3-5, add the BitBtn component and properties as shown in Table 3-6.

Table 3-6 BitBtn component and properties for the Panel specified in Table 3-5

COMPONENT	PROPERTY	SETTING
BitBtn	Height	25
	Kind	bkClose
	Left	8
	Top	4
	Width	81

5. Double-click the form's OnCreate event and enter code to load the specified file. The FormCreate procedure should look like this:

```
procedure TVReadme.FormCreate(Sender: TObject);
begin
  try
    Memo1.Lines.LoadFromFile(Memo1.Hint);
    Label1.Caption := Memo1.Hint;
  except
    on E:Exception do
      MessageDlg('Error Loading ' + Memo1.Hint + ': ' + E.Message,
       mtError, [mbok], 0);
```

```
  end;
end;
```

6. That's it! Run it and see your AUTOEXEC.BAT file. Try changing the Hint property of Memo1 to other file names. Try setting an invalid name.

How It Works

The TMemo component already knows how to load a text file and manage its scroll bars. All you have to do is direct it to open the desired file. Since there is no need to provide hint-style help in this application, the Hint property becomes a convenient place to store the name of the file to be opened (it's still functioning as a hint really, to the TMemo control itself).

Notice the use of the Exceptions feature of Delphi. Before attempting to open the file, the *try* keyword is encountered. This sets up an exception block. If anything goes wrong while trying to open the file, the assignment to Label1.Caption will be skipped and the code following the *except* keyword will be executed, resulting in a friendlier message to the user. Exception code such as this allows your program to handle errors gracefully instead of just terminating with a runtime error. If the LoadFromFile method is successful, the TMemo component immediately displays the loaded file.

Because you set the TMemo component's ReadOnly property to True, the user cannot edit or add any text. If you allowed the text to be changed onscreen, it still wouldn't change the actual data on disk since you've provided no code to write the changes back. Because changes can't be saved, it's wise to set the ReadOnly property to True; otherwise you could end up with a frustrated user!

Although the user cannot change the displayed data, it's still possible to highlight all or any portion of the text and copy it to the Clipboard. This functionality is built into Windows for all TEdit and TMemo components. You can use either the CTRL-INS or CTRL-C key sequences to copy selected text to the Clipboard. The ReadOnly property prevents the use of the standard Cut, Paste, and Delete key sequences.

You are also seeing another great use of TPanel components. You created Panel2 and made it effectively invisible by specifying bvNone for the BevelOuter property. Its sole purpose is to contain the Close button. Because Panel2 is set to be aligned with the right side of its owner (Panel1), it maintains this position no matter how you resize the form and in so doing, drags the Close button with it. This allows you to keep the Close button (or any other controls) right-aligned to the form without writing any code.

Comments

As easy as this How-To is, it demonstrates a couple of nifty features like exception handling and innovative use of a TPanel component. It also tips you to the idea of sometimes taking advantage of properties that would otherwise remain unused in a component and which, like the Hint property, have no function within the component itself.

3.4 How do I... Build a simple editor that remembers the last file opened?

COMPLEXITY: EASY

Problem

I'd like to create my own text editor. Notepad always opens in the Windows directory, and I'd like a similar editor that remembers the last file and directory it was in so users can get to those files faster. I also want to let users copy text between files. How difficult is this to do with Delphi?

Technique

Creating a basic text editor is only a little more involved than creating the ReadMe Viewer presented in the preceding How-To. Instead of predefining the file to be viewed, you'll let the user choose by adding a File Open dialog. Most of the code centers around making sure the user always gets a chance to save any changes made to the document. For Cut, Copy, and Paste, you simply need to make these elements available to users; TMemo already knows what to do with them! Finally, this How-To will introduce you to the TIniFile class, which makes creating and maintaining an initialization (.INI) file a snap.

Steps

Run EZEDIT.EXE. Open various text files. Try making changes to them and then immediately try to open another file. As with any good program, you are always given a chance to save your document if you've made any changes that haven't already been saved, as shown in Figure 3-4. Try the Clipboard menu items. Exit EZEDIT and start it again. Select File|Open; the File Open dialog will display the directory path and file name last used to open a file.

1. Create a new project. Save the default unit as EZEDIT1.PAS and the project as EZEDIT.DPR.

2. Add the components and settings as specified in Table 3-7.

Table 3-7 Components, properties, and settings for the EZEDIT project

COMPONENT	PROPERTY	SETTING
Form	Caption	Personal Editor
	Name	EZEdit

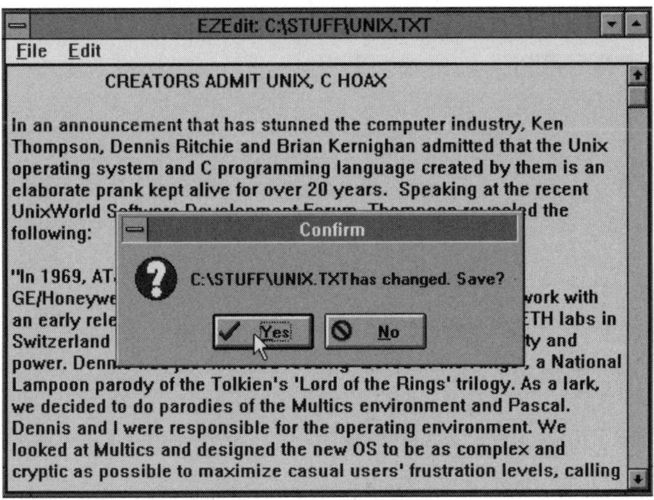

Figure 3-4 The EZEDIT editor in action

COMPONENT	PROPERTY	SETTING
MainMenu		
OpenDialog	DefaultExt	txt
	Filter	Text Files|*.txt
	+Options	
	-ofHideReadOnly	True
	-ofPathMustExist	True
	-ofFileMustExist	True
SaveDialog	DefaultExt	txt
	Filter	Text Files|*.txt
	+Options	
	-ofOverwritePrompt	True
	-ofPathMustExist	True
	-ofHideReadOnly	True
	-ofNoReadOnlyReturn	True
Memo	Align	alClient
	ScrollBars	ssVertical

3. Double-click the MainMenu component on the form and define MenuItems as shown in Table 3-8.

Table 3-8 MainMenu menu items for EZEDIT

MENU CAPTION	MENUITEM CAPTION	SHORTCUT
&File	&New	
	&Open	CTRL+O
	&Save	CTRL+S
	Save &As	
	-	
	E&xit	
&Edit	Cu&t	CTRL+X
	&Copy	CTRL+C
	&Paste	CTRL+V
	&Delete	CTRL+DEL
	Select &All	

4. Add **IniFiles** to the *uses* clause of the unit. This unit contains the TIniFile class you will use to maintain an initialization file for your editor.

5. EZEDIT needs a couple of string variables to store the name of the currently open file and a copy of the form's caption. It also needs an instance of the TIniFile class, and you will be adding a common procedure to be shared by some event handlers. Add the following declarations to the *private* section of the TEZEdit form object.

```
private
  { Private declarations }
  CurrentFile: String;
  SaveCaption: String;
  EZIni: TIniFile;
  procedure CheckFile;
```

6. Add a constant declaration just after the *implementation* statement as specified in the following code. It will be used as part of the form's caption when there is no existing file open.

```
implementation

const
  Untitled = ' [Untitled] ';
```

7. Now define the CheckFile procedure that was declared in the TEZEdit form object. This procedure checks whether the user has made any unsaved changes to the document. If so, it lets the user choose whether to save the changes or

discard them. Enter this entire procedure after the constant declaration you entered in step 6.

```
procedure TEZEdit.CheckFile;
begin
  if Memo1.Modified then begin
    if MessageDlg(CurrentFile + 'has changed. Save?',
      mtconfirmation,[mbyes, mbno], 0) = mb_ok
    then
      Save1Click(Self);
  end;
end;
```

8. Double-click the OnCreate event of the EZEdit form to enter the initialization code for the application. There is no file open when the application first runs, so the relevant variables are set accordingly. FormCreate then checks the initialization file in order to initialize the properties of the OpenDialog object. The complete FormCreate method should look like this:

```
procedure TEZEdit.FormCreate(Sender: TObject);
var
  Fname: string;
begin
  CurrentFile := Untitled;
  SaveCaption := Caption + ': ';
  Caption := SaveCaption + CurrentFile;
  EZIni := TIniFile.Create(ChangeFileExt(ParamStr(0), '.INI'));
  with OpenDialog1 do begin
    Fname := EZIni.ReadString('LastOpen', 'FileName', '*.TXT');
    InitialDir := ExtractFilePath(FName);
    FileName := ExtractFileName(FName);
  end;
end;
```

9. Double-click the OnClose event of the EZEdit form and enter the following cleanup code. It gives the user one last chance to save if there are any unsaved changes, and it updates the initialization file with the name of the last opened file. Note that it will not save "Untitled" to the EZINI.INI file; it will instead save a null file name.

```
procedure TEZEdit.FormClose(Sender: TObject; var Action: TCloseAction);
begin
  CheckFile;
  if CurrentFile = Untitled then CurrentFile := '';
  EZIni.WriteString('LastOpen', 'FileName', CurrentFile);
end;
```

10. Click on the New menu item and enter the code to start a new text file. This code checks for unsaved changes and then reinitializes the relevant variables to

indicate that the document has no file name yet. The TMemo object is cleared of its contents.

```
procedure TEZEdit.New1Click(Sender: TObject);
begin
  CheckFile;
  CurrentFile := UnTitled;
  Caption := SaveCaption + UnTitled;
  Memo1.Lines.Clear;
  Memo1.Modified := False;
end;
```

11. Click on the Open menu item and enter the following code. The current document is checked for unsaved changes, and then the standard Open dialog is executed. If a valid file is selected, it is loaded into the TMemo object and the form's caption is updated.

```
procedure TEZEdit.Open1Click(Sender: TObject);
begin
  CheckFile;
  if OpenDialog1.Execute then begin
    try
      Memo1.Lines.LoadfromFile(OpenDialog1.FileName);
      CurrentFile := OpenDialog1.FileName;
      Caption := SaveCaption + CurrentFile;
      with OpenDialog1 do
        InitialDir := ExtractFilePath(FileName);
    except
      on E:Exception do
        MessageDlg('Error loading ' + OpenDialog1.FileName + ': ' + E.Message,
          mtError, [mbok], 0);
    end;
  end;
end;
```

12. Click on the Save menu item and enter the following code to save the current document. This method is actually shared by the Save As event as well. If necessary, it requests a new file name from the user and then writes the document to disk.

```
procedure TEZEdit.Save1Click(Sender: TObject);
begin
  if (CurrentFile = Untitled) or (Sender = SaveAs1) then begin
    if SaveDialog1.Execute then begin
      CurrentFile := SaveDialog1.FileName;
      Caption := SaveCaption + CurrentFile;
    end else
      Exit;
  end;
  try
    Memo1.Lines.SavetoFile(CurrentFile);
```

```
    Memo1.Modified := False;
  except
    on E:Exception do
      MessageDlg('Error saving ' + OpenDialog1.FileName + ': ' + E.Message,
        mtError, [mbok], 0);
  end;
end;
```

13. Select the SaveAs1 TMenuItem in the Object Inspector and set its OnClick event to the Save1Click handler defined in step 12. They will both share this same handler.

14. Click on the Exit menu item and enter the following line to exit the application.

```
procedure TEZEdit.Exit1Click(Sender: TObject);
begin
 Close;
end;
```

15. Select the Cut1 menu item in the Object Inspector and, for the OnClick event, enter **EditMenuClick** as the event handler's name. Double-click on EditMenuClick and enter the following code to handle all the Edit menu items.

```
procedure TEZEdit.EditMenuClick(Sender: TObject);
begin
  if Sender = Cut1 then              Memo1.CutToClipboard
  else if Sender = Copy1 then       Memo1.CopyToClipboard
  else if Sender = Paste1 then      Memo1.PasteFromClipboard
  else if Sender = Delete1 then     Memo1.ClearSelection
  else if Sender = SelectAll1 then Memo1.SelectAll;
end;
```

16. Select EditMenuClick as the OnClick event handler for the Copy, Paste, Delete, and Select All menu items.

17. Compile and run the project.

How It Works

TMemo handles the bulk of the work for your text editor. TMemo knows how to read and write text files; you simply need to provide the file names. It also has the smarts to handle all Clipboard functions; you simply provide the connections to your menu commands. Most of the code you write in this How-To centers on managing the user's choices; in particular, always making sure the user has a chance to save any changed data before allowing another file to be opened or created.

Any time the user chooses to open or create a new document, or exit the application, it is necessary to check for unsaved changes so the user can be given a chance to save them. Rather than duplicating this code in several places, the necessary code has been placed in a separate procedure (CheckFile) that can be called by the various event handlers. This saves time, makes the code more readable, and results in a slightly smaller executable when compiled. Whenever possible, keep each of your procedures small—ideally no more than can fit on the screen at one time. If a procedure grows much beyond this, you should consider moving some of it to a separate procedure. On the other hand, there *is* such a thing as overkill! While you could define a separate handler for each of the Edit menu items, each of them would only consist of a single line of code to call a TMemo method. In this situation, it can make the code more readable and the resulting executable slightly smaller by *combining* these five events into a single procedure. The Sender parameter is tested to see which menu item called the handler, and the corresponding TMemo method is called in turn.

Another example of handler sharing is between the Save and Save As menu items. In the Save1Click event handler there are two conditions under which the SaveDialog object needs to be executed: when the user requests it directly and when the current document doesn't yet have a file name assigned. Since the latter case needs to be checked here anyway, it makes sense to check for both conditions at once. If there is already a file name assigned and the user didn't request Save As, then there is no need to call the SaveDialog object, and the handler simply saves the document immediately. Once saved, the Modified property of TMemo is updated to indicate that there are now no unsaved changes.

In the FormCreate method (step 8), a TIniFile object is created to manage the application's initialization file. The Create method for TIniFile takes the name of the initialization file as its parameter. Rather than hardcoding a file name here, the code creates a file name based on the program name. The ParamStr function (in the System unit) is used to return the program's command-line parameters. Passing 0 to ParamStr gets the fully qualified name of the program (drive name plus directory path plus executable name).

The string returned by ParamStr is then passed to ChangeFileExt along with '.INI' as the second parameter. ChangeFileExt (in the SysUtils unit) will replace the extension of the passed file name with this second parameter. In this case, the name EZEDIT.EXE is changed to EZEDIT.INI. The TIniFile.Create constructor will open or create the specified initialization file.

By using this method of creating and opening initialization files, you are assured that the initialization file name will always correspond to the program name, and will always be located in the same directory as the program itself.

Once opened, the initialization file can be managed using various methods of TIniFile. This How-To demonstrates the ReadString and WriteString methods. Both methods take a Section and a Key name as the first two parameters. For example, passing 'DeskTop' as the Section name will cause ReadString to look for a section in the file called '[DeskTop]'; a Key name of 'Pattern' will cause it to look for the key 'Pattern=' within the '[DeskTop]' section. The third parameter to ReadString is the default string you want returned if the Section or Key isn't found. For WriteString, the third parameter is the string you want written as the Key value.

The string returned from ReadString in this How-To is the name of the file last opened by EZEDIT, or '*.TXT' if none has been opened previously (or the initialization file is deleted). The OpenDialog component is then initialized with this information. When EZEDIT closes, the name of the file currently open is saved to the initialization file by WriteString.

Comments

Depending on the nature of your application, handling the different choices the user has can be the most difficult part of programming. One of Delphi's greatest strengths is that it removes so much of the mundane and tedious work from your hands and allows you to concentrate on these more important concerns. You do not have to worry about how to open, read, or write each line of a text file, nor about how to transfer data between your application and the Windows Clipboard. Instead you are free to think about what you want your users to be able to do and what they might do given those choices.

This How-To also shows valuable examples of sharing event handlers between different events. It also shows an example of isolating common code into a separate procedure. Both of these become more valuable as your applications become larger.

3.5 How do I... Add search and replace to my editor?

COMPLEXITY: INTERMEDIATE

Problem

My editor works great! Now I'd like to add the ability to search text documents for specific information. It would also be useful to provide search and replace, as in Notepad and other editors and word processors. Is this difficult in Delphi?

Technique

No editor is really complete without the ability to search for and optionally replace text within the document. Delphi provides easy access to the standard Find and Replace dialogs used by many programs. The dialogs are shown in Figures 3-5 and 3-6. All you have to do is write the code that actually performs the search and replace on the document. In this How-To you will add these enhancements to the editor you created in How-To 3.4. In so doing, you will learn a great deal about using PChar style strings and how to allocate memory for them.

Steps

Run FREDIT.EXE. Open different documents and search for various text. Check the Match Case check box and test the difference in results. Try replacing text. You can replace a single instance, or replace all instances with the Replace All button. Note

Figure 3-5 The standard Find dialog

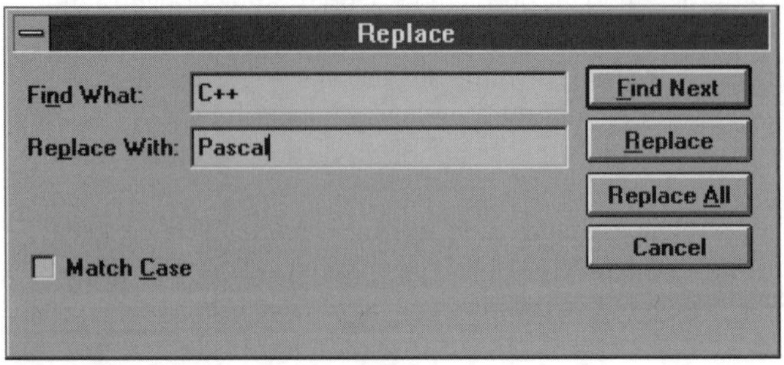

Figure 3-6 The standard Replace dialog

that the Find dialog disappears as soon as you press the Find Next button, while the Replace dialog stays onscreen until you close it.

1. Open EZEDIT.DPR. Save EZEDIT1.PAS as FREDIT1.PAS and EZEDIT.DPR as FREDIT.DPR.
2. Double-click on the MainMenu component and add to the existing menu items as specified in Table 3-9.

Table 3-9 Additional menu items for the FREDIT project

MENU CAPTION	MENUITEM CAPTION	SHORTCUT
&Search	&Find	CTRL+F
	Find &Next	CTRL+N
	&Replace	CTRL+R

3. You now need to declare additional variables and methods to the *private* section of the TEZEdit declaration. The following code shows the entire *private* section of TEZEdit.

Note: When you add entries to a class section, all variables must be declared before procedures and functions.

```
private
  { Private declarations }
  CurrentFile: String;
  EZIni: TIniFile;
  FStr, FPtr, FTarget: PChar;
  RStr: PChar;
  procedure CheckFile;
  procedure PrepareSearch(Sender: TObject);
  function DoSearch: Boolean;
  procedure DoReplace;
```

4. Just below the {$R *.DFM} statement, enter the following three procedure definitions. These will perform the searches and replacements on the currently open document.

```
{$R *.DFM}

procedure TEZEdit.PrepareSearch(Sender: TObject);
begin
  {If memory already allocated then release it}
  if Assigned(FStr) then StrDispose(FStr);
  if Assigned(FTarget) then StrDispose(FTarget);
  {Allocate new memory to hold the document}
  FStr := StrAlloc(Memo1.GetTextLen + 1);
  {Copy the document text into allocated memory}
  Memo1.GetTextBuf(FStr,Memo1.GetTextLen + 1);
  {Initialize the find pointer to the start of the document}
  FPtr := FStr;
  with (Sender as TFindDialog) do begin
    {Allocate memory for the user's search string}
    FTarget := StrAlloc(Length(FindText) + 1);
    {Copy search string, converting it to ASCIIZ}
    StrPCopy(FTarget,FindText);
    {If search is no case-sensitive, convert to all uppercase}
    if not (frMatchCase in Options) then begin
      StrUpper(FStr);
      StrUpper(FTarget);
    end;
  end;
end;

function TEZEdit.DoSearch: Boolean;
var
  ret: integer;
begin
  {While there is more text to search...}
  while FPtr <> nil do begin
    {Try to match first character of search string}
    FPtr := StrScan(FPtr, FTarget[0]);
    {Found 1st character, see if rest matches}
    if FPtr <> nil then begin
```

continued on next page

continued from previous page

```
      {Only compare up to length of search string}
      if StrLComp(FPtr, FTarget, StrLen(FTarget)) = 0 then begin
        {Found a match, set focus back to TMemo component}
        Memo1.SetFocus;
        {Calculate and assign position of found string}
        Memo1.SelStart := FPtr - FStr;
        {Length to highlight is always length of search string}
        Memo1.SelLength := StrLen(FTarget);
        {Set to next position ready for another search}
        Fptr := Fptr + 1;
        {Indicate success}
        DoSearch := True;
        exit;
      end;
    end else
      {No more occurrences left}
      Break;
    {Set to next position ready for another search}
    fptr := fptr + 1;
  end;
  {Nothing more found}
  DoSearch := False;
end;

procedure TEZEdit.DoReplace;
var
  ofs: integer;
begin
  {Replace highlighted on-screen text}
  Memo1.SetSelTextBuf(RStr);
  {Save offset of replacement position}
  ofs := FPtr - FStr - 1;
  {Dispose old copy of document}
  StrDispose(FStr);
  {Allocate memory for updated document}
  FStr := StrAlloc(Memo1.GetTextLen + 1);
  {Copy updated document}
  Memo1.GetTextBuf(FStr, Memo1.GetTextLen + 1);
  {If not case-sensitive, convert to uppercase}
  if not (frMatchCase in ReplaceDialog1.Options) then
    StrUpper(FStr);
  {Set find pointer to starting position of next search}
  FPtr := FStr + ofs + StrLen(RStr);
end;
```

5. Click on the Find menu item and enter this line to display the Find dialog for the user:

```
procedure TEZEdit.FindNext1Click(Sender: TObject);
begin
  FindDialog1.Execute;
end;
```

6. Click on the Find Next menu item and enter the following to allow the user to continue searching for more occurrences of the same string:

```
procedure TEZEdit.FindNext1Click(Sender: TObject);
begin
  if not DoSearch then
    {Let user know there was no match}
    MessageDlg('"' + FindDialog1.FindText + '" not found',
      mtinformation, [mbok], 0);
end;
```

7. On the Events page for FindDialog1, double-click the OnFind event and enter the following code to prepare for and perform a new search entered by the user.

```
procedure TEZEdit.FindDialog1Find(Sender: TObject);
begin
  FindDialog1.CloseDialog;
  PrepareSearch(FindDialog1);
  if not DoSearch then
    {No match was found}
    MessageDlg('"' + FindDialog1.FindText + '" not found',
      mtinformation, [mbok], 0);
end;
```

8. Click on the Replace menu item and enter this line to display the Replace dialog for the user:

```
procedure TEZEdit.Replace1Click(Sender: TObject);
begin
  ReplaceDialog1.Execute;
end;
```

9. On the Events page for ReplaceDialog1, double-click the OnFind event and enter the following to perform a Find without Replace.

```
procedure TEZEdit.ReplaceDialog1Find(Sender: TObject);
begin
  PrepareSearch(ReplaceDialog1);
  if not DoSearch then
    {No match was found}
    MessageDlg('"' + ReplaceDialog1.FindText + '" not found',
      mtinformation, [mbok], 0);
end;
```

10. On the Events page for ReplaceDialog1, double-click the OnReplace event and enter the following to perform both Replace and Replace All requests:

```
procedure TEZEdit.ReplaceDialog1Replace(Sender: TObject);
begin
  PrepareSearch(ReplaceDialog1);
```

continued on next page

continued from previous page

```
  with ReplaceDialog1 do begin
    {Allocate memory for search string}
    RStr := StrAlloc(Length(ReplaceText) + 1);
    {Copy replace string and convert to ASCIIZ}
    StrPCopy(RStr, ReplaceText);
    if frReplaceAll in Options then begin
      {Replace all occurrences of search string}
      while DoSearch do DoReplace;
    end else begin {frReplace}
      {Just replace next occurrence if found}
      if not DoSearch then
        MessageDlg('"' + ReplaceDialog1.FindText + '" not found',
          mtinformation, [mbok], 0)
      else
        DoReplace;
    end;
    {Free the memory holding the search string}
    StrDispose(RStr);
  end;
end;
```

11. Compile and run FREDIT.DPR. Open a text file and try out different searches and replaces. Notice that the Find dialog closes as soon as you enter your search string, while the Replace dialog stays open until you close it, as shown in Figure 3-7.

How It Works

The logic for handling the TFindDialog and TReplaceDialog components is a bit different from other common dialogs like TOpenDialog. When a TOpenDialog object returns from its Execute method, the user has already entered information and pressed the OK button. TOpenDialog is *modal*, meaning it does not return until the user has completed its use. TFindDialog and TReplaceDialog are *modeless*. They return immediately upon displaying the dialog onscreen even though the user has not yet entered any information. In other words, even while one of these dialogs is onscreen, the user can still continue to work within the application as if the dialog wasn't there. When the user does enter information, the dialog responds with either an OnFind or OnReplace event, and only then do you need to perform these functions.

When you handle the OnFind or OnReplace event, you have the choice of closing the dialog or leaving it open so the user can quickly enter more requests. This How-To demonstrates both options. The Find dialog is immediately closed upon receiving a request by calling TFindDialog's CloseDialog method, while the Replace dialog is left open until either the user closes it or the application is ended. Note that calling CloseDialog doesn't dispose of the TFindDialog object; it simply removes the dialog from the screen.

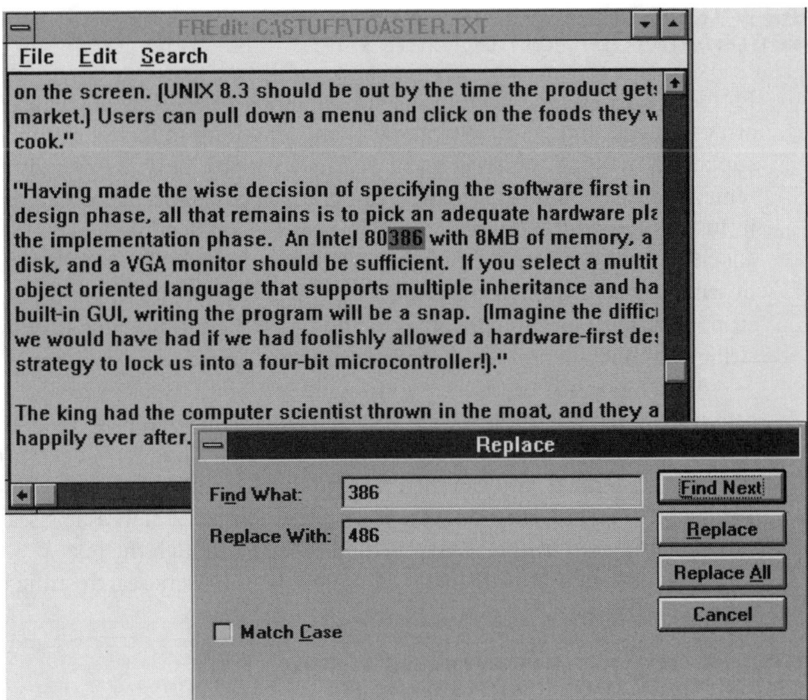

Figure 3-7 FREDIT during a Replace function

Preparing for a New Search

The preparation for a new search requires some explanation. TMemo allows you to access its text in different ways. Two of those ways, the Text and Lines properties, store the text as Pascal strings. This is not directly compatible with Windows, which stores text as ASCIIZ strings. The Lines property is very convenient for many purposes, so it may seem reasonable to simply construct a loop that iterates over each line to search for the text. However, there are some serious drawbacks to this. When you access the Lines property, TMemo has to load the single ASCIIZ string from Windows and then break it into separate Pascal strings for you. As each Pascal string is created, TMemo adds a carriage return and line feed, meaning it no longer matches the text as stored by Windows. If you now find the search string, it will be difficult to highlight it for the user because the position of the search string in the Lines property probably won't match its position in the Windows version of the text.

Fortunately, TMemo provides yet another way to access the text, and this method returns the ASCIIZ string to you exactly as stored by Windows. This method is demonstrated by the following two lines:

```
FStr := StrAlloc(Memo1.GetTextLen + 1);
Memo1.GetTextBuf(FStr,Memo1.GetTextLen + 1);
```

FStr is of type PChar, which means it is a pointer to an array of characters. Character arrays defined in this manner can be of any length up to the maximum of 64K as supported by Windows. When you declare a variable of type PChar, it's important to remember that you must actually point it at some memory before attempting to use it. In the preceding code fragment, FStr is assigned the address of a block of memory allocated using the StrAlloc function. The amount of memory needed is determined by calling TMemo's GetTextLen method, which returns the length of the ASCIIZ string. You must always remember to add one more to this value to allow for the string's terminating null (or zero) character.

Although it isn't done here, you should test FStr to make sure the memory allocation was successful. If it wasn't, FStr will equal Nil, which can be tested using the Assign function, as is done in the program prior to calling StrAlloc. Once the memory is allocated, you can then retrieve the text into this memory by calling TMemo's GetTextBuf method. FPtr is set equal to FStr to start a new search, and it is subsequently used by the Search method to track through the text.

Now that the text is available for searching, the user's search string needs some preparation:

```
FTarget := StrAlloc(Length(FindDialog1.FindText) + 1);
StrPCopy(FTarget,FindDialog1.FindText);
```

Since your copy of the Memo text is in ASCIIZ format, it will be much easier to perform the search if the user's search string is put into the same format. FTarget, another PChar, is allocated enough memory to contain the search string, and the string is then copied to FTarget using the StrPCopy function, which converts a Pascal string to an ASCIIZ string. The program now has its own internal copies of both the search string and the text. This becomes important in the event the user wants the search to be case-insensitive (by leaving the Match Case check box unchecked in the Find dialog). For a case-insensitive search, you need to make the case of the strings equal. The easiest way to do that is to use the StrUpper function:

```
if not (frMatchCase in FindDialog1.Options) then begin
  StrUpper(FStr);
  StrUpper(FTarget);
end;
```

Performing a Search

You are now ready to call the DoSearch method:

```
while FPtr <> nil do begin
  FPtr := StrScan(FPtr, FTarget[0]);
  if FPtr <> nil then begin
    if StrLComp(FPtr, FTarget, StrLen(FTarget)) = 0 then begin
      Memo1.SetFocus;
```

```
      Memo1.SelStart := FPtr - FStr;
      Memo1.SelLength := StrLen(FTarget);
      Fptr := Fptr + 1;
      DoSearch := True;
      exit;
    end;
  end else Break;
  fptr := fptr + 1;
end;
DoSearch := False;
```

The Search method is really quite simple. FPtr, which was set equal to FStr before calling Search, is used to navigate through the ASCIIZ string. As long as FPtr does not become Nil, you know there is more text to be searched. Search then uses StrScan to find the first occurrence of the first character of the search string. If StrScan is not able to find this single character, StrScan will set FPtr to Nil, which will cause a jump out of the *while* loop. If there is a match on this initial character, then a complete compare is performed using StrLComp. This function compares two complete strings up to the length you specify in the third parameter and returns zero if they are equal. If they are, then Search highlights the found text for the user.

To tell Windows where to start highlighting text, you need to pass it the offset into the ASCIIZ string. This is calculated by subtracting the memory address of the string (FStr) from the memory address of the found text (FPtr). The number of characters to be highlighted is always equal to the length of the user's search string. When these values are assigned to TMemo's SelStart and SelLength properties, TMemo automatically passes them on to Windows. If the found text is not currently visible in TMemo, TMemo automatically scrolls to make it visible.

Whether the search string is found or not, FPtr is always updated to point to the next character in the string with the following line:

```
fptr := fptr + 1;
```

The FPtr variable is a pointer into the text, therefore, incrementing it by 1 causes it to point to the next character in the string.

If the search is successful, the function is set to a True value and immediately exits. If the search string is not found, the *while* loop will end. If the *while* loop ends, it falls through to the next statement after the loop, which sets the function result to False.

Selecting the Next button simply calls the Search procedure directly. No other preparation is needed, as this was done on the initial search request from the user. If the search string was previously found, FPtr will already have been set to the next character and searching will automatically continue from that position.

Finally, the first two statements in the FindDialog1Find method can now be explained. If a previous search has been conducted, the PChar variables will be pointing at some allocated memory. Before you allocate more memory for the new search, you must be sure to release the previous allocation, otherwise your system will eventually run out of memory!

Replacing Text

The logic for the Replace request is similar, but you must process a little differently depending on whether the user requested a single replace or a Replace All request. In both cases you first prepare the search as is done for the OnFind event. In addition, the replacement text is converted into an ASCIIZ string (RStr) so that it is compatible with the text it will replace. If the request is for a single replace, DoSearch is called once and, if successful, DoReplace is called. For a multiple replace, DoReplace is executed for as long as the DoSearch function returns True. RStr is disposed of before exiting.

In the DoReplace procedure, TMemo's SetSelTextBuf method is all that's needed to replace the highlighted (found) text with the replacement text onscreen (this text was highlighted by the DoSearch function). However, if the length of the replacement text differs from the length of the search string, the internal copy and the onscreen text will no longer match. Therefore, in case there is another occurrence of the search string to be replaced, the internal copy must be updated. To do this, you first must save the current offset into the existing ASCIIZ string (this is the position where the next search would begin). We subtracted 1 from this position because FPtr has already been incremented one past where the string was found. The current copy is then disposed of and the new copy retrieved from the TMemo object. Again, a check must be made on whether the search is case-insensitive or not. Finally, FPtr is reset.

There are two important things to note here. First, the reason FPtr must be reset is because the new memory allocated may not be at the same address as the memory just disposed. Second, FPtr must be further adjusted so that it points to the first character *past* the replaced text. If you don't do this it would be possible for an infinite recursion to take place (resulting very quickly in a General Protection Fault). This would happen if the replacement text itself contained a copy of the replaced text (for example, replacing "bye" with "good-bye").

Comments

Object Pascal includes two completely different systems for handling text data. This may be confusing for many newcomers to Pascal and Delphi, but there are very good reasons for it. What's more, both systems offer certain advantages. If you have experience with C or C++, you are probably already familiar with pointers and with ASCIIZ strings. If your experience is with a language like Visual Basic, you will likely find it easier to understand Pascal strings. It is worth the time to get to know both systems and how they relate to one another.

When you are working within Delphi's various classes and components, you will almost always be able to use Pascal strings; but there are times, such as in this How-To, when it is necessary (and easier) to use ASCIIZ strings.

3.6 How do I...
Determine and modify the blink rate of the caret?

COMPLEXITY: EASY

Problem

How can I adjust the blink rate of the caret? I'd like to speed it up to draw attention to a particular edit box. It is also easier to find the caret on the screen if it blinks faster.

Technique

The Windows API includes functions to query and set the blink rate of the caret. You can use these to change the rate as often as you like. You can also make the change permanent by writing the new rate to WIN.INI.

Steps

Run BLINK.EXE and try different settings with the scroll bar, as shown in Figure 3-8. Notice how the thumb button of the scroll bar flashes according to the setting you specify. Windows uses the blink rate setting for both the caret and the thumb button of scroll bars.

1. Create a new project with a blank form. Save the default unit as BLINK1.PAS and the project as BLINK.DPR.

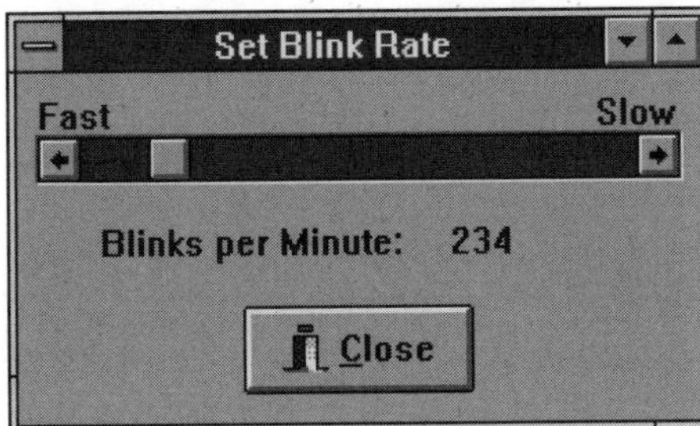

Figure 3-8 The BLINK utility

2. Add the components with the properties as shown in Table 3-10.

Table 3-10 Components, properties, and settings for the BLINK project

COMPONENT	PROPERTY	SETTING
Form	Caption	Set Blink Rate
	Height	159

continued on next page

continued from previous page

COMPONENT	PROPERTY	SETTING
	Width	273
ScrollBar	LargeChange	256
	Left	8
	Max	1024
	Min	1
	SmallChange	32
	Top	24
	Width	249
BitBtn	Kind	bkClose
	Left	88
	Top	88
Label	Caption	Fast
	Left	8
	Top	8
Label	Caption	Slow
	Left	224
	Top	8
Label	Caption	Blinks per Minute
	Left	32
	Top	56
Label	Caption	
	AutoSize	False
	Left	168
	Name	Blinks
	Top	56
	Width	56

3. In the *uses* clause of BLINK1.PAS, add **IniFiles**.
4. Just below the *implementation* statement, add the following declarations:

```
var
  WinIni: TIniFile;
  BlinkValue: integer;
```

5. On the Events page of Form1, double-click the OnCreate event and enter code to initialize the scroll bar position and Blinks label and save the current blink value:

```
procedure TForm1.FormCreate(Sender: TObject);
begin
  ScrollBar1.Position := GetCaretBlinkTime;
  BlinkValue := ScrollBar1.Position;
  Blinks.Caption := InttoStr(32768 div BlinkValue);
end;
```

6. On the Events page of ScrollBar1, double-click the OnScroll event and enter the following to set the Blink rate to the changed ScrollBar setting and update the Blinks label.

```
procedure TForm1.ScrollBar1Scroll(Sender: TObject; ScrollCode: TScrollCode;
  var ScrollPos: Integer);
begin
  If ScrollBar1.Position < 1 then ScrollBar1.Position := 1;
  SetCaretBlinkTime(ScrollBar1.Position);
  Blinks.Caption := InttoStr(32768 div ScrollBar1.Position);
end;
```

7. On the Events page of Form1, double-click the OnCloseQuery event and enter the following. This checks whether the value has been changed, and if so, changes the setting in WIN.INI.

```
procedure TForm1.FormCloseQuery(Sender: TObject; var CanClose: Boolean);
begin
  if BlinkValue <> ScrollBar1.Position then begin
    WinIni := TIniFile.Create('WIN.INI');
    WinIni.WriteInteger('Windows', 'CursorBlinkRate', ScrollBar1.Position);
    WinIni.Free;
    end;
  CanClose := True;
end;
```

8. Compile and test the project.

How It Works

GetCaretBlinkTime and SetCaretBlinkTime are Windows API functions. Windows allows a fair amount of flexibility for the programmer to query or change various system settings, and wherever this is permitted, you will find other similar API functions to do the job. For such system settings, Windows stores the values in various files, such as WIN.INI or SYSTEM.INI. To make a change permanent, you must write the setting to the correct section and key in these files. If you do not write the value out to the INI file, your setting will only last until the next time Windows is started.

TScrollBar components are excellent for setting ranges of values. You can set the Min and Max properties to any valid integer value, including negative values. The only rule is that Max must be greater than Min. The TScrollBar component will always return the correct relative value based on these properties regardless of the visual size of the TScrollBar. Very often you'll find, as in this How-To, that you can set the range so the Position property is directly usable as a value within your program. In this case, the range has been set to allow values from 1 to 1024. In fact, the setting for the caret's blink rate can range up to 65,535, but such a high value wouldn't make much sense. The rate represents the time in milliseconds between turning the caret on or off, so 65,535 would turn the caret on or off only once every 65 seconds! A setting of 1024 results in a cycle of about 65 blinks per minute. In the display of the blink rate, the setting is being divided into 32,768. This is so it will represent the number of complete blinks—once on and once off—per minute.

Note how important it is to ensure that the setting is not less than 1. A 0 or negative value would make no sense to Windows for this setting, and 0 would result in an EDivideByZero exception in the program, since the value is being used as a dividend. Although the Min property of the TScrollBar has been set to 1, it doesn't hurt to make an additional check in the code just in case. If the project was modified later and this setting was inadvertently changed to 0, this line of code would avoid an error.

Comments

You don't have to use GetCaretBlinkRate to determine the current value; you can get it from SetCaretBlinkRate when you assign your new value. This is handy when you only want to change the value temporarily, either for just your application, or for a specific control, such as an Edit box, in one of your forms. All visual components in Delphi have OnEnter and OnExit events that allow you to know when a form or component is getting the focus or losing it. This makes it easy to change a setting like the blink rate for a single control and restore it as soon as that control loses focus (whether to another control in the same form, another form, or another application).

It's important to note that when you change a setting such as the caret blink rate, you are changing it for all applications within Windows. If the user switches to another application while your setting is in effect, that application is also affected. Therefore, you should take great care when changing such settings. Unless you specifically intend for the new setting to be system-wide and/or permanent (as this How-To intends), you must be sure to make your application "Windows-Friendly" by restoring original settings whenever your application loses focus or closes.

3.7 How do I... Use scroll bars to select colors?

COMPLEXITY: EASY

Problem

Even though I understand how to use the RGB function to create a color value from the three primary colors, it's difficult to determine the values I want. How can I use

Delphi to write a utility that lets me visualize the result of combining different red, green, and blue values?

Technique

Colors are much easier to work with if you can see them. Using trial and error to set values for color properties can be frustrating. Why not find the color you like and let the computer tell you the RGB values? This How-To provides another perfect use for scroll bars, shown in Figure 3-9.

Steps

Run COLORS.EXE. Adjust the three scroll bars to see different color combinations. The TPanel behind each scroll bar displays the color intensity of the individual bar, while the form displays the combined color of all three scroll bars.

Note: Depending on the color resolution of your monitor, you may find that most colors are dithered (that is, the color is approximated by using two or three colors in various patterns). If you set your color resolution to 32K colors or greater, you will see mostly, or all, pure colors.

1. Create a new project with a blank form. Save the default unit as COLORS1.PAS and the project as COLORS.DPR.

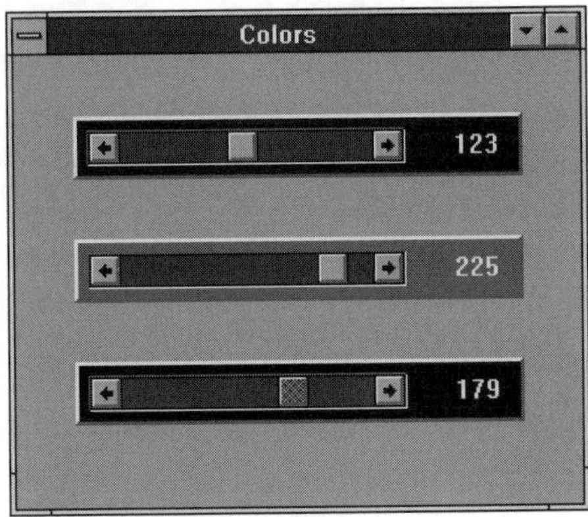

Figure 3-9 The COLORS utility

2. Add the components and properties as specified in Table 3-11.

Table 3-11 Components, properties, and settings for the COLORS project

COMPONENT	PROPERTY	SETTING
Form	Caption	Colors
	Height	263

continued on next page

continued from previous page

COMPONENT	PROPERTY	SETTING
	Width	312
Panel	BevelInner	bvRaised
	Caption	
	Height	33
	Left	32
	Name	RedPanel
	Top	32
	Width	241
Panel	BevelInner	bvRaised
	Caption	
	Height	33
	Left	32
	Name	GreenPanel
	Top	96
	Width	241
Panel	BevelInner	bvRaised
	Caption	
	Height	33
	Left	32
	Name	BluePanel
	Top	160
	Width	241

3. Add the components and properties as specified in Table 3-12 to the Panel named RedPanel.

Table 3-12 Components, properties, and settings for the RedPanel component

COMPONENT	PROPERTY	SETTING
ScrollBar	Height	17
	LargeChange	32
	Left	8
	Max	255
	Min	1
	Name	RedBar

COMPONENT	PROPERTY	SETTING
	SmallChange	1
	Top	8
	Width	169
Label	Alignment	taRightJustify
	Font.Color	White
	Height	16
	Left	220
	Name	RedNum
	Top	8

4. Add the components and properties as specified in Table 3-13 to the Panel named GreenPanel.

Table 3-13 Components, properties, and settings for the GreenPanel component

COMPONENT	PROPERTY	SETTING
ScrollBar	Height	17
	LargeChange	32
	Left	8
	Max	255
	Min	1
	Name	GreenBar
	SmallChange	1
	Top	8
	Width	169
Label	Alignment	taRightJustify
	Font.Color	White
	Height	16
	Left	220
	Name	GreenNum
	Top	8

5. Add the components and properties as specified in Table 3-14 to the Panel named BluePanel.

Table 3-14 Components, properties, and settings for the BluePanel component

COMPONENT	PROPERTY	SETTING
ScrollBar	Height	17
	LargeChange	32
	Left	8
	Max	255
	Min	1
	Name	BlueBar
	SmallChange	1
	Top	8
	Width	169
Label	Alignment	taRightJustify
	Font.Color	White
	Height	16
	Left	220
	Name	BlueNum
	Top	8

6. Select the Events page for RedBar and double-click the OnScroll event. Enter the following code to update the Red color level.

```
procedure TForm1.RedBarScroll(Sender: TObject; ScrollCode: TScrollCode;
  var ScrollPos: Integer);
begin
  RedPanel.Color := RGB(RedBar.Position,0,0);
  RedNum.Caption := IntToStr(RedBar.Position);
  RePaint;
end;
```

7. Select the Events page for GreenBar and double-click the OnScroll event. Enter the following code to update the Green color level.

```
procedure TForm1.GreenBarScroll(Sender: TObject; ScrollCode: TScrollCode;
  var ScrollPos: Integer);
begin
  GreenPanel.Color := RGB(0,GreenBar.Position,0);
  GreenNum.Caption := IntToStr(GreenBar.Position);
  RePaint;
end;
```

8. Select the Events page for BlueBar and double-click the OnScroll event. Enter the following code to update the Blue color level.

```
procedure TForm1.BlueBarScroll(Sender: TObject; ScrollCode: TScrollCode;
  var ScrollPos: Integer);
begin
  BluePanel.Color := RGB(0,0,GreenBar.Position);
  BlueNum.Caption := IntToStr(BlueBar.Position);
  RePaint;
end;
```

9. On the Events page of the form, double-click the OnCreate event and enter the following to initialize the ScrollBar and Color values.

```
procedure TForm1.FormCreate(Sender: TObject);
begin
  Redbar.Position := 0;
  Greenbar.Position := 0;
  Bluebar.Position := 0;
end;
```

10. Double-click the form's OnPaint event and enter the following code to repaint the form in the selected color.

```
procedure TForm1.FormPaint(Sender: TObject);
begin
  Form1.Color := RGB(RedBar.Position, GreenBar.Position, BlueBar.Position);
end;
```

11. Compile and run the project.

How It Works

Each time you adjust a scroll bar's position, the OnScroll event handler for that scroll bar resets the color of its TPanel component to the value of the current scroll bar position. The RePaint method of the form is then called, which in turn causes the form's OnPaint handler to be called, and the program sets the form's color to the combined values of the three scroll bars using the RGB function. The actual color values are displayed in the labels on the right side of the panels using the IntToStr function.

Comments

Although extremely easy to create, utilities like COLORS help you visualize things you might do in other applications. Delphi makes it easy to experiment in different areas of Windows functionality.

3.8 How do I... Limit text entry to certain characters?

COMPLEXITY: EASY

Problem

Delphi's useful TMaskEdit component takes care of things like phone numbers and zip codes, but there are times when I simply want to limit user entry to a certain range of characters. For instance, I want to allow only alphabetic characters when entering a name, or digits when entering a value. How can I do this with Delphi?

Technique

The easiest way to perform this kind of "masking" on a TEdit component is to handle the OnKeyPress event. Depending on the type of input check you want to do, you may also need to handle the OnChange event. Basically, the technique involves making the system forget that a character was entered if it's not one you want to allow.

Steps

Run EDITSPEC.EXE and try entering different characters in the two edit boxes. In the Numbers Only edit box try entering a minus sign in a position other than the first. Try entering more than one minus sign or decimal point. The EDITSPEC program is shown in Figure 3-10.

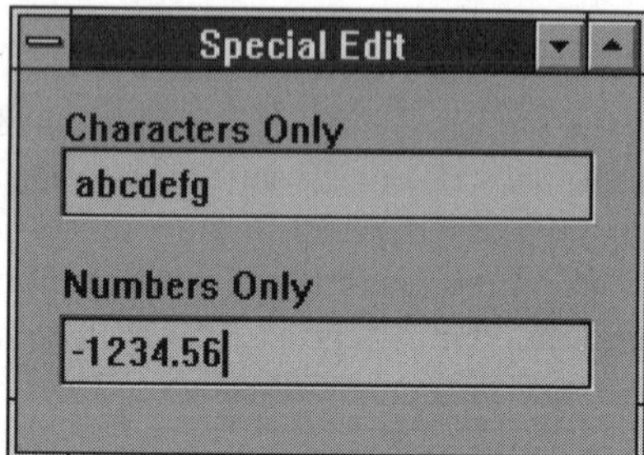

Figure 3-10 Running the EDITSPEC program

1. Create a new project. Save the default unit as EDITSPC1.PAS and the project as EDITSPEC.DPR.

2. Place two TEdit components on your form and remove the default text from the Text property.

3. Place a TLabel component above each TEdit. Enter **Characters Only** for the Caption property of one component and **Numbers Only** for the other.

4. In the TEdit labeled for characters only, double-click the OnKeyPress event and enter the following code.

```
procedure TForm1.Edit1KeyPress(Sender: TObject; var Key: Char);
begin
  if not (Key in ['a'..'z','A'..'Z',' ',#8]) then
    Key := #0;
end;
```

5. In the TEdit labeled for numbers only, double-click the OnKeyPress event and enter the following code.

```
procedure TForm1.Edit2KeyPress(Sender: TObject; var Key: Char);
begin
  if not (Key in ['0'..'9','-','.',#8]) then
    Key := #0;
  if (Key in ['.','-']) and (Pos(Key,Edit2.text) > 0) then
    Key := #0;
end;
```

6. Double-click the OnChange event for the Numbers Only TEdit and enter code to check for a valid negative value. The complete procedure should look like this:

```
procedure TForm1.Edit2Change(Sender: TObject);
var
  idx: word;
  bsp: String;
begin
  idx := Pos('-', Edit2.Text);
  if idx > 1 then begin
    bsp := Edit2.Text;
    System.Delete(bsp, idx, 1);
    Edit2.Text := bsp;
    MessageBeep(0);
  end;
end;
```

7. Compile and test the project.

How It Works

For both TEdit components, in the OnKeyPress event, you are checking for the particular characters you want to allow. This is an excellent use for Pascal sets. Notice how you can specify multiple characters or ranges of characters in the same set. If it's not a character you want to allow, you simply set the Key parameter to a null string, which can be specified by the notation #0. Also notice that in both cases, the value #8 has been specified as an allowable character. This is the character value of the backspace key. Most control characters only appear in the OnKeyDown and OnKeyUp events, but the backspace key is an exception and must be allowed to pass through.

Because Pascal is a strongly typed language, you can't simply assign a numeric value to a variable defined as a character. Whenever you want to assign a particular ASCII code value to a character variable, place the # symbol in front of the value, as you did here for the backspace key and the null character. This tells the compiler that you want the character represented by that value. The opposite is also true; if you want to assign the ASCII value of a character to a numeric variable (such as Byte, Word, or Integer), you would use the Ord function, for example:

```
Value := Ord('A');
```

The second test conducted for the Numbers Only TEdit is to make sure the user can only enter one minus sign and one decimal point. This is tested using the Pos function, which returns an offset where the specified character is found in the string, or zero if it is not found.

Some extra processing has been defined in the OnChange event for the Numbers Only TEdit. This code ensures that if a minus sign is entered, it is entered as the first character in the string. If the Pos function returns an offset greater than one, then there are other characters preceding the minus sign. This condition can't be easily checked in the OnKeyPress event because it's difficult to find out the user's current character position. Therefore, the user has to be allowed to enter the character before you can check it. After it has been entered, the character is present in the TEdit.Text property, so its position can be checked at this point. If found at any position past the first, the minus sign is deleted from the string. This requires three steps because the Delete function cannot be used directly on the Text property; therefore, you must make a copy of the Text property, process it, and then assign it back.

Comments

If all you need to do is check for particular characters or character ranges, but you don't otherwise need the user to enter data in a specific format or length, use the technique presented in this How-To. If you do require a specific format, such as a phone number, you should use Delphi's TMaskEdit component. Note the awkwardness of checking the validity of the position where the minus sign was entered; this is handled much better by the TMaskEdit component.

3.9 How do I...
Print simple text documents?

COMPLEXITY: EASY

Problem

I want users to be able to print the text documents they create with my editor. They should be able to choose and set up the printer. It would also be cool if they could choose their own font.

Technique

Delphi's TPrinter class (defined in the Printers unit) makes it easy to print text documents. With a combination of TPrinter, PrintDialog, and PrinterSetupDialog, Delphi handles most of the overhead associated with printing in Windows. In this How-To, you will pass the text from the TMemo component to a TPrinter object. In addition, you will use the FontDialog object to control the font used by both TMemo and TPrinter.

Steps

Run PREDIT.EXE on the demo disk. Open any text document. Click on Font in the Edit menu to try out different font styles, sizes, and colors. Figure 3-11 shows the standard Font dialog. From the File menu click on Printer Setup to choose a printer or to change settings for the printer. The Print Setup dialog is shown in Figure 3-12. Finally, click the Print item in the File menu to display the Print dialog and print your document (make sure your printer is on!). Figure 3-13 shows the standard Print dialog.

1. Open FREDIT.DPR. Save FREDIT1.PAS as PREDIT1.PAS and FREDIT.DPR as PREDIT.DPR.
2. Add the dialog components as shown in Table 3-15. The default property settings are fine for all three components except for the Device property of FontDialog.

Table 3-15 Additional dialog components and properties for the PREDIT project

COMPONENT	PROPERTY	SETTING
PrintDialog		Default settings
PrinterSetupDialog		Default settings
FontDialog	Device	prBoth

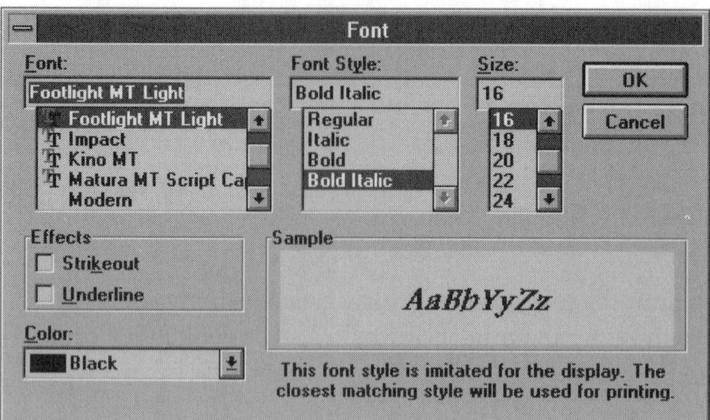

Figure 3-11 The standard Font dialog

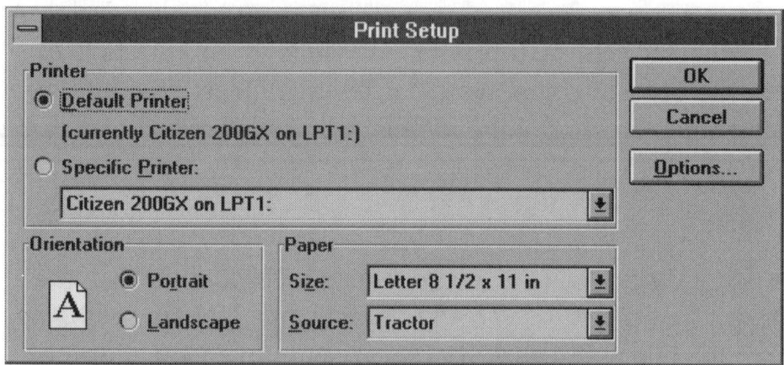

Figure 3-12 The standard Print Setup dialog

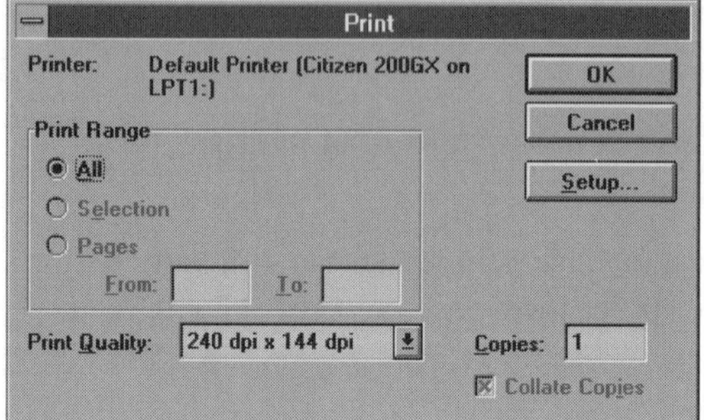

Figure 3-13 The standard Print dialog

3. Double-click the MainMenu component to bring up the Menu Designer. Insert another menu separator below the Save &As menu item in the &File menu and then insert two new menu items with the captions &Print and Printer Set&up. Append a separator and a new menu item with the caption &Font to the &Edit

menu. Table 3-16 shows the complete File and Edit menus. Close the Menu Designer when you are finished.

Table 3-16 File and Edit menus with new menu items added

MENU CAPTION	MENUITEM CAPTION	SHORTCUT
&File	&New	
	&Open	CTRL+O
	&Save	CTRL+S
	Save &As	
	-	
	&Print	
	Printer Set&up	
	-	
	E&xit	
&Edit	Cu&t	CTRL+X
	&Copy	CTRL+C
	&Paste	CTRL+V
	&Delete	CTRL+DEL
	Select &All	
	-	
	&Font	

4. In the PREDIT.PAS source code, add **Printers** to the *uses* clause. This gives your application access to the TPrinter object class.

5. Click on the new Font menu item in the form's menu and add the following code to assign the chosen font to the TMemo component.

```
procedure TEZEdit.Font1Click(Sender: TObject);
begin
  if FontDialog1.Execute then
    Memo1.Font := FontDialog1.Font;
end;
```

6. Click on the new Printer Setup menu item in the form's menu and add the following line to allow the user to choose or set up a printer.

```
procedure TEZEdit.PrintSetUp1Click(Sender: TObject);
begin
  PrinterSetupDialog1.Execute;
end;
```

7. Now click the new Print menu item in the form's menu and add code to print the currently displayed document. The entire Print1Click method should look like this:

```
procedure TEZEdit.Print1Click(Sender: TObject);
var
  TF: System.Text;
  i: integer;
begin
  if PrintDialog1.Execute then begin

    {create logical print file}
    AssignPRN(TF);
    {open the print file}
    Rewrite(TF);
    {use the same font}
    Printer.Canvas.Font := Memo1.Font;
    {a title for Print Manager to display}
    Printer.Title := Name;
    for i := 0 to Memo1.Lines.Count - 1 do
      {send each line to the printer}
      WriteLn(TF,Memo1.Lines[i]);
    {tell'em we're done}
    System.Close(TF);
  end;
end;
```

8. Compile and test the project.

How It Works

As with other common dialog objects such as TOpenDialog, the three common dialogs added here are very simple to use. If TFontDialog returns True, you simply assign the selected font to your TMemo component (or any other component that has a Font property directly or as part of a Canvas property), and the component will then redisplay itself with the selected font. The TPrinterSetupDialog component doesn't even need to be tested when executed. If you want to know whether the user changed any of the default settings, you can subsequently check the ChangeDefault property. If TPrintDialog returns True, the user has chosen to print. It also has a ChangeDefault property you can check to see whether any settings were changed.

Global Printer Object

You may notice that an object called Printer is being used to print the document, yet you have not declared this object anywhere. When you include the Printers unit in an application, it automatically creates an instance of the TPrinter class and assigns it to the variable Printer. Printer is declared in the *interface* section of the Printers unit and is therefore public to any other unit that includes Printers in the *uses* clause.

Both TPrinterSetupDialog and TPrintDialog have access to the global Printer object created in the Printers unit (because the Dialogs unit also specifies Printers in its *uses* clause). This makes it possible for these two dialog objects to automatically update the Printer object for you if the user makes any changes to the default printer settings. In particular, if the user selects a different printer, the Printer object is immediately informed of the change, so you don't have to worry about which printer was chosen. This information is available to you, though, should you have a need for it. You can check the PrinterIndex property of the Printer object to see which printer was selected. PrinterIndex is an index into the Printers property of TPrinter, which contains a list of strings naming all the selectable printers.

Note: When you access PrintDialog, you will see that it also gives you access to the PrinterSetup dialog. Therefore, you don't really need to provide a separate menu entry for PrinterSetup, but it can be a nice touch to do so.

Pascal Text Type

The System unit of Pascal contains a special file type called Text for reading and writing text files. Although normally used for disk files, it can also be used to reference a logical file such as the printer. The Print1Click method declares a variable of this type to print the document. To link this text variable to the printer, it is passed to the AssignPRN method (contained in the Printers unit). The printer file is then initialized by calling the Rewrite procedure. Rewrite actually opens the file link and prepares it to accept output. If this were a disk file, it would create the file, or if the file already existed, it would truncate it to zero length.

Before opening the printer file, the font currently in use by Memo1 is assigned to Printer's Canvas.Font property so the printed output will use the same font. Printer's Title property is assigned to the form's Name property. The Title property is used by Print Manager for display in its list of print jobs. Note that the Title property can only hold up to 30 characters.

Printing the Document

At this point, you are ready to send output to the printer. Because the Text variable TF is logically identified with the printer through the AssignPRN call, any output sent to TF will be captured by the Printer object and placed on its Canvas property. You now simply loop through the Lines property of Memo1 and send each line out with a call to WriteLn. WriteLn is also a standard Pascal System procedure for writing text.

After all lines have been written, the final step is to let Printer know that you're done. This is accomplished using the System unit's Close procedure. Printer intercepts this call and automatically performs the necessary calls to Windows (EndPage and EndDoc) to allow the document to be printed. Figure 3-14 shows the PREDIT project ready to print with a new font.

Comments

You will have noticed in this How-To that the TPrinter class contains its own Canvas property. When writing text using the WriteLn procedure, TPrinter intercepts these

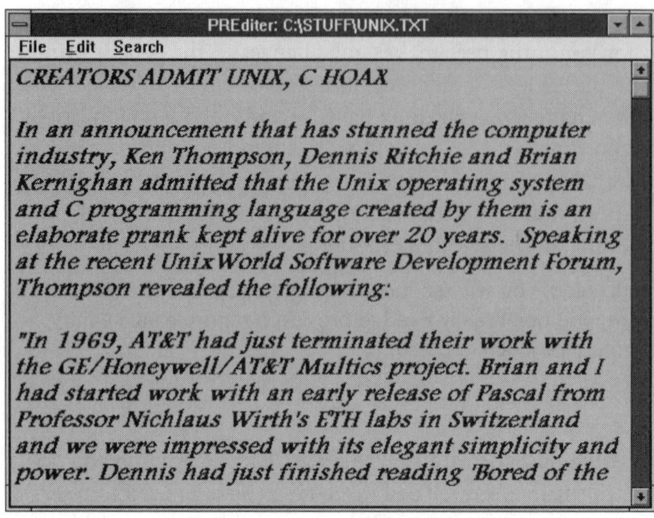

Figure 3-14 PREDIT.EXE sporting a different font style and size

procedure calls and arranges your text on its canvas. This Canvas property is the same as the Canvas properties used in other Delphi components, which means that, in addition to WriteLn, you can use the methods of Canvas to place text or graphics anywhere on the page. The advantage of using WriteLn for simple text files is that TPrinter handles paging for you as well. If you use other methods, you will need to handle paging yourself; however, this is fairly simple and the trade-off is complete freedom in what you print.

3.10 How do I...
Justify text within a specified frame?

COMPLEXITY: INTERMEDIATE

Problem

I often want to print text directly on a portion of a form or PaintBox, but it's very difficult to figure out how and where to break long lines of text so that it fits within a specific rectangular space. I'd also like to control alignment. Does Delphi provide an easy way to do this, and can it also be used for printing documents?

Technique

On a form or other container-type component, TLabels can take care of this for you automatically, but TLabels are limited to 255-character Pascal strings. If you have text longer than 255 characters, or if you want to format text on a page to be printed, TLabels are of no help.

Attempting to navigate through a long text string, calculating and manipulating the text so you can break it over several lines to fit within a certain space, is a tedious and difficult chore. Fortunately, you don't have to. Windows provides an API call that is custom-made for this very task. Using this call, you can format text to fit within any size rectangle anywhere on your form or printer page, and the text can be left, right, or center justified.

Steps

Run JUSTTEXT.EXE. Every time you select the Random button, a different size rectangle is drawn in a different position, but it's always exactly the right size to contain the entire sample text drawn within it. Try selecting the different radio buttons, as shown in Figure 3-15, to change the justification.

1. Create a new project with a blank form. Save the default unit as JUST1.PAS and the project as JUSTTEXT.DPR.

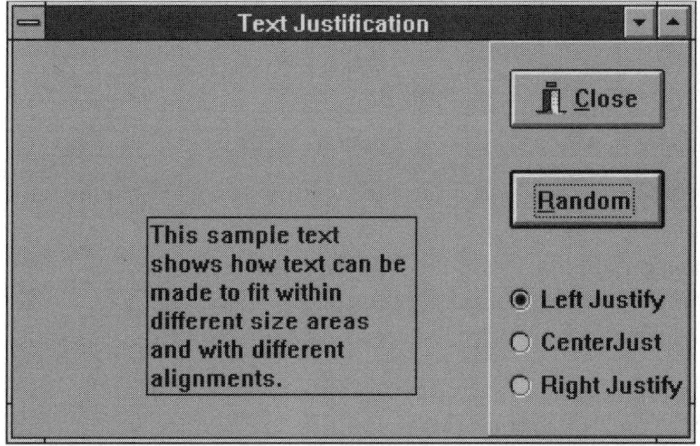

Figure 3-15 JUSTTEXT using the DrawText API function

2. Add the components and properties as shown in Table 3-17.

Table 3-17 Components, properties, and settings for the JUSTTEXT project

COMPONENT	PROPERTY	SETTING
Form	Caption	Text Justification
Panel	Align	alRight
	Caption	

continued on next page

continued from previous page

COMPONENT	PROPERTY	SETTING
	Left	305
BitBtn	Kind	bkClose
	Left	12
	Top	16
Button	Caption	&Random
	Left	12
	Top	72
RadioButton	Caption	Left Justify
	Checked	True
	Left	12
	Name	LeftJust
	Top	136
RadioButton	Caption	Center Just
	Left	12
	Name	CenterJust
	Top	160
RadioButton	Caption	Right Justify
	Left	12
	Name	RightJust
	Top	184

3. In the *private* section of Form1, add the following variable declarations. These are used for assigning the random position of the text.

```
private
  { Private declarations }
  LitTop, LitLeft, LitBottom, LitRight: Integer;
  TextJust: word;
```

4. Immediately following the *implementation* statement, add the following text constant.

```
implementation

const
  literal = 'This sample text shows how text can be made ' +
            'to fit within different size areas and with ' +
            'different alignments.';
```

5. On the Events page of the Object Inspector, double-click the OnCreate event for the form and enter the following code to seed the random number generator.

```
procedure TForm1.FormCreate(Sender: TObject);
begin
  Randomize;
end;
```

6. Click any one of the radio buttons. For the OnClick event, enter JustClick for the event handler name. Set the OnClick event for the other two radio buttons to this same event handler. Double-click this event handler and enter the following code to capture the alignment setting.

```
procedure TForm1.JustClick(Sender: TObject);
begin
  if LeftJust.Checked then TextJust := dt_Left
  else if CenterJust.Checked then TextJust := dt_Center
  else TextJust := dt_Right;
  Invalidate;
end;
```

7. Double-click the Random button and enter the following code to set a new random position and size for the rectangle.

```
procedure TForm1.Random1Click(Sender: TObject);
begin
  LitLeft := Random((ClientWidth - Panel1.Width) div 2);
  LitTop := Random(ClientHeight div 2);
  LitRight := Random(ClientWidth - Panel1.Width - LitLeft) - 1;
  if LitRight < 100 then LitRight := 100;
  inc(LitRight, LitLeft);
  Invalidate;
end;
```

8. Double-click the OnPaint event of the form and enter code to further adjust the rectangle, paint the rectangle and the text. The entire FormPaint procedure should look like this:

```
procedure TForm1.FormPaint(Sender: TObject);
var
  Tr, Rr: TRect;
begin
  Tr := Rect(LitLeft, LitTop, LitRight, 0);
  InflateRect(Tr, -2, -2);
  DrawText(Canvas.Handle, Literal, StrLen(Literal), Tr,
    dt_WordBreak or TextJust or dt_CalcRect);
  if Tr.Bottom >= ClientHeight then
    OffsetRect(Tr, 0, -(Tr.Bottom - ClientHeight));
  Rr := Tr;
  InflateRect(Rr, 2, 2);
  Canvas.Rectangle(Rr.Left, Rr.Top, Rr.Right, Rr.Bottom);
  DrawText(Canvas.Handle, Literal, StrLen(Literal), Tr,
    dt_WordBreak or TextJust);
end;
```

9. Double-click the OnResize event for the form and enter the following code to enforce a minimum size for the form.

```
procedure TForm1.FormResize(Sender: TObject);
begin
  if ClientWidth - Panel1.Width < 200 then
    ClientWidth := 200 + Panel1.Width;
  if ClientHeight < 200 then
    ClientHeight := 200;
  Invalidate;
end;
```

10. Compile and run the project.

How It Works

JUSTTEXT uses an API function called DrawText to do most of the work. DrawText is one of the more powerful and useful API text functions provided by Windows. Besides actually printing the text, it knows how to wrap text over multiple lines, justify the text both horizontally and vertically, and even calculate the required height of a rectangle for the specified text.

The first thing JUSTTEXT does when it starts is call the Randomize procedure (in the FormCreate method in step 5). This procedure seeds the random number generator. This is important; especially if you're developing games. If you don't do this, your program will generate the same pattern of "random" numbers every time it is run. Computers aren't able to generate a truly random number (if they could, you wouldn't be able to trust any of their arithmetic functions!). Randomize allows a series of seemingly random numbers to be generated by seeding the initial random value. This can be done many ways but is often done by performing various mathematical functions on the current time value.

When you press any of the three radio buttons, the event handler (see step 6) checks to see which one is checked and sets a variable to store the corresponding justification value used by the DrawText function. Whenever DrawText is called, this value is passed along too. The form's Invalidate method is called here to force an immediate update so the new justification is displayed.

Calculating the Rectangle

Clicking the Random button causes the program to use the Random function to generate a new starting position and size for the rectangle (shown in step 7). The top, left, and right borders are all calculated this way. Some additional limits are placed on the result of the random functions. The top and left borders are only allowed to be within the top-left quadrant of the available client area. The right border must be at least 100 positions to the right of the left border, but is allowed to extend to the edge of the TPanel. The bottom of the randomly generated rectangle is not set randomly because its value depends on how much vertical space is needed to display all the text within the left and right borders. Finally, the form's Invalidate method is called to force a repaint of the form.

The FormPaint method performs the actual painting (see step 8). Because DrawText requires a TRect structure to be passed with the rectangle coordinates, the first thing done is to assign the randomly assigned values to Tr using the Rect method. You pass 0 for the bottom value because it is not yet known what this value should be. The InflateRect API procedure is then called to shrink the rectangle by two pixels on all sides. This is done to allow a small space between the lines of the rectangle and the text within. DrawText is then called for the first time. On this call, a flag is passed called dt_CalcRect. This flag tells DrawText that it is not to actually paint the passed text; instead, DrawText calculates the vertical space required to contain all the text based on the top, left, and right values currently in the Tr structure. DrawText assigns the required value to Tr.Bottom. The other two flags passed are dt_WordBreak, which tells DrawText that it should break the text into lines that will fit within the left and right borders; and the TextJust variable, which was assigned in the JustClick method for the radio buttons, and will contain either dt_Left, dt_Center, or dt_Right.

Now that the bottom rectangle value is known, it can be checked to make sure it's within the client area of the form. If it isn't, the entire rectangle is adjusted upwards by the amount required to make it entirely visible using the OffsetRect API call. The finalized values in the Tr record are copied to the Rr record, which is then inflated by two pixels so it equals the size needed to paint the frame. The Rr values can then be passed to the form's Canvas.Rectangle method.

Drawing the Text

Finally, DrawText is called a second time with all the same parameters except for dt_CalcRect. DrawText will now actually paint the text within the rectangle specified by Tr. The DrawText API function requires you to pass a device context for the surface you wish to paint on. The TCanvas object stores this device context in its Handle property so it's always available to you whenever you want to use it directly. This applies to any component that contains a Canvas property, including the TPrinter object. The second parameter is the text to be printed; because this is an API call, the text must be an ASCIIZ string. Note that strings defined as constants, as Literal is, can be used as either Pascal or ASCIIZ strings. The third parameter is the length of the text to be printed. The fourth parameter is the TRect record containing the rectangle coordinates. The last parameter is a set of flags to control the functionality of DrawText.

Note: The flags used in this How-To are the most common ones you'll use, but there are also several others available. These are all well documented in Delphi's online help. You may want to look these up and experiment with them.

The FormResize method simply checks to make sure the form isn't allowed to be smaller than a specified size. This is so there is always enough room for the entire text string to be visible.

Revisiting PREDIT

Now that you've been introduced to the DrawText API function, you may want to revisit the Print1Click method you wrote in the PREDIT project from How-To 3.9. One of the limitations of the PREDIT printing function is that it will print on paper exactly as it is displayed onscreen in the TMemo component. If you size the PREDIT form so that only 20 characters can fit in a line, then it will also print with only 20 characters per line. The DrawText API function allows you to get around this limitation; you can format to any width anywhere on the printed page regardless of how it's displayed onscreen.

To use DrawText, you need to retrieve the ASCIIZ text from the TMemo component as you did for the Find and Replace functions. A sample Print1Click method for PREDIT, rewritten to use DrawText, is shown here. Note, however, that it's only sufficient for printing documents that can fit on a single page.

```
procedure TPREditer.Print1Click(Sender: TObject);
var
  MText: pchar;
  MLen: integer;
begin
  if PrintDialog1.Execute then begin
    with Printer do begin
      Canvas.Font := Memo1.Font;
      Title := Name;
      MLen := Memo1.GetTextLen;
      MText := StrAlloc(MLen + 1);
      Memo1.GetTextBuf(MText, MLen + 1);
      BeginDoc;
      DrawText(Canvas.Handle, MText, MLen, Canvas.ClipRect,
         dt_WordBreak);
      EndDoc;
      StrDispose(MText);
    end;
  end;
end;
```

This code is actually simpler to understand then the previous method of opening a logical file linked to the printer. In this version you are simply painting text directly on the Canvas property of the Printer object. When you are ready to paint the text for a new document, you first call BeginDoc to clear the canvas and set up the link to the printer. When you are finished painting the entire document, you call EndDoc to send the document off to the printer. If you have multiple pages to print, you must paint one page at a time and call NewPage before going on to the next page.

Comments

As mentioned, the sample Print1Click method shown in the "How It Works" section is only capable of painting a single page of text. If you attempt to print a document that spans more than one page, you will only get the first page. In order to print multipage documents, you must enhance this method further. The one shortcoming of DrawText is, given a specific rectangle to print in, it properly prints only as much text as can fit, but does not inform you how many characters were actually printed. This makes it difficult, for example, to break an ASCIIZ string over a page boundary; there is no easy way to determine where within the string to start printing on the next page.

4

4

MOUSE AND MENU

How do I...

Mouse control and the menu system tend to be taken for granted. Windows handles the movement of the mouse and the selection of menu items, and the application simply responds to messages sent to it by Windows. In Delphi, mouse and menu controls are available to you in the form of OnMouseDown, OnMouseUp, and OnMouseMove events for the mouse, and OnClick events for the menu. Delphi also provides methods for modifying menus and menu items and switching among the predefined cursors at run time. Although this is sufficient for most applications, you certainly aren't limited to static text menus and predefined mouse cursors!

In addition to using the standard mouse cursors, you can create your own. You can place the cursor anywhere on the screen at any time and even move the cursor under program control. For menus, you can replace the simple text items with bitmapped pictures, define your own custom check marks, or paint a menu item dynamically at run time. These features not only add sizzle to your application but also make your application more intuitive and friendly for the user.

4.1 Place the mouse cursor on a control

Using a simple Windows API function, you can place the mouse cursor anywhere at any time. The most common and useful purpose for this is to simultaneously highlight a particular control and allow the user to click on that control without moving the mouse.

4.2 Animate the mouse cursor

This How-To shows you how to animate the mouse. You will want to do this when creating tutorials for your application or writing presentations, games, or educational software in which the program must move the mouse.

4.3 Create and use my own mouse cursor

Delphi provides fourteen predefined mouse cursors. Any of these can be assigned to forms and controls at design time or run time. It's quite common, however, for applications to define additional cursors for special uses that the standard Delphi or Windows cursors don't cover. Delphi lets you add your own creations to its list of standard cursors and then lets you use them exactly as you would any other.

4.4 Modify the menu at run time

This How-To covers the Delphi methods for adding and removing menu items at run time and highlights the difference between main menus and menu items in performing these operations. These features are very useful for providing users with information about what options are available or are currently active at any moment during the use of your application.

4.5 Display a file history list in a menu

One common and useful feature employed by many applications is displaying a list of the most recently opened files as entries in a menu. This lets the user reopen these files with a single click and drag of the mouse or just two keystrokes instead of going through the steps of selecting a file from the Open dialog. This How-To shows you how to implement this feature.

4.6 Put pictures in menus

Menu items are not limited to text. Sometimes pictures are more informative in showing the purpose of the menu selection, and they can give your application a special flair. In this How-To you will install a picture in your menu to indicate whether sound is on or off.

4.7 Create and use custom check marks in menus

Windows' standard check mark for flagging a menu item as being checked is rather unremarkable. However, Windows allows you to define your own check marks. Not only that, but each menu item can be assigned two different check marks, one for selected and one for the unselected state.

4.8 Use a different font in a menu

Windows allows for a technique referred to as *Owner-Draw* that lets you take over the task of drawing various controls at run time. This How-To shows how to employ this technique to dynamically paint a menu item so that it changes according to user selections.

4.9 Modify the System menu

Although there are certain limits, Windows allows you to modify the application's System menu. Delphi helps out with a few built-in methods, and the rest can be done through the Windows API.

4.1 How do I...
Place the mouse cursor on a control?

COMPLEXITY: EASY

Problem

I've seen some applications that place the mouse cursor over a particular control, usually a button. This is great because it shows the preferred action and saves having to move the mouse at the same time. How do I do this in Delphi?

Technique

This is a very simple, yet often underused feature. Windows provides an API function to set the position of the mouse. All you need to do is decide where you want it and calculate the screen coordinates for that position.

Steps

Run PLACER.EXE. Use the cursor movement keys, TAB or SHIFT-TAB to switch focus to the different controls on the form. Each time the focus changes to a different control, the mouse cursor is placed at the exact center of that control, as shown in Figure 4-1. You are still free to move the mouse by hand and click on any control.

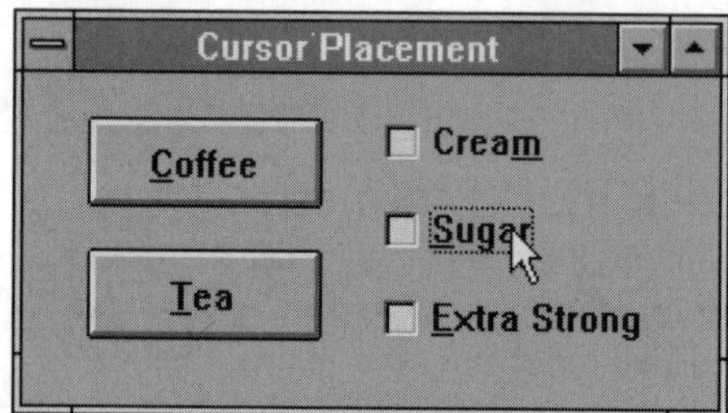

Figure 4-1 The PLACER application

1. Create a new project. Save the default unit as PLACER1.PAS and the project as PLACER.DPR.
2. Add the components, properties, and settings as shown in Table 4-1.

Table 4-1 Components, properties, and settings for the PLACER project

COMPONENT	PROPERTY	SETTING
Form	Caption	Cursor Placement
	ClientHeight	121
	ClientWidth	262
	KeyPreview	True
Button	Caption	&Coffee
	Left	24
	Top	16
Button	Caption	&Tea
	Left	24
	Top	64
CheckBox	Caption	Crea&m
	Left	136
	Top	16
CheckBox	Caption	&Sugar
	Left	136
	Top	48
CheckBox	Caption	&Extra Strong
	Left	136
	Top	80

3. Double-click the OnKeyUp event of Form1 on the Events page of the Object Inspector and enter the following code to change the mouse cursor's position.

```
procedure TForm1.FormKeyUp(Sender: TObject; var Key: Word;
  Shift: TShiftState);
var
  Mpt: TPoint;
begin
  Mpt := Point(ActiveControl.Width div 2, ActiveControl.Height div 2);
  Mpt := ActiveControl.ClientToScreen(Mpt);
  SetCursorPos(Mpt.x, Mpt.y);
end;
```

4. Compile and run the application.

How It Works

Every time a user presses a key, Windows sends messages to the active application. By default, Delphi doesn't bother passing messages for control keys on to your form. However, TForm provides a property called KeyPreview in case you want to receive these messages. If you set this property to True, Delphi will pass keyboard messages for such things as the TAB and cursor control keys to your form. By creating an event handler for OnKeyUp, you can then react to these events. Using the Key and Shift parameters, you can determine exactly what key or combination of keys was entered.

The order of events is important here. Before you receive the OnKeyUp event, Windows has already acted on the event—in this case, by changing the focus to another control. Therefore, the ActiveControl property of your form will yield the newly active control in the form. This allows you to perform any action you need based on which control is now active.

A variable, Mpt, of type TPoint is declared. TPoint, as its name implies, stores a point in the form of *x* and *y* coordinate values. It is an easy matter to calculate the center of the active control by dividing its Width and Height properties by two and assigning the results to the Mpt variable using the Point function. The values calculated here are, of course, only relative to the control itself. These values must now be converted into coordinates relative to the entire display screen in order to be used for placing the mouse cursor. Fortunately, Delphi simplifies this too! All visual components include a method called ClientToScreen (and a corresponding ScreenToClient method). ClientToScreen takes the TPoint value passed as being relative to the control and returns the equivalent screen TPoint value.

Note: The Windows API also has functions with the names ClientToScreen and ScreenToClient, but they require you to manually calculate the relative position within your form rather than within the particular control you're interested in. Therefore the Delphi methods are easier to use.

After the call to the ClientToScreen method, Mpt contains the correct *x* and *y* coordinates for the screen. These *x* and *y* values can now be passed to a simple Windows API function called SetCursorPos to actually move the mouse cursor to the desired position.

Comments

Although very simple, this How-To shows how seamlessly you can combine the advantages and power of Delphi objects, properties, and methods with direct access to Windows through its API. The advantages of this "best of both worlds" environment cannot be overemphasized.

4.2 How do I...
Animate the mouse cursor?

COMPLEXITY: EASY

Problem

I'm developing a tutorial for my application, and I'd like to have the program move the mouse across the screen from one control to another. How can I do this in Delphi?

Technique

In How-To 4.1, you learned how to place the mouse in any location on the screen. This How-To will build on this by using a similar API function to determine the current location of the mouse and repeatedly move it closer to the desired location using a system timer component.

Steps

Run FIDO.EXE. Move the mouse anywhere on the screen. The mouse will immediately begin to move back to the button in the Fido form, as shown in Figure 4-2. Notice how the button's caption changes between "Here Boy!" and "Good Mouse!". When you're done, you can close Fido by clicking the button.

1. Create a new project. Save the default unit as FIDO1.PAS and the project as FIDO.DPR.

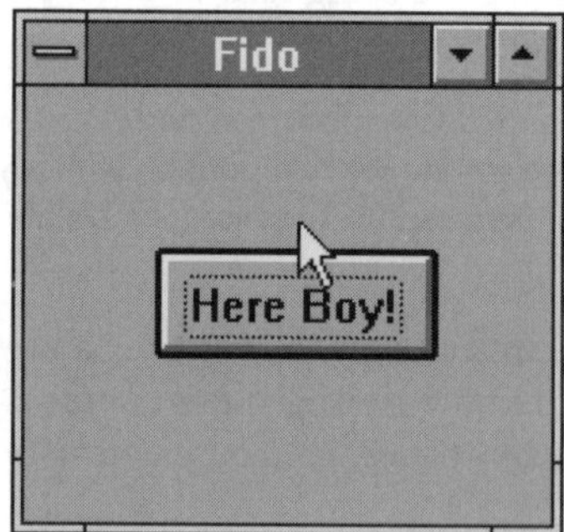

Figure 4-2 FIDO in action!

2. Add the components, properties, and settings as shown in Table 4-2.

Table 4-2 Components, properties, and settings for the FIDO project

COMPONENT	PROPERTY	SETTING
Form	Caption	Fido
	ClientHeight	130
	ClientWidth	164
	Position	poScreenCenter
Button	Left	40
	Top	48
Timer	Interval	25

3. In the *public* section of Form1, add the following variable declaration. This will be used to store the button control's center position.

```
public
  { Public declarations }
  Home: TPoint;
```

4. Just below the ***implementation*** statement, enter the following constant declarations. These will be used as captions for the button control.

```
implementation
{Define captions for button}
const
  Whistle = 'Here Boy!';
  Praise = 'Good Mouse!';
```

5. Double-click the form's OnCreate event and enter the following code. This code calculates the button's center position, converts it to screen coordinates, and places the mouse there as its initial position.

```
procedure TForm1.FormCreate(Sender: TObject);
begin
  {Calculate center of button relative to form}
  Home.x := Button1.Left + Button1.Width div 2;
  Home.y := Button1.Top + Button1.Height div 2;
  {Convert point to screen-relative Coordinates-ordinates}
  Home := ClientToScreen(Home);
  {Place the cursor there to start}
  SetCursorPos(Home.x, Home.y);
end;
```

6. Double-click the TTimer component and enter the following code to incrementally move the mouse closer to its home position at the center of the button control.

```
procedure TForm1.Timer1Timer(Sender: TObject);
var
  Mpt: TPoint;
  Dif: integer;
begin
  {Ask Windows where the cursor is}
  GetCursorPos(Mpt);
  if (Mpt.x = Home.x) and (Mpt.y = Home.y) then begin
    {Mouse is home}
    if Button1.Caption <> Praise then
      Button1.Caption := Praise;
  end else begin
    {"Call" the mouse home}
    If Button1.Caption <> Whistle then
      Button1.Caption := Whistle;
    {Get horizontal distance from home}
    Dif := Mpt.x - Home.x;
    {Move towards vertical center}
    if Dif > 8 then Dec(Mpt.x, 8)
    else if Dif < -8 then Inc(Mpt.x, 8)
    else Mpt.x := Home.x;
    {Get Vertical distance from home}
    Dif := Mpt.y - Home.y;
    {Move towards horizontal center}
    if Dif > 8 then Dec(Mpt.y, 8)
    else if Dif < -8 then Inc(Mpt.y, 8)
    else Mpt.y := Home.y;
    {Set new position}
    SetCursorPos(Mpt.x, Mpt.y);
  end;
end;
```

7. Finally, double-click the button control and enter the following statement to close the application.

```
procedure TForm1.Button1Click(Sender: TObject);
begin
  Close;
end;
```

8. Compile and run the application.

How It Works

Along with the SetCursorPos API function you learned about in How-To 4.1, Windows provides a corresponding GetCursorPos function to get the mouse cursor's current position. This position is returned in screen coordinates. Note the difference in the two functions: SetCursorPos requires you to pass the *x* and *y* coordinates as separate parameters, while GetCursorPos requires you to pass a single TPoint variable instead.

When the application begins, the center position of the button is calculated (relative to the form) and stored in the Home variable. Home is then converted to screen coordinates using the form's ClientToScreen method, and the mouse is moved to this home position. All this happens before the form is displayed on the screen.

On each tick of the timer, the current position of the mouse is retrieved using the GetCursorPos function. This position may differ from where you last placed it even while the animation is taking place. This is because the user is free to manually move the mouse at all times and can therefore "interfere" with the animation. (You could eliminate this interference by performing the animation in a loop that stepped by some increment to the target position. But this would be considered unfriendly in Windows since during such a loop, no other applications could execute. Windows would effectively be frozen until the animation completed.) The mouse position is then compared—first the *x* axis, then the *y* axis (the order is not important)—to determine the distance and direction from the home position. If the distance is greater then eight pixels, the mouse is moved eight pixels on that axis, otherwise it is set to the home position for that axis.

There is no need to perform any coordinate conversion in the Timer1Timer handler, because the home position was converted to screen coordinates when the application started. However, there is a flaw in this approach: if the position of the form changes, or it is maximized, the home position will no longer be valid. It is left as an exercise for the reader to decide how to handle this problem.

Finally, each time through the loop, the button's caption is updated, if necessary, according to whether the current mouse position is at the home position or not. Since it is known the program will be updating this caption whenever necessary, it wasn't necessary to assign any particular caption at design time.

Comments

Watch the route the animation takes from any given position back to the home position. If movement is required on both axes, the movement takes place at a 45 degree angle. Once either the *x* or *y* value matches the home *x* or *y* value, the mouse moves in a straight line for the remaining distance to the home position. If you would like the mouse to move in a single straight line back to the home position, you would need to calculate separate *x* and *y* movement factors based on the difference in distance on the two axes. This is fairly simple to calculate manually; however, if you're up to learning how to write Windows callback functions, then check out the LineDDA function in the Windows API. This function, via a callback function you define, will calculate every point on a line between the two points you specify. You can then store each of the returned Point values in an array and use these values to set each successive mouse position.

4.3 How do I...
Create and use my own mouse cursor?

COMPLEXITY: INTERMEDIATE

Problem

Delphi provides enough cursors for most needs, but I'm creating special tools for my application and I need to create my own cursors to represent these tools. Is there a way to add my own cursors to my Delphi application?

Technique

Delphi provides easy access to all the standard Windows cursors, plus it adds a few of its own. However, there is simply no way to foresee every possible need. To this end, Delphi has also been designed to allow easy addition of resources you create yourself. In this How-To, you will add a new cursor to your application's resources and then access this cursor within the application.

Steps

Run MYCURSOR.EXE. When you move the cursor within the form's client area, the cursor looks like a magnifying glass, as shown in Figure 4-3. In the upper-left corner of the cursor, you will see a tiny cross mark, this is the hot spot of the cursor. As soon as the hot spot moves outside the client area of the form, the cursor will change accordingly: the default arrow cursor if moved into the caption area, a sizing cursor if the hot spot is over one of the form's sizing borders, and so on.

Figure 4-3 MYCURSOR displaying its own cursor

1. Create a new project. Save the default unit as MYCURS1.PAS and the project as MYCURSOR.DPR.
2. Change the caption of the form to "Private Cursor" (or any caption you wish).
3. Just below the *implementation* statement, enter the following constant. This constant value will be used to represent the new cursor.

```
implementation
{Define a value for our cursor}
const
  crMagnify = 1;
```

4. Just below the first resource statement, add a second one to include the resource containing the new cursor.

```
{$R *.DFM}
{$R MYCURS1.RES}
```

5. On the Events page of the Object Inspector, double-click the OnShow event of the form and enter the following code to load the new cursor and assign it to Form1.

```
procedure TForm1.FormShow(Sender: TObject);
begin
  {Load new cursor into application's array}
  Screen.Cursors[crMagnify] := LoadCursor(HInstance, 'MAGNIFIER');
  {Now assign it to form}
  Form1.Cursor := crMagnify;
end;
```

6. Compile and run the application.

How It Works

As you can see, it's a snap to include any cursor resource into your application and use it. Once the cursor has been loaded, it can be used exactly like any of the predefined cursors Delphi provides—by assigning its constant value to the Cursor property of any form or control.

Creating Your Cursor

Naturally, before you can load your own cursor, you must create it. This can be done with Delphi's Image Editor utility or any other Windows resource utility, such as Borland's Resource Workshop. Whichever utility you use, you should create a resource file (.RES file extension) rather than just a cursor file (.CUR extension).

Note: Delphi creates a resource file with the same name as your project. When you create your own resource files, you must name them differently. For example, in this How-To, Delphi already uses the name MYCURSOR.RES and will overwrite any file you create with that name.

You can create as many separate cursors as you need in a single resource file. When you include that resource in your application, using the $R compiler directive, all the cursors are available to be loaded when needed by your application.

Note: In current versions of Windows, all cursors are 32-by-32 pixels in size and can only be black and white. When you design a cursor, don't forget to define a hot spot for it. Windows requires a hot spot in order to operate the cursor.

Delphi contains 15 predefined cursors for your use. These include all of the standard Windows cursors plus four included by Delphi itself. Each of these cursors is represented in Delphi by a constant value such as crArrow or crHourGlass. These predefined constants range in value from -1 to -15. All forms and controls start with a default cursor value of 0 (crDefault). Because Delphi uses this range of numbers for the predefined cursors, it is easy for you to select numbers for your own cursor constants—simply use positive numbers beginning with 1.

Loading Your Cursor

Every Delphi application you create includes a TScreen component (accessible through the global Screen variable). The TScreen component provides many things for your application, such as the current screen resolution and information about the application's forms. It also provides management of various resources, including available fonts and cursors. The Cursors property of TScreen is a simple array of type HCursor. HCursor is a variable type defined by Windows to represent a cursor resource. When you define a constant value to represent your cursor, you are simply defining an index position into the Cursors property that will be used to store the handle of your cursor.

To load a cursor from your application's resource, you use a Windows API function called LoadCursor. This function requires two parameters. The first parameter is the instance handle of your application. Whenever a Windows program is started, Windows assigns it an instance handle, which is always available to you in a global variable called HInstance. The second parameter to LoadCursor is the name of the particular cursor you want to load from your resource. The name you pass must exactly match the name you assigned to the cursor when you created and saved it in the resource file. LoadCursor stores the cursor image in memory and returns an HCursor handle to you. You can then assign this handle directly to the Cursors property using your defined constant value as the index value. Each cursor resource must be loaded with a different index value in the Cursors property.

Assigning Your Cursor

Now that your cursor has been loaded and has a reference in the Cursors property, you are free to assign that cursor to any form or control in your application at any time simply by assigning its constant value to the Cursor (or DragCursor) property of the form or control. When you assign a cursor constant to these properties, the property will perform the work required to make Windows use the corresponding cursor.

When you close your application, you do not have to worry about releasing the memory used by your cursors. Because you inserted references to your cursors into the Cursors property, the TScreen component will automatically delete the cursors for you before the application terminates.

Comments

It's quite a simple process to create cursor resources and store them in a resource file using the Image Editor or any other Windows resource utility. So you should feel free to create all the cursor resources you need or want for an application. Once created, as you can see, it's wonderfully simple to use them in your application.

4.4 How do I... Modify the menu at run time?

COMPLEXITY: EASY

Problem

I'm creating an application in which, depending on the situation, I'd like to add or remove menu items in the main menu rather than just disabling or graying them. This would also make it possible to let the user customize the menu to some extent. How is this done in Delphi?

Technique

All the methods and properties required for modifying menus at run time are built into the menu objects of Delphi. These methods and properties are documented, but the example presented in this How-To will demonstrate them and help clarify the differences in modifying TMainMenu and TMenuItem components. The methods shown here for TMainMenu also apply to TPopupMenu.

Steps

Run MODMENU.EXE. Under the Edit menu, you will find four menu items. These menu items allow you to add and remove additional top-level menus in the main menu, and add or remove additional menu items under the last top-level menu, as shown in Figure 4-4. Experiment with these. When you create new menus or menu items, try selecting them.

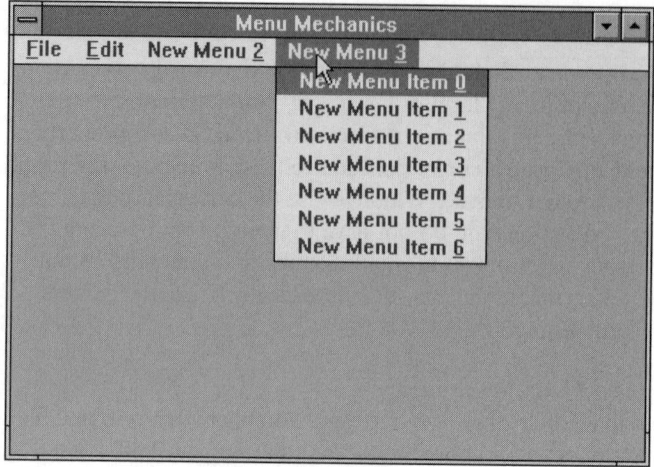

Figure 4-4 The MODMENU application

1. Create a new project. Save the default unit as MODMENU1.PAS and the project as MODMENU.DPR.
2. Add a TMainMenu component to the form and, using the Menu Designer, add the menus and menu items as shown in Table 4-3.

Table 4-3 Menu design for the MODMENU project

MENU	MENUITEM
&File	E&xit
&Edit	&Add Menu
	Add Menu &Item
	&Remove Menu
	Remove &Menu Item

3. In the *private* section of TForm1, add a declaration for the following menu event handler. This will be used to handle selection of the menu items you create at run time.

```
private
  { Private declarations }
  procedure DynaMenuClick(Sender: TObject);
```

4. Following the *implementation* and resource include statements, enter the definition for the DynaMenuClick event handler.

```
implementation

{$R *.DFM}

procedure TForm1.DynaMenuClick(Sender: TObject);
begin
  MessageDlg('You selected ' + (Sender as TMenuItem).Caption,
    mtInformation, [mbok], 0);
end;
```

5. Double-click the form's OnShow event in the Object Inspector and add the following code to disable three of the four Edit menu items.

```
procedure TForm1.FormShow(Sender: TObject);
begin
  AddMenuItem1.Enabled := False;
  RemoveMenu1.Enabled := False;
  RemoveMenuItem1.Enabled := False;
end;
```

6. Click on Edit|Add Menu and add the following code to create a new top-level menu in the main menu.

```
procedure TForm1.AddMenu1Click(Sender: TObject);
var
   NewItem: TMenuItem;
begin
  {Create a new menu item with main menu as owner}
  NewItem := TMenuItem.Create(MainMenu1);
  {Create caption for new menu item}
  NewItem.Caption := 'New Menu &' + IntToStr(MainMenu1.Items.Count);
  {Assign an event handler}
  NewItem.OnClick := DynaMenuClick;
  {Insert at end of main menu}
  MainMenu1.Items.Insert(MainMenu1.Items.Count, NewItem);
  {Ensure valid menu items are enabled}
  RemoveMenu1.Enabled := True;
  AddMenuItem1.Enabled := True;
end;
```

7. Click on Edit|Add Menu Item and enter the following code to add a new menu item under the last top-level menu.

```
procedure TForm1.AddMenuItem1Click(Sender: TObject);
var
   NewItem, ToItem: TMenuItem;
begin
```

continued on next page

continued from previous page

```
  {Don't add items to File or Edit menus}
  if MainMenu1.Items.Count > 2 then
    {Get reference to last main menu item}
    ToItem := MainMenu1.Items[MainMenu1.Items.Count - 1];
    {Create new menu item with last main menu item as owner}
    NewItem := TMenuItem.Create(ToItem);
    {Create caption relative to last main menu item's item count}
    NewItem.Caption := 'New Menu Item &' + IntToStr(ToItem.Count);
    {Assign an event handler}
    NewItem.OnClick := DynaMenuClick;
    {Ensure ToItem has no event handler}
    ToItem.OnClick := nil;
    {Insert under last main menu item}
    ToItem.Insert(ToItem.Count, NewItem);
    {Enable removal of items}
    RemoveMenuItem1.Enabled := True;  end;
end;
```

8. Click on Edit|Remove Menu and enter this code to remove the last top-level menu:

```
procedure TForm1.RemoveMenu1Click(Sender: TObject);
begin
  {Don't allow File or Edit menu to be deleted}
  if MainMenu1.Items.Count > 2 then
    {Delete the last item in the main menu}
    MainMenu1.Items.Delete(MainMenu1.Items.Count - 1);
  {Disable menu items}
  if MainMenu1.Items.Count = 2 then begin
    AddMenuItem1.Enabled := False;
    RemoveMenu1.Enabled := False;
    RemoveMenuItem1.Enabled := False;
  end;
end;
```

9. Click on Edit|Remove Menu Item and enter this code to remove the last menu item in the last top-level menu:

```
procedure TForm1.RemoveMenuItem1Click(Sender: TObject);
var
  ToItem: TMenuItem;
begin
  {Don't delete items from File or Edit menu}
  if MainMenu1.Items.Count > 2 then begin
    {Get reference to last main menu item}
    ToItem := MainMenu1.Items[MainMenu1.Items.Count - 1];
    {Make sure there's an item to delete}
    if ToItem.Count > 0 then
      {Delete the last item in the main menu's last item}
      ToItem.Delete(ToItem.Count - 1);
    {If no more items in this menu, disable item removal}
    if ToItem.Count = 0 then
```

```
    RemoveMenuItem1.Enabled := False;
  end;
end;
```

10. Click on File|Exit and enter the following line to close the application.

```
procedure TForm1.Exit1Click(Sender: TObject);
begin
  Close;
end;
```

11. Compile and run the application.

How It Works

The basic mechanics of adding and removing menu items and checking for their presence is quite simple. But it can get confusing because you're working with arrays of objects, and the technique is slightly different between the TMainMenu component and the TMenuItem components. The purpose of this How-To is to help clarify the techniques involved and get you more proficient with them.

If you've created and experimented with any menus yourself prior to this How-To, the code within the OnShow event handler probably doesn't need much explanation; you've probably already discovered how easy it is to disable or enable specific menu items. When the application first starts, the only valid menu item under the Edit menu is to add a new top-level menu, so the other three menu selections are disabled at this time. This could also be done at design time using the Menu Designer or the Object Inspector.

Adding Top-Level Menu Items

When Add Menu is selected, a new top-level menu is added to the main menu. It is important to understand at this point that all visible selections in a menu are TMenuItem components whether or not they are top-level menus. The TMainMenu component does not represent any selectable menu entries but only represents the menu as a whole. The following code is used to add a new top-level menu.

```
NewItem := TMenuItem.Create(MainMenu1);
NewItem.Caption := 'New Menu &' + IntToStr(MainMenu1.Items.Count);
NewItem.OnClick := DynaMenuClick;
MainMenu1.Items.Insert(MainMenu1.Items.Count, NewItem);
```

First, the new menu item is created, passing the main menu to the Create method to tell the item who its owner is to be. A caption is constructed complete with an accelerator key consisting of the new menu item's intended position as the last top-level item of the main menu. The new item's OnClick method is assigned to the event handler you defined for use by these dynamically created menu items. Finally, the new menu item is inserted into the main menu. In this case, new top-level items are always added at the end, but you can add them at any position from the first (position 0) to one past the last (indicated by the Count property of TMainMenu's Items property). As soon as the Insert method has completed, the new menu item will appear onscreen and be active. Selecting this new item from the menu will cause the DynaMenuClick handler to be called.

Removing a Top-Level Menu Item

Removing a top-level menu item is even easier:

```
if MainMenu1.Items.Count > 2 then
  MainMenu1.Items.Delete(MainMenu1.Items.Count - 1);
```

A check is first made to ensure there are dynamically created top-level menus that can be deleted before proceeding. Since there is code in this application to disable the RemoveMenu1 menu item at the correct time, this check is actually redundant, but it always pays to include extra checks in the code for safety.

The Delete method of TMainMenu's Items property only requires an index—the position number of the menu item you want deleted. This position number must range from 0 to one less than the current count of menu items in the main menu. In this How-To, only the last dynamically added top-level menu is deleted.

Note: If you choose to delete a top-level menu item that is not the last one, be sure to remember that all following top-level menu items will move down in position. For example, if there are five top-level menu items and you delete the fourth one, the one at the fifth position will move down to take the place of the deleted one and must now be addressed as the fourth item.

You do not have to be concerned with whether or not a top-level menu item contains submenu items. If there are any submenu items, they will be deleted by the top-level TMenuItem object when it is deleted.

Adding Menu Items to a Top-Level Menu Item

The code to add a menu item to a top-level menu is slightly more work since you must first address the desired top-level menu; other than that, it's almost the same as adding a top-level item:

```
if MainMenu1.Items.Count > 2 then begin
  ToItem := MainMenu1.Items[MainMenu1.Items.Count - 1];
  NewItem := TMenuItem.Create(ToItem);
  NewItem.Caption := 'New Menu Item &' + IntToStr(ToItem.Count);
  NewItem.OnClick := DynaMenuClick;
  ToItem.OnClick := nil;
  ToItem.Insert(ToItem.Count, NewItem);
```

First, a check is made to ensure that at least one dynamic top-level menu item has been added. This prevents new items from being added to the Edit menu. ToItem (of type TMenuItem) is then assigned to reference the last top-level menu item in the main menu. This is the menu to which a new item will be added. You then create NewItem, as is done for new top-level items. When the top-level menu referenced by ToItem was first created, its OnClick event was assigned to the DynaMenuClick handler. This was required in order to allow this top-level item to be handled directly when clicked. Now that a submenu item is being added to this top-level item, you must remove this handler reference from the top-level menu; otherwise, there will be no way to receive OnClick events for its submenu items. To do this, ToItem's OnClick property is assigned to Nil.

Finally, the new item can be inserted into the top-level menu item. The syntax of the Insert method of TMenuItem (referenced here by ToItem) is almost identical to the Insert method used to add a top-level menu item to the main menu. The difference is that this Insert method is a direct method of TMenuItem, whereas, for TMainMenu, Insert is a method of the Items property.

Removing Submenu Items

Removing a submenu item is almost as simple as removing a top-level item:

```
if MainMenu1.Items.Count > 2 then begin
  ToItem := MainMenu1.Items[MainMenu1.Items.Count - 1];
  if ToItem.Count > 0 then
    ToItem.Delete(ToItem.Count - 1);
```

Again, in order to protect the required functionality of the application, a check is made to ensure that there is at least one dynamic top-level menu. As in adding a new submenu item, a reference must first be made to the desired top-level menu item. The top-level item referenced by ToItem is then checked to make sure it contains at least one submenu item. If it has at least one, then the last one is deleted using the Delete method of TMenuItem. Once again, it should be noted that any submenu item can be deleted using this Delete method. If you delete any item but the last, all following items are moved down to fill the empty position.

If you create a menu with more than two levels (for example, a top-level menu item has a submenu item that, in turn, has its own submenu items), the logic for adding and removing these lower-level items is exactly the same as for the second level demonstrated in this How-To. The only difference is that there is one (or more) extra levels of reference you must make in order to address these lower-level items.

Comments

The menu objects provided by Delphi allow all the flexibility you need to create sophisticated menus, no matter how complex you need them to be. Besides the basic mechanics of adding and removing menus demonstrated in this How-To, the menu objects contain various other methods to allow you to manipulate your menus as needed.

4.5 How do I...
Display a file history list in a menu?

COMPLEXITY: INTERMEDIATE

Problem

Many applications provide a history of the most recently opened files within the File menu. This is a very convenient feature allowing users to reopen these files with a couple of mouse clicks or keystrokes rather than having to navigate the Open dialog every time. How can I implement this feature in my Delphi applications?

Technique

The techniques of adding and removing menu items, demonstrated in How-To 4.4, will be employed. In addition, a TStringList component will be used to manage the history and its storage to, and retrieval from, disk.

Steps

Run HISTORY.EXE. Under the File menu, you will see the typical menu selections found in most applications dealing with disk-based files. Experiment with the New, Open, and Save As menu entries. Open and Save As display the standard dialogs for selecting files. The file names you select won't actually be opened or saved, so you are free to select any names without damaging any data.

At first, there is no history displayed in the File menu. As you select different file names, this will quickly change, as shown in Figure 4-5. HISTORY.EXE will allow up

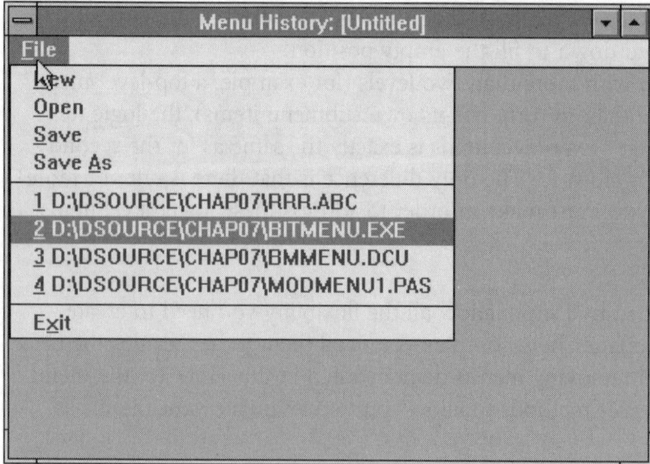

Figure 4-5 The HISTORY application

to nine file names to be displayed in the File menu. Note that when you select a file from this list, that file name disappears from the list until you open another file or save it under a different name.

1. Create a new project. Save the default unit as HISTORY1.PAS and the project as HISTORY.DPR.
2. Add the components, properties, and settings as shown in Table 4-4.

Table 4-4 Components, properties, and settings for the HISTORY project

COMPONENT	PROPERTY	SETTING
MainMenu		
OpenDialog	Filter	All Files|*.*
SaveDialog	Filter	All Files|*.*

3. Start the Menu Designer for the MainMenu component and add the menu items as shown in Table 4-5.

Table 4-5 Menu design for the project

MENU	MENUITEM
File	&New
	&Open
	&Save
	Save &As
	-
	Exit

4. Add the following declarations to the *private* section of TForm1. The comments included in the code describe the purpose of each declaration.

```
private
  { Private declarations }
  {List to store history of file names}
  History: TStringList;
  {A second menu separator when displaying history}
  N2: TMenuItem;
  {Name of currently open file, if any}
  CurName: string;
  {Procedure to rebuild history menu items}
  procedure RebuildHistory;
  {Event handler for dynamic history menu items}
  procedure ReOpenClick(Sender: TObject);
```

5. Just below the *implementation* statement, add the following constant definitions.

```
implementation

const
  {Used in caption when no existing file is open}
  UnTitled = '[Untitled]';
  {Maximum history menu items allowed}
  MaxHistory = 9;
```

6. Just below the resource compiler directive, add the code for the RebuildHistory procedure:

```
{$R *.DFM}

procedure TForm1.RebuildHistory;
var
  Item: TMenuItem;
  Pos, Idx1, Idx2: integer;
begin
  {History appears after existing separator}
  Idx1 := File1.IndexOf(N1) + 1;
  {If N2 exists then there are history items}
  if Assigned(N2) then begin
    {Use position of N2 as end of history range}
    Idx2 := File1.IndexOf(N2);
    {Delete all history elements including N2 separator}
    for Pos := Idx1 to Idx2 do File1.Delete(Idx1);
  end;
  {Trim list, if necessary, to maximum items allowed}
  if History.Count > MaxHistory then begin
    for Pos := MaxHistory to History.Count -1 do
      History.Delete(MaxHistory);
  end;
  {If there are history items then build menu items}
  if History.Count > 0 then begin
    {For each file name in history list}
    for Pos := 0 to History.Count -1 do begin
      {Create a new menu item}
      Item := TMenuItem.Create(File1);
      {Use position number as accelerator in front of file name}
      Item.Caption := '&' + IntToStr(Pos + 1) + ' ' + History[Pos];
      {Assign event handler}
      Item.OnClick := ReOpenClick;
      {Insert into File menu}
      File1.Insert(Idx1 + Pos, Item);
    end;
    {Create and insert a second separator following last item}
    N2 := TMenuItem.Create(File1);
    N2.Caption := '-';
    File1.Insert(Idx1 + History.Count, N2);
  end;
end;
```

7. Double-click Form1's OnCreate event in the Object Inspector and add the following code. This code will attempt to open and load the history file and initialize the application's caption.

```
procedure TForm1.FormCreate(Sender: TObject);
begin
  {Create the history list}
  History := TStringList.Create;
  try
    {Load stored history list from disk}
    History.LoadFromFile('HISTORY.HST');
    {Build menu items}
    RebuildHistory;
  except
    {Ignore exception, just means no history file created yet}
  end;
  {Save program caption in Hint property}
  Hint := Caption;
  {Update caption}
  Caption := Hint + ': ' + Untitled;
  {Initially no current file open}
  CurName := '';
end;
```

8. Click on File|New and enter the following code to prepare a new file.

```
procedure TForm1.New1Click(Sender: TObject);
begin
  {If a current file, add to history}
  if CurName <> '' then begin
    History.Insert(0, CurName);
    RebuildHistory;
  end;
  {Update caption and current file name}
  Caption := Hint + ': ' + Untitled;
  CurName := '';
end;
```

9. Click on File|Open and add the following code to prepare for the opened file.

```
procedure TForm1.Open1Click(Sender: TObject);
var
  Pos: integer;
begin
  if OpenDialog1.Execute then begin
    {If a current file, add to history}
    if (CurName <> '') then History.Insert(0, CurName);
    {See if newly selected file is in  history}
    Pos := History.IndexOf(OpenDialog1.FileName);
    {Selected file is in history so remove from history}
    if Pos >= 0 then History.Delete(Pos);
    RebuildHistory;
```

continued on next page

continued from previous page

```
    {Update caption and current file name}
    Caption := Hint + ': ' + OpenDialog1.FileName;
    CurName := OpenDialog1.FileName;
  end;
end;
```

10. Double-click the File|Save As menu item and add the following code to prepare for the saved file.

```
procedure TForm1.SaveAs1Click(Sender: TObject);
var
  Pos: integer;
begin
  if SaveDialog1.Execute then begin
    {If a current file, add to history}
    if (CurName <> '') then History.Insert(0, CurName);
    {See if newly selected file is in  history}
    Pos := History.IndexOf(SaveDialog1.FileName);
    {Selected file is in history so remove from history}
    if Pos >= 0 then History.Delete(Pos);
    RebuildHistory;
    {Update caption and current file name}
    Caption := Hint + ': ' + SaveDialog1.FileName;
    CurName := SaveDialog1.FileName;
  end;
end;
```

11. Double-click the form's OnDestroy event in the Object Inspector and add the following code to clean up before terminating the application.

```
procedure TForm1.FormDestroy(Sender: TObject);
begin
  {Update history list if a file still open}
  if CurName <> '' then History.Insert(0, CurName);
  {Save the history to disk}
  try
    History.SaveToFile('HISTORY.HST');
  except
    MessageDlg('Could not save History List',
      mtWarning, [mbOK], 0);
  end;
  {dispose list}
  History.Free;
end;
```

12. Enter the following procedure definition. This procedure will be the OnClick event handler for the history menu items.

```
procedure TForm1.ReOpenClick(Sender: TObject);
var
  Pos: integer;
```

```
  NewName: string;
begin
  {Calculate position in history list from
   relative menu position of selected file name.}
  Pos := File1.IndexOf(TMenuItem(Sender)) - File1.IndexOf(N1) - 1;
  {Get file name from history list}
  NewName := History[Pos];
  {If a current file, add to history}
  if CurName <> '' then History.Insert(0, CurName);
  {Remove the selected name from history}
  History.Delete(History.IndexOf(NewName));
  {Update the menu}
  RebuildHistory;
  {Update caption and current file name}
  Caption := Hint + ': ' + NewName;
  CurName := NewName;
end;
```

13. Finally, click on File|Exit and enter the following line to terminate the application.

```
procedure TForm1.Exit1Click(Sender: TObject);
begin
  Close;
end;
```

14. Compile and run the application.

How It Works

The key to implementing a feature such as this history list is to spend a little time up front to determine exactly what should happen for any possible related event. For each of the possible events available to the user through the File menu, the code required to correctly update the history list is slightly different. Once you figure out the requirements, the actual coding becomes fairly straightforward. For this sample application, forethought yielded the discovery that every time the history list is changed, the requirements for actually updating the File menu are the same; therefore, a separate procedure was written to perform the menu update, resulting in elimination of redundant code.

When the application is started, it immediately creates a TStringList object to act as the history list, as shown in step 7. An attempt is then made to load the history file from disk.

If TStringList's LoadFromFile procedure is successful, a call is made to RebuildHistory to update the File menu. By placing this code within an exception block, you prevent a runtime error from taking place should LoadFromFile not succeed in finding or reading the file. If such an error takes place, the call to RebuildHistory would be skipped and control directed to the *except* clause. The *except* clause specifies no error-handling code, but rather causes the error simply to be ignored. It is assumed that if the history list can't be found then one hasn't been created yet, and this is not an error that need concern the application's user.

When the user selects New from the File menu, the required action is to see if an existing file is open and, if so, add that name to the history list (see step 8).

The privately declared CurName variable is used to store the name of any currently open file. If CurName is a null string, then the currently open file is untitled (and therefore also unsaved), and there is no need to update the history list. If CurName is not null, then it is inserted as the first string of the History TStringList object. This causes the last opened file to always be first in the list. RebuildHistory is then called to update the File menu.

When File|Open is selected and OpenDialog returns True (step 9), the required action for CurName is the same as for File|New; it is added to the history list if not null. In addition, if the file name now being selected is already present in the history list, it needs to be removed.

To see if the selected file name is currently in the list, you use TStringList's IndexOf method, passing the string you want to search for. If the file name is present, IndexOf will return the index, or position number, in the list; otherwise it will return -1. This result is stored in Pos. Pos is then checked, and if it is greater than or equal to zero, the string at that position is deleted using TStringList's Delete method and passing Pos as the index of the string to be deleted. Now that the history list is up-to-date, RebuildHistory is called to update the File menu and CurName is assigned to the file name just selected.

If the user selects Save As (step 10), the required action is exactly the same as that for Open, except that the selected file name must be referenced from the SaveDialog component instead of from OpenDialog.

When the application is terminated by the user (step 11), CurName is checked once again and added to the history list if necessary. There is no need to call RebuildHistory since the menu doesn't need to be updated. Instead, the History list must be saved to disk.

The SaveToFile method of TStringList is called within an exception block to avoid any runtime errors if for any reason the save is not successful. If there is any error, a message is displayed to the user. You may want to enhance this by determining the kind of error encountered (for example, a full disk) and presenting a corresponding message to the user. Finally, the TStringList component is freed.

Updating the History List

The RebuildHistory procedure (step 6) is responsible for updating the history entries in the File menu. Because the history list can change in various ways (including the order of the entries), the easiest way to update the menu is simply to remove all existing history items and create them new each time.

Although you can place the history items anywhere within the menu, most applications place them at the bottom of the File menu just before the Exit menu item. They are normally set off visually by placing a menu separator both above and below the history items.

When you created the File menu with the Menu Designer, you inserted a single separator just before the Exit menu item. This separator, named N1 for you by Delphi, makes a convenient key with which you can determine the correct position where the history is to be placed. Using this method, you are free to change the File menu in any way; as long as the separator referenced by N1 remains immediately above the position where you want the history to appear.

The position of the N1 separator plus one represents the position of the first history menu item. The private N2 TMenuItem is used as the bottom separator for the history list. N2 is only created when there are history items to be displayed. Therefore, if N2 is assigned, the code loops through all menu positions between N1 and N2 and deletes the menu items at those positions. The N2 separator is also deleted.

Next, a check is made to ensure that the number of file names in the history list doesn't exceed the maximum allowed. The maximum set in this How-To is nine. You can set less if you want, but more than nine is not recommended for two reasons: Allowing too many entries will tend to make the menu too long and, eventually, may exceed the height of the screen. Second, you can only use single characters as accelerators. Since it's normal to use digits as accelerators for a history list, nine is a practical limit before accelerator characters start being duplicated. If you must allow more than nine, consider a separate top-level menu to contain just the history and only attempt to provide accelerators for the first nine.

The procedure then loops through each of the file names in the History string list to create the new menu items. An accelerator is created by prefixing the file name with an ampersand and the current string list position (plus one since the string list position is zero-based). The OnClick event property of each new menu item is assigned to the ReOpenClick handler. Finally, the menu item is inserted. After all of the history menu items have been added, a new menu item is created and assigned to N2 to act as the bottom separator.

Handling Click Events from the History Menu Items

When any of the history items are selected from the menu, the ReOpenClick handler is called (see step 12). The relative position of the selected item must be calculated in order to be able to retrieve the correct file name from the History string list. This can easily be accomplished using TMenuItem's IndexOf method. The position of the top separator (N1) simply needs to be subtracted from the position of whichever history item was selected. One more is subtracted to make the value zero-based, and this value represents the position in the History string list of the desired file name.

NewName, a string variable local to this procedure, is used to temporarily store the selected file name. This file name is then deleted from the History string list. As in the other menu event handlers, CurName is then checked and, if necessary, added to History. The File menu is then rebuilt and CurName is assigned to NewName.

Comments

Once you have worked your way through a couple of menu structures in which you need to handle such features as this, you should find working with Delphi's menu objects to be quite easy and even pleasurable. Hopefully, this How-To has helped to put you in that position.

4.6 How do I... Put pictures in menus?

COMPLEXITY: EASY

Problem

I've seen some applications that use pictures instead of text in their menus, and I think this is really cool! I find that a picture often works better than a small text label to indicate the purpose of a menu item. Is there any way to use pictures in the menu of a Delphi application?

Technique

Windows allows pictures, in the form of standard bitmaps, to be used as menu items. Therefore, it can also be done in Delphi. With the first release of Delphi, the menu components have no built-in support for this feature; it's possible, though not confirmed, that a later release may add this support. However, this simply means the Windows API must be used directly for now (and this method will still work even if Borland does add bitmap support later). This How-To features the ModifyMenu API function.

Steps

Run BITMENU.EXE. Click the Options menu. The first selection under Options is a normal text menu item labeled Normal Check. The second item is a bitmapped picture of a pair of speakers, as shown in Figure 4-6, and this item is currently checked. Both menu selections toggle their checked state each time they are selected; in addition, the second item toggles back and forth between pictures. Whenever it is selected to the unchecked state, the bitmap changes to contain a large red X (also shown in Figure 4-6) to indicate it is currently disabled. When selected again, the red X is removed.

1. Create a new project. Save the default unit as BITMENU1.PAS and the project as BITMENU.DPR.

2. Add a MainMenu component to the form and, using the Menu Designer, add the menu items as shown in Table 4-6.

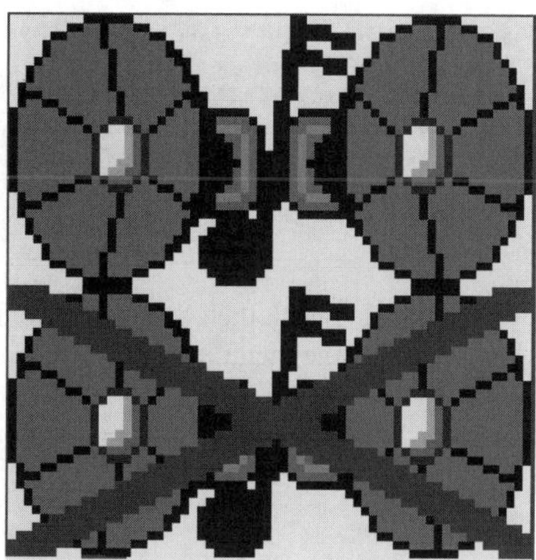

Figure 4-6 Sound bitmaps for the BITMENU project

Table 4-6 Menu design for the BITMENU project

MENU	MENUITEM
&Options	&Normal Check
	&Sound
	-
	E&xit

3. In the *private* section of Form1, add the following declarations to hold the menu bitmaps.

```
private
  { Private declarations }
  Sound, NoSound: TBitmap;
  SoundHandle: HBitmap;
```

4. Double-click the OnCreate event for Form1 in the Object Inspector and add the following code to load the menu bitmaps and initialize the Sound menu item with the Sound bitmap.

```
procedure TForm1.FormCreate(Sender: TObject);
begin
  {Create and load menu bitmaps}
  Sound := TBitmap.Create;
```

continued on next page

continued from previous page

```
  Sound.LoadFromFile('CHAP04\SOUND.BMP');
  NoSound := TBitmap.Create;
  NoSound.LoadFromFile('CHAP04\NOSOUND.BMP');
  {Tell Windows to use the sound picture}
  ModifyMenu(MainMenu1.Handle, Sound1.Command,
    mf_ByCommand or mf_Bitmap, Sound1.Command, PChar(Sound.Handle));
  SoundHandle := Sound.Handle;
end;
```

5. Double-click the OnDestroy event for Form1 and add the following code to delete the menu bitmaps.

```
procedure TForm1.FormDestroy(Sender: TObject);
begin
  Sound.Free;
  NoSound.Free;
end;
```

6. In the Object Inspector for the NormalCheck1 TMenuItem, enter **MenuClick** as the name of the OnClick event handler and press ENTER to create the handler. Enter the following code to handle the toggling of the check state for both NormalCheck1 and Sound1. When complete, set the OnClick event of Sound1 to MenuClick as well.

```
procedure TForm1.MenuClick(Sender: TObject);
begin
  if Sender = NormalCheck1 then
    {Handle check and uncheck for the normal menu item}
    NormalCheck1.Checked := not NormalCheck1.Checked
  else if Sender = Sound1 then begin
    {Switch the picture for the Sound menu item}
    if SoundHandle = Sound.Handle then
      SoundHandle := NoSound.Handle
    else
      SoundHandle := Sound.Handle;
  end;
  ModifyMenu(MainMenu1.Handle, Sound1.Command,
    mf_ByCommand or mf_Bitmap, Sound1.Command, PChar(SoundHandle));
end;
```

7. Click the Options|Exit menu item and enter the following line to close the application.

```
procedure TForm1.Exit1Click(Sender: TObject);
begin
  Close;
end;
```

8. Compile and run the application.

How It Works

The Windows API contains several procedures and functions to manage menus. Since the creation of menus and the addition and removal of menu items is much easier to do through the Delphi menu components, you will probably never have a need to use most of these API methods. If all of your menu items are to be standard text labels, there's no need ever to use an API function. However, if you wish to incorporate pictures into your menu, as in this How-To, you will need to use the API directly. Typically, the only API function you will need, as evidenced by this How-To, is the ModifyMenu function.

ModifyMenu is very flexible: with it, you can control the checked, disabled, or grayed states; change the text label; toggle between a text label and a bitmap; or change bitmaps. It will also allow you to combine multiple changes in a single call (as long as the requested changes don't conflict with one another).

Note: Bitmaps can only be used for submenu items. Windows will not allow a bitmap to be assigned to a top-level menu item (those appearing in the form's main menu bar).

Loading the Menu Bitmaps

When the application starts, it must first load the two bitmaps used for the checked and unchecked states of the Sound1 menu item (shown in step 4). For this How-To, these bitmaps are stored in their own separate files. They can easily be loaded using TBitmap's LoadFromFile method. Alternatively, you could include these two bitmaps in a resource (RES) file and include them as part of the program when compiled by using the $R compiler directive. (How-To 4.3 uses this method to include a programmer-defined cursor.) In this case, you wouldn't need any of the functionality of a TBitmap component; instead, you could define two variables of type HBitmap and assign these to the result of the LoadBitmap API calls. You would use the DeleteObject API function to free the bitmaps when done.

Using the ModifyMenu API

After loading the two bitmaps, the Sound bitmap is assigned to the Sound1 menu item using ModifyMenu. The first parameter to ModifyMenu must be the handle of the menu that contains the menu item you want to modify—in this case, MainMenu1.Handle. The second parameter depends on the method you want to use to identify the menu item. ModifyMenu allows two methods: a menu item can be identified by its command ID, or it can be identified by its position in the menu. Using the position method is more complicated and, since the command IDs of all your menu items are available to you via TMenuItem's Command property, you will always want to use the command ID method. All further descriptions of ModifyMenu in this How-To will use this method.

The third parameter must include the mf_ByCommand flag to indicate you are using the command ID method of identifying the menu item. Using the OR operator, other flags are included in the third parameter to indicate what actions are to be taken. In this case, ModifyMenu is being told that this menu item is to be displayed as a bitmap by passing mf_Bitmap. Sound1's Command property is passed again as the fourth parameter (always do this to preserve the current command ID value). Because mf_Bitmap was passed, ModifyMenu expects the handle of a bitmap to be passed as the fifth parameter; however, the type of the fifth parameter is a PChar. In order to pass the bitmap handle, it must be typecast as type PChar (typecasting is a frequent necessity when using the Windows API). The result of this call is, when you select the Options menu item the first time, the Sound1 menu item will display as a bitmap instead of the text label you assigned when you designed the menu. The last statement in the OnCreate method assigns the handle of the Sound bitmap to SoundHandle. The purpose of SoundHandle will become clear shortly.

Handling Menu Selections

When either Options|Normal Check or Options|Sound is selected, the MenuClick event handler will be called (see step 6). You need to check here to see if the menu item selected was either NormalCheck1 or Sound1, since in both cases you want to reverse the state of the item. For Normal Check, you simply want to reverse the state of the Checked property in order to cause the standard Windows check mark to appear or disappear from the menu; but for Sound, you want to reverse pictures instead. You could also turn the standard check mark on and off for Sound, as is done for Normal Check, but it would be redundant since the pictures say it all. This is where the variable SoundHandle comes in. It serves two purposes at once: it holds the current bitmap handle that is being displayed for the Sound menu item; and, by so doing, acts as a flag so the program knows what state the menu item is in, thereby taking the place of the Checked property, which is not being used.

Each time Options|Normal Check is selected, its checked state is reversed simply by using the NOT operator. For Options|Sound, SoundHandle has to be toggled between the two different bitmap handles. SoundHandle is then passed as the bitmap handle to ModifyMenu so that the Sound menu item is updated with the correct bitmap.

You will notice that ModifyMenu is called every time this method executes, even if the menu item selected is Normal Check. This is necessary because of the way the Delphi menu components operate. Every time you make a change to any property in any menu item component, Delphi performs a complete rebuild of the entire menu. Reversing the state of the Checked property of Normal Check results in such a rebuild and, because the menu components do not support bitmaps, the menu is rebuilt using only the text captions you assigned to the menu items during the design step. Therefore, you must call ModifyMenu for all menu items using bitmaps in order to restore the display of those bitmaps. With the current bitmap for the Sound menu item stored in SoundHandle, this task is easier since no further check is necessary to determine which bitmap to restore.

Comments

Using pictures in menus is never necessary, but they are often more self-explanatory than text labels, and besides, they are attractive and fun to use.

In this How-To you learned that you can not only use a bitmap for menu items, you can use any number of bitmaps for a single menu item, switching between them as needed during use of the application. In many cases, of course, you will only need a single bitmap to represent a menu item, where that menu item causes something to happen directly such as displaying another form or performing a task. The bitmaps you create for menu items can be pretty much any size you like, but you should try to keep them as compact as possible, especially in their height, in order to keep the overall menu more attractive and easy to use.

4.7 How do I...
Create and use custom check marks in menus?

COMPLEXITY: EASY

Problem

I've seen some applications that use a custom check mark in place of the standard, and rather plain, Windows check mark. Is it possible to do this in Delphi?

Technique

As with using bitmaps for menu items (shown in How-To 4.6), Windows also allows an application to assign a bitmap to be used as a custom check mark for a menu item. In fact, Windows allows two bitmaps to be assigned for each menu item, one for the checked state and one for the unchecked state (which is normally displayed as the absence of a check mark). This How-To features the Windows API function SetMenuItemBitmaps.

Steps

Run MENUCHK.EXE. Experiment by selecting the first three menu items under the Test menu to check and uncheck them. Note the use of the custom check marks for both the checked and unchecked states, as shown in Figure 4-7.

1. Create a new project. Save the default unit as MENUCHK1.PAS and the project as MENUCHK.DPR.

2. Add a TMainMenu component to the form and create the menu items as shown in Table 4-7.

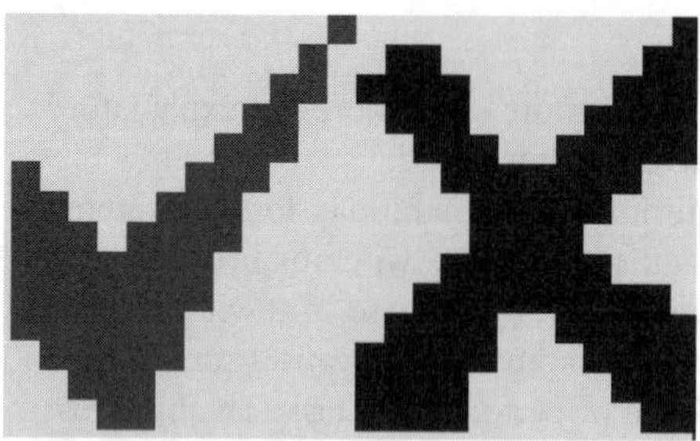

Figure 4-7 The MENUCHK project's custom check marks

Table 4-7 Menu design for the MENUCHK project

MENU	MENUITEM
&Test	Show &Checked
	Show &Unchecked
	Show &Both
	-
	E&xit

3. In the *private* section of Form1, define the following variables and procedure to be used to manage the bitmaps for the check mark.

```
private
  { Private declarations }
  BMCheck, BMUnCheck: TBitmap;
  procedure SetBitmaps;
```

4. After the *implementation* statement and $R compiler directive, define the SetBitmaps procedure. This procedure assigns the check mark's bitmaps to the menu items.

```
implementation

{$R *.DFM}

procedure TForm1.SetBitmaps;
begin
  {Assign only check bitmap to first menu item}
  SetMenuItemBitmaps(MainMenu1.Handle, ShowChecked1.Command,
    mf_ByCommand, 0, BMCheck.Handle);
  {Assign only uncheck bitmap to second menu item}
  SetMenuItemBitmaps(MainMenu1.Handle, ShowUnChecked1.Command,
```

```
    mf_ByCommand, BMUncheck.Handle, 0);
  {Assign both bitmaps to third menu item}
  SetMenuItemBitmaps(MainMenu1.Handle, ShowBoth1.Command,
    mf_ByCommand, BMUncheck.Handle, BMCheck.Handle);
end;
```

5. In the Object Inspector, double-click the OnCreate event for Form1 and add the following code to load the custom check marks and initialize the menu items with them.

```
procedure TForm1.FormCreate(Sender: TObject);
begin
  {Load menu bitmaps from disk}
  BMCheck := TBitmap.Create;
  BMCheck.LoadFromFile('CHAP04\CHECK.BMP');
  BMUnCheck := TBitmap.Create;
  BMUnCheck.LoadFromFile('CHAP04\UNCHECK.BMP');
  SetBitmaps;
end;
```

6. Double-click the OnDestroy event of Form1 and add the following code to free the memory used by the bitmaps.

```
procedure TForm1.FormDestroy(Sender: TObject);
begin
  {Dispose bitmaps}
  BMCheck.Free;
  BMUncheck.Free;
end;
```

7. For the OnClick event of ShowChecked1, enter MenuClick as the name of the event handler and press ENTER to create the handler. Enter the following code to check or uncheck the selected menu item. When finished, set the OnClick method of both ShowUnChecked1 and ShowBoth1 to the MenuClick event handler.

```
procedure TForm1.MenuClick(Sender: TObject);
begin
  {Reverse the checked state}
  with (Sender as TMenuItem) do Checked := not Checked;
  SetBitmaps;
end;
```

8. Click on Test|Exit and enter the following line to close the application.

```
procedure TForm1.Exit1Click(Sender: TObject);
begin
  Close;
end;
```

9. Compile and run the application.

How It Works

The two bitmaps used for the custom check marks are stored in individual bitmap (BMP) files and are loaded using TBitmap's LoadFromFile method. As was explained for the bitmaps in How-To 4.6, you could bind these bitmaps in a resource file and compile that resource into the program, then use the LoadBitmap and DeleteObject API functions to load and free the bitmaps.

Assigning the Check Marks

Once the bitmaps are loaded, a call is made to the private SetBitmaps procedure to actually assign these bitmaps to the menu items. The SetBitmaps procedure uses the SetMenuItemBitmaps API function.

As with the ModifyMenu API function used in How-To 4.6, SetMenuItemBitmaps requires the handle of the menu containing the target menu item to be passed as the first parameter and the menu item's command ID in the second parameter. The third parameter is set to mf_ByCommand to indicate the method by which Windows is to identify the menu item you wish to modify. Unlike ModifyMenu, no other flag values need to be passed. The fourth and fifth parameters are the bitmap handles to be used for, respectively, the unchecked state and the checked state.

You are free to assign bitmaps to either or both of the check states. If you do not wish to assign a bitmap for one of the states, simply pass zero. You can pass zero for both check states in order to stop the menu item from using your custom bitmaps (the checked state will revert to the standard Windows check mark).

Windows allows only a certain size of bitmap to be displayed as a check mark. You can assign any bitmap as a check mark, but if it's larger than the allowed size, Windows will only use the allowed portion. The allowed size changes according to the active display settings. For video settings that use Small Font, the check mark's size is 14-by-14 pixels. If the video setting specifies Large Font, the check mark's size is 12 pixels wide by 20 pixels high. If you want, you can design two sets of bitmaps, one set for each of these sizes, but it isn't really necessary. A good compromise is to make your custom check marks 12 pixels wide and 14 pixels high. Windows will display these at either video setting, and they will look fine.

When any of the three menu items employing custom check marks is clicked, the MenuClick event handler is called. The Sender parameter, although it will actually be referencing a TMenuItem component, is of type TObject, which means it needs to be typecast in order to reference properties or methods of the referenced TMenuItem:

```
with (Sender as TMenuItem) do Checked := not Checked;
SetBitmaps;
```

Once the check state of the selected menu item is reversed, a call to SetBitmaps is made.

It's important to understand that, with Windows itself, you are only required to assign the check mark's bitmaps to a menu item once. Windows will then continue to use the assigned bitmaps until you explicitly change them for that menu item. Windows knows which bitmap to display for either of the check states, so once assigned, you can forget about them (except to delete the bitmaps at program termination). However, as explained in How-To 4.6, Delphi's menu objects do not currently support the use of bitmaps, and every time you change a property of a menu item, Delphi rebuilds the entire menu. Because of this, any bitmap assignments you've made are lost and must be made again. To minimize this inconvenience, it is best to place the API calls to assign the bitmaps in a separate procedure as is done here, and then a simple call to this procedure is all that is necessary to reestablish the bitmap assignments. Although it is a slight inconvenience, it's a small price to pay for the other extensive conveniences provided to you by Delphi's menu components.

Comments

Note that for the ShowUnchecked1 menu item, when the item is checked, Windows displays its standard check mark. If you want a mark to be displayed only when the item is unchecked and to be blank when checked, you would need to create another bitmap that is simply a blank, or all white, rectangle and assign this to be used for the checked state of the menu item.

You can combine the techniques demonstrated here and in How-To 4.6 to provide completely customized menu items using your own bitmaps. This gives you great power over the look and feel of your application's menus. However, we're not done! There is yet another way to customize your menus using a technique known as Owner-Draw. This technique is presented next in How-To 4.8.

4.8 How do I...
Use a different font in a menu?

COMPLEXITY: ADVANCED

Problem

Windows always uses the System font for menus. It would be really cool if I could use a different font for the menus in my application and even cooler if I could allow users to choose the font. Is there a way to do this in Delphi?

Technique

Windows allows a technique for menus (and a few other standard controls) called Owner-Draw. The basic technique is to set your application up to handle two extra Windows messages that allow you to control the size and the actual painting of the menu item. Note that this technique, as with the technique of using bitmaps, is limited to submenu items; it cannot be used for top-level menu items. It also requires you to deal extensively with the Windows API and so is somewhat more complex than the methods presented so far.

Steps

Run ODMENU.EXE. Select Test|Font from the menu. You will be presented with the standard Font dialog. Choose any font on your system; choose any size, style, and color, and click the OK button. When you select the Test menu again, the Font menu item will be displayed using the font and attributes you selected. An example is shown in Figure 4-8. Try selecting the WingDings font!

1. Create a new project. Save the default unit as ODMENU1.PAS and the project as ODMENU.DPR.

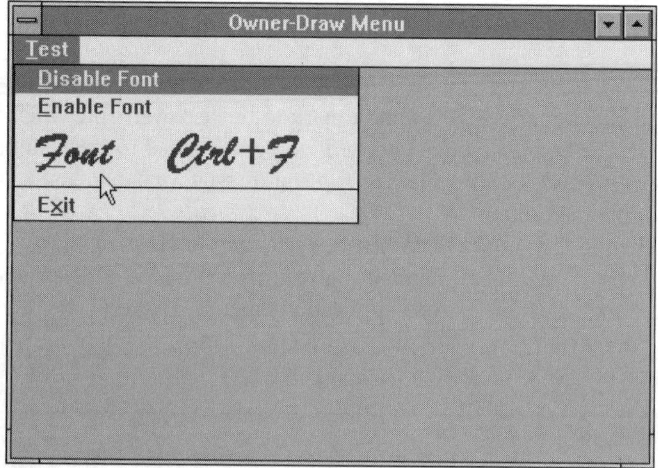

Figure 4-8 ODMENU showing its Owner-Draw menu item

2. Add a MainMenu and a FontDialog component to the form. Add menu items to the MainMenu component as shown in Table 4-8.

Table 4-8 Menu design for the ODMENU project

MENU	MENUITEM	SHORTCUT
&Test	&Disable Font	
	&Enable Font	
	&Font	Ctrl-F
	-	
	E&xit	

3. In the *private* section of Form1, add the following variable and procedure declarations to be used for handling the Owner-Draw menu item.

```
private
  { Private declarations }
  BM: TBitmap;
  MenuCap: array [0..255] of char;
  procedure WMMeasureItem(var MInfo: TMessage); message wm_MeasureItem;
  procedure WMDrawItem(var DInfo: TMessage); message wm_DrawItem;
```

4. Double-click the OnCreate event of Form1 in the Object Inspector and enter the following code to initialize the work variables, Font dialog, and menu item.

```
procedure TForm1.FormCreate(Sender: TObject);
begin
  {Create a work area}
  BM := TBitmap.Create;
  {Initialize current font to standard menu text color}
  FontDialog1.Font.Color := GetSysColor(color_MenuText);
  {Tell Windows this menu item is Owner-Draw}
  ModifyMenu(MainMenu1.Handle, Font1.Command,
    mf_ByCommand or mf_OwnerDraw, Font1.Command, nil);
  {Make a copy of menu caption now to save time}
  StrPCopy(MenuCap, Font1.Caption);
  {Does menu item have a shortcut assigned?}
  if Font1.ShortCut <> 0 then
    StrPCopy(StrEnd(MenuCap), #9 + ShortCutToText(Font1.ShortCut));
end;
```

5. Double-click the OnDestroy event of Form1 and enter the following code to free the TBitmap work variable.

```
procedure TForm1.FormDestroy(Sender: TObject);
begin
  {Dispose work area}
  BM.Free;
end;
```

6. Enter the following procedure definition. This procedure receives and handles wm_MeasureItem messages sent from Windows.

```
procedure TForm1.WMMeasureItem(var MInfo: TMessage);
const
  zero: integer = 0;
begin
  {Address the Windows supplied info}
  with PMeasureItemStruct(MInfo.LParam)^ do begin
    {Is message for a menu item}
    if CtlType = odt_Menu then begin
      {Is message for Font menu item}
```

continued on next page

continued from previous page

```
      if ItemID = Font1.Command then begin
        {Assign currently selected font to work space}
        BM.Canvas.Font := FontDialog1.Font;
        {Calculate needed height for current font}
        ItemHeight := BM.Canvas.TextHeight(Font1.Caption);
        {Calculate needed width for caption in current font}
        ItemWidth := LoWord(GetTabbedTextExtent(BM.Canvas.Handle, MenuCap,
          StrLen(MenuCap), zero, zero));
        {Tell Windows it's handled}
        MInfo.Result := 1;
      end;
    end;
  end;
end;
```

7. Enter the following procedure definition. This procedure receives and handles wm_DrawItem messages sent from Windows.

```
procedure TForm1.WMDrawItem(var DInfo: TMessage);
var
  oldFont: hFont;
begin
  {Address Windows supplied info}
  with PDrawItemStruct(DInfo.LParam)^ do begin
    {Is message for a menu item?}
    if CtlType = odt_Menu then begin
      {Is message for Font menu item?}
      if ItemID = Font1.Command then begin
        {Select current font into menu's device context}
        oldFont := SelectObject(HDC, FontDialog1.Font.Handle);
        {Set correct background color}
        if (ItemState and ods_Selected) <> 0 then
          BM.Canvas.Brush.Color := clHighlight
        else
          BM.Canvas.Brush.Color := clMenu;
        {Paint the background}
        FillRect(HDC, rcItem, BM.Canvas.Brush.Handle);
        {Adjust left bound of caption}
        Inc(rcItem.Left, LoWord(GetMenuCheckMarkDimensions));
        {Set text color according to state}
        if (ItemState and ods_disabled <> 0)
        or (ItemState and ods_Grayed <> 0) then
          {Use system's 'grayed' color}
          SetTextColor(HDC, GetSysColor(color_GrayText))
        else if (ItemState and ods_Selected <> 0) then
          {Use reverse of current font color}
          SetTextColor(HDC, not FontDialog1.Font.Color)
        else
          {Use selected font color}
          SetTextColor(HDC, FontDialog1.Font.Color);
        {Allow background color to surround characters}
        SetBkMode(HDC, Transparent);
        {Draw the menu's caption}
        DrawText(HDC, MenuCap, StrLen(MenuCap), rcItem,
```

```
        dt_Top or dt_SingleLine or dt_ExpandTabs);
      {Release current font handle}
      SelectObject(HDC, oldFont);
      {Tell Windows it's handled}
      DInfo.Result := 1;
    end;
  end;
 end;
end;
```

8. Click on Test|Enable Font and enter the following code to make the Font menu item active.

```
procedure TForm1.EnableFont1Click(Sender: TObject);
begin
  {Tell Windows this menu item is selectable again}
  ModifyMenu(MainMenu1.Handle, Font1.Command,
    mf_ByCommand or mf_Enabled or mf_OwnerDraw, Font1.Command, nil);
end;
```

9. Click on Test|Disable Font and enter the following code to disable the Font menu item.

```
procedure TForm1.DisableFont1Click(Sender: TObject);
begin
  {Tell Windows this menu item not selectable}
  ModifyMenu(MainMenu1.Handle, Font1.Command,
    mf_ByCommand or mf_Grayed or mf_OwnerDraw, Font1.Command, nil);
end;
```

10. Click on Test|Font and enter the following code to execute the Font dialog and force windows to send a new wm_MeasureItem message to the application.

```
procedure TForm1.Font1Click(Sender: TObject);
begin
  if FontDialog1.Execute then
    {Fool Windows into sending another wm_MeasureItem message
     so menu item can be sized for newly selected font.}
    ModifyMenu(MainMenu1.Handle, Font1.Command,
      mf_ByCommand or mf_OwnerDraw, Font1.Command, nil);
end;
```

11. Click on Test|Exit and enter the following line to close the application.

```
procedure TForm1.Exit1Click(Sender: TObject);
begin
  Close;
end;
```

12. Compile and run the application.

How It Works

The key to using the Owner-Draw technique is the ability to define message-response methods in your application. By default, messages sent from Windows that have any effect on your application are handled for you by Delphi. Those messages that do not need to be handled by your application are simply passed on to a default handler provided by Windows itself. By creating message-response methods, you are telling Delphi to pass specific Windows messages on to you for additional, or different, processing.

In the *private* section of the Form1 definition, you defined two procedure definitions. Each of these were followed by the keyword *message* and a constant value representing a Windows message. All possible messages that can be sent to your application have a corresponding constant defined in the Messages unit. The keyword *message* allows you to tell Delphi that you want to handle the named message yourself, and when this message is received by your application, it should be passed on to you by calling the defined procedure.

```
procedure WMMeasureItem(var MInfo: TMessage); message wm_MeasureItem;
procedure WMDrawItem(var DInfo: TMessage); message wm_DrawItem;
```

The two Windows messages being explicitly handled here by TForm1 are the two that Windows sends in order to allow an application to take over the painting of a standard Windows control.

Preparing for Owner-Draw

When the application starts, a few things must be done in order to prepare for painting the menu item. First, a work area is needed to perform the painting itself. A TBitmap component is created for this purpose. The font to be used by the Owner-Draw menu item will be stored in a TFontDialog component.

When a TFontDialog component is created, it defaults to the System font, which is correct for standard menus, but the color of the default font is not correct and must be changed before the menu can be allowed to display for the first time. To get the correct color for menu text (which you can choose by using the Color applet in Windows' Control Panel), an API function called GetSysColor is used and to this is passed the Windows constant color_MenuText. Windows defines a constant like this for every color that can be set by the user in the Color applet.

The ModifyMenu API function is then used to tell Windows that the painting of the Font1 menu item is to be handled by this application. This is done by including the mf_OwnerDraw constant as a flag in the third parameter (see How-To 4.6 for more information on ModifyMenu). Sending this message to Windows is what will cause Windows to start sending wm_MeasureItem and wm_DrawItem messages to the application:

```
ModifyMenu(MainMenu1.Handle, Font1.Command,
  mf_ByCommand or mf_OwnerDraw, Font1.Command, nil);
```

Finally, to make the coding easier in subsequent procedures, a copy of the caption to be painted in the menu item is constructed in the MenuCap string variable. Font1's ShortCut property is checked to see if a shortcut was defined for this menu item; if so, the shortcut text is appended to the caption with a preceding tab character.

The wm_MeasureItem Message Handler

In the definition for the WMMeasureItem procedure (see step 6), the first statement requires some explanation. MInfo, the parameter passed to the procedure, is of type TMessage, which is a record structure containing several fields of information that was passed to the application from Windows. The field in TMessage that has the needed information is named LParam. If and how LParam is used and what information it represents is dependent on the specific Windows message being received. For the wm_MeasureItem message, LParam is a memory pointer to another record structure defined by Windows. Delphi provides you with a record definition for this structure called TMeasureItemStruct and also defines a compatible pointer type called PMeasureItemStruct:

```
with PMeasureItemStruct(MInfo.LParam)^ do begin
```

Because LParam (whose actual type is LongInt) is actually a memory pointer, it must be typecast as such in order to address the fields of the record structure it points to and the pointer must be dereferenced using the ^ symbol (meaning "the contents at this address"). By typecasting and dereferencing this pointer in the *with* statement, the fields of the TMeasureItemStruct can now be accessed directly.

The variables CtlType, ItemID, ItemWidth, and ItemHeight are all fields of the TMeasureItemStruct record. CtlType and ItemID are already set by Windows to tell you which Owner-Draw control it is asking about. (Because there is only a single Owner-Draw control in this application, it isn't really necessary to check these fields, but it shows the technique required when you have multiple Owner-Draw controls). Windows expects you to fill in values for ItemWidth and ItemHeight (this is why MInfo is passed using the *var* keyword; so you can modify information in the passed record structure).

CtlType indicates the type of control (it will always equal the constant odt_Menu in this sample application). ItemID will be the specific command ID of the control to be measured (in this How-To it will always equal the command ID of the Font1 menu item).

Measuring the Menu Item

Once it's established that Windows is asking about the Font1 menu item, you need to provide Windows with the dimensions required for painting the control. This is where the TBitmap component, BM, comes in. This is used as a workspace to calculate the needed dimensions. First, the currently selected font is selected into BM's Canvas property. Next, the TextHeight method of TCanvas is used to determine the height needed for the menu item. Although TCanvas also has a TextWidth method, TextWidth cannot properly handle tab characters within a string. Therefore, the required width must be determined by using the API function GetTabbedTextExtent. GetTabbedTextExtent requires a device context to be passed as the first parameter. This can be accommodated by passing the Handle property of BM's Canvas property.

Note: In order for the Canvas.Handle property to be a valid device context, some function must first be performed on Canvas using one of its methods. This is accomplished here by first calling the TextHeight method of Canvas. If you do not first perform such a function, referencing the Handle property will return you a Windows *information context* instead of a device context. An information context is basically a read-only device context, and attempting to use it in an API function that requires a device context will fail.

The second and third parameters of GetTabbedTextExtent are the string to be measured and its character length. A variable initialized to zero is passed for the last two parameters to tell Windows it should use a default length for any tabs found in the string. The return value of GetTabbedTextExtent is a LongInt containing both the calculated width and height. Since you already have the height, all that's needed is the width, which is in the low word of the LongInt and can be extracted using the LoWord Pascal function.

Finally, the result field of MInfo is set to 1 in order to let Windows know this message was handled by the application. ItemWidth and ItemHeight are now available to Windows to use when it prepares the menu to be painted.

The wm_DrawItem Message Handler

Once Windows has called the WMMeasureItem procedure, it will then call the WMDrawItem procedure whenever the menu item needs to be painted. It's important to understand that when you choose to handle the painting of a control or menu item, you must take responsibility for painting it in all its required forms. Windows will inform you what state the item is to be painted in: Normal, Selected, Grayed, and so on; you must respond accordingly.

The explanation of typecasting and dereferencing the LParam field of MInfo in the WMMeasureItem procedure also applies to the DInfo variable passed to the WMDrawItem procedure. The record structure being addressed here, though, is of type TDrawItemStruct. The same checks are made on the same fields to determine that Windows is requesting the painting of the Font1 menu item.

Painting the Menu Item

The TDrawItemStruct record contains three important fields that are used to paint the item. ItemState tells you how the item should be painted, HDC is a device context supplied by Windows for you to paint on, and rcItem is the rectangular area within the device context where you should perform the painting.

First, the current font, stored in FontDialog1, is selected into the device context using the SelectObject API function. The font being replaced is saved in oldFont. Next, the background of the menu item is prepared. ItemState is consulted to decide what color the background should be, and the Brush.Color property of BM's Canvas property is set using the appropriate color as defined by the Windows constants clMenu and clHighlight. The Windows API version of the FillRect function is then called to paint the background of the menu item (not to be confused with the FillRect method of TCanvas).

The next statement uses the API function GetMenuCheckMarkDimensions. This function returns the width and height needed for a menu check mark, and these values are based on the current video mode. The width, extracted using the LoWord function, is added to the Left field of the supplied rcItem field (rcItem is of type TRect). This allows you to paint the menu item so as to allow for display of a check mark.

It is worth noting an inconsistency within Windows here. Windows' own programming documentation makes it clear that you should use this function in order to correctly paint a menu item, but Windows itself ignores it! If you change your video setting to use Large Font and run ODMENU.EXE, you will discover that the Owner-Draw menu item is painted 12 pixels from the left of the menu as per the value returned by this function, but all the other menu items, painted by Windows, continue to start 14 pixels from the left! The "correct" method is used in this How-To, but you will likely want to ignore this and just hardcode the magic value of 14 for your own Owner-Draw menu items. This inconsistency may, of course, change in the next version of Windows.

ItemState is consulted again to determine the correct text color for the menu item. There are three possibilities: Normal, Selected, or Grayed. Normally, in Windows, a disabled menu item is still painted in the normal state rather than grayed. This How-To has taken the position that a disabled menu item should be considered the same as a grayed menu item and both should be painted accordingly. If you disagree, simply remove the test for ods_Disabled and only test for ods_Grayed.

If it is to be painted as *grayed*, then the GetSysColor API function is used to get the currently defined gray color (as selected via the Color applet). If it's to be painted as *selected*, then the currently selected font color in FontDialog1 is reversed; otherwise, the currently selected font color is used directly.

When you draw text or lines in a Windows device context, you are using a pen resource. A pen has a foreground (or text) color, which you've already set using the SetTextColor API function. Its background color, used for painting the area behind text characters or in the spaces of patterned lines, can be set using the SetBKColor API function. However, if you want the background color to match the surface upon which the text is being drawn, the easier way is to use the SetBKMode API function passing the constant Transparent. This tells Windows not to use the background color at all but to let the current surface, whatever may be there, to show through instead. If you decide you subsequently want the background color to be used, you can call SetBKMode again, passing the constant Opaque.

You are now ready to draw the text of the menu item. This is done using a very powerful and flexible API function called DrawText. DrawText is passed the device context to draw on, the string to be drawn, and the string length. Following this, the rectangular area within the device context to be painted is passed. The last parameter is a set of flags to control how DrawText performs: dt_Top tells it to align the text with the top of the specified rectangle, dt_SingleLine tells it not to wrap text if the string width exceeds the width of the rectangle, and dt_ExpandTabs tells it to use the standard spacing for any tab characters in the string:

```
DrawText(HDC, MenuCap, StrLen(MenuCap), rcItem,
  dt_Top or dt_SingleLine or dt_ExpandTabs);
```

DrawText will automatically use all the other attributes you have selected into the device context, including all attributes of the selected font and color.

Once the text is drawn, you are finished. The original font must be selected back into the device context. This is done with another call to SelectObject passing the temporary oldFont variable. Finally, the Result field of DInfo is set to 1 to let Windows know the message was handled.

When you select the Font menu item, FontDialog1 is executed. If a new font was selected, a call to ModifyMenu is made. No changes are actually specified in this call; all parameters are exactly as were passed in the initial call to ModifyMenu made in the OnCreate event handler. The reason for this call is to trick Windows into sending the application another wm_MeasureItem message. This is necessary in order to give the application an opportunity to change the size of the menu item to accommodate the newly selected font. When you select the Disable Font menu item, ModifyMenu is called to set the menu to a grayed state. (The grayed state also includes the disabled attribute.) The purpose of this is so you can see the Owner-Draw menu item painted in this state. Selecting Enable Font also makes a call to ModifyMenu but passes mf_Enabled instead of mf_Grayed.

Comments

An outstanding feature of Delphi's design compared to other current development environments is that, for most applications, you will generally never have to worry about handling Windows messages directly. Delphi's components cover so many aspects of Windows programming and do it so well that, for many programmers, the need to understand the actual method of how Windows messages are received and handled by your application is virtually nonexistent. At the same time, the designers of Delphi recognized that there is simply no way they could build enough components, with enough flexibility and power, to handle every possible need of every programmer and application. With this in mind, they carefully designed Delphi in a way that minimizes, if not entirely eliminates, the limits many programmers run into when using other comparable development environments. Anytime you find a situation that Delphi can't handle for you, you simply use the Windows API. All API functions are available to you along with all Windows constants and data structures required to perform any desired programming task directly through the API.

In a great many of the How-Tos presented in this book, you have seen examples of sending messages to Windows to obtain information or perform some action. In this How-To, you are seeing an example of how you can define procedures specifically for the purpose of receiving messages sent to your application by Windows, and the elegant way in which Delphi allows you to do this.

The Owner-Draw technique may seem very complicated at first. This is because you are working primarily with the Windows API and its various requirements, data structures, and methods of operation. There is definitely a learning curve involved in mastering this kind of work, but as with most things, once you successfully make your way through it a time or two, it no longer seems so bad.

4.9 How do I... Modify the System menu?

COMPLEXITY: INTERMEDIATE

Problem

Some applications add their own items to the System menu and make modifications to the standard items. Can this be done in Delphi?

Technique

Within some limits, you can treat the System menu just like any other menu in Delphi. The difference is that there is no Delphi component representing the System menu; therefore, you must work through the Windows API, but this is reasonably simple. Windows will fight you in some cases—for example, it will not let you disable the Size menu item if your application is a resizeable form—but Delphi can help in some of these situations.

Steps

Run SYSMENU.EXE. As shown in Figure 4-9, there is a list of check boxes representing each standard System menu item, a set of radio buttons to let you select the action to be taken, a button to perform the selected actions on the selected menu items, and finally, another check box to allow Delphi to assist with the changes. Experiment with different selections to see what's possible, where Windows fights you, and how Delphi can lend support on certain items. For example, the only items Windows will allow you to gray or disable are the Close and Switch To items unless you allow Delphi to assist, in which case you can also gray the Size, Minimize, and Maximize items.

1. Create a new project. Save the default unit as SYSMENU1.PAS and the project as SYSMENU.DPR.

2. Add the components, properties, and settings as shown in Table 4-9.

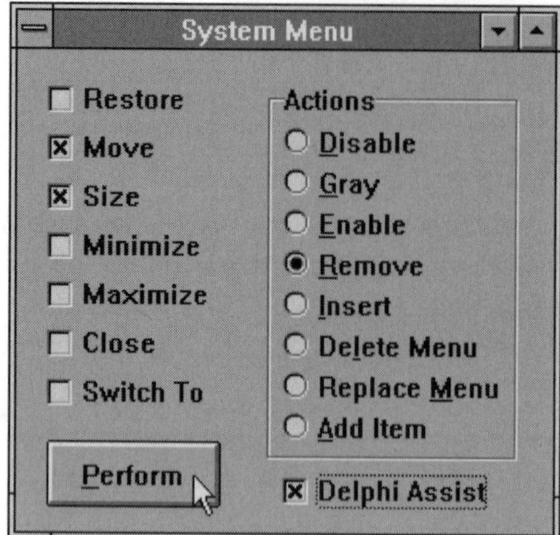

Figure 4-9 The SYSMENU application

Table 4-9 Components, properties, and settings for the SYSMENU project

COMPONENT	PROPERTY	SETTING
Form	Caption	System Menu
	ClientHeight	237
	ClientWidth	274
CheckBox	Caption	Restore
	Left	16
	Top	16
CheckBox	Caption	Move
	Left	16
	Top	40
CheckBox	Caption	Size
	Left	16
	Top	64
CheckBox	Caption	Minimize
	Left	16
	Top	88
CheckBox	Caption	Maximize
	Left	16
	Top	112
CheckBox	Caption	Close

COMPONENT	PROPERTY	SETTING
	Left	16
	Top	136
CheckBox	Caption	Switch To
	Left	16
	Top	160
Button	Caption	&Perform
	Left	16
	Top	192
RadioGroup	Caption	Actions
	Height	185
	Items	&Disable
		&Gray
		&Enable
		&Remove
		&Insert
		De&lete Menu
		Replace &Menu
		&Add Item
	Left	128
	Top	16
	Width	128
CheckBox	Caption	Delphi Assist
	Left	136
	Top	208

3. Following the *uses* clause, enter the type definitions as detailed here. These will be used to help manage the System menu.

```
uses
  SysUtils, WinTypes, WinProcs, Messages, Classes, Graphics, Controls,
  Forms, Dialogs, StdCtrls, ExtCtrls;

type
  {Enumerated type to represent each position in System Menu}
  SystemItems = (SRestore, SMove, SSize, SMin, SMax, S1, SClose, S2, SSwitch);
  {A set type to track presence of each standard system menu item}
  ItemSet = set of SystemItems;
```

4. In the *private* section of TForm1, add the following variable, procedure, and function declarations. Each of these is described by the accompanying comments.

```
private
    { Private declarations }
    {Handle for the System Menu}
    SysMenu: HMenu;
    {Set of System Menu items currently present}
    SItems: ItemSet;
    {Handles selected items for Enabled, Disabled, and Grayed}
    procedure Modify(Flag: integer);
    {Removes selected items}
    procedure RemoveItems;
    {Puts back selected items}
    procedure InsertItems;
    {Calculates position of standard item}
    function CalcPos(DefPos: SystemItems): Integer;
    {Handler for Windows wm_SysCommand message}
    procedure WMSysCommand(var SInfo: TMessage); message wm_SysCommand;
```

5. Following the *implementation* and resource compiler directive statements, enter the following constant definitions. These will be used to refer to the radio buttons within the RadioGroup1 object.

```
implementation

{$R *.DFM}

{Represents RadioButtons in RadioGroup1}
const
  RDisable = 0;
  RGray = 1;
  REnable = 2;
  RRemove = 3;
  RInsert = 4;
  RDelete = 5;
  RReplace = 6;
  RAdd = 7;
```

6. Enter the following definition for the Modify procedure. This should follow the constant definitions you just entered in step 5. Requests to enable, disable, or gray menu items are applied to the selected items by this procedure.

```
procedure TForm1.Modify(Flag: integer);
begin
  {Flag will equal one of: mf_Enabled, mf_Disabled, or mf_Grayed}
  if Assist.Checked then begin
    {Let Delphi help out with the change}
    if CBSize.Checked then
      {Change Form's sizeable attribute}
      if Flag = mf_Enabled then BorderStyle := bsSizeable
      else BorderStyle := bsSingle;
    if CBMin.Checked then
      {Add or Remove Minimize button from form}
```

```
      if Flag = mf_Enabled then BorderIcons := BorderIcons + [biMinimize]
      else BorderIcons := BorderIcons - [biMinimize];
    if CBMax.Checked then
      {Add or Remove Maximize button from form}
      if Flag = mf_Enabled then BorderIcons := BorderIcons + [biMaximize]
      else BorderIcons := BorderIcons - [biMaximize];
  end;
  {Attempt change via EnableMenuItem API call for each selected item}
  if CBRestore.Checked then
    EnableMenuItem(SysMenu, sc_Restore, mf_ByCommand or Flag);
  if CBMove.Checked then
    EnableMenuItem(SysMenu, sc_Move, mf_ByCommand or Flag);
  if CBSize.Checked then
    EnableMenuItem(SysMenu, sc_Size, mf_ByCommand or Flag);
  if CBMin.Checked then
    EnableMenuItem(SysMenu, sc_Minimize, mf_ByCommand or Flag);
  if CBMax.Checked then
    EnableMenuItem(SysMenu, sc_Maximize, mf_ByCommand or Flag);
  if CBClose.Checked then
    EnableMenuItem(SysMenu, sc_Close, mf_ByCommand or Flag);
  if CBSwitch.Checked then
    EnableMenuItem(SysMenu, sc_TaskList, mf_ByCommand or Flag);
end;
```

7. Following the Modify procedure, enter the definition for the RemoveItems procedure. This will remove selected items from the System menu and update the SItems set accordingly.

```
procedure TForm1.RemoveItems;
begin
  {Remove selected items via DeleteMenu API call and update SItems}
  if CBRestore.Checked then begin
    DeleteMenu(SysMenu, sc_Restore, mf_ByCommand);
    Exclude(SItems, SRestore);
  end;
  if CBMove.Checked then begin
    DeleteMenu(SysMenu, sc_Move, mf_ByCommand);
    Exclude(SItems, SMove);
  end;
  if CBSize.Checked then begin
    DeleteMenu(SysMenu, sc_Size, mf_ByCommand);
    Exclude(SItems, SSize);
  end;
  if CBMin.Checked then begin
    DeleteMenu(SysMenu, sc_Minimize, mf_ByCommand);
    Exclude(SItems, SMin);
  end;
  if CBMax.Checked then begin
    DeleteMenu(SysMenu, sc_Maximize, mf_ByCommand);
    Exclude(SItems, SMax);
  end;
  if CBClose.Checked then begin
    DeleteMenu(SysMenu, sc_Close, mf_ByCommand);
```

continued on next page

continued from previous page

```
    Exclude(SItems, SClose);
  end;
  if CBSwitch.Checked then begin
    DeleteMenu(SysMenu, sc_TaskList, mf_ByCommand);
    Exclude(SItems, SSwitch);
  end;
end;
```

8. Following the RemoveItems procedure, enter the CalcPos function definition as shown here. This simple little routine allows the program to place individual items into the System menu at the relative standard position.

```
function TForm1.CalcPos(DefPos: SystemItems): Integer;
var
  Item: SystemItems;
  Pos: Integer;
begin
  {This calculates the correct position to insert any standard
   System Menu item relative to the other items currently present.
   For example, if all items are removed, you can put each back
   one at a time in any order and they will all end up in the
   proper order for a standard system menu.}
  Pos := 0;
  {loop through all positions up to requested position}
  for Item := SRestore to DefPos do
    if Item in SItems then Inc(Pos);
  Result := Pos;
end;
```

9. Following CalcPos, enter the definition for the InsertItems procedure. This will return standard items to the System menu and update the SItems set accordingly.

```
procedure TForm1.InsertItems;
begin
  {For each selected item, only insert if not already there.
   For each item inserted, update the SItems set. For each
   selected item except Restore, the CalcPos function is used
   to determine the correct insert position, Restore is always
   inserted as the first item.}
  if (CBRestore.Checked) and not (SRestore in SItems) then begin
    InsertMenu(SysMenu, 0, mf_ByPosition, sc_Restore, '&Restore');
    Include(SItems, SRestore);
  end;
  if (CBMove.Checked) and not (SMove in SItems)  then begin
    InsertMenu(SysMenu, CalcPos(SMove), mf_ByPosition, sc_Move, '&Move');
    Include(SItems, SMove);
  end;
  if (CBSize.Checked) and not (SSize in SItems)  then begin
    InsertMenu(SysMenu, CalcPos(SSize), mf_ByPosition, sc_Size, '&Size');
    Include(SItems, SSize);
  end;
  if (CBMin.Checked) and not (SMin in SItems)  then begin
```

```
    InsertMenu(SysMenu, CalcPos(SMin), mf_ByPosition,
      sc_Minimize, 'Mi&nimize');
    Include(SItems, SMin);
  end;
  if (CBMax.Checked) and not (SMax in SItems)  then begin
    InsertMenu(SysMenu, CalcPos(SMax), mf_ByPosition,
      sc_Maximize, 'Ma&ximize');
    Include(SItems, SMax);
  end;
  if (CBClose.Checked) and not (SClose in SItems)  then begin
    InsertMenu(SysMenu, CalcPos(SClose), mf_ByPosition,
      sc_Close, '&Close'#9'Alt+F4');
    Include(SItems, SClose);
  end;
  if (CBSwitch.Checked) and not (SSwitch in SItems)  then begin
    InsertMenu(SysMenu, CalcPos(SSwitch), mf_ByPosition,
      sc_TaskList, 'S&witch...'#9'Ctrl+Esc');
    Include(SItems, SSwitch);
  end;
end;
```

10. Following InsertItems, enter the message handler for the wm_SysCommand message. This will respond to any extra menu items added to the System menu.

```
procedure TForm1.WMSysCommand(var SInfo: TMessage);
begin
  {Extract command ID assigned in AppendMenu}
  if (SInfo.WParam Shr 4) <= GetMenuItemCount(SysMenu) then
    {It's one of ours so respond to it}
    MessageDlg('Custom system menu item selected', mtInformation, [mbok], 0)
  else
    {Let Windows handle it}
    inherited;
end;
```

11. Double-click the form's OnCreate method and enter the following code to initialize the application.

```
procedure TForm1.FormCreate(Sender: TObject);
begin
  {Get handle to system menu}
  SysMenu := GetSystemMenu(Handle, False);
  {Initialize SItems: all items present}
  Sitems := [SRestore..SSwitch];
end;
```

12. Double-click the Perform button and enter the following code to carry out the selected action.

```
procedure TForm1.Button1Click(Sender: TObject);
var
```

continued on next page

continued from previous page

```
  Num: Integer;
  Cap: array [0..30] of char;
begin
  {ItemIndex indicates which radio button is selected}
  case RadioGroup1.ItemIndex of
    RDisable : Modify(mf_Disabled);
    RGray    : Modify(mf_Grayed);
    REnable  : Modify(mf_Enabled);
    RRemove  : RemoveItems;
    RInsert  : InsertItems;
    RDelete  :
      if Assist.Checked then
        {Remove system menu via Form property}
        BorderIcons := BorderIcons - [biSystemMenu]
      else
        {Tell Windows to delete menu from memory}
        DestroyMenu(SysMenu);
    RReplace : begin
      if Assist.Checked then
        {Add system menu via Form property}
        BorderIcons := BorderIcons + [biSystemMenu]
      else
        {Tell Windows to create new default system menu}
        GetSystemMenu(Handle, True);
      {Need to get handle of new system menu}
      SysMenu := GetSystemMenu(Handle, False);
    end;
    RAdd     : begin
      {Get current item count and add 1}
      Num := GetMenuItemCount(SysMenu) + 1;
      {Add to end of system menu with unique command ID and caption.
       Note that Windows reserves bottom 4 bits.}
      AppendMenu(SysMenu, mf_String, Num Shl 4,
        StrPCopy(Cap, IntToStr(Num) + ' New System Item'));
    end;
  end;
end;
```

13. Compile and run the application.

How It Works

Every menu in Windows has a handle assigned to it by Windows when it is created. When you create a menu in Delphi, the TMainMenu and TMenuItem components take care of the details for you in order to have the menus created and recognized in Windows. The returned handle is stored in the menu component's Handle property. Earlier in this chapter, there are examples of using the TMainMenu.Handle property (which is of type HMenu) to pass to various API functions such as ModifyMenu. For the System menu, there is no Delphi component to help you, so you must obtain and store the handle for the System menu yourself. This is done in the OnCreate event by using the GetSystemMenu API call and storing the returned handle in the SysMenu variable:

```
SysMenu := GetSystemMenu(Handle, False);
```

The Handle property passed as the first parameter to GetSystemMenu is the form's handle, which is of type HWindow. This tells Windows which System menu to return a handle for, since every application can have a separate System menu. The False parameter tells Windows that we do indeed want the handle of the current System menu. Passing True in this parameter would tell Windows that we want to assign a new System menu, with default settings, to our application; this would replace the current System menu, including any changes you may have made to it.

The following line of code initializes the SItems set to indicate that all standard menu items are currently present in the System menu. All enumerated values from SRestore to SSwitch are added to the SItems set.

```
Sitems := [SRestore..SSwitch];
```

Several private methods are defined in this application in order to break the program down into easier to understand steps. The first of these private methods, Modify, handles requests to disable, gray, or enable each of the selected menu items (see step 6).

Disabling, Enabling, and Graying System Menu Items

The Modify method first checks to see whether the user is requesting assistance from Delphi to perform the modifications. For disabling, enabling, and graying, Delphi can assist with three of the menu items. Without Delphi's help, requests to disable or gray the Size, Minimize, or Maximize menu items will be ignored by Windows. The reason is that Windows will see that the form has resizeable borders and Minimize and Maximize buttons. Using the BorderStyle property of the form, you can remove the resizeable border, and using the BorderIcons property, you can remove the Minimize and/or Maximize buttons. Making these changes through the form's properties will automatically cause the System menu to be updated appropriately.

The Flag parameter passed to Modify indicates the modification to be made. The Modify procedure then checks each check box in turn to see which menu items are selected for modification. For each one that is selected, Modify attempts to modify the menu item using the EnableMenuItem API function. The first parameter is the handle of the System menu retrieved from GetSystemMenu. The second parameter is the command ID of the menu item to be changed. The third parameter includes both the mf_ByCommand flag, which tells Windows to use this method to identify the menu item, and the value passed in Flag, which is one of mf_Disabled, mf_Grayed, or mf_Enabled.

As mentioned previously, for these modifications, Windows will only allow you to affect the Close and Switch To menu items; the others are ignored. They have all been coded in this How-To for demonstration, but in your own applications there is no point in coding the EnableMenuitem statements for any but the Close and Switch

To items. To disable or enable the Size, Minimize, and Maximize items, use the form's BorderStyle and BorderIcons properties.

Removing System Menu Items

The RemoveItems method (see step 7) does not need any extra assistance from Delphi. Even though Windows will not let you disable, gray, or enable certain items, it will let you remove them using the DeleteMenu API function.

Again, each check box is examined in turn to see if it was selected, and if so, that menu item is deleted from the System menu. The SItems set is updated in order to allow the program to keep track of which standard menu items are currently present in the System menu.

Adding Standard System Menu Items

When you want to add standard menu items back to the System menu, you will want to be sure they are added in the correct positions. It's very important that you retain this standard order. The menu will still work fine no matter which order the items are in, but you will confuse and frustrate users if your System menu items are ordered differently than other applications. The problem is, at any given moment, you do not know which items are present and which are not. For example, the Move menu item is normally the second item (following the Restore menu item), but you can't just tell Windows to add it in the second position; if you had removed all items except Minimize, then adding Move as the second item would place it under the Minimize item, when in fact it should be placed above.

The CalcPos function (defined in step 8) solves this positioning problem. In a complete System menu, you know the standard position each System menu item belongs in, so for any item to be added, you only need to find out which of the normally preceding items are currently present. CalcPos is passed the normal position for the item to be added (in DefPos). This value is zero-based so, when adding the Move item, 1 is passed to indicate it's normally the second item. CalcPos then loops through the standard item positions (SRestore being the first) up to the passed position. For each item currently present, which can be determined by checking the SItems set, the Pos value is incremented. At the end of the loop, Pos will indicate the actual position to insert the passed menu item. Note that this function must also take into account the separators that normally surround the Close menu item; that's why these were included in the SystemItems enumerated type as S1 and S2.

The InsertItems method, like the RemoveItems method, examines each check box to see if that item is to be inserted. It also checks to see whether or not this item is already present, because Windows will not prevent you from adding an item multiple times. If the item is already present, the selection is ignored. For each item, InsertItems uses the InsertMenu API function to add the item back to the System menu.

You need to tell Windows where to place the item, so mf_ByPosition is used with InsertMenu. The second parameter is the position to insert the item, and this is where the CalcPos function is used. The fourth parameter specifies the standard command ID to assign, and the last parameter is the text label to appear. SItems is then updated to indicate this item is once again present.

Handling System Menu Modification Requests

The event handler for the Perform button (step 12) determines what action has been selected and acts appropriately. Because various routines have been created to handle different actions, the code required here becomes simple and quite readable. The handler determines what action was selected from the list of radio buttons in RadioGroup1 by checking the ItemIndex property. The constants defined near the top of the unit are used here to test the possible action values in a *case* statement. For the first five possible values, a simple call to other routines is all that's necessary to carry out the action.

If the Delete Menu, Replace Menu, or Add Item actions are chosen, the work is performed directly within the Perform button's handler since the code is quite short. Two methods are demonstrated for deleting the System menu. The Delphi method is to remove biSystemMenu from the form's BorderIcons property. This causes TForm to re-create itself without a control button on the form. The API method is DestroyMenu. This also removes the menu completely; however, it does not remove the control button from the form—clicking on it displays a small empty menu rectangle.

The Replace Menu action, if the Delphi method is being used, is exactly opposite of the Delete Menu action: it adds biSystemMenu back to the BorderIcons property, causing the form to re-create itself with a new System menu in place. The API method must tell Windows to create and attach a new System menu by passing True as the second parameter to the GetSystemMenu function. Whichever method is used, the program must then call GetSystemMenu again (passing False) in order to get the handle for the new menu.

When the Add Item is selected, a new item is added to the System menu using the AppendMenu API function. AppendMenu, as its name implies, simply adds new items to the end of an existing menu, so no position parameter is required. The constant mf_String is passed to tell AppendMenu to expect the menu caption to be passed as the last parameter (which must be a PChar type string; StrPCopy is used to convert the constructed Pascal string into a PChar string).

When adding a new menu item, you must give the item a unique command ID (this is done for you when using Delphi's menu components, but these components can't easily be used here). For the System menu, all command IDs must have a value greater than 15 and less then 65280 (FF00 hex). This How-To simply takes the current count of items in the System menu (using the GetMenuItemCount API function) and performs a left shift of 4 bits to make it greater than 15. This method is fine for this demonstration, but is actually not a good method if you are allowing other menu items to be removed and re-added, as this could result in duplicate IDs for your custom menu items.

Responding to Clicks on the System Menu

Whenever a menu item on the System menu is selected, Windows sends a wm_SysCommand message. This applies to both the standard System menu items and any additional menu items you add to the System menu. Since you are not using TMenuItem components here, there is no way to attach an OnClick handler to these items, so you must handle the wm_SysCommand message in order to trap selection of these items. For demonstration purposes, WParam is checked to see if it is less than or equal to the current count of items in the System menu (after shifting right 4 bits to counter the left shift performed when adding the items). This works because all standard System menu item IDs (such as sc_Restore) are equal to or greater than 65280. In your own applications, you would compare WParam to the specific values you assigned when adding items.

If WParam does not equal one of your own added item command IDs, then you must call the default message handler (which can be done simply by using the keyword *inherit*); otherwise, Windows will not be able to perform the required actions for these items. You can, if you like, test WParam against standard IDs and perform your own additional work for the standard items. For example, if you'd like to perform some additional action whenever the user minimizes the application, simply compare WParam to sc_Minimize.

Comments

Although Windows enforces a few limits, you can wield a great deal of control over the System menu without much difficulty. As you can see, even though Delphi doesn't provide any direct help with the System menu, indirectly it still gives you additional control over it via a couple of standard form properties.

5

5

5

GRAPHICS

How do I...

Graphics have become an essential ingredient in many Windows applications, but writing such applications in Windows using Windows' APIs alone can be daunting (to say the least). For this reason, Delphi pays particular attention to these areas by providing a host of components and corresponding methods that allow you to build powerful graphical features into your application with very little effort. The topics in this chapter demonstrate many of Delphi's features and show you how to take full advantage of them. You'll be introduced to several Windows API functions that deal with graphics and learn how you can get the most from using a combination of Delphi's built-in methods and the Windows API. You will discover techniques for manipulating bitmaps and other objects. You'll see how to animate icons and create other animations and visual effects.

Note: Although the programs presented in this chapter will run fine in 16 color resolution, the bitmaps used will look their best at a video resolution of 256 colors or better.

5.1 Arrange the icons on the desktop

This simple How-To is an example of how easy it can be to tell Windows what to do via the Windows API (Application Programming Interface).

5.2 Autosize a form to fit a picture and autosize pictures to fit a form

Learn a useful technique for displaying pictures (bitmaps, icons, and metafiles). The form sizes itself to fit the picture you load. Once displayed, the form can be resized, and the picture will autosize itself to fit the form.

5.3 Visualize the pen mode settings

Using pens in Delphi is easy, but pens can do more than simply draw lines. The mode settings of a Delphi pen provide a variety of special effects. The problem is understanding what effect each different mode has. The utility presented in this How-To allows you to visualize all 16 mode settings for pens.

5.4 Draw a bounding box with the mouse

In many applications users must select a particular area of the form for various purposes. This may be to determine the size of an object to be drawn, or to group objects together for common processing. Building on the previous How-To, you will create a bounding box, or rubber-band effect, as you move the mouse.

5.5 Animate my minimized application's icon

You may be creating an application with the ability to inform users that some event has taken place, but a user may have minimized the application. Animating the icon is a great way to alert users without interrupting their active application.

5.6 Create hot spots in pictures

Delphi's TPaintBox component makes a terrific invisible hot spot that can be placed over parts of an image in order to trigger events as the mouse is passed over it. If you've ever tried to do this using *any* other language, you'll really appreciate how easy it is with Delphi!

5.7 Visualize the bitmap CopyMode settings

CopyMode settings control the effects that are produced when copying an image from one location to another. The utility in this How-To lets you experiment with the settings in order to gain an understanding of the different effects you can produce. You may want to invert all the colors of an image, or replace one color with another. Maybe you'd like to merge two pictures into one. See which settings accomplish these and more.

5.8 Create animation

Now that you've been introduced to the CopyMode settings, you're ready for some prime-time animation! In this How-To, you'll create an animated ball that bounces around a form containing a background image. If you would like to create games with Delphi, this is sure to get you started in the right direction. If you thought creating graphical games would be too complicated in Windows, this may change your mind.

5.9 Fade one picture into another

Some of the most popular applications on the market today are presentation packages. Such packages include the ability to perform various transitions between images. Building on the basics presented so far in this chapter, this How-To will not only show you a technique for merging images, but for fading one image out while another is fading in.

5.10 Fade text in and out over a background

You'll build on the technique used in How-To 5.9 to smoothly fade text into and out of an image. This is a particularly popular method of giving a professional look to presentations.

5.1 How do I...
Arrange the icons on the desktop?

COMPLEXITY: EASY

Problem

I'd like to create a utility to help me manage the Windows desktop. One of the things I'd like to do is to arrange the icons neatly on the desktop using a button in my utility rather than Program Manager's menu. Can I do this with Delphi?

Technique

This is one of the easier tasks to accomplish, but it's a good example of how you can control the Windows environment from within your own programs. To do this, you will make use of two simple Windows API functions combined into a single statement.

Note: Due to changes in the methods of managing icons in Windows 95, the application presented in this How-To only works with Windows 3.xx versions

Steps

Run ARRANGE.EXE. From Program Manager, start a few different applications and minimize each of them. Click and drag each of the minimized icons to different areas on the screen, as shown in Figure 5-1. You can also minimize Program Manager itself. Return to the ARRANGE.EXE application and click the Arrange Icons button. All the icons scattered around the desktop will line up neatly along the bottom of the desktop, just as they do when you select the Arrange Icons menu item in Program Manager.

1. Create a new project. Save the default unit as ARRANGE1.PAS and save the project as ARRANGE.DPR.

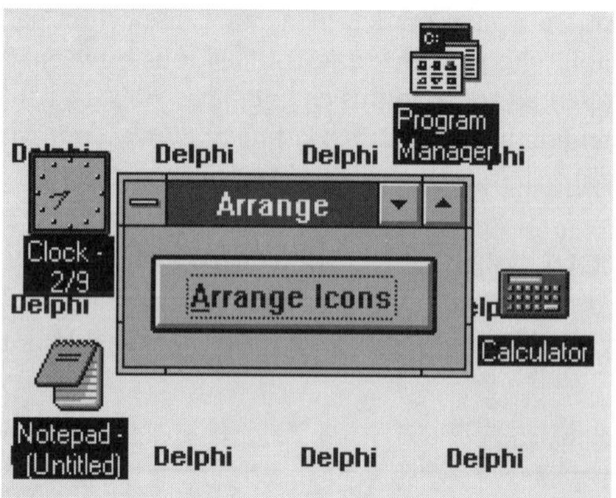

Figure 5-1 ARRANGE with icons scattered on desktop

2. Add the components and properties as shown in Table 5-1.

Table 5-1 Components, properties, and settings for the ARRANGE project

COMPONENT	PROPERTY	SETTING
Form	Caption	Arrange
	Height	76
	Width	148

COMPONENT	PROPERTY	SETTING
Button	Caption	&Arrange Icons
	Left	8
	Top	8
	Width	125

3. Double-click on the button and enter the following statement to arrange the desktop icons of all open applications.

```
procedure TForm1.Button1Click(Sender: TObject);
begin
  ArrangeIconicWindows(GetDesktopWindow);
end;
```

4. Compile and run the project. After clicking the Arrange Icons button, the desktop icons should be lined up, as shown in Figure 5-2.

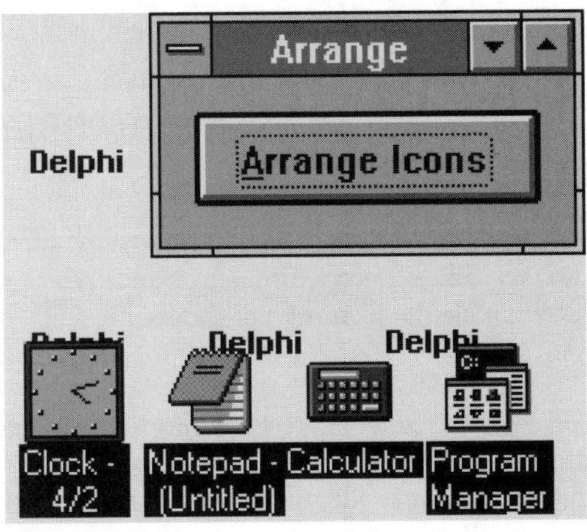

Figure 5-2 Desktop after clicking the Arrange Icons button

How It Works

The ArrangeIconicWindows function is one of the many API functions provided by Windows that allow you to emulate some of Windows' own abilities. GetDesktopWindow is another API function that returns a handle to the desktop. By embedding GetDesktopWindow directly as the parameter to ArrangeIconicWindows, you eliminate the need for declaring a variable to store the handle returned by GetDesktopWindow. Of course, if you plan to do more than one thing with the handle, it would be more efficient to store the returned handle in a variable and then use the variable in any calls that require that handle.

Note that ArrangeIconicWindows will also work if passed the handle of an MDI client window; any minimized forms will be lined up along the bottom of the MDI frame client window. If you are creating your own MDI application, you could do it this way, or you could use TForm's built-in ArrangeIcons method to arrange the icons within your MDI application window.

Comments

The Windows API is very large, but it can be fun as well as educational to browse through it (via Delphi's online help) to find different functions that control or query the Windows environment. You can then build these into your own application. Note that GetDesktopWindow is a good place to start if you want to create your own screen saver.

5.2 How do I...
Autosize a form to fit a picture and autosize pictures to fit a form?

COMPLEXITY: EASY

Problem

I want to create a form to display pictures, but I never know how large the picture will be until run time. Is there a way to make a Delphi form automatically size itself to the size of a picture and, conversely, scale the picture to fit the form?

Technique

With Delphi, just a few lines of code, combined with a few key property settings, will allow you to create a form that fits itself to the native size of a bitmap, icon, or metafile. Even better, with no additional lines of code, the form can then be resized and the picture will scale itself to fit. Cool!

Steps

Run PICTSIZE.EXE. It first appears simply as a caption bar with a menu. Click on the Load menu item to select a picture to display. Select any bitmap, icon, or Windows metafile. The form will immediately resize itself just enough to display the picture, and the picture will be painted in the client area of the form, as shown in Figure 5-3. Grab any of the sizing borders with the mouse and change the size of the form. Maximize, then restore the form. In each case, the picture is stretched to fill the new size of the form.

1. Create a new project. Save the default unit as PICTSIZ1.PAS and the project as PICTSIZE.DPR.

Figure 5-3 PICTSIZE displaying a picture

2. Add the components and properties as shown in Table 5-2.

Table 5-2 Components, properties, and settings for the PICTSIZE project

COMPONENT	PROPERTY	SETTING
Form	AutoScroll	False
	Caption	Picture Scale
	Position	poScreenCenter
	Scaled	False
MainMenu		
MenuItem	Caption	&Load
OpenDialog	Filter	All|*.bmp;*.ico;*.wmf
	+Options	
	-ofPathMustExist	True
	-ofFileMustExist	True
TImage	Align	alClient
	AutoSize	True
	Stretch	True

3. Click on the Load menu item and enter the following code in its event handler. This code loads the selected image, sizes the client area of the form precisely to fit the image, and recenters the form on the screen.

```
procedure TForm1.Load1Click(Sender: TObject);
begin
  if OpenDialog1.Execute then begin
    Image1.Picture.LoadFromFile(OpenDialog1.FileName);
    ClientWidth := Image1.Picture.Width;
    ClientHeight := Image1.Picture.Height;
    SetBounds((Screen.Width - Width) div 2,
      (Screen.Height - Height) div 2, Width, Height);
  end;
end;
```

4. Select the Events page of Form1 in the Object Inspector and double-click the OnCreate event. Enter the following lines to set an initial size for the empty form.

```
procedure TForm1.FormCreate(Sender: TObject);
begin
  ClientWidth := 200;
  Clientheight := 0;
end;
```

5. Compile and run the program. Load any bitmap, icon, or metafile you can find. Once displayed, try resizing the form, as shown in Figure 5-4.

Figure 5-4 PICTSIZE after resizing the form

How It Works

The Picture property of TImage is actually another component itself, complete with properties and methods. If you assign a file to the Picture property at design time, it is the Picture property that displays the Picture Editor dialog, which allows you to select a file to display. In this How-To, you don't need to assign anything at design time; instead, you use the standard OpenDialog component to select a file at run time. You then use the Picture component's LoadFromFile method to load the selected picture.

Certain property settings are crucial to make this form work the way you want. The AutoScroll and Scaled properties of Form1 are set to False, as these can get in the way when you want to set your Form manually to a specific size. For the Image component, setting the Align property to alClient allows it to automatically resize itself whenever the form is resized. Setting the Stretch property of Image1 is what causes the picture to be scaled to fit the form whenever it is manually resized.

Once a picture has been loaded into the Picture property of Image1, it is a simple matter to set the form's client dimensions equal to the Width and Height properties of the Picture property. Finally, even though you set the form's Position property to poScreenCenter, this only works on initial display; therefore the SetBounds method is used to recenter the form on the screen. When the application first starts, the Form1.FormCreate method is called and you set the form to a size just big enough to show the menu and the form's caption.

Comments

The TImage component is extremely powerful, flexible, and easy to use. You will typically need very little code, if any, to use this component to its best advantage.

5.3 How do I...
Visualize the pen mode settings?

COMPLEXITY: INTERMEDIATE

Problem

I know that pens have a Mode property, but I don't know what all these modes are or what effect they have when using the pen. How can I visualize the effects of each of the modes?

Technique

The best way to understand the effects of each of the 16 pen modes is by drawing all of them! You will create a form that first paints itself with the 16 basic Windows colors. These will be painted as vertical bars and act as the background in order to show the various effects. Then, starting with the pmBlack pen mode, 16 horizontal lines, one in each of the 16 basic colors, will be drawn. Using a button, you'll be able to click your way through each of the pen modes and see the effects on every color combination.

Steps

Run PENMODE.EXE. You can cycle through the 16 different modes using the Next button. The colors of the vertical lines are always the same. The horizontal lines are drawn using the same color assignments (and in the same order) as the vertical lines, but they are drawn using the currently selected pen mode. An example is shown in Figure 5-5.

1. Create a new project. Save the default unit as PENMODE1.PAS and the project as PENMODE.DPR.

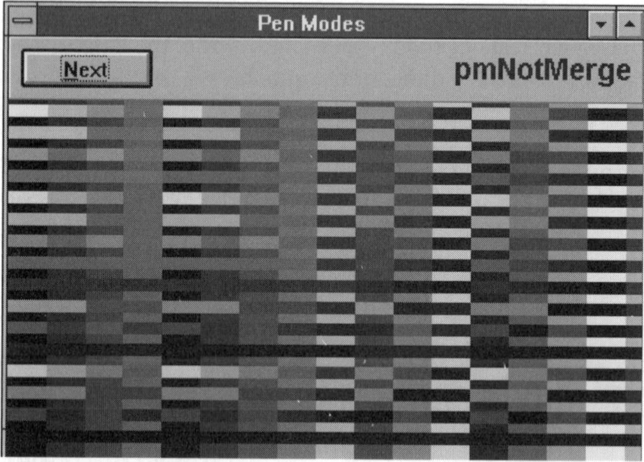

Figure 5-5 PENMODE showing the pmNotMerge setting

2. Add the components and properties as shown in Table 5-3.

Table 5-3 Components, properties, and settings for the PENMODE project

COMPONENT	PROPERTY	SETTING
Form	Caption	Pen Modes
Panel	Align	alTop
	Height	41

3. Place components on Panel1 as shown in Table 5-4.

Table 5-4 Components, properties, and settings to be placed on Panel1

COMPONENT	PROPERTY	SETTING
Button	Caption	&Next
	Height	25
	Left	24
	Top	8
Label	Alignment	taRightJustify
	Font.Color	clBlue
	Font.Name	Arial
	Font.Size	16
	Font.Style	fsBold

4. Immediately after the *implementation* statement, enter the following constant declarations. The Colors array is used to paint the lines on the form. The ModeNames array contains the captions displayed for each of the pen mode settings.

```
implementation
const
  Colors : array [0..15] of longint = (
    clBlack, clMaroon, clGreen, clOlive, clNavy,
    clPurple, clTeal, clGray, clSilver, clRed,
    clLime, clYellow, clBlue, clFuchsia, clAqua,
    clWhite);

  Cmode : TPenMode = pmblack;

  ModeNames : array [0..15] of string [13] = (
    'pmBlack', 'pmWhite', 'pmNop', 'pmNot', 'pmCopy',
    'pmNotCopy', 'pmMergePenNot', 'pmMaskPenNot',
    'pmMergeNotPen', 'pmMaskNotPen', 'pmMerge',
    'pmNotMerge', 'pmMask', 'pmNotMask', 'pmXor',
    'pmNotXor');
```

5. On the Events page of the form, double-click the OnPaint event. Enter code to paint the background vertical lines and the foreground horizontal lines featuring the current pen mode. The complete procedure should look like this:

```
procedure TForm1.FormPaint(Sender: TObject);
var
  cw, rw, i: integer;
begin
  cw := ClientWidth div 16;
  rw := (ClientHeight-Panel1.Height) div 16;
  with Canvas do begin
    Pen.Width := cw;
```

continued on next page

continued from previous page

```
      Pen.Mode := pmCopy;
      for i := 0 to 15 do begin
        Pen.Color := Colors[i];
        MoveTo(i * cw + cw div 2, 0);
        LineTo(i * cw + cw div 2, ClientHeight);
      end;
      Pen.Width := rw - 6;
      if Pen.Width < 1 then Pen.Width := 1;
      Pen.Mode := CMode;
      for i := 0 to 15 do begin
        Pen.Color := Colors[i];
        MoveTo(0,i * rw + rw div 2 + Panel1.Height);
        LineTo(ClientWidth, i * rw + rw div 2 + Panel1.Height);
      end;
    end;
end;
```

6. Next, double-click the form's OnResize event and enter the following code to cause a repaint whenever the form is resized.

```
procedure TForm1.FormResize(Sender: TObject);
begin
  Label1.Caption := ModeNames[ord(CMode)];
  Label1.left := Panel1.Width - 8 - Label1.Width;
  Invalidate;
end;
```

7. Finally, double-click on the Next button and enter the following code to cycle to the next pen mode.

```
procedure TForm1.Button1Click(Sender: TObject);
begin
  if CMode<>pmNotXor then inc(CMode) else CMode := pmBlack;
  Label1.Caption := ModeNames[ord(CMode)];
  Invalidate;
end;
```

8. Compile and run the project.

How It Works

Each of the 16 pen modes has a unique way of operating. Some of the pen modes ignore the current pen color and operate only on the colors currently on the screen. Other pen modes ignore the screen color and operate only using the pen color. Still others operate by combining the pen and screen colors in different ways.

No matter which pen mode is current, the program always paints a vertical line in each of the 16 basic colors (using the default pen mode of pmCopy). PENMODE then switches to the currently selected pen mode and draws a horizontal line in each of the 16 basic colors. The result is that you can see 256 different color interactions for each pen mode.

Each of the different modes deserves an explanation of what it's actually doing to achieve the effect you see. They are described in Table 5-5.

Table 5-5 The 16 pen modes

PEN MODE	DESCRIPTION
pmBlack	Tells Windows to ignore both the screen color and the pen color. The result is always a black line.
pmWhite	Ignores screen and pen color as with pmBlack, but always draws a white line.
pmNOP	"NOP" stands for No OPeration. It leaves the current screen contents unchanged.
pmNot	Pen color is ignored, the current screen color is inverted.
pmCopy	This is the default. Screen color is ignored, pen color is used.
pmNotCopy	Screen color is ignored, the inverted pen color is used.
pmMergePenNot	The screen color is inverted and then combined (logical OR) with pen color.
pmMaskPenNot	The screen color is inverted and then combined (logical AND) with pen color.
PmMergeNotPen	The pen color is inverted and then combined (logical OR) with screen.
pmMaskNotPen	The pen color is inverted and then combined (logical AND) with screen.
pmMerge	The pen color and screen color are combined (logical OR).
pmNotMerge	The result of pmMerge is inverted before use.
pmMask	The pen color and screen color are combined (logical AND).
pmNotMask	The result of pmMask is inverted before use.
pmXor	The pen color and screen color are Exclusive ORed. Only colors that are in either pen or screen but not both are used.
pmNotXor	The result of pmXor is inverted before use.

Comments

Although you will probably use only a few of the 16 pen modes, all of them have potential uses in various applications. By understanding the different effects that are possible, you may think of innovative ways to enhance your applications.

5.4 How do I...
Draw a bounding box with the mouse?

COMPLEXITY: EASY

Problem

OK, I have a much better idea of the power of the pen modes, but what I really need now is a way to let the user create a bounding box by dragging the mouse from one point to another on the form. I want the box to be visible no matter what colors are behind it on the form. How can I do this?

Technique

This How-To will feature one of the pen modes you learned in the previous How-To: pmNot. When the user clicks and holds a mouse button down, you will capture the mouse movements and draw a bounding box in response. This technique, often called *rubber-banding,* is shown in Figure 5-6. To show your rubber-banding to its best effect, this feature will be added to the PENMODE project you created in How-To 5.3.

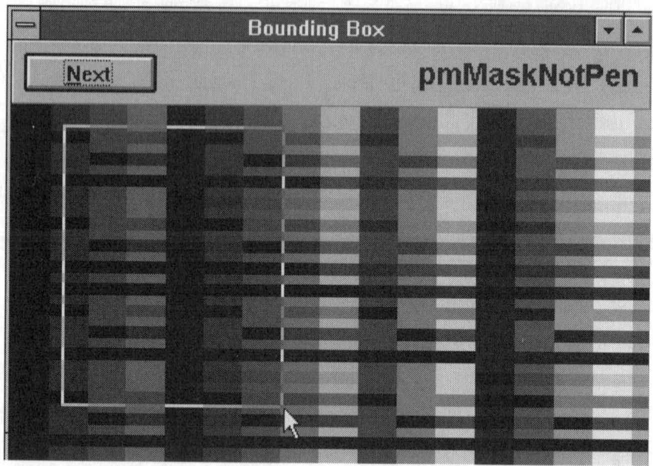

Figure 5-6 BOUNDER.EXE showing the rubber-band effect

Steps

Run BOUNDER.EXE. The program works identically to the PENMODE program created in How-To 5.3. Added to it is the bounding box that you can draw, beginning anywhere within the form's client area (the area painted with colored lines). To do so, click and hold either the left or right mouse button and drag the mouse. As long as you hold the mouse button down, the bounding box will stretch between the current position and the position you first clicked the mouse button. No matter what colors are currently onscreen, the bounding box is completely visible.

Note: You can even drag the mouse outside of the form; only the portion within the form will be visible, but it will still follow the movement of the mouse.

1. Open the PENMODE.DPR project. Save PENMODE1.PAS as BOUNDER1.PAS and save PENMODES.DPR as BOUNDER.DPR.

2. In the *private* section of Form1, add variable declarations for tracking the bounding box coordinates:

```
private
  { Private declarations }
  AnchorX, AnchorY,
  CurX, CurY: Integer;
  Bounding: Boolean;
```

3. Double-click the OnMouseDown event of the form and enter the following to initiate the bounding box. This code stores the current mouse position in two sets of variables. One set acts as the anchor or starting position of the mouse drag; the other tracks the movement of the mouse as it's dragged.

```
procedure TForm1.FormMouseDown(Sender: TObject; Button: TMouseButton;
  Shift: TShiftState; X, Y: Integer);
begin
  AnchorX := X; CurX := X;
  AnchorY := Y; CurY := Y;
  Bounding := true;
end;
```

4. Double-click the OnMouseMove event of the form. Enter code to update the current mouse position and draw the bounding box in its new position:

```
procedure TForm1.FormMouseMove(Sender: TObject; Shift: TShiftState; X,
  Y: Integer);
begin
  if Bounding then begin
    Canvas.Pen.Mode := pmNot;
    Canvas.Pen.Width := 2;
    Canvas.Brush.Style := bsClear;
    Canvas.Rectangle(AnchorX, AnchorY, CurX, CurY);
    CurX := X; CurY := Y;
    Canvas.Rectangle(AnchorX, AnchorY, CurX, CurY);
  end;
end;
```

5. Double-click the OnMouseUp event of the form and enter the following code to remove the bounding box:

```
procedure TForm1.FormMouseUp(Sender: TObject; Button: TMouseButton;
  Shift: TShiftState; X, Y: Integer);
begin
  if Bounding then begin
    Bounding := false;
    Canvas.Pen.Mode := pmNot;
    Canvas.Brush.Style := bsClear;
    Canvas.Rectangle(AnchorX, AnchorY, CurX, CurY);
  end;
end;
```

6. Compile and run the project.

How It Works

As you can see, the rubber-banding technique is very easy to achieve. Whenever the user clicks a button on the form's surface, the current mouse coordinates are stored in variables called AnchorX and AnchorY. A Boolean flag called Bounding is also set True so other event handlers know that bounding is currently in effect. CurX and CurY are set to the current mouse coordinates, effectively making the area of the bounding box exactly one pixel.

As long as the user continues to hold down the mouse button, the form continues to receive OnMouseMove events. If Bounding is True, the OnMouseMove handler first redraws the previous bounding box in the same place in order to erase it. Because pmNot has the effect of exactly inverting the screen colors, drawing the same line a second time with pmNot will restore the original screen colors. The variables CurX and CurY are then updated with the new mouse coordinates and the new bounding box is drawn.

When the user releases the mouse button, the OnMouseUp handler, if Bounding is True, draws the bounding box one last time at the last stored coordinates in order to erase it. It then sets Bounding to False so that the OnMouseMove handler will not continue to draw the bounding box.

The actual drawing of the bounding box is done using the Rectangle method of TCanvas. You could use MoveTo and four LineTo statements to draw the box instead, but it's obviously less code (and faster) to use the Rectangle method. The secret here is to be sure to set the Brush style to bsClear first in order to preserve the screen contents within the bounds of the box.

Note that you can easily check which mouse button was clicked in the OnMouseDown event handler and only initiate the bounding box if one or the other button was pressed, preserving the unused button for different uses.

Comments

The technique of handling the three mouse events (down, move, and up) is common to any interactive graphical process. You would handle these events in a similar way if you wanted to allow a user to move an object around the screen or actually draw lines and shapes on the screen. For drawing a shape, you typically use a bounding box like the one in this How-To. When the mouse is released, the bounding box is erased and the shape or object is drawn in its place.

If you plan to do a fair amount of such graphical work, it would be easy and worthwhile to create a component, most likely descended from TPaintBox, that has a rubber-banding technique built-in. Such a component would involve intercepting the mouse messages as they are received from Windows by overriding the corresponding *WMxxxx* methods for Mouse Down, Mouse Move, and Mouse Up events (there are separate routines for left, right, and middle mouse buttons). You would also need to add properties to enable or disable the feature and to hold the final coordinates of the bounding box. This would be a good introductory project if you want to learn how to create your own components. Or if you're in a hurry, you can use the one we've included on the companion disk!

5.5 How do I...
Animate my minimized application's icon?

COMPLEXITY: EASY

Problem

I would like to inform users that my application needs their attention, but I don't want to annoy them by popping up in front of whatever they are currently doing. How can I animate my application's minimized icon in Delphi?

Technique

There are a few ways to accomplish this. The method presented in this How-To involves loading multiple icons into your program; then when you need to alert the user, you simply switch between icons. The switching is queued by a timer.

Note: Due to changes in the methods of managing icons in Windows 95, the application presented in this How-To only works with Windows 3.xx versions

Steps

Run ICONANIM.EXE. It will look like Figure 5-7. If you minimize it without clicking the toggle button, you will see the standard default icon provided by Delphi. Clicking the toggle button to the On position will also minimize the program, but this time, the icon is a lightbulb that constantly switches on and off.

Figure 5-7 ICONANIM before being minimized

1. Create a new project. Save the default unit as ICONANI1 and save the project as ICONANIM.DPR.

2. Add the components and properties as shown in Table 5-6.

Table 5-6 Components, properties, and settings for the ICONANIM project

COMPONENT	PROPERTY	SETTING
Form	Caption	IconAnim
	Height	121
	Width	136
Timer	Interval	500
BiSwitch	Caption	
	Height	48

3. In the *private* section of the Form1 declaration add the following variables. BulbOn is a Boolean flag to indicate which icon is currently on display. OffIcon and OnIcon hold the two lightbulb icons.

```
private
  { Private declarations }
  BulbOn: boolean;
  OffIcon, OnIcon: TIcon;
```

4. Double-click the OnCreate event of Form1 and enter the following code to load the lightbulb icons.

```
procedure TForm1.FormCreate(Sender: TObject);
begin
  OffIcon:= TIcon.Create;
  OffIcon.LoadfromFile('CHAP05\BULBOFF.ICO');
  OnIcon := TIcon.Create;
  OnIcon.LoadfromFile('CHAP05\BULBON.ICO');
end;
```

5. Double-click the OnDestroy event of Form1 and enter code to free the icons:

```
procedure TForm1.FormDestroy(Sender: TObject);
begin
  OffIcon.Free;
  OnIcon.Free;
end;
```

6. Now double-click the OnTimer event of Timer1 and add the following code to allow the icons and the application's Title property to be switched when required.

```
procedure TForm1.IconTimerTimer(Sender: TObject);
begin
  if IsIconic(Application.handle) and BiSwitch1.Pon then begin
    if BulbOn then begin
      Form1.Icon.Assign(OffIcon);
      Application.Title := 'Bulb is Off';
    end else begin
      Form1.Icon.Assign(OnIcon);
      Application.Title := 'Bulb is On';
    end;
    BulbOn := not BulbOn;
    InvalidateRect(Application.Handle,nil,false);
  end else
    Application.Title := 'Icon Animation';
end;
```

7. Double-click the OnOn event of the BiSwitch VBX and enter the following line to automatically minimize the application when the switch is turned on.

```
Application.Minimize;
```

8. Double-click the BiSwitch OnOff event and enter this line to restore the application's normal icon:

```
Form1.Icon := Application.Icon;
```

9. Compile and run the project.

How It Works

When you click the toggle switch on, the program automatically minimizes itself and starts flashing between the two icons shown in Figure 5-8. You can also minimize the application the normal way via the minimize button; in this case the program only

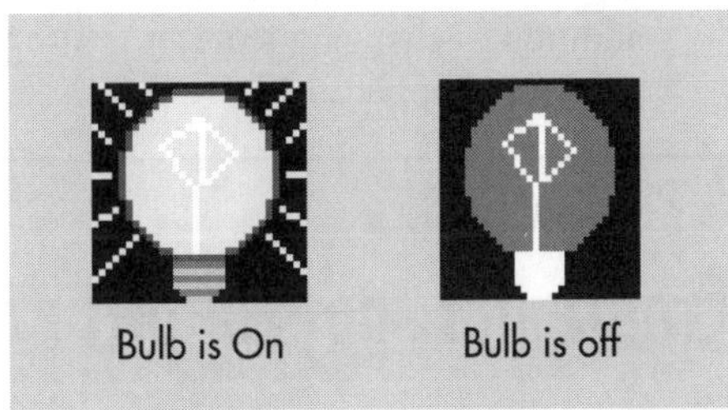

Figure 5-8 ICONANIM's lightbulb icons

flashes the icons if the switch is already turned on. Whenever the switch is turned off, the application's normal icon is reassigned.

It is important to note that both the application object itself and your main form can hold icons. Whenever the application needs to repaint its icon, it first checks to see whether the main form has an icon assigned; if so, it uses that icon instead of its own. This is why it's important to assign your flashing icons to the form's Icon property instead of the application's Icon property. Then, when you want to use the original icon for the application again, it's still available in the application's Icon property and can be assigned to the form's Icon property.

Note: This How-To also shows how to alter the application's title at run time. Windows uses this title as the icon caption whenever the application is minimized.

You will notice that the timer is enabled right from the start (at design time) and is left running during the life of the application. This is done in order to provide a place (in the TTimer's OnTimer event handler) to check whether or not the application is currently in a minimized state. The method to check this is through the Windows API IsIconic function. Note that the application's Handle property is passed, not the form's Handle property.

Finally, assigning a new icon to the form's Icon property is not sufficient to cause it to be displayed onscreen. Because the application is minimized, TForm's Refresh method also will not be effective. Therefore, we use another Windows API call, InvalidateRect, once again passing the application's Handle property. The second parameter to InvalidateRect is the area of the application we want repainted—in this case all of it. The third parameter tells Windows whether to first erase the area before painting. We pass False because the entire area of the icon needs to be painted anyway. Calling InvalidateRect causes a wm_Paint message to be sent to the application, which causes the application to repaint the icon.

Comments

Changing the application's icon is one of the most effective ways for a minimized application to get the user's attention. At the same time, it doesn't put users off by getting in the way of other work they may be doing on the screen at the time. In addition to changing icons, it is also possible to flash an icon and even to draw on a minimized application.

5.6 How do I...
Create hot spots in pictures?

COMPLEXITY: EASY

Problem

I want to be able to display a picture in my form that has hot spots. Then whenever a user drags the mouse over any of the hot spots, I'd like to pop up a small text window that describes that portion of the picture. This is difficult to do, even in Visual Basic. Is it any easier in Delphi?

Technique

Delphi has everything you need already built in to create and use hot spots. This How-To features an innovative use of the TPaintBox component and the Hint property found in all of Delphi's visual components.

Steps

Run HOTSPOTS.EXE. Move the mouse around the surface of the earth. As you do, small Hint windows will instantly appear naming the geographic feature currently under the mouse, as shown in Figure 5-9.

1. Create a new project. Save the default unit as HOTSPOT1.PAS and the project as HOTSPOTS.DPR.

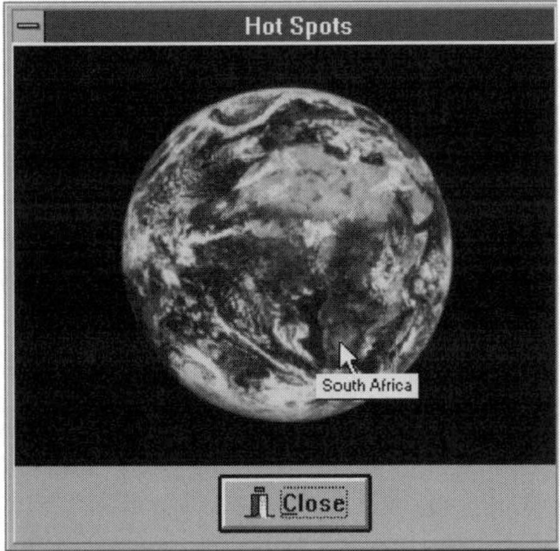

Figure 5-9 HOTSPOTS displaying a text pop-up

2. Add the components and properties as shown in Table 5-7.

Table 5-7 Components, properties, and settings for the HOTSPOTS project

COMPONENT	PROPERTY	SETTING
Form	BorderStyle	bsDialog
	Caption	HotSpots
	Height	312

continued on next page

continued from previous page

COMPONENT	PROPERTY	SETTING
	Width	327
Panel	Align	alClient
	ShowHint	True
Image	Align	alClient
	AutoSize	True
	Picture	CHAP05\SLIDE11.BMP
BitBtn	Kind	bkClose
	Left	120
	Top	244
PaintBox	Height	73
	Hint	South Atlantic
	Left	96
	Top	112
	Width	77
PaintBox	Height	61
	Hint	North Atlantic
	Left	72
	Top	32
	Width	61
PaintBox	Height	57
	Hint	North Africa
	Left	132
	Top	56
	Width	109
PaintBox	Height	69
	Hint	South Africa
	Left	176
	Top	112
	Width	53
PaintBox	Height	29
	Hint	Antarctica
	Left	100
	Top	184
	Width	121
PaintBox	Height	73
	Hint	South America

COMPONENT	PROPERTY	SETTING
	Left	56
	Top	96
	Width	37
PaintBox	Height	33
	Hint	Europe
	Left	132
	Top	24
	Width	105
PaintBox	Height	25
	Hint	South Atlantic
	Left	32
	Top	88
	Width	41

3. Compile and run the project. That's it. No code to write!

How It Works

All visual Delphi components have a Hint property. You can enter any text into this property up to 255 characters in length. For the hints to become active, they must be hosted by a TPanel component, and the TPanel's ShowHint property must be set to True.

By default, hints are displayed with a yellow background. You can change the background color of hints for your application by changing the HintColor property of TApplication like this:

```
Application.HintColor := clAqua;
```

You will also notice a small delay before the hint is shown the first time you move the mouse over the image. As long as the mouse remains over the image, subsequent hints appear immediately. If you move the mouse outside of the form, then back to the image, you will again see this delay. The amount of delay can also be controlled by changing the value of the HintPause property of TApplication.

Note: Every Delphi program predefines an instance of the TApplication object called Application.

TPaintBox components, by default, are completely invisible. They can only display if you actually paint something into them. However, being invisible doesn't prevent them from being active! Mouse movement over them is still detected, allowing the automatic hint actions to take place. You could easily write code for the OnMouseDown event for each of the TPaintBox components; so, in addition to the automatic hint when the mouse passes over, you could display additional information about the topic when the user clicks the mouse.

Comments

The hint mechanism built into Delphi makes it extremely convenient to provide context-sensitive help for all the controls in your form. This How-To shows how easy it is to extend this mechanism to be used with graphical images as well. The only limitation is that a TPaintBox component must be rectangular, making it difficult to place on irregular shapes. This can be overcome somewhat by placing multiple TPaintBoxes over an area, as was done here by splitting the South Atlantic region between two TPaintBoxes.

5.7 How do I...
Visualize the bitmap CopyMode settings?

COMPLEXITY: EASY

Problem

I know it's possible to create special effects when drawing bitmaps using the CopyMode property, but I don't understand the different settings or how they should be used. How can I visualize these when using Delphi?

Technique

As you did with the pen mode settings in How-To 5.3, you will create a utility to experiment with the CopyMode settings onscreen. The utility employs two bitmap images and allows you to copy one over the other using different CopyMode settings.

Steps

Run COPYMODE.EXE. On the right side of the form is a set of radio buttons, each representing a different CopyMode setting, as shown in Figure 5-10. Along the top, the Reset button paints the first image (always just copied), and the Morph! button performs the bitmap operation according to the currently set CopyMode radio button. The ColorGrid component allows you to set the Brush.Color property of the form's Canvas property. The brush color is used for some, though not all, of the CopyMode operations.

1. Create a new project. Save the default unit as CPYMODE1 and save the project as COPYMODE.DPR.

2. Add the components and properties as shown in Table 5-8.

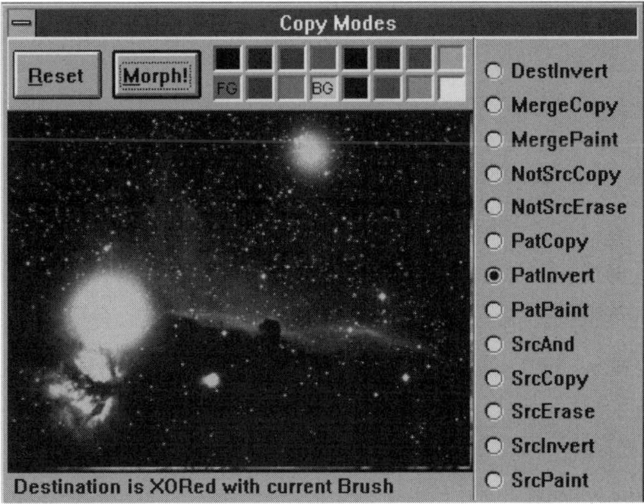

Figure 5-10 COPYMODE displaying one of the CopyMode settings

Table 5-8 Components, properties, and settings for Form1 of the COPYMODE project

COMPONENT	PROPERTY	SETTING
Form	BorderStyle	bsDialog
	Caption	Copy Modes
	Height	339
	Position	poScreenCenter
	Width	445
GroupBox	Caption	
	Height	321
	Left	320
	Top	-8
	Width	117
Panel	Caption	
	Height	49
	Left	0
	Top	0
	Width	321
Label	Caption	

continued on next page

continued from previous page

COMPONENT	PROPERTY	SETTING
	Left	4
	Top	292

3. On Panel1, add the components and properties as shown in Table 5-9.

Table 5-9 Components, properties, and settings for Panel1 of the COPYMODE project

COMPONENT	PROPERTY	SETTING
Button	Caption	&Reset
	Left	4
	Top	8
	Width	61
Button	Caption	&Morph!
	Left	72
	Top	8
	Width	61
ColorGrid	ForegroundEnabled	False
	Gridordering	go8x2
	Height	41
	Left	140
	Top	4
	Width	176

4. Add the radio button components and properties to GroupBox1 as shown in Table 5-10. The Left property for all radio buttons should be set to 8, and the Width property for all should be set to 100.

Table 5-10 Components, properties, and settings for GroupBox1 of the COPYMODE project

COMPONENT	PROPERTY	SETTING
RadioButton	Caption	DestInvert
	Hint	Destination bitmap is inverted
	Top	22
RadioButton	Caption	MergeCopy
	Hint	Brush is ANDed with source bitmap
	Top	45

COMPONENT	PROPERTY	SETTING
RadioButton	Caption	MergePaint
	Hint	Inverted source ORed into destination
	Top	68
RadioButton	Caption	NotSrcCopy
	Hint	Source is inverted
	Top	91
RadioButton	Caption	NotSrcErase
	Hint	Source ORed into destination, then inverted
	Top	113
RadioButton	Caption	PatCopy
	Hint	Current brush is copied
	Top	136
RadioButton	Caption	PatInvert
	Hint	Destination is XORed with current brush
	Top	159
RadioButton	Caption	PatPaint
	Hint	Inverted source OR brush OR destination
	Top	182
RadioButton	Caption	SrcAnd
	Hint	Source is ANDed with destination
	Top	205
RadioButton	Caption	SrcCopy
	Hint	Source is copied
	Top	228
RadioButton	Caption	SrcErase
	Hint	Inverted destination ANDed with source
	Top	250
RadioButton	Caption	SrcInvert
	Hint	Destination XORed with source
	Top	273
RadioButton	Caption	SrcPaint
	Hint	Destination ORed with source
	Top	296

5. Immediately after the *implementation* statement, enter the following variable declarations to hold the bitmap images.

```
implementation

var
  BMSrc, BMDest: TBitmap;
```

6. On the Events page for Form1, double-click the OnCreate event and enter the following code to load the two bitmaps and set the initial radio button on.

```
procedure Form1.FormCreate(Sender: TObject);
begin
  BMSrc := TBitmap.Create;
  BMSrc.LoadFromFile('CHAP05\SLIDE7.BMP');
  BMDest := TBitmap.Create;
  BMDest.LoadFromFile('CHAP05\SLIDE3.BMP');
  DestInvert.Checked := True;
end;
```

7. Double-click the TColorGrid component and enter a line as follows to set the brush color of the form.

```
procedure TForm1.ColorGrid1Change(Sender: TObject);
begin
  Canvas.Brush.Color := ColorGrid1.BackgroundColor;
end;
```

8. Click on the first of the 13 radio buttons. On the Events page, set the name of the event handler for the OnClick event to CopyModeClick. Then set the OnClick event for all 13 radio buttons to this event handler. Double-click one of the radio buttons and enter the following code for the CopyModeClick procedure. This code sets the CopyMode property of the form's Canvas property and copies the radio button's Hint property to the form's label component.

```
procedure TForm1.CopyModeClick(Sender: TObject);
begin
  if Sender = DestInvert then Canvas.CopyMode := cmDstInvert
  else if Sender = MergeCopy then Canvas.CopyMode := cmMergeCopy
  else if Sender = MergePaint then Canvas.CopyMode := cmMergePaint
  else if Sender = NotSrcCopy then Canvas.CopyMode := cmNotSrcCopy
  else if Sender = NotSrcErase then Canvas.CopyMode := cmNotSrcErase
  else if Sender = PatCopy then Canvas.CopyMode := cmPatCopy
  else if Sender = PatInvert then Canvas.CopyMode := cmPatInvert
  else if Sender = PatPaint then Canvas.CopyMode := cmPatPaint
  else if Sender = SrcAnd then Canvas.CopyMode := cmSrcAnd
  else if Sender = SrcCopy then Canvas.CopyMode := cmSrcCopy
  else if Sender = SrcErase then Canvas.CopyMode := cmSrcErase
  else if Sender = SrcInvert then Canvas.CopyMode := cmSrcInvert
  else if Sender = SrcPaint then Canvas.CopyMode := cmSrcPaint;
  Label1.Caption := TRadioButton(Sender).Hint;
end;
```

9. Double-click the Reset button and enter code as follows to copy the destination bitmap to the form's surface.

```
procedure TForm1.ResetClick(Sender: TObject);
var
  OldMode: TCopyMode;
begin
  OldMode := Canvas.CopyMode;
  Canvas.CopyMode := cmSrcCopy;
  Canvas.Draw(0, Panel1.Height, BMDest);
  Canvas.CopyMode := OldMode;
end;
```

10. Double-click the Morph! button and enter the following line. It copies the source bitmap over the destination using the currently selected CopyMode and brush color (as applicable).

```
procedure TForm1.MorphClick(Sender: TObject);
begin
  Canvas.Draw(0, Panel1.Height, BMSrc);
end;
```

11. Compile and run the project.

How It Works

The COPYMODE program first loads two bitmaps to use: one as a destination (to be copied to) and one as a source (to be copied from). During the use of the program, these two bitmaps are never modified directly. The destination bitmap is always copied to the screen in its normal form (using cmSrcCopy as the CopyMode setting). The source bitmap is always copied over the image currently on the form, using the currently selected CopyMode setting. The Draw method of the TCanvas component is used to copy the bitmaps to the form's surface. The Draw method always performs the drawing according to the currently selected CopyMode value and (if applicable) the currently selected Brush.Color value.

Each of the radio buttons has a brief description of its CopyMode setting in its Hint property. When you select a radio button, this Hint property is copied to the Label component on the form. From these (and from the results you see on the screen), you will see that there is a variety of different actions that can take place. Some settings only affect the destination bitmap, others only the source bitmap. Some combine both in some way, and still others include the current brush color in addition to one, both, or neither of the bitmaps. One feature not shown in this How-To is that the brush can also be assigned a bitmap pattern instead of a color. You will learn about this use of a brush next in How-To 5.8.

Note: Depending on the CopyMode selected, you can create many different effects compounded on top of each other. This is because the selected CopyMode setting interacts with whatever is currently on the form.

Comments

As with the pen mode settings, you will use only a few of the CopyMode settings to any great extent; but again, experimentation often leads to innovation. Note that only 13 different CopyMode settings are presented here. There are others, including cmBlackness and cmWhiteness. These are the settings that actually have names. In fact, there are 256 different settings for the CopyMode property (0 to 255). You may want to modify the program so you can experiment with all of them. What each of the unnamed settings does is beyond the scope of this book, but you may find it an enjoyable challenge to figure this out.

5.8 How do I... Create animation?

COMPLEXITY: INTERMEDIATE

Problem

I would like to write commercial-quality animated games. Naturally, performance is a big concern. Can I create professional-looking animation with Delphi?

Technique

Quality animation demands skills beyond the capabilities of a particular program, but Delphi reduces the complexity of building animations in Windows by providing components that encapsulate many of the details required to handle graphics. The TCanvas and TBitmap components are all that's needed to create animation.

The basic concept behind animation is simple: place an object at successive positions on the screen and, each time, remove it from the previous position. The technique for implementing this concept is somewhat more involved.

If your object happens to be a perfect rectangle, then placing your object onscreen is very easy. If you want an object of any other shape, the task becomes more complicated. This is because Windows can only perform bitmap operations in rectangular areas. Windows does provide other methods of drawing shapes, but they are relatively slow and unsuitable for animations. Even if the shape you want to animate is a circle, the bitmap containing that circle must be a rectangle.You use a special technique to place such a shape onscreen while preserving the portion of the background outside the shape but within the shape's rectangular bitmap. This technique involves merging the bitmap containing your shape with the background bitmap and requires the use of a another bitmap called a *mask*. Both the mask and the bitmap containing your shape must be created in a special way to allow this process to work.

Steps

Run BALL.EXE. You can control the horizontal and vertical speed of the ball using the scrollbars, shown on Figure 5-11. The ball bounces off the borders of the image. It will use the entire image no matter how you resize it.

1. Create a new project. Save the default unit as BALL1.PAS and save the project as BALL.DPR.

Figure 5-11 BALL.EXE displaying its bouncing ball

2. Add the components and properties as shown in Table 5-11.

Table 5-11 Components, properties, and settings for the BALL project

COMPONENT	PROPERTY	SETTING
Form	Caption	Bouncing Ball
	Position	poScreenCenter
Timer	Interval	5
Panel1	Align	alBottom
	Caption	
	Height	41
Panel2	Align	alRight
	Caption	
	Width	53
PaintBox	Align	alClient

3. Add the components and properties to Panel1 as shown in Table 5-12.

Table 5-12 Components, properties, and settings for Panel1

COMPONENT	PROPERTY	SETTING
ScrollBar	Height	149
	Kind	sbVertical
	LargeChange	8
	Left	20
	Max	64
	Name	ScrollBarY
	Top	28
Label	Caption	Slow
	Left	12
	Top	8
Label	Caption	Fast
	Left	12
	Top	180

4. Add the components and properties to Panel2 as shown in Table 5-13.

Table 5-13 Components, properties, and settings for Panel2

COMPONENT	PROPERTY	SETTING
Panel3	Align	alRight
	BevelOuter	bvNone
	Caption	
	Width	96
ScrollBar	LargeChange	8
	Left	48
	Max	64
	Name	ScrollBarX
	Top	12
	Width	189
Label	Caption	Slow
	Left	12
	Top	12

COMPONENT	PROPERTY	SETTING
Label	Caption	Fast
	Left	240
	Top	12

5. Add the BitBtn to Panel3 as shown in Table 5-14.

Table 5-14 BitBtn component for Panel3

COMPONENT	PROPERTY	SETTING
BitBtn	Kind	bkClose
	Left	4

6. In the *private* section of the Form1 declaration, add the following variable and procedure declarations. These are used for storing and manipulating bitmaps in order to move the ball around the image.

```
private
  { Private declarations }
  Ball, BallMask, Background, Saveback, WorkSpace: TBitmap;
  X, Y, Dx, Lx, Dy, Ly, SpeedX, SpeedY: Integer;
  procedure MoveBall;
```

7. Double-click Form1's OnCreate event and enter code as shown below. This code loads the required images, initializes the position, speed, and direction of the ball, and creates additional bitmap objects to be used as workspaces.

```
procedure TForm1.FormCreate(Sender: TObject);
begin
  Ball := TBitmap.Create;
  Ball.LoadFromFile('CHAP05\BALL.BMP');
  BallMask := TBitmap.Create;
  BallMask.LoadFromFile('CHAP05\BALLM.BMP');
  Background := TBitmap.Create;
  Background.LoadFromFile('CHAP05\SLIDE11.BMP');
  Saveback := TBitmap.Create;
  SaveBack.Width := Ball.Width;
  SaveBack.Height := Ball.Height;
  WorkSpace := TBitmap.Create;
  X := 0; Y := 0;
  Lx := X; Ly := Y;
  Dx := 1; Dy := 1;
  SpeedX := ScrollBarX.Position;
  SpeedY := ScrollBarY.Position;
end;
```

8. Double-click Form1's OnClose event and enter the following code to free all the bitmap objects.

```
procedure TForm1.FormClose(Sender: TObject; var Action: TCloseAction);
begin
  Ball.Free;
  BallMask.Free;
  Background.Free;
  SaveBack.Free;
  WorkSpace.Free;
end;
```

9. Immediately following the FormClose procedure created in step 8, define the MoveBall procedure as shown next. This procedure calculates the new ball position based on direction and speed.

```
procedure TForm1.MoveBall;
var
  i: integer;
begin
{Save the current ball position before moving it}
  Lx := X; Ly := Y;
  {Update the horizontal position}
  inc(X, SpeedX * Dx);
  {Check if past the left or right borders}
  if (X < 0) or (X + Ball.Width > PaintBox1.Width) then begin
    {If out of bounds, bounce back to correct position}
    if X < 0 then X := X * -1
    else X := (PaintBox1.Width shl 1) - X - (Ball.Width shl 1);
    Dx := Dx * -1;  {Reverse horizontal direction}
  end;
  {Update the vertical position}
  inc(Y, SpeedY * Dy);
  {Check if past top or bottom borders}
  if (Y < 0) or (Y + Ball.Height > PaintBox1.Height) then begin
    {If out of bounds, bounce back to correct position}
    if Y < 0 then Y := Y * -1
    else Y := (PaintBox1.Height shl 1) - Y - (Ball.Height shl 1);
    Dy := Dy * -1;  {Reverse vertical direction}
  end;
end;
```

10. Double-click the vertical scrollbar and enter the following line to update the vertical speed.

```
procedure TForm1.ScrollBarYChange(Sender: TObject);
begin
  SpeedY := ScrollBarY.Position;
end;
```

11. Double-click the horizontal scrollbar and enter the following line to update the horizontal speed.

```
procedure TForm1.ScrollBarXChange(Sender: TObject);
begin
  SpeedX := ScrollBarX.Position;
end;
```

12. Double-click the OnPaint event of PaintBox1. Enter the following code to repaint the background image. It also updates the in-memory copy of the background and the saved portion of the background from behind the ball's current position.

```
procedure TForm1.PaintBox1Paint(Sender: TObject);
begin
  {Resize the background}
  with PaintBox1.Canvas do
    StretchDraw(ClipRect, Background);
  {Capture to workspace too}
  with WorkSpace do begin
    Width := PaintBox1.Width;
    Height := PaintBox1.Height;
    Canvas.CopyMode := cmSrcCopy;
    Canvas.StretchDraw(Rect(0, 0, Width, Height), Background);
  end;
  {Update the saved background data}
  SaveBack.Canvas.CopyRect(Rect(0, 0, Ball.Width, Ball.Height),
    WorkSpace.Canvas, Rect(X, Y, X + Ball.Width, Y + Ball.Height));
end;
```

13. Double-click Timer1's OnTimer event and enter the following code. This is the heart of the animation. It does the actual bitmap manipulation to merge the ball image into the background image at each new position, and it erases the ball from the old position.

```
procedure TForm1.Timer1Timer(Sender: TObject);
var
  Fx, Tx, Fy, Ty: integer;
begin
  with WorkSpace.Canvas do begin
    {Erase ball by copying in saved background}
    CopyMode := cmSrcCopy;
    CopyRect(Rect(X, Y, X + Ball.Width, Y + Ball.Height),
      SaveBack.Canvas, Rect(0, 0, Ball.Width, Ball.Height));
    {set new ball position}
    MoveBall;
    {save background at new ball position}
    SaveBack.Canvas.CopyRect(Rect(0, 0, Ball.Width, Ball.Height),
      WorkSpace.Canvas, Rect(X, Y, X + Ball.Width, Y + Ball.Height));
    {Use ball mask to clear ball shape from work surface}
    CopyMode := cmSrcAnd;
    CopyRect(Rect(X, Y, X + Ball.Width, Y + Ball.Height),
      BallMask.Canvas, Rect(0, 0, Ball.Width, Ball.Height));
```

continued on next page

continued from previous page

```
    {Exclusive-OR the ball into place}
    CopyMode := cmSrcInvert;
    CopyRect(Rect(X, Y, X + Ball.Width, Y + Ball.Height),
      Ball.Canvas, Rect(0, 0, Ball.Width, Ball.Height));
  end;
  {Now blast the finished ball to the screen!}
  with PaintBox1.Canvas do begin
    if (Abs(X - Lx) <= Ball.Width)
    and (Abs(Y - Ly) <= Ball.Height) then begin
      {new and old positions within a ball diameter, so it's
       faster to display new and erase old position with a
       single operation}
      if Lx < X then Fx := Lx else Fx := X;
      if Ly < Y then Fy := Ly else Fy := Y;
      CopyRect(Rect(Fx, Fy, Fx + Ball.Width + SpeedX,
         Fy + Ball.Height + SpeedY), WorkSpace.Canvas, Rect(Fx, Fy,
         Fx + Ball.Width + SpeedX, Fy + Ball.Height + SpeedY))
    end else begin
      {old and new position more than a ball diameter apart,
       so it's better to perform separate copies}
      CopyRect(Rect(Lx, Ly, Lx + Ball.Width, Ly + Ball.Height),
        WorkSpace.Canvas, Rect(Lx, Ly, Lx + Ball.Width, Ly + Ball.Height));
      CopyRect(Rect(X, Y, X + Ball.Width, Y + Ball.Height),
        WorkSpace.Canvas, Rect(X, Y, X + Ball.Width, Y + Ball.Height));
    end;
  end;
end;
```

14. Double-click on Form1's OnResize event and enter the following code. This code is necessary to prevent the ball from being trapped should the form be resized so that the ball falls outside the form's boundaries.

```
procedure TForm1.FormResize(Sender: TObject);
begin
  {When resizing smaller, ball can get trapped beyond
   PaintBox borders, check and free if necessary.}
  if (X + Ball.Width > PaintBox1.Width) then
      X := PaintBox1.Width - Ball.Width - 1;
  if (Y + Ball.height > PaintBox1.Height) then
      Y := PaintBox1.Height - Ball.height - 1;
end;
```

15. Compile and run the project.

How It Works

Basic to any animation are the objects that move, and a surface, or background, to move them on. This How-To gives you a head start by providing these ingredients for you.

The three ingredients needed for this animation are all bitmaps. There is a bitmap to represent the background surface, a bitmap that contains the image of the ball, and a special bitmap that contains a masked version of the ball. The ball image contains the ball as it is seen in the animation. What's important for this image is that all areas of the bitmap that are not part of the ball are painted black, as shown on the left in Figure 5-12. The shape of the mask image is identical to the ball, but the interior of the ball is all black. All pixels not part of the ball image are painted white, as you can see on the right in Figure 5-12.

Whenever the ball is to be displayed at a new position on the background, all the work of painting it is done in memory, and only the result of this work is actually displayed to the screen. This is a very important consideration for two reasons: First is performance. Bitmap operations are much faster if done in memory; a bitmap operation to the screen is slower because it involves the video hardware. Second, because the painting of an animated object requires the use of the mask image, this would be visible as an ugly and annoying flicker if it were all done directly to the screen.

Another important consideration is the fact that this particular animation allows the background to be resized. Because of this, an additional workspace is needed for building the animation. The background image, stored in the TBitmap object named Background, is never altered; it always retains the image as it was loaded from disk. The image actually used for the animation is stored in the TBitmap object named WorkSpace. WorkSpace is updated every time the display surface changes size and always contains a copy of the background stretched to match the current dimensions of the display surface. If you plan on having an unchanging background for your animation, this extra workspace will not be necessary; you can perform all the work directly to the Background bitmap object instead.

When the program begins, it initializes all of the needed bitmaps and associated variables (in the FormCreate method shown in step 7). The timer placed on the form is already active, so the animation is already under way. However, since the vertical and horizontal speed values are initialized to zero, no movement takes place—the ball simply sits at its initial position until one or both scrollbars are moved.

Figure 5-12 The ball bitmap and its corresponding mask bitmap

Performing the Animation

Each time the program receives a timer tick, a new ball position is calculated and the ball is moved. This is done by first erasing the ball from its current position, calculating a new position, and then displaying the ball at the new position (refer to step 13).

Erasing the ball is the easiest part. The background from behind the ball's intended position is saved each time before placing the ball. When it's time to move the ball, this saved background image is simply copied back to WorkSpace at the ball's current position. Note that CopyMode is first set to cmSrcCopy in the workspace's Canvas property.

The MoveBall procedure is called to calculate the new position for the ball. The background at this new position must now be saved so the ball can be erased the next time through. This is done by copying the area from WorkSpace.Canvas to SaveBack.Canvas.

Now the ball can be painted at its new position. This is done in two steps. The first step sets CopyMode to cmSrcAnd, and then WorkSpace.Canvas copies the mask version of the ball into its image. The second step sets CopyMode to cmSrcPaint and WorkSpace.Canvas copies the actual ball bitmap into its image.

Painting the Ball Mask

The value, cmSrcAnd, specifies that each pixel from the mask bitmap is to be logically ANDed with the pixels in the workspace bitmap. Logical AND works as follows: if both corresponding bits are on, the result is a bit that is on; any other combination results in a bit that is off. Remember, in the mask, all pixels that are part of the ball are black and all surrounding pixels are white. The white pixels surrounding the ball (white equals all bits on) preserves the original bit settings in the workspace bitmap. Because the color black is represented by zero (all bits off), bits in the workspace bitmap ANDed with a black pixel will be turned off. This has the effect of punching a black hole into the workspace bitmap in the exact shape of the ball!

Painting the Ball

Now that a perfectly shaped hole exists in the workspace bitmap, all you have to do is fill it with the actual ball image. To do this, CopyMode is set to cmSrcPaint. This value specifies that each pixel in the ball bitmap is to be logically ORed with the pixels in the workspace bitmap. WorkSpace.Canvas then copies the ball image into itself.

Logical OR works as follows: if either or both corresponding bits are on, the result is a bit that is on; only if both bits are off will the result be a bit that is off. Because all bits in the workspace bitmap that lie within the shape of the ball have been turned off, they will be made equal to the corresponding bits in the ball image. Because all bits in the ball image that are not part of the ball are set to black, corresponding bits in the workspace bitmap will retain their current value. The ball image is now correctly merged into the background image and is ready to be displayed onscreen.

Moving the Completed Image to the Screen

Attention is now turned to PaintBox1. Its Canvas property copies the finished image from the workspace bitmap to the display. The code for this seems quite long but this is because of an effort to optimize performance (refer to step 13). This code must copy both the restored background from the ball's old position and the image of the ball at the new position. Before doing this it checks the distance between the old and new positions. If the distance the ball has moved is less than or equal to the diameter of the ball, then it performs a single copy that includes both old and new positions; otherwise, it performs two separate copies, rather than copying a large area to the screen.

The timer component has been set to an interval of 5. Although you could lower this if you want, you likely won't see any noticeable difference in performance—5 seems to be about optimum. Setting the timer to tick faster than the program can react is a waste and, in fact, could actually degrade performance. You will want to experiment with timer settings for your own animations.

Changing Backgrounds

Many games and simulations have backgrounds that constantly change in addition to the objects that move. What kind of changing background you need will determine the exact operations required; however, this How-To already includes some logic to help you. This animation is performed in a resizeable form. When the form is resized, the background bitmap is stretched to fill the new size. This means the background area saved before placing the ball at its current position is no longer valid, so it is copied again from the new background image. This same logic would apply if you had a moving background.

Comments

If you are serious about animation, you will want to take much of the code presented here and build it into component objects. This way, you will not have to continuously rewrite the same logic for every game and every object. A collection of such objects is often called a Sprite library. There will likely be Sprite libraries available for Delphi in a short time; perhaps yours will be one of them!

If you're *very* serious about animation, you may also want to investigate Microsoft's WinG graphics library. WinG is specifically aimed at increasing graphics performance so that even very complex animations will run well in Windows. WinG is available as a DLL (Dynamic Link Library) and it's free. All you need to use it in Delphi is an interface unit. Check the Delphi manuals for information on creating interface units for DLLs. Chances are also good that you'll be able to find such an interface unit, already written by someone else, on the Internet or in Borland's CompuServe forum for Delphi.

5.9 How do I... Fade one picture into another?

COMPLEXITY: ADVANCED

Problem

I have two pictures I want to display, and I'd like to create the effect of a gradual transition from one picture to the other rather than a sudden jump. Is this type of transition effect possible in Delphi?

Technique

You can use some of the same techniques employed in creating the animation in How-To 5.8 to create transition effects. In addition, a third ingredient is added to the operations between source and destination bitmaps: patterned brushes. In the COPY-MODE program presented in How-To 5.7, you saw the effects of a solid colored brush with some of the CopyMode settings. In this How-To, instead of simply setting the Brush property of a Canvas to a solid color, you will create patterned brushes from small bitmaps. These patterned brushes will be used much the same way as the mask version of the ball was used in How-To 5.8. You will also make extensive use of Windows' API functions for creating the transitions.

Steps

Run FADE.EXE. You will see a dialog with a picture displayed, as shown in Figure 5-13. Press the Fade Into button and watch as the picture fades out and a new picture fades in. You can continue pressing the Fade Into button; each time the current picture will be replaced with the other picture.

1. Create a new project. Save the default unit as FADE1.PAS and save the project as FADE.DPR.
2. Add the components and properties as shown in Table 5-15.

Table 5-15 Components, properties, and settings for the FADE project

COMPONENT	PROPERTY	SETTING
Form	BorderStyle	bsDialog
	Caption	Picture Fade
	Height	275
	Position	poScreenCenter
	Width	425
Panel	Align	alClient

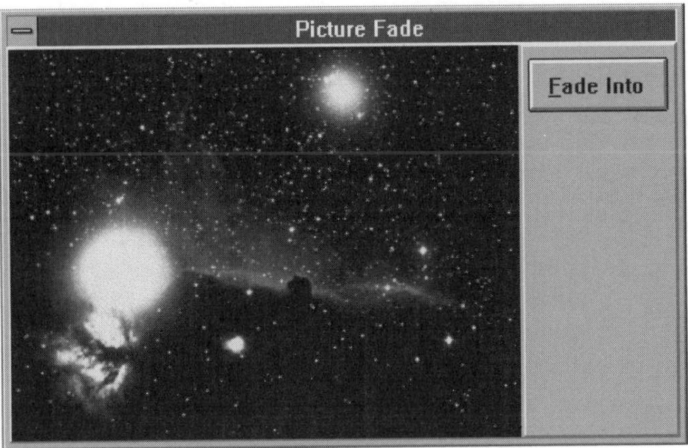

Figure 5-13 FADE.EXE with its initial picture

COMPONENT	PROPERTY	SETTING
	Caption	
Panel	Align	alRight
	Width	98
PaintBox	Align	alClient

3. On Panel2, add the button as shown in Table 5-16.

Table 5-16 Button component for Panel2

COMPONENT	PROPERTY	SETTING
Button	Caption	Fade Into
	Left	4
	Top	8

4. Before you begin to write code in FADE1.PAS, you will be creating a new object. This object will encapsulate all the actual code for performing transitions between bitmaps. If you have worked through the previous chapters, then you have already created and added some code to a unit called HOWUTILS.PAS. Open this unit file now (do not add to project).

5. First check the *uses* clause to make sure it contains references to all the necessary units. It should look like the following code. Make any necessary additions.

```
uses
  SysUtils, WinTypes, WinProcs, Messages, Classes, Graphics, Controls,
  Forms, Dialogs, StdCtrls, ExtCtrls, IniFiles;
```

6. Just above the *implementation* statement, add the following class declaration for TFadeEffect. TFadeEffect includes two private arrays of Windows brush handles and three public methods. The Create and Destroy methods are overrides to the inherited virtual class constructor and destructor. The FadeInto method performs the transitions.

```
type
  TFadeEffect = class
  private
    Masks: array [0..7] of hBrush;
    NegMasks: array [0..7] of hBrush;
  public
    constructor Create;
    destructor Destroy; override;
    procedure FadeInTo(Target: TCanvas; X, Y: integer; Pic: TBitmap);
end;

implementation
```

7. Move to the bottom of the unit, just above the final *end* statement, and add the following procedures. The $R directive tells Delphi to include a resource file called MERGE.RES. This resource file contains a set of bitmaps you will use to create brushes. Following that are the Create, Destroy, and FadeInto methods of the TFadeEffect object.

```
{$R merge.res}

constructor TFadeEffect.Create;
var
  m: integer;
  BrName: string[8];
  lb: TLogBrush;
  bm: hBitmap;
  Mask: TBitmap;
  r: TRect;
begin
  {used to create negative masks}
  Mask := TBitmap.Create;
  Mask.Width := 8;
  Mask.Height := 8;
  {load and create masks}
  for m := 0 to 7 do begin
    {load mask bitmap from resource}
```

```
    BrName := 'merge' + IntToStr(m); BrName[7] := #0;
    bm := LoadBitmap(HInstance, @BrName[1]);
    {create brush from bitmap}
    lb.lbStyle := bs_Pattern;
    lb.lbHatch := bm;
    Masks[m] := CreateBrushIndirect(lb);
    {create negative of same mask}
    Mask.Handle := bm;
    r := Rect(0, 0, 8, 8);
    InvertRect(Mask.Canvas.Handle, r);
    lb.lbHatch := Mask.Handle;
    NegMasks[m] := CreateBrushIndirect(lb);
    {dispose bitmap resource}
    DeleteObject(bm);
  end;
  Mask.Free;
end;

destructor TFadeEffect.Destroy;
var
  m: integer;
begin
  {dispose masks}
  for m := 0 to 7 do begin
    DeleteObject(Masks[m]);
    DeleteObject(NegMasks[m]);
  end;
end;

procedure TFadeEffect.FadeInTo(Target: TCanvas;
  X, Y: integer; Pic: TBitmap);
var
  m: integer;
  memDC1, memDC2: hDC;
  memBM1, memBM2, oldBM1, oldBM2: hBitmap;
  oldB1, oldB2: hBrush;
  URect: TRect;
begin
  {create memory DC and bitmap for target}
  memDC1 := CreateCompatibleDC(Target.Handle);
  memBM1 := CreateCompatibleBitmap(Target.Handle,
    Pic.Width, Pic.Height);
  oldBM1 := SelectObject(memDC1, memBM1);
  {copy picture to memory}
  BitBlt(memDC1, 0, 0, Pic.Width, Pic.Height,
    Target.Handle, X, Y, SrcCopy);
  {save original brush}
  oldB1 := Selectobject(memDC1, Masks[0]);

  {create memory DC and bitmap for picture}
  memDC2 := CreateCompatibleDC(Target.Handle);
  memBM2 := CreateCompatibleBitmap(Target.Handle,
    Pic.Width, Pic.Height);
  oldBM2 := SelectObject(memDC2, memBM2);
  {save original brush}
```

continued on next page

continued from previous page

```
  oldB2 := Selectobject(memDC2, NegMasks[0]);
  {perform a transition with each mask}
  for m := 0 to 7 do begin
    {Punch holes in current picture}
    SelectObject(memDC1, Masks[m]);
    BitBlt(memDC1, 0, 0, Pic.Width, Pic.Height,
      memDC1, 0, 0, MergeCopy);
    {Extract corresponding pixels in new picture}
    BitBlt(memDC2, 0, 0, Pic.Width, Pic.Height,
      Pic.Canvas.Handle, 0, 0, SrcCopy);
    SelectObject(memDC2, NegMasks[m]);
    BitBlt(memDC2, 0, 0, Pic.Width, Pic.Height,
      memDC2, 0, 0, MergeCopy);
    {Merge the two pictures}
    BitBlt(memDC1, 0, 0, Pic.Width, Pic.Height,
      memDC2, 0, 0, SrcPaint);
    {Blast it to the screen}
    BitBlt(Target.Handle, X, Y, Pic.Width, Pic.Height,
      memDC1, 0, 0, SrcCopy);
  end;
  {restore / dispose structures}
  SelectObject(memDC1, oldB1);
  SelectObject(memDC1, oldBM1);
  DeleteObject(memBM1);
  DeleteDC(memDC1);
  SelectObject(memDC2, oldB2);
  SelectObject(memDC2, oldBM2);
  DeleteObject(memBM2);
  DeleteDC(memDC2);
  {Paint full picture}
  Target.Draw(X, Y, Pic);
end;

end.
```

8. Now return to FADE.PAS and add HOWUTILS to the *uses* clause. The entire *uses* clause should look like this:

```
uses
  SysUtils, WinTypes, WinProcs, Messages, Classes, Graphics, Controls,
  Forms, Dialogs, StdCtrls, ExtCtrls, HowUtils;
```

9. In the *private* section of TForm1, add the following variables. This includes a variable of type TFadeEffect, which you have just defined in HOWUTILS.PAS.

```
private
  { Private declarations }
  Pic, Pic1, Pic2: TBitmap;
  Fader: TFadeEffect;
```

10. Double-click the OnCreate event of Form1 and enter the code below. This loads the two pictures that will be the subjects of the transition effects, adjusts the size

of the form and PaintBox to fit the pictures, and creates an instance of the TFadeEffect object.

```
procedure TForm1.FormCreate(Sender: TObject);
begin
  Pic1 := TBitmap.Create;
  Pic1.LoadFromFile('CHAP05\SLIDE7.BMP');
  Pic2 := TBitmap.Create;
  Pic2.LoadFromFile('CHAP05\SLIDE10.BMP');
  ClientWidth := Pic1.Width + Panel2.Width + 4;
  ClientHeight := Pic1.Height + 2;
  PaintBox1.Width := Pic1.Width;
  PaintBox1.Height := Pic1.Height;
  Fader := TFadeEffect.Create;
  Pic := Pic1;
end;
```

11. Double-click the OnDestroy event and add the following statements to free the objects.

```
procedure TForm1.FormDestroy(Sender: TObject);
begin
  Pic1.Free;
  Pic2.Free;
  Fader.Free;
end;
```

12. Double-click the OnPaint event of PaintBox1 and enter the following line to repaint the current image.

```
procedure TForm1.PaintBox1Paint(Sender: TObject);
begin
  PaintBox1.Canvas.Draw(0, 0, Pic);
end;
```

13. Double-click the Fade Into button and add the following. This executes the transition.

```
procedure TForm1.Button1Click(Sender: TObject);
begin
  if Pic = Pic1 then Pic := Pic2 else Pic := Pic1;
  Fader.FadeInTo(PaintBox1.Canvas, 0, 0, Pic);
end;
```

14. Compile and run the project. Figure 5-14 shows the second picture after a transition.

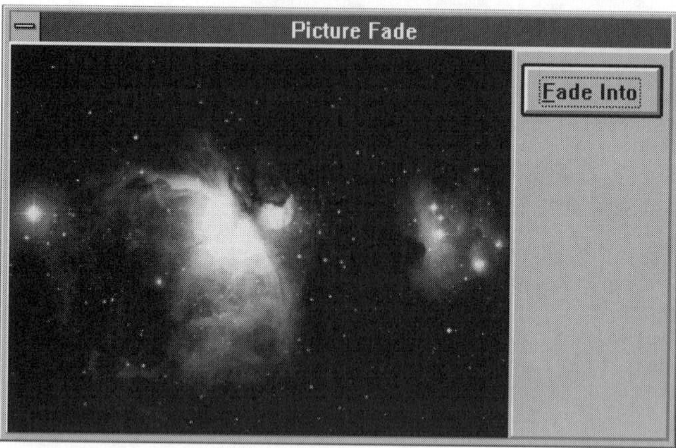

Figure 5-14 FADE.EXE after a complete transition

How It Works

Because the actual code to perform the transition effect has been placed in a separate unit, the code in FADE1.PAS becomes very simple. All FADE1.PAS needs to do is manage the actual pictures that are to be displayed. The FadeInto method of TFadeEffect will perform a transition between any TBitmap object passed to it and the current contents of the Canvas property of any visual component. Each time the Fade Into button is pressed, the pictures are reversed.

The FadeEffect Object

In the private section, two arrays are declared. Both of these arrays can hold eight elements of type HBrush. HBrush is a special type defined by Windows, and its purpose is to hold a handle to a Windows brush. It's this HBrush type and the corresponding Windows brush that Delphi's TBrush component encapsulates for you; however, in this particular application, it's easier to work with the Windows brushes directly.

```
Masks: array [0..7] of HBrush;
NegMasks: array [0..7] of HBrush;
```

The Create method (shown in step 7) does a great deal of work to initialize the object. Before any transitions can occur, the HBrush arrays must be loaded with actual brushes. This is where the resource file MERGE.RES comes into play. This resource file contains eight special bitmaps used to create brushes (shown in Figure 5-15). Each bitmap is used to create both a positive and a negative brush. All eight bitmaps are very small—only eight pixels in width and height. This is the size of a

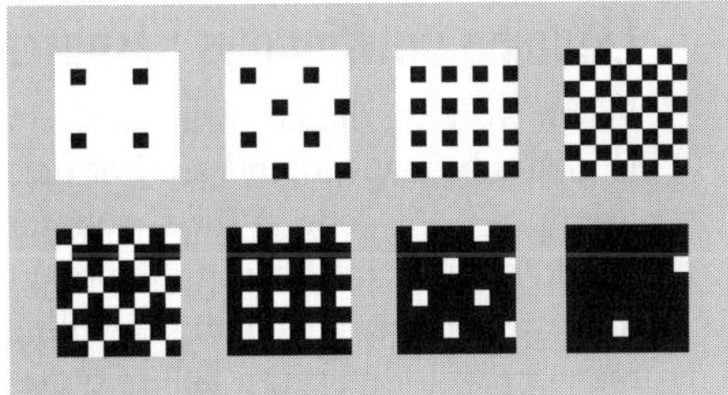

Figure 5-15 The eight positive brushes used in bitmap transitions

Windows brush. You can pass any bitmap to Windows to create a brush, but Windows will only use the upper-left eight-by-eight portion.

First, a temporary memory DC (device context) handle is created. This is necessary in order to create the negative versions of the bitmaps loaded from the resource file. A loop is then entered. This loop repeats eight times, once for each bitmap in the resource file. Each time through the loop, the next bitmap is retrieved from the resource using the LoadBitmap API function. LoadBitmap loads the specified bitmap into memory and returns a handle (HBitmap). This bitmap can now be used to create a brush. To do so, a special Windows structure called TLogBrush is used. By specifying various values for the fields in TLogBrush, you can create any kind of Windows brush. Here, only two fields are important: lbStyle is set to bs_Pattern, which tells Windows you're passing a bitmap; and lbHatch, which is assigned the handle of the bitmap. The TLogbrush structure is then passed to the API function CreateBrushIndirect. This function creates the actual brush in memory and returns a handle (HBrush), which is directly assigned to the Masks array.

Next, a negative version of the same brush is created. To do this, the bitmap is selected into the memory DC created at the beginning. This is done with the SelectObject API function. SelectObject returns the handle of the previously selected bitmap. It is important to save this handle as it needs to be selected back into the DC in order to release your own bitmap. Once the bitmap is selected into the DC, the Windows version of InvertRect is called to create a negative image. The bitmap handle is once again assigned to the lbHatch field of the TLogBrush structure, and another brush is created using the negative image.

Now that both versions of this brush are complete, cleanup must occur. Your bitmap must be released from the memory DC, and this is done by selecting the old bitmap (saved in oldbm) into the DC. Your bitmap is then deleted. At the end of the loop, 16 brushes have been created, 8 positive and 8 negative versions. The very last task in the Create function is to delete the memory DC that was created at the beginning.

Cleaning up Windows Resources

When working directly with the Windows API, it is imperative that all resources, like DCs and bitmaps, be released or deleted. This cannot be emphasized enough. For example, if the code in the Create method failed to delete the DC at the end, you would only be able to run the program four or five times before Windows would lock up or suffer a fatal abort. Failing to delete bitmaps or other objects that use memory wouldn't cause failure quite so quickly, but it would still be a very short time before Windows ran out of memory. When you use strictly the Delphi components and methods for performing graphics, as was done in How-To 5.8, you need not worry about this; Delphi components handle this cleanup for you. When working directly with the API though, managing resources becomes your responsibility. This fact will be even more clear as the FadeInto method is described next. As you will see, the code that performs the actual transition effect is quite short and straightforward; there is actually more code devoted to managing the resources needed for the transition.

The Transition Effect

First, the FadeInto method (in step 13) must allocate a DC and a bitmap in memory to represent the destination of the effect. The bitmap is selected into the DC and the previous bitmap handle is saved. The BitBlt API function then copies the current contents of the display from Target's Canvas object (the Handle property of a TCanvas component is a DC). Just as the original bitmap handle must be saved, so must the original brush handle when a new brush is selected, so this is done next.

Another DC and bitmap is created to represent the source for the transition. This is exactly the same as is done for the target DC and bitmap, except that no picture is copied to the bitmap. For this DC, the source picture will need to be copied in each time through the transition loop, so there is no need to do it yet. Again, a brush is selected into the DC, saving the original one. Note that at this point, it doesn't matter which brush is selected into the DC; the purpose here is only to save the handle of the original brush.

Now that the required memory resources have been created and prepared, the actual transition can take place. The transition consists of eight steps, each using a different brush pair. The positive brushes are used to gradually erase the current picture from the display, and the negative brushes are used to gradually fade the new picture in at the same time. Altogether, this requires five BitBlt operations (bitmap copies) using four different CopyMode settings each time through the loop.

To understand what is really happening, it will help to examine the brushes that are being used. Figure 5-15 shows the eight positive brushes from the MERGE.RES file. The negative brushes contain identical patterns but the black and white pixels are reversed. In each successive brush, additional pixels are colored black, but in each case, the black pixels from the previous brush remain black also. There is an obvious progression from mostly white to mostly black.

In the BitBlt calls, the last parameter is the CopyMode value. When using the API directly, the names for the CopyMode values are a little different than those used with the TCanvas object. When using the CopyMode property, the names begin with *cm*, with BitBlt the *cm* is dropped.

Each time through the loop, the next successive positive brush is selected into the memory DC containing the destination picture (the one to be faded out). The BitBlt then copies the picture onto itself but does so using the CopyMode value of MergeCopy. Remember from the COPYMODE project (How-To 5.7), that MergeCopy operates by ANDing the brush with the source bitmap. The result is that where there are black pixels in the brush, the corresponding pixels in the source bitmap are erased, effectively punching a bunch of tiny holes in the picture. The same operation is performed on the source picture (the one to be faded in), but a negative mask is used. This results in all of the pixels of the new picture being erased except those that match the position of the holes created in the destination picture. Each time through the loop, progressively more pixels are erased from the destination picture, and fewer pixels are erased from the source picture. Because more of the new picture needs to remain intact on each pass, it's necessary to copy the entire new picture back before erasing its pixels each time.

Now that the new picture contains just those pixels needed to fill the holes in the destination picture, the two pictures can be ORed together using the SrcPaint value for CopyMode. The result is then copied to the Handle property (DC) of the destination Canvas component, causing the merged picture to display on the screen.

Finally, it's time to clean up all the resources that were used in the transition. For both of the memory DCs, the original bitmap and original brush are selected back in, thus releasing your bitmaps and the last brushes used. The bitmaps and memory DCs are then deleted, releasing the memory and handles back to Windows. The brushes are *not* deleted—they are kept open for as long as the TFadeEffect object remains open. There is no need to repeatedly load and create these brushes each time the FadeInto method is called, because they will be properly deleted when the TFadeEffect object is freed.

The final act performed by TFadeEffect is to copy the entire new picture to the display. This is necessary as the image on display at this point still contains a few remnants of the old picture.

Comments

The big difference between using the Delphi component methods to perform bitmap operations and manually accessing the Windows API is the management of the device context (DC) handles, bitmap and brush handles, and being sure everything is cleaned up properly at the end. Despite the extra work this entails, there are times when it makes more sense to go directly to the API. Delphi does a terrific job of managing these resources for you, but Delphi's purpose is efficiency and performance (these are good things!), not special effects. When trying to create special effects such as this transition, it is often simpler to work directly with Windows. This How-To demonstrates very clearly though that you can quite freely mix direct API work with Delphi components and methods. It just takes a little time to learn the relationships that exist between the two in order to take best advantage of both.

An added tip that you may or may not have noticed during this How-To: during the progression, one of the brushes used is a perfect checkerboard pattern of black-and-white pixels. This brush represents the halfway point in the transition; both pictures are equally visible on the screen. If, rather than a transition, you want to display a translucent picture—one that is fully visible yet allows the background to show through in equal proportion—you would use this brush (and its negative counterpart) to produce the effect.

5.10 How do I... Fade text in and out over a background?

COMPLEXITY: INTERMEDIATE

Problem

Placing text over an image is easy, but it would be really cool if I could have the text fade in gradually instead of just appearing suddenly and, of course, have it fade out again as well. Can the techniques used to fade two pictures together also be used with text?

Technique

The technique to fade text in and out is definitely very similar to the technique used by the FadeInto method of the FadeEffect object you created in How-To 5.9. You turn the text into a bitmap and then fade that bitmap into the current display. In this How-To you will create two new methods and add them to the TFadeEffect object.

Steps

Run FADETEXT.EXE. Press the Fade In button. Now there's a classy "Hello World" program! Press the button again (note the button is now labeled Fade Out). The text fades away. The program is shown in Figure 5-16.

1. Create a new project. Save the default unit as FADETXT1.PAS and the project as FADETEXT.DPR.

2. Add the components and properties as shown in Table 5-17.

Table 5-17 Components, properties, and settings for the FADETEXT project

COMPONENT	PROPERTY	SETTING
Form	BorderStyle	bsDialog
	Caption	Text Fade
	Height	275

Figure 5-16 The FADETEXT program

COMPONENT	PROPERTY	SETTING
	Position	poScreenCenter
	Width	425
Panel	Align	alClient
	Caption	
Panel	Align	alRight
	Width	98
PaintBox	Align	alClient

3. Add a button to Panel2 as shown in Table 5-18.

Table 5-18 Button component for Panel2

COMPONENT	PROPERTY	SETTING
Button	Caption	Fade In
	Left	4
	Top	8

4. Open the HOWUTILS.PAS unit. Find the FadeEffect class declaration and add two more method declarations in the public section. The entire public section should look like this:

```
public
  constructor Create;
  destructor Destroy; override;
  procedure FadeInTo(Target: TCanvas; X, Y: integer;
    Pic: TBitmap);
  function FadeInText(Target: TCanvas; X, Y: integer;
    FText: String): TRect;
  procedure FadeOutText(Target: TCanvas; X, Y: integer;
    FText: String; Orig: TBitmap);
```

5. Now move to the bottom of the unit, just before the final *end* statement, and add the two new method definitions as shown here:

```
function TFadeEffect.FadeInText(Target: TCanvas;
  X, Y: integer; FText: String): TRect;
var
  Pic: TBitmap;
  W, H: integer;
  PicRect, TarRect: TRect;
begin
  Pic := TBitmap.Create;
  Pic.Canvas.Font := Target.Font;
  W := Pic.Canvas.TextWidth(FText);
  H := Pic.Canvas.TextHeight(FText);
  Pic.Width := W;
  Pic.Height := H;
  PicRect := Rect(0, 0, W, H);
  TarRect := Rect(X, Y, X + W, Y + H);
  Pic.Canvas.CopyRect(PicRect, Target, TarRect);
  SetBkMode(Pic.Canvas.Handle, Transparent);
  Pic.Canvas.TextOut(0, 0, FText);
  FadeInto(Target, X, Y, Pic);
  Pic.Free;
  FadeInText := TarRect;
end;

procedure TFadeEffect.FadeOutText(Target: TCanvas;
  TarRect: TRect; Orig: TBitmap);
var
  Pic: TBitmap;
  PicRect: TRect;
begin
  Pic := TBitmap.Create;
  Pic.Width := TarRect.Right - TarRect.Left;
  Pic.Height := TarRect.Bottom - TarRect.Top;
  PicRect := Rect(0, 0, Pic.Width, Pic.Height);
  Pic.Canvas.CopyRect(PicRect, Orig.Canvas, TarRect);
  FadeInto(Target, TarRect.Left, TarRect.Top, Pic);
  Pic.Free;
end;
```

6. Return to FADETXT1.PAS. Add a reference to HOWUTILS to the *uses* clause. Move down to the Form1 class declaration and add the following code to the *private* section.

```
private
  { Private declarations }
  Pic: TBitmap;
  Fader: TFadeEffect;
  IsFadeIn: Boolean;
  TR1, TR2: TRect;
```

7. Double-click the OnCreate event for Form1 and add the following code to load the background picture, create the FadeEffect object, and initialize the display.

```
procedure TForm1.FormCreate(Sender: TObject);
begin
  Pic := TBitmap.Create;
  Pic.LoadFromFile('CHAP05\SLIDE11.BMP');
  ClientWidth := Pic.Width + Panel2.Width + 4;
  ClientHeight := Pic.Height + 2;
  PaintBox1.Width := Pic.Width;
  PaintBox1.Height := Pic.Height;
  Fader := TFadeEffect.Create;
  IsFadeIn := True;
end;
```

8. Double-click the OnDestroy event of Form1 and enter the following code to free the allocated objects.

```
procedure TForm1.FormDestroy(Sender: TObject);
begin
  Pic.Free;
  Fader.Free;
end;
```

9. Double-click the OnPaint event of PaintBox1 and enter the line below to update the display.

```
procedure TForm1.PaintBox1Paint(Sender: TObject);
begin
  PaintBox1.Canvas.Draw(0, 0, Pic);
end;
```

10. Double-click the Fade In button and enter the following code to perform the text fade effect. Note that each time this is run, it sets itself to perform the opposite effect.

```
procedure TForm1.Button1Click(Sender: TObject);
begin
  PaintBox1.Canvas.Font.Name := 'Arial';
  PaintBox1.Canvas.Font.Size := 60;
  PaintBox1.Canvas.Font.Style := [fsItalic, fsBold];
  if IsFadeIn then begin
    PaintBox1.Canvas.Font.Color := clFuchsia;
```

continued on next page

continued from previous page

```
    TR1 := Fader.FadeInText(PaintBox1.Canvas, 60, 10, 'Hello');
    PaintBox1.Canvas.Font.Color := clLime;
    TR2 := Fader.FadeInText(PaintBox1.Canvas, 30, 140, 'World!');
    Button1.Caption := '&Fade Out';
  end else begin
    Fader.FadeOutText(PaintBox1.Canvas, TR1, Pic);
    Fader.FadeOutText(PaintBox1.Canvas, TR2, Pic);
    Button1.Caption := '&Fade In';
  end;
  IsFadeIn := not IsFadeIn;
end;
```

11. Compile and run the project.

How It Works

Both new methods, FadeInText and FadeOutText, make use of the existing FadeInto method to perform the actual transition. In other words, the actual transition works exactly the same as when fading from one picture to another. The difference in technique and resulting effect is in how the transition is prepared.

Before calling either of the new methods, you must first make sure to set up the desired Font property to be used for the effect. This is done with the following lines:

```
PaintBox1.Canvas.Font.Name := 'Arial';
PaintBox1.Canvas.Font.Size := 60;
PaintBox1.Canvas.Font.Style := [fsItalic, fsBold];
```

The font color is set before each of the calls to FadeInText. You are free to change any attributes of the font any way you like as often as you like for each call to FadeInText. The important thing is to set it. Since PaintBox1 will be passed to the FadeInText method, this font information becomes available to it.

If you intend to also fade out the text again, you must be sure to save the return value from the FadeInText method.

```
TR1 := Fader.FadeInText(PaintBox1.Canvas, 60, 10, 'Hello');
```

FadeInText returns a TRect structure. This structure returns the exact position and dimensions of the rectangle within the display that now contains the text. This structure needs to be passed to FadeOutText in order to erase it. Be sure the TRect structure you declare to hold this returned value is declared outside the method making the call to FadeInText, preferably in the private section of your TForm object. Remember that variables declared locally within a method do not hold their values after that method exits.

To prepare the transition, FadeInText first creates a temporary TBitmap object (Pic) to be used as the source picture. It then calculates the size needed for the bitmap to contain the text (refer to step 4). This allows it to perform the transition only on that part of the picture affected by the text. In order to do this, it first assigns

Pic's Canvas.Font property to the same font currently set in the passed Target parameter (which is PaintBox1 in this case). With the correct font set, it can calculate the needed size by calling two built-in methods of TCanvas: TextWidth returns the width in pixels needed to contain the entire text string; TextHeight returns the maximum height in pixels needed for the string. The dimensions of Pic are then set accordingly.

Next, two TRect objects are set up to be used with the CopyRect method. The first is set to match the dimensions just set for the Pic bitmap object. The second is set to the same size also, but is offset to represent the position within the target bitmap where the text is to appear. The CopyRect method then copies just that portion of the target bitmap into Pic.

```
PicRect := Rect(0, 0, W, H);
TarRect := Rect(X, Y, X + W, Y + H);
Pic.Canvas.CopyRect(PicRect, Target, TarRect);
```

To complete the preparation, you must actually paint the text into the source bitmap as it will appear at the end of the transition. One very important step to explain here is the call to the Windows API function SetBkMode. This function sets the background mode for the currently selected pen (pens are used both to write text and to draw lines). There are only two possible settings: Transparent and Opaque. Transparent means that Windows will draw the text leaving the background unchanged. Opaque means the rectangular area containing each character will be painted with the current background color first (which can be set with another API function called SetBkColor). For this effect, you want the characters to appear over the image without changing the image around the characters, so the constant value Transparent is selected.

Finally, the text can actually be painted into Pic. Since Pic already contains just that portion of the target image where the text is to be placed, the text is drawn at the very upper-left corner of Pic and will just perfectly fill the Pic bitmap. FadeInto can now be called. X and Y are passed to FadeInto to tell it where in the image to perform the transition. FadeInto is already smart enough to perform the transition only on an area the size of the source bitmap. Technically, the entire rectangular area in the image where the text is being placed is affected by the transition, but because the image under the text in the source bitmap is an exact copy of the target image, the effect is invisible except for the text itself.

The last acts performed by the FadeInText method are freeing the Pic bitmap object and assigning TarRect as the return value for the function.

The FadeOutText method functions almost exactly the same. Instead of passing it the position of the text and the text string, you pass it the TRect variable assigned as the return value of the FadeInText call and the original copy of the target image without the text.

```
Fader.FadeOutText(PaintBox1.Canvas, TR1, Pic);
```

As with FadeInText, FadeOutText creates a TBitmap object. It doesn't need to calculate the size of this bitmap itself as FadeInText does, it simply uses the values passed to it in the saved TRect variable. It copies the specified area from the passed original image and passes this as the source to the FadeInto method. The Pic bitmap object is freed and FadeOutText is finished.

Comments

The three methods you've created so far in the TFadeEffect object provide a great deal of power you can use in many different ways. Armed with the knowledge you've gained thus far, plus your imagination, you can probably come up with many other effects.

6

6

MULTIMEDIA

How do I...

Multimedia has rapidly become an accessory that just can't be ignored. There has been an explosion in multimedia use over the past couple of years. Virtually all new computers are being sold bundled with sound cards and CD-ROMs. Older machines that did not come with these features are quickly being upgraded.

Multimedia currently includes sight and sound. Sight includes pictures, animations, video, and even live, real-time motion. Sound includes sound effects, music, and voice recordings. It may not be long before developers find ways to include other senses as well; the Enterprise's Holodeck is the ultimate multimedia machine!

The best examples of multimedia use, naturally, are games. Besides combining just about every kind of multimedia data, they are also interactive. As hardware has become faster and more powerful, it has allowed games, and other applications such as online encyclopedias, to feature smooth, full-motion video. Many software developers now hire real actors and actresses to star in their applications.

Serious business applications can also benefit from the use of multimedia, whether in presentations and demonstrations or client and product databases. Even products such as tax-preparation software feature real people delivering advice.

In addition to standard multimedia on the PC, the new explosion of interest in *hypermedia* (defined as mixed text and graphics which are interactive and respond to user input in an informational fashion) has let to the creation of a standard, called HTML (HyperText Markup Language). This standard is used by viewers like Mosaic and Netscape on the Internet, but can also be used on a single PC or local network. Using HTML syntax, a complete multimedia viewer can be created in Delphi, supporting hypertext jump links, sound files, graphics (including GIF), sprite animations, and CD audio, MIDI, and even AVI video.

This chapter presents a few basics on playing and controlling multimedia and shows how easy it is to do with Delphi.

6.1 Play wave and midi files

This How-To uses Delphi's TMediaPlayer component to play music or other sounds stored as wave files or midi sequences. You can also program it to display the length of time that a file takes to play, and to use a TGauge component to track the progress of the file as it's playing.

6.2 Play video files in my form

In this How-To you will see how to display video animations; but unlike Windows' built-in MediaPlayer applet, this player will play the video on a TPanel within your form.

6.3 Play an audio CD

This How-To shows how to set up the MediaPlayer component to play an audio CD. In addition, it displays a list of audio tracks and their time lengths and allows users to select any track from the list as well as sequentially selecting them from the MediaPlayer component.

6.4 Create a multimedia player

The work you do in How-To's 6.1, 6.2, and 6.3 is combined into a single multimedia application. This How-To shows the beauty of building objects in separate units that can then be reused in any number of applications.

6.5 Create an HTML-based hypertext viewer

HTML is a text-based method for including control information in a document. This How-To will use Delphi's powerful string-manipulation functions to implement a basic subset of the HTML standard in a simple but effective hypertext viewer application.

6.6 Play sound files in an HTML document

Due to the nature of HTML, including special file formats is very simple. By adding a small number of elements to the application in How-To 6.5, sound file URL (Universal Resource Locators) can be processed with Delphi's TMediaPlayer component.

6.7 Show graphics files in an HTML document

Graphics are what set hypermedia apart from hypertext, and HTML includes the <IMG> tag to allow use of images both directly and as anchors and links. This How-To will demonstrate using TImage components together with TBitmaps to process and display .BMP, .ICO, .WMF, and .GIF file formats.

6.8 Display sprite animation in an HTML document

Powerful presentation engines often include support for moving complex bitmaps called sprites. An earlier How-To demonstrated the basic technique of sprite animation; this How-To will develop a sophisticated sprite object in Delphi which can be user-configured and invoked as a simple URL in the HTML viewer.

6.9 Create a multimedia HTML document display application

In addition to all the above formats, HTML can include any file type available on a PC. This How-To adds in the previous How-To's support for MIDI, CD Audio, and AVI video files to the finished hypermedia presentation application.

6.1 How Do I... Play wave and midi files?

COMPLEXITY: EASY

Problem

I would like users to be able to play wave sounds and midi sequences within my application, and they should be able to select the file they want to play at run time. It would also be cool if I could display the progress of the file as it plays. How do I do this with Delphi?

Technique

The basic ability to play multimedia files in Delphi is quite simple because most of what you need is already built into Delphi's TMediaPlayer and TOpenDialog components. It takes just a few lines of code to allow users to select a file and have it played. However, the TMediaPlayer component provides you with more than just a set of buttons to control the playing of multimedia files; it also provides information about the file being played. This information can be used in various ways to enhance the operation of your application.

In this How-To, you'll create a custom component, descended from the TPanel component, to display TMediaPlayer's additional information.

Steps

Run MIDI.EXE. The form is shown in Figure 6-1. Click the Open button and select any midi or wave file you have on your system. When you click the OK button on the Open dialog, the file is loaded and the play button on the MediaPlayer control becomes available. Click on this button to play the file. You can then let the entire file play, or you can use the pause or stop buttons. As the file plays, the progress gauge keeps track of the percentage complete.

1. Create a new project. Save the default unit as MIDI1.PAS and the project as MIDIPLAY.DPR.

2. Add the components, properties, and settings as shown in Table 6-1. The completed form as seen in the form designer is shown in Figure 6-2.

Figure 6-1 MIDIPLAY ready for action

Table 6-1 Components, properties, and settings for MIDIPLAY

COMPONENT	PROPERTY	SETTING
Form	BorderStyle	bsDialog
	Caption	Midi Player
	ClientHeight	146
	ClientWidth	174
	Name	MidiForm
	Position	poScreenCenter
Button	Caption	&Open
	Left	42
	Name	OpenButton
	Top	12
MediaPlayer	Left	16
	Top	52
	+VisibleButtons	
	- btStep	False
	- btBack	False
	- btRecord	False
	- btEject	False
OpenDialog	DefaultExt	MID
	Filter	Midi Sequencer|*.MID;*.RMI
	+Options	
	- ofFileMustExist	True

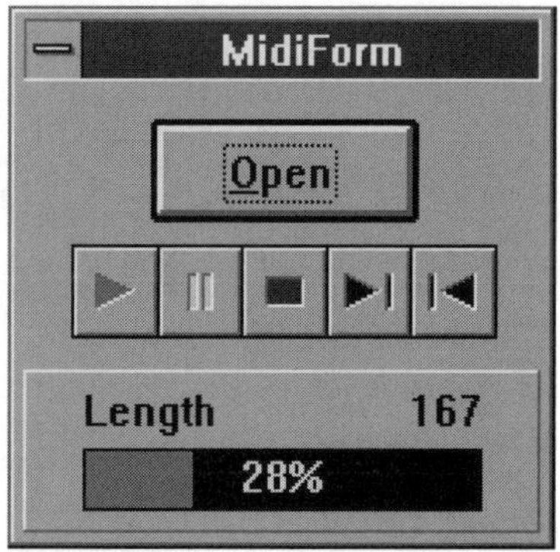

Figure 6-2 The MIDIPLAY form design

3. Create a new unit (select File|New Unit) and save it as IFMIDI.PAS. This unit implements a custom descendant of a TPanel component just for midi files.

4. Just below the *interface* statement, enter the uses clause as shown here:

```
uses
  SysUtils, WinTypes, WinProcs, Messages, Classes, Graphics, Controls,
  Forms, Dialogs, StdCtrls, MPlayer, ExtCtrls, Gauges;
```

5. Now you will declare a TPanel descendant called TMidiPanel. This descendant includes several other components and a few procedures, which will be created at run time rather than now, at design time. Enter the following declaration for TMidiPanel.

```
type
  TMidiPanel = class(TPanel)
    MP: TMediaPlayer;
    Timer: TTimer;
    Gauge: TGauge;
    LabLit, LabVal: TLabel;
    constructor Create(AOwner: TWinControl; Media: TMediaPlayer);
    procedure Open;
    procedure MPTime(Sender: TObject);
    procedure MPClick(Sender: TObject; Button: TMPBtnType;
      var DoDefault: Boolean);
    end;
```

6. Immediately following the *implementation* statement, enter the constructor method for TMidiPanel. This constructor first calls the inherited constructor, then creates all of its child components. This procedure is fairly long because it must set the desired properties for each of the child components.

```
constructor TMidiPanel.Create(AOwner: TWinControl; Media: TMediaPlayer);
begin
  {Create standard TPanel}
  inherited Create(AOwner);
  {Set the parent}
  Parent := AOwner;
  {Save a reference to the MediaPlayer control}
  MP := Media;
  {Assign handler for MediaPlayer component}
  MP.OnClick := MPClick;
  {Create timer}
  Timer := TTimer.Create(Self);
  Timer.Interval := 100;
  Timer.Enabled := False;
  Timer.OnTimer := MPTime;
  {Position self under the MediaPlayer control}
  Left := 0;
  Top := MP.Top + MP.Height + 10;
  Height := Parent.ClientHeight - Top;
```

```
  Width := Parent.ClientWidth;
  {Label for Midi file length}
  LabLit := TLabel.Create(Self);
  with LabLit do begin
    Parent := Self;
    Top := 5;
    Left := 20;
    Caption := 'Length';
  end;
  {Label to display Length value}
  LabVal := TLabel.Create(Self);
  with LabVal do begin
    Parent := Self;
    Top := 5;
    Left := Self.Width - 85;
    Alignment := taRightJustify;
    Caption := '0';
  end;
  {Create the progress Gauge}
  Gauge := TGauge.Create(Self);
  with Gauge do begin
    Parent := Self;
    Top := 25;
    Left := 20;
    Width := Self.Width - 40;
    Height := 20;
    BackColor := clNavy;
    ForeColor := clLime;
    Progress := 0;
  end;
end;
```

7. Now enter the code for the Open method. This method will be called by the application when it wants to play a midi file. Note that the TMediaPlayer's DeviceType property is set to dtAutoSelect. This allows other sound files, such as wave files, to be played.

```
procedure TMidiPanel.Open;
begin
  {Let MediaPlayer figure out the file type}
  MP.DeviceType := dtAutoSelect;
  {Call the MediaPlayer Open method}
  try
    MP.Open;
  except
    messagedlg('Could not open file', mtWarning, [mbOK], 0);
    exit;
  end;
  {Display length of this Midi file}
  LabVal.Caption := IntToStr(MP.Length);
end;
```

8. Next, enter the code for the MPTime event handler. This event handler is assigned at run time (in the TMidiPanel.Create constructor you entered in step 6) to the TTimer child component of TMidiPanel. It updates the progress gauge.

```
procedure TMidiPanel.MPTime(Sender: TObject);
begin
  {Update the progress gauge}
  Gauge.Progress := MP.Position *100 div MP.Length;
end;
```

9. The final method in this unit is the MPClick event handler. This handler is assigned at run time to the MediaPlayer component. The MediaPlayer component is actually owned by the application, but a reference to it was passed in the TMidiPanel.Create method so it could be handled by TMidiPanel.

```
procedure TMidiPanel.MPClick(Sender: TObject; Button: TMPBtnType;
  var DoDefault: Boolean);
begin
  if Button = btPlay then
    {Start timer for progress update}
    Timer.Enabled := True;
end;
```

10. Save IFMIDI.PAS, then return to MIDI1.PAS. In the *uses* clause, add a reference to the IFMIDI unit just created. The *uses* clause should look like this:

```
uses
  SysUtils, WinTypes, WinProcs, Messages, Classes, Graphics, Controls,
  Forms, Dialogs, StdCtrls, MPlayer, ExtCtrls, IFMidi;
```

11. In the *private* section of TMidiForm, add a variable of type TMidiPanel:

```
private
    { Private declarations }
    MPanel: TMidiPanel;
```

12. In the Object Inspector, double-click TMidiForm's OnCreate event and enter the following code to create the custom TMidiPanel component.

```
procedure TMidiForm.FormCreate(Sender: TObject);
begin
  {Create the custom TPanel for Midi info}
  MPanel := TMidiPanel.Create(Self, MediaPlayer1);
end;
```

13. Double-click the Open button on the TMidiForm and enter the following code. This displays the Open dialog, then opens and plays the selected file.

```
procedure TMidiForm.OpenButtonClick(Sender: TObject);
begin
```

```
  if OpenDialog1.Execute then begin
    with MediaPlayer1 do begin
      FileName := OpenDialog1.FileName;
      {Open the Midi file and display its length}
      MPanel.Open;
    end;
  end;
end;
```

14. Compile and run the application.

How It Works

As stated in the "Technique" section, only a few lines of code are essential to play a sound file: execute the OpenDialog, assign the selected file name to the TMediaPlayer component, then call TMediaPlayer's Open method. The rest of the code allows a dynamically created display to show the logical length of the selected file and its progress while playing.

This code would be simpler if the dynamic components were placed on the main form at design time—then it would only take a few more lines of code to make it all work. However, there are some good reasons for going to the extra trouble of creating a new custom class and placing it in a separate unit. The first is that you will need this same functionality again in How-To 6.4. By doing some extra work up front, you eliminate virtually all work when creating other applications that need this functionality. Second, building the new component provides an opportunity to show how to create and control components at run time rather than only at design time.

The IFMIDI unit you created (IF stands for InterFace) contains an object class descended from TPanel called TMidiPanel. The TPanel component is ideal for this type of work since it is a container type class that already knows how to display itself. Within TMidiPanel, you declare some extra variables. The variable MP (of type TMediaPlayer) will never actually become an object of its own; its purpose is to serve as a local access to the TMediaPlayer component that has already been created (at design time) in the parent form. The TTimer, TGauge, and TLabel components will all be created by TMidiPanel during its own creation.

Creating the TMidiPanel

TMidiPanel defines its own Create constructor. It is important to note that the Override directive is not used (see step 6). The reason for this is because the parameter list of this Create method differs from the TPanel version; you have added an extra parameter to allow passing of the form's TMediaPlayer component. If you were to add the Override directive, it would result in a compile error because overridden methods must maintain the same parameter list.

The other two methods are both event handlers. One is for the MediaPlayer component and one is for the Timer component. These handlers are assigned to the corresponding events during execution of TMidiPanel's Create constructor.

The Create constructor contains the most work in this unit. It must create and initialize all the child components and set up the event handlers. The first task that must be done is to call the inherited Create constructor, which in this case is the Create constructor of the TPanel component. This allows TPanel to perform all its necessary initialization. The first parameter to Create is AOwner (which is passed on to the inherited Create). This, as the name implies, is the windowed control that becomes the owner of the TMidiPanel component. This is very important; by assigning an owner, the disposal of this object becomes the responsibility of the owner. This means that, even though you've created this component manually, you do not need to be concerned with disposing of it when the application closes. The owner (in this case, the form) will dispose of it for you.

The next important step is to assign a parent. All windowed controls must have a parent. Without one, they will not be properly handled with regard to how Windows messages are routed through the application. Although the parent and the owner are very often the same, this does not have to be the case. Delphi's own documentation discusses this in more detail.

With the mandatory construction requirements safely dealt with, TMidiPanel can now turn its attention to the specific implementation. First, the value passed as the second parameter to Create (Media) must be saved by assigning it to the MP variable. This provides TMidiPanel with direct access to the TMediaPlayer component that is part of the design of the main form.

It's important to remember here that all such component variables are actually pointer variables. When you assign such a variable by calling the Create constructor of a component, you are actually assigning the address of the newly created component to your variable. In this case, the MP variable does not get assigned using the Create constructor, but instead is assigned the address of an already existing component. Both the MP variable and the MediaPlayer1 variable in the main form now point to the same address in memory; both are a reference to the same TMediaPlayer component object.

Now that MP points to something, it can be used. The first thing done with it is to assign a local method as its OnClick event handler. This means all clicks on the MediaPlayer1 component will be handled by a method of the TMidiPanel component instead of the main form. This ability to assign control of an event to any valid handler in any component is a very powerful feature of Delphi that provides incredible flexibility.

Next, the TTimer component is created and initialized. Note that TTimer does not have a Parent property; this is because TTimer is not a visual control. The TTimer's Interval property is set to 100 milliseconds to allow smooth update of media information, and its OnTimer event is assigned to the local MPTime event handler. It is disabled since there is currently no information from MediaPlayer1 that needs to be displayed.

Before creating the remaining controls, TMidiPanel sets up its own size and position within its parent (the main form). Since it has access to the TMediaPlayer component already on the main form through the MP variable, it's able to place itself precisely in relation to the MediaPlayer. It assigns itself all available client space below the MediaPlayer component as shown in the following code fragment.

```
Left := 0;
Top := MP.Top + MP.Height + 10;
Height := Parent.ClientHeight - Top;
Width := Parent.ClientWidth;
```

TMidiPlayer continues on to create and place the two TLabel components and the TGauge component. For all three of these, TMidiPanel assigns itself as both the owner and parent and sets their display positions and a few other properties such as the colors for the TGauge component. At the completion of the Create constructor, TMidiPanel and its child components will all be displayed on the main form.

Opening a Sound File

The Open method of TMidiPanel is quite simple. This method is called by the application when the user selects a file to be played. The first thing Open does is ensure that the TMediaPlayer's DeviceType property is set to dtAutoSelect (refer to step 7). Setting the value dtAutoSelect allows the user to select any type of multimedia file. It then calls the TMediaPlayer's Open method to actually open the selected file. This call to TMediaPlayer.Open is placed within an exception block in case the file cannot be read (the file does not exist or is not a valid file type). If there is an error, the exception block will display a message to the user and then exit from the block at that point. If successfully opened, the LabVal label component is set to display the logical length of the opened file (stored in the TMediaPlayer's Length property). Once the file is loaded, TMediaPlayer automatically updates its buttons to indicate the file can now be played.

Playing the Sound File

When the user clicks on the play button, a click event is triggered and control is passed to the MPClick method of TMidiPanel. All that needs to be done here is to start the timer for the progress gauge. TMediaPlayer will automatically start playing the file.

The MPTime handler receives all timer ticks from the Timer component. Each time it is called, it calculates the percentage of the sound file that has played so far and sets this value to the Gauge component's Progress property. The Gauge component automatically updates its display on the form. The Position property of the TMediaPlayer component keeps track of the current position in the sound file as it's playing, making it easy for you to use this information.

Main Form Logic

Because all the work has been done in the IFMIDI unit, there is very little that needs to be done by the main MIDI1 unit. The FormCreate method simply creates the TMidiPanel component, passing its Self property in order to assign itself as the parent and passing MediaPlayer1 in order to allow TMidiPanel to have access to it as shown below.

```
MPanel := TMidiPanel.Create(Self, MediaPlayer1);
```

The OpenButtonClick handler executes the OpenDialog, and if a file is selected, assigns the file name to MediaPlayer1. It then calls MPanel's (the TMidiPanel component) Open method.

Comments

This How-To demonstrates many features of Delphi that are extremely important to the creation of sophisticated applications. For starters, it shows an example of creating new units and adding them to an application. Furthermore, it shows that these units can be code only; there is no requirement for a unit to be paired with a form. This means you are free to create units for any purpose, and by keeping them separate from any particular form association, they become reusable in other applications simply by including a reference to them in an application's *uses* clause. You can then call any procedures or functions in that unit, or create and use any objects defined there.

Even if you're not yet ready to delve into the internal details of how Delphi components are programmed, you can create any number of components to suit your own purposes merely by creating a descendant of an existing component and changing one or more properties. As is done here with TMidiPanel, you can create components of any complexity by combining several components into one larger component. By placing these custom components into separate units (you can have more than one component in the same unit), you make your components easily reusable in any number of applications.

This example also shows that it is not necessary to place every component you create on Delphi's component palette. This is completely up to you. If you know you will be reusing a component over and over, then it definitely makes sense to do the little extra work needed to place your component on the palette. The IFMIDI unit can easily be added to the palette so that it can be added to a form at design time as well as at run time.

6.2 How Do I...
Play video files in my form?

COMPLEXITY: EASY

Problem

I want my application to play video files. I know the TMediaPlayer can play these just as easily as it plays sound files, but it plays the videos in a separate window (as does Windows' MediaPlayer applet). Is it possible to play the videos directly in my application, either on the form itself or on a TPanel?

Technique

Delphi's TMediaPlayer component operates by communicating with Microsoft's MMSYSTEM.DLL. By default, MMSYSTEM creates a separate window in which to play videos, so this is also the default for TMediaPlayer. However, you can specify your own window for playback. Any component that contains a window handle (and can therefore receive messages directly from Windows) can be used for playback. Naturally, you would not want to play a video on a specific control like a button or edit box, but both TForms and TPanels make suitable surfaces for video playback. TPanels are a good choice because they have built-in bevel properties allowing you to display an attractive frame around the video. You could also play the video directly on a form and use a TBevel component to create a frame around it.

As in How-To 6.1, you will create a descendant of TPanel. This descendant will specifically handle the details of hosting video playback.

Steps

Run VIDEO.EXE. Click the Open button and select any Windows animation (AVI) file you have on your system. When you click the OK button on the Open dialog, the file will be loaded and the video will automatically begin playing, as shown in Figure 6-3. You can let the entire file play, or you can use the pause or stop button at any time. The form and TPanel automatically resize as needed to play the selected video, and the form is always centered on the screen before commencing playback.

1. Create a new project. Save the default unit as VIDEO1.PAS and the project as VIDEO.DPR.

Figure 6-3 VIDEO in action

2. Add the components, properties, and settings as shown in Table 6-2.

Table 6-2 Components, properties, and settings for VIDEO

COMPONENT	PROPERTY	SETTING
Form	BorderStyle	bsDialog
	Caption	Media Player
	ClientHeight	100
	ClientWidth	213
	Name	VideoForm
	Position	poScreenCenter
	Scaled	False
Button	Caption	&Open
	Left	78
	Name	OpenButton
	Top	8
MediaPlayer	Left	8
	Top	48
	+VisibleButtons	
	- btRecord	False
	- btEject	False
OpenDialog	DefaultExt	AVI
	Filter	Windows Animation|*AVI
	+Options	
	- ofFileMustExist	True

3. Create a new unit (select File|New Unit) and save it as IFVIDEO.PAS. This unit implements a custom descendant of a TPanel component just for video files.
4. Just below the *interface* statement, enter the *uses* clause as shown here:

```
uses
  SysUtils, WinTypes, WinProcs, Messages, Classes, Graphics, Controls,
  Forms, Dialogs, StdCtrls, MPlayer, ExtCtrls;
```

5. You will now declare a TPanel descendant called TVideoPanel. This descendant will include several other components and a few procedures that will be created at run time rather than now, at design time. Enter the following declaration for TVideoPanel.

```
type
  TVideoPanel = class(TPanel)
    MP: TMediaPlayer;
    constructor Create(AOwner: TWinControl; Media: TMediaPlayer);
    procedure Open;
    end;
```

6. Immediately following the *implementation* statement, enter the constructor method for TVideoPanel. This constructor calls the inherited constructor of TPanel, assigns the parent, and sets up access for the form's TMediaPlayer component. It then hides itself, since there isn't yet any video to display.

```
constructor TVideoPanel.Create(AOwner: TWinControl; Media: TMediaPlayer);
begin
  {Create standard TPanel}
  inherited Create(AOwner);
  {Set the parent}
  Parent := AOwner;
  {Save a reference to the MediaPlayer component}
  MP := Media;
  {Make sure no OnClick method is assigned}
  MP.OnClick := nil;
  {No need to display yet}
  Visible := False;
end;
```

7. Now enter the code for the Open method, which will be called by the application when it wants to play a video file. Besides opening the video file, the Open method is responsible for resizing the TVideoPanel and the parent form so the video can be played.

```
procedure TVideoPanel.Open;
var
  fw, fh, fl, ft, pw, ph, pl: integer;
begin
  MP.DeviceType := dtAutoSelect;
  {Call the MediaPlayer Open method}
  try
    MP.Open;
  except
    messagedlg('Could not open the video file', mtwarning, [mbok], 0);
    exit;
  end;
  {Assign ourself as the video display window}
  MP.Display := Self;
  {Adjust display position to allow bevel to show,
   and request default video size be set.}
  MP.DisplayRect := Rect(2, 2, 0, 0);
  {Adjust panel size to accommodate video size}
  pw := MP.DisplayRect.Right - MP.DisplayRect.Left + 6;
  ph := MP.DisplayRect.Bottom - MP.DisplayRect.Top + 6;
```

continued on next page

continued from previous page

```
  {If width less then MediaPlayer component then center under it}
  if pw < MP.Width then pl := MP.Left + (MP.Width - pw) div 2
  {Otherwise align with left edge of MediaPlayer component}
  else pl := MP.Left;
  {Resize form to accommodate sized panel}
  fw := pw + pl * 2;
  fh := MP.Top + MP.Height + ph + 40;
  ft := (Screen.Height - fh) div 2;
  fl := (Screen.Width - fw) div 2;
  {Assign calculated values to the form and panel}
  Parent.ClientWidth := fw;
  Parent.ClientHeight := fh;
  Parent.SetBounds(fl, ft, Parent.Width, Parent.Height);
  Self.SetBounds(pl, MP.Top + MP.Height + 20, pw, ph);
  {now display it - ready for video}
  Visible := True;
end;
```

8. Save IFVIDEO.PAS, then return to VIDEO1.PAS. In the *uses* clause, add a reference to the IFVIDEO unit just created. The *uses* clause should look like this:

```
uses
  SysUtils, WinTypes, WinProcs, Messages, Classes, Graphics, Controls,
  Forms, Dialogs, StdCtrls, MPlayer, ExtCtrls, IFVideo;
```

9. In the *private* section of TVideoForm, add a variable of type TVideoPanel:

```
private
  { Private declarations }
  VideoPanel: TVideoPanel;
```

10. In the Object Inspector, double-click TVideoForm's OnCreate event and enter the following code to create the custom TVideoPanel component.

```
{Create the custom TPanel for Midi info}
VideoPanel := TVideoPanel.Create(Self, MediaPlayer1);
```

11. Double-click the Open button on the TVideoForm and enter the following code. This displays the Open dialog, then opens and plays the selected file.

```
procedure TMidiForm.OpenButtonClick(Sender: TObject);
begin
  if OpenDialog1.Execute then begin
    with MediaPlayer1 do begin
      {Assign the selected file}
      FileName := OpenDialog1.FileName;
      {Set up custom panel for video display}
      VideoPanel.Open;
    end;
  end;
end;
```

12. Compile and run the application.

How It Works

The IFVIDEO unit you create in this How-To contains an object class descended from TPanel called TVideoPanel. This component is very similar but, in fact, even simpler than the TMidiPanel component created in How-To 6.1.

Creating TVideoPanel

The Create constructor for TVideoPanel (shown in step 6) does very little work compared with TMidiPanel. As with TMidiPanel, it calls the inherited Create constructor of TPanel, assigns the Parent property, and saves the reference to the passed TMediaPlayer component. The most notable difference is that instead of assigning a local handler for the TMediaPlayer's OnClick method, TVideoPanel sets the method to nil. TVideoPanel does not define a handler for the TMediaPlayer component because TVideoPanel will not be displaying any information other than the video itself (this is also why it does not contain a TTimer component). It's an important safety measure to set the OnClick property to nil here because it's possible the event may have been previously assigned a handler by some other component that is no longer in use. The last action performed by the Create constructor is to set TVideoPanel's Visible property to False, as there is no need to display itself until a video file is opened.

While the Create constructor for TVideoPanel is much simpler than its counterpart in TMidiPanel, the Open method is more complicated (see step 7). This is because it must resize itself, and its parent form, each time a video file is played. The first part of Open is the same as the Open method of TMidiPanel. It sets the DeviceType property to dtAutoSelect so the user is not limited to AVI files, and then calls the TMediaPlayer component's Open method to load the selected file.

Directing Playback to Your Form

The next two statements in the Open method are the most important in this How-To:

```
MP.Display := Self;
MP.DisplayRect := Rect(2, 2, 0, 0);
```

These statements tell the TMediaPlayer component that the video file is to be played in a window of your choosing and where within that window it should be played. The first statement, assigning the Display property of TMediaPlayer to Self (the TVideoPanel object), causes TMediaPlayer to pass TVideoPanel's window handle on to MMSYSTEM. This causes MMSYSTEM to use TVideoPanel for playback instead of creating a separate window.

The second statement sets the DisplayRect property of the TMediaPlayer component. Passing the value of 2 for the Left and Top fields of the DisplayRect property causes the video to be placed two pixels in from the top-left corner of the panel, which allows TVideoPanel's border bevels to show. Passing 0 for the Right and Bottom fields tells TMediaPlayer to play the video at its native size, whatever that may be. TMediaPlayer's response to a 0 value for either Right or Bottom is to find out from MMSYSTEM how big the video is; it then replaces the 0 values in DisplayRect with that information.

Adjusting Positions and Size

As soon as DisplayRect has been assigned (passing 0 for the Right and Bottom), it can be used to find out the actual size of the video so the TVideoPanel can be resized accordingly. An important note here is that the Right and Bottom fields of DisplayRect provide you with the absolute width and height of the video, not the right and bottom pixel positions (in other words, they do not include the values passed for the Top and Left properties of DisplayRect). This is important to remember in order to correctly calculate the size needed for TVideoPanel. The Right and Bottom values are assigned to temporary variables and are further incremented by 4 in order to allow the panel's beveled border to show on all sides of the video:

```
pw := MP.DisplayRect.Right + 4;
ph := MP.DisplayRect.Bottom + 4;
```

The reason for using temporary variables is that if you assign the values directly to VideoPanel's properties, the panel will immediately attempt to resize itself. But there may not be enough room in the parent form to contain it at this point. Temporary variables are also used to hold calculated values for the parent form. Once all values are calculated, they are assigned to the form and the panel all at once, resulting in a much quicker and smoother-looking resize.

In order to make the screen more attractive no matter what size the video is, the video width is compared to the width of the TMediaPlayer component. If the video is smaller, TVideoPanel is centered under the MediaPlayer; otherwise, the left edge of TVideoPanel is lined up with the left edge of the MediaPlayer as shown in the following code fragment.

```
if pw < MP.Width then pl := MP.Left + (MP.Width - pw) div 2
else pl := MP.Left;
```

Next, the required size of the parent form is calculated so that it will allow the entire TVideoPanel to display. The width is set to the panel's width plus two times the current left value of the panel. The height takes into account the panel height and the space needed for the MediaPlayer and the OpenButton, plus a little extra to allow a border space:

```
fw := pw + pl * 2;
fh := MP.Top + MP.Height + ph + 30;
```

The form's screen position is then adjusted so it will be centered no matter what size it has been set to. This is done using the Screen component's properties. The

Screen component is always available in a Delphi application and provides information about the current video screen as you can see in the following code fragment.

```
ft := (Screen.Height - fh) div 2;
fl := (Screen.Width - fw) div 2;
```

Now that all the necessary values have been calculated, these values are assigned to the corresponding properties of the parent form and the TVideoPanel component. Finally, the TVideoPanel is made visible. The video is now ready to be played and will do so as soon as the user clicks the play button.

Using the Component

Once again, because the functionality has been built into a separate component, there is very little that needs to be done in the application to use it. The VideoPanel is created in the form's FormCreate method:

```
VideoPanel := TMidiPanel.Create(Self, MediaPlayer1);
```

The OpenButtonClick handler executes OpenDialog, assigns the selected file, and calls TVideoPanel's Open method:

```
if OpenDialog1.Execute then begin
  MediaPlayer1.FileName := OpenDialog1.FileName;
  VideoPanel.Open;
end;
```

Comments

As you can see, it's not hard to direct a video playback into your application, either on a TPanel or on the form itself, and it's also quite straightforward to find out the size of the video so you can prepare your playback surface accordingly.

It's also possible to scale the playback to suit yourself. Rather than sizing your surface to fit the video, you can fit the video to whatever space you want to grant it. This is accomplished by passing your own values for the Right and Bottom fields of TMediaPlayer's DisplayRect property. Note though that videos play best when allowed to play at their native size.

Like the TMidiPanel component created in How-To 6.1, TVideoPanel is able to get and set information in the TMediaPlayer component even though that component is owned by the parent form. In addition, TVideoPanel also controls the size and position of its parent form through the use of the Parent property.

Note that other animation files, besides Windows' AVI files, can also be played. In particular, this includes AutoDesk Animation files (which have the file extension of .FLC or .FLI). There is currently a catch however. TMediaPlayer controls multimedia files via Microsoft's MMSYSTEM, and this DLL does not know how to direct FLC or FLI files to a user-defined window. Therefore, if you play these files, they will play in their own separate window even though you have correctly specified your window control as the video surface. No doubt this will be fixed in a future version of MMSYSTEM.DLL.

6.3 How Do I...
Play an audio CD?

COMPLEXITY: INTERMEDIATE

Problem

I would like to create an application that can play audio CDs. How do I set up the TMediaPlayer component to do this? I would also like to display information about the CD, such as how many tracks it has and how long each track is. Can Delphi get this kind of information?

Technique

As with sound and video files, the TMediaPlayer component has no problem playing audio CDs. In fact, you can create an application to play an audio CD without writing a single line of code! All the necessary properties of the TMediaPlayer component can be set at design time. Playing an audio CD is easier than playing sound and video files because you don't have to worry about selecting a file; therefore, you don't need the OpenDialog component or an Open button.

Getting and displaying additional information about the CD is more complicated than either sound or video files, and this is where you will be writing some code. The main complication is that audio CDs can have a variable number of tracks, so it is more of a challenge to present this information onscreen. As you will see, however, Delphi makes it possible to develop an elegant solution to such a problem. This solution involves the use of a TScrollBox component and the Controls property shared by all TWinControl components.

Steps

Run CDAUDIO.EXE. When you click the Open CD button, CDAUDIO finds the CD player on your system and reads information about the currently loaded CD. If you switch to another CD, you need to click the Open button again to update the information. The total length of the CD in minutes and seconds and the current position will be displayed along with the number of tracks. Below these items, an entry for each track appears in the scroll box. You will see the track number and the time duration of each track. On the right side of the scroll box, beside track number one, you will see a blue number currently showing 0 for minutes and seconds (see Figure 6-4). This blue number will always display beside the currently playing track and show that track's current time position.

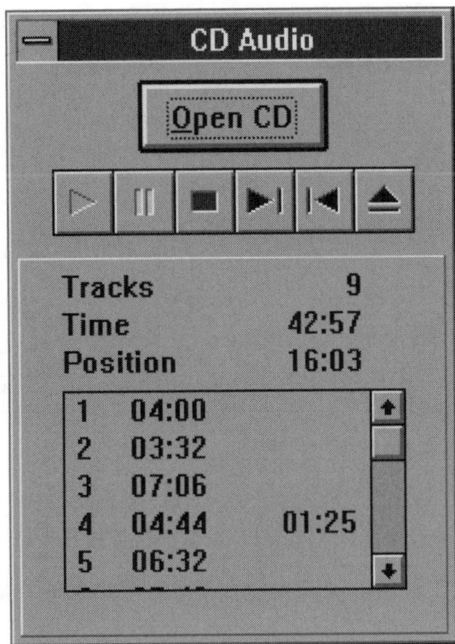

Figure 6-4 CDAUDIO in action

Click the play button to start the CD, and you will see the two time counters begin to count. You can press the next and previous buttons on the TMediaPlayer component to step back and forth through the various tracks. This ability is built into TMediaPlayer. More interesting, though, is that you can click on any track number within the scroll box (either the track number itself or the track length), and that track will immediately be played.

1. Create a new project. Save the default unit as CDAUDIO1.PAS and the project as CDAUDIO.DPR.
2. Add the components, properties, and settings as shown in Table 6-3.

Table 6-3 Components, properties, and settings for CDAUDIO

COMPONENT	PROPERTY	SETTING
Form	BorderStyle	bsDialog
	Caption	CD Audio
	ClientHeight	261
	ClientWidth	202
	Name	CDAudio

continued on next page

continued from previous page

COMPONENT	PROPERTY	SETTING
	Position	poScreenCenter
Button	Caption	&Open CD
	Left	56
	Name	OpenButton
	Top	8
MediaPlayer	AutoEnable	False
	Left	16
	Top	48
	+VisibleButtons	
	- btStep	False
	- btBack	False
	- btRecord	False

3. Create a new unit (select File|New Unit) and save it as IFAUDIO.PAS. This unit implements a custom descendant of a TPanel component just for audio CDs.
4. Just below the *interface* statement, enter the *uses* clause as shown here:

```
uses
  SysUtils, WinTypes, WinProcs, Messages, Classes, Graphics, Controls,
  Forms, Dialogs, StdCtrls, MPlayer, ExtCtrls;
```

5. You will now declare a TPanel descendant called TAudioPanel. This descendant will include several other components and procedures, which will be created at run time rather than now, at design time. Enter the following declaration for TAudioPanel.

```
type
  TAudioPanel = class(TPanel)
    MP: TMediaPlayer;
    Timer1: TTimer;
    ScrollBox: TScrollBox;
    Label1: TLabel;
    Label2: TLabel;
    Label3: TLabel;
    LTracks: TLabel;
    LTime: TLabel;
    LPosition: TLabel;
    CurPos: TLabel;
    TimeStr: String[10];
    MPButtons: TButtonSet;
    constructor Create(AOwner: TWinControl; Media: TMediaPlayer);
    procedure Open;
```

```
    procedure MPClick(Sender: TObject; Button: TMPBtnType;
      var DoDefault: Boolean);
    procedure Timer(Sender: TObject);
    procedure FormatTime(var s: String; t: Longint);
    function FormatTrack(var s: String; t: Longint): byte;
    procedure TrackSelect(Sender: TObject);
    end;
```

6. Following the declaration for TAudioPanel, you must define a special record type. This record will allow information received from the CD to be broken down into its time components (minutes and seconds). This type of record is called a variant record, meaning the same data in the record can be interpreted in different ways. This will be explained in greater detail in the "How It Works" section.

```
{Variant record to extract time info from CD}
TrackTime = record
  case byte of
  0: (Length: Longint);
  1: (Minutes:  Byte;
      Seconds:  Byte;
      Frames:   Byte;
      Extra:    Byte;
     );
  2: (Track:    Byte;
      Mins:     Byte;
      Secs:     Byte;
      Frms:     Byte;
     );
end;
```

7. Immediately following the *implementation* statement, enter the constructor method for TAudioPanel. This constructor first calls the inherited constructor, then creates all of its child components. This procedure is quite long, as it must create seven TLabel components and a TScrollBox component and set the properties for each of them.

```
constructor TAudioPanel.Create(AOwner: TWinControl; Media: TMediaPlayer);
begin
  {Create standard TPanel}
  inherited Create(AOwner);
  {Set the parent}
  Parent := AOwner;
  {Save a reference to the MediaPlayer control}
  MP := Media;
  {Turn off AutoEnabling of buttons}
  MP.AutoEnable := False;
  {Get initial set of enabled buttons}
  MPButtons := MP.EnabledButtons;
  {Now disable them all}
  MP.EnabledButtons := [];
```

continued on next page

continued from previous page

```
{Assign a handler for MediaPlayer clicks}
MP.OnClick := MPClick;
{Create a timer}
Timer1 := TTimer.Create(Self);
Timer1.Enabled := False;
Timer1.OnTimer := Timer;
{Position self under the MediaPlayer control}
Left := 0;
Top := MP.Top + MP.Height + 10;
Height := Parent.ClientHeight - Top;
Width := Parent.ClientWidth;
{Label for audio track count}
Label1 := TLabel.Create(Self);
with Label1 do begin
  Parent := Self;
  Top := 5;
  Left := 20;
  Caption := 'Tracks';
end;
{Label for time position}
Label2 := TLabel.Create(Self);
with Label2 do begin
  Parent := Self;
  Top := 22;
  Left := 20;
  Caption := 'Time';
end;
{Label for physical position}
Label3 := TLabel.Create(Self);
with Label3 do begin
  Parent := Self;
  Top := 39;
  Left := 20;
  Caption := 'Position';
end;
{Label for track value}
LTracks := TLabel.Create(Self);
with LTracks do begin
  Parent := Self;
  Top := 5;
  Left := 95;
  Alignment := taRightJustify;
  Caption := '0';
end;
{Label for time value}
LTime := TLabel.Create(Self);
with LTime do begin
  Parent := Self;
  Top := 22;
  Left := 95;
  Alignment := taRightJustify;
  Caption := '0';
end;
```

```
  {Label for position value}
  LPosition := TLabel.Create(Self);
  with LPosition do begin
    Parent := Self;
    Top := 39;
    Left := 95;
    Alignment := taRightJustify;
    Caption := '0';
  end;
  {Scrollbox for track details}
  ScrollBox := TScrollBox.Create(Self);
  with ScrollBox do begin
    Parent := Self;
    Top := 60;
    Left := 20;
    Width := Self.Width - 40;
    if Parent.Height < 140 then Parent.Height := 140;
    Height := Parent.Height - 80;
  end;
end;
```

8. Now enter the code for the Open method. This method will be called whenever you click the Open CD button. Note that TMediaPlayer's DeviceType property is set to dtCDAudio. TMediaPlayer must be told explicitly that this is the case; the dtAutoSelect value only works with sound or video files. In addition, the FileName property must be set to a null string, otherwise an attempt would be made to open the specified file. Each time Open is called, it updates its information about the CD and displays this information on the parent form by creating a set of dynamic TLabel components in the TScrollBox component.

```
procedure TAudioPanel.Open;
var
  i: Integer;
  Lab: TLabel;
begin
  with MP do begin
    {Ensure closed before attempt to open}
    if Mode = mpPlaying then Close;
    {dtAutoSelect only works on file-type data}
    DeviceType := dtCDAudio;
    {The entire CD is a nameless 'file'}
    FileName := '';
    {Force Open to complete before returning so
     needed information is available.}
    Wait := True;
    {Open access to the CD}
    try
      Open;
    except
      MessageDlg('Could not access CD, please check', mtWarning, [mbOK], 0);
      exit;
    end;
```

continued on next page

continued from previous page

```
    if Error  0 then begin
      MessageDlg(ErrorMessage, mtWarning, [mbOK], 0);
      exit;
    end;
    MP.EnabledButtons := [btPlay, btEject];
    {Display number of tracks}
    LTracks.Caption := IntToStr(Tracks);
    {Display total playing time}
    FormatTime(TimeStr, Length);
    LTime.Caption := TimeStr;
    {Remove and dispose any previous dynamic labels}
    for i := 0 to ScrollBox.ControlCount -1 do begin
      Lab := ScrollBox.Controls[0] as TLabel;
      ScrollBox.RemoveControl(Lab);
      Lab.Free;
    end;
    {Need two dynamic labels for each track}
    for i := 0 to Tracks -1 do begin
      {First of each pair just displays track number}
      Lab := TLabel.Create(ScrollBox);
      {Make a child of the ScrollBox}
      Lab.Parent := ScrollBox;
      Lab.Left := 5;
      Lab.Top := i * Lab.Height;
      Lab.Caption := IntToStr(i + 1); {Track #}
      {Assign to MouseClick event handler}
      Lab.OnClick := TrackSelect;
      {Second of each pair displays track length}
      Lab := TLabel.Create(ScrollBox);
      {Make a child of the ScrollBox}
      Lab.Parent := ScrollBox;
      Lab.Left := 30;
      Lab.Top := i * Lab.Height;
      {Extract TrackLength in MM:SS format}
      FormatTime(TimeStr, TrackLength[i + 1]);
      Lab.Caption := TimeStr;
      {Assign to MouseClick event handler}
      Lab.OnClick := TrackSelect;
    end;
    {Last dynamic control displays progress of
     currently playing track}
    CurPos := TLabel.Create(ScrollBox);
    CurPos.Parent := ScrollBox;
    CurPos.Left := 100;
    CurPos.Font.Color := clblue;
    {Position beside current track}
    CurPos.Top := CurPos.Height *
      (FormatTrack(TimeStr, Position) - 1);
  end;
end;
```

9. Next, enter the code for the MPClick event handler. All button clicks on the MediaPlayer component will come through this handler. The task of updating the TMediaPlayer's enabled buttons is done manually here.

```
{All button clicks on MediaPlayer component come through here,
 so we can update the enabled buttons}
procedure TAudioPanel.MPClick(Sender: TObject; Button: TMPBtnType;
  var DoDefault: Boolean);
begin
  case Button of
    btPlay: begin
      Timer1.Enabled := False;
      Open; {May have changed CDs!}
      MP.EnabledButtons := MPButtons - [btPlay];
      Timer1.Enabled := True;
    end;
    btPause: begin
      Timer1.Enabled := False;
      MP.EnabledButtons := MPButtons - [btPause] + [btPlay];
    end;
    btStop:  begin
      Timer1.Enabled := False;
      MP.EnabledButtons := [btEject, btPlay];
    end;
    btEject: begin
      Timer1.Enabled := False;
      MP.EnabledButtons := [];
    end;
  end;
  if MP.Error<>0 then
    MessageDlg(MP.ErrorMessage, mtWarning, [mbOK], 0);
end;
```

10. You must now enter the code for the timer's OnClick event handler. On each timer click, this handler updates the current time positions for the current track and the entire CD.

```
procedure TAudioPanel.Timer(Sender: TObject);
var
  i: Integer;
  Tot, Tr: TrackTime;
  CurT: Byte;

  {routine to add times together}
  procedure AddTime(var ToTime, FromTime: TrackTime);
  begin
    Inc(ToTime.Seconds, FromTime.Seconds);
    Inc(ToTime.Minutes, ToTime.Seconds div 60);
    ToTime.Seconds := ToTime.Seconds mod 60;
    Inc(ToTime.Minutes, FromTime.Minutes);
  end;
```

continued on next page

continued from previous page

```
begin
  with MP do begin
    {Get current track and its current position}
    CurT := FormatTrack(TimeStr, Position);
    {Display current position within current track}
    CurPos.Caption := TimeStr;
    {Position beside current track}
    CurPos.Top := ScrollBox.Controls[CurT * 2 - 1].Top;
    {Make sure it's visible}
    ScrollBox.ScrollInView(CurPos);
    {Add all prior track lengths}
    Tot.Length := 0;
    for i := 1 to CurT - 1 do begin
      Tr.Length := TrackLength[i];
      AddTime(Tot, Tr);
    end;
    {Get current track position again}
    Tr.Length := Position;
    {Transpose tfTMSF format to tfMSF format}
    Tr.Minutes := Tr.Mins;
    Tr.Seconds := Tr.Secs;
    Tr.Frames := Tr.Frms;
    {Add to total of prior tracks}
    AddTime(Tot, Tr);
    {Display current CD time position}
    FormatTime(TimeStr, Tot.Length);
    LPosition.Caption := TimeStr;
  end;
end;
```

11. Enter the TrackSelect method, which is an OnClick event handler shared by all the TLabel components that are created and placed in the scroll box. This method allows you to select and play any track from the displayed list.

```
procedure TAudioPanel.TrackSelect(Sender: TObject);
var
  Tr: TrackTime;
  i: Integer;
begin
  with MP do begin
    {Find out which line was clicked}
    for i := 1 to Tracks do begin
      {Allow click of either track # or time}
      if (Sender = ScrollBox.Controls[ 2 * i - 1])
      or (Sender = ScrollBox.Controls[ 2 * i - 2]) then begin
        {Stop timer to prevent 'bounce'}
        Timer1.Enabled := False;
        Tr.Length := 0;
        Tr.Track := i;
        {Set CD to start of selected track}
        Position := Tr.Length;
        {Restart display}
```

```
        Timer1.Enabled := True;
        {Play the track}
        Play;
        {Adjust the buttons}
        MP.EnabledButtons := MPButtons - [btPlay];
        {No need to search further}
        exit;
      end;
    end;
  end;
end;
```

12. The FormatTime method, entered next, is a helper routine that translates the time information from the long integer received from the CD into a time format that can be displayed.

```
{Extract time in tfMSF format. The elements of the
 TrackLength property are in this format.}
procedure TAudioPanel.FormatTime(var s: String; t: Longint);
var
  tt: TrackTime;
  tStr: String[10];
  i: Integer;
begin
  tt.Length := t;
  {Format as MM:SS}
  Str(tt.Minutes:2, tStr); s := tStr + ':';
  Str(tt.Seconds:2, tStr); s := s + tStr;
  {Replace blanks with zeros so column lines up}
  Repeat
    i := Pos(' ', s);
    if i > 0 then s[i] := '0';
  Until i = 0;
end;
```

13. The FormatTrack helper method is very much like the FormatTime method, but it handles a different format of information received from the CD that includes the currently playing track number. Here is the code for this method:

```
{Extract time in tfTMSF format. The Position property is
 in this format. Also return the extracted track number.}
function TAudioPanel.FormatTrack(var s: String; t: Longint): byte;
var
  tt: TrackTime;
  tStr: String[10];
  i: Integer;
begin
  {Format as MM:SS}
  tt.Length := t;
  Str(tt.Mins:2, tStr); s := tStr + ':';
  Str(tt.Secs:2, tStr); s := s + tStr;
```

continued on next page

continued from previous page

```
  {Replace blanks with zeros so column lines up}
  Repeat
    i := Pos(' ', s);
    if i > 0 then s[i] := '0';
  Until i = 0;
  {Return current track number}
  Result := tt.Track;
end;
```

14. Save IFAUDIO.PAS, then return to AUDIO1.PAS. In the *uses* clause, add a reference to the IFAUDIO unit just created. The *uses* clause should look like this:

```
uses
  SysUtils, WinTypes, WinProcs, Messages, Classes, Graphics, Controls,
  Forms, Dialogs, StdCtrls, MPlayer, ExtCtrls, IFAudio;
```

15. In the *private* section of TAudioForm, add a variable of type TAudioPanel:

```
private
    { Private declarations }
    CDPanel: TAudioPanel;
```

16. In the Object Inspector, double-click TCDAudio's OnCreate event and enter the following code to create the custom TAudioPanel component.

```
procedure TAudioForm.FormCreate(Sender: TObject);
begin
  {Create the custom TPanel for Audio info}
  CDPanel := TAudioPanel.Create(Self, MediaPlayer1);
end;
```

17. Double-click the Open CD button on the TAudioForm and enter the following code to open and display information about the CD.

```
procedure TMidiForm.OpenButtonClick(Sender: TObject);
begin
  CDPanel.Open;
end;
```

18. Compile and run the application.

How It Works

The IFAUDIO unit you create in this How-To contains an object class descended from TPanel called TAudioPanel. Like the TMidiPanel and TVideoPanel components, all the work of managing the information display for audio CDs is encapsulated in this class. In addition, for this class, updating the TMediaPlayer component's enabled buttons is also handled manually.

The first dramatically different ingredient in the IFAUDIO unit is the definition of a rather strange-looking record (if you're new to Pascal). This record structure is a variant record, so named because the same data space within the structure is defined in more than one way:

```
TrackTime = record
  case byte of
    0: (Length: Longint);
    1: (Minutes:  Byte;
        Seconds:  Byte;
        Frames:   Byte;
        Extra:    Byte;
       );
    2: (Track:    Byte;
        Mins:     Byte;
        Secs:     Byte;
        Frms:     Byte;
       );
  end;
end;
```

In the TrackTime record structure, there are three separate record definitions. If you add up the bytes taken by all the fields, you will get a total of 12. However, that is not the case. The total length of this record is really only 4 bytes (the size of the Longint field). The second field definition (containing the fields named Minutes, Seconds, Frames, and Extra) simply redefines the meaning of the same 4 bytes taken up by the Length field. The third definition (containing the Track, Mins, Secs, and Frms fields) redefines the same bytes again. At any time during execution of the program, you can refer to any one of these fields, and the data at that position will be interpreted according to the named field type. This record can therefore act as a translator. You can assign a value to the Length field (a Longint) and then extract the individual byte values from that Longint value, or set any of the byte fields and read it back out as a Longint. This kind of structure is often needed when dealing with data from another source, such as (in this case) a CD-ROM driver.

Creating TAudioPanel

The Create constructor of TAudioPanel is very long, but does mostly the same things as were done in the TMidiPanel and TVideoPanel Create constructors (see step 7). As in the others, the Create constructor first calls the inherited constructor for TPanel, assigns the Parent property, sets up access for the passed TMediaPlayer component, and assigns the OnClick event handler for TMediaPlayer. It also creates a timer and sets up the event handler for that. Three statements are worth noting:

```
MP.AutoEnable := False;
MPButtons := MP.EnabledButtons;
MP.EnabledButtons := [];
```

The first statement turns off TMediaPlayer's AutoEnable property. This means the application must handle the update of the valid TMediaPlayer buttons at all times. This is not difficult—it can all be handled quite simply within the OnClick method that is assigned to the TMediaPlayer. The next statement assigns the local variable, MPButtons, to the current set of enabled buttons in the MediaPlayer. This is actually relying on the fact that when the AutoEnable property is set to False, all buttons are initially set to an enabled state in the MediaPlayer. Therefore, MPButtons will equal the set of all buttons. MPButtons can now be used to simplify the updating of the enabled buttons elsewhere in the program. Finally, the EnabledButtons property is set to an empty set. Since the program has not yet opened a CD for playing, all buttons should start out as disabled.

The TAudioPanel constructor now sets up its own position and size. It will assign itself all available space under the position of the TMediaPlayer component. It then creates and initializes six TLabels and a TScrollBox. The first three TLabels are just that, labels to name the information the user will see. The next three TLabels are paired with the first three and will be used to display the specific information for any CD. The TScrollBox is sized and positioned under the six labels just created. The TScrollBox is left empty at this point, as there is no information to be displayed. When a CD is opened, the scroll box will contain information on the individual tracks found on the CD.

Opening a CD

The Open method of TAudioPanel is the most complex. This method is called by the application when the user clicks the Open CD button. Before attempting to access the CD, three things are done. The Mode property of the TMediaPlayer is checked to see if a CD is currently playing. If so, the CD is closed—otherwise an error might occur on the attempt to open it again. The DeviceType property is explicitly set to dtCDAudio, and the FileName property is set to a null string. Both of these are necessary to let TMediaPlayer know that it is a CD-ROM that is being accessed rather than a file structure (refer to step 8).

The Wait property is set to True so that the call to the TMediaPlayer's Open method will not return until access to the CD is complete. Doing this ensures that information you want about the CD will be available to the code immediately following a successful open. The TMediaPlayer Open method is then called (protected in an exception block), and a further check is made to see if any error occurred. If the Error property of TMediaPlayer is not 0, then an error of some sort occurred, and a corresponding error message is retrieved using the ErrorMessage method.

Preparing Display of CD Data

Now that a CD has been opened, the display can be updated. First, the play and eject buttons are enabled for the TMediaPlayer. The number of tracks and total running time of the CD are then displayed:

```
MP.EnabledButtons := [btPlay, btEject];
LTracks.Caption := IntToStr(Tracks);
FormatTime(TimeStr, Length);
LTime.Caption := TimeStr;
```

It is now time to create the dynamic TLabel components that will be used to display information on each track. Before doing this though, it must be remembered that this Open method can be called countless times during execution. Therefore, any dynamic TLabels that may have previously been created must first be disposed of as shown below.

```
for i := 0 to ScrollBox.ControlCount -1 do begin
  Lab := ScrollBox.Controls[0] as TLabel;
  ScrollBox.RemoveControl(Lab);
  Lab.Free;
end;
```

The code loops through each of the dynamic TLabel components that currently exist (if any), removes them from the TScrollBox component, and frees them. The ControlCount property, common to all windowed controls, keeps track of how many child windows a component has. Each of these child controls is accessible via the indexed Controls property. Since the only controls the TScrollBox component will have as children are the dynamic labels you create and assign to it, the Controls property makes a perfect mechanism for handling the requirements of this display. You do not need to be concerned with working out your own means of tracking these controls; it's already built in. Note that each time through the loop, the control that is assigned to Lab is the one at index zero; this is very important to remember when attempting to remove child controls from a component. Each time the child at index zero is removed, any following children are moved down to fill the space. In other words, as long as there are any children, there will always be one at index zero.

Now that the scroll box has been cleared of any existing TLabels, a new set can be created for the CD just opened. To do this, another loop is set up. This loop counts through the number of tracks currently indicated by the Track property of TMediaPlayer. Each time through the loop, two labels are created. The first one will simply be assigned the track number it represents. The second will be assigned the time value of that track. To do this, the time value is extracted from the indexed TrackLength property of the TMediaPlayer. This value is in the form of a Longint, and it is formatted into minutes and seconds using the FormatTime method. Each of the labels is positioned vertically by multiplying the current loop counter value (I) by the height of the TLabel. The complete loop is shown below.

```
for i := 0 to Tracks -1 do begin
  Lab := TLabel.Create(ScrollBox);
  Lab.Parent := ScrollBox;
  Lab.Left := 5;
  Lab.Top := i * Lab.Height;
  Lab.Caption := IntToStr(i + 1); {Track #}
  Lab.OnClick := TrackSelect;
```

continued on next page

continued from previous page

```
  {Second of each pair displays track length}
  Lab := TLabel.Create(ScrollBox);
  Lab.Parent := ScrollBox;
  Lab.Left := 30;
  Lab.Top := i * Lab.Height;
  FormatTime(TimeStr, TrackLength[i + 1]);
  Lab.Caption := TimeStr;
  Lab.OnClick := TrackSelect;
end;
```

Each of the TLabel controls created in the preceding loop has its OnClick property set to the TrackSelect event handler. This allows these TLabels to act as play buttons for the corresponding audio track. Finally, one more dynamic TLabel is created. This TLabel is used to track the time of the currently playing track and will always be displayed beside that track to act as an indicator of which track is playing. To format the time value for this label, the FormatTrack method is used instead of the FormatTime method. This is because the Position property is in a different format than the TrackLength value of each of the tracks.

Managing TMediaPlayer Buttons

When the user clicks on any TMediaPlayer button, a click event is triggered and control is passed to the MPClick method of TAudioPanel (see step 9). A *case* statement is used to test which button was clicked. Only four buttons need to be handled here. If play is clicked, the timer is temporarily stopped and the Open method (of TAudioPanel) is called to refresh all information. This is necessary in case there is a different CD present. The *case* statement then updates the TMediaPlayer buttons, enabling all but the play button and, finally, restarts the timer. When the pause button is clicked, the timer is disabled, the pause button is disabled, and the play button is enabled. For the stop button, all but the eject and play buttons are disabled; and for eject, all buttons are disabled. For both the stop and eject buttons, the timer is stopped.

Whichever button is clicked, a check is made following the *case* block to see if any error was encountered. If so, the appropriate error message is displayed to the user.

Updating Display During Play

The event handler for the timer must do quite a bit of work to format the current time values. Within this event handler, a local procedure has been defined called AddTime. This procedure only needs to be used by the Timer method, so it has been defined within the Timer method. No other code outside of Timer can "see" the AddTime procedure.

AddTime takes two parameters, both of which are of the type TrackTime. TrackTime is the variant record structure you have defined in the *interface* section of the unit. AddTime assumes the values passed in ToTime and FromTime are in the tfMSF format, meaning that the first three bytes represent minutes, seconds, and frames, respectively, and the fourth byte is unused. This is the format used by the values in the TrackLength property for each audio track. The ToTime parameter is passed by reference (specified using the *var* keyword). This allows the procedure to directly update the actual variable that ToTime represents. Without the *var* keyword, parameters are passed by value, meaning that (in the case of FromTime) it is only a local value and any changes made to it are not seen outside the procedure. AddTime adds the seconds and minutes in the FromTime record to the current time value in the ToTime record as shown below.

```
Inc(ToTime.Seconds, FromTime.Seconds);
Inc(ToTime.Minutes, ToTime.Seconds div 60);
ToTime.Seconds := ToTime.Seconds mod 60;
Inc(ToTime.Minutes, FromTime.Minutes);
```

In the main code of the Timer handler (shown in step 10), a call is made to FormatTrack to format a time value into a string using the current value of the Position property. The Position property is in tfTMSF format, meaning the first field is the track number followed by the minutes, seconds, and frames played so far within that track. In addition to formatting the minutes and seconds, FormatTrack returns the track number extracted from the Position property as can be seen below.

```
CurT := FormatTrack(TimeStr, Position);
CurPos.Caption := TimeStr;
CurPos.Top := ScrollBox.Controls[CurT * 2 - 1].Top;
ScrollBox.ScrollInView(CurPos);
```

The formatted string in TimeStr is then assigned to the CurPos TLabel component for display. The screen position of CurPos is updated using the saved track number in CurT. Finally, the ScrollInView method of TScrollBox is called to ensure that CurPos is visible.

Next, the value returned from FormatTrack (CurT) is used to control a loop that adds the lengths of all tracks prior to the current one. The loop assigns the TrackLength value to the Longint record variant of Tr, which is a TrackTime variable. Tr is then passed to AddTime, which extracts the time information from the Longint passed to it and adds it to the Tot variable (also of type TrackTime). This is shown in the code fragment below.

```
Tot.Length := 0;
for i := 1 to CurT - 1 do begin
  Tr.Length := TrackLength[i];
  AddTime(Tot, Tr);
end;
```

Now the current elapsed time of the currently playing track must be added. This information is available from the Position property, so it is assigned to the Tr variable. Since this is in tfTMSF format, it must be translated into tfMSF format before it can be passed to the AddTime procedure. Once done, the Tot variable is passed to

FormatTime to get a displayable string in TimeStr, which is then assigned to the LPosition TLabel component for display as shown below.

```
Tr.Length := Position;
Tr.Minutes := Tr.Mins;
Tr.Seconds := Tr.Secs;
Tr.Frames := Tr.Frms;
AddTime(Tot, Tr);
FormatTime(TimeStr, Tot.Length);
LPosition.Caption := TimeStr;
```

The TrackSelect handler (step 11), which was assigned to the dynamic TLabels in the Scrollbox, is an interesting method. Whenever one of the labels is clicked, TrackSelect must loop through them to find which one it was. Rather than loop once for all the TLabels, it loops once for each track and tests two TLabels at a time (because each pair of TLabels represents the same track). This is really a personal preference; it could be done either way with no clear advantage to either. The entire loop is shown below.

```
for i := 1 to Tracks do begin
  if (Sender = ScrollBox.Controls[ 2 * i - 1])
  or (Sender = ScrollBox.Controls[ 2 * i - 2]) then begin
    Timer1.Enabled := False;
    Tr.Length := 0;
    Tr.Track := i;
    Position := Tr.Length;
    Timer1.Enabled := True;
    Play;
    MP.EnabledButtons := MPButtons - [btPlay];
    exit;
  end;
end;
```

Each time through the loop, the Sender parameter is tested against the two TLabels representing that track. As soon as it matches one (which it must do for this procedure to have been called), you know which track was selected. The Longint field of the Tr variable is set to 0, and the selected track number is then assigned to Tr's Track field. Tr is then assigned to the Position property of TMediaPlayer, causing the CD player to be queued to the beginning of this track. TMediaPlayer is told to play the track, the TMediaPlayer buttons are updated, and the procedure exits.

The FormatTime method (in step 12) is quite simple. It assigns the passed Longint value to a local variable of type TrackTime and then formats a time string by extracting the Minutes and Seconds from the TrackTime record. The ":2" following the Minutes and Seconds values in the calls to the Str procedure tells Str to pad the value to two character positions even if the value is a single digit. However, Str will pad using blanks. In order to produce a consistent-looking display, the blanks need to be replaced with zeros. This is accomplished by using the Pos function. Pos searches for the specified character (a blank) in the specified string and returns the position. If the character is not found, Pos returns zero. It's an easy task to loop until no more blanks are found.

The FormatTrack function (see step 13) is almost identical to FormatTime, but it uses a different variant of the TrackTime variable to extract the minutes and seconds. It also returns the extracted track number as the function result.

Comments

As stated at the beginning of this How-To, the simple task of playing an audio CD can be accomplished without writing a single line of code. Considering that, you sure wrote a lot of code in this How-To! The result of this work, however, is a very complete and useful (and reusable) tool for playing and displaying audio CDs. As with How-To's 6.1 and 6.2, the functionality for audio CDs has been placed in a separate unit ready to be used in another application.

6.4 How Do I...
Create a multimedia player?

COMPLEXITY: EASY

Problem

Well, I now know how to play sound files, video files, and audio CDs. For each of these, I can create a separate unit with a descendant of TPanel to encapsulate the handling and display. I understand that these units are supposed to be reusable in Delphi. How is this done? Can I reuse all three of these units in the same application?

Technique

As stated in the first three How-To's, the reason for creating separate units, each with its own custom component, is to facilitate easy reuse and avoid doing all that work again for each new application. This How-To is the payoff. Here, with very little effort, you will create a single multimedia application that can handle all the multimedia types presented so far.

Steps

Run PLAYER.EXE. Click on File|Open to open a sound or video file, or click the Audio CD menu item if you have an audio CD inserted in your player. You can switch back and forth between any of these multimedia types, and each time you do, the form is redisplayed to accommodate the kind of object you are playing.
An example is shown in Figure 6-5.

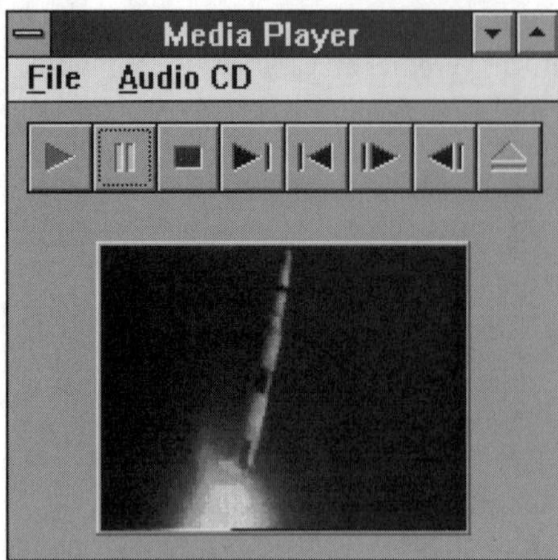

Figure 6-5 PLAYER in action

1. Create a new project. Save the default unit as PLAYER1.PAS and the project as PLAYER.DPR.
2. Add the components, properties, and settings as shown in Table 6-4.

Table 6-4 Components, properties, and settings for PLAYER

COMPONENT	PROPERTY	SETTING
Form	BorderStyle	bsDialog
	Caption	Media Player
	ClientHeight	251
	ClientWidth	241
	Name	MidiForm
	Position	poScreenCenter
MediaPlayer	Left	8
	Top	8
	+VisibleButtons	
	- btRecord	False
OpenDialog	DefaultExt	AVI
	Filter	Windows Animation|*.AVI
		Midi Sequencer|*.MID;*.RMI
	+Options	
	- ofFileMustExist	True
	- ofExtensionDifferent	True

3. Add a menu component to the form and create menu items for it as shown in Table 6-5.

Table 6-5 Menu components for PLAYER

MENU	MENUITEM
File	Open
	-
	Exit
Audio CD	

4. Add the units IFMIDI, IFVIDEO, and IFAUDIO to the *uses* clause of PLAYER1.PAS. The complete *uses* clause should look like this:

```
uses
  SysUtils, WinTypes, WinProcs, Messages, Classes, Graphics, Controls,
  Forms, Dialogs, StdCtrls, ExtCtrls, Menus, MPlayer, IFMidi, IFVideo,IFAudio;
```

5. In the *private* section of TForm1, add a variable of each type from the included units. Also add an extra variable of type TPanel.

```
private
    { Private declarations }
    AudioPanel: TAudioPanel;
    VideoPanel: TVideoPanel;
    MidiPanel:  TMidiPanel;
    CurPanel: TPanel;
```

6. Click the Audio CD menu item and add the following code to display and play the CD.

```
procedure TForm1.AudioCD1Click(Sender: TObject);
begin
  {Free current media panel object if any}
  CurPanel.Free;
  {Create the CD Display}
  AudioPanel := TAudioPanel.Create(Self, MediaPlayer1);
  {Open (and Play) the CD}
  AudioPanel.Open;
  {Assign common reference to open panel}
  CurPanel := AudioPanel;
end;
```

7. Click on File|Open and enter the following code to select and play a file.

```
procedure TForm1.Open1Click(Sender: TObject);
var
  FExt: String[4];
```

continued on next page

continued from previous page

```
begin
  {Get selected file}
  if Opendialog1.Execute then begin
    {Free current panel if any}
    CurPanel.Free;
    {Close anything currently open}
    MediaPlayer1.Stop;
    MediaPlayer1.Close;
    {Default to allowing buttons to be updated automatically}
    MediaPlayer1.AutoEnable := True;
    {Assign selected file}
    MediaPlayer1.FileName := OpenDialog1.FileName;
    {Extract the file extension}
    FExt := ExtractFileExt(MediaPlayer1.FileName);
    {If a sound file then create a MIDI panel}
    if (FExt = '.MID') or (FExt = '.RMI') or (FExt = '.WAV') then begin
      MidiPanel := TMidiPanel.Create(Self, MediaPlayer1);
      CurPanel := MidiPanel;
      MidiPanel.Open;
    end
    {Otherwise it must be a video file of some sort}
    else begin
      VideoPanel := TVideoPanel.Create(Self, MediaPlayer1);
      CurPanel := VideoPanel;
      VideoPanel.Open;
      MediaPlayer1.Play;
    end;
  end;
end;
```

8. Click on File|Exit and enter the following line to close the application.

```
procedure TForm1.Exit1Click(Sender: TObject);
begin
  Close;
end;
```

9. Compile and run the application.

How It Works

As promised, you have created a complete multimedia player that combines the functionality of the first three How-To's into a single application. Simply by including references to IFMIDI, IFVIDEO, and IFAUDIO in the *uses* clause, you can use the object classes defined in those units. There are no complicated requirements; as long as Delphi can find the units referenced, you can use whatever those units contain, just as if they were Delphi's own units.

In the declaration for TForm1, you create variables for each of the three classes defined in those units:

```
AudioPanel: TAudioPanel;
VideoPanel: TVideoPanel;
MidiPanel:  TMidiPanel;
CurPanel: TPanel;
```

The purpose of the CurPanel variable is to hold the reference for whichever of the other three is currently active. Because CurPanel is declared to be of type TPanel, which is the immediate ancestor of the three Panel descendants you have created, CurPanel can be used to point to any of them.

In the AudioCD1Click event handler, whatever is currently referenced by CurPanel is freed. AudioPanel is then created and its Open method is called. Just as in CDAUDIO, this is all that is needed to display the CD data and be able to play it. AudioPanel is then assigned to CurPanel. By doing this, you don't have to figure out which type of object is currently active in order to close it. Whichever one it is, it will be freed by calling CurPanel.Free, as in the following code fragment:

```
CurPanel.Free;
AudioPanel := TAudioPanel.Create(Self, MediaPlayer1);
AudioPanel.Open;
CurPanel := AudioPanel;
```

The Open1Click event handler handles both sound and video files. As in AudioCD1Click, CurPanel is freed, thereby freeing whatever object was currently active. In case a file is still playing, MediaPlayer1 is told to stop and close any open selection. The AutoEnable property is also set back to True in case it was left in a different state. The selected file name is assigned to TMediaPlayer1. At this point, you need to determine whether a sound file or a video file was selected in order to know whether to create a TMidiPanel component or a TVideoPanel component, as shown below.

```
MediaPlayer1.FileName := OpenDialog1.FileName;
FExt := ExtractFileExt(MediaPlayer1.FileName);
if (FExt = '.MID') or (FExt = '.RMI') or (FExt = '.WAV') then begin
  MidiPanel := TMidiPanel.Create(Self, MediaPlayer1);
  CurPanel := MidiPanel;
  MidiPanel.Open;
end
else begin
  VideoPanel := TVideoPanel.Create(Self, MediaPlayer1);
  CurPanel := VideoPanel;
  VideoPanel.Open;
  MediaPlayer1.Play;
end;
```

If it's a sound file, then a TMidiPanel component is created and its Open method called. Otherwise, a TVideoPanel component is created and both the Open and Play methods are called. In both cases, the newly created component is assigned to CurPanel, so it can easily be freed when no longer needed.

Comments

In the first three How-To's, you perform extra work in order to build descendant components to encapsulate the functionality desired for the different multimedia abilities. The purpose of this How-To is to let you enjoy the fruits of your labor by creating an application that includes all that previous functionality without nearly the effort that would be required had those custom components not been created. Whenever you create any sort of functionality, whether an object class, or just a set of procedures or functions, if you think they may be useful to you at a later time for a different application, it's a great idea to split them out into a separate unit.

6.5 How Do I...
Create an HTML-based hypertext viewer?

COMPLEXITY: ADVANCED

Problem

I need to create a presentation which includes hypertext links that jump to other files or different parts of my current document, as done by Windows Help files, for example. Is there a way to do this in Delphi?

Technique

While there are as many hypertext formats as there are viewers, one design is emerging rapidly to dominate the field: *HTML*, or HyperText Markup Language. Developed at CERN in Europe for use on the Internet, HTML has emerged as a simple but powerful standard for hypermedia files. The method behind HTML is called the Tag, and is a marked group of characters which tell the viewer how to handle included text. A viewer must be able to process these tags and understand how to interpret them visually and functionally. Using Delphi's string-manipulation routines, this can be done quickly and smoothly.

Steps

Run DHTMLVWR.EXE. in the CHAP06/HOWTO05 directory on the CD. Open the file TEST1.DHT and you will see a display similar to Figure 6-6. Click on the red text and you will jump to a new file, TEST2.DHT, as shown in Figure 6-7. Notice that when the mouse is near the red text, the cursor changes to the pointing finger used in Windows help files; this signifies an active jump link.

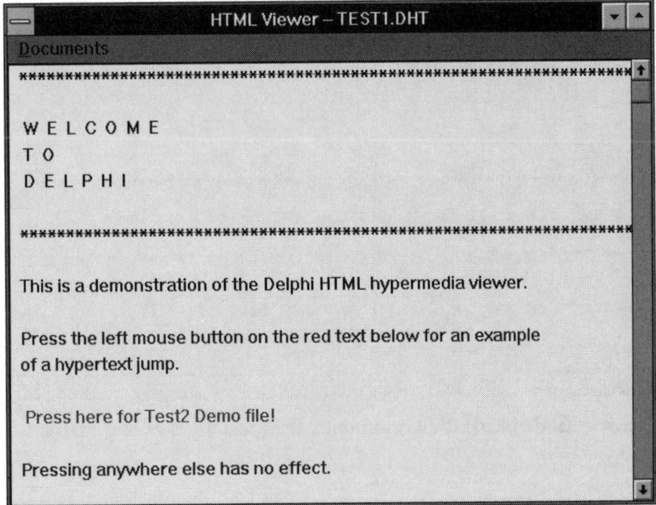

Figure 6-6 DHTMLVWR at run time showing a hypertext jump link

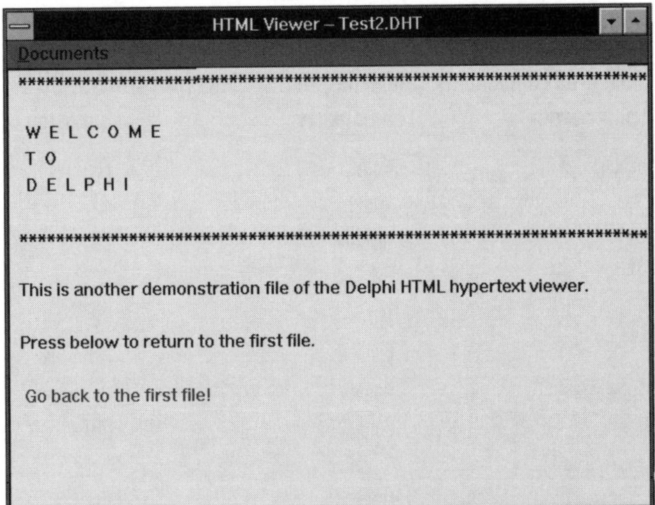

Figure 6-7 DHTMLVWR at run time showing the result of making a hypertext jump

Open TEST1.DHT in Notepad and you will see a display similar to Figure 6-8. Notice that the text which is red is surrounded by special characters. The application you are about to create will interpret those characters, called a *Tag*, as a hypertext link.

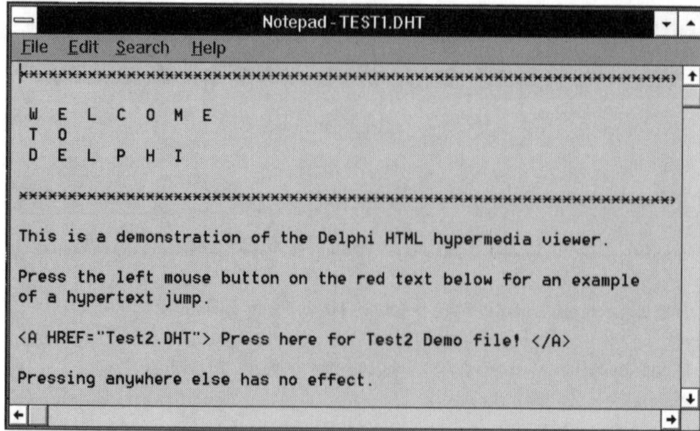

Figure 6-8 NOTEPAD open with TEST1.DHT, showing HTML syntax

1. Create a new project. Save the unit as DHTMLVWR.PAS and the project as DHTMLV1.DPR.
2. Add the components, properties, and settings as shown in Table 6-6.

Table 6-6 Components, properties, and settings for Form2 in DHTMLVWR

COMPONENT	PROPERTY	SETTING
TForm	Name	Form2
	Width	419
	Height	331
	Left	30
	Top	30
	Caption	HTML Viewer — No File
TOpenDialog	Name	OpenDialog1
	DefaultExt	DHT
	Filename	*.dht
	Filter	*.dht
TMainMenu	Name	MainMenu1
TMenuItem (Top Level)	Name	Document
	Caption	&Documents
TMenuItem (Under Doc)	Name	OpenDHTMLDocument1
	Caption	&Open DHTML Document
TMenuItem (Under Doc)	Name	Quit
	Caption	&Quit

3. Select the OnCreate event of Form2 and enter the following code to initialize the application.

```
procedure TForm2.FormCreate(Sender: TObject);
begin
  TotalLinkRecords := 0;
  LinkInsertPosition := 1;
  Screen.Cursors[ 5 ] := LoadCursor( HInstance , 'HTHAND' );
  DumpInvalidHTML := false;
  DocumentLoaded := false;
  TheStringList := TStringList.Create;
  TheScrollBox := NIL;
end;
```

4. Choose the OnDestroy event of Form2 and enter the following code to close the application.

```
procedure TForm2.FormDestroy(Sender: TObject);
var Counter_1 : Integer;
begin
  for Counter_1 := 1 to TotalLinkRecords do
  begin
    Dispose( TheLIArray[ Counter_1 ] );
  end;
end;
```

5. Select the OnClick event of the OpenDHTMLDocument menu item and enter the following code to load and display a new HTML document.

```
procedure TForm2.OpenDHTLDocument1Click(Sender: TObject);
var Counter_1 : Integer;
begin
  OpenDialog1.FileName := '*.DHT';
  if OpenDialog1.Execute then
  begin
    if DocumentLoaded then
    begin
      InitializeDHTMLFile( OpenDialog1.Filename , '' );
    end
    else
    begin
      TheHiddenMemo := TMemo.Create( Self );
      TheHiddenMemo.Parent := Self;
      TheHiddenMemo.Visible := false;
      TheHiddenMemo.Width := Form2.Width;
      TheHiddenMemo.Height := Form2.Height;
      TheHiddenMemo.Lines.LoadFromFile( OpenDialog1.Filename );
      For Counter_1 := 1 to TheHiddenMemo.Lines.Count do
      begin
        TheStringList.Add( TheHiddenMemo.Lines[ Counter_1 - 1 ] );
      end;
      TheHiddenMemo.Free;
      DocumentLoaded := true;
      CreateNewDHTDocument;
```

continued on next page

continued from previous page

```
      Caption := 'HTML Viewer -- ' + ExtractFilename( OpenDialog1.Filename );
    end;
  end;
end;
```

6. Select the OnClick event of the Quit menu item and enter the following code to exit the application.

```
procedure TForm2.Quit1Click(Sender: TObject);
begin
  if MessageDlg('Are you sure you want to quit?' ,
   mtConfirmation , [mbOK,mbCancel] , 0 ) = mrOK then
    Close;
end;
```

7. Go into the Code Editor and move up to the *type* keyword, then find the declaration for Form2 and its *public* keyword, and enter the following highlighted helper procedures and functions.

```
type
  TForm2 = class(TForm)
  public
    { Public declarations }
    procedure HotClick( Sender : TObject;
              Button: TMouseButton;
              Shift: TShiftState;
              X, Y: Integer );
    function GetStringToCharacter(     TheString    : String ;
                   TargetString : String;
                   GetTarget    : Boolean;
                  var ThePosition  : Integer  ) : String;
    function GetStringtoHTMLTag(     TheString       : String;
                  var EndingPosition : Integer ) : String;
    function GetHTMLTag(      TheString       : String;
              var EndingPosition : Integer ) : String;
    function ParseHTMLTag( TheString : String ) : Integer;
    function GetCompleteHTMLReference(     TheString      : String;
                    InputType      : Integer;
                   var EndingPosition,
                    OutputType     : Integer ) :
                                   String;
    function GetURL( TheString : String ) : String;
    function ParseURL(      TheString : String;
             var URL1,
             URL2       : String ) : Integer;
    function GetURLType( TheString : String ) : Integer;
    procedure ParseAnchor(      TheString      : String;
                AnchorType    : Integer;
             var DisplayedText,
                AnchorText    : String    );
    procedure ParseLink(      TheString      : String;
```

```
                LinkType       : Integer;
               var DisplayedText,
                LinkURL1,
                LinkURL2       : String;
               var LinkStatus    : Integer  );
    function CreateNewAnchorLink( AnchorName : String;
                 XPos,
                  YPos        : Integer ) : Integer;
    function CreateNewLocalLink( AnchorName,
                 FileName   : String;
                 TheType    : Integer ) : Integer;
    function CreateNewNonLocalLink( AnchorName ,
                  FileName     : String ) : Integer;
    procedure FindLocalAnchor(      TheAnchor : String;
                var XLoc,
                  YLoc       : Integer );
    procedure InitializeDHTMLFile( TheFileName , TheAnchorName : String );
    procedure CreateNewDHTDocument;
end;
```

8. Still in the Code Editor, move down below the *end* keyword for the Form2 type declaration, and enter the following highlighted assistant type definitions.

```
  HTMLLabel = class( TLabel )
    private
      LinkItem : Integer;
  end;
  PLinkItemRecord = ^LinkItemRecord;
  LinkItemRecord = record
    LinkFile : String;
    LinkAnchor : String;
    LinkType,
    XPosition ,
    YPosition   : Integer;
    HasLabel : Boolean;
    TheLabel : HTMLLabel;
  end;
  LinkItemArray = array[ 1 .. 255 ] of PLinkItemRecord;
```

9. Move down below the *var* keyword and type in the following highlighted helper variables.

```
var
  Form2: TForm2;
  TheHiddenMemo : TMemo;
  TheLIArray : LinkItemArray;
  LinkInsertPosition ,
  TotalLinkRecords         : Integer;
  PixelsPerLine : Integer;
  DumpInvalidHTML : Boolean;
  DocumentLoaded : Boolean;
  TheStringList : TStringList;
  TheScrollBox : TScrollBox;
```

10. Move down below the *implementation* keyword and type in the following assistant function to handle generic string manipulations.

```
function TForm2.GetStringToCharacter(     TheString     : String ;
                         TargetString : String;
                         GetTarget    : Boolean;
                       var ThePosition  : Integer  ) : String;
var TempString : String;
    Counter_1  : Integer;
begin
  { Clear the string to be returned }
  TempString := '';
  { Find the delimiter position; if not found will be 0 }
  Counter_1 := Pos( TargetString , TheString );
  if Counter_1 = 0 then
  begin
    Counter_1 := Length( TheString ) + 1;
  end
  else
  begin
    { If obtaining target token not desired, get up to it      }
    { Notice that if delimiter is first character, no result! }
    if not GetTarget then Counter_1 := Counter_1 - 1;
    { If the delimiter is found, get the string up to it }
    if Counter_1 <> 0 then
     TempString := Copy( TheString , 1 , Counter_1  );
    { Return either 0 or the position delimiter found at }
  end;
  ThePosition := Counter_1;
  { Return either the string to the delimiter or an empty one }
  GetStringToCharacter := TempString;
end;
```

11. Move down below the previous code and type in the following assistant function to handle pulling out non HTML text from a string.

```
function TForm2.GetStringtoHTMLTag(      TheString       : String;
                       var EndingPosition : Integer ) : String;
var TempString : String;
begin
  { Make the call to get up to HTML delimiter }
  TempString := GetStringToCharacter( TheString ,
   '<' , false , EndingPosition );
  { If empty string returned, input string has no HTML tag or it is first }
  if TempString = '' then
  begin
    if EndingPosition = 0 then
    begin  { First character is an HTML tag, so send back pos 1 & empty str }
      GetStringToHTMLTag := '';
      EndingPosition := 1;
    end
    else
    begin
      { Return entire input string }
```

```
      TempString := TheString;
      if TempString = '' then TempString := ' ';
      GetStringToHTMLTag := TempString;
      { Set next scan position past end of string to signal }
      { need for a new line                                 }
      EndingPosition := Length( TheString ) + 1;
    end;
  end
  else
  begin
    { Otherwise an HTML tag was found, return up to it }
    GetStringToHTMLTag := TempString;
    { Set the next scan position to the HTML tag opener }
    EndingPosition := EndingPosition + 1;
  end;
end;
```

12. Move down below the previous code and type in the following assistant function to handle getting an initial HTML tag (i.e. inside the first pair of angle brackets.)

```
function TForm2.GetHTMLTag(      TheString      : String;
                var EndingPosition : Integer ) : String;
var TempString : String;
begin
  { Make the call to find the end of the tag }
  TempString := GetStringToCharacter( TheString , '>' , true ,
   EndingPosition );
  if TempString = '' then
  begin { Malformed HTML token; signal error by empty string & -1 }
    GetHTMLTag := TempString;
    EndingPosition := -1;
  end
  else
  begin { Valid HTML tag; send back entire string & next scan pos }
    GetHTMLTag := TempString;
    EndingPosition := EndingPosition + 1;
  end;
end;
```

13. Move down below the previous code and type in the following assistant function to handle figuring out which HTML tag has been obtained to permit proper handling.

```
function TForm2.ParseHTMLTag( TheString : String ) : Integer;
begin
  case TheString[ 2 ] of
   'A' : begin { Anchor tag; check for type }
          case TheString[ 4 ] of
           'H' : begin
                  if Pos( 'HREF=' , TheString ) = 4 then
                  begin
```

continued on next page

continued from previous page

```
                 ParseHTMLTag := 1; { Valid Link Tag }
                end
                else
                 begin { Malformed tag; return -1 }
                  ParseHTMLTag := -1;
                end;
               end;
          'N' : begin
                if Pos( 'NAME=' , TheString ) = 4 then
                begin
                 ParseHTMLTag := 2; { Valid Anchor Tag }
                end
                else
                 begin { Malformed tag; return -1 }
                  ParseHTMLTag := -1;
                 end;
                end;
                 else
                  begin { Malformed tag; signal error with -1}
                  ParseHTMLTag := -1;
                 end;
                end
                end;
          '/' : begin { Terminator tag }
                 if Pos( '/A>' , TheString ) = 2 then
                 begin
             ParseHTMLTag := 4; { Valid Terminator Tag }
         end
        else
        begin { Malformed tag; return -1 }
        ParseHTMLTag := -1;
      end;
     end;
   else
    begin { Malformed tag; signal error by returning -1 }
     ParseHTMLTag := -1;
   end;
 end;
end;
```

14. Move down below the previous code and type in the following assistant function to handle getting the complete HTML reference (including intervening text).

```
function TForm2.GetCompleteHTMLReference(      TheString      : String;
                          InputType       : Integer;
                       var EndingPosition,
                          OutputType      : Integer ) : String;
var TempString ,
    TempString2 ,
    TempString3   : String;
    HTMLType      : Integer;
begin
```

```
OutputType := 0;
{ Get to first complete HTML Tag and then check }
TempString := GetHTMLTag( TheString , EndingPosition );
if TempString = '' then
begin { Invalid tag; signal error }
  GetCompleteHTMLReference := '';
  EndingPosition := 0;
end
else
begin
  { Find out which HTML Tag it is }
  HTMLType := ParseHTMLTag( TempString );
  case HTMLType of
    -1 : begin { Malformed HTML Tag; signal error }
           GetCompleteHTMLReference := '';
           EndingPosition := 0;
           OutputType := -1;
         end;
     1 : begin { Link Tag; recurse to get terminator }
           if InputType > 0 then
           begin { Inner link not allowed in recursion }
             EndingPosition := 0;
             GetCompleteHTMLReference := '';
             OutputType := -1;
             exit;
           end;
           { Call self with remaining string and recursion indicator }
           { This will get down to the ending </A>                  }
           TempString2 := Copy( TheString , EndingPosition , 255 );
           { Eat off any intervening text not in an HTML tag;  }
           TempString3 :=
            GetStringToCharacter( TempString2 , '<', false,EndingPosition);
           if TempString3 <> '' then
           begin
             TempString2 := Copy( TempString2 , EndingPosition + 1 , 255 );
             { Save the eaten off portion to return properly }
             TempString := TempString + TempString3;
           end;
           TempString3 := GetCompleteHTMLReference( TempString2 ,
            1 , EndingPosition , OutputType );
           { If a blank string is returned abort with error        }
           { otherwise add the returned string to saved first one }
           if Tempstring3 '' then TempString := TempString + TempString3
            else TempString := '';
           { Otherwise return the result }
           GetCompleteHTMLReference := TempString;
           { Output type will be 0;            }
           { by adding 2 signal a linked text }
           OutputType := OutputType + 2;
         end;
     2 : begin { Anchor Tag; recurse to get terminator }
           if InputType > 0 then
           begin { Inner anchor not allowed in recursion }
```

continued on next page

continued from previous page

```
          EndingPosition := 0;
          GetCompleteHTMLReference := '';
          OutputType := -1;
          exit;
        end;
        { Call self with remaining string and recursion indicator }
        { This will get down to the ending </A>                   }
        TempString2 := Copy( TheString , EndingPosition , 255 );
        { Eat off any intervening text not in an HTML tag; }
        TempString3 :=
         GetStringToCharacter( TempString2 , '<', false,EndingPosition);
        if TempString3 <> '' then
        begin
          TempString2 := Copy( TempString2 , EndingPosition + 1 , 255 );
          { Save the eaten off portion to return properly }
          TempString := TempString + TempString3;
        end;
        { If a blank string is returned abort with error         }
        { otherwise add the returned string to saved first one }
        TempString3 <> := GetCompleteHTMLReference( TempString2 ,
         1 , EndingPosition , OutputType );
        if Tempstring3 <> '' then TempString := TempString + TempString3
         else TempString := '';
        { Otherwise return the result }
        GetCompleteHTMLReference := TempString;
        { Output type will be 0;          }
        { by adding 4 signal anchored text }
        OutputType := OutputType + 4;
      end;
    4 : begin { Terminator Tag; valid only inside recursion }
        if InputType < 1 then
        begin { Naked Terminator not allowed (Arnold! Shame on you!) }
          EndingPosition := 0;
          GetCompleteHTMLReference := '';
          exit;
        end;
        { Otherwise just return the terminator symbol }
        GetCompleteHTMLReference := TempString;
      end;
    end;
  end;
  EndingPosition := Length( TempString ) + 1;
end;
```

15. Move down below the previous code and type in the following assistant function to handle obtaining a URL from a more complex string (easy due to bracketing “”).

```
function TForm2.GetURL( TheString : String ) : String;
var TempString : String;
    Counter_1 : Integer;
begin
  TempString := '';
```

```
  { Look for the start of the URL }
  Counter_1 := Pos( '"', TheString );
  if Counter_1 = 0 then
  begin { No valid URL; signal error by empty string }
    GetURL := TempString;
  end
  else
  begin
    { Chop off up through the first quote and get the rest }
    TempString := Copy( TheString , Counter_1 + 1, 255 );
    { Find ending quote }
    Counter_1 := Pos( '"' , TempString );
    if Counter_1 = 0 then
    begin { Malformed URL; signal error by empty string }
      GetURL := '';
    end
    else
    begin { Valid URL; send back without quotes }
      GetURL := Copy( TempString , 1 , Counter_1 - 1 );
    end;
  end;
end;
```

16. Move down below the previous code and type in the following assistant function to handle determining which of the three possible URL types the URL is.

```
function TForm2.ParseURL(      TheString : String;
                  var URL1,
                      URL2      : String ) : Integer;
var TempString : String;
    Counter_1  : Integer;
begin
  { Check the stripped URL for the local jump symbol }
  Counter_1 := Pos( '#' , TheString );
  case Counter_1 of
    0 : begin  { Not found; non-local URL }
          URL1 := TheString; { Send back whole string }
          URL2 := ''; { Null other string }
          ParseURL := 1; { Code for non-local URL}
        end;
    1 : begin  { First character; local URL }
          { Send back local anchor name without # }
          URL1 := Copy( TheString , 2 , 255 );
          URL2 := ''; { Null other string }
          ParseURL := 2; { Code for local URL }
        end;
    2..255 : begin { Later character; jump inside nl URL }
               { Put nonlocal URL in first string }
               URL1 := Copy( TheString , 1 , Counter_1 - 1 );
               { Put jump target in nl URL in second string }
               URL2 := Copy( TheString , Counter_1 + 1 , 255 );
               ParseURL := 3; { Code for nl URL w/link }
```

continued on next page

continued from previous page

```
                end;
   end;
end;
```

17. Move down below the previous code and type in the following assistant function to handle determining the URL type based on the extension of the file name.

```
function TForm2.GetURLType( TheString : String ) : Integer;
var ExtensionString : String;
begin
  { This function assumes a valid URL has been obtained }
  { It determines what type of data is acquired via URL }
  ExtensionString := Uppercase( ExtractFileExt( TheString ));
  if ExtensionString = '.DHT' then
  begin
    GetURLType := 11; { Standard delphi hypertext file }
    exit;
  end;
  GETURLType := -1; { File extension doesn't match known type; signal error }
end;
```

18. Move down below the previous code and type in the following assistant function to handle determining type of anchor reference has been obtained.

```
procedure TForm2.ParseAnchor(     TheString      : String;
                  AnchorType     : Integer;
                var DisplayedText,
                  AnchorText     : String    );
var TempString ,
    TempString2   : String;
    EndingPosition : Integer;
begin
  { Assume already have complete HTML reference; so peel off first tag }
  TempString := GetHTMLTag( TheString , EndingPosition );
  { Store the remaineder }
  TempString2 := Copy( TheString , EndingPosition , 255 );
  { If a text anchor pull out the non HTML string and dump rest }
  { If an image anchor pull out the image URL and dump rest      }
  case AnchorType of
    4 : DisplayedText := GetStringToHTMLTag( TempString2 , EndingPosition );
  end;
  { Pull the URL out of the first string }
  AnchorText := GetURL( TempString );
end;
```

19. Move down below the previous code and type in the following assistant function to handle obtaining the data from a link tag.

```
procedure TForm2.ParseLink(     TheString      : String;
                LinkType       : Integer;
              var DisplayedText,
                LinkURL1,
```

```
              LinkURL2       : String;
          var LinkStatus     : Integer   );
var TempString ,
    TempString2 : String;
    EndingPosition : Integer;
begin
  { Assume already have full HTML reference so pull out first tag }
  TempString := GetHTMLTag( TheString , EndingPosition );
  { Save the rest in a copy }
  TempString2 := Copy( TheString , EndingPosition , 255 );
  { If a text only trigger then get non HTML string }
  { Otherwise peel out the image URL                }
  case LinkType of
    2 : DisplayedText := GetStringToHTMLTag( TempString2 , EndingPosition );
  end;
  { Pull out the local jump , nonlocal jump, or nlj with anchor data }
  { Note that all special file calls are non-local jumps             }
  TempString2 := GetURL( TempString );
  LinkStatus := ParseURL( TempString2 , LinkURL1 , LinkURL2 );
end;
```

20. Move down below the previous code and type in the following assistant function to handle adding a new anchor hypertext link target.

```
function TForm2.CreateNewAnchorLink( AnchorName : String;
              XPos,
               YPos         : Integer ) : Integer;
begin
  { Add a new link record }
  New( TheLIArray[ LinkInsertPosition ] );
  with TheLIArray[ LinkInsertPosition ]^ do
  begin
    LinkType := 0;             { Anchor is 0; used for searching     }
    LinkAnchor := AnchorName;  { Store the target name for searches }
    LinkFile := '';            { No file name                        }
    XPosition := XPos;         { Store the character-based jump     }
    YPosition := YPos;         { position for scrolling (if any)    }
    HasLabel := false;
  end;
  { Send back the record id for use in link jumps }
  CreateNewAnchorLink := LinkInsertPosition;
  { Increment the pointers into the link array for next usage }
  LinkInsertPosition := LinkInsertPosition + 1;
  TotalLinkRecords := TotalLinkRecords + 1;
end;
```

21. Move down below the previous code and type in the following assistant function to handle creating a new hypertext link to a local file target anchor.

```
function TForm2.CreateNewLocalLink( AnchorName,
              FileName    : String;
               TheType     : Integer ) : Integer;
```

continued on next page

continued from previous page

```
begin
  { Add a new link record }
  New( TheLIArray[ LinkInsertPosition ] );
  with TheLIArray[ LinkInsertPosition ]^ do
  begin
    LinkType := TheType;        { Local Link = 1 - 10; 2-10 are special }
    LinkAnchor := AnchorName; { This is target anchor if simple link  }
    LinkFile := FileName;      { This is filename for special link     }
    XPosition := 0;             { These Fields are not used              }
    YPosition := 0;
    HasLabel := true;
  end;
  { Send back the record id for use in link jumps }
  CreateNewLocalLink := LinkInsertPosition;
  { Increment the pointers into the link array for next usage }
  LinkInsertPosition := LinkInsertPosition + 1;
  TotalLinkRecords := TotalLinkRecords + 1;
end;
```

22. Move down below the previous code and type in the following assistant function to handle creating a new hypertext link to a new file (or a special file later on).

```
function TForm2.CreateNewNonLocalLink( AnchorName ,
                      FileName     : String ) : Integer;
begin
  { Add a new link record }
  New( TheLIArray[ LinkInsertPosition ] );
  with TheLIArray[ LinkInsertPosition ]^ do
  begin
    LinkType := 11;             { Non-Local Link }
    LinkAnchor := AnchorName; { This is target anchor in new doc; may be '' }
    LinkFile := FileName;      { This is filename for new file    }
    XPosition := 0;             { These Fields are not used           }
    YPosition := 0;
    HasLabel := true;
  end;
  { Send back the record id for use in jump links }
  CreateNewNonLocalLink := LinkInsertPosition;
  { Increment the pointers into the link array for next usage }
  LinkInsertPosition := LinkInsertPosition + 1;
  TotalLinkRecords := TotalLinkRecords + 1;
end;
```

23. Move down below the previous code and type in the following assistant function to handle matching an anchor call to a specific hypertext record.

```
procedure TForm2.FindLocalAnchor(      TheAnchor : String;
                   var XLoc,
                       YLoc       : Integer );
var Counter_1 : Integer;
    Through   : Boolean;
begin
```

```
  { Use indeterminate loop to check records }
  Through := false;
  { Start at first record }
  Counter_1 := 1;
  { Loop through all current link records for document }
  while not Through do
  begin
    { If past end of the array signal error and exit }
    if Counter_1 > TotalLinkRecords then
    begin
      Counter_1 := -1;
      Through := true;
      XLoc := -1;
      YLoc := -1;
    end
    else
    begin
      { Otherwise grab current link }
      with TheLIArray[ Counter_1 ]^ do
      begin
        { If its an anchor and the name matches }
        if (( LinkAnchor = TheAnchor ) and ( LinkType = 0 )) then
        begin
          { Return its position and exit }
          XLoc := XPosition;
          YLoc := YPosition;
          Through := true;
        end
        else
        begin
          { Otherwise increment counter and keep going }
          Counter_1 := Counter_1 + 1;
        end;
      end;
    end;
  end;
end;
```

24. Move down below the previous code and type in the following assistant function to handle loading a new hypertext file.

```
procedure TForm2.InitializeDHTMLFile( TheFileName , TheAnchorName : String );
var Counter_1 ,
    WhichX    ,
    WhichY       : Integer;
begin
  TotalDisplayRecords := 0;
  for Counter_1 := 1 to TotalLinkRecords do
  begin
    Dispose( TheLIArray[ Counter_1 ] );
  end;
  TotalLinkRecords := 0;
  LinkInsertPosition := 1;
```

continued on next page

continued from previous page

```
  DumpInvalidHTML := false;
  DocumentLoaded := false;
  TheHiddenMemo := TMemo.Create( Self );
  TheHiddenMemo.Parent := Self;
  TheHiddenMemo.Visible := false;
  TheHiddenMemo.Width := Form2.Width;
  TheHiddenMemo.Height := Form2.Height;
  TheHiddenMemo.Lines.LoadFromFile( TheFileName );
  TheStringList.Clear;
  For Counter_1 := 1 to TheHiddenMemo.Lines.Count do
  begin
    TheStringList.Add( TheHiddenMemo.Lines[ Counter_1 - 1 ] );
  end;
  TheHiddenMemo.Free;
  DocumentLoaded := true;
  CreateNewDHTDocument;
    Caption := 'HTML Viewer -- ' + ExtractFileName( TheFilename );
  if TheAnchorName <> '' then
  begin
    FindLocalAnchor( TheAnchorName, WhichX , WhichY );
    TheScrollBox.VertScrollBar.Position := ( PixelsPerLine * WhichY ) -
     TheScrollBox.Height;
  end;
end;
```

25. Move down below the previous code and type in the following assistant function to handle responding to a mouse click on a hypertext link.

```
procedure TForm2.HotClick( Sender : TObject;
             Button: TMouseButton;
             Shift: TShiftState;
             X, Y: Integer );

var TheItem : Integer;
    TheLinkFile ,
    TheLinkAnchor : String;
begin
  { Do dynamic typecast to find out which type of object made call }
  if Sender is HTMLLabel then
  begin { Label hit; treat as text }
    TheItem := HTMLLabel( Sender ).LinkItem;
    { Grab the link record to work with }
    with TheLIArray[ TheItem ]^ do
    begin
      { Branch on type of link (note that 2-5 are not link ids & not used) }
      case LinkType of
        1 : begin { jump within current file }
              TheScrollBox.VertScrollBar.Position :=
               ( YPosition * PixelsPerLine ) - TheScrollBox.Height;
            end;
       11 : begin { jump to new file }
              InitializeDHTMLFile( LinkFile , LinkAnchor );
        end;
```

```
      end;
    end;
  end;
end;
```

26. Move down below the previous code and type in the following assistant function to handle displaying the hypertext in a new document.

```
procedure TForm2.CreateNewDHTDocument;
var TempString1   ,
    TempString2   ,
    TempURL1      ,
    TempURL2      ,
    WorkingString ,
    TheText           : String;
    TheLinkID ,
    TheURLType ,
    LStatus ,
    EndingPosition ,
    CurrentEnd ,
    Counter_1 ,
    CurrentXPosition ,
    CurrentYPosition ,
    CurrentLine       ,
    HTMLKind ,
    ValidResult          : Integer;
    Completed : Boolean;
    TheLabel : TLabel;
begin
  { Create the scrollbox to show the document on }
  TheScrollBox.Free;
  TheScrollBox := TScrollBox.Create( self );
  TheScrollBox.Parent := self;
  TheScrollBox.Align := alclient;
  { Find out height of a line in the document }
  PixelsPerLine := Form2.Canvas.TextHeight( 'W' ) + 2;
  { Set initial Drawing Positions }
  CurrentXPosition := 10;
  CurrentYPosition := 20;
  { Set the current line for line calculations }
  CurrentLine := 1;
  { Loop through the memo and display the lines as hypertext and graphics }
  for Counter_1 := 1 to TheStringList.Count do
  begin
    { Clear the flag to indicate completion of current line }
    Completed := false;
    { Start parsing at the first character }
    EndingPosition := 1;
    CurrentXPosition := 10;
    CurrentYPosition := (( CurrentLine - 1 ) * PixelsPerLine );
    { Get a working copy of the memo line }
    WorkingString := TheStringList.Strings[ Counter_1 - 1 ];
    { Work along the working string until done }
```

continued on next page

continued from previous page

```
    if DumpInvalidHTML then
    begin
      Completed := true;
      TheLabel := TLabel.Create( self );
      TheLabel.Parent := TheScrollBox;
      TheLabel.Font.Color := clBlack;
      TheLabel.Top := CurrentYPosition;
      TheLabel.Left := CurrentXPosition;
      TheLabel.Caption := WorkingString;
      TheLabel.Height := PixelsPerLine - 1;
      TheLabel.Width := Form2.Width - 5;
    end;
    while not Completed do
    begin
      { Eat off up to HTML command }
      TempString1 := GetStringToHTMLTag( WorkingString , CurrentEnd );
      if TempString1  '' then
      begin { Some text to show so show it}
        TheLabel := TLabel.Create( self );
        TheLabel.Parent := TheScrollBox;
        TheLabel.Font.Color := clBlack;
        TheLabel.Top := CurrentYPosition;
        TheLabel.Left := CurrentXPosition;
        TheLabel.Caption := TempString1;
        TheLabel.Height := PixelsPerLine - 1;
        TheLabel.Width := Form2.Width - 5;
        { Move the output pointer along }
        CurrentXPosition := CurrentXPosition +
         Form2.Canvas.TextWidth( TempString1 );
      end;
      { Check for the end of the working string }
      if CurrentEnd > Length( WorkingString ) then
      begin
        Completed := true;
        CurrentLine := CurrentLine + 1;
      end
      else
      begin
        { Chop off the parsed string portion and work with the rest }
        WorkingString := Copy( WorkingString , CurrentEnd , 255 );
        { Assume HTML tag next, so get it }
        TempString1 := GetCompleteHTMLReference( WorkingString , 0 ,
                           CurrentEnd , HTMLKind );
        if TempString1 = '' then
        begin { Bad or malformed HTML Tag; abort processing }
         MessageDlg( 'Bad or malformed HTML Tag! Aborting Processing...' ,
         mtError , [ mbOK ] , 0 );
        DumpInvalidHTML := true;
        TheLabel := TLabel.Create( self );
        TheLabel.Parent := TheScrollBox;
        TheLabel.Font.Color := clBlack;
        TheLabel.Top := CurrentYPosition;
        TheLabel.Left := CurrentXPosition;
```

```
    TheLabel.Caption := WorkingString;
    TheLabel.Height := PixelsPerLine - 1;
    TheLabel.Width := Form2.Width - 5;
    CurrentLine := CurrentLine + 1;
    Completed := true;
  end
  else
   begin { Possibly Valid HTML tag; process it to be sure }
    case HTMLKind of  { parse on type of tag }
      2 : begin { Jump reference; 2 is just text }
          ParseLink( TempString1 , 2 , TheText ,
          TempURL1 , TempURL2 , LStatus );
          case LStatus of { check for other processing }
           1 : begin { Jump link; check for special file type }
               TheURLType := GetURLType( TempURL1 );
               case TheURLTYpe of
                11 : begin { Standard DHT hypertext file }
                 TheLinkID := CreateNewNonLocalLink( '' ,
                 TempURL1 );
                 with TheLIArray[ TheLinkID ]^ do
                 begin
                   TheLabel := HTMLLabel.Create( self );
                   TheLabel.Parent := TheScrollBox;
                   TheLabel.Visible := true;
                   TheLabel.Top := CurrentYPosition;
                   TheLabel.Left := CurrentXPosition;
                   TheLabel.Width :=
                    Form2.Canvas.TextWidth( TheText ) + 2;
                    TheLabel.Height := PixelsPerLine;
                     TheLabel.OnMouseUp := HotClick;
                     TheLabel.Cursor := 5;
                     TheLabel.LinkItem := TheLinkID;
                     TheLabel.Font.Color := clRed;
                     TheLabel.Caption := TheText;
                     CurrentXPosition := CurrentXPosition +
                     Form2.Canvas.TextWidth( TheText );
                  end;
                 end;
              end;
           end;
           2 : begin { Local link; no special processing }
               TheLinkID := CreateNewLocalLink( TempURL1 ,
               '' , 1 );
               with TheLIArray[ TheLinkID ]^ do
               begin
                 TheLabel := HTMLLabel.Create( self );
                 TheLabel.Parent := TheScrollBox;
                 TheLabel.Visible := true;
                 TheLabel.Top := CurrentYPosition;
                 TheLabel.Left := CurrentXPosition;
                 TheLabel.Width :=
                 Form2.Canvas.TextWidth( TheText ) + 2;
                 TheLabel.Height := PixelsPerLine;
                 TheLabel.OnMouseUp := HotClick;
```

continued on next page

continued from previous page

```
                TheLabel.Cursor := 5;
                TheLabel.LinkItem := TheLinkID;
                TheLabel.Font.Color := clRed;
                TheLabel.Caption := TheText;
                CurrentXPosition := CurrentXPosition +
                Form2.Canvas.TextWidth( TheText );
             end;
            end;
           3 : begin { Non local URL with jump; check for DHT type }
               TheURLType := GetURLType( TempURL1 );
               if TheURLType <> 11 then
                begin { Attempt to do local jump in non HT file }
                 {Don't bother at this level; full app needs this}
              end;
               TheLinkID := CreateNewNonLocalLink( TempURL1 ,
               TempURL2 );
               with TheLIArray[ TheLinkID ]^ do
               begin
                TheLabel := HTMLLabel.Create( self );
                TheLabel.Parent := TheScrollBox;
                TheLabel.Visible := true;
                TheLabel.Top := CurrentYPosition;
                TheLabel.Left := CurrentXPosition;
                TheLabel.Width :=
                Form2.Canvas.TextWidth( TheText ) + 2;
                TheLabel.Height := PixelsPerLine;
                TheLabel.OnMouseUp := HotClick;
                TheLabel.Cursor := 5;
                TheLabel.LinkItem := TheLinkID;
                TheLabel.Font.Color := clRed;
                TheLabel.Caption := TheText;
                CurrentXPosition := CurrentXPosition +
                Form2.Canvas.TextWidth( TheText );
             end;
            end;
         end;
        end;
     4 : begin { Anchor reference; 4 is just text }
          ParseAnchor( TempString1 , 4 , TheText , TempURL1 );
          TheLinkID := CreateNewAnchorLink( TempURL1 ,
          CurrentXPosition , CurrentLine );
          TheLabel := TLabel.Create( self );
          TheLabel.Parent := TheScrollBox;
          TheLabel.Font.Color := clRed;
          TheLabel.Top := CurrentYPosition;
          TheLabel.Left := CurrentXPosition;
          TheLabel.Caption := TheText;
          TheLabel.Height := PixelsPerLine - 1;
          TheLabel.Width := Form2.Width - 5;
          CurrentXPosition := CurrentXPosition +
          Form2.Canvas.TextWidth( TheText );
       end;
    end;
 end;
```

```
      { Check for the end of the working string }
      if CurrentEnd > Length( WorkingString ) then
      begin
        CurrentLine := CurrentLine + 1;
        Completed := true;
      end
       else WorkingString := Copy( WorkingString , CurrentEnd , 255 );
     end;
    end;
  end;
  TheScrollBox.VertScrollbar.Visible := true;
  TheScrollBox.VertScrollbar.Range := ( CurrentLine * PixelsPerLine ) + 20;
  TheScrollBox.VertScrollBar.Increment := PixelsPerLine;
end;
```

27. Move back up to the {$R} directive line and add this code below it to load the custom cursor used for linked text..

```
{$R *.DFM}
{$R DHTCUR.RES}
```

28. Compile and test the project.

How it Works

Since most of the program involves string manipulation, there are copious comments in the code itself rather than extensive explanations here. Two points are worth noting however: the use of the TLabel component's OnMouseUp event to activate the hypertext links, and the nature of the URL concept.

Since most pages of hypertext are "sparse," that is they contain relatively few lines of text, it is safe to use the TLabel component to handle the chore of saving and displaying the text for each line, or part of a line. By changing the color of a linked text item to red, the user is shown that this is active text. Further emphasis is placed on the active text by having its Cursor property set to the Hand cursor loaded in the CreateForm method. (This in itself is a useful property of all Delphi components, not just TLabel.)

Once a user clicks on a linked item, however, a problem arises. If the link is within the existing file, things are simple; the scroll box which contains the labels is moved to center the new line of text, or at least place it on the screen. However, if the link is to another file several things have to be done. First, the existing Scrollbox, and its child controls, the label components, have to be removed from memory or they will rapidly eat up system resources and lock Windows. This is easily done with this line of code:

```
TheScrollBox.Free;
```

However, if this code is executed on, say, an OnClick event, a runtime error 210 will be encountered, which is called when an object without valid memory space is accessed. The reason is that after an OnClick, OnMouseDown, OnMouseMove, or similar mouse-based event is processed by the user procedure, the VCL running behind the scenes attempts to contact the component which initially received the message for final processing. Since in this situation, that component has been destroyed via the call to Free on its parent, the application encounters a GPF and the information from the new file is never displayed.

The solution is to use the OnMouseUp event. This event doesn't make the cleanup call, and so it is safe to destroy a calling component during handling of this message. This situation also applies generally, not just to TLabel components.

The URL concept is much more subtle than it might appear. In this simple version, all URLs are either an anchor in the same document (which allows fast scrolling within a given text file) or jumps to other text files. But because a URL is just a filename, it can theoretically be *any type of data the PC can process*. This capability is the basis for all the supercharged power in the applications that follow. It also is capable of almost unlimited expansion, as shown by its use in the HTTP system in use on the Internet with the World Wide Web.

Comments

A simple but effective hypertext editor, which has forms to create all the special HTML tags used in these applications, is found in the DHTEDIT.DPR project on the CD in the GOODIES/PROGRAMS directory.

For an excellent book on programming HTML and WWW applications using Winsock, see *The Internet Programmer's Bible*, by Nathan Wallace, from Waite Group Press.

6.6 How Do I... Play sound files in an HTML document?

COMPLEXITY: EASY

Problem

Now that I have a basic hypertext viewer, I'd like to add support for sound files. Can Delphi handle adding sound to HTML?

Technique

HTML's beauty lies in its ability to handle almost any data format. The core concept behind this capability is the URL, or Universal Resource Locator. A URL is, for purposes of a single PC or LAN application, simply a file name. By interpreting the file extension via more Delphi string manipulation, the viewer created in the previous How-To can add sound support to any HTML jump link.

Steps

Run DHTMLVWR.EXE in the CHAP06/HOWTO06 directory on the CD. Load TEST3.DHT; and you will see a display similar to Figure 6-9. Click on the Chimes

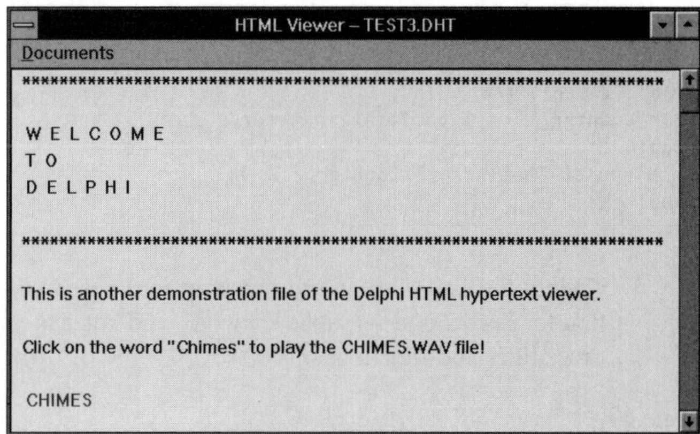

Figure 6-9 DHTMLV2 at run time showing a sound file link

jump link (denoted by red text and the change in the cursor). Assuming your PC has a sound card, you should hear the CHIMES.WAV file distributed with Windows 3.1 being played.

1. Copy the files from How-To 6.5 into a new directory. Rename the unit DHTVIEW2.PAS and the project DHTMLVWR.DPR.
2. Components, properties,and settings remain the same as from How-To 6.5.
3. Select the OnCreate event of Form1 and enter the following highlighted code to initialize the application.

```
procedure TForm2.FormCreate(Sender: TObject);
begin
  TotalLinkRecords := 0;
  LinkInsertPosition := 1;
  Screen.Cursors[ 5 ] := LoadCursor( HInstance , 'HTHAND' );
  DumpInvalidHTML := false;
  DocumentLoaded := false;
  TheStringList := TStringList.Create;
  MediaPlayer1 := TMediaPlayer.Create( Self );
  MediaPlayer1.Parent := self;
  MediaPlayer1.Visible := false;
  TheScrollBox := NIL;
end;
```

4. Select the OnDestroy event of Form2 and enter the following highlighted code to close the application.

```
procedure TForm2.FormDestroy(Sender: TObject);
var Counter_1 : Integer;
begin
  MediaPlayer1.Free;
  for Counter_1 := 1 to TotalLinkRecords do
  begin
    Dispose( TheLIArray[ Counter_1 ] );
  end;
end;
```

5. Go into the Code Editor and move up to the *type* keyword, then find the declaration for Form2 and its *public* keyword, and enter the following highlighted helper procedures and functions.

```
type
  TForm2 = class(TForm)
  public
    { Public declarations }
    procedure HotClick( Sender : TObject;
              Button: TMouseButton;
              Shift: TShiftState;
              X, Y: Integer );
    function GetStringToCharacter(      TheString     : String ;
                     TargetString : String;
                     GetTarget    : Boolean;
                    var ThePosition  : Integer  ) : String;
    function GetStringtoHTMLTag(      TheString       : String;
                    var EndingPosition : Integer ) : String;
    function GetHTMLTag(      TheString       : String;
                    var EndingPosition : Integer ) : String;
    function ParseHTMLTag( TheString : String ) : Integer;
    function GetCompleteHTMLReference(      TheString       : String;
                      InputType       : Integer;
                    var EndingPosition,
                      OutputType      : Integer ) : String;

    function GetURL( TheString : String ) : String;
    function ParseURL(      TheString : String;
             var URL1,
                 URL2      : String ) : Integer;
    function GetURLType( TheString : String ) : Integer;
    procedure ParseAnchor(      TheString      : String;
                 AnchorType     : Integer;
               var DisplayedText,
                 AnchorText     : String    );
    procedure ParseLink(      TheString      : String;
               LinkType       : Integer;
              var DisplayedText,
               LinkURL1,
               LinkURL2       : String;
              var LinkStatus     : Integer   );
    function CreateNewAnchorLink( AnchorName : String;
                XPos,
                YPos        : Integer ) : Integer;
```

```
    function CreateNewLocalLink( AnchorName,
                   FileName    : String;
                   TheType     : Integer ) : Integer;
    function CreateNewNonLocalLink( AnchorName ,
                    FileName     : String ) : Integer;
    procedure FindLocalAnchor(      TheAnchor : String;
                  var XLoc,
                    YLoc       : Integer );
    procedure PlayWaveAudio( TheWaveFile : String );
    procedure InitializeDHTMLFile( TheFileName , TheAnchorName : String );
    procedure CreateNewDHTDocument;
  end;
```

6. Move down below the *var* keyword and type in the following highlighted helper variables.

```
var
  Form2: TForm2;
  TheHiddenMemo : TMemo;
  TheLIArray : LinkItemArray;
  LinkInsertPosition ,
  TotalLinkRecords        : Integer;
  PixelsPerLine : Integer;
  DumpInvalidHTML : Boolean;
  DocumentLoaded : Boolean;
  TheStringList : TStringList;
  MediaPlayer1 : TMediaPlayer;
  TheScrollBox : TScrollBox;
```

7. Move down below the *implementation* keyword and enter this assistant procedure to handle playing a WAV audio file.

```
procedure TForm2.PlayWaveAudio( TheWaveFile : String );
begin
  MediaPlayer1.FileName := TheWaveFile;
  MediaPlayer1.Open;
  MediaPlayer1.Play;
  MediaPlayer1.Close;
end;
```

8. Find the function below and type in the highlighted text to handle determining the URL type based on the extension of the file name, including new types for this How-To.

```
function TForm2.GetURLType( TheString : String ) : Integer;
var ExtensionString : String;
begin
  { This function assumes a valid URL has been obtained }
  { It determines what type of data is acquired via URL }
  ExtensionString := Uppercase( ExtractFileExt( TheString ));
  if ExtensionString = '.DHT' then
```

continued on next page

continued from previous page

```
  begin
    GetURLType := 11; { Standard delphi hypertext file }
    exit;
  end;
  if ExtensionString = '.WAV' then
  begin
    GetURLType := 6; { Windows sound file }
    exit;
  end;
  GETURLType := -1; { File extension doesn't match known type; signal error }
end;
```

9. Find the function below and type in the highlighted text to handle responding to a hypertext link activation on the new file type.

```
procedure TForm2.HotClick( Sender : TOBject;
             Button: TMouseButton;
             Shift: TShiftState;
             X, Y: Integer );

var TheItem : Integer;
    TheLinkFile ,
    TheLinkAnchor : String;
begin
  { Do dynamic typecast to find out which type of object made call }
  if Sender is HTMLLabel then
  begin { Label hit; treat as text }
    TheItem := HTMLLabel( Sender ).LinkItem;
    { Grab the link record to work with }
    with TheLIArray[ TheItem ]^ do
    begin
      { Branch on type of link (note that 2-5 are not link ids & not used) }
      case LinkType of
        1 : begin { jump within current file }
              TheScrollBox.VertScrollBar.Position :=
               ( YPosition * PixelsPerLine ) - TheScrollBox.Height;
            end;
        6 : begin { wave file }
              PlayWaveAudio( LinkFile );
            end;
       11 : begin { jump to new file }
              InitializeDHTMLFile( LinkFile , LinkAnchor );
            end;
      end;
    end;
  end;
end;
```

10. Find the function below and type in the highlighted text to handle displaying hypertext links using the new URL type.

```
procedure TForm2.CreateNewDHTDocument;
var TempString1    ,
   TempString2    ,
   TempURL1       ,
   TempURL2       ,
    WorkingString ,
   TheText           : String;
   TheLinkID ,
   TheURLType ,
   LStatus ,
    EndingPosition ,
   CurrentEnd ,
   Counter_1 ,
   CurrentXPosition ,
   CurrentYPosition ,
   CurrentLine       ,
   HTMLKind ,
   ValidResult           : Integer;
   Completed : Boolean;
   TheLabel : TLabel;
begin
  { Create the scrollbox to show the document on }
  TheScrollBox.Free;
  TheScrollBox := TScrollBox.Create( self );
  TheScrollBox.Parent := self;
  TheScrollBox.Align := alclient;
 { Find out height of a line in the document }
  PixelsPerLine := Form2.Canvas.TextHeight( 'W' ) + 2;
  { Set initial Drawing Positions }
  CurrentXPosition := 10;
  CurrentYPosition := 20;
  { Set the current line for line calculations }
  CurrentLine := 1;
  { Loop through the memo and display the lines as hypertext and graphics }
  for Counter_1 := 1 to TheStringList.Count do
  begin
   { Clear the flag to indicate completion of current line }
   Completed := false;
   { Start parsing at the first character }
   EndingPosition := 1;
   CurrentXPosition := 10;
   CurrentYPosition := (( CurrentLine - 1 ) * PixelsPerLine );
   { Get a working copy of the memo line }
   WorkingString := TheStringList.Strings[ Counter_1 - 1 ];
   { Work along the working string until done }
   if DumpInvalidHTML then
   begin
    Completed := true;
    TheLabel := TLabel.Create( self );
    TheLabel.Parent := TheScrollBox;
    TheLabel.Font.Color := clBlack;
    TheLabel.Top := CurrentYPosition;
    TheLabel.Left := CurrentXPosition;
    TheLabel.Caption := WorkingString;
```

continued on next page

continued from previous page

```
    TheLabel.Height := PixelsPerLine - 1;
    TheLabel.Width := Form2.Width - 5;
   end;
    while not Completed do
    begin
     { Eat off up to HTML command }
     TempString1 := GetStringToHTMLTag( WorkingString , CurrentEnd );
     if TempString1  '' then
     begin { Some text to show so show it}
      TheLabel := TLabel.Create( self );
      TheLabel.Parent := TheScrollBox;
      TheLabel.Font.Color := clBlack;
      TheLabel.Top := CurrentYPosition;
      TheLabel.Left := CurrentXPosition;
      TheLabel.Caption := TempString1;
      TheLabel.Height := PixelsPerLine - 1;
      TheLabel.Width := Form2.Width - 5;
      { Move the output pointer along }
      CurrentXPosition := CurrentXPosition +
       Form2.Canvas.TextWidth( TempString1 );
    end;
     { Check for the end of the working string }
     if CurrentEnd > Length( WorkingString ) then
    begin
     Completed := true;
     CurrentLine := CurrentLine + 1;
    end
    else
    begin
     { Chop off the parsed string portion and work with the rest }
     WorkingString := Copy( WorkingString , CurrentEnd , 255 );
     { Assume HTML tag next, so get it }
     TempString1 := GetCompleteHTMLReference( WorkingString , 0 ,
                      CurrentEnd , HTMLKind );
     if TempString1 = '' then
     begin { Bad or malformed HTML Tag; abort processing }
      MessageDlg( 'Bad or malformed HTML Tag! Aborting Processing...' ,
      mtError , [ mbOK ] , 0 );
     DumpInvalidHTML := true;
     TheLabel := TLabel.Create( self );
     TheLabel.Parent := TheScrollBox;
     TheLabel.Font.Color := clBlack;
     TheLabel.Top := CurrentYPosition;
     TheLabel.Left := CurrentXPosition;
     TheLabel.Caption := WorkingString;
     TheLabel.Height := PixelsPerLine - 1;
     TheLabel.Width := Form2.Width - 5;
     CurrentLine := CurrentLine + 1;
     Completed := true;
   end
    else
    begin { Possibly Valid HTML tag; process it to be sure }
    case HTMLKind of  { parse on type of tag }
```

```
2 : begin { Jump reference; 2 is just text }
    ParseLink( TempString1 , 2 , TheText ,
    TempURL1 , TempURL2 , LStatus );
    case LStatus of { check for other processing }
            1 : begin { Jump link; check for special file type }
                TheURLType := GetURLType( TempURL1 );
                case TheURLTYpe of
                  6 : begin { Wave file }
                      TheLinkID := CreateNewLocalLink( '' ,
                      TempURL1 , TheURLType );
                      with TheLIArray[ TheLinkID ]^ do
                      begin
                        TheLabel := HTMLLabel.Create( self );
                        TheLabel.Parent := TheScrollBox;
                        TheLabel.Visible := true;
                        TheLabel.Top := CurrentYPosition;
                        TheLabel.Left := CurrentXPosition;
                        TheLabel.Width :=
                        Form2.Canvas.TextWidth( TheText ) + 2;
                        TheLabel.Height := PixelsPerLine;
                        TheLabel.OnMouseUp := HotClick;
                        TheLabel.Cursor := 5;
                        TheLabel.LinkItem := TheLinkID;
                        TheLabel.Font.Color := clRed;
                        TheLabel.Caption := TheText;
                        CurrentXPosition := CurrentXPosition +
                        Form2.Canvas.TextWidth( TheText );
                    end;
                  end;
                  11 : begin { Standard DHT hypertext file }
                       TheLinkID := CreateNewNonLocalLink( '' ,
                       TempURL1 );
                       with TheLIArray[ TheLinkID ]^ do
                       begin
                         TheLabel := HTMLLabel.Create( self );
                         TheLabel.Parent := TheScrollBox;
                         TheLabel.Visible := true;
                         TheLabel.Top := CurrentYPosition;
                         TheLabel.Left := CurrentXPosition;
                         TheLabel.Width :=
                          Form2.Canvas.TextWidth( TheText ) + 2;
                          TheLabel.Height := PixelsPerLine;
                          TheLabel.OnMouseUp := HotClick;
                          TheLabel.Cursor := 5;
                          TheLabel.LinkItem := TheLinkID;
                          TheLabel.Font.Color := clRed;
                          TheLabel.Caption := TheText;
                          CurrentXPosition := CurrentXPosition +
                          Form2.Canvas.TextWidth( TheText );
                       end;
                     end;
                  end;
                end;
              2 : begin { Local link; no special processing }
```

continued on next page

continued from previous page

```
          TheLinkID := CreateNewLocalLink( TempURL1 ,
          '' , 1 );
          with TheLIArray[ TheLinkID ]^ do
          begin
            TheLabel := HTMLLabel.Create( self );
            TheLabel.Parent := TheScrollBox;
            TheLabel.Visible := true;
            TheLabel.Top := CurrentYPosition;
            TheLabel.Left := CurrentXPosition;
            TheLabel.Width :=
             Form2.Canvas.TextWidth( TheText ) + 2;
            TheLabel.Height := PixelsPerLine;
            TheLabel.OnMouseUp := HotClick;
            TheLabel.Cursor := 5;
            TheLabel.LinkItem := TheLinkID;
            TheLabel.Font.Color := clRed;
            TheLabel.Caption := TheText;
            CurrentXPosition := CurrentXPosition +
            Form2.Canvas.TextWidth( TheText );
         end;
       end;
     3 : begin { Non local URL with jump; check for DHT type }
         TheURLType := GetURLType( TempURL1 );
         if TheURLType  11 then
          begin { Attempt to do local jump in non HT file }
           {Dont bother at this level; full app needs this}
         end;
          TheLinkID := CreateNewNonLocalLink( TempURL1 ,
          TempURL2 );
          with TheLIArray[ TheLinkID ]^ do
          begin
            TheLabel := HTMLLabel.Create( self );
            TheLabel.Parent := TheScrollBox;
            TheLabel.Visible := true;
            TheLabel.Top := CurrentYPosition;
            TheLabel.Left := CurrentXPosition;
            TheLabel.Width :=
             Form2.Canvas.TextWidth( TheText ) + 2;
            TheLabel.Height := PixelsPerLine;
            TheLabel.OnMouseUp := HotClick;
            TheLabel.Cursor := 5;
            TheLabel.LinkItem := TheLinkID;
            TheLabel.Font.Color := clRed;
            TheLabel.Caption := TheText;
            CurrentXPosition := CurrentXPosition +
             Form2.Canvas.TextWidth( TheText );
          end;
         end;
      end;
   end;
  4 : begin { Anchor reference; 4 is just text }
      ParseAnchor( TempString1 , 4 , TheText , TempURL1 );
```

```
                TheLinkID := CreateNewAnchorLink( TempURL1 ,
                CurrentXPosition , CurrentLine );
                TheLabel := TLabel.Create( self );
                TheLabel.Parent := TheScrollBox;
                TheLabel.Font.Color := clRed;
                TheLabel.Top := CurrentYPosition;
                TheLabel.Left := CurrentXPosition;
                TheLabel.Caption := TheText;
                TheLabel.Height := PixelsPerLine - 1;
                TheLabel.Width := Form2.Width - 5;
                CurrentXPosition := CurrentXPosition +
                 Form2.Canvas.TextWidth( TheText );
              end;
        end;
      end;
      { Check for the end of the working string }
      if CurrentEnd > Length( WorkingString ) then
      begin
       CurrentLine := CurrentLine + 1;
       Completed := true;
     end
      else WorkingString := Copy( WorkingString , CurrentEnd , 255 );
    end;
  end;
 end;
 TheScrollBox.VertScrollbar.Visible := true;
 TheScrollBox.VertScrollbar.Range := ( CurrentLine * PixelsPerLine ) + 20;
 TheScrollBox.VertScrollBar.Increment := PixelsPerLine;
end;
```

11. Compile and test the project.

How it Works

Due to the protean nature of the URL concept, adding .WAV file support to the viewer is almost trivial. All that is required is putting in a TMediaPlayer component and calling it with the filename of the URL.

There is one point of note, however; you may run the application and the .WAV file does not play. This is usually caused by the TMediaPlayer component being unable to create itself due to memory or resource limitations. If this happens, close some applications to free memory and/or resources, and the application should behave properly.

Comments

URLs are far more powerful than the current application indicates. The full specifications include Internet protocol elements which allow finding any file on any computer anywhere in the world. The same protocols can be adapted for use over LANs as well, or to make calls to remove servers for database uses.

6.7 How Do I...
Show graphics files in an HTML document?

COMPLEXITY: ADVANCED

Problem

Now for the hard part; I need to put graphical images in my presentation as part of the text. Also, I need to use the more common GIF format rather than the Windows BMP file type. Can Delphi deal with this additional complexity in an HTML file?

Technique

Since URLs can be any type of file, the HTML part of this How-To is easy. The complexity comes in due to the need to keep the images aligned with the text, and to handle the non-standard GIF format common on the Internet and commercial online services and bbs systems. Fortunately, Delphi's TImage component can handle all these problems, along with the TBitmap object for GIF conversion.

Steps

Run DHTMLVWR.EXE from the CHAP06\HOWTO07 directory and load TEST4.DHT; you should see a display similar to Figure 6-10. Click on the picture labeled "Delphi opens a universe of programming possibilities" and you will jump to

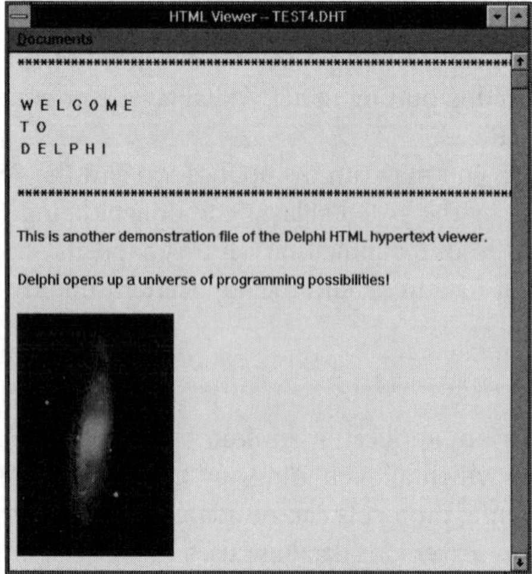

Figure 6-10 DHTMLVWR at run time showing a hypermedia graphics and text file

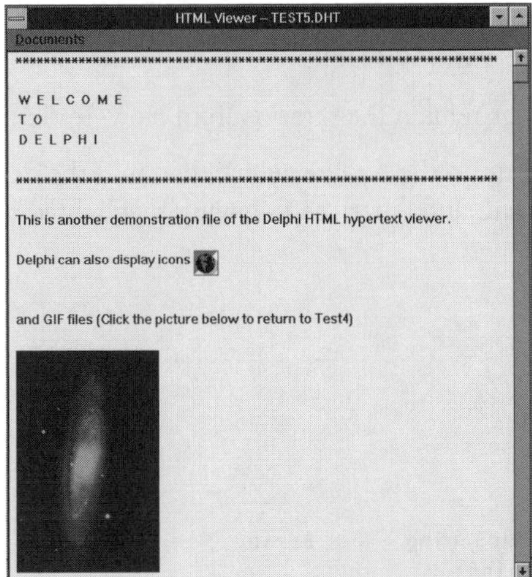

Figure 6-11 DHTMLVWR at run time showing another hypermedia file after a jump

TEST5.DHT, as shown in Figure 6-11. Open TEST4.DHT and TEST5.DHT in Notepad and you will see a display similar to Figure 6-12; notice that the documents use .ICO, .BMP, and .GIF file formats.

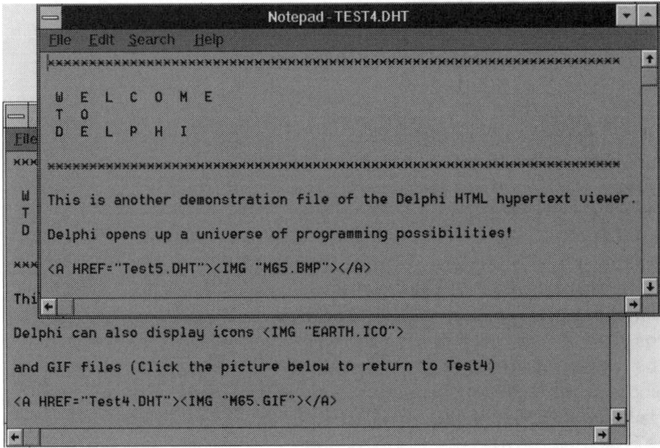

Figure 6-12 NOTEPAD open showing two HTML hypermedia files' syntax

1. Copy the files from How-To 6.6 into a new directory. Rename the unit DHTVIEW3.PAS and the project DHTMLVWR.DPR.
2. Components, properties, and settings remain the same as from How-To 6.5.
3. Go into the Code Editor and move up to the *type* keyword, then find the declaration for Form2 and its *public* keyword, and enter the following highlighted helper procedures and functions.

```
type
  TForm2 = class(TForm)
  public
    { Public declarations }
    procedure HotClick( Sender : TObject;
              Button: TMouseButton;
              Shift: TShiftState;
              X, Y: Integer );
    function GetStringToCharacter(     TheString     : String ;
                      TargetString : String;
                      GetTarget    : Boolean;
                  var ThePosition  : Integer  ) : String;
    function GetStringtoHTMLTag(      TheString       : String;
                     var EndingPosition : Integer ) : String;
    function GetHTMLTag(      TheString       : String;
                 var EndingPosition : Integer ) : String;
    function ParseHTMLTag( TheString : String ) : Integer;
    function GetCompleteHTMLReference(      TheString       : String;
                       InputType       : Integer;
                      var EndingPosition,
                       OutputType      : Integer ) :
                  String;
    function GetURL( TheString : String ) : String;
    function ParseURL(      TheString : String;
             var URL1,
                 URL2       : String ) : Integer;
    function GetURLType( TheString : String ) : Integer;
    procedure ParseAnchor(     TheString      : String;
                   AnchorType     : Integer;
                  var DisplayedText,
                   AnchorText     : String    );
    procedure ParseLink(      TheString      : String;
                  LinkType       : Integer;
                 var DisplayedText,
                  LinkURL1,
                  LinkURL2       : String;
                 var LinkStatus     : Integer  );
    function CreateNewAnchorLink( AnchorName : String;
                   XPos,
                   YPos          : Integer ) : Integer;
    function CreateNewLocalLink( AnchorName,
                   FileName    : String;
                   TheType     : Integer ) : Integer;
    function CreateNewNonLocalLink( AnchorName ,
                    FileName     : String ) : Integer;
    procedure FindLocalAnchor(      TheAnchor : String;
```

```
                var XLoc,
                 YLoc      : Integer );
    function CreateNewRawImage(      TheURL        : String;
                     CurrentX ,
                     CurrentY      : Integer;
                   var ImageWidth ,
                     ImageHeight   : Integer ) : Integer;
    procedure AddImage(     TheURL        : String;
                 CurrentX ,
                 CurrentY      : Integer;
               var ImageWidth ,
                 ImageHeight   : Integer );
    procedure PlayWaveAudio( TheWaveFile : String );
    procedure InitializeDHTMLFile( TheFileName , TheAnchorName : String );
    procedure CreateNewDHTDocument;
end;
```

4. Still in the Code Editor, move down below the *end* keyword for the Form2 type declaration, and enter the following highlighted assistant type definitions.

```
  HTMLLabel = class( TLabel )
    private
      LinkItem : Integer;
  end;
  HTMLImage = class( TImage )
    private
      LinkItem : Integer;
  end;
  PLinkItemRecord = ^LinkItemRecord;
  LinkItemRecord = record
    LinkFile : String;
    LinkAnchor : String;
    ImageFile : String;
    LinkType,
    XPosition ,
    YPosition    : Integer;
    HasImage ,
    HasLabel : Boolean;
    TheLabel : HTMLLabel;
    TheImage : HTMLImage;
  end;
  LinkItemArray = array[ 1 .. 255 ] of PLinkItemRecord;
```

5. Move down below the *implementation* keyword and enter this assistant procedure to handle obtaining a GIF file's image.

Note: The PGif type is declared in the CCGIF.PAS file which will be included in the Uses clause later.

```
procedure GetGifFile( TheBitmap : TBitmap; TheFileName : String );
var thebuffer : array[ 0..255] of char;
    TheGif : PGif;
```

continued on next page

continued from previous page

```
begin
  StrPCopy( TheBuffer , TheFilename );
  TheGif := NEW( PGif , Init( theBuffer ));
  TheBitmap.Width := TheGif^.ImageDescriptor.ImageWidth;
  TheBitmap.Height := TheGif^.ImageDescriptor.ImageHeight;
  TheGif^.Decode( false , TheBitmap );
  Dispose( TheGif , Done );
end;
```

6. Move down below the previous procedure and enter this assistant procedure to handle placing a new image on the display.

```
function TForm2.CreateNewRawImage(      TheURL          : String;
                    CurrentX ,
                    CurrentY      : Integer;
                  var ImageWidth ,
                    ImageHeight   : Integer ) : Integer;
var URLType : Integer;
   TemporaryBitmap : TBitmap;
begin
  URLType := GetURLType( TheURL );
  if (( URLType < 2 ) or ( URLType > 5 )) then
  begin  { Signal error on invalid image file format }
    CreateNewRawImage := -1;
    exit;
  end;
  { Add a new link record }
  New( TheLIArray[ LinkInsertPosition ] );
  with TheLIArray[ LinkInsertPosition ]^ do
  begin
   LinkType := 12;      { 12 is raw image without features        }
   LinkAnchor := '';   { This is target anchor if simple link  }
   LinkFile := '';     { This is filename for special link      }
   XPosition := 0;      { These Fields are not used               }
   ImageFile := TheURL;
   YPosition := 0;
   HasImage := true;
   HasLabel := false;
   TheImage := HTMLImage.Create( self );
   TheImage.Parent := TheScrollBox;
   case URLType of
     2..4 : begin { Windows compatible file format }
           TheImage.Picture.LoadFromFile( TheURL );
           TheImage.Visible := true;
           TheImage.Width := TheImage.Picture.Width;
           TheImage.Height := TheImage.Picture.Height;
           ImageWidth := TheImage.Picture.Width;
           ImageHeight := TheImage.Picture.Height;
           TheImage.Top := CurrentY;
           TheImage.Left := CurrentX;
            {TheScrollBox.InsertComponent( TheImage );}
         end;
    5     : begin { GIF format; add gif code }
```

```
          TemporaryBitmap := TBitmap.Create;
          GetGifFile( TemporaryBitmap , TheURL );
          TheImage.Top := CurrentY;
          TheImage.Left := CurrentX;
          TheImage.Picture.Bitmap.Height := TemporaryBitmap.Height;
          TheImage.Picture.Bitmap.Width := TemporaryBitmap.Width;
          TheImage.Picture.Bitmap.Canvas.Copyrect( Rect( 0 , 0 ,
          TemporaryBitmap.Width , TemporaryBitmap.Height ) ,
          TemporaryBitmap.Canvas , Rect( 0 , 0 ,TemporaryBitmap.Width,
          TemporaryBitmap.Height ));
          TemporaryBitmap.Free;
          TheImage.Height := TheImage.Picture.Bitmap.Height;
          TheImage.Width := TheImage.Picture.Bitmap.Width;
       end;
    end;
  end;
  { Send back the record id for use in paintboxes }
  CreateNewRawImage := LinkInsertPosition;
  { Increment the pointers into the link array for next usage }
  LinkInsertPosition := LinkInsertPosition + 1;
  TotalLinkRecords := TotalLinkRecords + 1;
end;
```

7. Move down below the previous procedure and enter this assistant procedure to handle adding an image to an existing hypertext link.

```
procedure TForm2.AddImage(     TheURL        : String;
               CurrentX ,
               CurrentY      : Integer;
             var ImageWidth ,
               ImageHeight   : Integer );
var URLType : Integer;
   TemporaryBitmap : TBitmap;
begin
 URLType := GetURLType( TheURL );
 if (( URLType < 2 ) or ( URLType > 5 )) then
 begin  { Signal error on invalid image file format }
   exit;
 end;
 { Add a new image }
 with TheLIArray[ TotalLinkRecords ]^ do
 begin
  ImageFile := TheURL;
  HasImage := true;
  TheImage := HTMLImage.Create( self );
  TheImage.Parent := TheScrollBox;
  case URLType of
   2..4 : begin { Windows compatible file format }
         TheImage.Picture.LoadFromFile( TheURL );
         TheImage.Visible := true;
         TheImage.Width := TheImage.Picture.Width;
         TheImage.Height := TheImage.Picture.Height;
         ImageWidth := TheImage.Picture.Width;
```

continued on next page

continued from previous page

```
          ImageHeight := TheImage.Picture.Height;
          TheImage.Top := CurrentY;
          TheImage.Left := CurrentX;
          {TheScrollBox.InsertComponent( TheImage );}
        end;
   5    : begin { GIF format; add gif code }
          TemporaryBitmap := TBitmap.Create;
          GetGifFile( TemporaryBitmap , TheURL );
          TheImage.Top := CurrentY;
          TheImage.Left := CurrentX;
          TheImage.Picture.Bitmap.Height := TemporaryBitmap.Height;
          TheImage.Picture.Bitmap.Width := TemporaryBitmap.Width;
          TheImage.Picture.Bitmap.Canvas.Copyrect( Rect( 0 , 0 ,
          TemporaryBitmap.Width , TemporaryBitmap.Height ) ,
          TemporaryBitmap.Canvas , Rect( 0 , 0 ,TemporaryBitmap.Width,
          TemporaryBitmap.Height ));
          TemporaryBitmap.Free;
          TheImage.Height := TheImage.Picture.Bitmap.Height;
          TheImage.Width := TheImage.Picture.Bitmap.Width;
          ImageWidth := TheImage.Width;
          ImageHeight := TheImage.Height;
        end;
    end;
  end;
end;
```

8. Find the following procedure in the code and add the highlighted items to allow recognition of image HTML tags.

```
function TForm2.ParseHTMLTag( TheString : String ) : Integer;
begin
 case TheString[ 2 ] of
 'A' : begin { Anchor tag; check for type }
      case TheString[ 4 ] of
      'H' : begin
           if Pos( 'HREF=' , TheString ) = 4 then
           begin
            ParseHTMLTag := 1; { Valid Link Tag }
          end
          else
           begin { Malformed tag; return -1 }
            ParseHTMLTag := -1;
          end;
         end;
      'N' : begin
           if Pos( 'NAME=' , TheString ) = 4 then
           begin
            ParseHTMLTag := 2; { Valid Anchor Tag }
           end
           else
            begin { Malformed tag; return -1 }
             ParseHTMLTag := -1;
            end;
```

```
          end;
       else
        begin { Malformed tag; signal error with -1}
        ParseHTMLTag := -1;
       end;
      end
     end;
 'I' : begin { Image tag }
       if Pos( 'IMG ' , TheString ) = 2 then
       begin
        ParseHTMLTag := 3; { Valid Image Tag }
       end
       else
        begin { Malformed tag; return -1 }
         ParseHTMLTag := -1;
       end;
     end;
 '/' : begin { Terminator tag }
       if Pos( '/A>' , TheString ) = 2 then
       begin
        ParseHTMLTag := 4; { Valid Terminator Tag }
      end
      else
       begin { Malformed tag; return -1 }
        ParseHTMLTag := -1;
       end;
      end;
    else
    begin { Malformed tag; signal error by returning -1 }
     ParseHTMLTag := -1;
   end;
 end;
end;
```

9. Find the following procedure in the code and add the highlighted items to handle getting the complete HTML reference (including intervening text and image tags).

```
function TForm2.GetCompleteHTMLReference(      TheString      : String;
                      InputType      : Integer;
                    var EndingPosition,
                      OutputType     : Integer ) : String;
var TempString ,
   TempString2 ,
   TempString3   : String;
   HTMLType      : Integer;
begin
 OutputType := 0;
 { Get to first complete HTML Tag and then check }
 TempString := GetHTMLTag( TheString , EndingPosition );
 if TempString = '' then
 begin { Invalid tag; signal error }
  GetCompleteHTMLReference := '';
  EndingPosition := 0;
end
```

continued on next page

continued from previous page

```
else
begin
 { Find out which HTML Tag it is }
 HTMLType := ParseHTMLTag( TempString );
 case HTMLType of
  -1 : begin { Malformed HTML Tag; signal error }
        GetCompleteHTMLReference := '';
        EndingPosition := 0;
        OutputType := -1;
     end;
   1 : begin { Link Tag; recurse to get terminator }
        if InputType > 0 then
        begin { Inner link not allowed in recursion }
        EndingPosition := 0;
        GetCompleteHTMLReference := '';
        OutputType := -1;
       exit;
    end;
     { Call self with remaining string and recursion indicator }
     { This will get down to the ending </A> including an IMG  }
     TempString2 := Copy( TheString , EndingPosition , 255 );
     { Eat off any intervening text not in an HTML tag; <IMG ok }
     TempString3 :=
      GetStringToCharacter( TempString2 ,'<',false ,EndingPosition );
     if TempString3 <> '' then
     begin
       TempString2 := Copy( TempString2 , EndingPosition + 1 , 255 );
       { Save the eaten off portion to return properly }
       TempString := TempString + TempString3;
     end;
      TempString3 := GetCompleteHTMLReference( TempString2 ,
      1 , EndingPosition , OutputType );
      { If a blank string is returned abort with error        }
      { otherwise add the returned string to saved first one }
      if Tempstring3 '' then TempString := TempString + TempString3
      else TempString := '';
      { Otherwise return the result }
      GetCompleteHTMLReference := TempString;
      { Output type will be 0 if not an image and 1 otherwise;  }
      { by adding 2 signal either a linked text or linked image }
      OutputType := OutputType + 2;
   end;
  2 : begin { Anchor Tag; recurse to get terminator }
       if InputType > 0 then
       begin { Inner anchor not allowed in recursion }
        EndingPosition := 0;
        GetCompleteHTMLReference := '';
        OutputType := -1;
       exit;
    end;
      { Call self with remaining string and recursion indicator }
      { This will get down to the ending </A> including an IMG  }
      TempString2 := Copy( TheString , EndingPosition , 255 );
      { Eat off any intervening text not in an HTML tag; <IMG ok }
```

```
TempString3 :=
 GetStringToCharacter( TempString2 , '<',false,EndingPosition );
if TempString3 <> '' then
begin
  TempString2 := Copy( TempString2 , EndingPosition + 1 , 255 );
  { Save the eaten off portion to return properly }
  TempString := TempString + TempString3;
end;
 { If a blank string is returned abort with error       }
 { otherwise add the returned string to saved first one }
 TempString3 := GetCompleteHTMLReference( TempString2 ,
 1 , EndingPosition , OutputType );
 if Tempstring3 <> '' then TempString := TempString + TempString3
 else TempString := '';
 { Otherwise return the result }
 GetCompleteHTMLReference := TempString;
 { Output type will be 0 if not an image and 1 otherwise;    }
 { by adding 4 signal either anchored text or anchored image }
 OutputType := OutputType + 4;
end;
3 : begin { Image Tag; may need to recurse to get terminator }
   if InputType = 0 then
    begin { not recursing,so won't have terminator; return current }
    GetCompleteHTMLReference := Tempstring;
    OutputType := 1;
    exit;
   end
   else
   begin
    if InputType = 2 then
     begin { In secondary recursion, so this is an error }
     GetCompleteHTMLReference := '';
     EndingPosition := 0;
     OutputType := -1;
     Exit;
   end
   else
   begin { Recursing inside Link or Anchor; get final terminator}
      TempString2 := Copy( TheString , EndingPosition , 255 );
     { Eat off any intervening text not in an HTML tag; <IMG ok }
     TempString3 :=
       GetStringToCharacter(TempString2,'<',false,EndingPosition);
    if TempString3 <> '' then
    begin
       TempString2 := Copy(TempString2 ,EndingPosition + 1 ,255);
     { Save the eaten off portion to return properly }
       TempString := TempString + TempString3;
    end;
     { Call self again with last string portion and level 2 flag}
     TempString3 := GetCompleteHTMLReference( TempString2 ,
      2 , EndingPosition , OutputType );
      { Signal error with empty string or put together last bit }
      if Tempstring3 <> '' then TempString :=
       TempString + TempString3 else TempString := '';
      { Return string and signal image output }
```

continued on next page

continued from previous page

```
            GetCompleteHTMLReference := TempString;
           OutputType := 1;
          end;
         end;
       end;
     4 : begin { Terminator Tag; valid only inside recursion }
        if InputType < 1 then
        begin { Naked Terminator not allowed (Arnold! Shame on you!) }
         EndingPosition := 0;
         GetCompleteHTMLReference := '';
         exit;
        end;
         { Otherwise just return the terminator symbol }
        GetCompleteHTMLReference := TempString;
      end;
    end;
  end;
 EndingPosition := Length( TempString ) + 1;
end;
```

10. Find the function below and type in the highlighted text to handle determining the URL type based on the extension of the file name, including new types for this How-To.

```
function TForm2.GetURLType( TheString : String ) : Integer;
var ExtensionString : String;
begin
  { This function assumes a valid URL has been obtained }
  { It determines what type of data is acquired via URL }
  ExtensionString := Uppercase( ExtractFileExt( TheString ));
  if ExtensionString = '.DHT' then
  begin
    GetURLType := 11; { Standard delphi hypertext file }
    exit;
  end;
  if ExtensionString = '.BMP' then
  begin
    GetURLType := 2; { Bitmap image file; only valid in IMG URL }
    exit;
  end;
  if ExtensionString = '.ICO' then
  begin
    GetURLType := 3; { Windows Icon image file; only valid in IMG URL }
    exit;
  end;
  if ExtensionString = '.WMF' then
  begin
    GetURLType := 4; { Windows Metafile image file; only valid in IMG URL }
    exit;
  end;
  if ExtensionString = '.GIF' then
  begin
    GetURLType := 5; { GIF image file; only valid in IMG URL }
```

```
    exit;
  end;
  if ExtensionString = '.WAV' then
  begin
    GetURLType := 6; { Windows sound file }
    exit;
  end;
  GETURLType := -1; { File extension doesn't match known type; signal error }
end;
```

11. Find the function below and type in the highlighted text to handle getting an image URL when parsing an anchor tag.

```
procedure TForm2.ParseAnchor(      TheString      : String;
                   AnchorType     : Integer;
                 var DisplayedText,
                   AnchorText     : String    );
var TempString ,
   TempString2  : String;
   EndingPosition : Integer;
begin
 { Assume already have complete HTML reference; so peel off first tag }
 TempString := GetHTMLTag( TheString , EndingPosition );
 { Store the remaineder }
 TempString2 := Copy( TheString , EndingPosition , 255 );
 { If a text anchor pull out the non HTML string and dump rest }
 { If an image anchor pull out the image URL and dump rest     }
 case AnchorType of
  4 : DisplayedText := GetStringToHTMLTag( TempString2 , EndingPosition );
  5 : DisplayedText := GetURL( TempString2 );
 end;
 { Pull the URL out of the first string }
 AnchorText := GetURL( TempString );
end;
```

12. Find the function below and type in the highlighted text to handle obtaining an image URL when parsing a link tag.

```
procedure TForm2.ParseLink(      TheString      : String;
                   LinkType       : Integer;
                 var DisplayedText,
                   LinkURL1,
                   LinkURL2       : String;
                 var LinkStatus     : Integer   );
var TempString ,
   TempString2 : String;
   EndingPosition : Integer;
begin
 { Assume already have full HTML reference so pull out first tag }
 TempString := GetHTMLTag( TheString , EndingPosition );
 { Save the rest in a copy }
 TempString2 := Copy( TheString , EndingPosition , 255 );
 { If a text only trigger then get non HTML string }
 { Otherwise peel out the image URL                 }
 case LinkType of
```

continued on next page

continued from previous page

```
    2 : DisplayedText := GetStringToHTMLTag( TempString2 , EndingPosition );
    3 : DisplayedText := GetURL( TempString2 );
  end;
  { Pull out the local jump , nonlocal jump, or nlj with anchor data }
  { Note that all special file calls are non-local jumps             }
  TempString2 := GetURL( TempString );
  LinkStatus := ParseURL( TempString2 , LinkURL1 , LinkURL2 );
end;
```

13. Find the function below and type in the highlighted text to handle adding a new anchor hypertext link target with image information.

```
function TForm2.CreateNewAnchorLink( AnchorName : String;
                  XPos,
                  YPos       : Integer ) : Integer;
begin
 { Add a new link record }
 New( TheLIArray[ LinkInsertPosition ] );
 with TheLIArray[ LinkInsertPosition ]^ do
 begin
  LinkType := 0;             { Anchor is 0; used for searching    }
  LinkAnchor := AnchorName;  { Store the target name for searches }
  LinkFile := '';            { No file name                       }
  XPosition := XPos;          { Store the character-based jump    }
  YPosition := YPos;          { position for scrolling (if any)   }
  ImageFile := '';
  HasImage := false;
  HasLabel := false;
 end;
 { Send back the record id for use in link jumps }
 CreateNewAnchorLink := LinkInsertPosition;
 { Increment the pointers into the link array for next usage }
 LinkInsertPosition := LinkInsertPosition + 1;
 TotalLinkRecords := TotalLinkRecords + 1;
end;
```

14. Find the function below and type in the highlighted text to handle adding a new hypertext link to a same file target anchor with image information.

```
function TForm2.CreateNewLocalLink( AnchorName,
                  FileName   : String;
                  TheType    : Integer ) : Integer;
begin
 { Add a new link record }
 New( TheLIArray[ LinkInsertPosition ] );
 with TheLIArray[ LinkInsertPosition ]^ do
 begin
   LinkType := TheType;       { Local Link = 1 - 10; 2-10 are special }
   LinkAnchor := AnchorName; { This is target anchor if simple link  }
   LinkFile := FileName;      { This is filename for special link     }
   XPosition := 0;             { These Fields are not used             }
   ImageFile := '';
   YPosition := 0;
```

```
    HasImage := false;
    HasLabel := true;
  end;
  { Send back the record id for use in link jumps }
  CreateNewLocalLink := LinkInsertPosition;
  { Increment the pointers into the link array for next usage }
  LinkInsertPosition := LinkInsertPosition + 1;
  TotalLinkRecords := TotalLinkRecords + 1;
end;
```

15. Find the function below and type in the highlighted text to handle adding a new hypertext link to different file (or a special file) with image information.

```
function TForm2.CreateNewNonLocalLink( AnchorName ,
                    FileName    : String ) : Integer;
begin
  { Add a new link record }
  New( TheLIArray[ LinkInsertPosition ] );
  with TheLIArray[ LinkInsertPosition ]^ do
  begin
    LinkType := 11;            { Non-Local Link }
    LinkAnchor := AnchorName; { This is target anchor in new doc; may be '' }
    LinkFile := FileName;      { This is filename for new file    }
    XPosition := 0;            { These Fields are not used         }
    YPosition := 0;
    HasImage := false;
    HasLabel := true;
  end;
  { Send back the record id for use in jump links }
  CreateNewNonLocalLink := LinkInsertPosition;
  { Increment the pointers into the link array for next usage }
  LinkInsertPosition := LinkInsertPosition + 1;
  TotalLinkRecords := TotalLinkRecords + 1;
end;
```

16. Find the function below and type in the highlighted text to handle responding to a hypertext link activation on images as well as text..

```
procedure TForm2.HotClick( Sender : TOBject;
              Button: TMouseButton;
              Shift: TShiftState;
              X, Y: Integer );

var TheItem : Integer;
    TheLinkFile ,
    TheLinkAnchor : String;
begin
 { Do dynamic typecast to find out which type of object made call }
 if Sender is HTMLLabel then
 begin { Label hit; treat as text }
  TheItem := HTMLLabel( Sender ).LinkItem;
  { Grab the link record to work with }
  with TheLIArray[ TheItem ]^ do
  begin
```

continued on next page

continued from previous page

```
    { Branch on type of link (note that 2-5 are not link ids & not used) }
    case LinkType of
     1 : begin { jump within current file }
          TheScrollBox.VertScrollBar.Position :=
          ( YPosition * PixelsPerLine ) - TheScrollBox.Height;
       end;
     6 : begin { wave file }
         PlayWaveAudio( LinkFile );
       end;
    11 : begin { jump to new file }
        InitializeDHTMLFile( LinkFile , LinkAnchor );
      end;
    end;
   end;
  end
  else
  begin { Image hit; treat as image }
    with Sender as HTMLImage do
    begin
     { Grab the link record to work with }
     with TheLIArray[ LinkItem ]^ do
     begin
       { Branch on type of link(note that 2-5 are not link ids & not used) }
       case LinkType of
        1 : begin { jump within current file }
            VertScrollBar.Position :=
            ( YPosition * PixelsPerLine ) - Self.Height;
          end;
        6 : begin { wave file }
            PlayWaveAudio( LinkFile );
          end;
       11 : begin { jump to new file }
            InitializeDHTMLFile( LinkFile , LinkAnchor );
          end;
       end;
    end;
   end;
  end;
end;
```

17. Find the function below and type in the highlighted text to handle displaying hypertext links using graphics as well as text.

```
procedure TForm2.CreateNewDHTDocument;
var TempString1    ,
    TempString2    ,
    TempURL1       ,
    TempURL2       ,
    WorkingString ,
    TheText           : String;
    TheLinkID ,
    TheURLType ,
    LStatus ,
```

```
  EndingPosition ,
  CurrentEnd ,
  Counter_1 ,
  CurrentXPosition ,
  CurrentYPosition ,
  CurrentLine       ,
  IH ,
  ImageX ,
  ImageY ,
  HTMLKind ,
  ValidResult          : Integer;
  ImageShownOnLine ,
  Completed : Boolean;
  TheLabel :TLabel;
begin
 { Create the scrollbox to show the document on }
 TheScrollBox.Free;
 TheScrollBox := TScrollBox.Create( self );
 TheScrollBox.Parent := self;
 TheScrollBox.Align := alclient;
 { Find out height of a line in the document }
 PixelsPerLine := Form2.Canvas.TextHeight( 'W' ) + 2;
 { Set initial Drawing Positions }
 CurrentXPosition := 10;
 CurrentYPosition := 20;
 { Set the current line for line calculations }
 CurrentLine := 1;
 { Loop through the memo and display the lines as hypertext and graphics }
 for Counter_1 := 1 to TheStringList.Count do
 begin
  { Clear the flag to indicate completion of current line }
  Completed := false;
  ImageShownOnLine := false;
  { Start parsing at the first character }
  EndingPosition := 1;
  CurrentXPosition := 10;
  CurrentYPosition := (( CurrentLine - 1 ) * PixelsPerLine );
  { Get a working copy of the memo line }
  WorkingString := TheStringList.Strings[ Counter_1 - 1 ];
  { Work along the working string until done }
  if DumpInvalidHTML then
  begin
   Completed := true;
   TheLabel := TLabel.Create( self );
   TheLabel.Parent := TheScrollBox;
   TheLabel.Font.Color := clBlack;
   TheLabel.Top := CurrentYPosition;
   TheLabel.Left := CurrentXPosition;
   TheLabel.Caption := WorkingString;
   TheLabel.Height := PixelsPerLine - 1;
   TheLabel.Width := Form2.Width - 5;
  end;
  while not Completed do
  begin
   { Eat off up to HTML command }
```

continued on next page

continued from previous page

```
  TempString1 := GetStringToHTMLTag( WorkingString , CurrentEnd );
  if TempString1 <> '' then
  begin { Some text to show so show it}
   TheLabel := TLabel.Create( self );
   TheLabel.Parent := TheScrollBox;
   TheLabel.Font.Color := clBlack;
   TheLabel.Top := CurrentYPosition;
   TheLabel.Left := CurrentXPosition;
   TheLabel.Caption := TempString1;
   TheLabel.Height := PixelsPerLine - 1;
   TheLabel.Width := Form2.Width - 5;
   { Move the output pointer along }
   CurrentXPosition := CurrentXPosition +
     Form2.Canvas.TextWidth( TempString1 );
  end;
   { Check for the end of the working string }
   if CurrentEnd > Length( WorkingString ) then
   begin
   Completed := true;
   CurrentLine := CurrentLine + 1;
   if ImageShownOnLine then
   begin
     ImageShownOnLine := false;
      CurrentLine := CurrentLine - 1 + (( IH div PixelsPerLine ) + 1 );
   end;
   end
   else
   begin
    { Chop off the parsed string portion and work with the rest }
    WorkingString := Copy( WorkingString , CurrentEnd , 255 );
    { Assume HTML tag next, so get it }
    TempString1 := GetCompleteHTMLReference( WorkingString , 0 ,
                     CurrentEnd , HTMLKind );
    if TempString1 = '' then
    begin { Bad or malformed HTML Tag; abort processing }
     MessageDlg( 'Bad or malformed HTML Tag! Aborting Processing...' ,
     mtError , [ mbOK ] , 0 );
    DumpInvalidHTML := true;
    TheLabel := TLabel.Create( self );
    TheLabel.Parent := TheScrollBox;
    TheLabel.Font.Color := clBlack;
    TheLabel.Top := CurrentYPosition;
    TheLabel.Left := CurrentXPosition;
    TheLabel.Caption := WorkingString;
    TheLabel.Height := PixelsPerLine - 1;
    TheLabel.Width := Form2.Width - 5;
     {TheScrollBox.InsertComponent( TheLabel );}
     if not ImageShownOnLine then
     begin
      Completed := true;
      CurrentLine := CurrentLine + 1;
    end
    else
    begin
```

```
    ImageShownOnLine := false;
    CurrentLine := CurrentLine + (( IH div PixelsPerLine ) + 1 );
    Completed := true;
   end;
  end
  else
   begin { Possibly Valid HTML tag; process it to be sure }
    case HTMLKind of  { parse on type of tag }
     1 : begin { Raw image without anchor or jump attached }
         TempString2 := GetURL( TempString1 );
         ValidResult := CreateNewRawImage( TempString2 ,
          CurrentXPosition , CurrentYPosition , ImageY, ImageX );
         if ValidResult < 0 then
         begin { Bad image file; signal and abort }
           MessageDlg( 'Invalid Image! Aborting Processing...' ,
         mtError , [ mbOK ] , 0 );
         DumpInvalidHTML := true;
         TheLabel := TLabel.Create( self );
         TheLabel.Parent := TheScrollBox;
         TheLabel.Font.Color := clBlack;
         TheLabel.Top := CurrentYPosition;
         TheLabel.Left := CurrentXPosition;
         TheLabel.Caption := WorkingString;
         TheLabel.Height := PixelsPerLine - 1;
         TheLabel.Width := Form2.Width - 5;
         if not ImageShownOnLine then
        begin
          Completed := true;
          CurrentLine := CurrentLine + 1;
        end
        else
        begin
          ImageShownOnLine := false;
          CurrentLine := CurrentLine +
          (( IH div PixelsPerLine ) + 1 );
          Completed := true;
        end;
        end
        else
        begin
          ImageShownOnLine := true;
          CurrentXPosition := CurrentXPosition + ImageX;
          IH := ImageY;
       end;
      end;
     2 : begin { Jump reference; 2 is just text }
         ParseLink( TempString1 , 2 , TheText ,
         TempURL1 , TempURL2 , LStatus );
         case LStatus of { check for other processing }
          1 : begin { Jump link; check for special file type }
              TheURLType := GetURLType( TempURL1 );
              case TheURLTYpe of
               6 : begin { Wave file }
                   TheLinkID := CreateNewLocalLink( '' ,
```

continued on next page

continued from previous page

```
                    TempURL1 , TheURLType );
                    with TheLIArray[ TheLinkID ]^ do
                    begin
                    TheLabel := HTMLLabel.Create( self );
                    TheLabel.Parent := TheScrollBox;
                    TheLabel.Visible := true;
                    TheLabel.Top := CurrentYPosition;
                    TheLabel.Left := CurrentXPosition;
                    TheLabel.Width :=
                     Form2.Canvas.TextWidth( TheText ) + 2;
                    TheLabel.Height := PixelsPerLine;
                    TheLabel.OnMouseUp := HotClick;
                    TheLabel.Cursor := 5;
                    TheLabel.LinkItem := TheLinkID;
                    TheLabel.Font.Color := clRed;
                    TheLabel.Caption := TheText;
                    CurrentXPosition := CurrentXPosition +
                     Form2.Canvas.TextWidth( TheText );
                 end;
                end;
            11 : begin { Standard DHT hypertext file }
                  TheLinkID := CreateNewNonLocalLink( '' ,
                  TempURL1 );
                  with TheLIArray[ TheLinkID ]^ do
                  begin
                   TheLabel := HTMLLabel.Create( self );
                   TheLabel.Parent := TheScrollBox;
                   TheLabel.Visible := true;
                   TheLabel.Top := CurrentYPosition;
                   TheLabel.Left := CurrentXPosition;
                   TheLabel.Width :=
                    Form2.Canvas.TextWidth( TheText ) + 2;
                   TheLabel.Height := PixelsPerLine;
                   TheLabel.OnMouseUp := HotClick;
                   TheLabel.Cursor := 5;
                   TheLabel.LinkItem := TheLinkID;
                   TheLabel.Font.Color := clRed;
                   TheLabel.Caption := TheText;
                   CurrentXPosition := CurrentXPosition +
                    Form2.Canvas.TextWidth( TheText );
                end;
               end;
           end;
          end;
        2 : begin { Local link; no special processing }
             TheLinkID := CreateNewLocalLink( TempURL1 ,
             '' , 1 );
             with TheLIArray[ TheLinkID ]^ do
             begin
               TheLabel := HTMLLabel.Create( self );
               TheLabel.Parent := TheScrollBox;
               TheLabel.Visible := true;
               TheLabel.Top := CurrentYPosition;
               TheLabel.Left := CurrentXPosition;
```

```
          TheLabel.Width :=
           Form2.Canvas.TextWidth( TheText ) + 2;
          TheLabel.Height := PixelsPerLine;
          TheLabel.OnMouseUp := HotClick;
          TheLabel.Cursor := 5;
          TheLabel.LinkItem := TheLinkID;
          TheLabel.Font.Color := clRed;
          TheLabel.Caption := TheText;
          CurrentXPosition := CurrentXPosition +
           Form2.Canvas.TextWidth( TheText );
        end;
       end;
    3 : begin { Non local URL with jump; check for DHT type }
         TheURLType := GetURLType( TempURL1 );
         if TheURLType  11 then
         begin { Attempt to do local jump in non HT file }
           {Dont bother at this level; full app needs this}
         end;
         TheLinkID := CreateNewNonLocalLink( TempURL1 ,
          TempURL2 );
         with TheLIArray[ TheLinkID ]^ do
         begin
           TheLabel := HTMLLabel.Create( self );
           TheLabel.Parent := TheScrollBox;
           TheLabel.Visible := true;
           TheLabel.Top := CurrentYPosition;
           TheLabel.Left := CurrentXPosition;
           TheLabel.Width :=
            Form2.Canvas.TextWidth( TheText ) + 2;
           TheLabel.Height := PixelsPerLine;
           TheLabel.OnMouseUp := HotClick;
           TheLabel.Cursor := 5;
           TheLabel.LinkItem := TheLinkID;
           TheLabel.Font.Color := clRed;
           TheLabel.Caption := TheText;
           CurrentXPosition := CurrentXPosition +
            Form2.Canvas.TextWidth( TheText );
         end;
        end;
     end;
   end;
   3 : begin { Jump reference; 3 is linked bitmap }
       ParseLink( TempString1 , 3 , TheText ,
       TempURL1 , TempURL2 , LStatus );
       case LStatus of { check for other processing }
        1 : begin { Jump link; check for special file type }
            TheURLType := GetURLType( TempURL1 );
            case TheURLTYpe of
             6 : begin { Wave file }
                  TheLinkID := CreateNewLocalLink( '' ,
                  TempURL1 , TheURLType );
                  AddImage( TheText , CurrentXPosition ,
                  CurrentYPosition , ImageY , ImageX );
```

continued on next page

continued from previous page

```
                ImageShownOnLine := true;
               IH := ImageX;
               with TheLIArray[ TheLinkID ]^ do
               begin
                TheImage.OnMouseUp := HotClick;
                TheImage.Cursor := 5;
                TheImage.LinkItem := TheLinkID;
             end;
                CurrentXPosition:=CurrentXPosition+ImageY;
          end;
       11 : begin { Standard DHT hypertext file }
          TheLinkID := CreateNewNonLocalLink( '' ,
          TempURL1 );
          AddImage( TheText , CurrentXPosition ,
          CurrentYPosition , ImageX , ImageY );
          ImageShownOnLine := true;
          IH := ImageY;
          with TheLIArray[ TheLinkID ]^ do
          begin
           TheImage.OnMouseUp := HotClick;
           TheImage.Cursor := 5;
           TheImage.LinkItem := TheLinkID;
         end;
           CurrentXPosition:=CurrentXPosition+ImageX;
        end;
      end;
     end;
     2 : begin { Local link; no special processing }
        TheLinkID := CreateNewLocalLink( TempURL1 ,
        '' , 1 );
        AddImage( TheText , CurrentXPosition ,
          CurrentYPosition , ImageY , ImageX );
         ImageShownOnLine := true;
        IH := ImageY;
        with TheLIArray[ TheLinkID ]^ do
        begin
          TheImage.OnMouseUp := HotClick;
          TheImage.Cursor := 5;
          TheImage.LinkItem := TheLinkID;
        end;
          CurrentXPosition := CurrentXPosition + ImageX;
      end;
     3 : begin { Non local URL with jump; check for DHT type }
         TheURLType := GetURLType( TempURL1 );
         if TheURLType <> 11 then
         begin { Attempt to do local jump in non HT file }
          {Dont bother at this level; full app needs this}
        end;
        TheLinkID := CreateNewNonLocalLink( TempURL1 ,
        TempURL2 );
        AddImage( TheText , CurrentXPosition ,
        CurrentYPosition , ImageY , ImageX );
        ImageShownOnLine := true;
        IH := ImageY;
```

```
          with TheLIArray[ TheLinkID ]^ do
          begin
            TheImage.OnMouseUp := HotClick;
            TheImage.Cursor := 5;
            TheImage.LinkItem := TheLinkID;
           end;
            CurrentXPosition := CurrentXPosition + ImageX;
          end;
       end;
      end;
    4 : begin { Anchor reference; 4 is just text }
          ParseAnchor( TempString1 , 4 , TheText , TempURL1 );
          TheLinkID := CreateNewAnchorLink( TempURL1 ,
           CurrentXPosition , CurrentLine );
          TheLabel := TLabel.Create( self );
          TheLabel.Parent := TheScrollBox;
          TheLabel.Font.Color := clRed;
          TheLabel.Top := CurrentYPosition;
          TheLabel.Left := CurrentXPosition;
          TheLabel.Caption := TheText;
          TheLabel.Height := PixelsPerLine - 1;
          TheLabel.Width := Form2.Width - 5;
          CurrentXPosition := CurrentXPosition +
           Form2.Canvas.TextWidth( TheText );
      end;
    5 : begin { Anchor reference; 5 is just image }
          ParseAnchor( TempString1 , 5 , TheText , TempURL1 );
          TheLinkID := CreateNewAnchorLink( TempURL2 ,
           CurrentXPosition , CurrentLine );
          AddImage( TheText , CurrentXPosition ,
           CurrentYPosition , ImageY , ImageX );
          ImageShownOnLine := true;
        IH := ImageY;
           CurrentXPosition := CurrentXPosition + ImageX;
      end;
   end;
  end;
   { Check for the end of the working string }
   if CurrentEnd > Length( WorkingString ) then
   begin
    if not ImageShownOnLine then
    begin
     CurrentLine := CurrentLine + 1;
     Completed := true;
   end
   else
   begin
    ImageShownOnLine := false;
    CurrentLine := CurrentLine + (( IH div PixelsPerLine ) + 1 );
    Completed := true;
  end;
 end
  else WorkingString := Copy( WorkingString , CurrentEnd , 255 );
end;
end;
```

continued on next page

continued from previous page

```
  end;
    TheScrollBox.VertScrollbar.Visible := true;
    TheScrollBox.VertScrollbar.Range := ( CurrentLine * PixelsPerLine ) + 20;
    TheScrollBox.VertScrollBar.Increment := PixelsPerLine;
end;
```

18. Move back up to the *uses* keyword and enter the following unit to allow using GIF files.

```
uses
  SysUtils, WinTypes, WinProcs, Messages, Classes, Graphics, Controls,
  Forms, Dialogs, Menus, StdCtrls, ExtCtrls, MPlayer, CCGif;
```

19. Compile and test the project.

How it Works

The raw power of HTML is clearly visible in this How-To. Images are added simply by putting in an additional allowed tag type (for the <IMG > construct) and then allowing an image to replace a line of text in a link or anchor tag.

The images are shown directly on the scrollbox component via the TImage components. By making their parent the Scrollbox, when it is deleted they are deleted as well. This allows freeing their memory and resources without having to explicitly keep track of them, an advantage the VCL provides.

Comments

The GIF unit is included despite an ongoing legal battle in the computer community over who, if anyone, owns the patent on the LZW compression algorithm used in the GIF standard.

6.8 How Do I... Display sprite animation in an HTML document?

COMPLEXITY: ADVANCED

Problem

Some commercial presentation programs have cute little moving bitmaps that respond to mouse actions. Can Delphi add this to the HTML viewer?

Technique

The small moving bitmaps with non-rectangular shapes are called *Sprites*; How-To 5.8 demonstrated the basic technique for showing a sprite. Using URL syntax and a custom Delphi Object Pascal file type, the HTML viewer has no problem including user-created sprite animations in its presentations.

Steps

Run DHTMLVWR.EXE from CHAP06\HOWTO08 directory on the CD, and load TEST6.DHT. Click on the "Unleashing the Power of Objects!" red text and a little fireball will streak across the screen and explode (as shown in Figure 6-13).

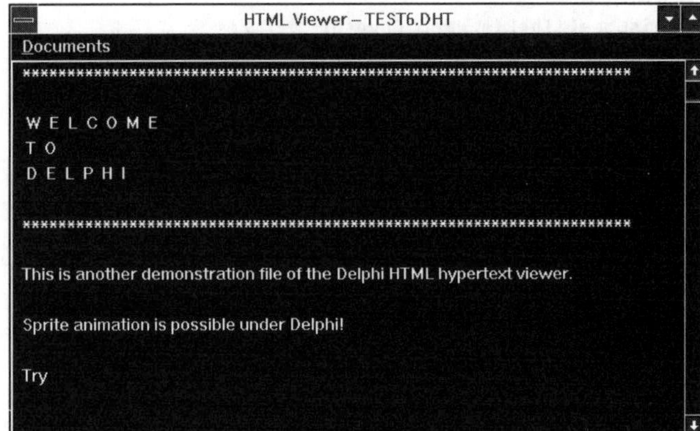

Figure 6-13 DHTMLVWR at run time showing a sprite fireball animation triggered by a hypertext link

1. Copy the files from How-To 6.7 into a new directory. Rename the unit DHTVIEW4.PAS and the project DHTMLVWR.DPR.
2. Components, properties,and settings remain the same as from How-To 6.5.
3. Select the OnCreate event of Form1 and enter the following highlighted code to initialize the application.

```
procedure TForm2.FormCreate(Sender: TObject);
begin
  TotalLinkRecords := 0;
  LinkInsertPosition := 1;
  Screen.Cursors[ 5 ] := LoadCursor( HInstance , 'HTHAND' );
  TotalSprites := 0;
  DumpInvalidHTML := false;
  DocumentLoaded := false;
  TheStringList := TStringList.Create;
  MediaPlayer1 := TMediaPlayer.Create( Self );
  MediaPlayer1.Parent := self;
  MediaPlayer1.Visible := false;
  TheScrollBox := NIL;
end;
```

4. Select the OnDestroy event of Form2 and enter the following highlighted code to close the application.

```
procedure TForm2.FormDestroy(Sender: TObject);
var Counter_1 : Integer;
begin
  MediaPlayer1.Free;
  for Counter_1 := 1 to TotalLinkRecords do
  begin
    Dispose( TheLIArray[ Counter_1 ] );
  end;
  for Counter_1 := 1 to TotalSprites do
  begin
    TheSpritesArray[ Counter_1 ]^.TheSprite.Free;
  end;
end;
```

5. Still in the Code Editor, move down below the *end* keyword for the Form2 type declaration, and enter the following highlighted assistant type definitions.

```
HTMLLabel = class( TLabel )
    private
      LinkItem : Integer;
  end;
  HTMLImage = class( TImage )
    private
      LinkItem : Integer;
  end;
  PLinkItemRecord = ^LinkItemRecord;
  LinkItemRecord = record
    LinkFile : String;
    LinkAnchor : String;
    ImageFile : String;
    LinkType,
    XPosition ,
    YPosition   : Integer;
    HasImage ,
    HasLabel : Boolean;
    TheLabel : HTMLLabel;
    TheImage : HTMLImage;
  end;
  LinkItemArray = array[ 1 .. 255 ] of PLinkItemRecord;
  TNamesArray = array[ 1 .. 20 , 1 .. 2 ] of String;
  TDeltasArray = array [ 1 .. 20 , 1 .. 2 ] of Integer;
  TObjectArray = array [ 1 .. 20 , 1 .. 2 ] of TObject;
  TSpriteRecord = record
      TotalImages : Integer;
      TheNamesArray : TNamesArray;
      DeltasArray   : TDeltasArray;
      StartingX ,
      StartingY ,
      NewSpriteInterval,
      TimerInterval       : Integer;
  end;
```

```
  ASprite = class( TObject )
    private
      TheSpriteRecord : TSpriteRecord;
      SpriteTimer : TTimer;
      TheSpriteBitmaps : TObjectArray;
      CurrentSpriteX ,
      CurrentSpriteY ,
      CurrentImage ,
      CurrentDelayInterval : Integer;
      constructor Create( TheFileName : String );
      procedure LoadFromFile( TheFileName : String );
      procedure Play;
      procedure Free;
      procedure SpriteOnTimer(Sender: TObject);
      procedure DrawCurrentSprite;
  end;
  pSprite = ^TSprite;
  TSprite = record
    TheSprite : ASprite;
  end;
```

6. Move down below the *var* keyword and type in the following highlighted helper variables.

```
var
  Form2: TForm2;
  TheHiddenMemo : TMemo;
  TheLIArray : LinkItemArray;
  LinkInsertPosition ,
  TotalLinkRecords        : Integer;
  PixelsPerLine : Integer;
  WhichSprites : array[ 1 .. 255 ] of Integer;
  TheSpritesArray : array[ 1 .. 50 ] of PSprite;
  DumpInvalidHTML : Boolean;
  TotalSprites : Integer;
  DocumentLoaded : Boolean;
  TheStringList : TStringList;
  MediaPlayer1 : TMediaPlayer;
  SaveBackgroundBitmap,
  WorkspaceBitmap : TBitmap;
  TheScrollBox : TScrollBox;
  GlobalCanvas : TCanvas;
  OldHandle : HDC
```

7. Move down below the *implementation* keyword and type in the following assistant procedure to play a sprite file on demand.

```
procedure ASprite.Play;
begin
  CurrentSpriteX := TheSpriteRecord.StartingX;
  CurrentSpriteY := TheSpriteRecord.StartingY;
  SaveBackgroundBitmap := TBitmap.Create;
  SaveBackgroundBitmap.Width := TBitmap( TheSpriteBitmaps[ 1 , 1 ]).Width;
```

continued on next page

continued from previous page

```
  SaveBackgroundBitmap.Height := TBitmap( TheSpriteBitmaps[ 1 , 1 ]).Height;
  GlobalCanvas := TCanvas.Create;
  GlobalCanvas.Handle := GetDC( 0 );
  WorkSpaceBitmap := TBitmap.Create;
  with WorkSpaceBitmap do begin
    Width := Form2.Width;
    Height := Form2.Height;
    Canvas.CopyMode := cmSrcCopy;
    Canvas.CopyRect(Rect(0, 0, Width, Height),
     GlobalCanvas , Rect(TheScrollBox.Left,TheScrollBox.Top,Width,Height));
  end;
  {Update the saved background data}
  SaveBackgroundBitmap.Canvas.CopyRect(
   Rect(0, 0, TBitmap( TheSpriteBitmaps[ 1 , 1 ]).Width,
    TBitmap( TheSpriteBitmaps[ 1 , 1 ]).Height ),
     WorkSpaceBitmap.Canvas,
      Rect(CurrentSpriteX, CurrentSpriteY,
       CurrentSpriteX + TBitmap( TheSpriteBitmaps[ 1 , 1 ]).Width,
        CurrentSpriteY + TBitmap( TheSpriteBitmaps[ 1 , 1 ]).Height));
  CurrentImage := 1;
  CurrentDelayInterval := TheSpriteRecord.NewSpriteInterval;
  SpriteTimer.Interval := TheSpriteRecord.TimerInterval;
  SpriteTimer.Enabled := true;
  DrawCurrentSprite;
end;
```

8. Move down below the previous procedure and type in the following assistant procedure to load a sprite file.

```
procedure ASprite.LoadFromFile( TheFileName : String );
var TheFile : File of TSpriteRecord;
    Counter_1 : Integer;
begin
  Assign( TheFile , TheFilename );
  Reset( TheFile );
  Seek( TheFile , 0 );
  Read( TheFile , TheSpriteRecord );
  CloseFile( TheFile );
  for Counter_1 := 1 to TheSpriteRecord.TotalImages do
  begin
    TBitmap( TheSpriteBitmaps[ Counter_1 , 1 ] ) := TBitmap.Create;
    TBitmap( TheSpriteBitmaps[ Counter_1 , 2 ] ) := TBitmap.Create;
    TBitmap( TheSpriteBitmaps[ Counter_1 , 1 ] )
     .LoadFromFile( TheSpriteRecord.TheNamesArray[ Counter_1 , 2 ] );
    TBitmap( TheSpriteBitmaps[ Counter_1 , 2 ] )
     .LoadFromFile( TheSpriteRecord.TheNamesArray[ Counter_1 , 1 ] );
  end;
end;
```

9. Move down below the previous procedure and type in the following assistant procedure to create a sprite object, including loading its data from a file.

```
constructor ASprite.Create( TheFileName : String );
```

```
begin
  inherited Create;
  SpriteTimer := TTimer.Create( Form2 );
  SpriteTimer.Enabled := false;
  SpriteTimer.OnTimer := SpriteOnTimer;
  LoadFromFile( TheFileName );
end;
```

10. Move down below the previous procedure and type in the following assistant procedure to handle removing a sprite from memory, including all its component bitmaps.

```
procedure ASprite.Free;
var Counter_1 : Integer;
begin
  SpriteTimer.Free;
  SpriteTimer := NIL;
  for Counter_1 := 1 to TheSpriteRecord.TotalImages do
  begin
    TBitmap( TheSpriteBitmaps[ Counter_1 , 1 ]).Free;
    TBitmap( TheSpriteBitmaps[ Counter_1 , 2 ]).Free;
  end;
  inherited Free;
end;
```

11. Move down below the previous procedure and type in the following assistant procedure to handle drawing the current bitmaps of the active sprite.

```
procedure ASprite.DrawCurrentSprite;
var OldX, OldY : Integer;
begin
 with WorkSpaceBitmap.Canvas do
 begin
  {Erase by copying in saved background}
  CopyMode := cmSrcCopy;
  CopyRect(Rect( CurrentSpriteX,
        CurrentSpriteY,
        CurrentSpriteX + TBitmap( TheSpriteBitmaps[1 , 1 ]).Width,
        CurrentSpriteY + TBitmap( TheSpriteBitmaps[1,1 ]).Height),
      SaveBackgroundBitmap.Canvas,
      Rect(0, 0, TBitmap( TheSpriteBitmaps[ 1 , 1 ]).Width,
        TBitmap( TheSpriteBitmaps[ 1 , 1 ]).Height));
  OldX := CurrentSpriteX;
  OldY := CurrentSpriteY;
  CurrentSpriteX:=CurrentSpriteX + TheSpriteRecord.DeltasArray[ CurrentImage ,1];
  CurrentSpriteY := CurrentSpriteY + TheSpriteRecord.DeltasArray[ CurrentImage , 2 ];
  {save background at new position}
  SaveBackgroundBitmap.Canvas.CopyRect(
  Rect(0, 0, TBitmap( TheSpriteBitmaps[ 1 , 1 ]).Width,
  TBitmap( TheSpriteBitmaps[ 1 , 1 ]).Height),
  WorkSpaceBitmap.Canvas,
  Rect(CurrentSpriteX,
```

continued on next page

continued from previous page

```
    CurrentSpriteY,
     CurrentSpriteX + TBitmap( TheSpriteBitmaps[ 1 , 1 ]).Width,
     CurrentSpriteY + TBitmap( TheSpriteBitmaps[ 1 , 1 ]).Height));
  {Use sprite mask to clear sprite shape from work surface}
  CopyMode := cmSrcAnd;
  CopyRect(Rect(CurrentSpriteX,
       CurrentSpriteY,
       CurrentSpriteX + TBitmap( TheSpriteBitmaps[ 1 , 1 ]).Width,
       CurrentSpriteY + TBitmap( TheSpriteBitmaps[1 ,1 ]).Height),
      TBitmap( TheSpriteBitmaps[ CurrentImage , 1 ]).Canvas,
      Rect(0, 0, TBitmap( TheSpriteBitmaps[ 1 , 1 ]).Width,
      TBitmap( TheSpriteBitmaps[ 1 , 1 ]).Height));
  {paint the sprite into place}
  CopyMode := cmSrcPaint;
  CopyRect(Rect(CurrentSpriteX,
            CurrentSpriteY,
            CurrentSpriteX + TBitmap( TheSpriteBitmaps[ 1 , 1 ]).Width,
            CurrentSpriteY + TBitmap(TheSpriteBitmaps[1 , 1 ]).Height),
           TBitmap( TheSpriteBitmaps[ CurrentImage , 2 ]).Canvas,
           Rect(0, 0, TBitmap( TheSpriteBitmaps[ 1 , 1 ]).Width,
           TBitmap( TheSpriteBitmaps[ 1 , 1 ]).Height));
 end;
 {Now blast the finished sprite image to the screen!}
 with GlobalCanvas do
 begin
  CopyRect(Rect(OldX, OldY,
         OldX + TBitmap( TheSpriteBitmaps[ 1 , 1 ]).Width + 10,
         OldY + TBitmap( TheSpriteBitmaps[ 1 , 1 ]).Height ),
       WorkSpaceBitmap.Canvas,
     Rect(OldX, OldY,
         OldX + TBitmap( TheSpriteBitmaps[ 1 , 1 ]).Width + 10,
         OldY + TBitmap( TheSpriteBitmaps[ 1 , 1 ]).Height));
  end;
end;
```

12. Move down below the previous procedure and type in the following assistant procedure to handle moving sprites and changing the active bitmap on timer events, as well as cleaning up afterwards..

```
procedure ASprite.SpriteOnTimer(Sender: TObject);
var OldX , OldY : Integer;
begin
 DrawCurrentSprite;
 CurrentDelayInterval := CurrentDelayInterval - 1;
 if CurrentDelayInterval = 0 then
 begin
  CurrentDelayInterval := TheSpriteRecord.NewSpriteInterval;
  CurrentImage := CurrentImage + 1;
  if CurrentImage > TheSpriteRecord.TotalImages then
  begin
   SpriteTimer.Enabled := false;
   with WorkSpaceBitmap.Canvas do
   begin
```

```
    {Erase by copying in saved background}
    CopyMode := cmSrcCopy;
    CopyRect(Rect( CurrentSpriteX,
               CurrentSpriteY,
                CurrentSpriteX+TBitmap(TheSpriteBitmaps[1, 1 ]).Width,
                CurrentSpriteY+TBitmap(TheSpriteBitmaps[1,1]).Height),
          SaveBackgroundBitmap.Canvas,
           Rect(0, 0, TBitmap( TheSpriteBitmaps[ 1 , 1 ]).Width,
             TBitmap( TheSpriteBitmaps[ 1 , 1 ]).Height));
   OldX := CurrentSpriteX;
   OldY := CurrentSpriteY;
  end;
   {Now blast the finished sprite image to the screen!}
   with GlobalCanvas do
   begin
    CopyRect(Rect(OldX, OldY,
           OldX + TBitmap( TheSpriteBitmaps[ 1 , 1 ]).Width + 10,
           OldY + TBitmap( TheSpriteBitmaps[ 1 , 1 ]).Height ),
          WorkSpaceBitmap.Canvas,
        Rect(OldX, OldY,
           OldX + TBitmap( TheSpriteBitmaps[ 1 , 1 ]).Width + 10,
           OldY + TBitmap( TheSpriteBitmaps[ 1 , 1 ]).Height));
  end;
   WorkSpaceBitmap.Free;
   SaveBackgroundBitmap.Free;
   ReleaseDC( 0 , GlobalCanvas.Handle );
   GlobalCanvas.Handle := OldHandle
   GlobalCanvas.Free;
  end;
 end;
end;
```

13. Find the function below and type in the highlighted text to handle determining the URL type based on the extension of the file name, including new types for this How-To.

```
function TForm2.GetURLType( TheString : String ) : Integer;
var ExtensionString : String;
begin
  { This function assumes a valid URL has been obtained }
  { It determines what type of data is acquired via URL }
  ExtensionString := Uppercase( ExtractFileExt( TheString ));
  if ExtensionString = '.DHT' then
  begin
    GetURLType := 11; { Standard delphi hypertext file }
    exit;
  end;
  if ExtensionString = '.BMP' then
  begin
    GetURLType := 2; { Bitmap image file; only valid in IMG URL }
    exit;
  end;
  if ExtensionString = '.ICO' then
```

continued from previous page

```
  begin
    GetURLType := 3; { Windows Icon image file; only valid in IMG URL }
    exit;
  end;
  if ExtensionString = '.WMF' then
  begin
    GetURLType := 4; { Windows Metafile image file; only valid in IMG URL }
    exit;
  end;
  if ExtensionString = '.GIF' then
  begin
    GetURLType := 5; { GIF image file; only valid in IMG URL }
    exit;
  end;
  if ExtensionString = '.WAV' then
  begin
    GetURLType := 6; { Windows sound file }
    exit;
  end;
  if ExtensionString = '.SPR' then
  begin
    GetURLType := 7; { Delphi sprite file }
    exit;
  end;
  GETURLType := -1; { File extension doesn't match known type; signal error }
end;
```

14. Find the function below and type in the highlighted text to handle loading a new hypertext file, first clearing previous sprite files.

```
procedure TForm2.InitializeDHTMLFile( TheFileName , TheAnchorName : String );
var Counter_1 ,
    WhichX    ,
    WhichY      : Integer;
begin
  for Counter_1 := 1 to TotalLinkRecords do
  begin
    Dispose( TheLIArray[ Counter_1 ] );
  end;
  for Counter_1 := 1 to TotalSprites do
  begin
    TheSpritesArray[ Counter_1 ]^.TheSprite.Free;
  end;
  TotalSprites := 0;
  TotalLinkRecords := 0;
  LinkInsertPosition := 1;
  DumpInvalidHTML := false;
  DocumentLoaded := false;
  TheHiddenMemo := TMemo.Create( Self );
  TheHiddenMemo.Parent := Self;
  TheHiddenMemo.Visible := false;
  TheHiddenMemo.Width := Form2.Width;
  TheHiddenMemo.Height := Form2.Height;
```

```
  TheHiddenMemo.Lines.LoadFromFile( TheFileName );
  TheStringList.Clear;
  For Counter_1 := 1 to TheHiddenMemo.Lines.Count do
  begin
    TheStringList.Add( TheHiddenMemo.Lines[ Counter_1 - 1 ] );
  end;
  TheHiddenMemo.Free;
  DocumentLoaded := true;
  CreateNewDHTDocument;
    Caption := 'HTML Viewer -- ' + ExtractFileName( TheFilename );
  if TheAnchorName <> '' then
  begin
    FindLocalAnchor( TheAnchorName, WhichX , WhichY );
    TheScrollBox.VertScrollBar.Position := ( PixelsPerLine * WhichY ) -
     TheScrollBox.Height;
  end;
end;
```

15. Find the function below and type in the highlighted text to handle responding to a hypertext link activation including the new file type.

```
procedure TForm2.HotClick( Sender : TObject;
             Button: TMouseButton;
             Shift: TShiftState;
             X, Y: Integer );

var TheItem : Integer;
    TheLinkFile ,
    TheLinkAnchor : String;
begin
 { Do dynamic typecast to find out which type of object made call }
 if Sender is HTMLLabel then
 begin { Label hit; treat as text }
  TheItem := HTMLLabel( Sender ).LinkItem;
  { Grab the link record to work with }
  with TheLIArray[ TheItem ]^ do
  begin
   { Branch on type of link (note that 2-5 are not link ids & not used) }
   case LinkType of
    1 : begin { jump within current file }
         TheScrollBox.VertScrollBar.Position :=
         ( YPosition * PixelsPerLine ) - TheScrollBox.Height;
       end;
    6 : begin { wave file }
         PlayWaveAudio( LinkFile );
       end;
    7 : begin { sprite file }
        TheSpritesArray[ WhichSprites[ TheItem ]]^.TheSprite.Play;
       end;
   11 : begin { jump to new file }
        InitializeDHTMLFile( LinkFile , LinkAnchor );
       end;
   end;
```

continued on next page

continued from previous page

```
  end;
 end
  else
  begin { Image hit; treat as image }
   with Sender as HTMLImage do
   begin
    { Grab the link record to work with }
    with TheLIArray[ LinkItem ]^ do
    begin
     { Branch on type of link(note that 2-5 are not link ids & not used) }
     case LinkType of
      1 : begin { jump within current file }
          VertScrollBar.Position :=
          ( YPosition * PixelsPerLine ) - Self.Height;
        end;
      6 : begin { wave file }
          PlayWaveAudio( LinkFile );
        end;
      7 : begin { sprite file }
           TheSpritesArray[ WhichSprites[ LinkItem ]]^.TheSprite.Play;
        end;
     11 : begin { jump to new file }
          InitializeDHTMLFile( LinkFile , LinkAnchor );
        end;
     end;
    end;
  end;
 end;
end;
```

16. Find the function below and type in the highlighted text to handle displaying hypertext links using the new URL types.

```
procedure TForm2.CreateNewDHTDocument;
var TempString1   ,
    TempString2   ,
    TempURL1      ,
    TempURL2      ,
    WorkingString ,
    TheText           : String;
    TheLinkID ,
    TheURLType ,
    LStatus ,
    EndingPosition ,
    CurrentEnd ,
    Counter_1 ,
    CurrentXPosition ,
    CurrentYPosition ,
    CurrentLine       ,
    IH ,
    ImageX ,
    ImageY ,
    HTMLKind ,
```

```
    ValidResult         : Integer;
    ImageShownOnLine ,
    Completed : Boolean;
    TheLabel :TLabel;
begin
  { Create the scrollbox to show the document on }
  TheScrollBox.Free;
  TheScrollBox := TScrollBox.Create( self );
  TheScrollBox.Parent := self;
  TheScrollBox.Align := alclient;
 { Find out height of a line in the document }
  PixelsPerLine := Form2.Canvas.TextHeight( 'W' ) + 2;
  { Set initial Drawing Positions }
  CurrentXPosition := 10;
  CurrentYPosition := 20;
  { Set the current line for line calculations }
  CurrentLine := 1;
  { Loop through the memo and display the lines as hypertext and graphics }
  for Counter_1 := 1 to TheStringList.Count do
  begin
    { Clear the flag to indicate completion of current line }
    Completed := false;
    ImageShownOnLine := false;
    { Start parsing at the first character }
    EndingPosition := 1;
    CurrentXPosition := 10;
    CurrentYPosition := (( CurrentLine - 1 ) * PixelsPerLine );
    { Get a working copy of the memo line }
    WorkingString := TheStringList.Strings[ Counter_1 - 1 ];
    { Work along the working string until done }
    if DumpInvalidHTML then
    begin
      Completed := true;
      TheLabel := TLabel.Create( self );
      TheLabel.Parent := TheScrollBox;
      TheLabel.Font.Color := clBlack;
      TheLabel.Top := CurrentYPosition;
      TheLabel.Left := CurrentXPosition;
      TheLabel.Caption := WorkingString;
      TheLabel.Height := PixelsPerLine - 1;
      TheLabel.Width := Form2.Width - 5;
     end;
    while not Completed do
    begin
      { Eat off up to HTML command }
      TempString1 := GetStringToHTMLTag( WorkingString , CurrentEnd );
      if TempString1 <> '' then
      begin { Some text to show so show it}
        TheLabel := TLabel.Create( self );
        TheLabel.Parent := TheScrollBox;
        TheLabel.Font.Color := clBlack;
        TheLabel.Top := CurrentYPosition;
        TheLabel.Left := CurrentXPosition;
        TheLabel.Caption := TempString1;
        TheLabel.Height := PixelsPerLine - 1;
```

continued on next page

continued from previous page

```
     TheLabel.Width := Form2.Width - 5;
    { Move the output pointer along }
     CurrentXPosition := CurrentXPosition +
      Form2.Canvas.TextWidth( TempString1 );
   end;
   { Check for the end of the working string }
   if CurrentEnd > Length( WorkingString ) then
   begin
     Completed := true;
     CurrentLine := CurrentLine + 1;
     if ImageShownOnLine then
     begin
       ImageShownOnLine := false;
       CurrentLine := CurrentLine - 1 + (( IH div PixelsPerLine ) + 1 );
     end;
   end
   else
   begin
     { Chop off the parsed string portion and work with the rest }
     WorkingString := Copy( WorkingString , CurrentEnd , 255 );
     { Assume HTML tag next, so get it }
     TempString1 := GetCompleteHTMLReference( WorkingString , 0 ,
                    CurrentEnd , HTMLKind );
     if TempString1 = '' then
     begin { Bad or malformed HTML Tag; abort processing }
       MessageDlg( 'Bad or malformed HTML Tag! Aborting Processing...' ,
        mtError , [ mbOK ] , 0 );
       DumpInvalidHTML := true;
       TheLabel := TLabel.Create( self );
       TheLabel.Parent := TheScrollBox;
       TheLabel.Font.Color := clBlack;
       TheLabel.Top := CurrentYPosition;
       TheLabel.Left := CurrentXPosition;
       TheLabel.Caption := WorkingString;
       TheLabel.Height := PixelsPerLine - 1;
       TheLabel.Width := Form2.Width - 5;
       if not ImageShownOnLine then
       begin
         Completed := true;
         CurrentLine := CurrentLine + 1;
       end
       else
       begin
         ImageShownOnLine := false;
         CurrentLine := CurrentLine + (( IH div PixelsPerLine ) + 1 );
         Completed := true;
       end;
     end
     else
     begin { Possibly Valid HTML tag; process it to be sure }
       case HTMLKind of  { parse on type of tag }
         1 : begin { Raw image without anchor or jump attached }
               TempString2 := GetURL( TempString1 );
               ValidResult := CreateNewRawImage( TempString2 ,
```

```
          CurrentXPosition , CurrentYPosition , ImageY, ImageX );
         if ValidResult < 0 then
         begin { Bad image file; signal and abort }
           MessageDlg( 'Invalid Image! Aborting Processing...' ,
            mtError , [ mbOK ] , 0 );
           DumpInvalidHTML := true;
           TheLabel := TLabel.Create( self );
           TheLabel.Parent := TheScrollBox;
           TheLabel.Font.Color := clBlack;
           TheLabel.Top := CurrentYPosition;
           TheLabel.Left := CurrentXPosition;
           TheLabel.Caption := WorkingString;
           TheLabel.Height := PixelsPerLine - 1;
           TheLabel.Width := Form2.Width - 5;
           if not ImageShownOnLine then
           begin
             Completed := true;
             CurrentLine := CurrentLine + 1;
           end
           else
           begin
             ImageShownOnLine := false;
             CurrentLine := CurrentLine +
              (( IH div PixelsPerLine ) + 1 );
             Completed := true;
           end;
         end
         else
         begin
           ImageShownOnLine := true;
           CurrentXPosition := CurrentXPosition + ImageX;
           IH := ImageY;
         end;
       end;
   2 : begin { Jump reference; 2 is just text }
         ParseLink( TempString1 , 2 , TheText ,
          TempURL1 , TempURL2 , LStatus );
         case LStatus of { check for other processing }
           1 : begin { Jump link; check for special file type }
                 TheURLType := GetURLType( TempURL1 );
                 case TheURLTYpe of
                   6 : begin { Wave file }
                         TheLinkID := CreateNewLocalLink( '' ,
                          TempURL1 , TheURLType );
                         with TheLIArray[ TheLinkID ]^ do
                         begin
                           TheLabel := HTMLLabel.Create( self );
                           TheLabel.Parent := TheScrollBox;
                           TheLabel.Visible := true;
                           TheLabel.Top := CurrentYPosition;
                           TheLabel.Left := CurrentXPosition;
                           TheLabel.Width :=
                            Form2.Canvas.TextWidth( TheText ) + 2;
                           TheLabel.Height := PixelsPerLine;
```

continued on next page

continued from previous page

```
                  TheLabel.OnMouseUp := HotClick;
                  TheLabel.Cursor := 5;
                  TheLabel.LinkItem := TheLinkID;
                  TheLabel.Font.Color := clRed;
                  TheLabel.Caption := TheText;
                  CurrentXPosition := CurrentXPosition +
                   Form2.Canvas.TextWidth( TheText );
                end;
              end;
           7 : begin { Sprite file }
                TheLinkID := CreateNewLocalLink( '' ,
                 TempURL1 , TheURLType );
                with TheLIArray[ TheLinkID ]^ do
                begin
                  TheLabel := HTMLLabel.Create( self );
                  TheLabel.Parent := TheScrollBox;
                  TheLabel.Visible := true;
                  TheLabel.Top := CurrentYPosition;
                  TheLabel.Left := CurrentXPosition;
                  TheLabel.Width :=
                   Form2.Canvas.TextWidth( TheText ) + 2;
                  TheLabel.Height := PixelsPerLine;
                  TheLabel.OnMouseUp := HotClick;
                  TheLabel.Cursor := 5;
                  TheLabel.LinkItem := TheLinkID;
                  TheLabel.Font.Color := clRed;
                  TheLabel.Caption := TheText;
                  CurrentXPosition := CurrentXPosition +
                   Form2.Canvas.TextWidth( TheText );
                end;
                TotalSprites := TotalSprites + 1;
                New( TheSpritesArray[ TotalSprites ] );
                WhichSprites[ TheLinkID ] := TotalSprites;
                with TheSpritesArray[ TotalSprites ]^ do
                begin
                  TheSprite := ASprite.Create( TempURL1 );
                end;
              end;
          11 : begin { Standard DHT hypertext file }
                TheLinkID := CreateNewNonLocalLink( '' ,
                 TempURL1 );
                with TheLIArray[ TheLinkID ]^ do
                begin
                  TheLabel := HTMLLabel.Create( self );
                  TheLabel.Parent := TheScrollBox;
                  TheLabel.Visible := true;
                  TheLabel.Top := CurrentYPosition;
                  TheLabel.Left := CurrentXPosition;
                  TheLabel.Width :=
                   Form2.Canvas.TextWidth( TheText ) + 2;
                  TheLabel.Height := PixelsPerLine;
                  TheLabel.OnMouseUp := HotClick;
                  TheLabel.Cursor := 5;
                  TheLabel.LinkItem := TheLinkID;
```

```
                    TheLabel.Font.Color := clRed;
                    TheLabel.Caption := TheText;
                    CurrentXPosition := CurrentXPosition +
                     Form2.Canvas.TextWidth( TheText );
                  end;
                end;
          end;
        end;
     2 : begin { Local link; no special processing }
           TheLinkID := CreateNewLocalLink( TempURL1 ,
           '' , 1 );
           with TheLIArray[ TheLinkID ]^ do
           begin
             TheLabel := HTMLLabel.Create( self );
             TheLabel.Parent := TheScrollBox;
             TheLabel.Visible := true;
             TheLabel.Top := CurrentYPosition;
             TheLabel.Left := CurrentXPosition;
             TheLabel.Width :=
              Form2.Canvas.TextWidth( TheText ) + 2;
             TheLabel.Height := PixelsPerLine;
             TheLabel.OnMouseUp := HotClick;
             TheLabel.Cursor := 5;
             TheLabel.LinkItem := TheLinkID;
             TheLabel.Font.Color := clRed;
             TheLabel.Caption := TheText;
             CurrentXPosition := CurrentXPosition +
              Form2.Canvas.TextWidth( TheText );
           end;
         end;
     3 : begin { Non local URL with jump; check for DHT type }
           TheURLType := GetURLType( TempURL1 );
           if TheURLType <> 11 then
           begin { Attempt to do local jump in non HT file }
             {Don't bother at this level; full app needs this}
           end;
           TheLinkID := CreateNewNonLocalLink( TempURL1 ,
            TempURL2 );
           with TheLIArray[ TheLinkID ]^ do
           begin
             TheLabel := HTMLLabel.Create( self );
             TheLabel.Parent := TheScrollBox;
             TheLabel.Visible := true;
             TheLabel.Top := CurrentYPosition;
             TheLabel.Left := CurrentXPosition;
             TheLabel.Width :=
              Form2.Canvas.TextWidth( TheText ) + 2;
             TheLabel.Height := PixelsPerLine;
             TheLabel.OnMouseUp := HotClick;
             TheLabel.Cursor := 5;
             TheLabel.LinkItem := TheLinkID;
             TheLabel.Font.Color := clRed;
             TheLabel.Caption := TheText;
             CurrentXPosition := CurrentXPosition +
              Form2.Canvas.TextWidth( TheText );
```

continued on next page

continued from previous page

```
                        end;
                      end;
                  end;
                end;
            3 : begin { Jump reference; 3 is linked bitmap }
                  ParseLink( TempString1 , 3 , TheText ,
                   TempURL1 , TempURL2 , LStatus );
                  case LStatus of { check for other processing }
                    1 : begin { Jump link; check for special file type }
                          TheURLType := GetURLType( TempURL1 );
                          case TheURLTYpe of
                            6 : begin { Wave file }
                                  TheLinkID := CreateNewLocalLink( '' ,
                                   TempURL1 , TheURLType );
                                  AddImage( TheText , CurrentXPosition ,
                                   CurrentYPosition , ImageY , ImageX );
                                  ImageShownOnLine := true;
                                  IH := ImageX;
                                  with TheLIArray[ TheLinkID ]^ do
                                  begin
                                    TheImage.OnMouseUp := HotClick;
                                    TheImage.Cursor := 5;
                                    TheImage.LinkItem := TheLinkID;
                                  end;
                                  CurrentXPosition:=CurrentXPosition+ ImageY;
                                end;
                            7 : begin { Sprite file }
                                  TheLinkID := CreateNewLocalLink( '' ,
                                   TempURL1 , TheURLType );
                                  AddImage( TheText , CurrentXPosition ,
                                   CurrentYPosition , ImageY , ImageX );
                                  ImageShownOnLine := true;
                                  IH := ImageY;
                                  with TheLIArray[ TheLinkID ]^ do
                                  begin
                                    TheImage.OnMouseUp := HotClick;
                                    TheImage.Cursor := 5;
                                    TheImage.LinkItem := TheLinkID;
                                  end;
                                  TotalSprites := TotalSprites + 1;
                                  New( TheSpritesArray[ TotalSprites ] );
                                  WhichSprites[ TheLinkID ] := TotalSprites;
                                  with TheSpritesArray[ TotalSprites ]^ do
                                  begin
                                    TheSprite := ASprite.Create(TempURL1 );
                                  end;
                                  CurrentXPosition:=CurrentXPosition+ ImageX;
                                end;
                           11 : begin { Standard DHT hypertext file }
                                  TheLinkID := CreateNewNonLocalLink( '' ,
                                   TempURL1 );
                                  AddImage( TheText , CurrentXPosition ,
                                   CurrentYPosition , ImageX , ImageY );
                                  ImageShownOnLine := true;
```

```
                        IH := ImageY;
                        with TheLIArray[ TheLinkID ]^ do
                        begin
                          TheImage.OnMouseUp := HotClick;
                          TheImage.Cursor := 5;
                          TheImage.LinkItem := TheLinkID;
                        end;
                        CurrentXPosition:= CurrentXPosition+ImageX;
                      end;
                  end;
                end;
            2 : begin { Local link; no special processing }
                  TheLinkID := CreateNewLocalLink( TempURL1 ,
                   '' , 1 );
                  AddImage( TheText , CurrentXPosition ,
                   CurrentYPosition , ImageY , ImageX );
                  ImageShownOnLine := true;
                  IH := ImageY;
                  with TheLIArray[ TheLinkID ]^ do
                  begin
                    TheImage.OnMouseUp := HotClick;
                    TheImage.Cursor := 5;
                    {TheImage.OnMouseMove := HTMLMouseMove;}
                    TheImage.LinkItem := TheLinkID;
                  end;
                  CurrentXPosition := CurrentXPosition + ImageX;
                end;
            3 : begin { Non local URL with jump; check for DHT type }
                  TheURLType := GetURLType( TempURL1 );
                  if TheURLType <> 11 then
                  begin { Attempt to do local jump in non HT file }
                    {Don't bother at this level; full app needs this}
                  end;
                  TheLinkID := CreateNewNonLocalLink( TempURL1 ,
                   TempURL2 );
                  AddImage( TheText , CurrentXPosition ,
                   CurrentYPosition , ImageY , ImageX );
                  ImageShownOnLine := true;
                  IH := ImageY;
                  with TheLIArray[ TheLinkID ]^ do
                  begin
                    TheImage.OnMouseUp := HotClick;
                    TheImage.Cursor := 5;
                    TheImage.LinkItem := TheLinkID;
                  end;
                  CurrentXPosition := CurrentXPosition + ImageX;
                end;
          end;
        end;
    4 : begin { Anchor reference; 4 is just text }
          ParseAnchor( TempString1 , 4 , TheText , TempURL1 );
          TheLinkID := CreateNewAnchorLink( TempURL1 ,
           CurrentXPosition , CurrentLine );
          TheLabel := TLabel.Create( self );
          TheLabel.Parent := TheScrollBox;
```

continued on next page

continued from previous page

```
                    TheLabel.Font.Color := clRed;
                    TheLabel.Top := CurrentYPosition;
                    TheLabel.Left := CurrentXPosition;
                    TheLabel.Caption := TheText;
                    TheLabel.Height := PixelsPerLine - 1;
                    TheLabel.Width := Form2.Width - 5;
                    CurrentXPosition := CurrentXPosition +
                     Form2.Canvas.TextWidth( TheText );
                  end;
              5 : begin { Anchor reference; 5 is just image }
                    ParseAnchor( TempString1 , 5 , TheText , TempURL1 );
                    TheLinkID := CreateNewAnchorLink( TempURL2 ,
                     CurrentXPosition , CurrentLine );
                    AddImage( TheText , CurrentXPosition ,
                     CurrentYPosition , ImageY , ImageX );
                    ImageShownOnLine := true;
                    IH := ImageY;
                    CurrentXPosition := CurrentXPosition + ImageX;
                  end;
          end;
        end;
        { Check for the end of the working string }
        if CurrentEnd > Length( WorkingString ) then
        begin
          if not ImageShownOnLine then
          begin
            CurrentLine := CurrentLine + 1;
            Completed := true;
          end
          else
          begin
            ImageShownOnLine := false;
            CurrentLine := CurrentLine + (( IH div PixelsPerLine ) + 1 );
            Completed := true;
          end;
        end
        else WorkingString := Copy( WorkingString , CurrentEnd , 255 );
      end;
    end;
  end;
  TheScrollBox.VertScrollbar.Visible := true;
  TheScrollBox.VertScrollbar.Range := ( CurrentLine * PixelsPerLine ) + 20;
  TheScrollBox.VertScrollBar.Increment := PixelsPerLine;
end;
```

17. Compile and test the project.

How It Works

The key in this How-To lies in using a combination of a timer object with an array of TObjects to allow array-indexed access to TBitmap objects for drawing the sprites.

Had the application attempted to create an array of forty TBitmaps, the compiler would have been unable to do so since this would violate the 64K segmented memory architecture of 16-bit Windows.

Another critical point this application has to overcome is that to show the sprite properly, the handle to the DC for the entire screen is needed, but attached to a TCanvas object so that the CopyRect property can be used. The solution is in these lines of code:

```
GlobalCanvas := TCanvas.Create;
OldHandle := GlobalCanvas.Handle
GlobalCanvas.Handle := GetDC( 0 );
```

OldHandle is of type HDC, which is a handle to a Device Context. At first glance this might seem dangerous, since the DC obtained with GetDC is not created by the VCL. However, it turns out from studying the VCL source code that the handle of a TCanvas is a cached DC and once a valid DC is assigned to one it will work fine, as illustrated in these lines of code.

```
WorkspaceBitmap.Canvas.CopyRect(Rect(0, 0, Width, Height),
GlobalCanvas , Rect(TheScrollBox.Left,TheScrollBox.Top,Width,Height));
```

Notice that passing in the GlobalCanvas object with its handle to the screen DC works just fine! The only potential problem is disposing of a cached DC which may have lived in OldHandle, and that is taken care of here:

```
ReleaseDC( 0 , GlobalCanvas.Handle );
GlobalCanvas.Handle := OldHandle
GlobalCanvas.Free;
```

By resetting the handle property of the GlobalCanvas object prior to calling Free, any cached DC is released. The call to ReleaseDC is made to free up the DC obtained outside the VCL system.

Comments

Included on the CD is another Delphi project, SPRITEDIT.DPR. It gives the source code for a form which allows creating .SPR files interactively.

6.9 How Do I...
Create a complete multimedia HTML document display application?

COMPLEXITY: INTERMEDIATE

Problem

Well, why not go for broke, and put every multimedia format on my PC into the HTML viewer. Can Delphi let me add MIDI files, CD Audio tracks, even AVI video to the HTML display application?

Technique

Delphi is up to the challenge, using techniques from previous How-To's in this chapter and one object developed earlier. When it's done, DHTMLVWR.EXE is a full-blown hypermedia demonstration program!

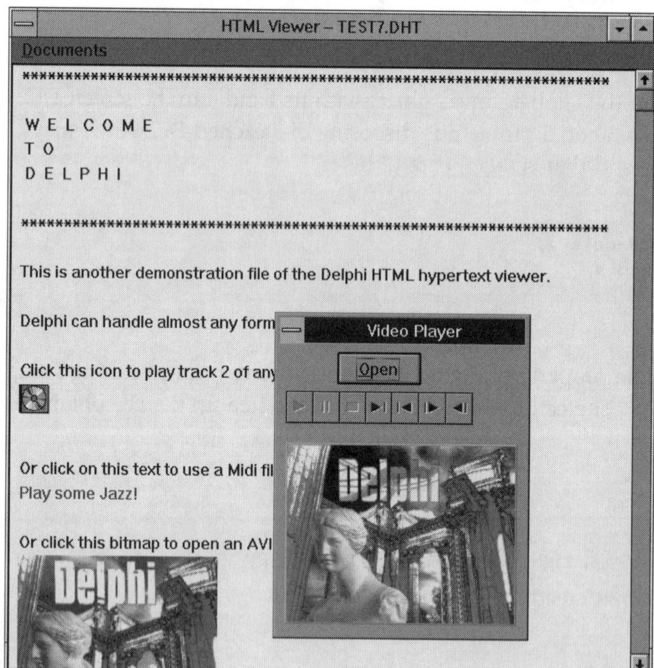

Figure 6-14 DHTMLVWR at run time showing an AVI video link being displayed

Steps

Run DHTMLVWR.EXE from the CHAP06/HOWTO09 directory, and load TEST7.DHT. Assuming you have a CD player on your PC and an audio CD, place it in the PC CD tray and then click on the "Play CD" icon, and the second track of the CD will play. Click on the "Play Some Jazz" red text line and a jazz midi file will play. Or Click on the "Show a Delphi Video" bitmap and a window will open with the Delphi AVI file loaded, as shown in Figure 6-14.

1. Copy the files from How-To 6.8 into a new directory. Rename the unit DHTVIEW5.PAS and the project DHTMLVWR.DPR.
2. Components, properties,and settings remain the same as from How-To 6.5.
3. Go into the Code Editor and move up to the *type* keyword, then find the declaration for Form2 and its *public* keyword, and enter the following highlighted helper procedures and functions.

```
type
 TForm2 = class(TForm)
 public
  { Public declarations }
procedure HotClick( Sender : TObject;
            Button: TMouseButton;
            Shift: TShiftState;
            X, Y: Integer );
  function GetStringToCharacter(   TheString    : String ;
                   TargetString : String;
                    GetTarget    : Boolean;
                  var   ThePosition  : Integer  ) : String;
  function GetStringtoHTMLTag(   TheString       : String;
                  var   EndingPosition : Integer ) : String;
  function GetHTMLTag(   TheString       : String;
              var   EndingPosition : Integer ) : String;
  function ParseHTMLTag(   TheString : String ) : Integer;
  function GetCompleteHTMLReference(   TheString      : String;
                     InputType      : Integer;
                    var   EndingPosition,
                     OutputType     : Integer ) : String;
    function GetURL(   TheString : String ) : String;
    function ParseURL(   TheString : String;
              var   URL1,
                  URL2       : String ) : Integer;
    function GetURLType(   TheString : String ) : Integer;
    procedure ParseAnchor(   TheString      : String;
                  AnchorType     : Integer;
                var   DisplayedText,
                  AnchorText     : String    );
    procedure ParseLink(   TheString      : String;
                  LinkType       : Integer;
               var   DisplayedText,
                  LinkURL1,
```

continued on next page

continued from previous page

```
                    LinkURL2        : String;
                var   LinkStatus     : Integer   );
  function CreateNewAnchorLink(   AnchorName : String;
                    XPos,
                    YPos         : Integer ) : Integer;
  function CreateNewLocalLink(   AnchorName,
                    FileName    : String;
                    TheType     : Integer ) : Integer;
  function CreateNewNonLocalLink(   AnchorName ,
                    FileName     : String ) : Integer;
  procedure FindLocalAnchor(   TheAnchor : String;
                var  XLoc,
                    YLoc     : Integer );
  function CreateNewRawImage(   TheURL         : String;
                    CurrentX  ,
                    CurrentY      : Integer;
                var  ImageWidth  ,
                    ImageHeight  : Integer ) : Integer;
  procedure AddImage(   TheURL          : String;
              CurrentX  ,
              CurrentY      : Integer;
          var  ImageWidth  ,
              ImageHeight  : Integer );
  procedure PlayWaveAudio(   TheWaveFile : String );
  procedure PlayAviVideo(   TheAviFile : String );
  procedure PlayMidiAudio(   TheMidiFile : String );
  procedure PlayCDAudio(   TheCDReferenceFile : String );
  procedure InitializeDHTMLFile(   TheFileName , TheAnchorName : String );
  procedure CreateNewDHTDocument;
end;
```

4. Still in the Code Editor, move down below the *end* keyword for the Form2 type declaration, and enter the following highlighted assistant type definitions.

```
HTMLLabel = class( TLabel )
  private
    LinkItem : Integer;
end;
HTMLImage = class( TImage )
  private
    LinkItem : Integer;
end;
PLinkItemRecord = ^LinkItemRecord;
LinkItemRecord = record
  LinkFile : String;
  LinkAnchor : String;
  ImageFile : String;
  LinkType,
  XPosition ,
  YPosition    : Integer;
  HasImage ,
```

```
    HasLabel : Boolean;
    TheLabel : HTMLLabel;
    TheImage : HTMLImage;
  end;
  LinkItemArray = array[ 1 .. 255 ] of PLinkItemRecord;
  TNamesArray = array[ 1 .. 20 , 1 .. 2 ] of String;
  TDeltasArray = array [ 1 .. 20 , 1 .. 2 ] of Integer;
  TObjectArray = array [ 1 .. 20 , 1 .. 2 ] of TObject;
  TSpriteRecord = record
       TotalImages : Integer;
       TheNamesArray : TNamesArray;
       DeltasArray   : TDeltasArray;
       StartingX ,
       StartingY ,
       NewSpriteInterval,
       TimerInterval       : Integer;
  end;
  ASprite = class( TObject )
    private
       TheSpriteRecord : TSpriteRecord;
       SpriteTimer : TTimer;
       TheSpriteBitmaps : TObjectArray;
       CurrentSpriteX ,
       CurrentSpriteY ,
       CurrentImage ,
       CurrentDelayInterval : Integer;
       constructor Create( TheFileName : String );
       procedure LoadFromFile( TheFileName : String );
       procedure Play;
       procedure Free;
       procedure SpriteOnTimer(Sender: TObject);
       procedure DrawCurrentSprite;
  end;
  pSprite = ^TSprite;
  TSprite = record
    TheSprite : ASprite;
  end;
  CDARecord = record
    TrackToPlay : Integer;
  end;
```

5. Move down below the *implementation* keyword and enter this assistant procedure to handle playing an AVI video file.

```
procedure TForm2.PlayAviVideo( TheAviFile : String );
begin
  StoredAVIFilename := TheAviFile;
  VideoForm := TVideoForm.Create( Self );
  VideoForm.OpenButtonClick( Self );
end;
```

continued on next page

6. Move down below the previous procedure and enter this assistant procedure to deal with playing a MIDI audio file.

```
procedure TForm2.PlayMidiAudio( TheMidiFile : String );
begin
  MediaPlayer1.FileName := TheMidiFile;
  MediaPlayer1.Open;
  MediaPlayer1.Play;
  MediaPlayer1.Close;
end;
```

7. Move down below the previous procedure and enter this assistant procedure to take care of playing an audio CD track from a description file.

```
procedure TForm2.PlayCDAudio( TheCDReferenceFile : String );
var Counter_1 : Integer;
    TheFile : File of CDARecord;
    TheCDARecord : CDARecord;
begin
  AssignFile( TheFile , TheCDReferenceFile );
  Reset( TheFile );
  Seek( TheFile , 0 );
  Read( TheFile , TheCDARecord );
  CloseFile( TheFile );
  with MediaPlayer1 do
  begin
    {Ensure closed before attempt to open}
    if Mode = mpPlaying then Close;
    {dtAutoSelect only works on file-type data}
    DeviceType := dtCDAudio;
    {The entire CD is a nameless 'file'}
    FileName := '';
    { Open The CD }
    Open;
    { Move to the Desired track }
    for Counter_1 := 1 to TheCDARecord.TrackToPlay do
     Next;
    { And Play it! }
    Play;
    { Close the Player }
    Close;
  end;
end;
```

8. Find the function below and type in the highlighted text to handle determining the URL type based on the extension of the file name, including new types for this How-To.

```
function TForm2.GetURLType( TheString : String ) : Integer;
var ExtensionString : String;
begin
  { This function assumes a valid URL has been obtained }
  { It determines what type of data is acquired via URL }
```

```
  ExtensionString := Uppercase( ExtractFileExt( TheString ));
  if ExtensionString = '.DHT' then
  begin
    GetURLType := 11; { Standard delphi hypertext file }
    exit;
  end;
  if ExtensionString = '.BMP' then
  begin
    GetURLType := 2; { Bitmap image file; only valid in IMG URL }
    exit;
  end;
  if ExtensionString = '.ICO' then
  begin
    GetURLType := 3; { Windows Icon image file; only valid in IMG URL }
    exit;
  end;
  if ExtensionString = '.WMF' then
  begin
    GetURLType := 4; { Windows Metafile image file; only valid in IMG URL }
    exit;
  end;
  if ExtensionString = '.GIF' then
  begin
    GetURLType := 5; { GIF image file; only valid in IMG URL }
    exit;
  end;
  if ExtensionString = '.WAV' then
  begin
    GetURLType := 6; { Windows sound file }
    exit;
  end;
  if ExtensionString = '.SPR' then
  begin
    GetURLType := 7; { Delphi sprite file }
    exit;
  end;
  if ExtensionString = '.AVI' then
  begin
    GetURLType := 8; { Windows video image file }
    exit;
  end;
  if ExtensionString = '.MID' then
  begin
    GetURLType := 9; { Windows MIDI sound file }
    exit;
  end;
  if ExtensionString = '.CDA' then
  begin
    GetURLType := 10; { CD Audio sound track DHT reference file }
    exit;
  end;
  GETURLType := -1; { File extension doesn't match known type; signal error }
end;
```

continued on next page

9. Find the function below and type in the highlighted text to handle responding to a hypertext link activation including the new file types.

```
procedure TForm2.HotClick( Sender : TOBject;
             Button: TMouseButton;
             Shift: TShiftState;
             X, Y: Integer );

var TheItem : Integer;
   TheLinkFile ,
   TheLinkAnchor : String;
begin
 { Do dynamic typecast to find out which type of object made call }
 if Sender is HTMLLabel then
 begin { Paintbox hit; treat as text }
  TheItem := HTMLLabel( Sender ).LinkItem;
  { Grab the link record to work with }
  with TheLIArray[ TheItem ]^ do
  begin
   { Branch on type of link (note that 2-5 are not link ids & not used) }
   case LinkType of
    1 : begin { jump within current file }
          TheScrollBox.VertScrollBar.Position :=
          ( YPosition * PixelsPerLine ) - TheScrollBox.Height;
       end;
    6 : begin { wave file }
          PlayWaveAudio( LinkFile );
       end;
    7 : begin { sprite file }
          TheSpritesArray[ WhichSprites[ TheItem ]]^.TheSprite.Play;
       end;
    8 : begin { avi file }
          PlayAviVideo( LinkFile );
       end;
    9 : begin { midi file }
          PlayMidiAudio( LinkFile );
       end;
    10 : begin { cd audio ref file }
          PlayCDAudio( LinkFile );
       end;
    11 : begin { jump to new file }
          InitializeDHTMLFile( LinkFile , LinkAnchor );
       end;
    end;
   end;
 end
 else
 begin { Image hit; treat as image }
  with Sender as HTMLImage do
  begin
   { Grab the link record to work with }
   with TheLIArray[ LinkItem ]^ do
   begin
```

```
    { Branch on type of link(note that 2-5 are not link ids & not used) }
    case LinkType of
     1 : begin { jump within current file }
         VertScrollBar.Position :=
         ( YPosition * PixelsPerLine ) - Self.Height;
        end;
      6 : begin { wave file }
          PlayWaveAudio( LinkFile );
        end;
      7 : begin { sprite file }
          TheSpritesArray[ WhichSprites[ LinkItem ]]^.TheSprite.Play;
        end;
      8 : begin { avi file }
          PlayAviVideo( LinkFile );
        end;
      9 : begin { midi file }
          PlayMidiAudio( LinkFile );
        end;
      10 : begin { cd audio ref file }
           PlayCDAudio( LinkFile );
        end;
      11 : begin { jump to new file }
           InitializeDHTMLFile( LinkFile , LinkAnchor );
        end;
      end;
     end;
   end;
 end;
end;
```

10. Find the function below and type in the highlighted text to handle displaying hypertext links using the new URL types.

```
procedure TForm2.CreateNewDHTDocument;
var TempString1    ,
  TempString2   ,
  TempURL1      ,
  TempURL2      ,
  WorkingString ,
  TheText          : String;
  TheLinkID ,
  TheURLType ,
  LStatus ,
  EndingPosition ,
  CurrentEnd ,
  Counter_1 ,
  CurrentXPosition ,
  CurrentYPosition ,
  CurrentLine       ,
  IH ,
  ImageX ,
  ImageY ,
  HTMLKind ,
```

continued on next page

continued from previous page

```
  ValidResult         : Integer;
  ImageShownOnLine ,
  Completed : Boolean;
  TheLabel :TLabel;
begin
 { Create the scrollbox to show the document on }
 TheScrollBox.Free;
 TheScrollBox := TScrollBox.Create( self );
 TheScrollBox.Parent := self;
 TheScrollBox.Align := alclient;
 { Find out height of a line in the document }
 PixelsPerLine := Form2.Canvas.TextHeight( 'W' ) + 2;
 { Set initial Drawing Positions }
 CurrentXPosition := 10;
 CurrentYPosition := 20;
 { Set the current line for line calculations }
 CurrentLine := 1;
 { Loop through the memo and display the lines as hypertext and graphics }
 for Counter_1 := 1 to TheStringList.Count do
 begin
  { Clear the flag to indicate completion of current line }
  Completed := false;
  ImageShownOnLine := false;
  { Start parsing at the first character }
  EndingPosition := 1;
  CurrentXPosition := 10;
  CurrentYPosition := (( CurrentLine - 1 ) * PixelsPerLine );
  { Get a working copy of the memo line }
  WorkingString := TheStringList.Strings[ Counter_1 - 1 ];
  { Work along the working string until done }
  if DumpInvalidHTML then
  begin
   Completed := true;
   TheLabel := TLabel.Create( self );
   TheLabel.Parent := TheScrollBox;
   TheLabel.Font.Color := clBlack;
   TheLabel.Top := CurrentYPosition;
   TheLabel.Left := CurrentXPosition;
   TheLabel.Caption := WorkingString;
   TheLabel.Height := PixelsPerLine - 1;
   TheLabel.Width := Form2.Width - 5;
   { TheScrollBox.InsertComponent( TheLabel );}
  end;
  while not Completed do
  begin
   { Eat off up to HTML command }
   TempString1 := GetStringToHTMLTag( WorkingString , CurrentEnd );
   if TempString1 <> '' then
   begin { Some text to show so show it}
    TheLabel := TLabel.Create( self );
    TheLabel.Parent := TheScrollBox;
    TheLabel.Font.Color := clBlack;
    TheLabel.Top := CurrentYPosition;
    TheLabel.Left := CurrentXPosition;
```

```
   TheLabel.Caption := TempString1;
   TheLabel.Height := PixelsPerLine - 1;
   TheLabel.Width := Form2.Width - 5;
   { Move the output pointer along }
   CurrentXPosition := CurrentXPosition +
    Form2.Canvas.TextWidth( TempString1 );
end;
 { Check for the end of the working string }
 if CurrentEnd > Length( WorkingString ) then
 begin
  Completed := true;
  CurrentLine := CurrentLine + 1;
  if ImageShownOnLine then
  begin
   ImageShownOnLine := false;
   CurrentLine := CurrentLine - 1 + (( IH div PixelsPerLine ) + 1 );
 end;
end
else
 begin
  { Chop off the parsed string portion and work with the rest }
  WorkingString := Copy( WorkingString , CurrentEnd , 255 );
  { Assume HTML tag next, so get it }
  TempString1 := GetCompleteHTMLReference( WorkingString , 0 ,
                     CurrentEnd , HTMLKind );
  if TempString1 = '' then
  begin { Bad or malformed HTML Tag; abort processing }
   MessageDlg( 'Bad or malformed HTML Tag! Aborting Processing...' ,
   mtError , [ mbOK ] , 0 );
   DumpInvalidHTML := true;
   TheLabel := TLabel.Create( self );
   TheLabel.Parent := TheScrollBox;
   TheLabel.Font.Color := clBlack;
   TheLabel.Top := CurrentYPosition;
   TheLabel.Left := CurrentXPosition;
   TheLabel.Caption := WorkingString;
   TheLabel.Height := PixelsPerLine - 1;
   TheLabel.Width := Form2.Width - 5;
   if not ImageShownOnLine then
   begin
    Completed := true;
    CurrentLine := CurrentLine + 1;
  end
  else
  begin
   ImageShownOnLine := false;
   CurrentLine := CurrentLine + (( IH div PixelsPerLine ) + 1 );
   Completed := true;
 end;
end
 else
 begin { Possibly Valid HTML tag; process it to be sure }
  case HTMLKind of  { parse on type of tag }
   1 : begin { Raw image without anchor or jump attached }
       TempString2 := GetURL( TempString1 );
```

continued on next page

continued from previous page

```
          ValidResult := CreateNewRawImage( TempString2 ,
          CurrentXPosition , CurrentYPosition , ImageY, ImageX );
          if ValidResult < 0 then
          begin { Bad image file; signal and abort }
           MessageDlg( 'Invalid Image! Aborting Processing...' ,
           mtError , [ mbOK ] , 0 );
          DumpInvalidHTML := true;
          TheLabel := TLabel.Create( self );
          TheLabel.Parent := TheScrollBox;
          TheLabel.Font.Color := clBlack;
          TheLabel.Top := CurrentYPosition;
          TheLabel.Left := CurrentXPosition;
          TheLabel.Caption := WorkingString;
          TheLabel.Height := PixelsPerLine - 1;
          TheLabel.Width := Form2.Width - 5;
          if not ImageShownOnLine then
          begin
           Completed := true;
           CurrentLine := CurrentLine + 1;
         end
         else
         begin
          ImageShownOnLine := false;
          CurrentLine := CurrentLine +
          (( IH div PixelsPerLine ) + 1 );
          Completed := true;
        end;
       end
       else
       begin
        ImageShownOnLine := true;
        CurrentXPosition := CurrentXPosition + ImageX;
        IH := ImageY;
       end;
      end;
    2 : begin { Jump reference; 2 is just text }
        ParseLink( TempString1 , 2 , TheText ,
        TempURL1 , TempURL2 , LStatus );
        case LStatus of { check for other processing }
         1 : begin { Jump link; check for special file type }
            TheURLType := GetURLType( TempURL1 );
            case TheURLTYpe of
             6 : begin { Wave file }
                  TheLinkID := CreateNewLocalLink( '' ,
                  TempURL1 , TheURLType );
                  with TheLIArray[ TheLinkID ]^ do
                 begin
                  TheLabel := HTMLLabel.Create( self );
                  TheLabel.Parent := TheScrollBox;
                  TheLabel.Visible := true;
                  TheLabel.Top := CurrentYPosition;
                  TheLabel.Left := CurrentXPosition;
                  TheLabel.Width :=
                  Form2.Canvas.TextWidth( TheText ) + 2;
```

```
      TheLabel.Height := PixelsPerLine;
      TheLabel.OnMouseUp := HotClick;
      TheLabel.Cursor := 5;
      TheLabel.LinkItem := TheLinkID;
      TheLabel.Font.Color := clRed;
      TheLabel.Caption := TheText;
      CurrentXPosition := CurrentXPosition +
       Form2.Canvas.TextWidth( TheText );
    end;
  end;
 7 : begin { Sprite file }
      TheLinkID := CreateNewLocalLink( '' ,
      TempURL1 , TheURLType );
      with TheLIArray[ TheLinkID ]^ do
      begin
       TheLabel := HTMLLabel.Create( self );
       TheLabel.Parent := TheScrollBox;
       TheLabel.Visible := true;
       TheLabel.Top := CurrentYPosition;
       TheLabel.Left := CurrentXPosition;
       TheLabel.Width :=
       Form2.Canvas.TextWidth( TheText ) + 2;
       TheLabel.Height := PixelsPerLine;
       TheLabel.OnMouseUp := HotClick;
       TheLabel.Cursor := 5;
       TheLabel.LinkItem := TheLinkID;
       TheLabel.Font.Color := clRed;
       TheLabel.Caption := TheText;
       CurrentXPosition := CurrentXPosition +
       Form2.Canvas.TextWidth( TheText );
    end;
      TotalSprites := TotalSprites + 1;
      New( TheSpritesArray[ TotalSprites ] );
      WhichSprites[ TheLinkID ] := TotalSprites;
      with TheSpritesArray[ TotalSprites ]^ do
     begin
      TheSprite := ASprite.Create( TempURL1 );
    end;
  end;
 8 : begin { AVI file }
       TheLinkID := CreateNewLocalLink( '' ,
       TempURL1 , TheURLType );
       with TheLIArray[ TheLinkID ]^ do
       begin
        TheLabel := HTMLLabel.Create( self );
        TheLabel.Parent := TheScrollBox;
        TheLabel.Visible := true;
        TheLabel.Top := CurrentYPosition;
        TheLabel.Left := CurrentXPosition;
        TheLabel.Width :=
        Form2.Canvas.TextWidth( TheText ) + 2;
        TheLabel.Height := PixelsPerLine;
        TheLabel.OnMouseUp := HotClick;
        TheLabel.Cursor := 5;
        TheLabel.LinkItem := TheLinkID;
```

continued on next page

continued from previous page

```
          TheLabel.Font.Color := clRed;
          TheLabel.Caption := TheText;
          CurrentXPosition := CurrentXPosition +
          Form2.Canvas.TextWidth( TheText );
       end;
     end;
   9 : begin { MIDI file }
        TheLinkID := CreateNewLocalLink( '' ,
        TempURL1 , TheURLType );
        with TheLIArray[ TheLinkID ]^ do
        begin
         TheLabel := HTMLLabel.Create( self );
         TheLabel.Parent := TheScrollBox;
         TheLabel.Visible := true;
         TheLabel.Top := CurrentYPosition;
         TheLabel.Left := CurrentXPosition;
         TheLabel.Width :=
         Form2.Canvas.TextWidth( TheText ) + 2;
         TheLabel.Height := PixelsPerLine;
         TheLabel.OnMouseUp := HotClick;
         TheLabel.Cursor := 5;
         TheLabel.LinkItem := TheLinkID;
         TheLabel.Font.Color := clRed;
         TheLabel.Caption := TheText;
         CurrentXPosition := CurrentXPosition +
         Form2.Canvas.TextWidth( TheText );
      end;
    end;
   10 : begin { CD Audio file }
        TheLinkID := CreateNewLocalLink( '' ,
        TempURL1 , TheURLType );
        with TheLIArray[ TheLinkID ]^ do
        begin
         TheLabel := HTMLLabel.Create( self );
         TheLabel.Parent := TheScrollBox;
         TheLabel.Visible := true;
         TheLabel.Top := CurrentYPosition;
         TheLabel.Left := CurrentXPosition;
         TheLabel.Width :=
         Form2.Canvas.TextWidth( TheText ) + 2;
         TheLabel.Height := PixelsPerLine;
         TheLabel.OnMouseUp := HotClick;
         TheLabel.Cursor := 5;
         TheLabel.LinkItem := TheLinkID;
         TheLabel.Font.Color := clRed;
         TheLabel.Caption := TheText;
         CurrentXPosition := CurrentXPosition +
         Form2.Canvas.TextWidth( TheText );
     end;
   end;
   11 : begin { Standard DHT hypertext file }
        TheLinkID := CreateNewNonLocalLink( '' ,
        TempURL1 );
        with TheLIArray[ TheLinkID ]^ do
```

```
            begin
             TheLabel := HTMLLabel.Create( self );
             TheLabel.Parent := TheScrollBox;
             TheLabel.Visible := true;
             TheLabel.Top := CurrentYPosition;
             TheLabel.Left := CurrentXPosition;
             TheLabel.Width :=
             Form2.Canvas.TextWidth( TheText ) + 2;
             TheLabel.Height := PixelsPerLine;
             TheLabel.OnMouseUp := HotClick;
             TheLabel.Cursor := 5;
             TheLabel.LinkItem := TheLinkID;
             TheLabel.Font.Color := clRed;
             TheLabel.Caption := TheText;
             CurrentXPosition := CurrentXPosition +
             Form2.Canvas.TextWidth( TheText );
          end;
         end;
     end;
   end;
  2 : begin { Local link; no special processing }
      TheLinkID := CreateNewLocalLink( TempURL1 ,
      '' , 1 );
      with TheLIArray[ TheLinkID ]^ do
      begin
       TheLabel := HTMLLabel.Create( self );
       TheLabel.Parent := TheScrollBox;
       TheLabel.Visible := true;
       TheLabel.Top := CurrentYPosition;
       TheLabel.Left := CurrentXPosition;
       TheLabel.Width :=
       Form2.Canvas.TextWidth( TheText ) + 2;
       TheLabel.Height := PixelsPerLine;
       TheLabel.OnMouseUp := HotClick;
       TheLabel.Cursor := 5;
       TheLabel.LinkItem := TheLinkID;
       TheLabel.Font.Color := clRed;
       TheLabel.Caption := TheText;
       CurrentXPosition := CurrentXPosition +
       Form2.Canvas.TextWidth( TheText );
    end;
   end;
  3 : begin { Non local URL with jump; check for DHT type }
      TheURLType := GetURLType( TempURL1 );
      if TheURLType <> 11 then
      begin { Attempt to do local jump in non HT file }
       {Don't bother at this level; full app needs this}
     end;
      TheLinkID := CreateNewNonLocalLink( TempURL1 ,
      TempURL2 );
      with TheLIArray[ TheLinkID ]^ do
      begin
       TheLabel := HTMLLabel.Create( self );
       TheLabel.Parent := TheScrollBox;
       TheLabel.Visible := true;
```

continued on next page

continued from previous page

```
            TheLabel.Top := CurrentYPosition;
            TheLabel.Left := CurrentXPosition;
            TheLabel.Width :=
            Form2.Canvas.TextWidth( TheText ) + 2;
            TheLabel.Height := PixelsPerLine;
            TheLabel.OnMouseUp := HotClick;
            TheLabel.Cursor := 5;
            TheLabel.LinkItem := TheLinkID;
            TheLabel.Font.Color := clRed;
            TheLabel.Caption := TheText;
            CurrentXPosition := CurrentXPosition +
            Form2.Canvas.TextWidth( TheText );
          end;
         end;
      end;
     end;
    3 : begin { Jump reference; 3 is linked bitmap }
        ParseLink( TempString1 , 3 , TheText ,
        TempURL1 , TempURL2 , LStatus );
        case LStatus of { check for other processing }
         1 : begin { Jump link; check for special file type }
            TheURLType := GetURLType( TempURL1 );
            case TheURLTYpe of
             6 : begin { Wave file }
                 TheLinkID := CreateNewLocalLink( '' ,
                 TempURL1 , TheURLType );
                 AddImage( TheText , CurrentXPosition ,
                 CurrentYPosition , ImageY , ImageX );
                 ImageShownOnLine := true;
                 IH := ImageX;
                 with TheLIArray[ TheLinkID ]^ do
                 begin
                  TheImage.OnMouseUp := HotClick;
                  TheImage.Cursor := 5;
                  TheImage.LinkItem := TheLinkID;
                end;
                  CurrentXPosition:=CurrentXPosition+ ImageY;
               end;
             7 : begin { Sprite file }
                 TheLinkID := CreateNewLocalLink( '' ,
                 TempURL1 , TheURLType );
                 AddImage( TheText , CurrentXPosition ,
                 CurrentYPosition , ImageY , ImageX );
                 ImageShownOnLine := true;
                 IH := ImageY;
                 with TheLIArray[ TheLinkID ]^ do
                 begin
                  TheImage.OnMouseUp := HotClick;
                  TheImage.Cursor := 5;
                  {TheImage.OnMouseMove := HTMLMouseMove;}
                  TheImage.LinkItem := TheLinkID;
                end;
                  TotalSprites := TotalSprites + 1;
```

```
  New( TheSpritesArray[ TotalSprites ] );
  WhichSprites[ TheLinkID ] := TotalSprites;
  with TheSpritesArray[ TotalSprites ]^ do
  begin
   TheSprite := ASprite.Create( TempURL1 );
 end;
   CurrentXPosition:=CurrentXPosition+ ImageX;
 end;
8 : begin { AVI file }
     TheLinkID := CreateNewLocalLink( '' ,
     TempURL1 , TheURLType );
      AddImage( TheText , CurrentXPosition ,
     CurrentYPosition , ImageY , ImageX );
     ImageShownOnLine := true;
     IH := ImageY;
     with TheLIArray[ TheLinkID ]^ do
     begin
      TheImage.OnMouseUp := HotClick;
      TheImage.Cursor := 5;
      TheImage.LinkItem := TheLinkID;
    end;
      CurrentXPosition:=CurrentXPosition+ ImageX;
  end;
9 : begin { MIDI file }
     TheLinkID := CreateNewLocalLink( '' ,
     TempURL1 , TheURLType );
     AddImage( TheText , CurrentXPosition ,
     CurrentYPosition , ImageY , ImageX );
     ImageShownOnLine := true;
     IH := ImageY;
     with TheLIArray[ TheLinkID ]^ do
     begin
      TheImage.OnMouseUp := HotClick;
      TheImage.Cursor := 5;
      TheImage.LinkItem := TheLinkID;
    end;
      CurrentXPosition:=CurrentXPosition+ ImageX;
  end;
10 : begin { CD Audio file }
     TheLinkID := CreateNewLocalLink( '' ,
     TempURL1 , TheURLType );
     AddImage( TheText , CurrentXPosition ,
     CurrentYPosition , ImageY , ImageX );
     ImageShownOnLine := true;
     IH := ImageY;
     with TheLIArray[ TheLinkID ]^ do
     begin
      TheImage.OnMouseUp := HotClick;
      TheImage.Cursor := 5;
      TheImage.LinkItem := TheLinkID;
    end;
      CurrentXPosition:=CurrentXPosition+ ImageX;
  end;
```

continued on next page

continued from previous page

```
          11 : begin { Standard DHT hypertext file }
              TheLinkID := CreateNewNonLocalLink( '' ,
              TempURL1 );
              AddImage( TheText , CurrentXPosition ,
              CurrentYPosition , ImageX , ImageY );
              ImageShownOnLine := true;
              IH := ImageY;
              with TheLIArray[ TheLinkID ]^ do
              begin
               TheImage.OnMouseUp := HotClick;
               TheImage.Cursor := 5;
               TheImage.LinkItem := TheLinkID;
             end;
               CurrentXPosition:=CurrentXPosition+ ImageX;
           end;
        end;
       end;
       2 : begin { Local link; no special processing }
           TheLinkID := CreateNewLocalLink( TempURL1 ,
           '' , 1 );
           AddImage( TheText , CurrentXPosition ,
           CurrentYPosition , ImageY , ImageX );
           ImageShownOnLine := true;
           IH := ImageY;
           with TheLIArray[ TheLinkID ]^ do
           begin
            TheImage.OnMouseUp := HotClick;
            TheImage.Cursor := 5;
            TheImage.LinkItem := TheLinkID;
         end;
            CurrentXPosition := CurrentXPosition + ImageX;
        end;
       3 : begin { Non local URL with jump; check for DHT type }
           TheURLType := GetURLType( TempURL1 );
           if TheURLType <> 11 then
           begin { Attempt to do local jump in non HT file }
            {Dont bother at this level; full app needs this}
         end;
           TheLinkID := CreateNewNonLocalLink( TempURL1 ,
           TempURL2 );
           AddImage( TheText , CurrentXPosition ,
           CurrentYPosition , ImageY , ImageX );
           ImageShownOnLine := true;
           IH := ImageY;
           with TheLIArray[ TheLinkID ]^ do
           begin
            TheImage.OnMouseUp := HotClick;
            TheImage.Cursor := 5;
            TheImage.LinkItem := TheLinkID;
          end;
            CurrentXPosition := CurrentXPosition + ImageX;
         end;
      end;
```

```
          end;
         4 : begin { Anchor reference; 4 is just text }
             ParseAnchor( TempString1 , 4 , TheText , TempURL1 );
             TheLinkID := CreateNewAnchorLink( TempURL1 ,
              CurrentXPosition , CurrentLine );
              TheLabel := TLabel.Create( self );
              TheLabel.Parent := TheScrollBox;
              TheLabel.Font.Color := clRed;
              TheLabel.Top := CurrentYPosition;
              TheLabel.Left := CurrentXPosition;
              TheLabel.Caption := TheText;
              TheLabel.Height := PixelsPerLine - 1;
              TheLabel.Width := Form2.Width - 5;
              CurrentXPosition := CurrentXPosition +
              Form2.Canvas.TextWidth( TheText );
            end;
          5 : begin { Anchor reference; 5 is just image }
               ParseAnchor( TempString1 , 5 , TheText , TempURL1 );
               TheLinkID := CreateNewAnchorLink( TempURL2 ,
               CurrentXPosition , CurrentLine );
               AddImage( TheText , CurrentXPosition ,
               CurrentYPosition , ImageY , ImageX );
               ImageShownOnLine := true;
               IH := ImageY;
                CurrentXPosition := CurrentXPosition + ImageX;
             end;
          end;
       end;
        { Check for the end of the working string }
        if CurrentEnd > Length( WorkingString ) then
        begin
         if not ImageShownOnLine then
         begin
           CurrentLine := CurrentLine + 1;
           Completed := true;
         end
         else
         begin
          ImageShownOnLine := false;
          CurrentLine := CurrentLine + (( IH div PixelsPerLine ) + 1 );
          Completed := true;
        end;
       end
        else WorkingString := Copy( WorkingString , CurrentEnd , 255 );
     end;
   end;
 end;
  TheScrollBox.VertScrollbar.Visible := true;
 TheScrollBox.VertScrollbar.Range := ( CurrentLine * PixelsPerLine ) + 20;
 TheScrollBox.VertScrollBar.Increment := PixelsPerLine;
end;
```

11. Compile and test the project.

continued on next page

How It Works

This How-To is fairly simple. It employes the code-reuse capabilities inherent in the object metaphor, by creating the TVideoPanel object from How-To 6.2 to display the AVI file. The TMediaplayer component handles the playing of both audio CD tracks and MIDI files.

Comments

Notice that the code closes each media device after it is finished playing. This prevents multimedia collisions which might cause unpredictable behavior.

7

7 ENVIRONMENT AND SYSTEM

How Do I...

As a programmer, you have probably discovered the importance of knowing what is going on in the world around your application. This is especially true in Windows programming, because several processes can be happening at the same time. The good news is that Windows gives you fairly good facilities in the way of API functions to find out much of the information that you may want. The bad news is that Delphi does not encapsulate many of these functions, so you have to use the Windows API. As previous chapters have shown, however, this really isn't bad news because Delphi makes it so easy to use Windows API functions. The toughest thing about using API functions is knowing which ones to use, and that is what this chapter is all about!

7.1 Run another application from my application

There will be times when you need to run another program from your application. This may be another Windows program, but it could also be a DOS program. Whatever the need, this How-To gives ideas on how to accomplish this. It also shows how to cause your program to wait until the other program has completed its processing. This is helpful for running DOS file decompression programs, for example.

7.2 Exit Windows and return to DOS

The Windows API gives you the power to take control of Windows and exit to DOS. You can also run a program while in DOS and then return to Windows, or even reboot the user's computer. These functions are commonly used in installation programs and could certainly be used elsewhere.

7.3 Delay my application for a specified period of time

Some of the other programming environments have a command such as SLEEP or PAUSE that causes program execution to pause for a specified period of time. Delphi does not have a command designed specifically for this purpose, but of course there are ways to do it. This How-To shows one method to pause program execution without using a timer.

7.4 Prevent Windows from shutting down during an operation

When the user tries to exit Windows, each running program is queried as to whether it is ready to shut down. You can take advantage of this query to stop

Windows from shutting down or at least inform the user that some action should be taken prior to shutting down Windows.

7.5 Search an entire disk for a file

During the installation process it is often necessary to find a particular file. There are other times when this ability might be useful, such as in utilities that search a drive for duplicate files. This How-To shows you the basics of searching through all the directories and subdirectories on a drive.

7.6 Disable the Windows screen saver

The Windows screen saver is a handy feature that saves the computer's monitor from getting burned in and provides a welcome diversion. There are times when the screen saver is not so welcome, such as during long operations that are CPU intensive. The screen saver can make these operations take longer to complete. This How-To demonstrates how to disable the screen saver when necessary.

7.7 Prevent multiple instances of my program from being loaded

Windows' ability to run several instances of a program at once is usually considered an advantage, but problems can result if a program is not designed to be run this way. The best way to protect against these problems is simply not to allow multiple instances of your program to be run.

7.8 Determine how many function keys are on the user's keyboard

When you add support for function keys, you must take into account that the user may not have some of the keys that your program requires. Determining the number of function keys that a user has is fairly easy with the right Windows API call.

7.9 Determine the directory where Windows is located

The Windows directory is an important one to keep track of on the user's system. There are times, especially when installing files, that it is essential to know where the Windows directory is. You can't assume that it is on the C: drive. It might be on another drive or maybe even on another computer. Luckily, a Windows API function will track it down for you.

7.10 Determine system resources and display them in a form

If system resources get too low, Windows can grind to a screeching halt with little or no warning. If your application is in the middle of an important process when

Windows runs out of resources, data loss or corruption can result. This How-To shows you how to keep tabs on these resources.

7.11 Determine how much memory is available

Usually Windows does a pretty good job of making sure ample memory is available, but there are situations that can get you and your program in trouble. This How-To shows how to monitor the memory available to your application.

7.12 Determine the correct version of Windows that is running on the user's machine

The Windows API function that returns the version of Windows your application is running on doesn't always give you the correct information. This How-To shows how to get the correct version every time.

7.13 Find out if the user's machine has a defective Pentium processor

You may have heard that a flaw was found in many of the new Pentium processors. The flaw is not a big one and isn't likely to affect most users. If you develop applications that could be affected by this flaw, however, it may be a good idea to give your users a warning if they are unknowingly running a defective Pentium-based computer.

7.14 Simulate SPY in Delphi

SPY is a utility included with the Windows Software Development Kit (SDK) that allows you to get information about the various windows on your system. Delphi includes a similar program called WinSight. This How-To demonstrates some of the techniques used in these programs and builds a helpful utility that you can add to your collection.

7.15 Time functions in my application

There is often more than one way to achieve the same result while writing a program. One way to decide which algorithm is best is to time it. Many functions will be far too fast to time with a stopwatch, so this How-To shows you how to add code to your programs and time whatever you want down to the millisecond.

7.16 Set a file's date and time

The date and time stamps of a file are normally set by DOS to the last time the file was updated. You can set the time and date yourself, and this can make it easier to recognize when files have been changed. This How-To shows you how to modify the date and time stamp of files—and develop a handy utility in the process.

7.1 How Do I...
Run another application from my application?

COMPLEXITY: INTERMEDIATE

Problem

I often need to run another program from my Delphi application, but I'm not sure how to do this. In addition, it would be helpful if I could cause my application to wait until the other program finishes processing before my program continues with what it is doing. How can I do this with Delphi?

Technique

Running another program from your Delphi application isn't too difficult. It involves the use of either the ShellExecute or WinExec Windows API functions. There is no facility in these functions to wait for an application to complete its processing though, so you'll see how to add this capability yourself.

Steps

Run DELSHELL.EXE. Notice the options offered by the check boxes on the form, as shown in Figure 7-1. Experiment with the various options while running several DOS or Windows programs. The printing option works for files that have been associated with a Windows program capable of directly printing a file.

1. Create a new project with a blank form and name it DELSHELL.DPR. Name the unit DELSHEL.PAS.

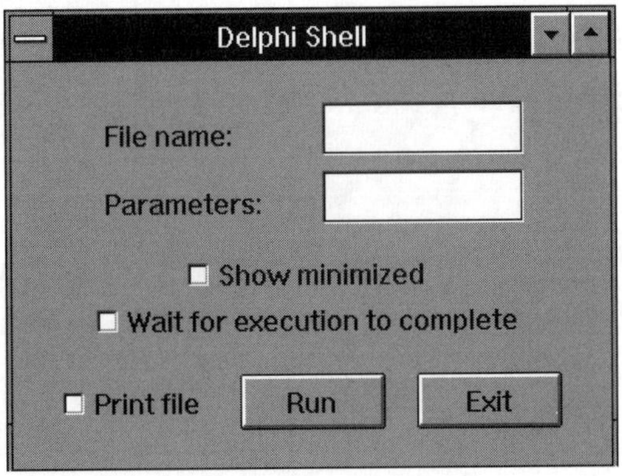

Figure 7-1 DELSHELL at run time

2. Add components and set their properties as shown in Table 7-1.

Table 7-1 Components, properties, and settings for Form1 in the DELSHELL project

COMPONENT	PROPERTY	SETTING
Form1	Left	200
	Top	116
	Width	376
	Height	274
	Caption	Delphi Shell
Label1	Left	56
	Top	34
	Width	80
	Height	20
	Caption	File name:
Label2	Left	56
	Top	74
	Width	98
	Height	20
	Caption	Parameters:
Edit1	Left	192
	Top	26
	Width	121
	Height	29
Edit2	Left	192
	Top	66
	Width	121
	Height	29
CheckBox1	Left	108
	Top	117
	Width	153
	Height	17
	Caption	Show minimized
CheckBox2	Left	52
	Top	144
	Width	265
	Height	17
	Caption	Wait for execution to complete

COMPONENT	PROPERTY	SETTING
CheckBox3	Left	31
	Top	192
	Width	90
	Height	17
	Caption	Print file
Button1	Left	140
	Top	184
	Width	89
	Height	33
	Caption	Run
Button2	Left	248
	Top	184
	Width	89
	Height	33
	Caption	Exit
Timer1	Enabled	False
	Interval	500

3. Double-click on CheckBox3 (the Print file check box) and add the following code to the resulting OnClick event handler.

```
{ Manage print mode and Button1's caption }
procedure TForm1.CheckBox3Click(Sender: TObject);
begin
  if Checkbox3.Checked then
    Button1.Caption := 'Print'
  else Button1.Caption := 'Run';
end;
```

4. Double-click on Button1 (the Run button) and add the following code to the resulting OnClick event handler.

```
procedure TForm1.Button1Click(Sender: TObject);
var
  ActiveWindow: HWnd;
  HowShow: integer;
  WindowList: Pointer;
begin
  if Checkbox1.Checked then
    HowShow := SW_SHOWMINIMIZED
  else HowShow := SW_SHOWNORMAL;
  { Start flashing form's caption }
```

continued on next page

continued from previous page

```
  Timer1.Enabled := True;
  { Don't allow input while waiting }
  WindowList := DisableTaskWindows(0);
  ActiveWindow := GetActiveWindow;
  try
    if not ShellExec(Edit1.Text, Edit2.Text, '', Checkbox3.Checked,
      HowShow, CheckBox2.Checked) then
    MessageDlg('Could not run file', mtInformation, [mbOK], 0);
  finally
    { Ensure we return to pre-waiting state }
    EnableTaskWindows(WindowList);
    SetActiveWindow(ActiveWindow);
    Timer1.Enabled := False;
    Caption := 'Delphi Shell';
  end;
end;
```

5. Double-click on Button2 (the Exit button) and add the following code to the resulting OnClick event handler.

```
{ Close application }
procedure TForm1.Button2Click(Sender: TObject);
begin
  Close;
end;
```

6. Double-click on Timer1 and add the following code to the resulting OnTimer event handler.

```
{ Change form's caption to 'Waiting' and flash }
procedure TForm1.Timer1Timer(Sender: TObject);
begin
  if Caption = 'Waiting' then
    Caption := ''
  else Caption := 'Waiting';
end;
```

7. While still in the Code Editor, move up to the *implementation* keyword and add a *uses* clause as shown here:

```
implementation

uses HowUtils;

{$R *.DFM}
```

8. Next you're going to add a function to the HowUtils unit. If you have been building this unit as you go along, add it to the project using the File|Add File menu option in Delphi. If you do not yet have a HowUtils unit, you can create one using the File|New Unit menu option in Delphi. Add the following function declaration to the unit's *interface* section.

```
unit HowUtils;

interface

uses
  SysUtils, WinTypes, WinProcs, Messages, Classes, Controls,
  Forms, IniFiles, ToolHelp, ShellAPI;

function ShellExec(const PathStr, CmdStr, DirStr: String;
  PrintIt: boolean; Show: word; Wait: Boolean): boolean;

implementation
```

9. Add the ShellExec function to the HowUtils unit's *implementation* section as shown here:

```
function ShellExec(const PathStr, CmdStr, DirStr: string;
  PrintIt: boolean; Show: word; Wait: boolean): boolean;
var
  Inst: THandle;
  Path, CmdLine, Dir: PChar;
  Op: array[0..5] of Char;
  AppWin: hWnd;
  Valid: Bool;
begin
  if PrintIt then StrPCopy(Op, 'print') else StrPCopy(Op, 'open');
  { Get memory for PChars }
  GetMem(Path, Length(PathStr)+1);
  GetMem(CmdLine, Length(CmdStr)+1);
  GetMem(Dir, Length(DirStr)+1);
  try
    { Copy strings to PChars }
    StrPCopy(Path, PathStr);
    StrPCopy(CmdLine, CmdStr);
    StrPCopy(Dir, DirStr);
    { Execute file }
    Inst := ShellExecute(0, Op, Path, CmdLine, Dir, Show);
    { If 32 or less, an error occurred }
    if Inst <= 32 then Result := False else
    begin
      if Wait then
      begin
        { Loop while program is running }
        while GetModuleUsage(Inst)  0 do
          Application.ProcessMessages;
        { Acknowledge error from last iteration of loop }
        OutputDebugString('--> Please ignore the previous error'#10#13);
      end;
      Result := True;
    end;
  finally
    { Ensure memory is freed }
```

continued on next page

continued from previous page

```
    FreeMem(Path, Length(PathStr)+1);
    FreeMem(CmdLine, Length(CmdStr)+1);
    FreeMem(Dir, Length(DirStr)+1);
  end;
end;
```

10. Compile and test the project.

How It Works

This How-To is centered around the ShellExecute API function, which is an improvement over the WinExec function. ShellExecute is smarter about finding your applications—in most cases, you won't have to supply a path for the file name. ShellExecute can also open documents that are associated with programs and optionally print them. The ShellExec function in this How-To is a wrapper around the ShellExecute API function.

Normally, if you execute a program using the WinExec or ShellExecute API function, your program will continue with what it was doing after the program starts. In order to get the program to wait for the spawned program to complete its processing, you have to take a few extra steps. Our ShellExec function adds the necessary functionality to support waiting for a program to complete its execution. First, there is a loop in the ShellExec function that continuously calls GetModuleUsage and Application.ProcessMessages. The calls to GetModuleUsage check whether the program is still running, and the calls to ProcessMessages allow other Windows messages to be processed while in the loop. Note also that you take a few steps before and after the call to ShellExec in the program to ensure that the form will not accept user input during the waiting process.

Comments

There is more than one way to wait while an application is running. Each method has its advantages and disadvantages. Looping while checking GetModuleUsage is used in this How-To because it is fairly easy to implement and works well with both DOS and Windows programs. This method has two drawbacks that you should be aware of. First, the final iteration of the loop will make a call to GetModuleUsage with an invalid handle because the instance no longer exists. This does not cause a problem, but does cause the debug version of Windows to generate an error message. The OutputDebugString API call is there to let any potential user know that the error is expected. This API displays a string on the device that monitors messages from the debug version of Windows.

The other issue that you should be aware of is that the WIN32 API does not support the GetModuleUsage function. This means that if you use the WIN32 version of Delphi when it becomes available to compile a 32-bit program for Windows NT or Windows 95, you will need to find another way of monitoring the running program.

7.2 How Do I...
Exit Windows and return to DOS?

COMPLEXITY: EASY

Problem

During a portion of the setup routine of some of my Delphi applications, I want to exit Windows in order to install some drivers. I also sometimes need to reboot the user's computer from Windows. I've noticed that other Windows applications can do this, so it must be possible. How do I do this with my Delphi applications?

Technique

Delphi does not provide any direct functions to exit Windows, but this is easy enough to do using the Windows API. You can choose between two functions that provide this capability, depending on the options needed. The ExitWindows API function causes Windows to exit and gives you the option to stay in DOS, to return to Windows, or to reboot the computer. The ExitWindowsExec API function quits Windows, then runs a DOS program. When the DOS program has finished, Windows restarts.

Steps

Run EXITWIN.EXE. Make sure you don't have any unsaved work in any of your open applications. Then try exiting Windows using the different options presented by the radio buttons, as shown in Figure 7-2.

1. Create a new project with a blank form and name it EXITWIN.DPR. Name the unit EXITWIN1.PAS.

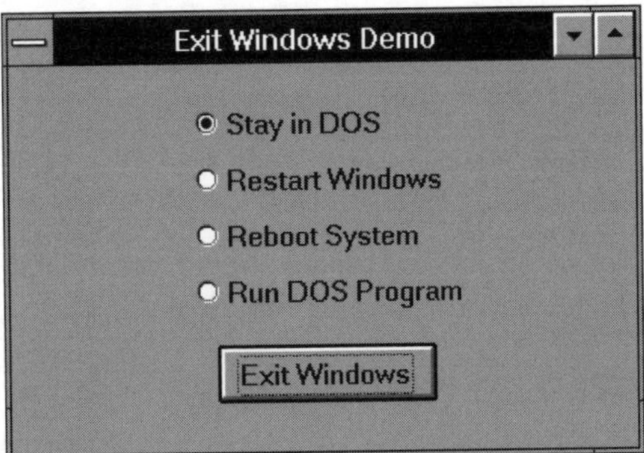

Figure 7-2 EXITWIN at run time

2. Add components to Form1 and set their properties as shown in Table 7-2.

Table 7-2 Components, properties, and settings for Form1 in the EXITWIN project

COMPONENT	PROPERTY	SETTING
Form1	Left	257
	Top	141
	Width	378
	Height	256
	Caption	Exit Windows Demo
	+Font	
	-Color	clBlack
	-Name	MS Sans Serif
	-Size	10
Button1	Left	121
	Top	160
	Width	129
	Height	33
	Caption	Exit Windows
RadioButton1	Left	109
	Top	24
	Width	148
	Height	20
	TabStop	True
	Caption	Stay in DOS
	Checked	True
RadioButton2	Left	109
	Top	56
	Width	153
	Height	20
	Caption	Restart Windows
RadioButton3	Left	109
	Top	88
	Width	145
	Height	20
	Caption	Reboot System
RadioButton4	Left	109
	Top	120

COMPONENT	PROPERTY	SETTING
	Width	169
	Height	20
	Caption	Run DOS Program
OpenDialog1	DefaultExt	exe
	Filter	Dos Program|*.exe
	+Options	
	-ofHideReadOnly	True
	-ofFileMustExist	True
	Title	Run DOS Program

3. Double-click on the button and add the following code to the resulting OnClick event handler.

```
procedure TForm1.Button1Click(Sender: TObject);
var
  ExitCode: Integer;
  S: Array[0..127] of char;
begin
  { Stay in DOS }
  if Radiobutton1.Checked then ExitCode := 0
    { Exit Windows and return to Windows }
    else if RadioButton2.Checked then ExitCode := ew_RestartWindows
    { Exit Windows and reboot the computer }
    else if RadioButton3.Checked then ExitCode := ew_RebootSystem
    { Exit Windows, run a DOS program }
    else if RadioButton4.Checked then
      if OpenDialog1.Execute then
        ExitWindowsExec(StrPCopy(S, OpenDialog1.FileName), nil)
        else Exit;
  ExitWindows(ExitCode, 0);
end;
```

4. Compile and test the program.

How It Works

When Button1 is clicked, checks are made to determine which radio button is selected. The appropriate value is then loaded into the ExitCode variable, which is used for the call to the ExitWindows API function. You must use a different API function, ExitWindowsExec, if the user wants to exit Windows and run a DOS program.

Comments

This code is normally used in installation programs, but may certainly be useful at any time. If you want to restart your program when Windows restarts, you can add your program to the Load or Run entries in the [windows] section of the WIN.INI file prior to exiting Windows. Be sure to remove it once the program is restarted unless you want your program to run every time the user starts Windows.

7.3 How Do I...
Delay my application for a specified period of time?

COMPLEXITY: INTERMEDIATE

Problem

There are many occasions when I want to pause my Delphi application for a given period of time. I know I can do this with a timer component, but sometimes a timer may not work—such as when fairly high accuracy is required. I would also like to avoid using a limited resource such as a timer. Is there a way I can pause execution in my Delphi application without using a timer?

Technique

Windows provides a time standard in TOOLHELP.DLL that is accurate to the millisecond. The main purpose of this is to time events or functions, which you will do in How-To 7.15, later in this chapter. It is also possible to put your program in a loop that continuously checks this time standard for a certain value, effectively causing your program to delay.

Steps

Run SLEEP.EXE. Enter a value in the edit box and click the Start button. Note that the application pauses for the specified number of milliseconds and displays the results, as shown in Figure 7-3. If you have a way of timing the pause, you'll find that it is fairly accurate.

1. Create a new project with a blank form and name it SLEEP.DPR. Name the unit SLEEP1.PAS.

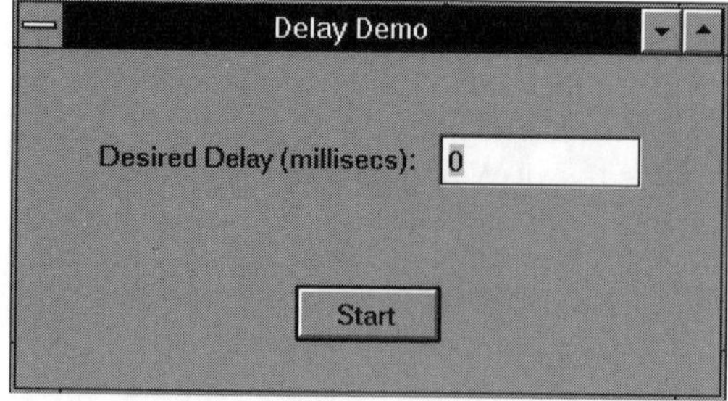

Figure 7-3 SLEEP at run time

2. Add components to Form1 and set their properties as shown in Table 7-3.

Table 7-3 Components, properties, and settings for Form1 in the SLEEP project

COMPONENT	PROPERTY	SETTING
Form1	Left	200
	Top	118
	Width	435
	Height	233
	Caption	Delay Demo
	+Font	
	-Color	clBlack
	-Name	MS Sans Serif
	-Size	10
Label1	Left	49
	Top	52
	Width	193
	Height	20
	Caption	Desired Delay (millisecs):
Label2	Left	181
	Top	96
	Width	64
	Height	20
	Caption	Sleeping
	+Font	
	-Color	clRed
	-Name	MS Sans Serif
	-Size	10
	ParentFont	False
	Visible	False
Edit1	Left	257
	Top	136
	Width	121
	Height	29
	Text	0
Button1	Left	169
	Top	136

continued on next page

continued from previous page

COMPONENT	PROPERTY	SETTING
	Width	89
	Height	33
	Caption	Start
	Default	True
Timer1	Enabled	False
	Interval	500

3. Double-click on Button1 and write the following code in the resulting OnClick event handler.

```
procedure TForm1.Button1Click(Sender: TObject);
var
  TimeRec: TTimerInfo;
  TimeStart: LongInt;
begin
  { Initialize buffer }
  TimeRec.dwSize := SizeOf(TimeRec);
  { Get starting time }
  TimerCount(@TimeRec);
  TimeStart := TimeRec.dwmsSinceStart;
  { Start flashing the "sleeping" label }
  Timer1.Enabled := True;
  repeat
    { Let other applications work while checking time }
    Application.ProcessMessages;
    TimerCount(@TimeRec);
  until TimeRec.dwmsSinceStart >= (TimeStart + StrToInt(Edit1.Text));
  { Stop flashing label }
  Timer1.Enabled := False;
  { Make sure label is invisible }
  Label2.Visible := False;
  Messagebeep(0);
  MessageDlg('The '+Edit1.Text+' mSec delay is complete', mtInformation,
    [mbOk], 0);
end;
```

4. Double-click on Timer1 and write the following code in the resulting OnTimer event handler.

```
{ Flash label while sleeping }
procedure TForm1.Timer1Timer(Sender: TObject);
begin
  Label2.Visible := not(Label2.Visible);
end;
```

5. While still in the Code Editor, move up to the *implementation* keyword and add a *uses* clause as shown here. This tells the compiler where to look for some of the structures and functions used in your code.

```
implementation

uses Toolhelp;

{$R *.DFM}
```

6. Compile and test the program.

How It Works

TOOLHELP has a counter that keeps track of the number of milliseconds since the computer was started and also since the current virtual machine was started. This counter is maintained to ensure its advertised accuracy to the millisecond. In this How-To, you simply check this counter at the beginning of the pause—then continuously check the counter against a calculated value that signals the end of the delay. Note that there is a timer component on the form, but this timer has nothing to do with the pause of the program itself. It is only used to create a flashing indicator that shows when the program is pausing.

Comments

If the computer running this application is left on for long periods of time, it is possible that TOOLHELP's counter will roll over. It would probably be a good idea to add code to cover this possibility. Since a LongInt is used to keep track of milliseconds, it would take something on the order of 24 days to roll over the counter.

7.4 How Do I... Prevent Windows from shutting down during an operation?

COMPLEXITY: EASY

Problem

Some of my Delphi applications have routines such as sorting that really shouldn't be interrupted. Is there a way to prevent users from shutting down Windows before these routines are complete?

Technique

When a user tries to quit Windows, each running application is sent a wm_QueryEndSession message. This message basically asks the application if it's okay to shut down. When a Delphi application receives this message, the OnCloseQuery event for the main form is fired—so you can use the OnCloseQuery event handler to control whether Windows shuts down.

Steps

Run SHUTDOWN.EXE. Try to shut down Windows. Note that Windows will not shut down unless the Can Close check box, shown in Figure 7-4, is checked. Open Form2. It also has a Can Close check box. If both forms are open, both Can Close check boxes must be checked to allow Windows to shut down.

1. Create a new project with a blank form and name it SHUTDOWN.DPR. Name the unit SHUTDWN1.PAS.

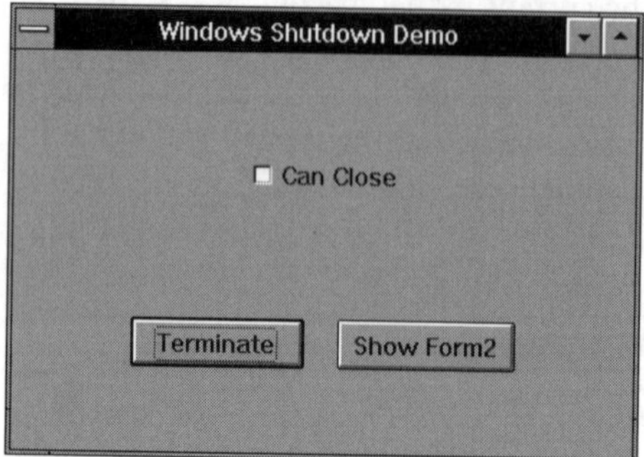

Figure 7-4 SHUTDOWN at run time

2. Add components to Form1 and set their properties as shown in Table 7-4.

Table 7-4 Components, properties, and settings for Form1 in the SHUTDOWN project

COMPONENT	PROPERTY	SETTING
Form1	Left	200
	Top	118
	Width	435
	Height	300
	Caption	Windows Shutdown Demo
Button1	Left	81
	Top	176
	Width	121
	Height	33
	Caption	Terminate
Button2	Left	225
	Top	176
	Width	121

COMPONENT	PROPERTY	SETTING
	Height	33
	Caption	Show Form2
CheckBox1	Left	165
	Top	72
	Width	108
	Height	17
	Caption	Can Close

3. Click on Form1 so it is selected in the Object Inspector. Select the Events page of the Object Inspector and double-click in the right-hand column of the OnCloseQuery event. Add the following code to the resulting OnCloseQuery event handler.

```
procedure TForm1.FormCloseQuery(Sender: TObject; var CanClose: Boolean);
begin
  CanClose := CheckBox1.Checked;
end;
```

4. Double-click on Button1 (the Terminate button) and add the following code to the resulting OnClick event handler.

```
procedure TForm1.Button1Click(Sender: TObject);
begin
  Application.Terminate;
end;
```

5. Double-click on Button2 (the Show Form2 button) and add the following code to the resulting OnClick event handler.

```
procedure TForm1.Button2Click(Sender: TObject);
begin
  Form2.Show;
end;
```

6. While still in the Code Editor, move up to the *implementation* keyword and add a *uses* clause as shown here:

```
implementation

uses Shutdwn2;

{$R *.DFM}
```

7. Add a new blank form to the project. Name the unit SHUTDWN2.PAS.
8. Add the components and set their properties as shown in Table 7-5.

Table 7-5 Components, properties, and settings for Form2 in the SHUTDOWN project

COMPONENT	PROPERTY	SETTING
Form2	Left	224
	Top	146
	Width	326
	Height	185
	Caption	Form2
CheckBox1	Left	111
	Top	66
	Width	97
	Height	17
	Caption	Can Close

9. Click on Form2 so it is selected in the Object Inspector. Select the Events page of the Object Inspector and double-click in the right-hand column of the OnCloseQuery event. Add the following code to the resulting OnCloseQuery event handler.

```
procedure TForm2.FormCloseQuery(Sender: TObject; var CanClose: Boolean);
begin
  CanClose := Checkbox1.Checked;
end;
```

10. Compile and test the project.

How It Works

When a Delphi application receives a wm_QueryEndSession message, the OnCloseQuery event is fired. In the event handler, you can set the value of the CanClose variable depending on the state of your program. If CanClose is set to False, Windows will abort the shutdown procedure.

Comments

It is a good idea to keep the OnCloseQuery event in mind. The typical use for it is if data on the form has been changed and needs to be modified. While not shown in this example, the user is typically asked whether to save the data. The code for showing a message box would also be included in the OnCloseQuery event handler.

There are other occasions where you might consider setting the CanClose variable to False—possibly when you are in the middle of a long process that shouldn't be interrupted, such as a sort or backup operation. In this case, you could loop using Application.ProcessMessages until the operation was complete, and then set the CanClose variable to True.

7.5 How Do I...
Search an entire disk for a file?

COMPLEXITY: ADVANCED

Problem

I need a function that can search an entire disk drive for a given file specification. Delphi has a routine that will search through the path for a file, but I need to search the entire disk. How do I do this in Delphi?

Technique

Delphi's two functions—FindFirst and FindNext—work together to let you search for files. The tricky part is walking through the hierarchy of directories and subdirectories on the hard drive. This is accomplished in this How-To by using a recursive procedure.

Steps

Run FINDER.EXE. Select a drive to search, type the desired file specification in the edit box, and click on the OK button. The list box will fill with files that meet your criteria. Figure 7-5 shows an example.

1. Create a new project with a blank form and name it FINDER.DPR. Name the unit FINDER1.PAS.

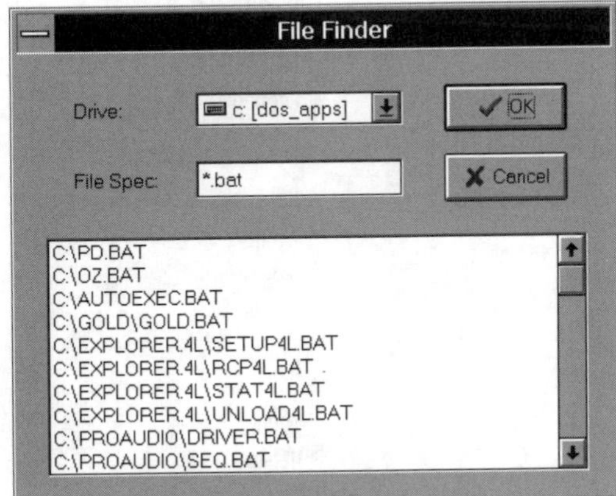

Figure 7-5 FINDER at run time

2. Add components to Form1 and set their properties as shown in Table 7-6.

Table 7-6 Components, properties, and settings for Form1 in the FINDER project

COMPONENT	PROPERTY	SETTING
Form1	Left	200
	Top	118
	Width	435
	Height	343
	+BorderIcons	
	-biSystemMenu	True
	-biMinimize	True
	-biMaximize	False
	BorderStyle	bsDialog
	Caption	File Finder
	+Font	
	-Color	clBlack
	-Name	MS Sans Serif
	-Size	8
Label1	Left	40
	Top	32
	Width	35
	Height	16
	Caption	Drive:
Label2	Left	40
	Top	80
	Width	60
	Height	16
	Caption	File Spec:
DriveComboBox1	Left	128
	Top	29
	Width	145
	Height	22
Edit1	Left	128
	Top	76
	Width	145
	Height	24
	Text	*.*
BitBtn1	Left	304

COMPONENT	PROPERTY	SETTING
	Top	24
	Width	89
	Height	33
	Kind	bkOK
BitBtn2	Left	304
	Top	72
	Width	89
	Height	33
	Kind	bkCancel
ListBox1	Left	21
	Top	128
	Width	385
	Height	162
	IntegralHeight	True

3. Double-click on BitBtn1 (the OK button) and add the following code to the resulting OnClick event handler. This is the recursive procedure that does the file search.

```
procedure TForm1.BitBtn1Click(Sender: TObject);

  { Recursive Procedure }
  procedure SearchTree;
  var
    SR: TSearchRec;
    DosError: integer;
    Dir: String;
  begin
    { Find first file matching spec }
    DosError := FindFirst(Edit1.Text, 0, SR);
    GetDir(0, Dir);
    if Dir[Length(Dir)]  '\' then Dir := Dir + '\';
    { Find all files in directory matching spec }
    while DosError = 0 do
    begin
      try
        Listbox1.Items.Add(Dir+SR.Name);
      except
        { If list box gets full... }
        on EOutOfResources do
        begin
          { Show messagebox and... }
          MessageDlg('Number of files exceeds list box capacity.',
            mtInformation, [mbOk], 0);
          { Raise Abort exception to quit procedure }
```

continued on next page

continued from previous page

```
          Abort;
        end;
      end;
      DosError := FindNext(SR);
    end;
    { Find first subdirectory in directory }
    DosError := FindFirst('*.*', faDirectory, SR);
    { Find all subdirectories in directory }
    while DosError = 0 do
    begin
      if ((SR.Attr and faDirectory = faDirectory) and
        (SR.Name  '.') and (SR.Name  '..')) then
      begin
        { Switch to subdirectory }
        ChDir(SR.Name);
        { Recurse }
        SearchTree;
        { Drop back to parent directory }
        ChDir('..');
      end;
      DosError := FindNext(SR);
    end;
  end;

begin
  { Clear before each search }
  Listbox1.Clear;
  ChDir(DriveComboBox1.Drive+':\');
  SearchTree;
  if Listbox1.Items.Count = 0 then
    Listbox1.Items.Add('No matching files found');
end;
```

4. Double-click on BitBtn2 (the Cancel button) and add the following code to the resulting OnClick event handler.

```
procedure TForm1.BitBtn2Click(Sender: TObject);
begin
  Close;
end;
```

5. Compile and test the project.

How It Works

Delphi's FindFirst function must always be called first in order to properly initialize the TSearchRec structure. Each time either the FindFirst or FindNext function returns a zero DosError value, a file matching the file specification has been found. There is other information, such as file size, available in the TSearchRec structure—refer to Delphi's documentation for details if necessary.

A recursive function is typically difficult to follow in code. Basically, the order of events is as follows: First, the main OnClick event handler procedure clears any items out of the list box, moves to the desired directory, and calls the SearchTree procedure. The first portion of the SearchTree procedure searches the directory for any files that match the file specification. If any are found, they are added to the list box. Once the directory has been completely searched for files, it is then searched for subdirectories. Once a subdirectory is found, the ChDir procedure is used to move to that directory and SearchTree is called—this is the recursion part.

The first instance of SearchTree is still running; it is just in suspension for the time being. The second instance of SearchTree repeats the actions of the first, but in the new directory. It then moves to a deeper directory if one is available and starts another copy of SearchTree. This continues until the deepest directory is reached and searched, so there may be several copies of the SearchTree procedure running at any given time.

The deepest directory has no subdirectories, so that copy of SearchTree terminates, and the previous copy of SearchTree becomes active at the line following the call to SearchTree, which moves the search back to the previous directory to look for more subdirectories to conquer. This process is continued until the entire drive has been searched, or until the list box is full.

When a string is added to a full list box, an EOutOfResources exception is generated. This exception is handled, and a message box is displayed showing the error. At this point, you are presented with the problem of having to shut down all of the SearchTree procedures that are still running recursively. Calling Exit will only exit the current procedure; the remaining procedures would run—causing more exceptions. The Halt procedure would effectively and abruptly stop the program, but this isn't considered good manners. Reraising the EOutOfResources exception would work, but the default exception message box would be shown in addition to the one you already showed, possibly confusing the user.

The answer to this problem is the Abort procedure. This procedure raises a silent exception, which acts exactly like a regular exception but does not display a message box. Raising an exception in this way efficiently shuts down all of the recursive SearchTree procedures and returns control to the user with the program in a stable state.

Comments

This How-To effectively shows a searching technique that can be used in anything that is maintained in a hierarchical way, such as family trees or electronic mail messages.

If you are running this program under Delphi, keep in mind that the exception caused by the Abort procedure will trigger Delphi's integrated debugger if you have the Break on Exceptions option enabled on the Preferences page of your Environment Options dialog.

7.6 How Do I...
Disable the Windows screen saver?

COMPLEXITY: EASY

Problem

I have a Delphi application that takes a while to do some processing. Occasionally, the delay is long enough to allow the Windows screen saver to start. If this happens, my processing can really get slowed down. I know enough to turn off the screen saver on my computer, but some of my users may not realize this should be done. Is there a way I can automatically stop the screen saver from coming on while my application is running?

Technique

Windows posts a wm_Syscommand message to the active application prior to starting the screen saver. You can handle this message using the OnMessage event handler of TApplication. Returning a nonzero value in response to the message prevents the screen saver from running.

Steps

Run SAVENOT.EXE. The form is shown in Figure 7-6. Ensure that your Windows screen saver has been enabled. Allow the system to remain idle long enough for the screen saver to come on. Note that when the check box is checked, the screen saver will not come on.

1. Create a new project with a blank form and name it SAVENOT.DPR. Name the unit SAVENOT1.PAS.

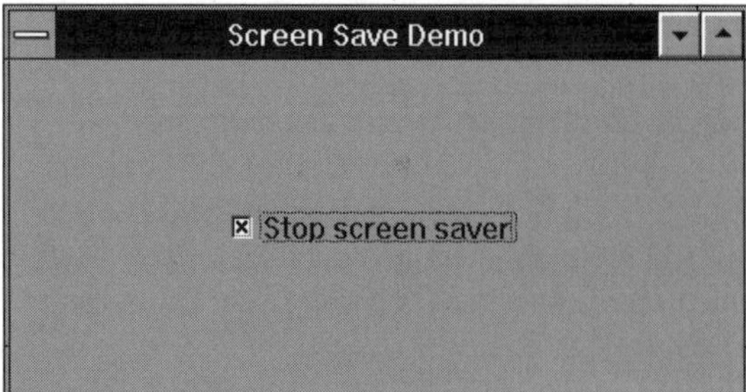

Figure 7-6 SAVENOT at run time

2. Add components and set their properties as shown in Table 7-7.

Table 7-7 Components, properties, and settings for Form1 in the SAVENOT project

COMPONENT	PROPERTY	SETTING
Form1	Left	199
	Top	117
	Width	435
	Height	222
	Caption	Screen Save Demo
CheckBox1	Left	129
	Top	85
	Width	169
	Height	17
	Caption	Stop screen saver

3. Double-click on Form1. Add the following code to the resulting OnCreate event handler.

```
procedure TForm1.FormCreate(Sender: TObject);
begin
  Application.OnMessage := AppMessage;
end;
```

4. While still in the Code Editor, move up to the object declaration for Form1. Add a method declaration for AppMessage as shown here:

```
type
  TForm1 = class(TForm)
    CheckBox1: TCheckBox;
    procedure FormCreate(Sender: TObject);
  private
    { Private declarations }
    procedure AppMessage(var Msg: TMsg; var Handled: Boolean);
 public
    { Public declarations }
  end;
```

5. While still in the Code Editor, add the AppMessage procedure to the *implementation* section of the unit as follows:

```
implementation

{$R *.DFM}

procedure TForm1.AppMessage(var Msg: TMsg; var Handled: Boolean);
```

continued on next page

continued from previous page

```
begin
  if (Msg.Message = wm_Syscommand) and (Msg.wParam = sc_Screensave)
    and Checkbox1.Checked then Handled := True;
end;

procedure TForm1.FormCreate(Sender: TObject);
```

6. Compile and test the project.

How It Works

Windows constantly watches the system for user activity, such as usage of the mouse and keyboard. If the keyboard and mouse are inactive for a period of time, Windows takes steps to run the selected screen saver. Prior to running the screen saver, Windows posts a wm_Syscommand message to the active application with the wParam parameter set to a value of sc_Screensave.

You can respond to messages that are posted to your application by providing an event handler for the OnMessage event. In the event handler, you test to see if the message is the one you are looking for—if it is, you set the Handled variable to True if the criteria to disable the screen saver is True. Windows will not run the screen saver if it sees that the message was handled by the active application.

Comments

For this example, the only criterion used to determine whether the screen saver should be disabled is the state of the check box. In most cases, the criterion will be something different, such as whether a certain process is running or not. It is recommended that this technique be used only if side effects of the screen saver must be avoided during a certain process. Disabling the screen saver indiscriminately during your application's operation would not be welcomed by many users.

7.7 How Do I...
Prevent multiple instances of my program from being loaded?

COMPLEXITY: INTERMEDIATE

Problem

I just wrote a Delphi application that may not work properly if more than one instance is running at the same time. In order to protect the user from possible problems, I'd like to prevent more than one instance of the application from being started. How can I do this with a Delphi application?

Technique

Delphi applications have a built-in global variable that allows you to check how many instances of the program are running. In order to find out if two instances of the same program are running, all you have to do is check this variable. You can then take appropriate action during startup of the program based on the value of the variable.

Steps

Run ONEINST.EXE. With the first instance of the program still running, as shown in Figure 7-7, try to start another. Note that a message box is shown and the second instance is aborted. If the first instance of the program is overlapped by other windows, it will be brought to the top.

1. Create a new project with a blank form and name it ONEINST.DPR. Name the unit ONEINST1.PAS.

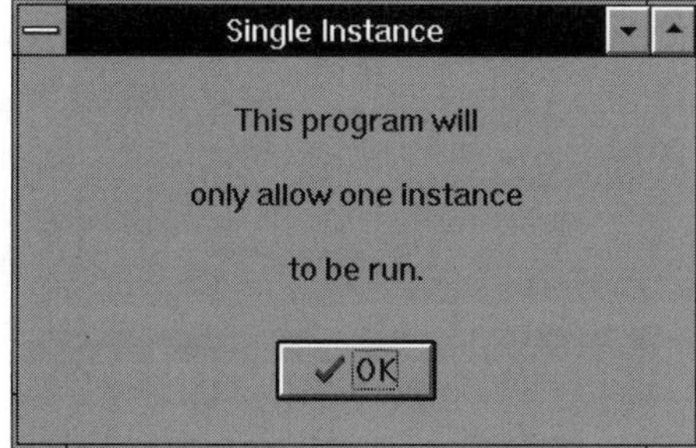

Figure 7-7 ONEINST at run time

2. Add components and set their properties as shown in Table 7-8.

Table 7-8 Components, properties, and settings for Form1 in the ONEINST project

COMPONENT	PROPERTY	SETTING
Form1	Name	SingInst
	Left	253
	Top	118
	Width	382
	Height	243
	Caption	Single Instance
Label1	Left	120
	Top	24

continued on next page

continued from previous page

COMPONENT	PROPERTY	SETTING
	Width	135
	Height	20
	Caption	This program will
Label2	Left	95
	Top	64
	Width	135
	Height	20
	Caption	only allow one instance
Label3	Left	150
	Top	104
	Width	75
	Height	20
	Caption	to be run.
BitBtn1	Left	143
	Top	152
	Width	89
	Height	33
	Kind	bkOK

3. Double-click on BitBtn1 (the OK button) and add the following code to the resulting OnClick event handler.

```
procedure TSingInst.BitBtn1Click(Sender: TObject);
begin
  Close;
end;
```

4. Now you need to add some code to the project file. Select View|Project Source in Delphi's main menu to show the project file in the Code Editor. Add the following code.

```
begin
  if HPrevInst = 0 then
  begin
    Application.CreateForm(TSingInst, SingInst);
    Application.Run;
  end
  else
  begin
    MessageBox(0, 'This application is already running',
      'Single Instance', mb_OK);
    if SetFocus(FindWindow('TSingInst', nil)) = 0 then
```

```
      MessageBox(0, 'The window handle is invalid',
        'Single Instance', mb_OK);
  end;
end.
```

5. Compile and test the project.

How It Works

Every Delphi application has a global variable, HPrevInst, that contains a pointer to the previous instance of the application if one exists. This variable is tested at the very beginning of the startup code. If the value is zero (meaning there is no previous instance), normal startup continues. If HPrevInst contains something other than zero, a previous instance of the program exists, so the normal application startup code is not run. Instead, a message box indicates that the application is already running and sets the focus to the previous instance's main form.

The SetFocus API function brings the previous instance's main form to the top. In order to do this, you need to obtain the window handle for the form. The FindWindow API function works fairly well for this purpose. You can use FindWindow to search for a window with a given caption or window class.

Comments

You will need to weigh the advantages and disadvantages of searching for a window's caption or window class with FindWindow. The example in this How-To searches for the window class, which turns out to be the same as the class name of a Delphi form. If you use this method, be sure to change your form's name to a unique one. Using Form1 would not be a very good idea. If you decide to search for the form's caption, make sure you don't change the caption during the operation of the program (to indicate an open file, for instance).

This is a powerful technique. Make sure you really need it before you use it though. There are many times that a user may want to have more than one instance of your application running. To be a Windows-friendly programmer, you should allow the user to do this unless there is a good reason not to.

7.8 How Do I...
Determine how many function keys are on the user's keyboard?

COMPLEXITY: EASY

Problem

I've added the ability to use function keys for several of the functions in my Delphi application, but some users may not have as many function keys as other users. I need to account for this and offer alternate keys. Is there a way that I can find out how many keys are on the user's keyboard?

Technique

With a call to a single API function you can find out what type of keyboard the user has and the number of function keys on the keyboard.

Steps

Run KEYDEMO.EXE. The program's form displays the type of keyboard and number of function keys available on the keyboard, as shown in Figure 7-8.

1. Create a new project with a blank form and name it KEYDEMO.DPR. Name the unit KEYDEMO1.PAS.

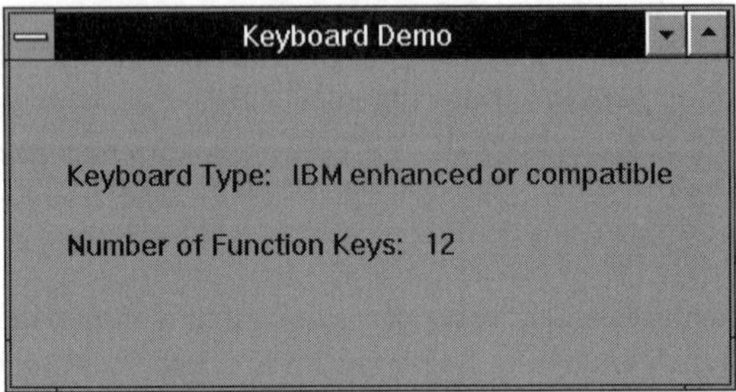

Figure 7-8 KEYDEMO at run time

2. Add components and set their properties as shown in Table 7-9.

Table 7-9 Components, properties, and settings for Form1 in the KEYDEMO project

COMPONENT	PROPERTY	SETTING
Form1	Left	200
	Top	118
	Width	435
	Height	222
	Caption	Keyboard Demo
Label1	Left	32
	Top	56
	Width	124
	Height	20
	Caption	Keyboard Type:
Label2	Left	168
	Top	56

COMPONENT	PROPERTY	SETTING
	Width	53
	Height	20
	Caption	Label2
	+Font	
	-Color	clNavy
	-Name	System
	-Size	10
	ParentFont	False
Label3	Left	32
	Top	96
	Width	203
	Height	20
	Caption	Number of Function Keys:
Label4	Left	248
	Top	96
	Width	53
	Height	20
	Caption	Label4
	+Font	
	-Color	clNavy
	-Name	System
	-Size	10
	ParentFont	False

3. Click Form1 so it is selected in the Object Inspector. On the Events page of the Object Inspector, double-click in the right-hand column of the OnCreate event. Add the following code to the resulting OnCreate event handler.

```
procedure TForm1.FormCreate(Sender: TObject);
begin
  case GetKeyboardType(0) of
    1: Label2.Caption := 'IBM PC/XT or compatible';
    2: Label2.Caption := 'Olivetti M24';
    3: Label2.Caption := 'IBM AT or compatible';
    4: Label2.Caption := 'IBM enhanced or compatible';
    5: Label2.Caption := 'Nokia 1050 or compatible';
    6: Label2.Caption := 'Nokia 9140 or compatible'
    else Label2.Caption := 'Unrecognized keyboard type';
  end;
  Label4.Caption := IntToStr(GetKeyboardType(2));
end;
```

4. Compile and test the project.

How It Works

Windows queries the installed keyboard driver to determine which type of keyboard is installed. This information is obtained from the GetKeyboardType API function, which takes a single parameter to determine the return. If a 0 is passed, GetKeyboardType returns an integer describing the type of keyboard installed. If a 1 is passed, the return is an integer relating to the keyboard subtype.

Comments

Users always appreciate it when the fancy keyboard they paid for is fully supported. The majority of programs do not use all of the function keys available. The GetKeyboardType API has somewhat limited use, but it is important if you want to tailor your program dynamically to the user's keyboard.

7.9 How Do I... Determine the directory where Windows is located?

COMPLEXITY: EASY

Problem

During the startup phase of one of my Delphi applications, I like to check whether certain files exist. These files are located in the WINDOWS and WINDOWS\SYSTEM directories. I'd rather not take the time to search the entire drive for these files. Is there an easier way to look for them?

Technique

The location of both directories could certainly be found by searching the various drives on the user's machine, but this can be time-consuming if there are several drives to search. The problem is further complicated if the user's machine is connected to a network. Fortunately, there are Windows API functions that make finding the Windows directories a simple matter.

Steps

Run DIRDEMO.EXE. The form should correctly identify the location of your WINDOWS and WINDOWS/SYSTEM directories, as shown in Figure 7-9.

1. Create a new project with a blank form and name it DIRDEMO.PRJ. Name the unit DIRDEMO1.PAS.

2. Add components and set their properties as shown in Table 7-10.

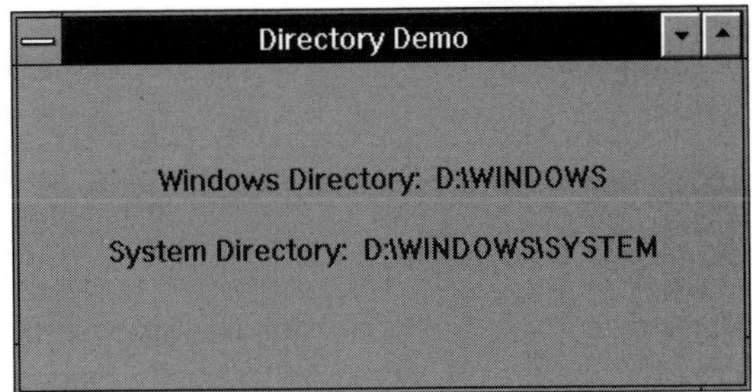

Figure 7-9 DIRDEMO at run time

Table 7-10 Components, properties, and settings for Form1 in the DIRDEMO project

COMPONENT	PROPERTY	SETTING
Form1	Left	200
	Top	118
	Width	435
	Height	220
	Caption	Directory Demo
Label1	Left	37
	Top	56
	Width	353
	Height	20
	Alignment	taCenter
	AutoSize	False
	Caption	Label1
Label2	Left	37
	Top	96
	Width	353
	Height	20
	Alignment	taCenter
	AutoSize	False
	Caption	Label2

3. Click on Form1 so it is selected in the Object Inspector. On the Events page of the Object Inspector, double-click in the right-hand column of the OnCreate property and add the following code to the resulting OnCreate event handler.

```
procedure TForm1.FormCreate(Sender: TObject);
const
  Text1 = 'Windows Directory:  ';
  Text2 = 'System Directory:  ';
var
  WinDir, SysDir: array [0..144] of char;
begin
  GetWindowsDirectory(WinDir, 144);
  GetSystemDirectory(SysDir, 144);
  Label1.Caption := Text1+StrPas(WinDir);
  Label2.Caption := Text2+StrPas(SysDir);
end;
```

4. Compile and test the project.

How It Works

The GetWindowsDirectory and GetSystemDirectory API functions return the respective directories in the form of a null-terminated string. The string must be converted into the form that Delphi normally uses. This conversion is accomplished by the StrPas function.

Comments

Keep in mind that the user's machine might be on a network. It's fairly common to find the WINDOWS directory on the local hard drive and the SYSTEM directory on a remote hard drive.

7.10 How Do I...
Determine system resources and display them in a form?

COMPLEXITY: EASY

Problem

I've noticed that some programs display system resources in their About boxes. I'd like to add a professional touch to my Delphi applications by displaying system resources in one of my forms. How can I do this?

Technique

You can determine the amount of available system resources by making a couple of calls to Windows API functions. Once you get the values, it's fairly easy to format them in an appropriate way and display them wherever you like.

Steps

Run RESMON.EXE. The Resource Monitor form has two gauge components that display the available user and GDI resources, as shown in Figure 7-10. Try minimizing the form to see how the available resources are shown in the icon's caption.

1. Create a new project with a blank form and name it RESMON.DPR. Name the unit RESMON1.PAS.

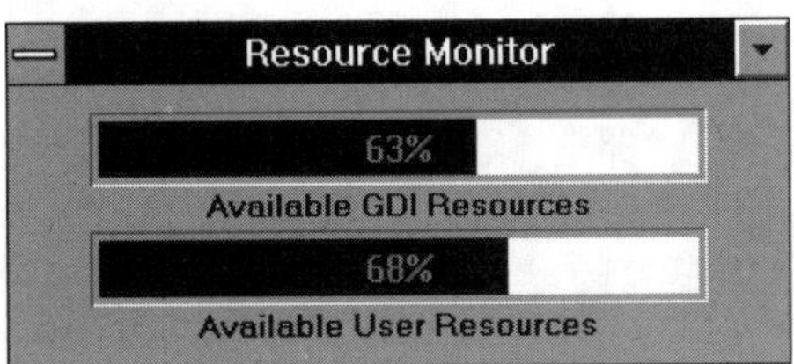

Figure 7-10 RESMON at run time

2. Add components and set their properties as shown in Table 7-11.

Table 7-11 Components, properties, and settings for Form1 in the RESMON project

COMPONENT	PROPERTY	SETTING
Form1	Left	226
	Top	224
	Width	357
	Height	154
	AutoScroll	False
	+BorderIcons	
	-biSystemMenu	True
	-biMinimize	True
	-biMaximize	False
	BorderStyle	bsSingle
	Caption	Resource Monitor
	+Font	
	-Color	clGray
	-Name	System
	-Size	10
	-Style	[fsBold]

continued on next page

continued from previous page

COMPONENT	PROPERTY	SETTING
Bevel1	Left	37
	Top	12
	Width	281
	Height	33
Bevel2	Left	37
	Top	65
	Width	281
	Height	33
Gauge1	Name	GDI
	Left	41
	Top	16
	Width	273
	Height	25
	+Font	
	-Color	clBlue
	-Name	System
	-Size	10
	-Style	[fsBold]
	BorderStyle	bsNone
	ForeColor	clBlue
	ParentFont	False
	Progress	0
Gauge2	Name	User
	Left	41
	Top	69
	Width	273
	Height	25
	+Font	
	-Color	clBlue
	-Name	System
	-Size	10
	-Style	[fsBold]
	BorderStyle	bsNone
	ForeColor	clBlue
	ParentFont	False

COMPONENT	PROPERTY	SETTING
	Progress	0
Label1	Left	90
	Top	46
	Width	176
	Height	16
	Caption	Available GDI Resources
	+Font	
	-Color	clBlack
	-Name	MS Sans Serif
	-Size	8
	-Style	[fsBold]
	ParentFont	False
Label2	Left	86
	Top	99
	Width	183
	Height	16
	Caption	Available User Resources
	+Font	
	-Color	clBlack
	-Name	MS Sans Serif
	-Size	8
	-Style	[fsBold]
	ParentFont	False
Timer1	Interval	1000

3. Click on Form1 so it is selected in the Object Inspector. On the Events page of the Object Inspector, double-click in the right-hand column of the OnCreate event. Add the following code to the resulting OnCreate event handler.

```
procedure TForm1.FormCreate(Sender: TObject);
begin
  DefaultTitle := Application.Title;
  { Fire OnTimer event to initialize gauges }
  Timer1Timer(Self);
end;
```

4. Double-click the timer component on Form1. Add the following code to the resulting OnTimer event handler.

```
procedure TForm1.Timer1Timer(Sender: TObject);
begin
  GDI.Progress  := GetFreeSystemResources(gfsr_GDIResources);
  { If resources get low, make gauge color red }
  if GDI.Progress < 10 then
    GDI.ForeColor := clRed
    else GDI.ForeColor := clBlue;
  User.Progress := GetFreeSystemResources(gfsr_UserResources);
  { If resources get low, make gauge color red }
  if User.Progress < 10 then
    User.ForeColor := clRed
    else User.ForeColor := clBlue;
  { Only update if values have changed }
  if (GDI.Progress = LastGDI) and (User.Progress = LastUser) then Exit;
  LastGDI := GDI.Progress;
  LastUser := User.Progress;
  { Update caption incase form is minimized }
  Application.Title := DefaultTitle+' User: '+IntToStr(User.Progress)+'%'+
    ' GDI: '+IntToStr(GDI.Progress)+'%';
end;
```

5. While still in the Code Editor, move up to the Form1 type declaration and add the following code to the *private* section.

```
type
  TForm1 = class(TForm)
    Timer1: TTimer;
    Bevel1: TBevel;
    Bevel2: TBevel;
    GDI: TGauge;
    User: TGauge;
    Label1: TLabel;
    Label2: TLabel;
    procedure Timer1Timer(Sender: TObject);
    procedure FormCreate(Sender: TObject);
  private
    { Private declarations }
    DefaultTitle: string;
    LastGDI: LongInt;
    LastUser: LongInt;
  public
    { Public declarations }
  end;
```

6. Compile and test the project.

How It Works

This How-To makes use of the GetFreeSystemResources API function to determine the free user and GDI resources. These values are fed directly to the TGauge components, which visually represent the system resources. A timer is used to periodically update the gauges. The application's title property is also updated with the resource information so the information can be seen if the resource monitor's form is minimized.

Comments

Resources are a very precious commodity in the Windows environment. If you aren't careful, errors in a program can cause the available resources to continuously be reduced. If the resources are allowed to get to a critical level, Windows could crash without warning.

7.11 How Do I... Determine how much memory is available?

COMPLEXITY: ADVANCED

Problem

I know that keeping track of system memory is important. How can I find out how much memory is available on the user's machine? Also, I've heard that it is important to keep track of low memory. What is low memory and why is this important? I thought I didn't have to worry about low memory in Windows applications.

Technique

It's easy to determine the total amount of memory available by making a call to a Windows API function. Determining the amount of low memory (memory below 1MB) is a little more involved. It requires some special calls and calculations.

Steps

Run WINMEM.EXE. Total available memory and available low memory are displayed on the form, as shown in Figure 7-11. Experiment by opening and closing applications and noting the changes in the available memory.

1. Create a new project with a blank form and name it WINMEM.DPR. Name the unit WINMEM1.PAS.

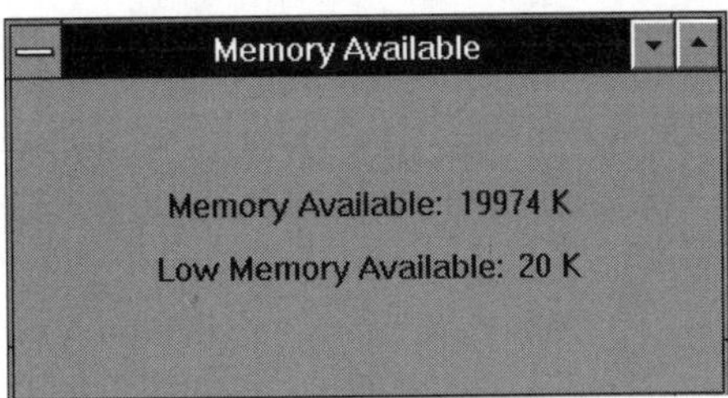

Figure 7-11 WINMEM at run time

2. Add components and set their properties as shown in Table 7-12.

Table 7-12 Components, properties, and settings for Form1 in the WINMEM project

COMPONENT	PROPERTY	SETTING
Form1	Left	242
	Top	160
	Width	382
	Height	197
	Caption	Memory Available
Label1	Left	50
	Top	55
	Width	273
	Height	20
	Alignment	taCenter
	AutoSize	False
	Caption	Memory Available:
Label2	Left	50
	Top	87
	Width	273
	Height	20
	Alignment	taCenter
	AutoSize	False
	Caption	Low Memory Available:
Timer1	Interval	1000

3. Double-click on Timer1 and add the following code to the resulting OnTimer event handler.

```
procedure TForm1.Timer1Timer(Sender: TObject);
const
  Text1 = 'Memory Available:';
  Text2 = 'Low Memory Available:';
begin
  Label1.Caption := Text1+'  '+IntToStr(GetFreeSpace(0) div 1024)+' K';
  Label2.Caption := Text2+'  '+IntToStr(GetLowMem div 1024)+' K';
end;
```

4. While still in the Code Editor, move up to the *implementation* keyword and add a *uses* clause as shown here:

```
implementation

uses HowUtils;

{$R *.DFM}
```

5. Next you're going to add a function to the HowUtils unit. If you have been building this unit as you go along, add it to the project using the File|Add File menu option in Delphi. If you do not yet have a HowUtils unit, you can create one using the File|New Unit menu option in Delphi. Add the following function declaration to the unit's *interface* section.

```
unit HowUtils;

interface

uses
  SysUtils, WinTypes, WinProcs, Messages, Classes, Controls,
  Forms, IniFiles, ToolHelp, ShellAPI;

function GetLowMem: LongInt;
```

6. Add the GetLowMem function to the HowUtils unit's *implementation* section as shown here:

```
implementation

function GetLowMem: LongInt;
var
  GlobalEntry:    TGlobalEntry;
  Walking:        Bool;
  EndOfLastBlock: LongInt;
  EndOfMem:       LongInt;
  Total:          LongInt;
begin
  { Initialize }
  Result := 0;
  EndOfLastBlock := $7FFFFFFF;
  GlobalEntry.dwSize := Sizeof(GlobalEntry);
  { Fill GlobalEntry with info on first object }
  Walking := GlobalFirst(@GlobalEntry, Global_All);
  with GlobalEntry do
    while Walking do
    begin
      { Clear high bit of dwAddress }
      dwAddress := dwAddress and $7FFFFFFF;
      { If address is > 1 meg fake a FIXED block at end of heap }
      if dwAddress > $100000 then
      begin
        dwAddress := EndOfMem;
        hBlock    := $FFFF;
```

continued on next page

continued from previous page

```
      wType     := GT_SENTINEL;
    end;
    { These are all cases where the block can't be moved. If we  }
    { find any such case, we need to check if there is any free  }
    { memory prior to the block.                                   }
    if (wType  GT_FREE) and (hBlock <> 0) and (((hBlock and 1) <> 0)
      or (wcLock  0) or (wcPageLock <> 0)) then
    begin
      { If true, there was a gap of free memory, add the size of the }
      { free space to result }
      if dwAddress > EndOfLastBlock then
        Inc(Result, dwAddress - EndOfLastBlock);
      if hBlock = $FFFF then Break;
      { Update EndOfLastBlock }
      EndOfLastBlock := dwAddress + dwBlockSize;
    end;
    EndOfMem := dwAddress + dwBlockSize;
    { Fill GlobalEntry with info on next object }
    Walking := GlobalNext(@GlobalEntry, Global_All);
  end;
end;
```

7. Compile and test the project.

How It Works

You call the GetFreeSpace Windows API function to obtain the available Windows memory. This API function returns the total amount of memory available to your application—including virtual memory. Once you have this value, it is simply a matter of converting it into a format suitable for display and displaying it, as shown in step 3.

Finding out the available low memory (memory below 1MB) is more difficult. In order to get this information, you use the GlobalFirst and GlobalNext API functions to walk the global heap. As you do this, you make note of the free memory in the low memory area and add it up. Once you have the information you are interested in, you convert it to a format suitable for display.

Comments

Low memory is often overlooked, but can be very important. Some programs require a certain amount of low memory to run successfully. Delphi applications sometimes fall into this category. The Borland Database Engine (BDE) requires some low memory, and some of the functions in the SysUtils unit specifically require low memory.

If there isn't enough low memory for the program to run, and a shortage of low memory is not considered, the results can be confusing because the About box reports plenty of system memory available.

7.12 How Do I...
Determine the correct version of Windows that is running on the user's machine?

COMPLEXITY: EASY

Problem

I've noticed that many Windows applications display the version of Windows that is running on the user's machine. I've also noticed that some programs report this incorrectly. Microsoft Word 6.0, for example, shows the version of Windows to be 3.10, and the About box for File Manager shows the version to be 3.11. Why is there a difference, and how can I show the correct version?

Technique

A Windows API function shows the version of Windows that is running on the machine, but it isn't always correct. When Microsoft developed Windows 3.11 and Windows for Workgroups 3.11, they discovered that many existing programs were looking for the Windows version to be 3.10. These programs reported errors or refused to run with version 3.11. In order to provide compatibility with the maximum number of programs, Microsoft decided to make the API function return 3.10 instead of 3.11. You can determine the correct version by using an alternate method—however, you'll see how to use both the API function and the alternate method here and then compare the output.

Steps

Run WINVER.EXE. The top label component on the form will show the correct version of Windows even if you are running Windows 3.11 or Windows for Workgroups 3.11, as shown in Figure 7-12. The lower label component shows the version being returned by the GetVersion API function.

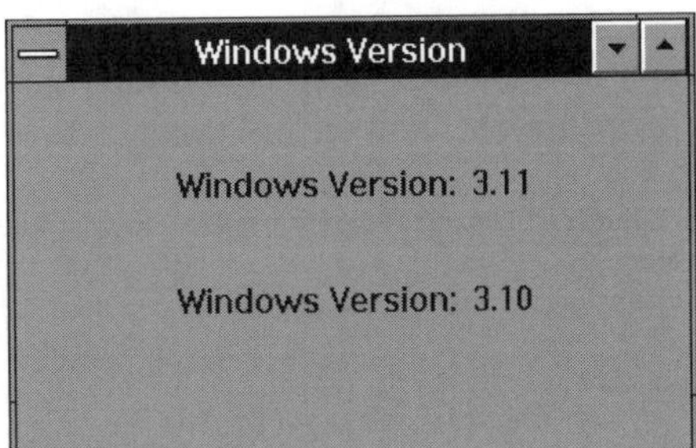

Figure 7-12 WINVER at run time

1. Create a new project with a blank form and name it WINVER.DPR. Name the unit WINVER1.PAS.
2. Add components and set their properties as shown in Table 7-13.

Table 7-13 Components, properties, and settings for Form1 in the WINVER project

COMPONENT	PROPERTY	SETTING
Form1	Left	200
	Top	118
	Width	346
	Height	215
	Caption	Windows Version
Label1	Left	41
	Top	40
	Width	257
	Height	20
	Alignment	taCenter
	AutoSize	False
	Caption	Label1
Label2	Left	41
	Top	96
	Width	257
	Height	20
	Alignment	taCenter
	AutoSize	False
	Caption	Label2

3. Click on Form1 so it is selected in the Object Inspector. On the Events page of the Object Inspector, double-click in the right-hand column of the OnCreate event. Add the following code to the resulting OnCreate event handler.

```
procedure TForm1.FormCreate(Sender: TObject);
const
  Text = 'Windows Version:  ';
var
  Buffer: Pointer;
  FileInfo: Pvs_FixedFileInfo;
  BufHandle, BufferSize: LongInt;
  Ver, Len: Word;
begin
```

```
  Buffer := nil;
  { Get buffer size }
  BufferSize := GetFileVersionInfoSize('USER.EXE', BufHandle);
  { Create buffer }
  GetMem(Buffer, BufferSize);
  try
    { Fill buffer with version resource }
    GetFileVersionInfo('USER.EXE', BufHandle, BufferSize, Buffer);
    { Read desired file version info from buffer }
    VerQueryValue(Buffer, '\', Pointer(FileInfo), Len);
    { Convert to string format }
    Label1.Caption := Text+IntToStr(HiWord(FileInfo^.dwFileVersionMS))+
      '.'+IntToStr(LoWord(FileInfo^.dwFileVersionMS));
  finally
    FreeMem(Buffer, BufferSize);
  end;
  { Get Windows version the API way }
  Ver := GetVersion;
  Label2.Caption := Text+IntToStr(Lo(Ver))+'.'+IntToStr(Hi(Ver));
end;
```

4. Compile and test the project.

How It Works

Many Windows programs have file version information embedded in them in a version resource. Version information can also be found in other files such as DLLs, VBXs, and so on. This version information follows a standard format, so you can use the GetFileVersionInfo and VerQueryValue Windows API functions to read and interpret the version directly from the file. The GetVersion API function does not get the Windows version information in this way. As stated in the "Technique" section of this How-To, the GetVersion API will return 3.10 in both 3.10 and 3.11 versions of Windows.

This How-To reads the version information from the USER.EXE file. This file has the correct version information and is required for Windows to run. A buffer is established to hold the resource and load it using the GetFileVersionInfo API function. The buffer is then read by the VerQueryValue API function to give the desired values. Once these values are obtained, it's simply a matter of converting them to a format suitable for display.

Note: Getting version information from the GetVersion API function is a bit easier—unfortunately, the information cannot be counted on as correct.

Comments

The technique used to get version information out of USER.EXE can also be used to get version information from other files. This might be useful in an installation program, for example. If you use this technique on unknown files, you should be prepared for the possibility of the file not containing version information.

7.13 How Do I...
Find out if the user's machine has a defective Pentium processor?

COMPLEXITY: EASY

Problem

I've read that many of the Pentium processors found in computers today may be defective. Is this something I should be concerned about? Is there a way I can detect whether my user's machine has a defective Pentium processor?

Technique

Delphi automatically protects your programs against defective Pentium processors if you have the Pentium-safe FDIV option enabled in the compiler options page of the Project Options dialog. Even though this option is available, you may need to check for the flaw.

The flaw found in some Pentium processors is specific to the floating point FDIV function. The vast majority of programs and users will not be affected by this flaw, but in case you think you may be—or are just curious as to whether you have a flawed Pentium chip in your computer—detecting one is simply a matter of knowing what to look for.

Steps

Run PENTIUM.EXE. The test for a flawed Pentium processor is completed when the form is created. Results of the test are displayed in Label1 on the form, as shown in Figure 7-13.

1. Create a new project with a blank form and name it PENTIUM.DPR. Name the unit PENT.PAS.

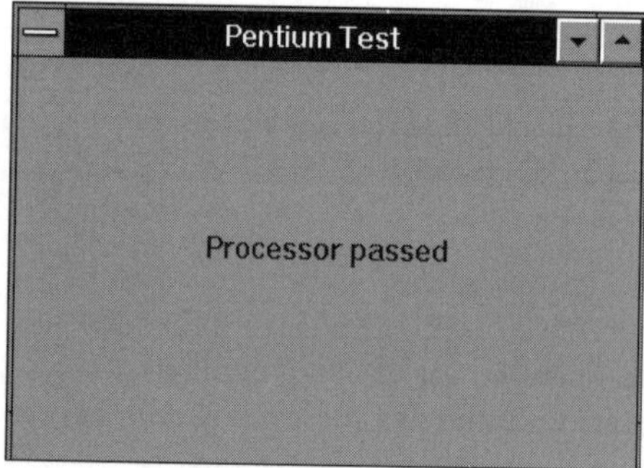

Figure 7-13 PENTIUM at run time

2. Add components and set their properties as shown in Table 7-14.

Table 7-14 Components, properties, and settings for Form1 in the PENTIUM project

COMPONENT	PROPERTY	SETTING
Form1	Left	200
	Top	118
	Width	369
	Height	259
	Caption	Pentium Test
Label1	Left	16
	Top	94
	Width	329
	Height	20
	Alignment	taCenter
	AutoSize	False

3. Double-click on Form1 and add the following code to the resulting OnCreate event handler.

```
procedure TForm1.FormCreate(Sender: TObject);
const
  a_bug: single = 4195835.0;
  b_bug: single = 3145727.0;
var
  r: double;
begin
{$U-}
  r := a_bug / b_bug;
{$U+}
  if a_bug - r * b_bug > 1.0 then
    Label1.Caption := 'Flawed Pentium detected'
  else Label1.Caption := 'Processor passed';
end;
```

4. Compile and test the project.

How It Works

The Pentium flaw only affects certain combinations of numbers when using the floating point FDIV function. This How-To specifically tests one of the known bad combinations while the form is being created. The results are then displayed when the form is shown.

Comments

The {$U-} compiler directive is used in the code to ensure that the Pentium Save FDIV option is off during the test of the processor.

If you find that you have a defective Pentium processor, you should evaluate whether you need a replacement or not. The vast majority of users will not be affected by the defect. Even so, many computer users get annoyed by the fact that their computer isn't perfect.

7.14 How Do I...
Simulate SPY in Delphi?

COMPLEXITY: INTERMEDIATE

Problem

The Windows Software Development Kit (SDK) includes a program called SPY that gives information about other programs' windows. WinSight, which is included with Delphi, serves a similar purpose. I want to write my own utility that does the same thing. How do I do this in Delphi?

Technique

This How-To requires the coordination of a few Windows API functions and some knowledge of how things interact in Windows. You call the SetCapture API to tell Windows that you want mouse messages sent to your form instead of the window that the cursor is over. You then process the mouse messages to determine which window the mouse is over and get the desired information about that window by calling a few more Windows APIs.

Steps

Run DELSPY.EXE. Click on the Spy button, then move the mouse cursor over other windows on your computer's desktop. Note that DELSPY highlights each window as the mouse cursor passes over it. Useful information about the highlighted window is displayed on the Delspy form, as shown in Figure 7-14. If you wish to freeze the information, you can exit the spy mode at any time by clicking the mouse button.

1. Create a new project with a blank form and name it DELSPY.DPR. Name the unit DELSPY1.PAS.

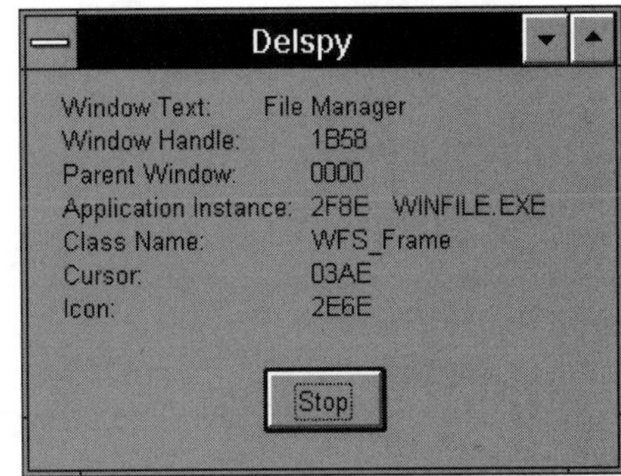

Figure 7-14 DELSPY at run time

2. Add components and set their properties as shown in Table 7-15.

Table 7-15 Components, properties, and settings for Form1 in the DELSPY project

COMPONENT	PROPERTY	SETTING
Form1	Left	304
	Top	132
	Width	317
	Height	238
	Caption	Delspy
Panel1	Left	0
	Top	0
	Width	309
	Height	203
	Align	alClient
	BevelOuter	bvNone
	+Font	
	-Color	clBlack
	-Size	8
	-Name	Arial
	ParentFont	False
Label1	Left	18
	Top	11
	Width	79
	Height	16

continued on next page

continued from previous page

COMPONENT	PROPERTY	SETTING
	Caption	Window Text:
Label2	Left	18
	Top	28
	Width	94
	Height	16
	Caption	Window Handle:
Label3	Left	18
	Top	45
	Width	92
	Height	16
	Caption	Parent Window:
Label4	Left	18
	Top	62
	Width	121
	Height	16
	Caption	Application Instance:
Label5	Left	18
	Top	79
	Width	75
	Height	16
	Caption	Class Name:
Label6	Left	18
	Top	96
	Width	42
	Height	16
	Caption	Cursor:
Label7	Left	18
	Top	113
	Width	28
	Height	16
	Caption	Icon:
Label8	Left	123
	Top	11
	Width	4
	Height	16
	+Font	

COMPONENT	PROPERTY	SETTING
	-Color	clBlue
	-Size	8
	-Name	Arial
	ParentFont	False
Label9	Left	148
	Top	28
	Width	28
	Height	16
	Caption	0000
	+Font	
	-Color	clBlue
	-Size	8
	-Name	Arial
	ParentFont	False
Label10	Left	148
	Top	45
	Width	28
	Height	16
	Caption	0000
	+Font	
	-Color	clBlue
	-Size	8
	-Name	Arial
	ParentFont	False
Label11	Left	148
	Top	62
	Width	28
	Height	16
	Caption	0000
	+Font	
	-Color	clBlue
	-Size	8
	-Name	Arial
	ParentFont	False
Label12	Left	148
	Top	79

continued on next page

continued from previous page

COMPONENT	PROPERTY	SETTING
	Width	4
	Height	16
	+Font	
	-Color	clBlue
	-Size	8
	-Name	Arial
	ParentFont	False
Label13	Left	148
	Top	96
	Width	28
	Height	16
	Caption	0000
	+Font	
	-Color	clBlue
	-Size	8
	-Name	Arial
	ParentFont	False
Label14	Left	148
	Top	113
	Width	28
	Height	16
	Caption	0000
	+Font	
	-Color	clBlue
	-Size	8
	-Name	Arial
	ParentFont	False
Label15	Left	191
	Top	62
	Width	4
	Height	16
	+Font	
	-Color	clBlue
	-Size	8
	-Name	Arial
	ParentFont	False

COMPONENT	PROPERTY	SETTING
Button1	Left	122
	Top	152
	Width	65
	Height	33
	Caption	Spy

3. Double-click on Button1 and add the following code to the resulting OnClick event handler.

```
{ Start spying }
procedure TForm1.Button1Click(Sender: TObject);
begin
  OldWnd := 0;
  SetCapture(Handle);
  Button1.Caption := 'Stop';
end;
```

4. Click on Form1 and ensure that it is selected in the Object Inspector. On the Events page, double-click in the right-hand column of the OnMouseDown event. Add the following code to the resulting OnMouseDown event handler.

```
{ Stop spying }
procedure TForm1.FormMouseDown(Sender: TObject; Button: TMouseButton;
  Shift: TShiftState; X, Y: Integer);
begin
  ReleaseCapture;
  FrameWindow(OldWnd);
  Button1.Caption := 'Spy';
end;
```

5. Click on Form1 and ensure that it is selected in the Object Inspector. On the Events page, double-click in the right-hand column of the OnMouseMove event. Add the following code to the resulting OnMouseMove event handler.

```
procedure TForm1.FormMouseMove(Sender: TObject; Shift: TShiftState; X,
  Y: Integer);
var
  MousePos: LongInt;
  MousePoint: TPoint;
  TextBuf: array[0..255] of char;
  Wnd: hWnd;
begin
  { Find the window under the cursor }
  MousePos := GetMessagePos;
  MousePoint := MakePoint(MousePos);
  Wnd := WindowFromPoint(MousePoint);
  { If this is a new window, continue }
```

continued on next page

continued from previous page

```
  if Wnd  OldWnd then
  begin
    { Caption }
    GetWindowText(Wnd, @TextBuf, 255);
    Label8.Caption := StrPas(TextBuf);
    { hWnd }
    Label9.Caption := IntToHex(Wnd,4);
    { Parent hWnd }
    Label10.Caption := IntToHex(GetParent(Wnd),4);
    { Instance handle
    Label11.Caption := IntToHex(GetWindowWord(Wnd, GWW_HINSTANCE), 4);
    { Class name }
    GetClassName(Wnd, @TextBuf, 255);
    Label12.Caption := StrPas(TextBuf);
    { Cursor handle }
    Label13.Caption := IntToHex(GetClassWord(Wnd, GCW_HCURSOR), 4);
    { Icon handle }
    Label14.Caption := IntToHex(GetClassWord(Wnd, GCW_HICON), 4);
    { File name of instance }
    GetModuleFileName(GetWindowWord(Wnd, GWW_HINSTANCE), @TextBuf, 255);
    Label15.Caption := ExtractFileName(StrPas(TextBuf));
    { Remove highlight from old window }
    if OldWnd  0 then FrameWindow(OldWnd);
    { Highlight new window }
    FrameWindow(Wnd);
    OldWnd := Wnd;
  end;
end;
```

6. While still in the Code Editor, add the following variable and procedure after the *implementation* keyword as shown.

```
implementation

{$R *.DFM}

var
  OldWnd: hWnd;

procedure FrameWindow(Wnd: HWnd);
var
  Rect: TRect;
  DC: hDC;
  OldPen, Pen: hPen;
  OldBrush, Brush: hBrush;
  X2, Y2: Integer;
begin
  { Get the target window's rect and DC }
  GetWindowRect(Wnd, Rect);
  DC := GetWindowDC(Wnd);
  { Set ROP appropriately for highlighting }
  SetROP2(DC, R2_NOT);
```

```
  { Select brush and pen }
  Pen := CreatePen(PS_InsideFrame, 4, 0);
  OldPen := SelectObject(DC, Pen);
  Brush := GetStockObject(Null_Brush);
  OldBrush := SelectObject(DC, Brush);
  { Set dimensions of highlight }
  X2 := Rect.Right - Rect.Left;
  Y2 := Rect.Bottom - Rect.Top;
  { Draw highlight box }
  Rectangle(DC, 0, 0, X2, Y2);
  { Clean up }
  SelectObject(DC, OldBrush);
  SelectObject(DC, OldPen);
  ReleaseDC(Wnd, DC);
  { Do NOT delete the brush, because it was a stock object }
  DeleteObject(Pen);
end;
```

7. Compile and test the project.

How It Works

Normally, Windows sends mouse messages to the window under the mouse cursor. By using the SetCapture Windows API function, you receive all messages while you are spying. The GetMessagePos and WindowFromPoint API functions give you the location of the cursor at the time the message was sent and which window is located under the mouse cursor.

Once the window handle (hWnd) of the window under the cursor is determined, it is compared with the previous hWnd, which was stored as OldWnd. If these window handles match, no further action is taken.

Note: You can reduce flicker by updating the screen only when you need to.

If the window handles do not match, several API functions are used to update the parameters shown on the Delspy form. The GetWindowText API obtains the caption of the window, the GetParent API gets the handle of the window's parent window, and GetWindowWord gets the window's instance handle. Some functions tell you more than one thing. The GetClassWord API gives you the cursor handle and the icon handle. The GetModuleFileName API gives you the file name of the window's program.

The user knows which window is being spied on by the highlighted borders. The FrameWindow procedure does this using a raster operation (ROP) to invert the border of the window. Notice that the drawing in this procedure is done with direct calls to the Windows GDI functions. This is necessary because the windows being highlighted do not necessarily belong to your application, so you cannot use Delphi functions to do the highlighting.

In order to highlight the window, you get the window's size by calling GetWindowRect. A device context (DC) can be obtained by using the GetWindowDC

API function. The necessary tools are assembled to do the drawing. A pen is used to draw the actual outline of the window, and a Null_Brush is used so the rectangle does not get filled in. Note that this particular brush is a stock object and does not get deleted when you are finished with it.

Comments

This How-To creates a useful tool that you may choose to add to Delphi's Tools menu. Although the techniques used here lend themselves particularly well to utilities such as this one, you may find other uses for the individual API functions.

7.15 How Do I...
Time functions in my application?

COMPLEXITY: INTERMEDIATE

Problem

I'm going through my program trying to optimize various functions. It's difficult to tell whether my improvements are making a difference. Is there a way that I can time various sections of code in my Delphi programs?

Technique

It's fairly common to use a utility called a *profiler* to time various functions in your program. Delphi does not include a profiler, so in order to see how efficient your functions are, you'll have to time them individually using the time standard introduced in How-To 7.3.

Steps

Run STPWTCH.EXE. Select a function that you want to time. Enter a value such as 10,000 in the edit box for the number of iterations you want to test.. Click on the Start Timing button to time the function. The program iterates through the selected function and displays the elapsed time, as shown in Figure 7-15. Experiment with other values and functions.

Note: Entering a large number can tie up the computer for a long time, and there is no mechanism in this project that allows you to quit the timing or switch to other programs once you have started.

1. Create a new project with a blank form and name it STPWTCH.DPR. Name the unit STPWTCH1.PAS.

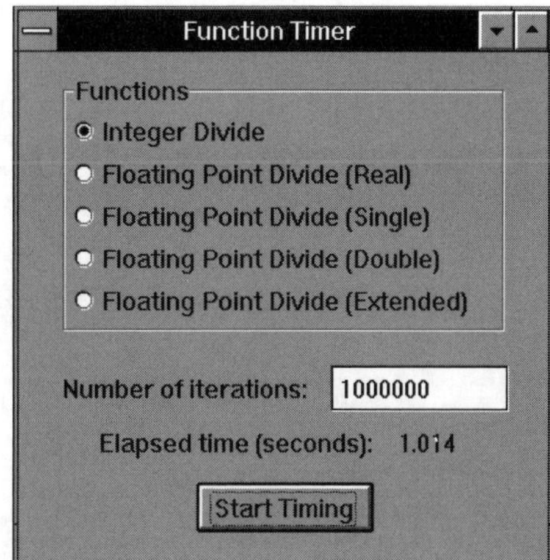

Figure 7-15 STPWTCH at run time

2. Add components and set their properties as shown in Table 7-16.

Table 7-16 Components, properties, and settings for Form1 in the STPWTCH project

COMPONENT	PROPERTY	SETTING
Form1	Left	200
	Top	118
	Width	371
	Height	374
	Caption	Function Timer
Label1	Left	29
	Top	213
	Width	167
	Height	20
	Caption	Number of iterations:
Label2	Left	54
	Top	249
	Width	187
	Height	20
	Caption	Elapsed time (seconds):
Label3	Left	259
	Top	249

continued on next page

continued from previous page

COMPONENT	PROPERTY	SETTING
	Width	9
	Height	20
	Caption	0
	+Font	
	-Color	clBlue
	-Size	10
	-Name	System
	-Style	[fsBold]
	ParentFont	False
RadioGroup1	Left	30
	Top	16
	Width	302
	Height	169
	Caption	Functions
	Items	Integer Divide
		Floating Point Divide (Real)
		Floating Point Divide (Single)
		Floating Point Divide (Double)
		Floating Point Divide (Extended)
Edit1	Left	213
	Top	208
	Width	121
	Height	29
	Text	0
Button1	Left	121
	Top	285
	Width	121
	Height	33
	Caption	Start Timing

3. Double-click on Button1 and add the following code to the resulting OnClick event handler.

```
procedure TForm1.Button1Click(Sender: TObject);
const
  Dividend = 731;
  Divisor = 639;
```

```
var
  IDividend, IDivisor, IQuotient: Integer;
  RDividend, RDivisor, RQuotient: Real;
  SDividend, SDivisor, SQuotient: Single;
  DDividend, DDivisor, DQuotient: Double;
  EDividend, EDivisor, EQuotient: Extended;
  I, Start: LongInt;
begin
  case RadioGroup1.ItemIndex of
    0 : begin { Integer }
          { Initialize }
          IDividend := Dividend;
          IDivisor := Divisor;
          { Set cursor to indicate busy }
          Screen.Cursor := crHourGlass;
          try
            { Get beginning time }
            Start := StartTimer;
            { Loop through function }
            for I := 1 to StrToInt(Edit1.Text) do
              IQuotient := IDividend div IDivisor;
            { Get and display elapsed time }
            Label3.Caption := FloatToStr(ElapsedTime(Start) / 1000);
          finally
            { Ensures cursor is returned to default }
            Screen.Cursor := crDefault;
          end;
        end;
    1 : begin { Real }
          RDividend := Dividend;
          RDivisor := Divisor;
          Screen.Cursor := crHourGlass;
          try
            Start := StartTimer;
            for I := 1 to StrToInt(Edit1.Text) do
              RQuotient := RDividend / RDivisor;
            Label3.Caption := FloatToStr(ElapsedTime(Start) / 1000);
          finally
            Screen.Cursor := crDefault;
          end;
        end;
    2 : begin { Single }
          SDividend := Dividend;
          SDivisor := Divisor;
          Screen.Cursor := crHourGlass;
          try
            Start := StartTimer;
            for I := 1 to StrToInt(Edit1.Text) do
              SQuotient := SDividend / SDivisor;
            Label3.Caption := FloatToStr(ElapsedTime(Start) / 1000);
          finally
            Screen.Cursor := crDefault;
          end;
        end;
```

continued on next page

continued from previous page

```
    3 : begin { Double }
          DDividend := Dividend;
          DDivisor := Divisor;
          Screen.Cursor := crHourGlass;
          try
            Start := StartTimer;
            for I := 1 to StrToInt(Edit1.Text) do
              DQuotient := DDividend / DDivisor;
            Label3.Caption := FloatToStr(ElapsedTime(Start) / 1000);
          finally
            Screen.Cursor := crDefault;
          end;
        end;
    4 : begin { Extended }
          EDividend := Dividend;
          EDivisor := Divisor;
          Screen.Cursor := crHourGlass;
          try
            Start := StartTimer;
            for I := 1 to StrToInt(Edit1.Text) do
              EQuotient := EDividend / EDivisor;
            Label3.Caption := FloatToStr(ElapsedTime(Start) / 1000);
          finally
            Screen.Cursor := crDefault;
          end;
        end;
  end;
end;
```

4. While still in the Code Editor, move up to the *interface* keyword and add a *uses* clause as shown here:

```
implementation

uses HowUtils;

{$R *.DFM}
```

5. Next you're going to add a function to the HowUtils unit. If you have been building this unit as you go along, add it to the project using the File|Add File menu option in Delphi. If you do not yet have a HowUtils unit, you can create one using the File|New Unit menu option in Delphi. Add the following function declarations to the unit's *interface* section.

```
unit HowUtils;

interface

uses
  SysUtils, WinTypes, WinProcs, Messages, Classes, Controls,
  Forms, IniFiles, ToolHelp, ShellAPI;
```

```
function StartTimer: LongInt;
function ElapsedTime(Start: LongInt): LongInt;
```

6. Add the StartTimer function to the HowUtils unit's *implementation* section as shown here:

```
function StartTimer: LongInt;
var
  TimeRec: TTimerInfo;
  TimeStart: LongInt;
begin
  { Initialize buffer }
  TimeRec.dwSize := SizeOf(TimeRec);
  { Get starting time }
  TimerCount(@TimeRec);
  Result := TimeRec.dwmsSinceStart;
end;
```

7. Add the ElapsedTime function to the HowUtils unit's *implementation* section:

```
function ElapsedTime(Start: LongInt): LongInt;
var
  TimeRec: TTimerInfo;
  TimeStart: LongInt;
begin
  { Initialize buffer }
  TimeRec.dwSize := SizeOf(TimeRec);
  { Get starting time }
  TimerCount(@TimeRec);
  Result := TimeRec.dwmsSinceStart - Start;
end;
```

8. Compile and test the project.

How It Works

You use the same TOOLHELP functions that you used in How-To 7.3 to accomplish the timing. The StartTimer function gets the timer count at the beginning of the function. When the function is complete, a call to the ElapsedTime function gives you the difference between the starting time and ending time in milliseconds.

Comments

Since Delphi lacks a profiler, timing functions such as these can come in very handy. As stated in How-To 7.3, this technique is accurate to the millisecond. There is some overhead involved in calling the functions, but since the overhead will be the same for each call, comparisons are very accurate.

7.16 How Do I...
Set a file's date and time?

COMPLEXITY: INTERMEDIATE

Problem

I'd like to be able to set the time and date of several files to a given value. Delphi's TOUCH.COM utility sets all files in a directory to the current date and time, but it won't let me specify a date and time if I want to. How can I do this with Delphi?

Technique

Delphi has several built-in functions that set the time and date of a file. You can expand on this capability to create a utility that lets you select one or more files in a directory to be updated.

Steps

Run FDATE.EXE. Navigate as necessary using the file and directory list boxes and the drive combo box. Try selecting some files and setting the date and time using one of the custom options, as shown in Figure 7-16.

Note: You can select multiple files by holding the SHIFT or CTRL key down while clicking on the items in the file list box.

1. Create a new project with a blank form and save it as FDATE.DPR. Name the unit FDATE1.PAS.

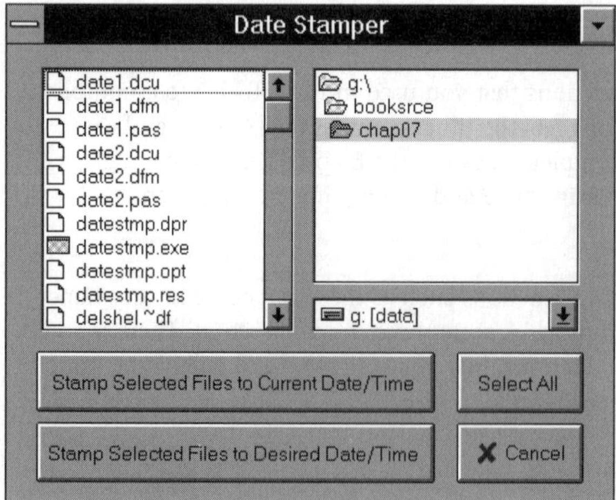

Figure 7-16 FDATE at run time

2. Add components to Form1 and set their properties as shown in Table 7-17.

Table 7-17 Components, properties, and settings for Form1 in the FDATE project

COMPONENT	PROPERTY	SETTING
Form1	Left	235
	Top	116
	Width	396
	Height	326
	Caption	Date Stamper
	+Font	
	-Color	clBlack
	-Size	8
	-Name	Arial
	Scaled	False
FileListBox1	Left	15
	Top	15
	Width	170
	Height	161
	ItemHeight	16
	MultiSelect	True
	ShowGlyphs	True
DirectoryListBox1	Left	199
	Top	15
	Width	175
	Height	130
	FileList	FileListBox1
	ItemHeight	16
DriveComboBox1	Left	199
	Top	154
	Width	175
	Height	22
	DirList	DirectoryListBox1
Button1	Left	288
	Top	190
	Width	89
	Height	41
	Caption	Select All

continued on next page

continued from previous page

COMPONENT	PROPERTY	SETTING
Button2	Left	11
	Top	240
	Width	270
	Height	41
	Caption	Stamp Selected Files to Desired Date / Time
Button3	Left	11
	Top	190
	Width	270
	Height	41
	Caption	Stamp Selected Files to Current Date / Time
BitBtn1	Left	288
	Top	240
	Width	89
	Height	41
	Kind	bkCancel

3. Create an OnClick event handler for Button1. Type the following code in the resulting Button1Click event handler. This code provides the user with a quick way of selecting all of the files in the file list box.

```
procedure TForm1.Button1Click(Sender: TObject);
var
  I: integer;
begin
  { Hide the listbox so the user doesn't see the changes }
  FileListbox1.Visible := False;
  try
    { Select all items in the listbox }
    for I := FileListbox1.Items.Count - 1 downto 0 do
      FileListbox1.Selected[I] := True;
  finally
    { Show the listbox }
    FileListbox1.Visible := True;
  end;
end;
```

4. Create an OnClick event handler for Button2. Type the following code in the resulting Button2Click event handler. This allows the user to set the file time stamps to a specific date and time.

```
procedure TForm1.Button2Click(Sender: TObject);
var
  FHandle: THandle;
```

```
  I: integer;
  DT: TDateTime;
begin
{ Show a modal dialog - if the OK button is pressed, do the following }
if DateDlg.ShowModal = mrOk then
  begin
    { Get the desired date and time from the modal dialog }
    DT := StrToDateTime(DateDlg.Edit1.Text);
    for I := 0 to FileListbox1.Items.Count - 1 do
    begin
      if FileListbox1.Selected[I] = True then
      begin
        FHandle := FileOpen(FileListbox1.Items.Strings[I], $0002);
        try
          { Set the date and time of the selected files }
          FileSetDate(FHandle, DateTimeToFileDate(DT));
        finally
          { Make sure the file gets closed }
          FileClose(FHandle);
        end;
      end;
    end;
  end;
end;
```

5. Create an OnClick event handler for Button3. Type the following code in the resulting Button3Click event handler. This allows the user to set the file time stamps to the current date and time.

```
procedure TForm1.Button3Click(Sender: TObject);
var
  FHandle: THandle;
  I: integer;
  DT: TDateTime;
begin
  { Save the current date/time so all files get set the same }
  DT := Now;
  for I := 0 to FileListbox1.Items.Count - 1 do
  begin
    if FileListbox1.Selected[I] = True then
    begin
      FHandle := FileOpen(FileListbox1.Items.Strings[I], $0002);
      try
        { Set the date and time }
        FileSetDate(FHandle, DateTimeToFileDate(DT));
      finally
        { Make sure the file gets closed }
        FileClose(FHandle);
      end;
    end;
  end;
end;
```

6. Create an OnClick event handler for BitBtn1. Type the following code in the resulting BitBtn1Click event handler.

```
procedure TForm1.BitBtn1Click(Sender: TObject);
begin
  Close;
end;
```

7. While still in the Code Editor, add a *uses* clause after the *implementation* keyword as shown here:

```
implementation

uses FDate2;

{$R *.DFM}
```

8. Add a new blank form to the project and name the unit FDATE2.PAS.

9. Add components and set their properties as shown in Table 7-18.

Table 7-18 Components, properties, and settings for Form2 in the FDATE project

COMPONENT	PROPERTY	SETTING
Form2	Name	DateDlg
	Left	263
	Top	115
	BorderStyle	bsDialog
	Caption	Enter Date / Time
	ClientHeight	140
	ClientWidth	349
	+Font	
	-Color	clBlack
	-Size	8
	-Name	Arial
	Position	poScreenCenter
	Scaled	False
Bevel1	Left	11
	Top	10
	Width	327
	Height	71
	Shape	bsFrame
Label1	Left	32

COMPONENT	PROPERTY	SETTING
	Top	37
	Width	106
	Height	16
	Caption	Enter Date / Time:
Edit1	Left	156
	Top	32
	Width	161
	Height	24
	Text	MM/DD/YY HH:MM:SS
BitBtn1	Name	OKBtn
	Left	24
	Top	94
	Width	95
	Height	33
	Kind	bkOK
BitBtn2	Name	CancelBtn
	Left	127
	Top	94
	Width	95
	Height	33
	Kind	bkCancel
BitBtn3	Name	HelpBtn
	Left	231
	Top	94
	Width	94
	Height	33
	Kind	bkHelp

10. Compile and test the project.

How It Works

This How-To demonstrates the power available with Delphi's existing components and routines. FileListbox, DirectoryListbox, and DriveCombobox are all designed to work together. As long as they are connected, they will automatically update each other as required.

The date and file management routines are taken from the SYSUTILS unit provided with Delphi. The routines make it easy to do things like changing the date stamp of a file, determining the current date and time, and making the necessary conversions between the different data formats used in this project.

Comments

A utility such as this can come in handy if you are developing software or working with large numbers of files on a computer. If you stamp all files of a project to a single date and time, it is easy to tell if any files have been changed.

In order to mold this How-To into a full blown utility, you'll probably want to add some data validation and other things to make it a bit more user friendly. The string that currently needs to be entered for the user-defined date and time is controlled by the StrToDateTime function in the SYSUTILS unit. If the string does not match the required format, an exception will occur.

8

8

PERIPHERALS

How Do I...

The PC environment is very successful for a number of reasons, and one of them is that it is an open system: There are literally tens of thousands of possible combinations of monitors, graphics cards, printers, modems, sound cards, and other peripherals. As a programmer, you need to be able to determine which hardware configuration a PC is using, and be able to utilize its various peripherals in your applications. Delphi includes powerful features that allow you to determine the configuration of a computer, control numerous aspects of printing, and access the serial port for modems and other devices. Also included are multimedia extensions and DOS access to permit use of an installed sound card and the internal speaker. The How-To's in this chapter take you step by step through programming these features into your applications.

8.1 Determine the color capabilities of a monitor or printer

Many applications require a color monitor or printer, and sometimes even a specific resolution or color range. With Delphi you can access the Windows API to obtain complete information about a given computer's monitor and default printer.

8.2 Control the size of a printed page

There are times when you want to dynamically set the number of lines printed on a page rather than use the normal printer page size. You can use Delphi's Printer object to obtain this level of control over printed output.

8.3 Maintain the same look on the printed page as on the screen

Another problem with printing is that due to differing screen and printer resolutions, what appears as one size on the screen looks very different when printed "as is." You can use the Delphi Printer object to allow a close match between what you see and what you get.

8.4 Maintain the 3D look in the printer options dialog

Some dialog boxes supplied by printer manufacturers don't have the 3D look common in modern Windows applications. You can use Delphi to make any dialog box conform to the new sculptured look.

8.5 Control the modem on a PC

Many PCs have modems installed. Delphi can use Windows API functions together with DOS file I/O to create a simple but powerful phone dialer application.

8.6 Send and receive data through the serial port

Sometimes you may need to exchange data with your application over a serial port using the modem. Rather than buy an expensive communications add-in, you can use Delphi to create a complete terminal emulator using DOS and Windows API function calls.

8.7 Control the speaker as the SOUND function did in Turbo Pascal

Some PCs don't have sound cards installed. You can use Windows multimedia functions in Delphi to access the speaker and reproduce the power of the SOUND function in Turbo Pascal.

8.8 Play music with the PC speaker

Not every PC has a sound card, but there is still a way to create simple musical effects. The PC speaker can be controlled via Delphi thanks to the Sound functions of the Windows API.

8.1 How do I... Determine the color capabilities of a monitor or printer?

COMPLEXITY: INTERMEDIATE

Problem

Modern applications often require color capabilities for the monitor and printer, sometimes at a given resolution or color level. Is there an easy way to determine the hardware configuration of a PC without having to ask the user?

Technique

The Windows API has a powerful function called GetDeviceCaps, which returns a vast quantity of information about the supported capabilities of a given display device. To get this information you use the Handle property built into all Delphi forms to obtain the screen display context, and then call GetDeviceCaps to find out the color capabilities of the monitor and graphics card.

Steps

Run DEVCOLOR.EXE. You will see a display similar to Figure 8-1, depending on your monitor and printer configuration. Switch to the printer color page, and you will see the color information for your default printer (if you have one enabled.)

1. Create a new project with a tabbed notebook form and name it DEVCOLOR.DPR. Name the unit DEVCAPFM.PAS.
2. Add components to TabbedNotebookDlg and set their properties as shown in Table 8-1.

Note: The GroupBox2 and GroupBox4 components go inside the GroupBox1 and GroupBox3 components to ensure proper display.

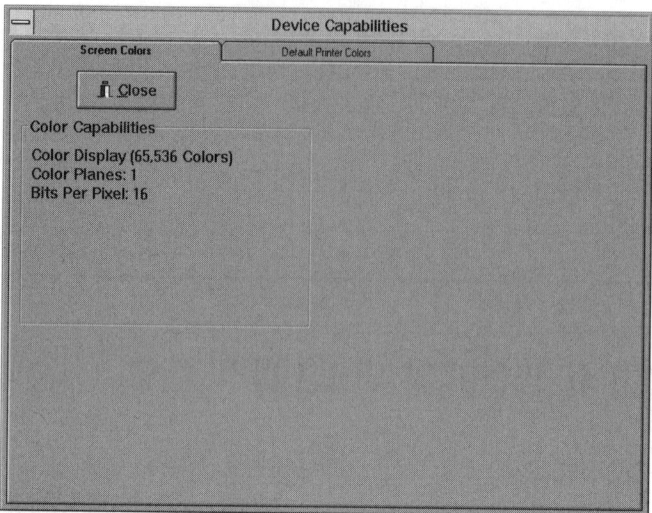

Figure 8-1 DEVCOLOR at run time showing screen color information

Table 8-1 Components, properties, and settings for TabbedNotebookDlg in DEVCOLOR

COMPONENT	PROPERTY	SETTING
TabbedNotebookDlg	Type	Application Main Form
	Width	571
	Height	431
	Left	30
	Top	29
	Caption	Device Capabilities
TabbedNotebook1	Type	TTabbedNotebook
	Width	563
	Height	396
	Left	0
	Top	0
	Pages	Screen Colors
		Default Printer Colors
GroupBox1	Type	TGroupBox (on page 0)
	Left	8
	Top	48
	Width	257

COMPONENT	PROPERTY	SETTING
	Height	177
	Caption	Color Capabilities
GroupBox2	Type	TGroupBox (inside GroupBox1)
	Left	8
	Top	80
	Width	241
	Height	81
	Caption	Palette Device
GroupBox3	Type	TGroupBox (on page 1)
	Left	8
	Top	48
	Width	257
	Height	177
	Caption	Color Capabilities
GroupBox4	Type	TGroupBox (inside GroupBox3)
	Left	8
	Top	80
	Width	241
	Height	81
	Caption	Palette Device
BitBtn1	Type	TBitBtn
	Left	56
	Top	8
	Width	89
	Height	33
	Kind	bkClose
Label1	Type	Tlabel (page 1)
	Left	24
	Top	16
	Width	4
	Height	20
	Caption	(blank)
Label3	Type	Tlabel (page 0 GroupBox1)
	Left	8
	Top	24
	Width	168

continued on next page

continued from previous page

COMPONENT	PROPERTY	SETTING
	Height	16
	Caption	Color Display (256 Colors)
Label4	Type	Tlabel (page 0 GroupBox1)
	Left	8
	Top	40
	Width	91
	Height	16
	Caption	Color Planes
Label5	Type	Tlabel (page 0 GroupBox1)
	Left	8
	Top	56
	Width	97
	Height	16
	Caption	Bits Per Pixel
Label6	Type	Tlabel (page 0 GroupBox2)
	Left	8
	Top	24
	Width	171
	Height	16
	Caption	Maximum Palette Entries
Label7	Type	Tlabel (page 0 GroupBox2)
	Left	8
	Top	40
	Width	206
	Height	16
	Caption	Total Reserved Palette Entries
Label8	Type	Tlabel (page 0 GroupBox2)
	Left	8
	Top	56
	Width	150
	Height	16
	Caption	Total Available Colors
Label9	Type	Tlabel (page 1 GroupBox3)
	Left	8
	Top	24
	Width	168

COMPONENT	PROPERTY	SETTING
	Height	16
	Caption	Color Display (256 Colors)
Label10	Type	Tlabel (page 1 GroupBox3)
	Left	8
	Top	40
	Width	91
	Height	16
	Caption	Color Planes
Label11	Type	Tlabel (page 1 GroupBox3)
	Left	8
	Top	56
	Width	97
	Height	16
	Caption	Bits Per Pixel
Label12	Type	Tlabel (page 1 GroupBox4)
	Left	8
	Top	24
	Width	171
	Height	16
	Caption	Maximum Palette Entries
Label13	Type	Tlabel (page 1 GroupBox4)
	Left	8
	Top	40
	Width	206
	Height	16
	Caption	Total Reserved Palette Entries
Label14	Type	Tlabel (page 1 GroupBox4)
	Left	8
	Top	56
	Width	150
	Height	16
	Caption	Total Available Colors

3. Select the OnClick event of BitBtn1 and enter the following line of code to close the form when you're done.

```
procedure TTabbedNotebookDlg.BitBtn1Click(Sender: TObject);
```

```
begin
  Close;
end;
```

4. Now activate the OnCreate event of the TabbedNotebookDlg form and enter the following code to be executed on startup of the program. The unfamiliar procedures are helpers you will enter in a moment.

```
procedure TTabbedNotebookDlg.FormCreate(Sender: TObject);
begin
  GetScreenColorCaps;
  GetPrinterColorCaps;
end;
```

5. While still in the Code Editor, move up to the *private* keyword and enter the following two lines, which allow Delphi to recognize your helper procedures later.

```
private
    { Private declarations }
    procedure GetScreenColorCaps;
    procedure GetPrinterColorCaps;
```

6. Now drop down to just below the *implementation* keyword and enter this helper function, which manipulates a Windows-style PChar string.

```
{ Function to work along a PChar String until the next delimiter is found }
function GetPCharAtom( ThePChar : PChar; TheDelimiter : Char ) : PChar;
const NextElement : PChar = nil;
begin
  if ThePChar = nil then ThePChar := NextElement;
  { Call the StrScan pascal function to return a pointer to the    }
  { position where the delimiter character is first found, or nil }
  { if it wasnÆt found                                             }
  NextElement := StrScan( ThePChar , TheDelimiter );
  if NextElement  nil then
  begin
    NextElement^ := #0;
    NextElement := @NextElement[ 1 ];
  end;
  GetPCharAtom := ThePChar;
end;
```

7. Under the previous function, insert the following assistant function, which makes up for the lack of a power (exponentiation) operator in Pascal.

```
{ Add a power function since pascal doesn't support this operator }
function Power( TheBase , TheExponent : Longint ) : Longint;
var ReturnVal : Longint;
    Counter_1 : Longint;

begin
  { Initialize the return value to 1 because anything to 0 power is 1 }
  { The loop multiplies TheBase times itself for Counter_1 - 1 times   }
```

```
  ReturnVal := 1;
  for Counter_1 := 1 to TheExponent do
  begin
    ReturnVal := ReturnVal * TheBase;
  end;
  Power := ReturnVal;
end;
```

8. Below the Power function enter the helper function listed next. This handles calling the GetDeviceCaps function in the Windows API and decoding and storing the results in your form.

```
procedure TTabbedNotebookDlg.GetScreenColorCaps;
var The_Integer : Integer;
    Total_Colors ,
    Total_Color_Shades : Longint;
begin
  {************************************************}
  {*    Get the device capabilities for the screen *}
  {*    using the GETDEVICECAPS API function       *}
  {************************************************}
  { BITSPIXEL determines the number of colors in the device }
  The_Integer := GetDeviceCaps( TabbedNotebookDlg.Canvas.Handle , BITSPIXEL );
  Total_Color_Shades := Power( 2 , The_Integer );
  Label5.Caption := Label5.Caption + IntToStr( The_Integer );
  { PLANES determines the number of color planes }
  The_Integer := GetDeviceCaps( TabbedNotebookDlg.Canvas.Handle , PLANES );
  Label4.Caption := Label4.Caption + IntToStr( The_Integer );
  Total_Colors := Power( Total_Color_Shades , The_Integer );
  if Total_Colors < 3 then Label3.Caption := 'Monochrome Display' else
   Label3.Caption := 'Color Display (' + IntToStr( Total_Colors ) + ' Colors)';
  { RASTERCAPS uses ANDing to determine if the device is a palette device }
  The_Integer := GetDeviceCaps( TabbedNotebookDlg.Canvas.Handle , RASTERCAPS );
  if ( The_Integer and rc_PALETTE ) = rc_PALETTE then
  begin
       { SIZEPALETTE gets the number of palette entries }
    The_Integer := GetDeviceCaps( TabbedNotebookDlg.Canvas.Handle , SIZEPALETTE );
    Label6.Caption := Label6.Caption + IntToStr( The_Integer );
    { NUMRESERVED gets the number of reserved palette entries }
    The_Integer := GetDeviceCaps( TabbedNotebookDlg.Canvas.Handle , NUMRESERVED );
    Label7.Caption := Label7.Caption + IntToStr( The_Integer);
    { COLORRES gets the number of available colors }
    The_Integer := GetDeviceCaps( TabbedNotebookDlg.Canvas.Handle , COLORRES );
    Total_Colors := Power( 2 , The_Integer );
    Label8.Caption := Label8.Caption + IntToStr( Total_Colors );
  end
  else
  begin
    Groupbox2.Visible := false;
  end;
end;
```

9. Beneath the previous function type in the following helper function, which gets the device capabilities for the printer.

```
procedure TTabbedNotebookDlg.GetPrinterColorCaps;

var The_DC : HDC;
    The_Integer : Integer;
    PrinterBuffer : array[ 0 .. 80 ] of Char;
    TheDriverName ,
    TheDeviceName ,
    TheOutputName    : Pchar;
    Total_Colors ,
    Total_Color_Shades : Longint;

begin
  {**************************************************}
  {*     Get the device capabilities for the printer *}
  {*     using the GetDeviceCaps function of the API *}
  {**************************************************}
  GetProfileString( 'windows' , 'device' , ',,' , PrinterBuffer ,
    SizeOf( PrinterBuffer ));
  TheDeviceName := GetPCharAtom( PrinterBuffer , ',' );
  TheDriverName := GetPCharAtom( nil , ',' );
  TheOutputName := GetPCharAtom( nil , ',' );
  The_DC := CreateDC(  TheDriverName , TheDeviceName , TheOutputName , nil );
  { Alternatively, could have used the Printer.Canvas.Handle instead of  }
  { going through CreateDC; above illustrates alternate method           }
  If The_DC  0 then
  begin
    { BITSPIXEL determine the number of colors in the device }
    The_Integer := GetDeviceCaps( The_DC , BITSPIXEL );
    Total_Color_Shades := POWER( 2 , The_Integer );
    Label11.Caption := Label11.Caption + IntToStr( The_Integer );
    { PLANES determine the number of color planes }
    The_Integer := GetDeviceCaps( The_DC , PLANES );
    Label10.Caption := Label10.Caption + IntToStr( The_Integer );
    Total_Colors := Power( Total_Color_Shades , The_Integer );
    if Total_Colors < 3 then Label9.Caption := 'Monochrome Printer' else
     Label9.Caption := 'Color Printer (' + IntToStr( Total_Colors ) +
       ' Colors)';
    { RASTERCAPS uses ANDing to determine if the device is a palette device }
    The_Integer := GetDeviceCaps( The_DC , RASTERCAPS );
    if ( The_Integer and rc_PALETTE ) = rc_PALETTE then
    begin
      { SIZEPALETTE gets the number of palette entries }
      The_Integer := GetDeviceCaps( The_DC , SIZEPALETTE );
      Label12.Caption := Label12.Caption + IntToStr( The_Integer );
      { NUMRESERVED gets the number of reserved palette entries }
      The_Integer := GetDeviceCaps( The_DC , NUMRESERVED );
      Label13.Caption := Label13.Caption + IntToStr( The_Integer );
      { COLORRES gets the number of available colors }
      The_Integer := GetDeviceCaps( The_DC , COLORRES );
      Total_Colors := Power( 2 , The_Integer );
      Label14.Caption := Label14.Caption + IntToStr( Total_Colors );
    end
    else
    begin
      Groupbox4.Visible := false;
```

```
    end;
    {VERY IMPORTANT STEP! DC's must be quickly released or Windows hangs!}
    DeleteDC( The_DC );
  end
  else
  begin
    Label1.Caption := 'No default printer selected.';
    GroupBox3.Visible := false;
  end;
end;
```

10. Compile and test the project.

How It Works

The key to the project is the GetDeviceCaps function, but before you can get the information, you need to obtain a display context, which is a Windows data structure used to construct the images that will be displayed. Windows creates this data structure based on one of two things: a *handle*, which is a pointer to a window of some sort, or a set of strings that allow the system to access the driver, device, and type of output. The Canvas.Handle property, built into all Delphi forms, contains the screen display context (DC); GetDeviceCaps is called with this DC and various constants to find out the color capabilities of the monitor and graphics card. The constants are defined by Windows and can be studied in the online help for the GetDeviceCaps function. These constants are used in Boolean operations to check for a specific "flag" in a stored value. This flag is a single bit in the stored value, which is 1 if True and 0 if False.

To test whether a flag is True, you can use a bitwise AND operation. A bitwise AND operation makes use of a Windows test constant in which the bit you want to test is set to 1 and all other bits are set to 0. Any bit value ANDed with 1 results in the original value—zero remains zero and one remains one. Thus when a test constant for a single flag is ANDed with a number that stores a group of such flags, if the flag is 1 (True) in the storage number, the output of the AND operation will equal the test constant, as shown here:

```
Stored Number        1010

Test Constant        0010

AND Result           0010
```

This test constant tests the second bit of the stored number. Because this bit is set to 1, the result is equal to the test constant.

If the flag is 0 (False) in the storage number, the result is 0, as shown here.

```
Stored Number        1000

Test Constant        0010
```

```
AND Result              0000
```

In this case the second bit in the stored number is set to 0, which when ANDed with the test constant gives a result of 0.

In step 9 we used the test constant rc_Palette to test a storage value returned by GetDeviceCaps:

```
The_Integer := GetDeviceCaps( The_DC , RASTERCAPS );
    if ( The_Integer and rc_PALETTE ) = rc_PALETTE then
```

The rc_Palette constant has a bit set to 1 in the flag position of the Rastercaps storage number used to denote whether a hardware item uses the palette method of color determination (in which a color value is a number that points to an entry in the palette, or list of available colors; this entry gives the actual color information to Windows) or whether the hardware item accepts direct color information using the RGB (red green blue) system.

Obtaining the printer information is more challenging. Fortunately, Windows always sets the value of the default printer in a string in the WIN.INI file. The GetProfileString API call obtains a string from WIN.INI with the three names needed to create a display context for the default printer. The helper function GetPCharAtom parses the Pchar string and splits out the device, driver, and output names. CreateDC can then use these strings to synthesize a display context for the printer.

An alternate, and simpler, method is to use the Printer.Canvas.Handle property of the Printer object in Delphi, as was done for the screen. However, the Printer object has limitations, and you may want to implement your own print capabilities, in which case the GetProfileString approach will always work.

The color information is a bit complicated. Color is displayed in Windows using two pieces of data: the number of bits per pixel and the number of color planes. The number of bits per pixel determines how many shades of a color are possible, using the formula ($2^{\text{BitsPerPixel}}$). For example, if a graphics card has 8 bits per pixel, it can display 256 shades (2^8) of any color. The number of color planes determines how many colors a device can show, using the formula ((Total Shades per Color)$^{\text{Number of Color Planes}}$). For example, if a graphics card has 8 shades per color and 3 color planes, it can display 256 total colors (8^3). (These are issues of how the physical memory is arranged to drive the electron guns in the monitor or the color mixing in a printer.)

Notice that at the end of the printer procedure DeleteDC is called. This is critical, because there are a very small number of display (or device) contexts in Windows. One of the reasons for putting in the two helper functions to do the actual form setup is that due to the limitations of Windows DC resources, putting the capabilities acquisition functions in the FormCreate procedure directly could cause Windows to lock up when it runs out of display contexts. Similarly, not releasing a DC when its calling procedure is finished will eventually prevent other routines and programs from drawing, and thus freeze Windows in its tracks.

Comments

Another Delphi project, DEVCPADV.DPR, provides a wealth of information about the GetDeviceCaps function. Run it to see an amazing portrait of the capabilities of your system's hardware. With a little tweaking, you could modify this application to show information about any printer on the system, as well as plotters, metafiles, and other esoteric display systems.

8.2 How do I... Control the size of a printed page?

COMPLEXITY: EASY

Problem

Sometimes I don't want to use a fixed page size for my printed output. Is there a way in Delphi to dynamically control the number of lines on a page of hard copy?

Technique

Delphi's Printer object allows fast and user-friendly printing of forms and data. The NewPage method of the Printer object gives you control over how many lines of text are printed on a single page.

Steps

Run PRINTER1.EXE and load a text file. You will see a display similar to Figure 8-2, depending on your system's default font. Now pull down the File menu and select Print with User Pages. The dialog box shown in the figure will appear, letting you set the number of text lines per page. The normal printer dialog box will then appear; you can cancel and close the program, or allow the file to print to observe how the page count you entered affects the final output.

1. Open the TEXTEDIT sample program from the Delphi \DEMOS\DOC directory. Save it to a new directory as PRINTER1.DPR. Save the MAIN.PAS file as PRNCTRL1.PAS; save the MDIEDIT.PAS file as MDIEDIT1.PAS.
2. Add a new bottom-button dialog form; name its unit PGCNTDLG.PAS and set its properties as shown in Table 8-2.

Note: Remove the Help button but leave the panel component, which isn't shown in the table.

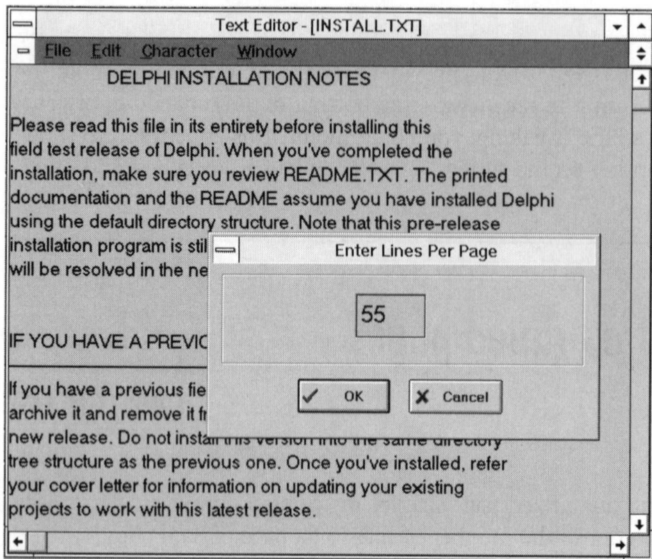

Figure 8-2 PRINTER1 at run time showing the lines per page dialog box

Table 8-2 Components, properties, and settings for LinesPerPageDlg in PRINTER1

COMPONENT	PROPERTY	SETTING
LinesPerPageDlg	Type	Main Form
	Width	325
	Height	166
	Left	121
	Top	233
	Caption	Enter Lines Per Page
Edit1	Type	TEdit
	Width	57
	Height	34
	Left	120
	Top	24
	Text	55

3. Return to the EditForm component and activate its MainMenu component. Add the menu item in Table 8-3 to the end of the File menu.

Table 8-3 Additional menu item for the MainMenu component of EditForm in PRNCTRL1

COMPONENT	PROPERTY	SETTING
Print2	Type	TMenuItem
	Caption	Print with &User Pages

4. Activate the OnClick property of the Print2 menu item and enter the following code, which allows users to control page size during printing.

```
procedure TEditForm.Print2Click(Sender: TObject);
var
  TheText: System.Text;
  Counter_1 ,
  TotalLines : Integer;
begin
  { Display the modal dialog box for number of lines per page }
  LinesPerPageDlg.ShowModal;
  if Linebreak = 0 then Linebreak := 55;
  if PrintDialog1.Execute then
  begin
    { Use DOS to send output to printer instead of a file }
    AssignPrn( TheText );
    Rewrite( TheText );
    Printer.Canvas.Font := Memo1.Font;
    TotalLines := 0;
    for Counter_1 := 0 to Memo1.Lines.Count - 1 do
    begin
      Writeln( TheText , Memo1.Lines[ Counter_1 ] );
      { Increase the line count for every line printed }
      TotalLines := TotalLines + 1;
      if TotalLines = LineBreak then
      begin
        { This procedure sends a form feed to the printer }
        Printer.NewPage;
        TotalLines := 0;
      end;
    end;
    System.Close( TheText );
  end;
end;
```

5. Next, select the OK button from the LinesPerPageDlg form and select its OnClick event handler. Type in the following code to set the Linebreak variable (which you will create next) after user input.

```
procedure TLinesPerPageDlg.OKBtnClick(Sender: TObject);
begin
  Linebreak := StrToInt( Edit1.Text);
  Close;
end;
```

6. Now select the MDIEdit1 unit and move to the *var* keyword. Enter this helper variable to hold the value entered in the dialog box.

```
var
  Linebreak : Integer;
```

7. Return to the LinesPerPageDlg form, activate the Cancel button, and enter the following code to close the dialog if the user elects to cancel instead of accepting a value.

```
procedure TLinesPerPageDlg.CancelBtnClick(Sender: TObject);
begin
  Close;
end;
```

8. Go to the PGCNTDLG.PAS unit and enter the following *uses* clause under the *implementation* keyword. This allows use of the Linebreak variable in MDIEdit1 without a circular unit reference during compiling. (Circular reference problems occur because two units each refer to each other in their respective *uses* clauses. The compiler has no way normally to decide which to compile first. By placing the reference to a calling unit in the *implementation* section, the compiler knows to compile that unit first and thus avoids the problem.)

```
implementation
{ Put this here to avoid circular unit references }
uses mdiedit1;
```

9. Compile and test the project.

How It Works

Delphi's object for controlling printers, named simply Printer, has a number of powerful features, two of which are the ability to assign a DOS text file to the selected Windows printer, and a device-independent form-feed method.

AssignPrn is the redirection procedure for printing DOS text files under Windows in Delphi. It allows use of the standard Pascal Writeln procedure to print to a Windows output device, similar to the WinCRT unit in Turbo Pascal for Windows. Notice, however, that you can use the Printer object's canvas during Writeln printing to change the font.

The exact escape sequence sent to a printer to produce a form feed varies widely. The Printer object encapsulates this variability through calls to the Windows device driver for the selected printer; all you need to do is make the NewPage method call to eject the current page and start a new one.

Comments

This How-To implements one simple form of page control. It does not deal with problems caused by differences in printer and screen resolution.This is a more challenging task, to change the font during printing to produce a WYSIWYG appearance. The next How-To shows you how it's done.

8.3 How do I...
Maintain the same appearance on the printed page as on the screen?

COMPLEXITY: EASY

Problem

Since the resolution on my screen and my printer may be very different, sometimes hard copy doesn't format correctly. Is there a way in Delphi to make sure that what I see on the screen is what I get on the printed copy?

Technique

In this How-To you turn again to the Printer object, which Delphi uses to encapsulate control over Windows printing. The Printer has a Canvas property, which has methods that allow determination of the relative size of a font. This can be used to resize the printed font to make hard copy output very close to what is shown on the monitor.

Steps

Run PRINTER2.EXE and load a text file. You will see a display similar to Figure 8-3, depending on your system's default font. Now pull down the Printer menu from the

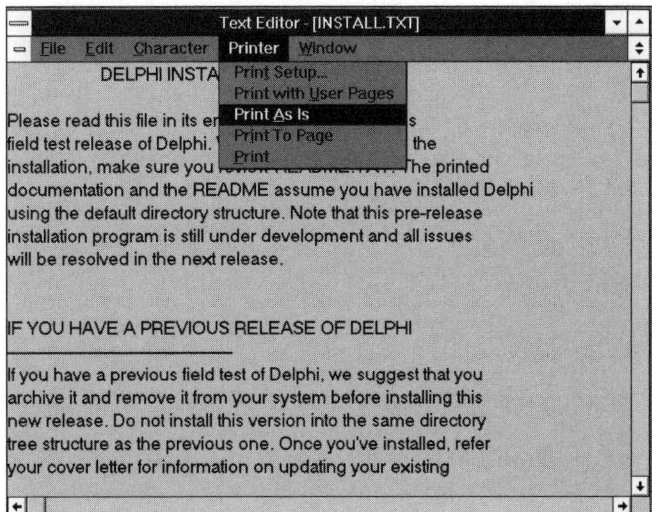

Figure 8-3 PRINTER2 at run time displaying the printer options menu

top-level menu. Notice the two items that are different from the PRINTER1 application: Print As Is and Print To Page. If you wish, select either and observe the results. You will find that Print As Is may produce a printed copy which is very different than what appears on the monitor, while Print To Page comes very close to reproducing the visual look on the hard copy.

1. Open the PRINTER1 project and save it to a new directory as PRINTER2. Rename the PRNCTRL1.PAS file to PRNCTRL2.PAS and MDIEDIT1.PAS to MDIEDIT2.PAS to avoid confusion. You don't need to rename the PGCNTDLG.PAS unit since it doesn't change.
2. Modify the MainMenu component of the EditForm as shown in Table 8-4.

Note: Move the Print, Print with User Pages, and Print Setup items from the File menu to the new Printer menu.

Table 8-4 Additional menu items for the MainMenu component of EditForm in PRNCTRL2

COMPONENT	PROPERTY	SETTING
Print1	Type	TMenuItem (top level)
	Caption	Printer
PrintAsIs1	Type	TMenuItem (under Printer)
	Caption	Print &As Is
	Checked	True
PrintToPage1	Type	TMenuItem (under Printer)
	Caption	Pr&int To Page

3. Activate the Print1 menu item's OnClick property and enter the following code to print the text in the memo component either without changes or to match the screen display.

```
procedure TEditForm.Print1Click(Sender: TObject);
var
  Line: Integer;
  PrintText: System.Text;
  TheScreenWidth ,
  ThePrinterWidth : Integer;
begin
  if PrintDialog1.Execute then
  begin
    AssignPrn(PrintText);
    Rewrite(PrintText);
    Printer.Canvas.Font := Memo1.Font;
    { These lines convert the printer font to an approximation }
    { of the screen font.                                      }
    if PrintToFit then
```

```
    begin
      TheScreenWidth := FrameForm.Canvas.TextWidth( 'W' );
      ThePrinterWidth := Printer.Canvas.TextWidth( 'W' );
      if TheScreenWidth < ThePrinterWidth then
      begin
        Printer.Canvas.Font.Size := Printer.Canvas.Font.Size +
        Round( Printer.Canvas.Font.Size *
        ( TheScreenWidth / ThePrinterWidth )) - 1;
      end
      else
      begin
        Printer.Canvas.Font.Size := Printer.Canvas.Font.Size -
        Round( Printer.Canvas.Font.Size *
        ( TheScreenWidth / ThePrinterWidth )) - 1;
      end;
    end;
    for Line := 0 to Memo1.Lines.Count - 1 do
    begin
      Writeln(PrintText, Memo1.Lines[Line]);
    end;
     System.Close(PrintText);
  end;
end;
```

4. Now choose the Print With User Pages menu item's OnClick event handler, and set it to likewise match display to printer output.

```
procedure TEditForm.Print2Click(Sender: TObject);
var
  Line: Integer;
  PrintText: System.Text;
  TotalLines : Integer;
  TheScreenWidth ,
  ThePrinterWidth : Integer;
begin
  LinesPerPageDlg.ShowModal;
  exit;
  if Linebreak = 0 then Linebreak := 55;
  if PrintDialog1.Execute then
  begin
    AssignPrn(PrintText);
    Rewrite(PrintText);
    Printer.Canvas.Font := Memo1.Font;
    { These lines convert the printer font to an approximation }
    { of the screen font.                                      }
    if PrintToFit then
    begin
      TheScreenWidth := FrameForm.Canvas.TextWidth( 'W' );
      ThePrinterWidth := Printer.Canvas.TextWidth( 'W' );
      if TheScreenWidth < ThePrinterWidth then
      begin
        Printer.Canvas.Font.Size := Printer.Canvas.Font.Size +
        Round( Printer.Canvas.Font.Size *
        ( TheScreenWidth / ThePrinterWidth )) - 1;
      end
```

continued on next page

continued from previous page

```
      else
      begin
        Printer.Canvas.Font.Size := Printer.Canvas.Font.Size -
        Round( Printer.Canvas.Font.Size *
        ( TheScreenWidth / ThePrinterWidth )) - 1;
      end;
    end;
    TotalLines := 0;
    for Line := 0 to Memo1.Lines.Count - 1 do
    begin
      Writeln(PrintText, Memo1.Lines[Line]);
      TotalLines := TotalLines + 1;
      if TotalLines = LineBreak then
      begin
        Printer.NewPage;
        TotalLines := 0;
      end;
    end;
    System.Close(PrintText);
  end;
end;
```

5. Select the MDIEdit2 unit and move to the *implementation* keyword, then enter these two extra *uses* references to prevent circular unit reference compilation errors.

```
implementation

{$R *.DFM}

{ add these two units to prevent circular references }
uses Prnctrl2 , Pgcntdlg , SysUtils;
```

6. While still in the Code Editor, move to the *var* keyword and add this helper flag variable.

```
var Linebreak : Integer;
    PrintToFit : Boolean;
```

7. Compile and test the project.

How It Works

The Canvas property of the main form and of the Printer are both wrappers around the Windows GDI interface. By using their built-in TextWidth methods, the application can determine whether it needs to increase or reduce the size of the font on the printer to match that of the screen. The Font object's Size property is then modified by an appropriate amount to come as close as possible to matching the ratio of screen to printer displays.

Comments

In addition to text output, Delphi can also print its graphical images directly, via the Print method available on all TForm objects and their descendants. The PrintScale property of the TForm object determines a similar scaling ability to that shown above. It has settings of PrintAsIs, which tries to exactly reproduce the screen image on the printer but without taking size into account, and PrintToPage, which attempts to use all the available page space for the image.

8.4 How do I... Maintain the 3D look in the printer options dialog?

COMPLEXITY: EASY

Problem

I like the new sculptured look of Delphi and Windows 95. But some older printer drivers were written before 3D dialog boxes became available. Is there a way to make older controls look like the rest of my application?

Technique

Because Windows uses a lot of information from the source application in creating dialog boxes, you can trick it into making any dialog box from a program look sculptured, even if it wasn't originally compiled that way.

Steps

Run PRINTER3.EXE and load a text file. Choose Print Setup from the Printer menu and select a driver you know wasn't 3D when you last used it. Activating the dialog now will produce a display similar to Figure 8-4, depending on the specific printer you choose.

1. Open the PRINTER2 project and save it to a new directory as PRINTER3. Rename the PRNCTRL2.PAS file to PRNCTRL3.PAS and MDIEDIT2.PAS to MDIEDIT3.PAS to avoid confusion.
2. Select EditForm from MDIEDIT3 and activate its OnCreate event handler. Add the single line of code shown here, which is all that is needed to produce a sculptured dialog box from a flat one.

```
procedure TEditForm.FormCreate(Sender: TObject);
begin
  ParentCtl3d := true;
end;
```

3. Go into the code of the PGCNTDLG.PAS unit and, under the *implementation* keyword, add this *uses* clause to prevent circular unit references.

```
implementation
{ Add this clause to prevent circular reference errors }
uses mdiedit3;
```

4. Compile and test the project.

How It Works

Yes, that's all there is to it. By setting the ParentCtl3d property of the base form for all the editing forms to True, any printer dialog box you activate takes on the sculptured look.

Comments

This trick also works on other dialogs and even programs. Try adding some older code with "flat" dialogs or child windows to a Delphi form with this property set to True, and they will take on the modern 3D look without any further changes to their code. Remember, however, that while the common dialogs of Windows 3.1 are automatically set to the 3D style, your code, and code from third-party applications, requires setting the ParentCtl3d property.

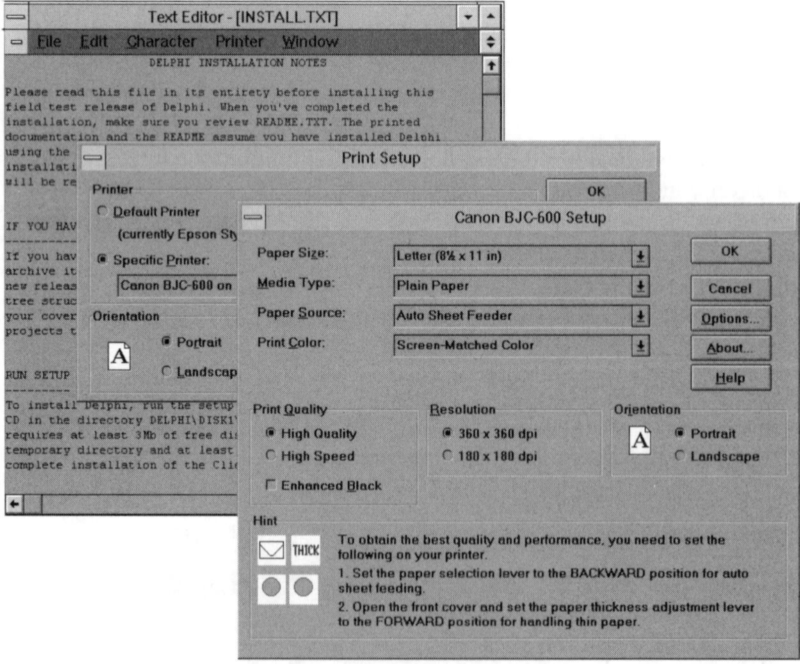

Figure 8-4 PRINTER3 at runtime showing a 3D Canon options dialog box

Note: To use this technique with Windows 3.1 common dialogs, make sure that the CTL3DV2.DLL included with Delphi is in the WINDOWS\SYSTEM directory.

8.5 How do I... Control the modem on a PC?

COMPLEXITY: EASY

Problem

Sometimes I need to access my modem from a program. Is there an easy way to control a modem from Delphi?

Technique

Despite rumors to the contrary, accessing a modem from a program doesn't require black art. All that's required is an understanding of how DOS uses files to redirect output coupled with a little knowledge of standard modem control strings, and you can create your own phone dialer in Delphi.

Steps

Run PHONDIAL.EXE. You will see a display similar to Figure 8-5. Select one of the two numbers from the combo boxes and, with your phone down, press Dial The Number. Your modem will sound and dial the listed number. As soon as you hear a ring, pick up the phone and press Hang Up The Modem. You'll be ready to talk to whoever answers.

1. Create a new project with a blank form and name it PHONDIAL.DPR. Name the unit PHDIAL.PAS.
2. Add the following components to Form1 and set their properties as shown in Table 8-5.

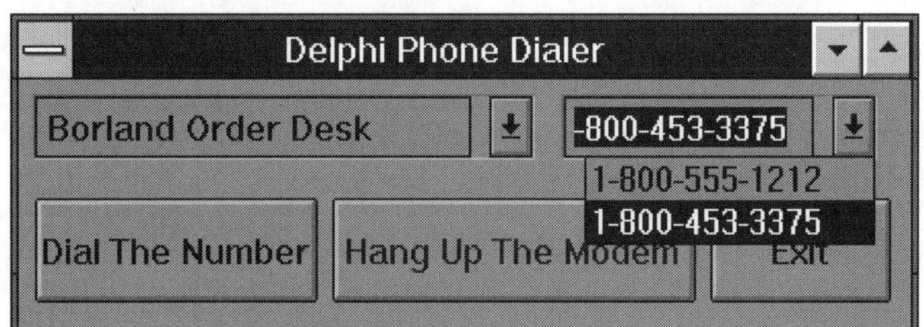

Figure 8-5 PHONDIAL at run time showing linked phone number and name comboboxes

Table 8-5 Components, properties, and settings for Form1 of PHONDIAL

COMPONENT	PROPERTY	SETTING
Form1	Type	Application Main Form
	Width	443
	Height	153
	Left	42
	Top	85
	Caption	Delphi Phone Dialer
ComboBox1	Type	TComboBox
	Left	8
	Top	8
	Width	241
	Height	29
	Text	800 Information
	Items	800 Information
		Borland Order Desk
ComboBox2	Type	TComboBox
	Left	264
	Top	8
	Width	153
	Height	29
	Text	1-800-555-1212
	Items	1-800-555-1212
		1-800-453-3375
Button1	Type	TButton
	Left	8
	Top	56
	Width	137
	Height	49
	Caption	Dial The Number
	Enabled	True
Button2	Type	TButton
	Left	152
	Top	56
	Width	177
	Height	49
	Caption	Hang Up The Modem

COMPONENT	PROPERTY	SETTING
	Enabled	False
Button3	Type	TButton
	Left	336
	Top	56
	Width	89
	Height	49
	Caption	Exit
	Enabled	True

3. Select the OnClick event of Button1 and enter the following lines of code to dial the currently selected number. (Don't worry about the undeclared File1 variable; you'll add it in a moment.)

```
procedure TForm1.Button1Click(Sender: TObject);
var The_String : String;
    TheIndex : Integer;
begin
  TheIndex := ComboBox2.ItemIndex;
  if TheIndex < 0 then TheIndex := 0;
  { Trick DOS by telling it that COM2 is really a text file }
  AssignFile( File1 , 'COM2' );
  ReWrite( File1 );
  { Build the modem command string with the Hayes-compatible syntax     }
  { ATDT for dial prefix, number from the combobox and ASCII 13 for CR }
  The_String := 'ATDT' + ComboBox2.Items[ TheIndex ] + #13;
  { Send the command string to the modem via Write }
  Write( File1 , The_String );
  { Then call Flush to send the data to the modem }
  Flush( File1 );
  Button2.Enabled := True;
  Button1.Enabled := False;
end;
```

4. Move to just below the *var* keyword and add this helper File variable, which lets DOS treat the modem as a text file.

```
var
  Form1: Tform1;
  File1 : TextFile;
```

5. Select the OnClick event of Button2 and enter the following code to hang up the modem once the conversation has begun.

```
procedure TForm1.Button2Click(Sender: TObject);
begin
{ Send a literal command string ATH to hang up the Hayes-compatible modem }
  Writeln( File1 , 'ATH' );
  CloseFile( File1 );
```

continued on next page

continued from previous page

```
  Button1.Enabled := True;
  Button2.Enabled := False;
end;
```

6. Select the OnClick event of Button3 and enter this code to close the application.

```
procedure TForm1.Button3Click(Sender: TObject);
begin
  Close;
end;
```

7. Select the OnChange event of ComboBox1 and enter this next line of code. It links any selection of ComboBox1 to the selection of ComboBox2 to maintain synchronization.

```
procedure TForm1.ComboBox1Change(Sender: TObject);
begin
  { Make sure the comboboxes are synchronized }
  ComboBox2.ItemIndex := ComboBox1.ItemIndex;
end;
```

8. Select the OnChange event of Button1 and enter the following code to maintain synchronization of ComboBox1 to ComboBox2.

```
procedure TForm1.ComboBox2Change(Sender: TObject);
begin
{ Make sure the comboboxes are synchronized }
  ComboBox1.ItemIndex := ComboBox2.ItemIndex;
end;
```

9. Compile and test the project.

How It Works

This trick is an old DOS programmer's dodge. You tell DOS that the COM port is actually a text file, and DOS believes it because file redirection is a key part of old DOS and the pre-PC operating systems DOS was based on. Then all you need to do is write some command strings to the "file," which represents the modem, and it dials the number.

Two points of interest here. First, notice that the dial string for a Hayes-compatible modem is "ATDT" and that the hang-up string is "ATH". If a modem is not Hayes-compatible this won't work. In such rare cases you can obtain the modem's control strings from the manufacturer and change the code appropriately. Also, COM2 is assumed for the modem since most mice live on COM1 these days. Again, if a different COM port has the modem, the code can be easily altered.

Finally, notice that the two combo boxes are rigged to reset each other. This way, selecting a name gives the user the number, and vice versa. This is a user-interface issue, which might easily be overlooked.

Comments

A few modems (including the author's) don't allow you to keep the line open after you hang up the modem. This makes them unusable for phone dialer applications, and is not the fault of Delphi or the code. Such modems can sometimes be configured to avoid this problem, but this *is* black art!

A useful enhancement to the application would be fields to enter new numbers and names and the ability to save and load them with text files. The OOP design of Delphi contains LoadFromFile and SaveToFile capabilities for Edit controls and string lists such as those used by the combo boxes, so implementing this would be straightforward.

Finally, it's a good idea to set the modem to 2400 baud when using it as a phone dialer; DOS doesn't buffer its output, and at speeds higher than 2400, characters may be lost, resulting in incorrect dialing.

8.6 How do I...
Send and receive data through the serial port?

COMPLEXITY: ADVANCED

Problem

I want to exchange data within my application using the modem. Do I have to buy an expensive terminal emulation package to do this, or is there a way in Delphi to do simple serial input and output?

Technique

Fortunately, Windows 3.1 includes a fairly sophisticated set of API functions for controlling serial I/O. You can use Delphi and these functions to create a "dumb" but fully working terminal that can contact local dial-up servers in text mode.

Steps

Run DLTERMNL.EXE. Set the communications parameters for your modem and a simple local dial-up server—a BBS or similar system. Then select Open Port from the Communications menu. Type in an initialization string (**AT&F** is standard for Hayes-compatible modems) and when you see the OK, type in **ATDT** and a phone number. The modem will dial the server, and then you respond in the same way you would with a commercial communications package. Log off the server, and you will see a screen similar to the one shown in Figure 8-6. You can then close the COM port and the application.

1. Create a new project with a blank form and name it DLTERMNL.DPR. Name the unit TERMPROG.PAS.

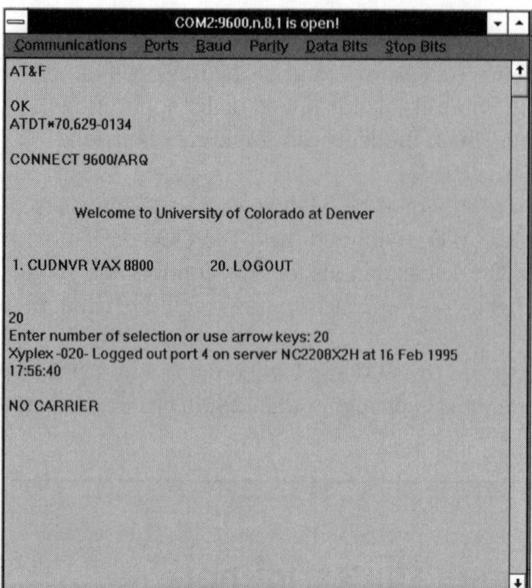

Figure 8-6 DLTERMNL at run time showing a session with a university terminal server

2. Add components to Form1 and set their properties as shown in Table 8-6.

Table 8-6 Components, properties, and settings for Form1 in DLTERMNL

COMPONENT	PROPERTY	SETTING
Form1	Type	Application Main Form
	Width	552
	Height	293
	Left	29
	Top	44
	Caption	Communications Port Closed
Memo1	Type	TMemo
	Left	0
	Top	0
	Width	532
	Height	231
	Align	alClient

COMPONENT	PROPERTY	SETTING
	ScrollBar	sbVertical
MainMenu1	Type	TMainMenu
	AutoMerge	False
Timer1	Type	TTimer
	Enabled	True
	Interval	100

3. Select the MainMenu1 component and enter the menu settings shown in Table 8-7.

Table 8-7 Menu items for the MainMenu component of Form1 in TERMPROG

COMPONENT	PROPERTY	SETTING
Communications1	Type	TMenuItem (top level)
	Caption	&Communications
	Checked	False
OpenPort1	Type	TMenuItem (under Communications)
	Caption	Open Port
	Checked	False
ClosePort1	Type	TMenuItem (under Communications)
	Caption	Close Port
	Checked	False
Exit1	Type	TMenuItem (under Communications)
	Caption	E&xit
	Checked	False
Ports1	Type	TMenuItem (top level)
	Caption	&Ports
	Checked	False
CommPort11	Type	TMenuItem (under Ports)
	Caption	Comm Port &1
	Checked	False
CommPort21	Type	TMenuItem (under Ports)
	Caption	Comm Port &2
	Checked	True
CommPort31	Type	TMenuItem (under Ports)
	Caption	Comm Port &3
	Checked	False

continued on next page

continued from previous page

COMPONENT	PROPERTY	SETTING
Baud1	Type	TMenuItem (top level)
	Caption	&Baud
	Checked	False
N24001	Type	TMenuItem (under Baud)
	Caption	2400
	Checked	False
N96001	Type	TMenuItem (under Baud)
	Caption	9600
	Checked	True
N144001	Type	TMenuItem (under Baud)
	Caption	14400
	Checked	False
Parity1	Type	TMenuItem (top level)
	Caption	Par&ity
	Checked	False
None1	Type	TMenuItem (under Parity)
	Caption	None
	Checked	True
Even1	Type	TMenuItem (under Parity)
	Caption	Even
	Checked	False
Odd1	Type	TMenuItem (under Parity)
	Caption	Odd
	Checked	False
DataBits1	Type	TMenuItem (top level)
	Caption	&Data Bits
	Checked	False
N7DataBits	Type	TMenuItem (under Data Bits)
	Caption	7 Data Bits
	Checked	False
N8DataBits	Type	TMenuItem (under Data Bits)
	Caption	8 Data Bits
	Checked	True
StopBits1	Type	TMenuItem (top level)
	Caption	&Stop Bits
	Checked	False

COMPONENT	PROPERTY	SETTING
N0StopBits1	Type	TMenuItem (under Stop Bits)
	Caption	0 Stop Bits
	Checked	False
N1StopBits1	Type	TMenuItem (under Stop Bits)
	Caption	1 Stop Bits
	Checked	True
N2StopBits1	Type	TMenuItem (under Stop Bits)
	Caption	2 Stop Bits
	Checked	False

4. Select the OnClick event of OpenPort1 and enter the following code to open the selected COM port.

```
procedure TForm1.OpenPort1Click(Sender: TObject);
begin
  Open_Communications;
  { If the procedure above set nCid to >= 0 operation was OK }
  if nCid >= 0 then
  begin
    caption := Communications_String + ' is open!';
    Comm_Port_Open := true;
  end;
end;
```

5. Select the OnClick event of ClosePort1 and enter the following code to close the COM port.

```
procedure TForm1.ClosePort1Click(Sender: TObject);
begin
  Close_Communications;
end;
```

6. Select the OnClick event of Exit1 and enter the following code to close the application gracefully.

```
procedure TForm1.Exit1Click(Sender: TObject);
begin
  if Comm_Port_Open then Close_Communications;
  Close;
end;
```

7. Select the OnClick event of CommPort11 and set the Port data string to COM1.

```
{ Set the Port_String (note no closing :) }
procedure TForm1.CommPort11Click(Sender: TObject);
begin
  Port_String := 'COM1';
end;
```

8. Select the OnClick event of CommPort21 and set the Port data string to COM2.

```
procedure TForm1.CommPort21Click(Sender: TObject);
begin
  Port_String := 'COM2';
end;
```

9. Select the OnClick event of CommPort31 and set the Port data string to COM3.

```
procedure TForm1.CommPort31Click(Sender: TObject);
begin
  Port_String := 'COM3';
end;
```

10. Select the OnClick event of N24001 and set the Baud data string to 2400 baud.

```
{ Set the Baud_String to (note the leading :) }
procedure TForm1.N24001Click(Sender: TObject);
begin
  Baud_String := ':2400';
end;
```

11. Select the OnClick event of N96001 and set the Baud data string to 9600 baud.

```
procedure TForm1.N96001Click(Sender: TObject);
begin
  Baud_String := ':9600';
end;
```

12. Select the OnClick event of N144001 and set the Baud data string to 14400 baud.

```
procedure TForm1.N144001Click(Sender: TObject);
begin
  Baud_String := ':14400';
end;
```

13. Select the OnClick event of None1 and set the Parity data string to no parity.

```
{ Set the Parity_String to (note the leading ,) }
procedure TForm1.None1Click(Sender: TObject);
begin
  Parity_String := ',n';
end;
```

14. Select the OnClick event of Even1 and set the Parity data string to odd parity.

```
procedure TForm1.Even1Click(Sender: TObject);
begin
  Parity_String := ',e';
end;
```

15. Select the OnClick event of Odd1 and set the Parity data string to even parity.

```
procedure TForm1.Odd1Click(Sender: TObject);
begin
```

```
  Parity_String := ',o';
end;
```

16. Select the OnClick event of N7DataBits and set the Data Bits data string to 7 bits.

```
{ Set the Data_Bits_String (note the leading ,) }
procedure TForm1.N7DataBitsClick(Sender: TObject);
begin
  Data_Bits_String := ',7';
end;
```

17. Select the OnClick event of N8DataBits and set the Data Bits data string to 8 bits.

```
procedure TForm1.N8DataBitsClick(Sender: TObject);
begin
  Data_Bits_String := ',8';
end;
```

18. Select the OnClick event of N0StopBits1 and set the Stop Bits data string to no stop bits.

```
{ Set the Stop_Bits_String (note the leading ,) }
procedure TForm1.N0StopBits1Click(Sender: TObject);
begin
  Stop_Bits_String := ',0';
end;
```

19. Select the OnClick event of N1StopBits1 and set the Stop Bits data string to 1 stop bit.

```
procedure TForm1.N1StopBits1Click(Sender: TObject);
begin
  Stop_Bits_String := ',1';
end;
```

20. Select the OnClick event of N2StopBits1 and set the Stop Bits data string to 2 stop bits.

```
procedure TForm1.N2StopBits1Click(Sender: TObject);
begin
  Stop_Bits_String := ',2';
end;
```

21. While still in the Code Editor, move up under the *var* keyword and add the following assistant variables.

```
var
  Form1: TForm1;
  Communications_String : String;
  Port_String : String;
  Parity_String : String;
  Baud_String : String;
  Data_Bits_String : String;
  Stop_Bits_String : String;
```

continued on next page

continued from previous page

```
Comm_Port_Open    : Boolean;
Input_Buffer_String ,
Output_Buffer_String : Pchar;
nCid : Integer;
The_Display_String : String;
```

22. Staying in the Code Editor, move up to the *private* keyword and add the following helper function declarations so Delphi can recognize them later.

```
private
    { Private declarations }
    procedure Open_Communications;
    procedure Close_Communications;
    procedure Poll_Communications;
```

23. Move down under the *implementation* keyword and add the following assistant procedure to handle the complexities of opening the COM port under Windows.

Note: This and the following procedures use strange variable names and unusual procedure calls. These are due to the nature of the Windows communications API. As far as possible, each variable and API procedure/function call is explained by comments just before it is used or called.

```
{ This procedure opens the COM port using the Windows communications API }
procedure TForm1.Open_Communications;
{ LpDCB is a pointer to a Device Control Block. DCB data structures hold a   }
{ great deal of information used by Windows to deal with the wide variety of }
{ modems and similar serial communications devices on the market.            }
var LpDCB : TDCB;
    Return_Value : Integer;
    The_Buffer : array[ 0 .. 256 ] of char;
    The_Pchar : PChar;
begin
  StrPCopy( The_Buffer , Port_String );
  { Call the OpenComm Windows API function with two black-art buffer sizes }
  nCid := OpenComm( The_Buffer , 1024 , 1024 );
  { If nCid is a negative number the COM port was not available or missing }
  if nCid < 0 then
  begin
    MessageDlg( 'Unable to Open Comm Port ' + Port_String ,
    mtError, [mbOk], 0 );
    Exit;
  end;
  { Copy the Communications data string (everything else but the COM id)    }
  { into a buffer Windows likes using the null-terminated string procedure }
  StrPCopy( The_Buffer , Communications_String );
  { Store the return from the BuildCommDCB function to see if there is }
  { enough memory to build the Device Control Block and no bad data     }
  Return_Value := BuildCommDCB( The_Buffer , LpDCB );
  { If a negative number was returned the DCB could not be built }
  if Return_Value < 0 then
  begin
    MessageDlg( 'Unable to Build Comm DCB as ' + Communications_String ,
```

```
      mtError, [mbOk], 0 );
      Close_Communications;
      { Set nCid to a negative number to inform the calling procedure it failed }
      nCid := -1;
      Exit;
    end;
    { Set the Id field of the DCB to the byte value of nCid (COM port value) }
    LpDCB.Id := BYTE( nCid );
    { Make the final API call to set up the initial state of the modem }
    Return_Value := SetCommState( LpDCB );
    { If the returned value is negative then something else went wrong }
    if Return_Value < 0 then
    begin
      MessageDlg( 'Unable to Use Comm DCB as ' + Communications_String ,
      mtError, [mbOk], 0 );
      Close_Communications;
      nCid := -1;
      EXIT;
    end;
end;
```

24. Now move down under the previous procedure and add the following assistant procedure to handle the complexities of closing the COM port under Windows.

```
{ This procedure handles closing the COM port using the Windows comm API }
procedure TForm1.Close_Communications;
var Return_Value : Integer;
begin
  { Call the CloseComm API function with the port id value in nCid }
  Return_Value := CloseComm( nCid );
  { If the return value is negative the port either was not open or       }
  { our process didnÆt have control over it or the modem malfunctioned. }
  if Return_Value < 0 then
  begin
    MessageDlg( 'Unable to Close Comm Port!',
    mtError, [mbOk], 0 );
    { Set the nCid to a negative number to stop the polling function }
    nCid := -1;
  end
  else
  begin
    caption := 'Communications Port Closed';
    Comm_Port_Open := false;
  end;
end;
```

25. Still in the Code Editor, move down under the previous procedure and add this next assistant procedure to handle the complexities of polling the COM port (checking for input data) under Windows.

```
{ This procedure handles checking for asynchronous input to the COM port  }
{ It is triggered by a call from a Timer compoenent but could also be run }
```

continued on next page

continued from previous page

```
{ continuously using a ProcessMessages call.                               }
procedure TForm1.Poll_Communications;
{ LpStat is a pointer to a Windows Comm API data struncture for modem status }
var LpStat : TComStat;
    Return_Value : Integer;
    NChars : Integer;
    CommError : Integer;
    Counter_1 : Integer;
begin
  { Call ReadComm with the active port number, a buffer, and buffer size }
  { Nchars will hold the number of characters waiting in the buffer      }
  NChars := ReadComm( nCid , Input_Buffer_String , 1024 );
  { If Nchars is negative this is an error and so ignore it and set }
  { the value to its positive state to read in the input characters }
  if NChars < 0 then NChars := NChars * -1;
  if NChars > 0 then
  begin
    for Counter_1 := 1 to NChars do
    begin
      { filter out control characters (less than 32) and ignore them }
      if Ord( Input_Buffer_String[ Counter_1 - 1 ] ) > 31 then
      { Add any non-control charactes to the buffer until a CR is read }
      The_Display_String :=
       The_Display_String + Input_Buffer_String[ Counter_1 - 1 ];
      { If a CR is read then dump the buffer into the Memo field }
      if Ord( Input_Buffer_String[ Counter_1 - 1 ]) = 13 then
      begin
        { Doing it this way prevents unwanted scrolling }
        Memo1.Lines.Add( The_Display_String );
        The_Display_String := '';
      end;
    end;
    { Clear the Input_Buffer_String from windows for next time }
    StrCopy( Input_Buffer_String , '' );
    { Get any comm errors but ignore them for this simple application  }
    { In a more detailed application the LpStat variable would be used }
    { along with the error code for trouble shooting.                  }
    CommError := GetCommError( nCid , LpStat );
  end;
end;
```

26. Select the OnCreate event handler for Form1 and add the following initialization code, which sets the default COM values.

```
procedure TForm1.FormCreate(Sender: TObject);
begin
  Port_String := 'COM2';
  Parity_String := ',n';
  Baud_String := ':9600';
  Data_Bits_String := ',8';
  Stop_Bits_String := ',1';
{ Set the Communications_String to the concatenation of the other strings }
  Communications_String := Port_String +
   Baud_String + Parity_String + Data_Bits_String +
    Stop_Bits_String;
```

```
  Comm_Port_Open := false;
  GetMem( Output_Buffer_String , 1025 );
  GetMem( Input_Buffer_String , 1025 );
  Output_Buffer_String := '';
{ Set the active port id to negative to indicate not in use }
  nCid := -1;
  The_Display_String := '';
end;
```

27. Choose the OnKeyPress event handler for Memo1 and add the following code, which sends typed characters to the modem for dispatch to the remote computer.

```
procedure TForm1.Memo1KeyPress(Sender: TObject; var Key: Char);
{ LpStat is a pointer to a Windows comm API data structure }
var LpStat : TComStat;
    Return_Value : Integer;
    Holder : array[ 0 .. 2 ] of Char;
    PHolder : array[ 0 .. 1025 ] of Char;
    Hold_Output_Buffer_String : PChar;
begin
  { Only send characters if the COM port is opened }
  if Comm_Port_Open then
  begin
    StrPCopy( Holder , Key );
    Output_Buffer_String := StrCat( Output_Buffer_String , Holder );
    { Call GetCommError just to clear the output flag; ignore any result }
    GetCommError( nCid , LpStat );
    { The major reason for this call is to find out if the comm output }
    { buffer has overflowed. If it has not we try to send more data    }
    if LpStat.cbOutQue < 1024 then
    begin
      { Try to send the waiting characters through the modem }
      { using STRLEN to tell how many to send }
      Return_Value := WriteComm( nCid , Output_Buffer_String ,
       StrLen( Output_Buffer_String ));
      { The Return_Value is how many characters were successfully sent   }
      { If it is negative there was an error but this simple application }
      { will ignore that and set it to its positive value                 }
      if Return_Value < 0 then Return_Value := Return_Value * -1;
      { This step preserves the initial pointer to the output buffer }
      Hold_Output_Buffer_String := Output_Buffer_String;
      { Use pointer arithmetic to move up the original pointer as many }
      { characters as were successfully sent                           }
      Output_Buffer_String := Output_Buffer_String + Return_Value;
      { Then copy the modified string into a holding variable }
      StrCopy( PHolder , Output_Buffer_String );
      { Assign the stored pointer location to the original pointer variable }
      Output_Buffer_String := Hold_Output_Buffer_String;
      { Copy back the shortened string to the original memory location }
      StrCopy( Output_Buffer_String , PHolder );
    end;
  end;
end;
```

28. Activate the OnTimer event for the Timer1 component and add the following code, which triggers an asynchronous communications polling procedure call.

```
procedure TForm1.Timer1Timer(Sender: TObject);
begin
  if Comm_Port_Open then Poll_Communications;
end;
```

29. Compile and test the project.

How It Works

Handling asynchronous communications under DOS normally requires a third-party function library. Windows provides this library in its Communication API, but there are two major tasks that the API functions don't cover: communications polling and keyboard intercept.

Communications polling is required because of the asynchronous nature of the serial input; there is no way to predict when characters will arrive at the port, or how many will be sent at a given time. Under DOS, an application would establish a loop to check for arriving data and then handle it. But due to the multiple application nature of Windows, this design would effectively bring the system to a halt, as no other program could run. The solution is a buffering system, in which a Timer signals every few hundred milliseconds for a polling procedure to check for incoming data and dispatch it. An alternative approach in standard Windows API programming would be to place a polling loop inside a single event handler, and interrupt it with a PeekMessage or WaitMessage call to hand control to other applications; however, Delphi has placed a wrapper around standard message handling, making this infeasible. (Delphi does provide similar functionality in its OnIdle and ProcessMessages procedures, however. For an example of using ProcessMessages, see How To 2-5.)

Likewise, when a key is entered, an OnKeyPress event handler intercepts it and adds it to an outgoing data buffer being sent to the serial port. What makes this process nontrivial is the need to continually "loop" the string buffer of 1K characters. The procedure must reset the buffer's head to the next nontransmitted character and then copy the new string back to the buffer's starting point. This process is complicated still further by the requirement that the buffers being manipulated be the PChar ASCIIZ null-terminated string type required by Windows, rather than the normal Pascal string type. The solution is a set of buffers and pointers as described in the code given in the steps.

Comments

This application is just about as "dumb" as a terminal can get, but it illustrates the basics of serial input and output in the Windows 3.1 environment. Enhancements such as file capture, sending binary files over the modem, and so on, can easily be added by simply redirecting the stream of characters from Poll_Communications.

A final word to the wise. Serial I/O in Windows 3.1 has a number of hidden bugs, which can trip up even experienced communications developers. An excellent article by Mike Sax, titled "Communications Gotchas," clearly outlines the problems and their solutions. It appeared in the December 1994 issue of *Windows Tech Journal*.

8.7 How do I... Control the speaker as the SOUND function did in Turbo Pascal?

COMPLEXITY: INTERMEDIATE

Problem

Not everyone who uses my applications has a sound card in their PC. Can I still gain access to the speaker to create tones for my program?

Technique

Technically, the Multimedia Extensions of Windows 3.1 replaced the Sound functions of Windows 2.0 and 3.0. However, if the computer running Windows doesn't have a sound card, the SOUND.DRV module is loaded. You can gain access to it via the older API routines to create a simple tone generator using Delphi.

Steps

Run SOUNDER.EXE. You will see a display similar to Figure 8-7. Press the Open the Speaker button; if you get an error dialog, check the "Comments" section on how to

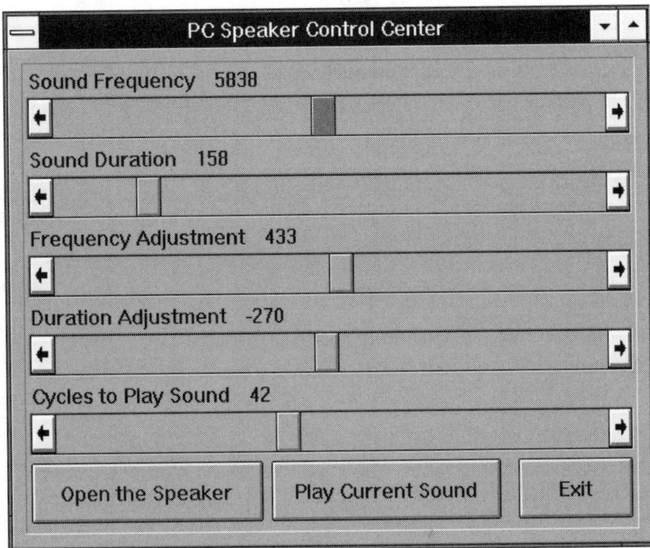

Figure 8-7 SOUNDER at run time showing a sample tone

proceed. Otherwise use the five slider bars to set up sound parameters, and then test the tones by pressing the Play Current Sound button. When you are ready, click on Exit to end the program.

1. Create a new project with a blank form and name it SOUNDER.DPR. Name the unit SOUND1.PAS.
2. Add components to Form1 and set their properties as shown in Table 8-8.

Table 8-8 Components, properties, and settings for Form1 in SOUNDER

COMPONENT	PROPERTY	SETTING
Form1	Type	Application Main Form
	Width	545
	Height	440
	Left	40
	Top	29
	Caption	PC Speaker Control Center
Panel1	Type	TPanel
	Left	0
	Top	0
	Width	537
	Height	405
	Align	alClient
	BevelInner	bvLowered
	BevelOuter	bvRaised
	BorderWidth	10
Label1	Type	Tlabel
	Left	16
	Top	16
	Width	156
	Height	20
	Caption	Sound Frequency
Label2	Type	Tlabel
	Left	16
	Top	80
	Width	128
	Height	20
	Caption	Sound Duration

COMPONENT	PROPERTY	SETTING
Label3	Type	Tlabel
	Left	16
	Top	144
	Width	200
	Height	20
	Caption	Frequency Adjustment
Label4	Type	Tlabel
	Left	16
	Top	208
	Width	168
	Height	20
	Caption	Duration Adjustment
Label5	Type	Tlabel
	Left	16
	Top	272
	Width	174
	Height	20
	Caption	Cycles to Play Sound
ScrollBar1	Type	TScrollbar
	Left	16
	Top	40
	Width	505
	Height	33
	Position	1
	Kind	sbHorizontal
	Min	1
	Max	100
ScrollBar2	Type	TScrollbar
	Left	16
	Top	104
	Width	505
	Height	33
	Kind	sbHorizontal
	Position	1
	Min	1
	Max	100

continued on next page

continued from previous page

COMPONENT	PROPERTY	SETTING
ScrollBar3	Type	TScrollbar
	Left	16
	Top	168
	Width	505
	Height	33
	Kind	sbHorizontal
	Position	50
	Min	1
	Max	100
ScrollBar4	Type	TScrollBar
	Left	16
	Top	232
	Width	505
	Height	33
	Kind	sbHorizontal
	Position	50
	Min	1
	Max	100
ScrollBar5	Type	TScrollBar
	Left	16
	Top	296
	Width	505
	Height	33
	Kind	sbHorizontal
	Position	50
	Min	1
	Max	100
Button3	Type	TButton
	Left	16
	Top	336
	Width	193
	Height	49
	Caption	Open the Speaker
	Enabled	True
Button1	Type	TButton
	Left	224

COMPONENT	PROPERTY	SETTING
	Top	336
	Width	193
	Height	49
	Caption	Play Current Sound
	Enabled	False
Button2	Type	TButton
	Left	424
	Top	336
	Width	97
	Height	49
	Caption	Exit
	Enabled	False

3. Select the OnClick event of Button3 and enter the following code to open the speaker driver under Windows.

```
procedure TForm1.Button3Click(Sender: TObject);
var The_Result : Integer;
begin
  { Call OpenSound to attempt to open the speaker }
  The_Result := OpenSound;
  { If don't get at least 1 voice then abort; some other app }
  { is using the speaker or SOUND.DRV is not installed       }
  if The_Result < 1 then
  begin
    MessageDlg( 'Unable to Open Speaker!' ,
     mtError , [mbOK] , 0 );
    Close;
  end
  else
  begin
    Button3.Enabled := false;
    Button1.Enabled := true;
    Button2.Enabled := true;
  end;
end;
```

4. Activate the OnClick event of Button1 and enter the following code to play the current tone settings via the SetVoiceSound and StartSound API calls.

```
procedure TForm1.Button1Click(Sender: TObject);
var Working_Frequency : Longint;
    Working_Duration  : Integer;
    Counter_1          : Integer;
begin
  Working_Frequency := Current_Frequency;
  Working_Duration := Current_Duration;
```

continued on next page

continued from previous page

```
  { Run the loop to play the current value of freq and time }
  for Counter_1 := 1 to Current_Play_Length do
  begin
    { Set Working_Frequency to the previous value +- adjustment }
    Working_Frequency := Working_Frequency +
     Current_Frequency_Adjustment;
    { Don't let the working frequency go below zero }
    if Working_Frequency < 0 then Working_Frequency := 0;
    { Set Working_Duration to the previous value +- adjustment }
    Working_Duration := Working_Duration +
      Current_Duration_Adjustment;
    { Don't let the working duration go below zero }
    if Working_Duration < 0 then Working_Duration := 0;
    { Call SetVoiceSound to set up our desired tone }
    SetVoiceSound( 1 ,
      (Working_Frequency * 65536),  Working_Duration );
    { Call StartSound to actually play the tone }
    StartSound;
  end;
end;
```

5. Move to the OnClick event of Button2 and enter the following code, which will close the speaker driver and the program.

```
procedure TForm1.Button2Click(Sender: TObject);
begin
  CloseSound;
  Close;
end;
```

6. Choose the OnCreate Event of Form1 and enter these lines of code to initialize the application.

```
procedure TForm1.FormCreate(Sender: TObject);
var TheString : String;
begin
  Current_Frequency := ScrollBar1.Position;
  Current_Duration  := ScrollBar2.Position;
  Current_Frequency_Adjustment := ScrollBar3.Position - 1000;
  Current_Duration_Adjustment := ScrollBar4.Position - 1000;
  Current_Play_Length := ScrollBar5.Position;
  Label1.Caption := 'Sound Frequency      ' +
   IntToStr( ScrollBar1.Position );
  Label2.Caption := 'Sound Duration       ' +
   IntToStr( ScrollBar2.Position );
  Label3.Caption := 'Frequency Adjustment      ' +
   IntToStr( ScrollBar3.Position - 12000 );
  Label4.Caption := 'Duration Adjustment       ' +
   IntToStr( ScrollBar4.Position - 12000 );
  Label5.Caption := 'Cycles To Play Sound      ' + IntToStr( ScrollBar5.Position );
end;
```

7. Activate the OnChange Event of ScrollBar1 and enter the following code to respond to the user setting the value of the played frequency.

```
procedure TForm1.ScrollBar1Change(Sender: TObject);
begin
  Current_Frequency := Scrollbar1.Position;
  Label1.Caption := 'Sound Frequency      ' +
   IntToStr( ScrollBar1.Position );
end;
```

8. Select the OnChange event of ScrollBar2 and enter the following code. It handles user changes to the duration of the played tone.

```
procedure TForm1.ScrollBar2Change(Sender: TObject);
begin
  Current_Duration := Scrollbar2.Position;
  Label2.Caption := 'Sound Duration      ' +
   IntToStr( ScrollBar2.Position );
end;
```

9. Move to the OnChange event of ScrollBar3 and enter the following code to process changes to the frequency during play of the tone.

```
procedure TForm1.ScrollBar3Change(Sender: TObject);
begin
  Current_Frequency_Adjustment := Scrollbar3.Position - 12000;
  Label3.Caption := 'Frequency Adjustment      ' +
   IntToStr( ScrollBar3.Position - 12000 );
end;
```

10. Go to the OnChange event of ScrollBar4 and enter the following code. This takes care of adjustments to how long a tone is played during each loop.

```
procedure TForm1.ScrollBar4Change(Sender: TObject);
begin
  Current_Duration_Adjustment := Scrollbar4.Position - 12000;
  Label4.Caption := 'Duration Adjustment      ' +
   IntToStr( ScrollBar4.Position - 12000 );
end;
```

11. Shift to the OnChange event of ScrollBar5 and enter the following code to respond to user changes in the number of loops a tone is played.

```
procedure TForm1.ScrollBar5Change(Sender: TObject);
begin
  Current_Play_Length := Scrollbar5.Position;
  Label5.Caption := 'Cycles to Play Sound      ' +
   IntToStr( ScrollBar5.Position );
end;
```

12. Compile and test the project.

How It Works

The four key functions in the Windows sound API—OpenSound, CloseSound, SetVoiceSound, and StartSound—are explained in some detail here.

OpenSound is the API call to determine whether the SOUND.DRV file is available (either directly or via emulation from a sound card) and whether any other application is currently using the speaker. OpenSound must be called before any further sound API calls are made or they will fail. If the call succeeds, it returns the number of "voices" available from the device, normally 1. A zero or a negative number indicates another application is using the speaker, or that SOUND.DRV or its emulation is not available.

CloseSound simply releases control of the speaker driver so another application can use it. Calling CloseSound without a successful call to OpenSound does not produce a runtime error, but in this application it is not allowed because it is not user friendly.

SetVoiceSound is the most important sound API call used here. It sends in the voice to use (1 for the speaker), the frequency of the sound (multiplied by 65,536 to move it to the high word of the parameter), and how many cycles to sound the tone. As this is a Windows 2.0 API call, documentation is scarce, but experimentation indicates that each unit of frequency is about 10 hertz, and each unit of duration is about a millisecond.

StartSound is the call that tells the operating system to start playing its sound queue. Windows stores sounds in a list and plays them until the queue is empty. This is important for applications that produce music, such as MUSICBOX, described in the next How-To.

Comments

If OpenSound can't get access to the speaker, it means that either SOUND.DRV is not loaded (or an equivalent driver for a sound card), or another application acquired the speaker and didn't release it. To solve the problem, check your CONFIG.SYS file to be sure the line "DEVICE=SOUND.DRV" or a similar driver is present; if it isn't, add it and reboot the computer. Otherwise, exit and restart Windows. The form should work correctly then. Be sure you click Exit to leave SOUNDER, or the problem will reoccur the next time you use the program.

One small warning is in order; in the strict sense, the Sound API is no longer supported as of Windows 3.1. Therefore, some recent models of PCs, particularly laptops, may not support the SOUND.DRV module completely, resulting in EMM or other exceptions when Sound API calls are made. In these cases, this and the next How-To will unfortunately not function.

Note: You could enhance this form by adding the ability to save all the parameters into a record and put one or more such records into a file. Then a loading module could be added to load the preset tones and play them in sequence, creating sound effects for an application.

8.8 How do I...
Play music with the PC speaker?

COMPLEXITY: ADVANCED

Problem

I want some simple musical effects in my application, but not everyone has a sound card in their PC. Is there a way to produce speaker-based music in Windows with Delphi?

Technique

As in How-To 8.7, you can use the Windows API sound functions to create simple musical effects with the PC speaker. Unlike the previous program, however, you can use a function that reproduces specific musical effects.

Steps

Run MUSICBOX.EXE. You will see a display similar to Figure 8-8. Press the Load Music String button and select GRNSLEEV.MUS from the dialog box. Then press Play

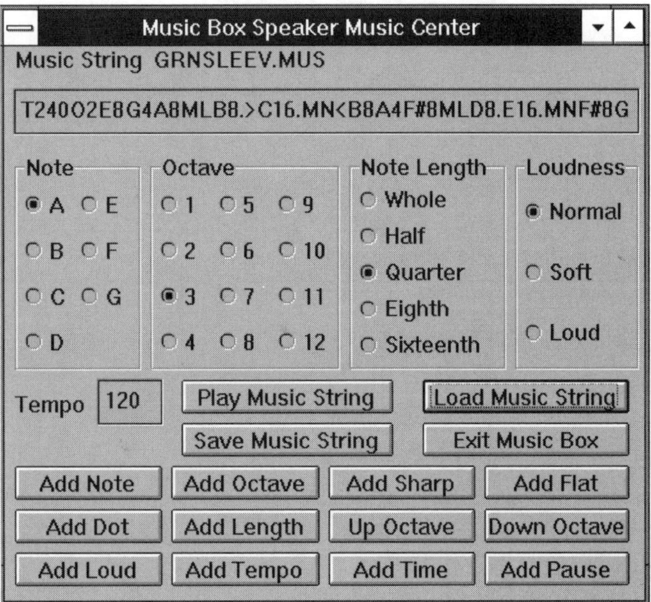

Figure 8-8 MUSICBOX at run time with the Greensleeves music string loaded

Music String and you will hear a somewhat tinny version of "Greensleeves" on your PC speaker. Press the Exit Music Box button to close the program.

1. Create a new project with a blank form and name it MUSICBOX.DPR. Name the unit SPMUSIC.PAS.
2. Add components to Form1 and set their properties as shown in Table 8-9.

Table 8-9 Components, properties, and settings for Form1 in MUSICBOX

COMPONENT	PROPERTY	SETTING
Form1	Type	Application Main Form
	Width	501
	Height	447
	Left	43
	Top	31
	Caption	Music Box Speaker Music Center
Edit1	Type	TEdit
	Left	481
	Top	33
	Width	8
	Height	32
	Text	(blank)
Edit2	Type	TEdit
	Left	72
	Top	248
	Width	49
	Height	33
	Text	120
Label1	Type	Tlabel
	Left	8
	Top	0
	Width	98
	Height	20
	Caption	Music String
Label2	Type	Tlabel
	Left	8
	Top	256
	Width	54

COMPONENT	PROPERTY	SETTING
	Height	20
	Caption	Tempo
RadioGroup1	Type	TRadioGroup
	Left	8
	Top	80
	Width	97
	Height	161
	ItemIndex	0
	Columns	2
	Items	A
		B
		C
		D
		E
		F
		G
	Caption	Note
RadioGroup2	Type	TRadioGroup
	Left	112
	Top	80
	Width	145
	Height	161
	ItemIndex	2
	Columns	3
	Items	1
		2
		3
		4
		5
		6
		7
		8
		9
		10
		11
		12

continued on next page

continued from previous page

COMPONENT	PROPERTY	SETTING
	Caption	Octave
RadioGroup3	Type	TRadioGroup
	Left	264
	Top	80
	Width	121
	Height	161
	ItemIndex	2
	Items	Whole
		Half
		Quarter
		Eighth
		Sixteenth
	Caption	Note Length
RadioGroup4	Type	TRadioGroup
	Left	392
	Top	80
	Width	97
	Height	161
	ItemIndex	0
	Items	Normal
		Soft
		Loud
	Caption	Loudness
Button1	Type	TButton
	Left	8
	Top	312
	Width	113
	Height	25
	Caption	Add Note
Button2	Type	TButton
	Left	128
	Top	312
	Width	113
	Height	25
	Caption	Add Octave
Button3	Type	TButton

COMPONENT	PROPERTY	SETTING
	Left	248
	Top	312
	Width	113
	Height	25
	Caption	Add Sharp
Button4	Type	TButton
	Left	368
	Top	312
	Width	113
	Height	25
	Caption	Add Flat
Button5	Type	TButton
	Left	8
	Top	344
	Width	113
	Height	25
	Caption	Add Dot
Button6	Type	TButton
	Left	128
	Top	344
	Width	113
	Height	25
	Caption	Add Length
Button7	Type	TButton
	Left	248
	Top	344
	Width	113
	Height	25
	Caption	Up Octave
Button8	Type	TButton
	Left	368
	Top	344
	Width	113
	Height	25
	Caption	Down Octave
Button9	Type	TButton

continued on next page

continued from previous page

COMPONENT	PROPERTY	SETTING
	Left	8
	Top	376
	Width	113
	Height	25
	Caption	Add Loud
Button10	Type	TButton
	Left	128
	Top	376
	Width	113
	Height	25
	Caption	Add Tempo
Button11	Type	TButton
	Left	248
	Top	376
	Width	113
	Height	25
	Caption	Add Time
Button12	Type	TButton
	Left	368
	Top	376
	Width	113
	Height	25
	Caption	Add Pause
Button13	Type	TButton
	Left	136
	Top	248
	Width	161
	Height	25
	Caption	Play Music String
Button14	Type	TButton
	Left	320
	Top	248
	Width	161
	Height	25
	Caption	Load Music String
Button15	Type	TButton

COMPONENT	PROPERTY	SETTING
	Left	136
	Top	280
	Width	161
	Height	25
	Caption	Save Music String
Button16	Type	TButton
	Left	320
	Top	280
	Width	161
	Height	25
	Caption	Exit Music Box
OpenDialog1	Type	TOpenDialog
	DefaultExt	mus
	FileName	*.mus
	Filter	*.mus
SaveDialog1	Type	TSaveDialog
	DefaultExt	mus
	FileName	*.mus
	Filter	*.mus

3. Select the OnClick event of Button1 and enter the following code to set the string value of the base note currently entered.

```
procedure TForm1.Button1Click(Sender: TObject);
begin
{ Convert the radio button in the radiogroup to a note letter }
  case RadioGroup1.ItemIndex of
    0 : Edit1.Text := Edit1.Text + 'A';
    1 : Edit1.Text := Edit1.Text + 'B';
    2 : Edit1.Text := Edit1.Text + 'C';
    3 : Edit1.Text := Edit1.Text + 'D';
    4 : Edit1.Text := Edit1.Text + 'E';
    5 : Edit1.Text := Edit1.Text + 'F';
    6 : Edit1.Text := Edit1.Text + 'G';
  end;
end;
```

4. Activate the OnClick event of Button2 and enter the following code to enter the current octave setting into the music string.

```
procedure TForm1.Button2Click(Sender: TObject);
begin
  { Add an octave token to the music string with its value }
```

continued on next page

continued from previous page

```
  Edit1.Text := Edit1.Text + 'O' + IntToStr( RadioGroup2.ItemIndex + 1 );
end;
```

5. Choose the OnClick event of Button3 and enter this code to put a sharp symbol in the music string.

```
procedure TForm1.Button3Click(Sender: TObject);
begin
  { Put a sharp symbol in the music string }
  Edit1.Text := Edit1.Text + '#';
end;
```

6. Go to the OnClick event of Button4 and enter this code to put a flat symbol in the music string.

```
procedure TForm1.Button4Click(Sender: TObject);
begin
  { Add a flat symbol to the music string }
  Edit1.Text := Edit1.Text + '-';
end;
```

7. Move to the OnClick event of Button5 and enter this code to add a dotted note to the music string.

```
procedure TForm1.Button5Click(Sender: TObject);
begin
  { Increase the dot count in the music string }
  Edit1.Text := Edit1.Text + '.';
end;
```

8. Select the OnClick event of Button6 and enter the following code. This handles putting the speed of the note into the music string.

```
procedure TForm1.Button6Click(Sender: TObject);
var NoteType  : Integer;
begin
  { Select a note value for the current speed setting }
  case RadioGroup3.ItemIndex of
    0 : NoteType := 1;
    1 : NoteType := 2;
    2 : NoteType := 4;
    3 : NoteType := 8;
    4 : NoteType := 16;
  end;
  { Put the note speed in the music string }
  Edit1.Text := Edit1.Text + 'L' + IntToStr( NoteType );
end;
```

9. Activate the OnClick event of Button7 and enter the following code to enter an octave number increase.

```
procedure TForm1.Button7Click(Sender: TObject);
begin
{ As long as the octave is below ten allow an increase of 1 }
```

```
  If RadioGroup2.ItemIndex < 10 then
  begin
    { Add the octave increase symbol to the music string }
    Edit1.Text := Edit1.Text + '>';
    { Increment the octave value shown in the octave display }
    RadioGroup2.ItemIndex := RadioGroup2.ItemIndex + 1;
  end;
end;
```

10. Choose the OnClick event of Button8 and enter this code to deal with decreasing the octave setting by one.

```
procedure TForm1.Button8Click(Sender: TObject);
begin
  { If the octave setting is above 1 then decrease it by 1 }
  If RadioGroup2.ItemIndex > 0 then
  begin
    { Add an octave decrease symbol to the music string }
    Edit1.Text := Edit1.Text + '<'
    { Decrease the setting of the octave display };
    RadioGroup2.ItemIndex := RadioGroup2.ItemIndex - 1;
  end;
end;
```

11. Move to the OnClick event of Button9 and enter the following code to set the playback tempo.

```
procedure TForm1.Button9Click(Sender: TObject);
begin
  { use the setting of the tempo radiogroup to put the appropriate symbols }
  { in the music string; MN=normal, MS=soft, ML=Loud                       }
  case RadioGroup4.ItemIndex of
    0 : Edit1.Text := Edit1.Text + 'MN';
    1 : Edit1.Text := Edit1.Text + 'MS';
    2 : Edit1.Text := Edit1.Text + 'ML';
  end;
end;
```

12. Activate the OnClick event of Button10 and enter this code, which sets the tempo numerically.

```
procedure TForm1.Button10Click(Sender: TObject);
var TheValue : Integer;
begin
  TheValue := StrToInt( Edit2.Text );
  { If the number is outside the allowable range set it to the default }
  if (( TheValue < 32 ) or ( TheValue > 255 )) then
  begin
    Edit2.Text := '120';
  end
  else
  begin
   { Otherwise set it to the entered value with the numerical tempo symbol }
   Edit1.Text := Edit1.Text + 'T' + Edit2.Text;
```

continued on next page

continued from previous page

```
  end;
end;
```

13. Move to the OnClick event of Button11 and enter this code, which sets the note length numerically.

```
procedure TForm1.Button11Click(Sender: TObject);
begin
  { Enter a note value directly from the radiogroup to the music string }
  case RadioGroup3.ItemIndex of
    0 : Edit1.Text := Edit1.Text + '1';
    1 : Edit1.Text := Edit1.Text + '2';
    2 : Edit1.Text := Edit1.Text + '4';
    3 : Edit1.Text := Edit1.Text + '8';
    4 : Edit1.Text := Edit1.Text + '16';
  end;
end;
```

14. Select the OnClick event of Button12 and enter the following code to place a pause in the music string.

```
procedure TForm1.Button12Click(Sender: TObject);
begin
  { Enter a pause symbol in the music string }
  Edit1.Text := Edit1.Text + 'P';
end;
```

15. Bring up the OnClick event of Button13 and enter the following code. This handles parsing the music string and converting it into music. (This is a very long procedure due to the complexity of the string that it needs to analyze.)

```
procedure TForm1.Button13Click(Sender: TObject);
begin
{ Check to see that there is music to play }
  TotalCharacters := Length( Edit1.Text );
  if TotalCharacters = 0 then
  begin
    MessageDlg( 'No music string to play!' ,
    mtError , [mbOK] , 0 );
    Exit;
  end;
  { Otherwise move down the string to its end and parse for music symbols }
  repeat
    case Edit1.Text[ CharacterPosition ] of
      { An explicit musical note }
      'A'..'G','P' : begin
                  AddTheCurrentNote;
                   { Parse the string to see what pitch the new note is }
                   case Edit1.Text[ CharacterPosition ] of
                   'A' : ThePitch := 10;
                   'B' : ThePitch := 12;
                   'C' : ThePitch := 1;
                   'D' : ThePitch := 3;
                   'E' : ThePitch := 5;
```

```
                'F' : ThePitch := 6;
                'G' : ThePitch := 8;
                'P' : ThePitch := 0;
              end;
              NoteIsNew := true;
              CharacterPosition := CharacterPosition + 1;
            end;
    { A sharp symbol }
    '#'          : begin
              { Increase the pitch by 1; note this parallels piano kb }
              ThePitch := ThePitch + 1;
              CharacterPosition := CharacterPosition + 1;
            end;
    { A flat symbol }
    '-'          : begin
              { Decrease the pitch by 1; note this parallels piano kb }
              ThePitch := ThePitch - 1;
              CharacterPosition := CharacterPosition + 1;
            end;
    { A dot symbol }
    '.'          : begin
               { Increase dot count; this is note's quickness }
               TotalDots := TotalDots + 1;
               CharacterPosition := CharacterPosition + 1;
            end;
    { An unsymbolized number }
    '1'..'9'     : begin
               { Set a notelength directly via the GetNumber }
               { assistant function                        }
               TheNoteLength := GetNumber( CharacterPosition );
            end;
    { An octave increase symbol }
    '>'          : begin
               AddTheCurrentNote;
               { Increase the new octave setting }
               TheOctave := TheOctave + 1;
               CharacterPosition := CharacterPosition + 1;
            end;
    { An octave decrease symbol }
    '<'          : begin
               AddTheCurrentNote;
               { Decrease the new octave setting }
               TheOctave := TheOctave - 1;
               CharacterPosition := CharacterPosition + 1;
            end;
    { A mode token }
    'M'          : begin
               AddTheCurrentNote;
               CharacterPosition := CharacterPosition + 1;
               { Set the loudness variable depending on the }
               { token: N=normal=0,S=soft=2,L=loud=1        }
               case Edit1.Text[ CharacterPosition ] of
                 'N' : TheLoudness := 0;
                 'S' : TheLoudness := 2;
                 'L' : TheLoudness := 1;
```

continued on next page

continued from previous page

```
                    end;
                    CharacterPosition := CharacterPosition + 1;
                    AccentIsNew := true;
                  end;
      { A numerical octave token }
      'O'           : begin
                    AddTheCurrentNote;
                    CharacterPosition := CharacterPosition + 1;
                    { Call GetNumber to obtain the new octave value }
                    TheOctave := GetNumber( CharacterPosition );
                  end;
      { A numerical tempo token }
      'T'           : begin
                    AddTheCurrentNote;
                    CharacterPosition := CharacterPosition + 1;
                    { Call the helper function GetNumber for the new tempo }
                    TheTempo := GetNumber( CharacterPosition );
                    AccentIsNew := true;
                  end;
      { A numerical notelength token }
      'L'           : begin
                    AddTheCurrentNote;
                    CharacterPosition := CharacterPosition + 1;
                    { Use the GetNumber function to obtain the new speed }
                    TheLength := GetNumber( CharacterPosition );
                  end;
    end;
  until ( CharacterPosition > TotalCharacters );
  AddTheCurrentNote;
  { And start playing the music with a sound API call }
  StartSound;
  { Reset CharacterPosition to the beginning of the string for a new playing }
  CharacterPosition := 1;
end;
```

16. Choose the OnClick event of Button14 and enter this code to load a music string.

```
procedure TForm1.Button14Click(Sender: TObject);
var TheMemo : TMemo;
begin
  if OpenDialog1.Execute then
  begin
    Filename := OpenDialog1.Filename;
    Label1.Caption := 'Music String  ' +
     ExtractFilename(Filename);
    { Create the dommy memo component }
    TheMemo := TMemo.Create( self );
    { Load the string from the text file }
    TheMemo.Lines.LoadFromFile( Filename );
    { Set the music string's edit control to the text just read in }
    Edit1.Text := TheMemo.Text;
    TheMemo.Destroy;
  end;
end;
```

17. Go to the OnClick event of Button15 and enter the following code to save the music string to a file.

```
procedure TForm1.Button15Click(Sender: TObject);
var TheMemo : TMemo;
begin
  SaveDialog1.Filename := Filename;
  if SaveDialog1.Execute then
  begin
    Filename := SaveDialog1.Filename;
    Label1.Caption := 'Music String  ' +
     ExtractFilename(Filename);
    { Create the dummy memo component }
    TheMemo := TMemo.Create( self );
    TheMemo.Text := Edit1.Text;
    { Get the music string from the edit control to the text to read out }
    { Save the string to the text file }
    TheMemo.Lines.SaveToFile(Filename);
    TheMemo.destroy;
  end;
end;
```

18. Move to the OnClick event of Button16 and enter this code to close the application.

```
procedure TForm1.Button16Click(Sender: TObject);
begin
  CloseSound;
  Close;
end;
```

19. Bring up the OnCreate Event of Form1 and enter the following code to initialize the application.

```
procedure TForm1.FormCreate(Sender: TObject);
var TheResult : Integer;
begin
  { Call the OpenSound API function to acquire the speaker driver }
  TheResult := OpenSound;
  { If did not get at least 1 voice then either another app is using speaker }
  { or SOUND.DRV is not loaded                                               }
  if TheResult < 1 then
  begin
   MessageDlg( 'Unable to Open Speaker! Exiting...' ,
   mtError , [mbOK] , 0 );
   Close;
  end;
  TotalDots := 0;
  ThePitch := 0;
  FileName := '';
  TheTempo := 120;
  TheLoudness := 0;
  TheOctave := 3;
  TheLength := 4;
  TheNoteLength := 0;
```

continued on next page

continued from previous page

```
  SetVoiceQueueSize( 1 , 1024 );
  NoteIsNew := false;
  AccentIsNew := true;
  CharacterPosition := 1;
  TotalCharacters := 0;
end;
```

20. Go into the Code Editor, move up to the keyword *private*, and enter the following two lines. They allow Delphi to recognize your helper functions, which you will add in a moment.

```
private
    { Private declarations }
    procedure AddTheCurrentNote;
    function GetNumber( var ThePosition : Integer ) : Integer;
```

21. Drop down to the *var* keyword and add these helper variable declarations.

```
var
  Form1: TForm1;
  TotalDots : Integer;
  ThePitch  : Integer;
  FileName  : String;
  TheTempo : Integer;
  TheLoudness : Integer;
  TheOctave : Integer;
  TheLength : Integer;
  TheNoteLength : Integer;
  NoteIsNew : Boolean;
  AccentIsNew : Boolean;
  CharacterPosition : Integer;
  TotalCharacters : Integer;
```

22. While still in the Code Editor, move up to the beginning of the code just under the *implementation* keyword and type in the following helper function to add a new note to the play list.

```
procedure TForm1.AddTheCurrentNote;
var ThePlayLength : Integer;
begin
  { If the new accent flag is set then send through a new accent setting }
  { (the 1 and 0 are unused settings)                                     }
  if AccentIsNew then SetVoiceAccent( 1 , TheTempo , 1 , TheLoudness , 0 );
  { if the new note flag is set then also add a new note to the queue }
  if NoteIsNew then
  begin
    { Make sure a valid pitch is set }
    if ThePitch > 0 then
    begin
      { Determine the actual note setting by multiplying the pitch times }
      { the octave times 12; this reproduces the piano keyboard          }
      ThePitch := (( ThePitch + ( TheOctave * 12 )) - 1 );
      { If the explicit note length variable is set }
      if TheNoteLength > 0 then
```

```
      begin
        { Set the play length to that value }
        ThePlayLength := TheNoteLength;
        { And clear the explicit length holder }
        TheNoteLength := 0;
      end
      else
      begin
        { Otherwise pick up the note-based speed }
        ThePlayLength := TheLength;
      end;
      { Enter the new note in the play list }
      SetVoiceNote( 1 , ThePitch , ThePlayLength , TotalDots );
      { And clear the dots holder for the next note }
      TotalDots := 0;
    end;
  end;
  { Clear the new accent and new note flags }
  AccentIsNew := false;
  NoteIsNew := false;
end;
```

23. Move down and type in the following helper function to obtain a number from the music string.

```
{ Obtain a number from the music string, moving the global pointer along }
function TForm1.GetNumber( var ThePosition : Integer ) : Integer;
var Through : Boolean;
    NumberString : String;
    TempNumber ,
    HoldCode     : Integer;
begin
  { Set the flag to loop until done }
  Through := false;
  { Clear the number string }
  NumberString := '';
  { Loop until out of numbers }
  while not Through do
  begin
    { Put the current number on the accumulated string }
    NumberString := NumberString + Edit1.Text[ ThePosition ];
    ThePosition := ThePosition + 1;
    { Exit if at the end of the string }
    if ThePosition > Length( Edit1.Text ) then Through := true
    else
    begin
      { Otherwise check for another number and if not exit }
      case Edit1.Text[ ThePosition ] of
        '0' : Through := false;
        '1'..'9' : Through := false;
        else Through := true;
      end;
    end;
  end;
  { Evaluate the accumulated number string }
```

continued on next page

continued from previous page

```
  Val( NumberString , TempNumber , HoldCode );
  GetNumber := TempNumber;
end;
```

24. Compile and test the project.

How It Works

The keys to the entire program are the two functions SetVoiceAccent and SetVoiceNote. SetVoiceAccent controls the tempo of the notes played after a call, and whether they are loud, normal, or soft. SetVoiceNote enables specifying the musical note (determined as on the piano keyboard as 1 to 88, with 0 being a rest note.) The letter notes are augmented by an octave setting; sharps and flats are added due to the spacing of the letter notes on the numbered keyboard. The length of the note is the length parameter ranging from a whole note to a sixteenth note. The dots are for quick, "dotted" notes.

Having determined how to make the sounds, you need a way to represent them. For some years BASIC has had the ON PLAY statement with a macro language for notes. Windows 2.0 implemented this language in the sound API, and it is reproduced here via the string system.

Note: Duration is entered in the string as the inverse of the time, for example, a quarter, or ¼th note, is a 4 in the string.

Notice the use of the SetVoiceQueueSize statement in the form's OnCreate handler. This is needed because Windows queues notes while one is playing. The SetVoiceQueueSize call decides how much memory Windows will save to hold its notes; 1024 is a "black art" number that seems to work in most cases.

Comments

The Load and Save options are not strictly necessary, but they make MUSICBOX a much friendlier program. By adding a music box component to an application, any number of windows events can now have associated speaker-music cues. (Darth Vader's theme for an error dialog, perhaps...)

9

9

DATABASE

How do I...

Despite its many other powerful features, Delphi is primarily intended as a tool for creating front-end display applications for database systems. For this reason, support for database programming is the most extensive and powerful feature of the program. From simple Paradox or dBASE tables through complex client/server SQL queries, Delphi has built-in components that automate much of the process.

The How-To's in this chapter cover linking Delphi's forms to record-oriented and SQL-type databases, using the many data-aware VCL components provided, and exploiting the power of OOP in the database objects provided with Delphi. Also covered are techniques for controlling the layout of database displays, both in the Delphi IDE and at run time.

This chapter is written at a more basic level than some of the others in the book. This is due to the unique way in which Delphi combines visual design with OOP flexibility and then adds compiled runtime programming. The end result is a database development environment like no other, and even long-time pros in the field can find unsuspected and surprising results lurking under Delphi's hood!

9.1 View the contents of a database in Delphi

Delphi provides a powerful component for database access called TTable. Combined with built-in editors in the Delphi IDE, this VCL element allows swift and easy access to any record-oriented database (such as Paradox or dBASE).

9.2 View the contents of an SQL-based database in Delphi

While single-user databases such as Paradox tend to be record oriented, larger and more complex ones are based on a query language concept, which keeps data in sets. The most common way to access such data is SQL (Structured Query Language), which has been standardized. Delphi provides a TQuery component to complement the TTable element for easy SQL access.

9.3 Use VCL components to automatically display database info

Rather than having to program data transfer from the TTable or TQuery objects into VCL display components at run time, Delphi programmers can access a large array of "data-aware" VCL components, which are counterparts to standard displays but automatically update their information when a new database element is selected by the user.

9.4 Use VCL components to navigate a database

One of the more tedious database programming chores is navigation: moving from one record to another in the table. Delphi has automated this task with its powerful TDBNavigator component.

9.5 Search a database in Delphi

The principal reason for having databases is to be able to search them for desired information. Delphi's OOP encapsulation of its TTable component allows easy and intuitive access to the searching capabilities of the underlying database.

9.6 Edit a database in Delphi

Although displaying data is often the most needed element of database programming, being able to make changes on the display and have them reflected in the underlying data is a feature of commercial database front-end programs and has created an industry all of its own. Delphi uses OOP to make performing this task both easy and user-friendly.

9.7 Control the layout of database table displays at design time

Many databases are large both in terms of size and in number of data fields. Sometimes it is confusing to show all the available data at once. Delphi has an IDE tool called Fields Editor that allows complete control over which fields of the underlying database are shown in the visible form.

9.8 Control the layout of database table displays at run time

Just as the Fields Editor allows design time control over the amount of data shown on the form, Delphi's TField objects use OOP capabilities to allow equal control and flexibility at run time.

9.9 Link data-aware VCL components to automate responses

As a "put it all together" How-To, this application shows the way data-aware VCL components can use Object Pascal to manipulate one another and produce a seamless, user-friendly front end for a complex database.

9.1 How do I... View the contents of a database in Delphi?

COMPLEXITY: EASY

Problem

I need to create a quick application that displays some data from a Paradox or dBASE database, but I have virtually no experience in database programming. Does Delphi have a way to easily show the contents of a record-oriented database?

Technique

Delphi provides a VCL component called TTable, which automates the process of opening and obtaining data from a record-oriented database such as Paradox. Along with the TDBGrid display component (which will be covered in much more detail throughout the chapter), this makes showing the information in a database quite easy.

Steps

Run TTABDEMO.EXE. You will see a display similar to Figure 9-1. This form displays an orders database in Paradox format from the MAST (Marine Adventures and Sunken Treasures) fictional company included with the DEMOS directory in the full installation of Delphi.

Note: If your version of the program doesn't run properly, it is likely that you have either not installed the DEMOS directory with its database components (or the IDAPI runtime module) or have removed them since installation. All of the demos in this chapter require the DEMOS directory and the IDAPI runtime unit; in order to use them, you will need to reinstall these files.

1. Create a new blank project and name it TTABDEMO.DPR. Name the unit TTDMAIN.PAS.

TTable Demo

OrderNo	CustNo	PaymentMethod	ItemsTotal	SaleDate
1003	1510	Credit	$1,250.00	4/12/88
1004	2156	Check	$7,885.00	4/17/88
1005	1356	Visa	$4,807.00	4/20/88
1006	1380	Visa	$31,987.00	11/6/94
1007	1384	Visa	$6,500.00	5/1/88
1008	1510	Visa	$1,449.50	5/3/88
1009	1513	COD	$5,587.00	5/11/88
1010	1551	COD	$4,996.00	5/11/88
1011	1560	COD	$2,679.85	5/18/88
1012	1563	Credit	$5,201.00	5/19/88
1013	1624	Credit	$3,115.00	5/25/88
1014	1645	Credit	$134.85	5/25/88
1015	1651	MC	$20,321.75	5/25/88
1016	1680	AmEx	$2,605.00	6/2/88
1017	1984	Check	$10,195.00	6/12/88
1018	2118	Check	$5,256.00	6/18/88

Figure 9-1 TTABDEMO at run time showing the MAST orders database in Paradox

2. Add the components to Form1 and set their properties as shown in Table 9-1.

Table 9-1 Components, properties, and settings for Form1 of TTABDEMO

COMPONENT	PROPERTY	SETTING
Form1	Type	Application Main Form
	Width	437
	Height	416
	Left	37
	Top	32
	Caption	TTable Demo
Table1	Type	TTable
	Active	False
	DatabaseName	DBDEMOS
	ReadOnly	True
	TableName	ORDERS.DB
	TableType	ttDefault
DataSource1	Type	TDataSource
	AutoEdit	False
	DataSet	Table1
	Enabled	True
DBGrid1	Type	TDBGrid
	Align	alClient
	DataSource	DataSource1
	Options:dgEditing	False
	Visible	True

3. Activate the OnCreate event handler for Form1 and add the following code to display the database when the application runs.

```
procedure TForm1.FormCreate(Sender: TObject);
begin
  Table1.Open;
end;
```

4. Compile and test the project.

How It Works

Despite its apparent simplicity, this How-To provides the core of all that will follow, through use of the linked TTable, TDataSource, and TDBGrid components. Each is explained in detail here.

The TTable component is an abstraction of a record-oriented database. It connects to the actual database using a variety of drivers provided with Delphi. For more details on these, see the *Database Application Developer's Guide*. The DatabaseName property normally contains a BDE "alias," which uses the Borland database engine to allow variation in the actual path to the database from user to user. The end user sets up the real path name in the BDE as an alias, and Delphi communicates with the BDE at run time to find it.

The TableName property is the actual database table file name to be used by the component. TTable automatically configures itself depending on the file extension of the file name; this is the ttDefault TableType property. Alternatively, if the database file has a nonstandard name, the TableType property can explicitly set the data type to a variety of recognized formats.

The ReadOnly and Active properties are extremely important because they control two major elements: whether the table's underlying data is shown at design time, and whether the data can be modified by the application during run time. If Active is False, the underlying data is not shown at design time. Also, in order to show the table's data at run time, an explicit call must be made in the OnCreate event handler to open the table. If Active is True, data is available at design time and will automatically be shown at run time as well. ReadOnly is automatically True if Active is True; if Active is False, ReadOnly can be either True or False. This property controls whether the user can alter the data in the underlying table.

Although the TTable component gives complete access to the database table, it has no way to communicate that information to the user. The TDataSource component serves as the bridge for this requirement. An "invisible" component, TDataSource is nonetheless essential, because without it none of the data-aware VCL controls can function. The component's most important property is DataSet, which is set to Table1. This tells it where to obtain the information requested by higher level objects. Its AutoEdit property, if True, automatically handles posting changes made in data-aware controls that accept user input to the underlying table. It is therefore important to set this property to False if the TTable component is set to ReadOnly. The Enable property is normally True; the only need to set it to False is to prevent redrawing of data-aware components, which might slow down a complex manipulation of the database itself.

The TDBGrid component completes the chain, showing on the form all the fields of the database table and their information. Its most vital property is DataSource, which is set to DataSource1. This tells it where to obtain the information to set itself up and display its data. All this is done behind the scenes and needs no programmer intervention. The Options:dgEditing setting is to maintain consistency with the ReadOnly property of the TTable. If True, this component allows users to directly alter displayed values in the grid and have them posted to the underlying table.

That's all there is to it! With one line of code (which is only needed due to the desire to have a read-only database), all the records of the orders table are available for display. In the following How-To's, this baseline will expand into truly awesome functionality.

Comments

When you add the TTable component and set its DatabaseName and TableName properties, Delphi immediately adds a slew of data types to the main form, as shown here:

```
Table1OrderNo: TFloatField;
Table1CustNo: TFloatField;
Table1ItemsTotal: TCurrencyField;
Table1PaymentMethod: TStringField;
Table1SaleDate: TDateTimeField;
Table1ShipDate: TDateTimeField;
Table1EmpNo: TIntegerField;
Table1ShipToContact: TStringField;
Table1ShipToAddr1: TStringField;
Table1ShipToAddr2: TStringField;
Table1ShipToCity: TStringField;
Table1ShipToState: TStringField;
Table1ShipToZip: TStringField;
Table1ShipToCountry: TStringField;
Table1ShipToPhone: TStringField;
Table1ShipVIA: TStringField;
Table1PO: TStringField;
Table1Terms: TStringField;
Table1TaxRate: TFloatField;
Table1Freight: TCurrencyField;
Table1AmountPaid: TCurrencyField;
```

These TField entries are not used in code anywhere, and you might be tempted to delete them. If you do, however, Delphi will signal an exception at run time from the DBGrid component. These data elements are used by DBGrid to format and display the information in the table via the DataSource component. In point of fact, the TField object is probably the most important database element in Delphi, and it will be the subject of considerable discussion in the How-To's that follow.

9.2 How do I... View the contents of an SQL-based database in Delphi?

COMPLEXITY: INTERMEDIATE

Problem

I have a database that is in SQL rather than record-oriented format. Can Delphi access this type of data?

Technique

The TQuery component replaces the TTable component for access to SQL-oriented data. Although TTable components can access SQL-oriented databases, they cannot perform SQL operations on them. TQuery handles this chore, and very nicely at that.

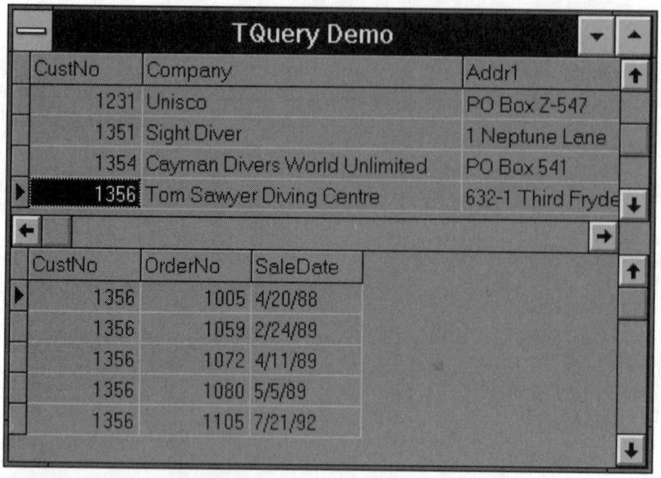

Figure 9-2 TQRYDEMO at run time showing the MAST customers and orders databases in SQL

Steps

Run TQRYDEMO.EXE. You will see a display similar to Figure 9-2. This form displays a customers database in SQL format from the MAST (Marine Adventures and Sunken Treasures) fictional company included with the DEMOS directory in the full installation of Delphi. The first pane is the customers database; the second is an SQL query on the orders made by a given customer selected in the first pane.

1. Create a new blank project and name it TQRYDEMO.DPR. Name the unit TQRYMAIN.PAS.
2. Add the components to Form1 and set their properties as shown in Table 9-2.

Table 9-2 Components, properties, and settings for Form1 of TQRYDEMO

COMPONENT	PROPERTY	SETTING
Form1	Type	Application Main Form
	Width	435
	Height	300
	Left	25
	Top	54
	Caption	TQuery Demo
CustomerTable	Type	TTable
	Active	True
	DatabaseName	DBDEMOS

COMPONENT	PROPERTY	SETTING
	ReadOnly	False
	TableName	CUSTOMER
	TableType	ttDefault
OrdersQuery	Type	TQuery
	Active	True
	DatabaseName	DBDEMOS
	DataSource	CustomerDataSource
	RequestLive	False
	Params: ParameterName	CustNo
	ParameterType	Float
	SQL	select Orders.CustNo, Orders.OrderNo,
		Orders.SaleDate
		from Orders
		where Orders.CustNo = :CustNo
CustomerDataSource	Type	TDataSource
	AutoEdit	True
	DataSet	CustomerTable
	Enabled	True
OrdersDataSource	Type	TDataSource
	AutoEdit	True
	DataSet	OrdersQuery
	Enabled	True
CustomerGrid	Type	TDBGrid
	Align	alTop
	DataSource	CustomerDataSource
	Visible	True
	Width	427
	Height	127
OrdersGrid	Type	TDBGrid
	Align	alClient
	DataSource	OrdersDataSource
	Visible	True

Note: The Params and SQL properties are entered by bringing up two different property editors via the ellipsis buttons in their respective Object Inspector fields. In the editors, the information in Table 9-2 is simple to enter. (Be sure, however, to include the RETURN (ascii 13 carriage return/linefeed) characters in the SQL statements, as they are important!)

3. Activate the OnCreate event handler for Form1 and add the following code to display the database when the application runs.

```
procedure TForm1.FormCreate(Sender: TObject);
begin
  CustomerTable.Open;
end;
```

4. Compile and test the project.

How It Works

The TQuery object used here has two major elements not found in the TTable object—Params and SQL. These elements are required because of the differences between a record- and a set-oriented database.

Params (short for Parameters) are used to bind fields from a data source to runtime parameters in an accompanying SQL statement. A value can be entered via the Parameters Editor, or it can be fixed at run time by the compiler. It is used here to allow setting the value of the CustNo parameter to that of the selected field in the first pane.

SQL is the query to be used to fill the fields of the second DBGrid component. SQL queries are strings of text that are interpreted by the underlying database engine and used to determine which information in the database meets the stated requirements. While the complexities of SQL are far beyond the scope of this book, this particular query is easily seen to request the customer number, order number, and order date for all records that have a customer number equal to that selected in the top pane.

Comments

Notice that the TTable component does not add a large number of TField components as it did in How-To 9.1. This is because the underlying database is SQL-based rather than record oriented.

9.3 How do I...
Use VCL components to automatically display database information?

COMPLEXITY: EASY

Problem

Now that I can access my databases, am I going to have to write tons of code just to display the information in anything but a grid?

Technique

Although DBGrid is arguably the most powerful component in Delphi, additional controls are provided which, like DBGrid, are "data aware." This means they will automatically update themselves as the underlying database selections or data change.

Steps

Run DAWCDEMO.EXE. You will see a display similar to Figure 9-3. This form displays an orders database in SQL format from the MAST (Marine Adventures and Sunken Treasures) fictional company included with the DEMOS directory in the full installation of Delphi. As selections are made in the grid, the information in the label, edit control, combo box, and list box is automatically updated.

1. Create a new blank project and name it DAWCDEMO.DPR. Name the unit DAWCMAIN.PAS.

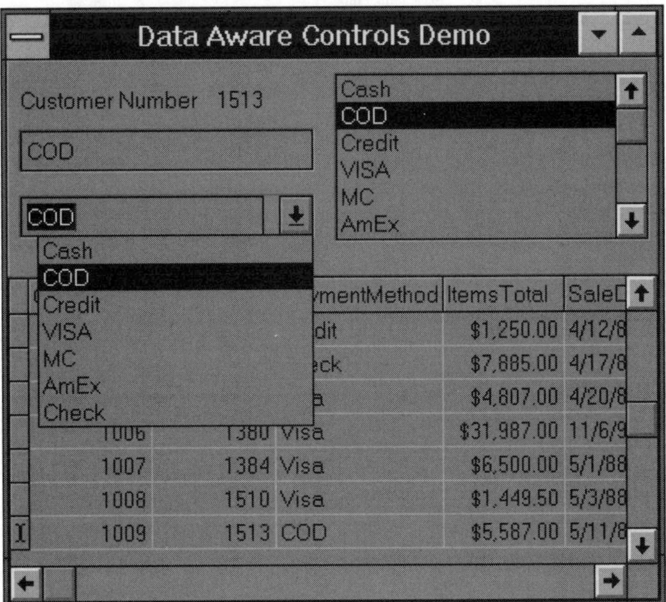

Figure 9-3 DAWCDEMO at run time showing data-aware controls on the MAST database

2. Add the components to Form1 and set their properties as shown in Table 9-3.

Table 9-3 Components, properties, and settings for Form1 of DAWCDEMO

COMPONENT	PROPERTY	SETTING
Form1	Type	Application Main Form
	Width	407
	Height	357
	Left	52
	Top	50
	Caption	Data Aware Controls Demo
Table1	Type	TTable
	Active	True
	DatabaseName	DBDEMOS
	ReadOnly	False
	TableName	ORDERS.DB
	TableType	ttDefault
DataSource1	Type	TDataSource
	AutoEdit	True
	DataSet	Table1
	Enabled	True
DBGrid1	Type	TDBGrid
	Align	alClient
	DataSource	DataSource1
	Visible	True
Panel1	Type	TPanel
	Width	399
	Height	129
	Left	0
	Top	0
	BevelOuter	bvRaised
Label1	Type	TLabel
	Width	108
	Height	16
	Left	8
	Top	16
	Caption	Customer Number
DBText1	Type	TDBText

COMPONENT	PROPERTY	SETTING
	Width	65
	Height	17
	Left	128
	Top	16
	DataSource	DataSource1
	DataField	CustNo
DBListBox1	Type	TDBListBox
	Width	193
	Height	99
	Left	200
	Top	9
	DataSource	DataSource1
	DataField	PaymentMethod
DBEdit1	Type	TDBEdit
	Width	178
	Height	24
	Left	8
	Top	42
	DataSource	DataSource1
	DataField	PaymentMethod
DBComboBox1	Type	TDBComboBox
	Width	178
	Height	24
	Left	8
	Top	81
	DataSource	DataSource1
	DataField	PaymentMethod
	Style	csDropDown
	DropDownCount	8

3. Compile and test the project.

How It Works

The key functionality of this application lies in its four data-aware VCL components: TDBText, DBListBox, DBComboBox, and DBEdit. They all have a common DataSource field, which connects them to a TDataSource component that in turn links back to a TTable or TQuery. Each is considered in some detail here.

The simplest DAC (data-aware component) is the TDBText element. This variation of TLabel has a DataField property. This variable is set to one of the available fields of the underlying table for the data source (as can be seen in the drop-down list in the Object Inspector). The component itself handles any data-type conversion problems (such as a number to a string). What makes this and all the other DACs powerful is that when the "cursor" (or active record) in the database changes, the value in the DataField changes automatically.

The DBListBox component is a standard VCL list box, with two major differences. First, once its DataField property is added, it automatically fills up its Items property with the available data values for the selected field. (This limits the use of this component to data fields with enumerated types that can be converted into strings.) Second, when the value of DataField changes due to moving the cursor in the underlying table, the selected item in the list box changes automatically.

DBComboBox is similar to DBListBox except that it displays the list of available choices as a drop-down list. It otherwise functions the same as a normal VCL ComboBox component.

The DBEdit component has a unique capability. In addition to changing whenever the underlying cursor moves, it can also be used to enter a new value for the field, provided the database is available for editing and the appropriate settings are made in the VCL components to permit it.

Comments

Notice that there is not a single line of user-written code in this How-To. Delphi produces all the power of this application itself. The equivalent functionality developed in Clipper or C++ would require hundreds of lines of program code. As more and more powerful DACs become available for the Delphi environment, look for this capability to become even more amazing.

9.4 How do I...
Use VCL components to navigate a database?

COMPLEXITY: EASY

Problem

I would like to allow users to quickly move around in my database by using onscreen button controls like the directional buttons on a VCR. Does Delphi have any functionality to handle this?

Technique

Delphi includes the highly sophisticated TDBNavigator component. This How-To demonstrates its use on a simple database, allowing the user to move forward and backward as well as to the start and end of the database.

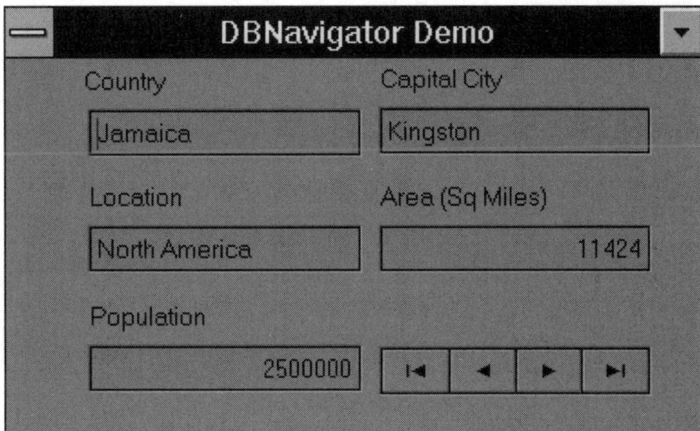

Figure 9-4 DBNAVDEM at run time showing a geographical database and navigator component

Steps

Run DBNAVDEM.EXE. You will see a display similar to Figure 9-4. This form displays a database of geographical data included with the DEMOS directory in the full installation of Delphi. The buttons on the lower right are the navigator. The inner buttons move the position up or down one record, while the leftmost goes to the start and the rightmost to the end of the database. Note that when a given action is inappropriate, the navigator button displays a disabled color.

1. Create a new blank project and name it DBNAVDEM.DPR. Name the unit DBND-MAIN.PAS.

2. Add the components to Form1 and set their properties as shown in Table 9-4.

Table 9-4 Components, properties, and settings for Form1 of DBNAVDEM

COMPONENT	PROPERTY	SETTING
Form1	Type	Application Main Form
	Width	393
	Height	237
	Left	81
	Top	84
	Caption	DBNavigator Demo
Table1	Type	TTable

continued on next page

continued from previous page

COMPONENT	PROPERTY	SETTING
	Active	True
	DatabaseName	DBDEMOS
	ReadOnly	False
	TableName	COUNTRY
	TableType	ttDefault
DataSource1	Type	TDataSource
	AutoEdit	True
	DataSet	Table1
	Enabled	True
DBNavigator1	Type	TDBNavigator
	Width	149
	Height	25
	Left	206
	Top	155
	DataSource	DataSource1
	VisibleButtons	
	nbFirst	True
	nbPrior	True
	nbNext	True
	nbLast	True
	nbInsert	False
	nbDelete	False
	nbEdit	False
	nbPost	False
	nbCancel	False
	nbRefresh	False
DBEdit1	Type	TDBEdit
	Width	149
	Height	24
	Left	46
	Top	28
	DataSource	DataSource1
	DataField	Name
Label1	Type	TLabel
	Width	45
	Height	16
	Left	43

COMPONENT	PROPERTY	SETTING
	Top	4
	Caption	Country
DBEdit2	Type	TDBEdit
	Width	149
	Height	25
	Left	206
	Top	27
	DataSource	DataSource1
	DataField	Capital
Label2	Type	TLabel
	Width	67
	Height	16
	Left	206
	Top	3
	Caption	Capital City
DBEdit3	Type	TDBEdit
	Width	149
	Height	25
	Left	46
	Top	90
	DataSource	DataSource1
	DataField	Continent
Label3	Type	TLabel
	Width	51
	Height	16
	Left	46
	Top	66
	Caption	Location
DBEdit4	Type	TDBEdit
	Width	149
	Height	25
	Left	206
	Top	90
	DataSource	DataSource1
	DataField	Area
Label4	Type	TLabel
	Width	92

continued on next page

continued from previous page

COMPONENT	PROPERTY	SETTING
	Height	16
	Left	206
	Top	66
	Caption	Area (Sq Miles)
DBEdit5	Type	TDBEdit
	Width	149
	Height	25
	Left	46
	Top	154
	DataSource	DataSource1
	DataField	Population
Label5	Type	TLabel
	Width	64
	Height	16
	Left	46
	Top	130
	Caption	Population

3. Compile and test the project.

How It Works

TDBNavigator is a simple wrapper around an enormously complex object. This set of button controls gives users (and programmers) quick and powerful control over all types of databases accessible in Delphi.

The DBNavigator component is actually a visual envelope around an Object Pascal object, which has a number of very powerful methods that manipulate the TTable components that control access to the physical database file(s). These methods include moving to the end or beginning of the database, moving forward or backward one record, changing edit mode, posting edited changes, inserting or deleting data, canceling previously made (but not posted) changes, and refreshing the database (useful for shared data over a network).

All of these methods have a representative button that will be displayed if its corresponding VisibleButtons field is set in the Object Inspector. The buttons automatically invalidate when their function would not be appropriate and validate when it would.

Comments

The only major element missing from the TDBNavigator object is a variable that holds the actual cursor position in the database. This is presumably hidden for consistency purposes, since altering it directly might lead to unpredictable and destructive consequences—but at least a read-only property would have been nice.

9.5 How do I...
Search a database in Delphi?

COMPLEXITY: INTERMEDIATE

Problem

Users often need to search the database interactively. Is there a way to handle this in Delphi without extensive programming?

Technique

Due to its OOP nature, Delphi's database components provide some remarkable functionality for tiny amounts of code. Using the SetKey and GotoKey methods of the TTable object, you can quickly search any database for a given index key.

Steps

Run SRCHDEMO.EXE. You will see a display similar to Figure 9-5. This form displays an orders database from the MAST (Marine Adventures and Sunken Treasures) fictional company included with the DEMOS directory in the full installation of Delphi. Enter a valid customer number in the edit box and press the Perform the Search button. The selected row of the grid will move to that customer. If you

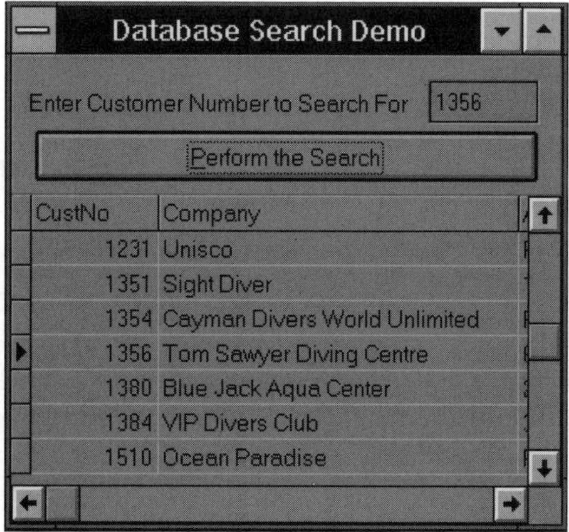

Figure 9-5 SRCHDEMO at run time showing a successful customer number search

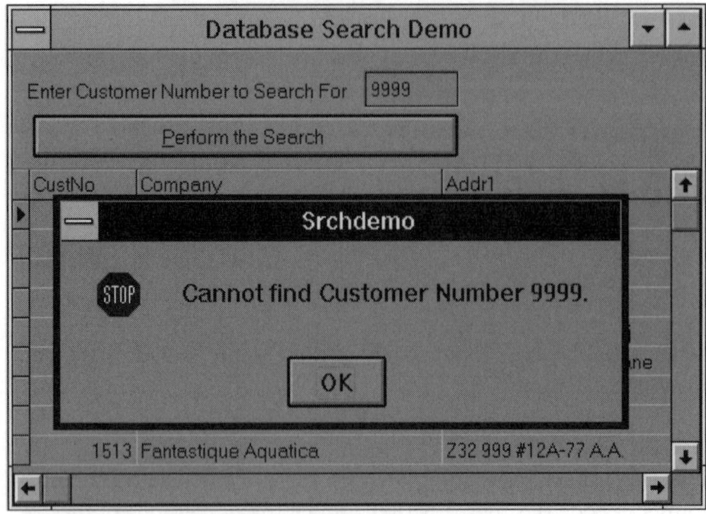

Figure 9-6 SRCHDEMO at run time showing an unsuccessful customer number search

enter an invalid number, you will see a display similar to Figure 9-6, which illustrates the built-in exception handler for the TTable object.

1. Create a new blank project and name it SRCHDEMO.DPR. Name the unit SRCHMAIN.PAS.

2. Add the components to Form1 and set their properties as shown in Table 9-5.

Table 9-5 Components, properties, and settings for Form1 of SRCHDEMO

COMPONENT	PROPERTY	SETTING
Form1	Type	Application Main Form
	Width	336
	Height	305
	Left	21
	Top	36
	Caption	Database Search Demo
CustomerTable	Type	TTable
	Active	True
	DatabaseName	DBDEMOS

COMPONENT	PROPERTY	SETTING
	ReadOnly	False
	TableName	CUSTOMER
	TableType	ttDefault
DataSource1	Type	TDataSource
	AutoEdit	False
	DataSet	CustomerTable
	Enabled	True
DBGrid1	Type	TDBGrid
	Align	alClient
	DataSource	DataSource1
	Visible	True
CustomerNumberEdit	Type	TEdit
	Width	65
	Height	24
	Left	248
	Top	15
	Text	(blank)
Label1	Type	TLabel
	Width	225
	Height	16
	Left	10
	Top	20
	Caption	Enter Customer Number to Search For
Panel1	Type	TPanel\
	align	taCenter
	Width	328
	Height	81
	BevelOuter	bvRaised
SearchButton	Type	TButton
	Width	299
	Height	29
	Left	14
	Top	44
	Caption	&Perform the Search

3. Activate the OnCreate event handler for Form1 and add the following code to display the database when the application runs.

```
procedure TForm1.FormCreate(Sender: TObject);
begin
  CustomerTable.Open;
end;
```

4. Activate the OnClick event handler for SearchButton and add these lines of code to perform the actual search at run time:

```
procedure TForm1.SearchButtonClick(Sender: TObject);
var
  CustomerNumber: Double;
begin
  { Get the number to search for }
  CustomerNumber := StrToFloat(CustomerNumberEdit.Text);
  { This method sets the database into search mode }
  CustomerTable.SetKey;
  { Set the first index key to a float equal to entered number }
  CustomerTable.IndexFields[0].AsFloat := CustomerNumber;
  { If search is successful GotoKey will return true        }
  { Otherwise raise an exception to handle aborting safely }
  { Note the use of the formatted output string!            }
  if not CustomerTable.GotoKey then
    raise Exception.CreateFmt('Cannot find Customer Number %g',
         [CustomerNumber]);
end;
```

5. Compile and test the project.

How It Works

There is a set of powerful methods in the TTable object that involve searching; this demonstration covers SetKey and GotoKey, the most commonly used.

SetKey is a method that tells the TTable object that, until execution of a search function, all assignment statements are to be taken as entries to search against. This is called being in SetKey mode. Once a search command is issued, SetKey mode is automatically canceled.

Once SetKey mode is established, a search target must be entered. TTable components have two arrays, Fields and IndexFields, that are used to store information about the database. The 0th element in either array is normally used for the search target; however, if multiple keys are desired, multiple entries in the array can be assigned prior to executing the search.

Note the use of the AsFloat element of the TField object. This call performs implicit typecasting on the imported variable; there are a number of built-in AsXXXX methods for the TField component to allow importing various kinds of data. If no typecast is needed, a variable can be directly assigned by setting the Value element.

Finally, the GotoKey method is called. This performs the actual search and returns a Boolean value as to whether the search succeeded; if the search fails, it will return False. If the search succeeds, the cursor for the TTable is moved to the row containing the first matching value (which may update any data-aware controls linked to the TTable). In the example in this How-To, an exception is raised to inform the user that an invalid search was requested. An invalid search does not change the cursor's position.

Comments

In addition to GotoKey, TTable has a substring search function, GotoNearest. In addition, two other methods spare a programmer even more work by encapsulating the SetKey, search target assignment, and GotoKey statements in one: these are FindKey and FindNearest.

There are even more sophisticated search methods available in TTable; if you are interested, you can read about them in the *Database Application Developer's Guide*.

9.6 How do I... Edit a database in Delphi?

COMPLEXITY: EASY

Problem

Sometimes users want to be able to update their database while viewing it. Can Delphi do both things at once?

Technique

Delphi allows two different ways to edit a database, one implicit and one explicit. The implicit method is contained in the Active, AutoEdit, and dgEditing properties of the TTable, TDataSource, and TDBGrid components, respectively; the explicit method is contained in TTable's Post and Edit methods.

Steps

Run EDITDEMO.EXE. You will see a display similar to Figure 9-7. This form displays an orders database from the MAST (Marine Adventures and Sunken Treasures) fictional company included with the DEMOS directory in the full installation of Delphi. Select a field in the DBGrid and enter a reasonable value (the company names are a good choice), and then press ENTER. The database will update and the new value will be shown. Alternatively, select a record with the mouse, enter a value in the edit control, and press the Update the Database button. A similar change will occur (only to the company name), as shown in Figure 9-8.

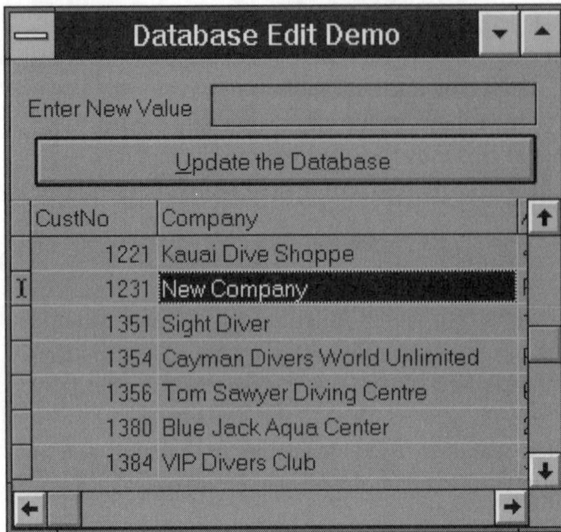

Figure 9-7 EDITDEMO at run time showing DBGrid implicit editing

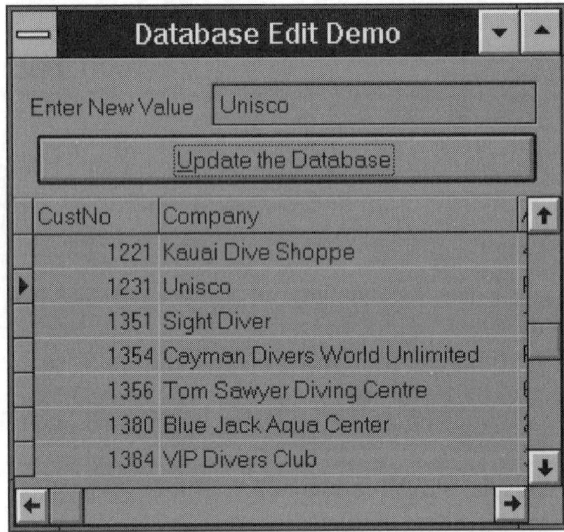

Figure 9-8 EDITDEMO at run time showing TEdit explicit editing

1. Create a new blank project and name it EDITDEMO.DPR. Name the unit EDITMAIN.PAS.
2. Add the components to Form1 and set their properties as shown in Table 9-6.

Table 9-6 Components, properties, and settings for Form1 of EDITDEMO

COMPONENT	PROPERTY	SETTING
Form1	Type	Application Main Form
	Width	336
	Height	305
	Left	21
	Top	36
	Caption	Database Search Demo
CustomerTable	Type	TTable
	Active	True
	DatabaseName	DBDEMOS
	ReadOnly	False
	TableName	CUSTOMER
	TableType	ttDefault
DataSource1	Type	TDataSource
	AutoEdit	False
	DataSet	CustomerTable
	Enabled	True
DBGrid1	Type	TDBGrid
	Align	alClient
	DataSource	DataSource1
	Visible	True
Edit1	Type	TEdit
	Width	193
	Height	24
	Left	120
	Top	15
	Text	(blank)
Label1	Type	TLabel
	Width	225
	Height	16
	Left	10
	Top	20
	Caption	Enter New Value
Panel1	Type	TPanel\
	align	taCenter
	Width	328

continued on next page

continued from previous page

COMPONENT	PROPERTY	SETTING
	Height	81
	BevelOuter	bvRaised
UpdateButton	Type	TButton
	Width	299
	Height	29
	Left	14
	Top	44
	Caption	&Update the Database

3. Activate the OnCreate event handler for Form1 and add the following code to display the database when the application runs.

```
procedure TForm1.FormCreate(Sender: TObject);
begin
  CustomerTable.Open;
end;
```

4. Activate the OnClick event handler for UpdateButton and add these lines of code to perform the explicit database update from the edit control:

```
procedure TForm1.UpdateButtonClick(Sender: TObject);
begin
  { Put the database in Edit mode to be sure }
  CustomerTable.Edit;
  { Assign the company name value from edit control }
  CustomerTable.Fields[ 1 ].AsString := Edit1.Text;
  { Tell the TTable object to really update the database }
  { Alternatively could cancel with no changes.          }
  CustomerTable.Post;
  { After this point changes are final! }
end;
```

5. Compile and test the project.

How It Works

In order to understand what happens in this application, some discussion of the three levels of Delphi's database components is needed. The TTable object is the real key to editing, since it is the ultimate gatekeeper. If it is set to Active, it is automatically possible to edit it (although it may not be in edit mode at a given time). If TTable is not Active, and is set to ReadOnly, then no editing is possible. However, if ReadOnly is False, even an inactive table can be edited.

What all this boils down to is that, normally, anything a user wants to enter in displayed database data is automatically accepted by Delphi and updated to the underlying database. However, at either design time or run time, properties can be set to prevent this for security reasons or to preserve data integrity.

The runtime calls needed to allow editing of data all reside in the TTable object. The application in this How-To shows the two most important: Edit and Post. Edit is a method which, when called, sets the database into edit mode if it is not already in edit mode and if it is not read-only. If editing is already allowed, no exception is raised; but if the database is read-only, an exception will occur.

Post is a method that tells the TTable component to send the changes stored in the TField objects that are part of the TTable to the underlying database file. Once this is done, the changes cannot be undone. However, until Post is called, a call to the Cancel method will return all altered fields to their stored values. (This is not an undo function; the values restored are those in the underlying file, not unsaved previous entries.)

Comments

This How-To illustrates editing in a TTable environment. Alternatively, SQL editing is also possible with TQuery components. This is covered in considerable detail in the *Database Application Developer's Guide*, pages 135 to 180.

The TDataSource component has a property called AutoEdit, which sets TTable into edit mode (if it is not read-only) as soon as any data-aware control receives an OnChange message, meaning user input has begun. If AutoEdit is False, then explicit program statements must be made to set the edit mode or changes to data-aware controls will not be kept. Finally, TDBGrid has a dbEditing option that is True by default; however, if manually set to False, changes in the displayed data are not allowed.

9.7 How do I...
Control the layout of database table displays at design time?

COMPLEXITY: EASY

Problem

My database has too many fields for easy display, and users get confused. Is there a way to limit the fields displayed by data-aware components at design time in Delphi?

Technique

Just as properties have specialized editors in Delphi, several of the database components also have such helper dialogs. The one that gives design time control over the fields displayed in a TTable is the Fields Editor.

Steps

Run FIELDEMO.EXE. You will see a display similar to Figure 9-9. This form displays an orders database from the MAST (Marine Adventures and Sunken Treasures) fictional company included with the DEMOS directory in the full installation of Delphi. Notice that only three fields are showing: the order number, customer number, and payment method. This is due to intervention at design time.

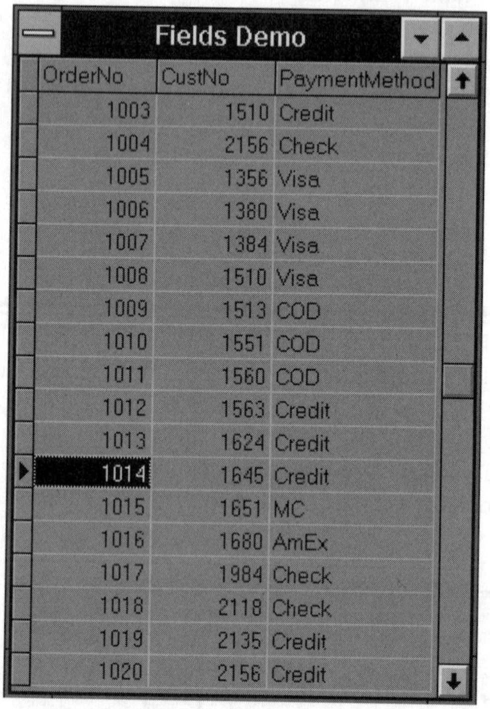

Figure 9-9 FIELDEMO at run time showing design time field display control

1. Copy the project from How-To 9.1 to a new directory. Rename it FIELDEMO.DPR. Rename the unit FLD1MAIN.PAS.

2. Change the Form1 component's caption as shown in Table 9-7.

Table 9-7 Modification to Form1 of FIELDEMO

COMPONENT	PROPERTY	SETTING
Form1	Type	Application Main Form
	Caption	Fields Demo

Figure 9-10 The Fields Editor at design time showing highlighted fields to be removed

3. Double-click the TTable component and the Fields Editor will appear, as shown in Figure 9-10. Select all but the CustNo, OrderNo, and PaymentMethod fields and remove them. Close the Fields Editor.
4. Compile and test the project.

How It Works

The Fields Editor works with the TTable component to determine the available fields for display. By default they are all available, but with the Fields Editor it is possible to change which ones are shown at run time.

Comments

The Fields Editor can do a great deal more than this simple application illustrates. It also can create calculated fields that appear only on the Delphi form and that are determined by user-input formulas. This is covered in more detail in the *Database Application Developer's Guide*, pages 68 to 83.

9.8 How do I...
Control the layout of database table displays at run time?

COMPLEXITY: INTERMEDIATE

Problem

At times I need to reconfigure my displayed fields during the operation of my application. Is there a way to duplicate the effects of the Fields Editor at run time?

Technique

The TTable object maintains a list of its available fields at run time. This list can be accessed and the display properties of the data controlled by programming.

Steps

Run FIELDEM2.EXE. You will see a display similar to Figure 9-11. This form displays an orders database from the MAST (Marine Adventures and Sunken Treasures) fictional company included with the DEMOS directory in the full installation of Delphi. It shows only the first four fields of the database, which was configured at design time to show all of its fields.

1. Copy the FIELDEMO project to a new directory and rename it FIELDEM2.DPR. Rename the unit FLD2MAIN.PAS.
2. Activate the Fields Editor by double-clicking the TTable component. Select Add and add all the listed fields. The forms display then returns to the normal state of the component.
3. Activate the OnCreate event handler for Form1 and add the following code to display the database with limited fields shown when the application runs.

```
procedure TForm1.FormCreate(Sender: TObject);
var Counter_1 : Integer;
begin
  { Open the table explicitly }
  Table1.Open;
  { Run a loop to set the visible property of all but }
  { the first four fields to false, controlling their }
  { display. Could reset them later if desired!       }
  for Counter_1 := 4 to Table1.FieldCount - 1 do
  begin
    Table1.Fields[ Counter_1 ].Visible := false;
  end;
end;
```

4. Compile and test the project.

How It Works

This How-To uses the Fields property of all TTable objects to access the underlying data fields used by the Delphi data-aware components at run time. Since these TField components are based on the standard TComponent object, they have a Visible property, which when set to False means the system cannot display them. In this case, this includes using them in higher level components such as TDBGrid; thus, simply by setting the underlying TFields to Invisible, the application also removes them from runtime access.

Notice the use of the FieldCount property to determine how many fields are available at run time. In this case, this wasn't necessary, since the total fields available could have been counted and a number specified. However, in a more robust appli-

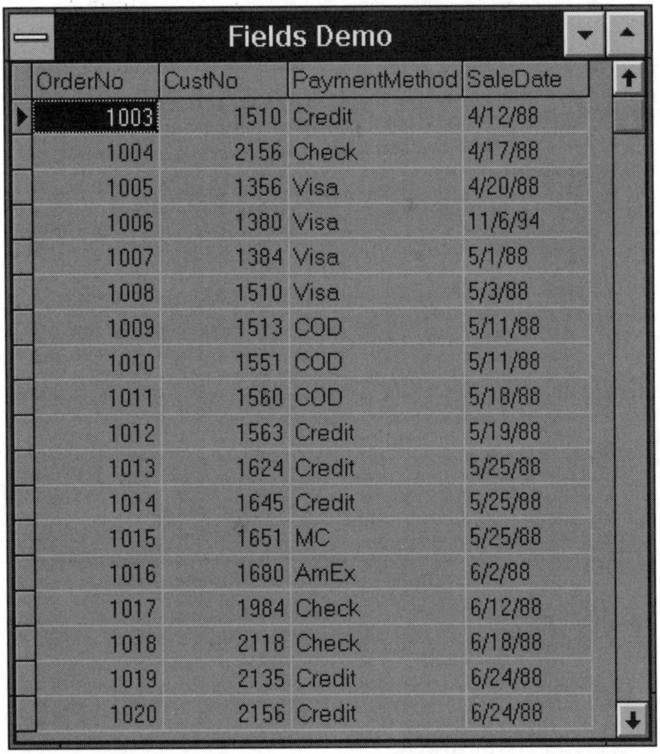

Fields Demo

OrderNo	CustNo	PaymentMethod	SaleDate
1003	1510	Credit	4/12/88
1004	2156	Check	4/17/88
1005	1356	Visa	4/20/88
1006	1380	Visa	11/6/94
1007	1384	Visa	5/1/88
1008	1510	Visa	5/3/88
1009	1513	COD	5/11/88
1010	1551	COD	5/11/88
1011	1560	COD	5/18/88
1012	1563	Credit	5/19/88
1013	1624	Credit	5/25/88
1014	1645	Credit	5/25/88
1015	1651	MC	5/25/88
1016	1680	AmEx	6/2/88
1017	1984	Check	6/12/88
1018	2118	Check	6/18/88
1019	2135	Credit	6/24/88
1020	2156	Credit	6/24/88

Figure 9-11 FIELDEM2 at run time showing runtime field display control

cation, this number might change due to changes in the underlying database, and so making the loop based on a runtime variable makes the application a little sturdier.

Comments

There are an enormous number of capabilities hiding inside the TField component. Aside from its dynamic typecasting abilities, it also includes methods for doing input validation and for creating "virtual" fields that are calculated at run time. Getting to know TField is the first priority of anyone planning to use Delphi for serious database work.

9.9 How do I...
Link data-aware VCL components to automate responses to user requests?

COMPLEXITY: ADVANCED

Problem

I'd like to make my database application as user-friendly as possible. Is there a way to avoid making explicit search requests using data-aware components in Delphi?

Technique

Delphi provides a mechanism by which one database can control the display of another. One of the components using this mechanism is TDBLookupCombo, which is a special combo box control that takes data from one database and uses it to set a value from another.

Steps

Run LDAWDEMO.EXE. You will see a display similar to Figure 9-12. This form displays an orders database from the MAST (Marine Adventures and Sunken Treasures) fictional company included with the DEMOS directory in the full installation of Delphi. When you select a field in the grid display, the name of the company that placed that order appears in the DBLookupCombo above. You can also drop down a list of all companies that have placed orders.

1. Create a new blank project and name it LDAWDEMO.DPR. Name the unit LDAWMAIN.PAS.

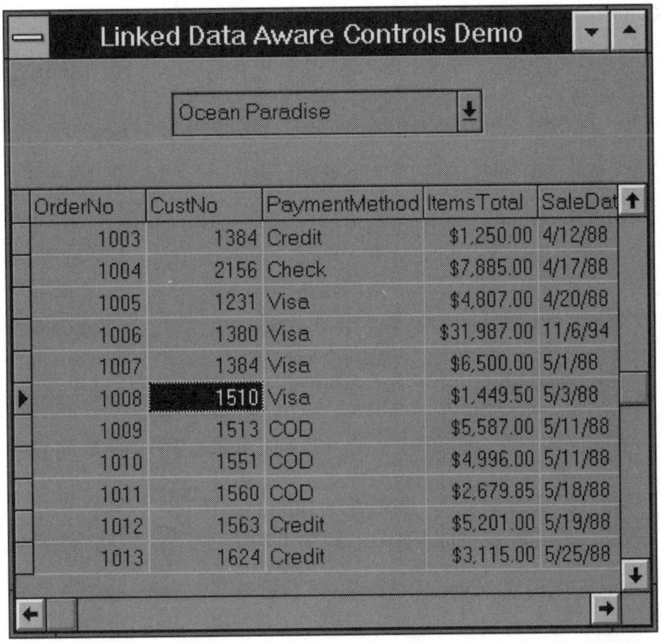

Figure 9-12 LDAWDEMO at run time showing linking of two data-aware controls

2. Add the components to Form1 and set their properties as shown in Table 9-8.

Table 9-8 Components, properties, and settings for Form1 of LDAWDEMO

COMPONENT	PROPERTY	SETTING
Form1	Type	Application Main Form
	Width	421
	Height	394
	Left	33
	Top	21
	Caption	Linked Data Aware Controls Demo
CustomerTable	Type	TTable
	Active	True
	DatabaseName	DBDEMOS
	ReadOnly	False
	TableName	CUSTOMER.DB

continued on next page

continued from previous page

COMPONENT	PROPERTY	SETTING
	TableType	ttDefault
OrdersTable	Type	TTable
	Active	True
	DatabaseName	DBDEMOS
	ReadOnly	False
	TableName	ORDERS.DB
	TableType	ttDefault
CustomerDataSource	Type	TDataSource
	AutoEdit	True
	DataSet	CustomerTable
	Enabled	True
OrdersDataSource	Type	TDataSource
	AutoEdit	True
	DataSet	OrdersTable
	Enabled	True
DBGrid1	Type	TDBGrid
	Align	alClient
	DataSource	OrdersDataSource
	Visible	True
Panel1	Type	TPanel
	align	taCenter
	Width	413
	Height	81
	BevelOuter	bvRaised
DBLookupCombo1	Type	TDBLookupCombo
	Width	200
	Height	27
	Left	105
	Top	22
	Style	csDropDown
	DataSource	OrdersDataSource
	DropDownCount	8
	LookupDisplay	Company
	LookupField	CustNo
	LookupSource	CustomerDataSource

3. Compile and test the project.

How It Works

TDBLookupCombo is one of two controls provided with Delphi that link two or more databases together to make searching more user-friendly. Both controls work on the principle of a linked field, that is, a data field in common between two database tables.

The mechanism that makes the Lookup objects useful is their ability to automatically take a number or other key and use it to obtain the value from another field in the target database and then display that value rather than the one they were originally sent by the source table. In this case, the DataSource component is the OrdersDataSource, while the target (LookupSource) is the CustomerDataSource. The LookupField is the shared key (CustNo in this case), and the LookupDisplay is the actual field whose value is to be shown in the combo box—here, it is the company's name.

Comments

The nine How-To's in this chapter have barely scratched the surface of Delphi's database functionality. Aside from its likely niche as a premier RAD tool, Delphi will certainly find a lasting place designing database front ends and maintenance tools.

10

10

OLE AND DDE

How Do I...

Windows' multiple application environment requires that applications communicate with one another. Two mechanisms provide for this communication: DDE (Dynamic Data Exchange) and OLE (Object Linking and Embedding). Delphi has automated DDE completely and OLE partially. With the components provided in the first release of Delphi, you can give your applications powerful functionality previously reserved for programs written with Software Development Kits (SDKs) in C or C++. The tricks and techniques in this chapter show you how to take full advantage of DDE to control other applications and exchange data with them. You'll also learn how to create a professional installation utility that interacts with the Windows Program Manager, and how to manage information among any number of running applications. Finally, you'll discover how OLE can save you from writing complex display code in applications and even save space by using linked rather than embedded objects.

10.1 Create a new program group in Program Manager

New Windows applications often require more than simply copying files from a disk. To manage them effectively, users will want to create new directories and add Program Manager groups. This How-To demonstrates a number of Delphi functions that allow almost complete automation of the installation process.

10.2 Use drag-and-drop in my applications

One of the most impressive and time-saving features of Windows is the ability to drag-and-drop files and other information on the desktop. Under Windows 3.1, this feature was limited to working with the File Manager applet; with the advent of OLE 2.0, Delphi allows any two components to use drag-and-drop to communicate.

10.3 Exchange data between two applications simultaneously

UNIX systems have a very powerful little application called "Chat." With this program, users on different machines linked over a network can type text to each other instantly—a sort of instant e-mail. Using Delphi and NetDDE, you can reproduce a Chat client for Windows.

10.4 Control another application from the current application

Sometimes you need to use an application which is not currently running, or which is being used by someone else. DDE allows one program to activate and control another. This How-To demonstrates this by using Delphi's DDE components to fully automate the Chat client created in How-To 10.3.

10.5 Manage communication among any number of applications

Once applications start communicating with one another, electronic traffic jams occur. Rather than hardwiring each communications link, this How-To uses DDE to permit any number of Chat clients (created in How-To 10.4) to be active and talk to each other at once; but it adds a way to find out whether the line is busy.

10.6 View the contents of an OLE 2.0 file

Object Linking and Embedding (OLE) is the metaphor for the future in Windows, creating files that contain not only data but information to allow the creating application to display and edit the data. The first release of Delphi has automated the process of using OLE 2.0 containers, and this How-To creates a component that permits easy viewing of any OLE file.

10.7 Create documents with text, graphics, and sound

The modern Windows environment is rich with sound, graphics, and formatted text. Instead of writing all the code to handle these diverse formats, you can use OLE 2.0 containers in your Delphi applications to provide complex information in documents.

10.1 How do I... Create a new program group in Program Manager?

COMPLEXITY: ADVANCED

Problem

Windows applications require more than simply copying files from a disk to the hard drive. Users need to choose which files to install, where to install them, and whether or not to create a new group in Program Manager for the application. Does Delphi have an easy way to handle all these tasks for my program?

Technique

A full-featured installation utility needs two special capabilities: copying a file (potentially a compressed file) and creating a new Program Manager group. The LZExpand unit of Delphi's Windows API calls, coupled with DDE, can perform both these tasks.

Steps

Run INSTALLR.EXE. Notice that it gives the location of the installation files as drive A; if you have installed them to your hard drive, change this entry to the new directory for the How-To example files. Click on the Install MyApp button. Then open Program Manager, and you will see that a new program group has been created with all the files checked on the MyApp Installation form, as shown in Figure 10-1. Delete the new group from Program Manager by selecting it and choosing Delete from the File menu. Open File Manager, select the MYAPPDIR directory, and then choose Delete from the File menu. If you like, experiment with deselecting the Create Program Manager Group check box and various file check boxes, or with giving a different target drive/directory. When you are finished experimenting, be sure to delete any Program Manager group you installed and any directory placed on your hard drive.

1. Create a new project with a blank form and name it INSTALLR.DPR. Name the unit INSTALLR.PAS.

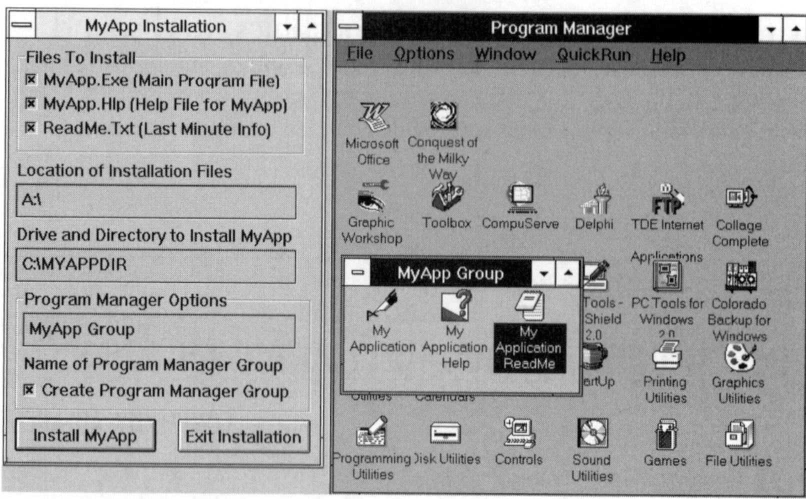

Figure 10-1 INSTALLR at run time

2. Add components to Form1 and set their properties as shown in Table 10-1.

Note: Be careful to add the two GroupBox components first, and place the check boxes inside them to ensure that the form displays correctly.

Table 10-1 Components, properties, and settings for Form1 in INSTALLR

COMPONENT	PROPERTY	SETTING
Form1	Type	Application Main Form
	Width	331
	Height	455
	Left	44
	Top	17
GroupBox1	Type	TGroupBox
	Left	8
	Top	8
	Width	297
	Height	105
	Caption	Files To Install
GroupBox2	Type	TGroupBox
	Left	8

COMPONENT	PROPERTY	SETTING
	Top	248
	Width	305
	Height	121
	Caption	Program Manager Options
Button1	Type	TButton
	Left	8
	Top	376
	Width	145
	Height	33
	Caption	Install MyApp
Button2	Type	TButton
	Left	176
	Top	376
	Width	137
	Height	33
	Caption	Exit Installation
Label1	Type	TLabel
	Left	8
	Top	120
	Width	222
	Height	20
	Caption	Location of Installation Files
	Alignment	taLeftJustify
Label2	Type	TLabel
	Left	8
	Top	184
	Width	285
	Height	20
	Caption	Drive and Directory to Install MyApp
	Alignment	taLeftJustify
Label3	Type	TLabel
	Left	8
	Top	64
	Width	268
	Height	20
	Caption	Name of Program Manager Group

continued on next page

continued from previous page

COMPONENT	PROPERTY	SETTING
	Alignment	taLeftJustify
CheckBox1	Type	TCheckBox
	Left	8
	Top	16
	Width	273
	Height	33
	Caption	MyApp.Exe (Main Program File)
	State	cbChecked
	Alignment	taRightJustify
	Ctl3D	True
CheckBox2	Type	TCheckBox
	Left	8
	Top	40
	Width	273
	Height	33
	Caption	MyApp.Hlp (Help File for MyApp)
	State	cbChecked
	Alignment	taRightJustify
	Ctl3D	True
CheckBox3	Type	TCheckBox
	Left	8
	Top	64
	Width	281
	Height	33
	Caption	ReadMe.Txt (Last Minute Info)
	State	cbChecked
	Alignment	taRightJustify
	Ctl3D	True
CheckBox4	Type	TCheckBox
	Left	16
	Top	336
	Width	289
	Height	25
	Caption	Create Program Manager Group
	State	cbChecked
	Alignment	taRightJustify

COMPONENT	PROPERTY	SETTING
	Ctl3D	True
Edit1	Type	TEdit
	Left	8
	Top	144
	Width	289
	Height	33
	Text	A:\
	Ctl3D	True
Edit2	Type	TEdit
	Left	8
	Top	208
	Width	289
	Height	33
	Text	C:\MYAPPDIR
	Ctl3D	True
Edit3	Type	TEdit
	Left	8
	Top	124
	Width	281
	Height	33
	Text	MyApp Group
	Ctl3D	True
DdeClientConv1	Type	TDdeClientConv
	ConnectMode	ddeAutomatic
	ddeService	PROGMAN
	ddeTopic	PROGMAN
	FormatChars	False

3. Activate the OnCreate event handler of Form1 and add the following code to initialize the application. Don't be concerned if some of the functions are unfamiliar; they are helper functions you will add later on in this How-To.

```
procedure TForm1.FormCreate(Sender: TObject);
begin
  {Initialize the data records for the installation}
  CreateInstallationRecord( 'A:\' , 'C:\MYAPPDIR' , 'MyApp Group' , 3 , True);
  AddFileToInstall( 1 , 'MyApp.Exe' , 'My Application' , 'MyAppExe.Ico' , 1 ,
   True );
  AddFileToInstall( 2 , 'MyApp.Hlp' , 'My Application Help' , 'MyAppHlp.Ico' ,
   0 , True );
```

continued on next page

continued from previous page

```
  AddFileToInstall( 3 , 'ReadMe.Txt' , 'My Application ReadMe' , 'ReadMe.Ico' ,
    1 , True );
end;
```

4. Go to the OnClick event of Button2 and type in this code, which prevents your program from being closed by mistake:

```
{Warn the user that installation is not finished and}
{exit if still desired.                              }
procedure TForm1.Button2Click(Sender: TObject);
begin
  if MessageDlg('Installation is not complete!  Exit now?',
    mtInformation, [mbYes, mbNo], 0) = mrYes then
  begin
    Close;
  end;
end;
```

5. To handle the selection or deselection of the check boxes, each one must be linked to a field in the installation record. Choose each check box's OnClick event handler, and then type in the code shown under its procedure name. When these handlers are clicked, they flip the on-off state of the attached record variable.

```
{Flip the state of a file to install}
procedure TForm1.CheckBox1Click(Sender: TObject);
begin
  The_Installation_Record.File_Array[ 1 ].Install_OK :=
   not( The_Installation_Record.File_Array[ 1 ].Install_OK );
end;

{Flip the state of a file to install}
procedure TForm1.CheckBox2Click(Sender: TObject);
begin
  The_Installation_Record.File_Array[ 2 ].Install_OK :=
   not( The_Installation_Record.File_Array[ 2 ].Install_OK );
end;

{Flip the state of a file to install}
procedure TForm1.CheckBox3Click(Sender: TObject);
begin
  The_Installation_Record.File_Array[ 3 ].Install_OK :=
   not( The_Installation_Record.File_Array[ 3 ].Install_OK );
end;

{Flip the state of permission to create a new ProgMan group}
procedure TForm1.CheckBox4Click(Sender: TObject);
begin
  The_Installation_Record.Install_PM_Group_OK :=
   not( The_Installation_Record.Install_PM_Group_OK );
end;
```

6. Next you set up the procedures to update the three information fields contained in the edit controls. Unlike the check boxes, you attach the code for the edit controls to the OnChange event. Select each edit control's OnChange event handler and fill in the code for that handler. Now whenever the user changes the text in the edit controls the underlying data used to install the program will change as well.

```
{Record any change in the startup directory}
procedure TForm1.Edit1Change(Sender: TObject);
begin
  The_Installation_Record.Starting_Directory :=
   Edit3.Text;
end;

{Record any change in the target directory}
procedure TForm1.Edit2Change(Sender: TObject);
begin
  The_Installation_Record.Installation_Directory :=
   Edit1.Text;
end;

{Record any change in the ProgMan group name}
procedure TForm1.Edit3Change(Sender: TObject);
begin
  The_Installation_Record.Group_Name :=
   Edit3.Text;
end;
```

7. To handle the installation procedure itself, go to the OnClick event of Button1 and type the following lines. Your application will install the desired files and optionally create a Program Manager group when the first button is clicked. Again, don't worry about unfamiliar function names, as you will enter these specialized assistant functions and procedures shortly.

```
procedure TForm1.Button1Click(Sender: TObject);
var  Counter_1 : Integer;
begin
  {if the installation directory cannot be created abort}
  if not CreateInstallDirectory then Close;
  for Counter_1 := 1 to
   The_Installation_Record.Total_Files_To_Install do
  begin
    with The_Installation_Record.File_Array[ Counter_1 ] do
    begin
      if Install_OK then
      begin
        {if a file is flagged to install, install it and its icon file}
        if not InstallFile( File_Name ) then Close;
        if not InstallFile( Icon_File_Name ) then Close;
      end;
    end;
  end;
  {if the user wishes to create the Program Manager group do so}
```

continued on next page

continued from previous page

```
  if The_Installation_Record.Install_PM_Group_OK then
  begin
    {abort if unable to contact ProgMan}
    if not CreateDDELinkToProgMan then Close;
    begin
      {abort if unable to create new group}
      if not CreateProgramGroup then Close;
      for Counter_1 := 1 to
       The_Installation_Record.Total_Files_To_Install do
      begin
        if The_Installation_Record.File_Array[ Counter_1 ].
         Install_OK then
        begin
          {if a file was installed add it to the ProgMan group}
          if not CreateProgramItem( Counter_1 ) then Close;
        end;
      end;
    end;
  end;
  {if nothing went wrong exit here}
  Close;
end;
```

8. Now give Delphi the specifications for the data records you will use to store information from the user and for your own needs. Go into the Code Editor and move up through the code until you find a line near the keyword *type*. Right after that line, add the following code to tell Delphi the structure of the records you will use in this program.

```
{ Record to hold basic installation information }
  Installation_File_Record = record
    File_Name: String;
    Icon_File_Name: String;
    Display_Name: String;
    File_State: Integer;
    Install_OK: boolean;
  end;
  { Central Record to hold indiviual file records and common info }
  Installation_Record = record
    Installation_Directory: String;
    Starting_Directory: String;
    Install_PM_Group_OK : Boolean;
    Group_Name: String;
    Total_Files_To_Install: Integer;
    File_Array: array [1 .. 3] of Installation_File_Record;
  end;
```

9. Move down through the code until you find the keyword *var*. Add the following code, which lets Delphi create the variable needed to store the installation information.

```
var
  Form1: TForm1;
  The_Installation_Record : Installation_Record;
```

10. Here's where you add a number of helper functions that allow Delphi to create and install the desired files. Move down in the Code Editor until you find the keyword *implementation*. Just below it add the following two procedures, which you called in step 7, to allow initialization of the installation records.

```
{ procedure to handle setting up default installation information }
procedure CreateInstallationRecord( StartingDirectory ,
           InstallingDirectory , GroupName : String;
            Total_Files : Integer; PMGroupOK : Boolean );

begin
  with The_Installation_Record do
  begin
    Starting_Directory := StartingDirectory;
    Installation_Directory := InstallingDirectory;
    Group_Name := GroupName;
    Total_Files_To_Install := Total_Files;
    Install_PM_Group_OK := PMGroupOK;
  end;
end;

{ procedure to add a file to be installed }
procedure AddFileToInstall( FileNumber : Integer;
           FileName , DisplayName , IconFileName : String;
            State : Integer; DoInstall : Boolean );

begin
  with The_Installation_Record.File_Array[ FileNumber ] do
  begin
    File_Name := FileName;
    Display_Name := DisplayName;
    Icon_File_Name := IconFileName;
    File_State := State;
    Install_OK := DoInstall;
  end;
end;
```

11. Now add the helper function to create the installation directory on the hard disk.

```
{ function to create installation directory and handle errors }
{ returns true if succeeded, false otherwise.                 }
function CreateInstallDirectory : Boolean;
begin
  CreateInstallDirectory := True;
  try
    MkDir( The_Installation_Record.Installation_Directory );
  except
    on EFCreateError do
    begin
      MessageDlg('Unable To Create Installation Directory!', mtError,
       [mbOk], 0);
      CreateInstallDirectory := False;
    end;
  end;
end;
```

12. The next helper function handles the complex code to copy a file from one place to another. It uses the LZExpand unit, which you will add to the *uses* clause in step 15.

```
{ procedure to install a file, using LZ unit functions }
{ returns false if didn't succeed, true otherwise       }
Function InstallFile( Filename : String ) : Boolean;

var TheName          : PChar;
    DDE_String       : String;
    The_Style        : Word;
    File1 ,
    File2             : Integer;
    The_TOFS         : TOFStruct;
    LZResult         : Longint;

begin
  InstallFile := True;
  GETMEM( TheName , 256 );
  TheName := '';
  DDE_String := '';
  DDE_String :=
   The_Installation_Record.Starting_Directory;
  DDE_String := DDE_String + FileName;
  StrPCopy( TheName , DDE_String );
  The_Style := OF_READWRITE;
  {Open the source file for reading}
  File1 := LZOpenFile( TheName , The_TOFS , The_Style );
  if File1 < 0 then { Unable to open source file }
  begin
    MessageDlg('Unable To Install File ' + FileName , mtError,[mbOk], 0);
    InstallFile := False;
    Exit;
  end;
  DDE_String := '';
  DDE_String :=
   The_Installation_Record.Installation_Directory;
  DDE_String := DDE_String + '\' + FileName;
  TheName := '';
  StrPCopy( TheName , DDE_String );
  The_Style := OF_CREATE;
  {Create the destination file as new}
  File2 := LZOpenFile( TheName , The_TOFS , The_Style );
  if File2 < 0 then { Unable to create destination file }
  begin
    MessageDlg('Unable To Install File ' + FileName , mtError,[mbOk], 0);
    InstallFile := False;
    Exit;
  end;
  {Copy the file over}
  LZResult := LZCopy( File1 , File2 );
  {Close all files}
  _LCLOSE( File1 );
  _LCLOSE( File2 );
  If LZResult < 0 then
```

```
  begin
    MessageDlg('Unable To Install File ' + FileName , mtError,[mbOk], 0);
    InstallFile := False;
  end;
end;
```

13. Now you can set up the functions to call Program Manager. First, enter the following helper procedure to make it simpler to create the complicated character groups that Program Manager's interface uses.

```
{ procedure to assemble the installation strings for Program Manager }
procedure CreateProgmanInstallStrings( var CommandLine , IconPath , Minimized ,
            X_Position , Y_Position : String; Item : Integer );

begin
  {To maintain icon spacing in the group display give each icon some room}
  STR( ( 20 + (( Item - 1 ) * 80 )) , X_Position );
  Y_Position := '20';
  {The command line must include the directory where the file exists}
  CommandLine := The_Installation_Record.
   Installation_Directory + '\' +
    The_Installation_Record.File_Array[ Item ].
     File_Name;
  {To display an icon the path to the icon file must be included}
  IconPath := The_Installation_Record.
   Installation_Directory + '\' +
    The_Installation_Record.File_Array[ Item ].
     Icon_File_Name;
  {An empty string indicates a normal program startup while anything}
  {else begins the program as an icon.                               }
  if The_Installation_Record.File_Array[ Item ].
   File_State > 0 then Minimized := ''
    else Minimized := '1';
end;
```

14. Enter the three specialized functions that establish the link to Program Manager and install a new group and new program items in that group. Rather than explain the process here, detailed comments in each helper function explain key elements of the code.

```
{ function to open the DDE Link to Progman. Returns true unless }
{ the link could not be opened.                                 }
function CreateDDELinkToProgMan : Boolean;

var DDE_OK : Boolean;

begin
  CreateDDELinkToProgMan := True;
  {Both the server and the topic for Program Manager are PROGMAN}
  DDE_OK := Form1.DdeClientConv1.SetLink ('PROGMAN','PROGMAN');
  if not DDE_OK then
  begin
    MessageDlg('Unable To Contact Program Manager!', mtError ,[mbOk], 0);
    CreateDDELinkToProgMan := False;
```

continued on next page

continued from previous page

```
  end;
end;

{ function to create a new Program Manager group. Returns true unless }
{ contact is lost or the group name exists or is invalid.            }
function CreateProgramGroup : Boolean;

var DDE_String : String;
    DDE_Data   : PChar;
    DDE_OK     : Boolean;

begin
  CreateProgramGroup := True;
  {Assemble the data for the new group in a string and copy it to a Pchar}
  DDE_String := '[CreateGroup("' +
   The_Installation_Record.Group_Name + '")]';
  GetMem ( DDE_Data , Length( DDE_String ) + 1 );
  StrPCopy ( DDE_Data , DDE_String );
  {Program Manager accepts DDE commands only via ExecuteMacro()}
  DDE_OK := Form1.DdeClientConv1.ExecuteMacro( DDE_Data , False);
  FreeMem ( DDE_Data , Length( DDE_String ) + 1 );
  if not DDE_OK then
  begin
    MessageDlg('Unable To Create Program Group ' +
     The_Installation_Record.Group_Name , mtError ,[mbOk], 0);
    CreateProgramGroup := False;
  end;
end;

{ Function to create a Program Manager Group Item. It returns true}
{ unless the item cannot be added.                               }
function CreateProgramItem( ItemNumber : Integer ) : Boolean;

var Current_X_Position_String ,
    Current_Y_Position_String ,
    Command_Line_String       ,
    Icon_Path_String          ,
    Minimized_String          ,
    DDE_String                  : String;
    DDE_Data                    : PChar;
    DDE_OK                      : Boolean;

begin
  CreateProgramItem := True;
  {Obtain current item data strings}
  CreateProgManInstallStrings( Command_Line_String , Icon_Path_String ,
   Minimized_String , Current_X_Position_String , Current_Y_Position_String ,
    ItemNumber );
  {Assemble the data as a string. separate individual items by "" and ,    }
  {,, indicates an unused position in the command string to Program Manager}
  DDE_String :=
   '[AddItem("' + Command_Line_String + '","' +
    The_Installation_Record.File_Array[ ItemNumber ].
     Display_Name + '","' + Icon_Path_String + '",,"'
     + Current_X_Position_String + '","' +
```

```
        Current_Y_Position_String + '","' +
      The_Installation_Record.Installation_Directory +
        '",,"' + Minimized_String + '")]';
  GETMEM ( DDE_Data , Length( DDE_String ) + 1 );
  StrPCopy ( DDE_Data , DDE_String );
  DDE_OK := Form1.DdeClientConv1.ExecuteMacro( DDE_Data , False );
  FREEMEM ( DDE_Data , Length( DDE_String ) + 1 );
  if not DDE_OK then
  begin
    MessageDlg('Unable To Create Program Item ' + Command_Line_String ,
      mtError ,[mbOk], 0);
    CreateProgramItem := False;
  end;
end;
```

15. Move up to the very top of the code until you see the first *uses* clause. At the very end, add LZExpand before the final semicolon.

```
uses
  SysUtils, WinTypes, WinProcs, Messages, Classes, Graphics, Controls,
  Forms, Dialogs, DdeMan, StdCtrls, LZExpand;
```

16. Compile and test the project.

How It Works

Delphi has automated much of the complexity of DDE behind the DDEClientConv object's interface. You can establish a full DDE conversation with any other application provided two critical pieces of data are known: the Service, which is normally the application's executable name, and its Topic—that is, the file of data to be used in the exchange. For Program Manager, research shows that both the Service and Topic are PROGMAN. The SetLink method of DDEClientConv establishes the conversation if Program Manager is available. There are then several possible methods of sending information to the DDE server, including PokeData and ExecuteMacro. Further checking into the Windows SDK reveals that Program Manager accepts data via ExecuteMacro, with specific and complex string formats. These formats are explained in detail in the CreateProgmanInstallStrings procedure. Once the data is transferred to Program Manager, closing the application automatically ends the DDE link due to the destructor functionality of the DDEClientConv object.

Standard Pascal does not provide file-copying capabilities. Fortunately, the LZExpand unit ships with Delphi, and it provides API calls that allow not only direct file copying, but file decompression using the Lempel-Ziv algorithm popular in the "zip" file formats. (However, LZ functions are not compatible with the PKZip program's files.) To use LZExpand, first a source file is opened with LZOpen set to read and write. Then the target file is created with LZOpen set to create. Using stored file handles, LZCopy is then called and does the actual data transfer. Had the source file been a compressed file, it could have decompressed as well during the process.

Comments

The application in this How-To spends considerable time trapping errors—a user-friendly trait that is often overlooked in program design.

Also, it is important to notice the setting of ddeAutomatic in the design of the DDEClientConv object. If this property is set to ddeManual, an additional call to OpenLink is required to establish the conversation, and to CloseLink when closing the application. Delphi's documentation is not entirely clear on this point.

10.2 How do I... Use drag-and-drop in my applications?

COMPLEXITY: INTERMEDIATE

Problem

One of the principal advantages of the Windows desktop environment is the ability to move information around by simply clicking the mouse on an item and dragging it to another location. This drag-and-drop functionality is actually part of the OLE system; is there an easy way to give my application access to such cutting-edge power?

Technique

Drag-and-drop was initially available in Windows as part of the File Manager applet using standard Windows messages and API functions. Later, OLE was developed and this capability became available to other applications. Delphi has partially automated the OLE 2.0 standard, allowing programs to use drag-and-drop both with File Manager and to exchange information between any two controls of any forms within the same Delphi application.

Steps

Run TRASHIT.EXE. Its main form will appear, as shown in Figure 10-2. Using the directory outline, move to a directory with several unnecessary files; then click on one in the file list window, drag it down to the trash can icon you see on the bottom of the desktop, and let go of the mouse. A dialog box appears, asking if you wish to delete the dragged file. Say yes, and it will disappear, deleted normally but retrievable via standard undelete utilities, such as those from Central Point Software or DOS 6.x. Double-click on the trash can icon, and a configuration form similar to the one in Figure 10-3 will appear. You can choose from three types of deletions and whether or not to confirm each deletion. Click on OK to keep any changes you make or Cancel to leave the settings the way they were. Select multiple items with the mouse and drag them to the trash can (or one of the other icons if you changed the deletion method). If Confirm is active, you will be asked to approve each removal; if Confirm is off, the files will simply be deleted.

Note: Normal undelete utilities cannot restore the Shredder (Reset Deletion) option, but sophisticated tools like DiskFix from Central Point Systems can; *no* utility will recover a file deleted with the Incinerator (Overwrite Deletion) option! For this reason, these two functions are turned off in the version shipped with the book. If you wish to activate them, follow the instructions in the note following the last step.

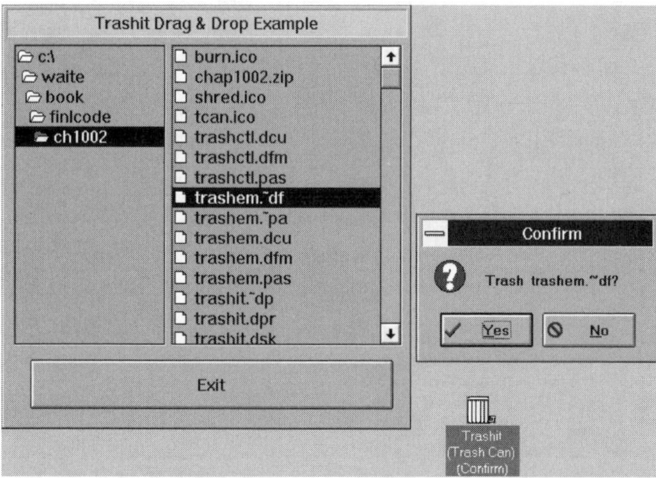

Figure 10-2 TRASHIT at run time, showing a file deletion

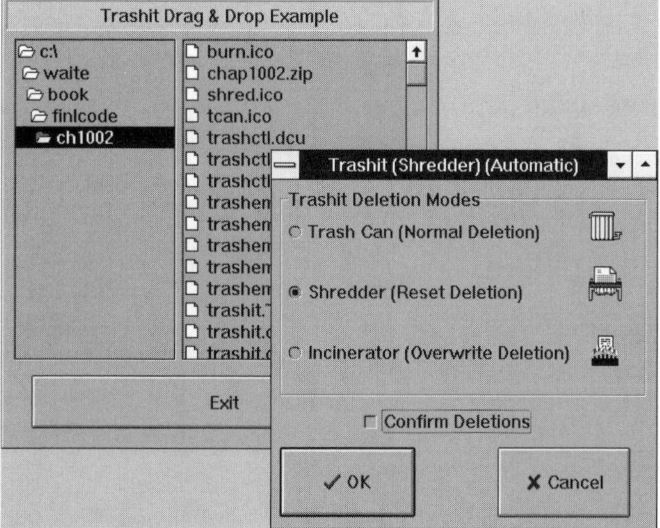

Figure 10-3 TRASHIT's control panel at run time, showing confirmation off and reset delete selected

1. Create a new project with a blank form and save it as TRASHIT.DPR. Name the unit TRASHEM.PAS.
2. Add components to Form1 and set properties as shown in Table 10-2.

Table 10-2 Components, properties, and settings for FMForm in TRASHIT

COMPONENT	PROPERTY	SETTING
FMForm	Type	Main Application Form
	Left	31
	Top	13
	Width	415
	Height	419
	+BorderIcons	
	-biSystemMenu	False
	-biMaximize	False
	-biMinimize	False
	BorderStyle	bsDialog
	Caption	Trashit Drag & Drop Example
Button1	Type	TButton
	Left	24
	Top	320
	Width	369
	Height	49
	Caption	Exit
DirectoryListBox1	Type	TDirectoryListBox
	Left	8
	Top	8
	Width	153
	Height	297
	FileList	FileListBox1
FileListBox1	Type	TFileListBox
	Left	168
	Top	8
	Width	233
	Height	297
	ShowGlyphs	True
	MultiSelect	True

3. Go to Delphi's File menu and choose New Form. Select a blank form. Then rename the new unit TRASHCTL.PAS. Add the controls with properties set as in Table 10-3.

Table 10-3 Components, properties, and settings for TrashitControlForm in TRASHCTL

COMPONENT	PROPERTY	SETTING
TrashitControlForm	Type	BlankForm
	Left	96
	Top	31
	Width	379
	Height	361
	+BorderIcons	
	-biSystemMenu	False
	-biMaximize	False
	-biMinimize	False
	BorderStyle	bsSingle
	Visible	True
	Caption	Trashit (Shredder) (Automatic)
	WindowState	wsMinimized
GroupBox1	Type	TGroupBox
	Left	8
	Top	8
	Width	353
	Height	193
	Caption	Trashit Deletion Modes
RadioButton1	Type	TRadioButton
	Left	8
	Top	24
	Width	257
	Height	33
	Caption	Trash Can (Normal Deletion)
	Checked	True
RadioButton2	Type	TRadioButton
	Left	8
	Top	80
	Width	265

continued on next page

continued from previous page

COMPONENT	PROPERTY	SETTING
	Height	33
	Caption	Shredder (Reset Deletion)
	Checked	False
RadioButton3	Type	TRadioButton
	Left	8
	Top	136
	Width	289
	Height	33
	Caption	Incinerator (Overwrite Deletion)
	Checked	False
Image1	Type	TImage
	Left	296
	Top	16
	Width	33
	Height	41
	Visible	True
Image2	Type	TImage
	Left	296
	Top	72
	Width	33
	Height	41
	Visible	True
Image3	Type	TImage
	Left	296
	Top	136
	Width	33
	Height	33
	Visible	True
CheckBox1	Type	TCheckBox
	Left	88
	Top	208
	Width	169
	Height	33
	Caption	Confirm Deletions
	Checked	True
BitBtn1	Type	TButton

COMPONENT	PROPERTY	SETTING
	Left	8
	Top	248
	Width	129
	Height	65
	Kind	bkOK
BitBtn2	Type	TButton
	Left	216
	Top	248
	Width	129
	Height	65
	Kind	bkCancel

4. Select the Image1 component and go to the Picture property in the Object Inspector. Click on the ellipsis (...) button, and then select Load from the Picture Editor that appears. Type in **TCAN.ICO** for the file name, with any necessary directory information for the example files from the CD. Select OK, and the trash can icon appears in the control. Do the same for the Image2 component, using the file name **SHRED.ICO**, and the Image3 component using **BURN.ICO**. Now the icons are in place for the form. Click on the drop-down box for components and select TrashitControlForm. Select its Icon property and enter **TCAN.ICO** again. This will start the form with the trash can as its icon, which is what you want since the default deletion mode is normal.

5. Now select the OnClick event of the Button1 component of FMForm and add the following code to close the application.

```
procedure TFMForm.Button1Click(Sender: TObject);
begin
  Close;
end;
```

6. Select the FileListBox1 component and activate its OnMouseDown event box. Add these lines to handle Delphi component-based dragging and dropping.

```
procedure TFMForm.FileListMouseDown(Sender: TObject; Button: TMouseButton;
  Shift: TShiftState; X, Y: Integer);
begin
  {check for left button}
  if Button = mbLeft then
    {check for the sending object to be a filelistbox using special   }
    {as operator which will not process the loop if the typecast fails}
    with Sender as TFileListBox do
    begin
      {if the listbox is not currently empty then start dragging}
      if ItemAtPos(Point(X, Y), True) >= 0 then
```

continued on next page

continued from previous page

```
        BeginDrag(False);
    end;
end;
```

7. Go to the OnEndDrag event for the same control and enter these two lines to handle a successful Delphi component drag-and-drop operation:

```
procedure TFMForm.FileListEndDrag(Sender, Target: TObject; X, Y: Integer);
begin
  {if the user dragged a file to the trashcan do an update}
  if Target  nil then FileListBox1.Update;
end;
```

8. Select the TrashitControlForm and activate its OnCreate event handler; type in the following program lines to take care of initializing the form.

```
procedure TTrashitControlForm.FormCreate(Sender: TObject);
begin
  {create the three icons for our display}
  TrashCanIcon := TIcon.Create;
  ShredderIcon := TIcon.Create;
  IncineratorIcon := TIcon.Create;
  {set them to our display files; use your examples directory in the name!}
  TrashCanIcon.LoadFromFile( 'TCan.Ico' );
  ShredderIcon.LoadFromFile( 'Shred.Ico' );
  IncineratorIcon.LoadFromFile( 'Burn.Ico' );
  {set up the state variables for normal deletion and confirmation}
  DeletionType := 1;
  ConfirmState := True;
  {set up the "memory" variables so we can restore the old state}
  OldDeletionType := DeletionType;
  OldConfirmState := ConfirmState;
  {set up our user-friendly caption strings}
  StateString := 'Trashit (Trash Can) ';
  ConfirmString := '(Confirm)';
{ Tell File Manager to accept dragged files }
  DragAcceptFiles( Handle , true );
  { Set up the message handler for the dropfiles message }
  Application.OnMessage := AppMessage;
  { Minimize the window }
  WindowState := wsMinimized;
end;
```

9. Staying in the code, move up to just under the *type* keyword and add the following line, so that Delphi can recognize a helper variable.

```
type
  SelectionArray = array[ 1 .. 256 ] of Integer;
  TTrashitControlForm = class(TForm)
```

10. Move down in the code to the keyword *var* and add the following lines to declare other helper variables.

```
var
  TrashitControlForm: TTrashitControlForm;
```

```
  OldDeletionType ,
  DeletionType : Integer;
  ConfirmState ,
  OldConfirmState : Boolean;
  TrashCanIcon ,
  ShredderIcon ,
  IncineratorIcon : TIcon;
  StateString ,
  ConfirmString  : String;
```

11. Next, select each of the radio buttons in turn on the form. Activate their OnClick handlers and type in the appropriate code to handle user changes in the deletion mode.

```
{set the trashit icon to a trashcan and its state to normal}
procedure TTrashitControlForm.RadioButton1Click(Sender: TObject);
begin
  TrashitControlForm.Icon := TrashcanIcon;
  DeletionType := 1;
  StateString := 'Trashit (Trash Can) ';
  {reset the form caption for user-friendliness}
  TrashitControlForm.Caption := StateString + ConfirmString;
end;

{set the trashit icon to a shredder and its state to reset}
procedure TTrashitControlForm.RadioButton2Click(Sender: TObject);
begin
  TrashitControlForm.Icon := ShredderIcon;
  DeletionType := 2;
  StateString := 'Trashit (Shredder) ';
  {reset the form caption for user-friendliness}
  TrashitControlForm.Caption := StateString + ConfirmString;
end;

{set the trashit icon to an incinerator and its state to overwrite}
procedure TTrashitControlForm.RadioButton3Click(Sender: TObject);
begin
  TrashitControlForm.Icon := IncineratorIcon;
  DeletionType := 3;
  StateString := 'Trashit (Incinerator) ';
  {reset the form caption for user-friendliness}
  TrashitControlForm.Caption := StateString + ConfirmString;
end;
```

12. Select the check box and activate its OnClick handler; add these lines of code to take care of user changes in the confirmation option.

```
{toggle the confirmation state of the form}
procedure TTrashitControlForm.CheckBox1Click(Sender: TObject);
begin
  ConfirmState := Not( ConfirmState );
  if ConfirmState then ConfirmString := '(Confirm)'
   else ConfirmString := '(Automatic)';
  {reset the form caption for user-friendliness}
```

continued on next page

continued from previous page

```
  TrashitControlForm.Caption := StateString + ConfirmString;
end;
```

13. Now select the OK button's OnClick event handler and type in the following code, which saves information needed to reset a previous state from a cancel selection and reminimizes the form.

```
procedure TTrashitControlForm.BitBtn1Click(Sender: TObject);
begin
  {set the old states to remember the new states}
  OldDeletionType := DeletionType;
  OldConfirmState := ConfirmState;
  {minimize the form so it goes back to its icon}
  TrashitControlForm.WindowState := wsMinimized;
end;
```

14. Choose the Cancel button and enter the following lines in its OnClick handler. This allows user-friendly cancellation of control form choices by restoring the original states.

```
procedure TTrashitControlForm.BitBtn2Click(Sender: TObject);
begin
  {use the saved previous deletion state to reset the icons,}
  {radio buttons, and caption strings.                      }
  case OldDeletionType of
    1 : begin
          TrashitControlForm.Icon := TrashcanIcon;
          DeletionType := OldDeletionType;
          RadioButton1.Checked := True;
          StateString := 'Shreddem (Trash Can) ';
        end;
    2 : begin
          TrashitControlForm.Icon := ShredderIcon;
          DeletionType := OldDeletionType;
          RadioButton2.Checked := True;
          StateString  := 'Shreddem (Shredder) ';
      end;
    3 : begin
          TrashitControlForm.Icon := IncineratorIcon;
          DeletionType := OldDeletionType;
          RadioButton3.Checked := True;
          StateString := 'Shreddem (Incinerator) ';
        end;
  end;
  {reset the confirmation state and the checkbox; double code is a}
  {possible Delphi memory bug; remove it if not needed            }
  ConfirmState := OldConfirmState;
  CheckBox1.Checked := OldConfirmState;
  {this is the bug line}
  ConfirmState := OldConfirmState;
  {reset the caption string}
  if ConfirmState then ConfirmString := '(Confirm)' else
   ConfirmString := '(Automatic)';
  {reset the form's caption and minimize it back to its old icon}
  TrashitControlForm.Caption := StateString + ConfirmString;
```

```
  TrashitControlForm.WindowState := wsMinimized;
end;
```

15. You're ready to set up the form to handle deleting items that are dragged and dropped onto it. Select the main form in the Object Inspector and activate its OnDragOver event handler. Type in this code to allow the form to accept dragged items.

```
procedure TTrashitControlForm.GroupBox1DragOver(Sender, Source: TObject; X, Y:
Integer;
  State: TDragState; var Accept: Boolean);
begin
  {ignore drags from non-file listboxes}
  if Source is TFileListBox then
  Accept := True;
end;
```

16. You must now tell your form how to actually do the deletions for dropped files. Move to the Object Inspector and select the OnDragDrop event handler. Type in the following lines of code. Don't worry if they contain unfamiliar functions and procedures; these are more helper functions you'll add in a moment.

```
procedure TTrashitControlForm.GroupBox1DragDrop(Sender, Source: TObject; X, Y:
Integer);
var TypeString ,
    CurrentFileName : String;
    Counter_1 ,
    TotalItems   : Integer;
    TheSelections : SelectionArray;
begin
  {make sure our source is a filelistbox}
  if Source is TFileListBox then
  begin
    {set our deletion type in a user-friendly string}
    case DeletionType of
      1 : TypeString := 'Trash ';
      2 : TypeString := 'Shred ';
      3 : TypeString := 'Incinerate ';
    end;
    {get one or more dragged files}
    GetMultipleDraggedFiles( Source , TotalItems , TheSelections );
    for Counter_1 := 1 to TotalItems do
    begin
      {do the typecast on our source}
      with (Source as TFileListBox) do
      begin
        {get the current file from our list}
        CurrentFileName := Items[ TheSelections[ Counter_1 ]];
        {if we are set to confirm deletes do so}
        if ConfirmState then
        begin
          {only delete an entry if dialog says to}
          if ConfirmFileDeletion( TypeString , CurrentFileName ) then
          begin
```

continued on next page

continued from previous page

```
            {use type setting to choose delete type; note that for}
            {this example the dangerous ones are turned off!      }
            case DeletionType of
              1 : NormalFileDelete( CurrentFileName );
              2 : {ResetFileDelete( CurrentFilename )};
              3 : {OverwriteFileDelete( CurrentFileName )};
            end;
          end;
        end
        else
        begin
          {if confirmation is off just delete each file in sequence}
          case DeletionType of
            1 : NormalFileDelete( CurrentFileName );
            2 : {ResetFileDelete( CurrentFilename )};
            3 : {OverwriteFileDelete( CurrentFileName )};
          end;
        end;
        {update our filelistbox before we leave just in case!}
        Update;
      end;
    end;
  end;
end;
```

17. Now the helper functions listed in the procedure above must be added. There are several of them, and the code is listed below. Pay particular attention to the comments, as some of these functions can be very dangerous! First, add this procedure to obtain a list of multiple file names from the dragged object.

```
procedure GetMultipleDraggedFiles( var Source : TObject; var Total_Files : Integer;
                                   var Selections : SelectionArray );
var Counter_1 ,
    Index_Number : Integer;

begin
  {convert our generic source to filelistbox}
  with Source as TFileListBox do
  begin
    {index our array from 1}
    Index_Number := 1;
    {check the total items}
    for Counter_1 := 1 to Items.Count do
    begin
      {if an item is selected put its position in the array}
      if Selected[ Counter_1 - 1 ] then
      begin
        Selections[ Index_Number ] := Counter_1 - 1;
        Index_Number := Index_Number + 1;
      end;
    end;
    {store the total selections even if it's just 1}
    Total_Files := Index_Number - 1;
  end;
end;
```

18. Next, add this function to obtain user confirmation prior to deleting a file.

```
function ConfirmFileDeletion( DeleteTypeString , FileName : String ) : Boolean;

begin
  {use a message dialog to confirm a deletion}
  if MessageDlg( DeleteTypeString + ' ' + FileName + '?',
      mtConfirmation, [mbYes, mbNo], 0) = idYes then ConfirmFileDeletion := True
        else ConfirmFileDeletion := False;
end;
```

19. This procedure handles normal file deletions.

```
procedure NormalFileDelete( FileName : String );

begin
  {standard delete call. can be undone with undelete; safe to use}
  DeleteFile( FileName );
end;
```

20. The next procedure is the reset delete; it can only be activated by the method described in the note at the end of these steps.

```
procedure ResetFileDelete( FileName : String );

var The_File : Integer;

begin
  {secure deletion; CANNOT be undone with undelete, requires diskfix tool}
  {use carefully!                                                                }
  {this call resets the file size to 0 so that normal undelete can't fix }
  The_File := FileOpen( FileName , fmCreate );
  FileClose( The_File );
  DeleteFile( FileName);
end;
```

21. This procedure is the overwrite delete and is *extremely* dangerous. It can only be activated as explained in the endnote.

```
procedure OverwriteFileDelete( FileName : String );

var The_File : File of Byte;
    Counter_1 ,
    The_Size : Longint;
    The_Byte : Byte;

begin
  {*******************************************************************}
  {*                                                                 *}
  {*    THIS IS A VERY VERY DANGEROUS FUNCTION! USE IT WITH EXTREME   *}
  {*    CAUTION!!!! A FILE DELETED THIS WAY CAN ONLY BE RESTORED FROM *}
  {*    TAPE BACKUP!!!                                               *}
  {*                                                                 *}
  {*******************************************************************}
```

continued on next page

continued from previous page

```
   The_Byte := 255;
   AssignFile( The_File , FileName );
   Reset( The_File );
   The_Size := FileSize( The_File );
   {loop through here and write a random number to the file over its     }
   {entire length. This makes it effectively impossible to recover it!  }
   For Counter_1 := 0 to The_Size - 1 do
   begin
     Seek( The_File , Counter_1 );
     Write( The_File , The_Byte );
   end;
   Close( The_File );
end;
```

22. Now enter this assistant procedure, which takes care of messages from File Manager involving dragging and dropping files from it to TRASHIT.

```
procedure TTrashitControlForm.AppMessage(var Msg: TMsg; var Handled: Boolean);

var TheDropHandle : THandle;
    The_PChar        : array[ 0 ..79 ] of char;
    Counter_1    ,
    TotalFiles      : Integer;
    TypeString ,
    CurrentFileName : String;
begin
  { Check for a dropfiles message }
  if Msg.Message = WM_DROPFILES then
  begin
    { Set handled to true to stop further message passing }
    Handled := true;
    { Get the handle from the dropped file }
    TheDropHandle := THandle( Msg.wParam );
    { Obtain the total files from the File Manager }
    TotalFiles := DragQueryFile( TheDropHandle ,
                                 65535          ,
                                 The_PChar      ,
                                 80               );
    { Determine each file's name and its status for deletion }
    For Counter_1 := 0 to TotalFiles - 1 do
    begin
      DragQueryFile( TheDropHandle ,
                     Counter_1      ,
                     The_PChar      ,
                     80               );
      {set our deletion type in a user-friendly string}
      case DeletionType of
        1 : TypeString := 'Trash ';
        2 : TypeString := 'Shred ';
        3 : TypeString := 'Incinerate ';
      end;
      CurrentFileName := StrPas( The_PChar );
      {if we are set to confirm deletes do so}
      if ConfirmState then
      begin
```

```
        {only delete an entry if dialog says to}
        if ConfirmFileDeletion( TypeString , CurrentFileName ) then
        begin
          {use type setting to choose delete type; note that for}
          {this example the dangerous ones are turned off!      }
          case DeletionType of
            1 : NormalFileDelete( CurrentFileName );
            2 : {ResetFileDelete( CurrentFilename )};
            3 : {OverwriteFileDelete( CurrentFileName )};
          end;
        end;
      end
      else
      begin
        {if confirmation is off just delete each file in sequence}
        case DeletionType of
          1 : NormalFileDelete( CurrentFileName );
          2 : {ResetFileDelete( CurrentFilename )};
          3 : {OverwriteFileDelete( CurrentFileName )};
        end;
      end;
    end;
  end;
end;
```

23. Finally, move to the very end of the list of procedures for the TrashitControlForm and add this procedure declaration, which allows Delphi to use the assistant procedure you just entered.

```
    procedure CheckBox1Click(Sender: TObject);
    procedure AppMessage(var Msg: TMsg; var Handled: Boolean);
  private
```

24. Compile and test the program.

Note: Setting the trash can to anything but normal deletions does nothing; this is a protection for novice users. If you wish to use the more powerful deletion functions, remove the "comment" brackets ({}) from the second and third function calls in the two sections of the OnDragDrop and AppMessage event handlers. Remember, it is *difficult* to recover files from the reset delete and **impossible** from overwrite!

How It Works

The key technology that makes TRASHIT work is built into every control in Delphi, through its event handlers for dragging. Setting the BeginDrag handler in the FileListBox control tells FileListBox to allow dragging its file names to other controls. (The false parameter tells Delphi not to start a drag operation until the move has advanced five pixels, thus allowing mouse clicks to avoid the overhead of starting and stopping a drag operation.) Putting in the OnEndDrag handler is not strictly required for this example but it might be in a more complex application—one that re-sorts a database, for example.

The workhorse routines are in the control panel, which handles the actual file deletion. First the OnDragOver event handler is used to accept only drags from file list boxes. Nothing else is going to be processed. Instead, it could have accepted only Tbitmap objects, dragged from a picture control and sent to the printer; the beauty of the Delphi system is that it can send any control to any other control using the *as* and *is* keywords. Then to actually delete the files sent to the control, a call is made to the OnDragDrop handler. Again the key functionality is in the ability to turn the generic Source parameter into a TFileListBox with the *same information* as the one in the other form. It is difficult to overstate the power this gives programmers, since an arbitrarily complex object can exchange information this way provided it is a descendant of the generic Tobject object. The extra functions, such as having the form minimize itself and show a different icon depending on its state, are chrome, but they make the applet much more user friendly.

For completeness, a message handling routine for the older WM_DROPFILES message from the File Manager applet is also included. This allows TRASHIT to work by itself on the desktop as well as with the companion list boxes.

Comments

There is a price to pay for the amazing power of Delphi's drag-and-drop; it currently only works with other forms compiled in the same Delphi application. It will not work with other Delphi applications or with non-Delphi programs at this time. Borland has indicated it plans to include full support for OLE 2.0 servers and automation in a future release, at which point these limitations will cease to exist. But even now, consider how powerful this functionality is: with one mouse action a user can transfer as much information as programmers can stuff into a Delphi object.

10.3 How do I... Exchange data between two applications simultaneously?

COMPLEXITY: EASY

Problem

The growth of networked computing has made it more and more essential that applications be able to communicate with one another. Does this mean I'll have to learn complex modem and LAN protocols to add this capability to my programs?

Technique

So far you've used OLE and DDE only with highly specialized or built-in functions. In this How-To you will combine Delphi's functionality with DDE on a single user system or NetDDE under Windows for Workgroups to create a Windows version of the popular UNIX Chat client.

Steps

Run HARRYCHT.EXE. If you press the Chat With Tom button, either on the same PC or with TOMCHT.EXE installed on another computer linked to yours via NetDDE, the TOMCHT screen will appear on your monitor (or the networked computer's monitor). Tom can press the Chat With Harry button, and the two of you can type text in the boxes labeled Talk To Tom/Harry. The text will appear in the Tom/Harry's Replies memo fields. Figure 10-4 shows the two-way conversation.

Note: Pressing ENTER doesn't carry over—a small bug in Delphi.

1. Create a new project with a blank form and name the project HARRYCHT.DPR. Name the unit HARCCLI.PAS.
2. Add components and set their properties as shown in Table 10-4.

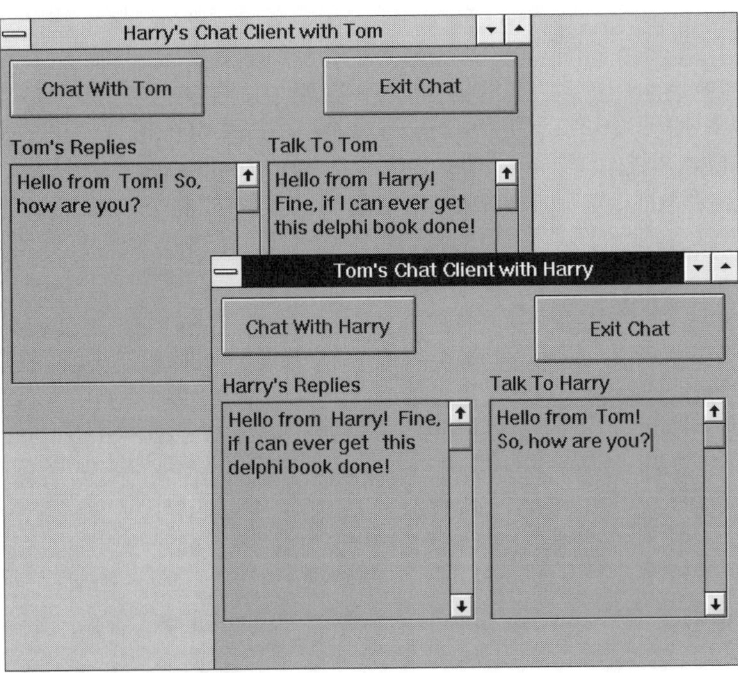

Figure 10-4 HARRYCHT and TOMCHT at run time showing two-way networked conversation

Table 10-4 Components, properties, and settings of HarrysChatForm in HARRYCHT

COMPONENT	PROPERTY	SETTING
HarrysChatForm	Type	Application Main Form
	Left	33
	Top	38
	Width	470
	Height	358
	Caption	Harry's Chat Client with Tom
	BorderStyle	bsSingle
Button1	Type	TButton
	Left	8
	Top	8
	Width	297
	Height	49
	Caption	Chat With Tom
Button2	Type	TButton
	Left	280
	Top	8
	Width	169
	Height	49
	Caption	Exit Chat
TomsRepliesMemo	Type	TMemo
	Left	8
	Top	96
	Width	217
	Height	185
	Lines	(blank)
HarrysTalkMemo	Type	TMemo
	Left	232
	Top	96
	Width	217
	Height	185
	Lines	Hello from Harry!
Label1	Type	TLabel
	Left	8
	Top	72
	Width	129

COMPONENT	PROPERTY	SETTING
	Height	25
	Caption	Tom's Replies
Label2	Type	TLabel
	Left	232
	Top	72
	Width	121
	Height	25
	Caption	Talk To Tom
DdeClientItem	Type	TDdeClientItem
	Lines	(blank)
DdeClient	Type	TDdeClientConv
	ConnectMode	ddeAutomatic
	FormatChars	False
HarrysChatLines	Type	TDdeServerItem
	ServerConv	HarrysChatServer
	Lines	Hello from Harry!
HarrysChatServer	Type	TDdeServerConv

3. Select the Button1 OnClick event handler and enter this code to set up the DDE link with TOMCHT.EXE.

```
procedure THarrysChatForm.Button1Click(Sender: TObject);
begin
  {set up the link with the Tomcht app to its dde server}
  DdeClient.SetLink ('Tomcht', 'TomsChatServer' );
  {if we had not set the mode to ddeAutomatic we would}
  {need to call DdeClient.OpenLink here!              }
  {set up the field for automatic updating}
  DdeClientItem.DdeConv := DdeClient;
  {establish which data item of his we wish to get}
  DdeClientItem.DdeItem := 'TomsChatLines';
  {turn off the chat button to avoid confusion!}
  Button1.Enabled := False;
end;
```

4. Choose Button2's OnClick event handler and enter this program line to close the application.

```
procedure THarrysChatForm.Button2Click(Sender: TObject);
begin
  Close;
end;
```

5. Select the DdeClientItem component and activate its OnChange event. Add the following line to the event handler, which displays incoming data from the link to Tom.

```
procedure THarrysChatForm.DdeClientItemChange(Sender: TObject);
begin
  {Whenever we get new data from Tom update his memo field}
  TomsRepliesMemo.Lines := DdeClientItem.Lines;
end;
```

6. Now select the HarrysTalkMemo component and activate its OnChange event handler; add this line of code to send Harry's input to Tom.

```
procedure THarrysChatForm.HarrysTalkMemoChange(Sender: TObject);
begin
  {Whenever we type something send it to Tom}
  HarrysChatLines.Lines := HarrysTalkMemo.Lines;
end;
```

7. Create the duplicate application, TOMCHT. Save the HARRYCHT application and repeat the steps above to create a new application named TOMCHT and TOMCCLI.PAS. Add the components listed in Table 10-5.

Table 10-5 Components, properties, and settings of TomsChatForm in TOMCHT

COMPONENT	PROPERTY	SETTING
TomsChatForm	Type	Application Main Form
	Left	33
	Top	38
	Width	470
	Height	358
	Caption	Tom's Chat Client with Harry
	BorderStyle	bsSingle
Button1	Type	TButton
	Left	8
	Top	8
	Width	297
	Height	49
	Caption	Chat With Harry
Button2	Type	TButton
	Left	280
	Top	8
	Width	169

COMPONENT	PROPERTY	SETTING
	Height	49
	Caption	Exit Chat
HarrysRepliesMemo	Type	TMemo
	Left	8
	Top	96
	Width	217
	Height	185
	Lines	(blank)
TomsTalkMemo	Type	TMemo
	Left	232
	Top	96
	Width	217
	Height	185
	Lines	Hello from Tom!
Label1	Type	TLabel
	Left	8
	Top	72
	Width	129
	Height	25
	Caption	Harry's Replies
Label2	Type	TLabel
	Left	232
	Top	72
	Width	121
	Height	25
	Caption	Talk to Harry
DdeClientItem	Type	TDdeClientItem
	Lines	(blank)
DdeClient	Type	TDdeClientConv
	ConnectMode	ddeAutomatic
	FormatChars	False
TomsChatLines	Type	TDdeServerItem
	ServerConv	TomsChatServer
	Lines	Hello from Tom!
TomsChatServer	Type	TDdeServerConv

8. Type in the code for the four event handlers listed below, using the same steps as for HARRYCHT.

```
procedure TTomsChatForm.DdeClientItemChange(Sender: TObject);
begin
  {whenever we get new data from harry update his memo field}
  HarrysRepliesMemo.Lines := DdeClientItem.Lines;
end;

procedure TTomsChatForm.Button1Click(Sender: TObject);
begin
  {set up the link with the Tomcht app to its dde server}
  DdeClient.SetLink ('Harrycht', 'HarrysChatServer' );
  {if we had not set the mode to ddeAutomatic we would}
  {need to call DdeClient.OpenLink here!              }
  {set up the field for automatic updating}
  DdeClientItem.DdeConv := DdeClient;
  {establish which data item of his we wish to get}
  DdeClientItem.DdeItem := 'HarrysChatLines';
  {turn off the chat button to avoid confusion!}
  Button1.Enabled := False;
end;

procedure TTomsChatForm.Button2Click(Sender: TObject);
begin
  Close;
end;

procedure TTomsChatForm.TomsTalkMemoChange(Sender: TObject);
begin
  {Whenever we type something send it to Harry}
  TomsChatLines.Lines := TomsTalkMemo.Lines;
end;
```

9. Compile and test the project.

How It Works

It is a testament to the power "under the hood" in Delphi that an application this sophisticated can be written with so few lines of code. There are two major tricks here, both of which are worth discussing. First, notice the comment about ddeAutomatic and OpenLink. The power of the Delphi DDE system lies in the fact that once a component is told to set up its link, it does so automatically, with no further commands from the programmer. If ddeManual is turned on for the client, the OpenLink and CloseLink methods must be used to manually create and close the conversation. The fields of the linked conversation are the name of the target EXE (TOMCHT/HARRYCHT) for the Service and the name of the DDE server component on each application for the Topic. While technically there is no need to add a server for an application this simple, it will be important in the two versions of Windows Chat clients described in How-Tos 10.4 and 10.5.

The second and more subtle trick in this application is coordinating the two memo fields. Just establishing the link on the receiving end isn't sufficient. It is also necessary to set the OnChange event for the source Memo fields in each application to update their DdeServer whenever some new text is entered. If this is not done, the server never gets the new data and the connection seems not to be working.

Comments

At this point, your Chat client is little more than a demo toy. Particularly annoying is the requirement that the recipient of a chat request manually establish his or her own link back to the sender. Also, each application is hardwired to another client, which limits the usefulness of the system. Fortunately, there is still more functionality in the Delphi DDE toolbox. The next How-To will let you turn Chat into a truly useful application.

10.4 How do I...
Control another application from the current application?

COMPLEXITY: INTERMEDIATE

Problem

There are times when I want my running application to change the state or behavior of another program without the user having to start the program and enter commands. Does Delphi have a simple method for doing this?

Technique

Dynamic Data Exchange can do more than just update data fields between programs. It also has macro-language capabilities that you can use to activate and control one program from another.

Steps

Run DIANNE.EXE. Select Chat with Tom from the drop-down list, then click on Establish Conversation. Tom's chat client appears. Type in some text in either Talk field, and it will appear in the other application's Replies field. An example is shown in Figure 10-5.

1. Create a new project with a blank form. Name the project DIANNE.DPR and name the unit DCHTCLSV.PAS.

2. Add components and properties as shown in Table 10-6.

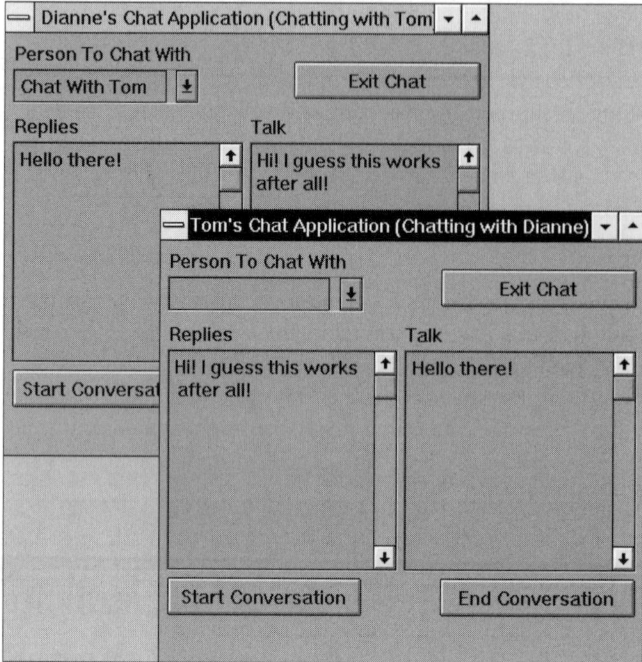

Figure 10-5 DIANNE and TOM at run time showing multiuser networked chat

Table 10-6 Components, properties, and settings of ChatForm in DIANNE

COMPONENT	PROPERTY	SETTING
ChatForm	Type	Application Main Form
	Left	55
	Top	39
	Width	448
	Height	406
	Caption	Dianne's Chat Application
	BorderStyle	bsSingle
Button1	Type	TButton
	Left	8
	Top	296
	Width	169
	Height	33
	Enabled	True

COMPONENT	PROPERTY	SETTING
	Caption	Start Conversation
Button2	Type	TButton
	Left	264
	Top	296
	Width	169
	Height	33
	Enabled	False
	Caption	End Conversation
Button3	Type	TButton
	Left	264
	Top	24
	Width	169
	Height	33
	Enabled	True
	Caption	Exit Chat
ClientData	Type	TMemo
	Left	8
	Top	96
	Width	209
	Height	193
	Lines	(blank)
ServerData	Type	TMemo
	Left	224
	Top	96
	Width	209
	Height	193
	Lines	(blank)
ClientLabel	Type	TLabel
	Left	8
	Top	72
	Width	89
	Height	25
	Caption	Replies
ServerLabel	Type	TLabel
	Left	224
	Top	72

continued on next page

continued from previous page

COMPONENT	PROPERTY	SETTING
	Width	33
	Height	20
	Caption	Talk
	Left	8
	Top	8
	Width	162
	Height	20
	Caption	Person To Chat With
ConversationComboBox	Type	TComboBox
	Left	8
	Top	32
	Width	169
	Height	29
	Style	csDropDown
ChatClientItem	Type	TDdeClientItem
	Lines	(blank)
ChatClient	Type	TDdeClientConv
	ConnectMode	ddeAutomatic
	FormatChars	False
ChatServerItem	Type	TDdeServerItem
	ServerConv	ChatServer
	Lines	(blank)
ChatServer	Type	TDdeServerConv

3. Select the combo box component in the Object Inspector, click on the Items property, and then on the ellipsis. Enter the following two lines in the String Editor to hold the names of Dianne's Chat targets.

```
Chat with Tom
Chat with Harry
```

4. Select the Button3 component's OnClick property and enter the following code in the Code Editor to close the application.

```
procedure TChatForm.Button3Click(Sender: TObject);
begin
  Close;
end;
```

5. Move up to the keyword *var*; enter the following two lines under it to declare helper variables.

```
var
  ChatForm: TChatForm;
  HoldCaption ,
  ServiceString : String;
```

6. Now return to the Object Inspector and select the ComboBox component's OnChange event. Type in these lines of code to set the current Chat target.

```
procedure TChatForm.ConversationComboBoxChange(Sender: TObject);
begin
  {set the string used to initiate a DDE conversation based on}
  {which item is selected in the combobox.                    }
  case ConversationComboBox.ItemIndex of
    0 : ServiceString := 'Tom';
    1 : ServiceString := 'Harry';
  end;
end;
```

7. Choose the Button1 component and select its OnClick event handler. Enter the following code to establish a DDE conversation with a selected target.

```
procedure TChatForm.Button1Click(Sender: TObject);
var MacroPChar : PChar;
begin
  {save the old caption string}
  HoldCaption := ChatForm.Caption;
  {if the user hasn't selected a callee set default}
  if ServiceString = '' then ServiceString := 'Tom';
  {set up the PChar for our server name}
  GetMem( MacroPChar , 80 );
  MacroPChar := 'Dianne';
  {set up the link to our callee}
  ChatClient.SetLink ( ServiceString , 'ChatServer' );
  {ddeAutomatic means we don't need to do OpenLink}
  {set up our client field}
  ChatClientItem.DdeConv := ChatClient;
  {all our callees will have the same server name}
  ChatClientItem.DdeItem := 'ChatServerItem';
  {now we control our callee's application to get it}
  {to turn on its chat link to us!                  }
  ChatClient.ExecuteMacro( MacroPChar , False );
  {Turn off the start conversation button and turn on the}
  {end conversation button                               }
  Button1.Enabled := False;
  Button2.Enabled := True;
  {change the caption of our form to indicate who we're talking with}
  ChatForm.Caption := HoldCaption + ' (Chatting with ' + ServiceString + ')';
end;
```

8. Now choose the Button2 component and select its OnClick event handler. Enter these lines in the Code Editor to terminate a DDE conversation.

```
procedure TChatForm.Button2Click(Sender: TObject);
var MacroPChar : PChar;
begin
```

continued on next page

continued from previous page

```
  {set up our command PChar for ending the conversation}
  GetMem( MacroPChar , 80 );
  MacroPChar := 'End Conversation';
  {call our callee's application and tell it to end our conversation}
  ChatClient.ExecuteMacro( MacroPChar , False );
  {close the link on our end}
  ChatClient.CloseLink;
  {change the buttons back to the starting state}
  Button1.Enabled := True;
  Button2.Enabled := False;
  {return the form's caption to the default state}
  ChatForm.Caption := HoldCaption;
end;
```

9. Activate the OnChange event handler of the ServerData memo field and type in this code to send data to the target application.

```
procedure TChatForm.ServerDataChange(Sender: TObject);
begin
  {when we type something to our callee send it over}
  ChatServerItem.Lines := ServerData.Lines;
end;
```

10. Select the ChatClientItem's OnChange event handler and enter the following code to receive data from a caller.

```
procedure TChatForm.ChatClientItemChange(Sender: TObject);
begin
  {update our display when we get something from our callee}
  ClientData.Lines := ChatClientItem.Lines;
end;
```

11. Choose the ChatServer component's OnExecuteMacro event handler and add this program code to respond to macro language calls from the caller.

```
procedure TChatForm.ChatServerExecuteMacro(Sender: TObject; Msg: TStrings);
begin
  {check our message to see if we are being told to shut down}
  if Msg.Strings[ 0 ] = 'End Conversation' then
  begin
    {if so shut our link to the caller and reset our buttons and caption}
    ChatClient.CloseLink;
    Button1.Enabled := True;
    Button2.Enabled := False;
    ChatForm.Caption := HoldCaption;
  end
  else
  begin
    {otherwise we assume we're being given the name of the person calling}
    {us and so set up a dde link to their server                          }
    HoldCaption := ChatForm.Caption;
    ChatClient.SetLink ( Msg.Strings[ 0 ] , 'ChatServer' );
    ChatClientItem.DdeConv := ChatClient;
    ChatClientItem.DdeItem := 'ChatServerItem';
```

```
    Button1.Enabled := False;
    Button2.Enabled := True;
    ChatForm.Caption := HoldCaption + ' (Chatting with ' + Msg.Strings[ 0 ] +
     ')';
  end;
end;
```

12. To complete the project, duplicate the code in DIANNE.DPR, making appropriate changes in TOM.DPR and HARRY.DPR. They are already supplied with the CD; their components are listed in Tables 10-7 and 10-8.

Table 10-7 Components, properties, and settings of ChatForm in TOM

COMPONENT	PROPERTY	SETTING
ChatForm	Type	Application Main Form
	Left	55
	Top	39
	Width	448
	Height	406
	Caption	Tom's Chat Application
	BorderStyle	bsSingle
Button1	Type	TButton
	Left	8
	Top	296
	Width	169
	Height	33
	Enabled	True
	Caption	Start Conversation
Button2	Type	TButton
	Left	264
	Top	296
	Width	169
	Height	33
	Enabled	False
	Caption	End Conversation
Button3	Type	TButton
	Left	264
	Top	24
	Width	169
	Height	33

continued on next page

continued from previous page

COMPONENT	PROPERTY	SETTING
	Enabled	True
	Caption	Exit Chat
ClientData	Type	TMemo
	Left	8
	Top	96
	Width	209
	Height	193
	Lines	(blank)
ServerData	Type	TMemo
	Left	224
	Top	96
	Width	209
	Height	193
	Lines	(blank)
ClientLabel	Type	TLabel
	Left	8
	Top	72
	Width	89
	Height	25
	Caption	Replies
ServerLabel	Type	TLabel
	Left	224
	Top	72
	Width	33
	Height	20
	Caption	Talk
ConversationLabel	Type	TLabel
	Left	8
	Top	8
	Width	162
	Height	20
	Caption	Person To Chat With
ConversationComboBox	Type	TComboBox
	Left	8
	Top	32
	Width	169

COMPONENT	PROPERTY	SETTING
	Height	29
	Style	csDropDown
	Lines	Chat With Dianne
		Chat With Harry
ChatClientItem	Type	TDdeClientItem
	Lines	(blank)
ChatClient	Type	TDdeClientConv
	ConnectMode	ddeAutomatic
	FormatChars	False
ChatServerItem	Type	TDdeServerItem
	ServerConv	ChatServer
	Lines	(blank)
ChatServer	Type	TDdeServerConv

Table 10-8 Components, properties, and settings of ChatForm in HARRY

COMPONENT	PROPERTY	SETTING
ChatForm	Type	Application Main Form
	Left	55
	Top	39
	Width	448
	Height	406
	Caption	Harry's Chat Application
	BorderStyle	bsSingle
Button1	Type	TButton
	Left	8
	Top	296
	Width	169
	Height	33
	Enabled	True
	Caption	Start Conversation
Button2	Type	TButton
	Left	264
	Top	296
	Width	169

continued on next page

continued from previous page

COMPONENT	PROPERTY	SETTING
	Height	33
	Enabled	False
	Caption	End Conversation
Button3	Type	TButton
	Left	264
	Top	24
	Width	169
	Height	33
	Enabled	True
	Caption	Exit Chat
ClientData	Type	TMemo
	Left	8
	Top	96
	Width	209
	Height	193
	Lines	(blank)
ServerData	Type	TMemo
	Left	224
	Top	96
	Width	209
	Height	193
	Lines	(blank)
ClientLabel	Type	TLabel
	Left	8
	Top	72
	Width	89
	Height	25
	Caption	Replies
ServerLabel	Type	TLabel
	Left	224
	Top	72
	Width	33
	Height	20
	Caption	Talk
ConversationLabel	Type	TLabel
	Left	8

COMPONENT	PROPERTY	SETTING
	Top	8
	Width	162
	Height	20
	Caption	Person To Chat With
ConversationComboBox	Type	TComboBox
	Left	8
	Top	32
	Width	169
	Height	29
	Style	csDropDown
	Lines	Chat With Dianne
		Chat With Tom
ChatClientItem	Type	TDdeClientItem
	Lines	(blank)
ChatClient	Type	TDdeClientConv
	ConnectMode	ddeAutomatic
	FormatChars	False
ChatServerItem	Type	TDdeServerItem
	ServerConv	ChatServer
	Lines	(blank)
ChatServer	Type	TDdeServerConv

13. The following is the code for the TCHTCLSV unit in TOM.

```
unit Tchtclsv;

interface

uses WinTypes, WinProcs, Classes, Graphics, Forms, Controls, StdCtrls, Menus,
     DdeMan;

type
  TChatForm = class(TForm)
    ClientLabel: TLabel;
    ClientData: TMemo;
    ServerData: TMemo;
    ServerLabel: TLabel;
    ConversationComboBox: TComboBox;
    ConversationLabel: TLabel;
    Button1: TButton;
    Button2: TButton;
    Button3: TButton;
    ChatServerItem: TDdeServerItem;
```

continued on next page

continued from previous page

```
    ChatServer: TDdeServerConv;
    ChatClient: TDdeClientConv;
    ChatClientItem: TDdeClientItem;

    procedure ChatClientItemChange(Sender: TObject);
    procedure Button1Click(Sender: TObject);
    procedure Button2Click(Sender: TObject);
    procedure ServerDataChange(Sender: TObject);
    procedure ConversationComboBoxChange(Sender: TObject);
    procedure Button3Click(Sender: TObject);
    procedure ChatServerExecuteMacro(Sender: TObject; Msg: TStrings);
  private
    { Private declarations }
  public
    { Public declarations }
  end;

var
  ChatForm: TChatForm;
  HoldCaption ,
  ServiceString : String;

implementation

uses Dialogs, SysUtils;

{$R *.DFM}

procedure TChatForm.ChatClientItemChange(Sender: TObject);
begin
  {update our display when we get something from our callee}
  ClientData.Lines := ChatClientItem.Lines;
end;

procedure TChatForm.Button1Click(Sender: TObject);
var MacroPChar : PChar;
begin
  {save the old caption string}
  HoldCaption := ChatForm.Caption;
  {if the user hasn't selected a callee set default}
  if ServiceString = '' then ServiceString := 'Dianne';
  {set up the PChar for our server name}
  GetMem( MacroPChar , 80 );
  MacroPChar := 'Tom';
  {set up the link to our callee}
  ChatClient.SetLink ( ServiceString , 'ChatServer' );
  {ddeAutomatic means we don't need to do OpenLink}
  {set up our client field}
  ChatClientItem.DdeConv := ChatClient;
  {all our callees will have the same server name}
  ChatClientItem.DdeItem := 'ChatServerItem';
  {now we control our callee's application to get it}
  {to turn on its chat link to us!                    }
  ChatClient.ExecuteMacro( MacroPChar , False );
  {Turn off the start conversation button and turn on the}
```

```
  {end conversation button                                     }
  Button1.Enabled := False;
  Button2.Enabled := True;
  {change the caption of our form to indicate who we're talking with}
  ChatForm.Caption := HoldCaption + ' (Chatting with ' + ServiceString + ')';
end;

procedure TChatForm.Button2Click(Sender: TObject);
var MacroPChar : PChar;
begin
  {set up our command PChar for ending the conversation}
  GetMem( MacroPChar , 80 );
  MacroPChar := 'End Conversation';
  {call our callee's application and tell it to end our conversation}
  ChatClient.ExecuteMacro( MacroPChar , False );
  {close the link on our end}
  ChatClient.CloseLink;
  {change the buttons back to the starting state}
  Button1.Enabled := True;
  Button2.Enabled := False;
  {return the form's caption to the default state}
  ChatForm.Caption := HoldCaption;
end;

procedure TChatForm.ServerDataChange(Sender: TObject);
begin
  {when we type something to our callee send it over}
  ChatServerItem.Lines := ServerData.Lines;
end;

procedure TChatForm.ConversationComboBoxChange(Sender: TObject);
begin
  {set the string used to initiate a DDE conversation based on}
  {which item is selected in the combobox.                    }
  case ConversationComboBox.ItemIndex of
    0 : ServiceString := 'Dianne';
    1 : ServiceString := 'Harry';
  end;
end;

procedure TChatForm.Button3Click(Sender: TObject);
begin
  Close;
end;

procedure TChatForm.ChatServerExecuteMacro(Sender: TObject; Msg: TStrings);
begin
  {check our message to see if we are being told to shut down}
  if Msg.Strings[ 0 ] = 'End Conversation' then
  begin
    {if so shut our link to the caller and reset our buttons and caption}
    ChatClient.CloseLink;
    Button1.Enabled := True;
    Button2.Enabled := False;
    ChatForm.Caption := HoldCaption;
```

continued on next page

continued from previous page

```
  end
  else
  begin
    {otherwise we assume we're being given the name of the person calling}
    {us and so set up a dde link to their server                         }
    HoldCaption := ChatForm.Caption;
    ChatClient.SetLink ( Msg.Strings[ 0 ] , 'ChatServer' );
    ChatClientItem.DdeConv := ChatClient;
    ChatClientItem.DdeItem := 'ChatServerItem';
    Button1.Enabled := False;
    Button2.Enabled := True;
    ChatForm.Caption := HoldCaption + ' (Chatting with ' + Msg.Strings[ 0 ] +
     ')';
  end;
end;

end.
```

14. The following is the code for the HCHTCLSV unit in HARRY.

```
unit Hchtclsv;

interface

uses WinTypes, WinProcs, Classes, Graphics, Forms, Controls, StdCtrls, Menus,
     DdeMan;

type
  TChatForm = class(TForm)
    ClientLabel: TLabel;
    ClientData: TMemo;
    ServerData: TMemo;
    ServerLabel: TLabel;
    ConversationComboBox: TComboBox;
    ConversationLabel: TLabel;
    Button1: TButton;
    Button2: TButton;
    Button3: TButton;
    ChatServerItem: TDdeServerItem;
    ChatServer: TDdeServerConv;
    ChatClient: TDdeClientConv;
    ChatClientItem: TDdeClientItem;

    procedure ChatClientItemChange(Sender: TObject);
    procedure Button1Click(Sender: TObject);
    procedure Button2Click(Sender: TObject);
    procedure ServerDataChange(Sender: TObject);
    procedure ConversationComboBoxChange(Sender: TObject);
    procedure Button3Click(Sender: TObject);
    procedure ChatServerExecuteMacro(Sender: TObject; Msg: TStrings);
  private
    { Private declarations }
  public
    { Public declarations }
  end;
```

```
var
  ChatForm: TChatForm;
  HoldCaption ,
  ServiceString : String;

implementation

uses Dialogs, SysUtils;

{$R *.DFM}

procedure TChatForm.ChatClientItemChange(Sender: TObject);
begin
  {update our display when we get something from our callee}
  ClientData.Lines := ChatClientItem.Lines;
end;

procedure TChatForm.Button1Click(Sender: TObject);
var MacroPChar : PChar;
begin
  {save the old caption string}
  HoldCaption := ChatForm.Caption;
  {if the user hasn't selected a callee set default}
  if ServiceString = '' then ServiceString := 'Dianne';
  {set up the PChar for our server name}
  GetMem( MacroPChar , 80 );
  MacroPChar := 'Harry';
  {set up the link to our callee}
  ChatClient.SetLink ( ServiceString , 'ChatServer' );
  {ddeAutomatic means we don't need to do OpenLink}
  {set up our client field}
  ChatClientItem.DdeConv := ChatClient;
  {all our callees will have the same server name}
  ChatClientItem.DdeItem := 'ChatServerItem';
  {now we control our callee's application to get it}
  {to turn on its chat link to us!                  }
  ChatClient.ExecuteMacro( MacroPChar , False );
  {Turn off the start conversation button and turn on the}
  {end conversation button                               }
  Button1.Enabled := False;
  Button2.Enabled := True;
  {change the caption of our form to indicate who we're talking with}
  ChatForm.Caption := HoldCaption + ' (Chatting with ' + ServiceString + ')';
end;

procedure TChatForm.Button2Click(Sender: TObject);
var MacroPChar : PChar;
begin
  {set up our command PChar for ending the conversation}
  GETMEM( MacroPChar , 80 );
  MacroPChar := 'End Conversation';
  {call our callee's application and tell it to end our conversation}
  ChatClient.ExecuteMacro( MacroPChar , False );
  {close the link on our end}
```

continued on next page

continued from previous page

```
  ChatClient.CloseLink;
  {change the buttons back to the starting state}
  Button1.Enabled := True;
  Button2.Enabled := False;
  {return the form's caption to the default state}
  ChatForm.Caption := HoldCaption;
end;

procedure TChatForm.ServerDataChange(Sender: TObject);
begin
  {when we type something to our callee send it over}
  ChatServerItem.Lines := ServerData.Lines;
end;

procedure TChatForm.ConversationComboBoxChange(Sender: TObject);
begin
  {set the string used to initiate a DDE conversation based on}
  {which item is selected in the combobox.                   }
  case ConversationComboBox.ItemIndex of
    0 : ServiceString := 'Dianne';
    1 : ServiceString := 'Tom';
  end;
end;

procedure TChatForm.Button3Click(Sender: TObject);
begin
  Close;
end;

procedure TChatForm.ChatServerExecuteMacro(Sender: TObject; Msg: TStrings);
begin
  {check our message to see if we are being told to shut down}
  if Msg.Strings[ 0 ] = 'End Conversation' then
  begin
    {if so shut our link to the caller and reset our buttons and caption}
    ChatClient.CloseLink;
    Button1.Enabled := True;
    Button2.Enabled := False;
    ChatForm.Caption := HoldCaption;
  end
  else
  begin
    {otherwise we assume we're being given the name of the person calling}
    {us and so set up a dde link to their server                         }
    HoldCaption := ChatForm.Caption;
    ChatClient.SetLink ( Msg.Strings[ 0 ] , 'ChatServer' );
    ChatClientItem.DdeConv := ChatClient;
    ChatClientItem.DdeItem := 'ChatServerItem';
    Button1.Enabled := False;
    Button2.Enabled := True;
    ChatForm.Caption := HoldCaption + ' (Chatting with ' + Msg.Strings[ 0 ] +
     ')';
  end;
end;

end.
```

15. Compile and test the project.

How It Works

The key to the application is the ExecuteMacro DDE function. The previous How-To demonstrated initiating a DDE conversation from a Chat application once the application was started. ExecuteMacro adds the ability to build command and control strings into an application to respond to messages via the DDE connection. Thus a program can send a name to the target server over the macro link and tell its target to start a conversation with itself in return. Then by checking the same string for the "End Conversation" keywords, the applications know when their caller is asking them to terminate the conversation and automatically shut down.

The True/False flag sent in each of the ExecuteMacro functions tells Delphi whether or not to send any further OnExecuteMacro events to the server. If a program sends a command string that requires a lengthy execution process, which it doesn't want interrupted, it could set this flag to True. Then any other DDE macro strings that might be sent would be ignored. The application would test for this by checking the optional Boolean return value of all DDE functions in Delphi until it returned True, indicating the server was free to accept commands again.

Comments

This is a simple example, but in practice the number of macro strings that you can process is limited only by your willingness to write the code. Since PChar strings can be as large as available memory, your applications can include a rich set of macro-language features, thanks to Delphi and ExecuteMacro.

10.5 How do I...
Manage communication among any number of applications?

COMPLEXITY: EASY

Problem

Now that it's so easy for my applications to talk to each other, I'm discovering problems with message traffic jams. How can I keep track of my communicating programs in a simple but powerful way?

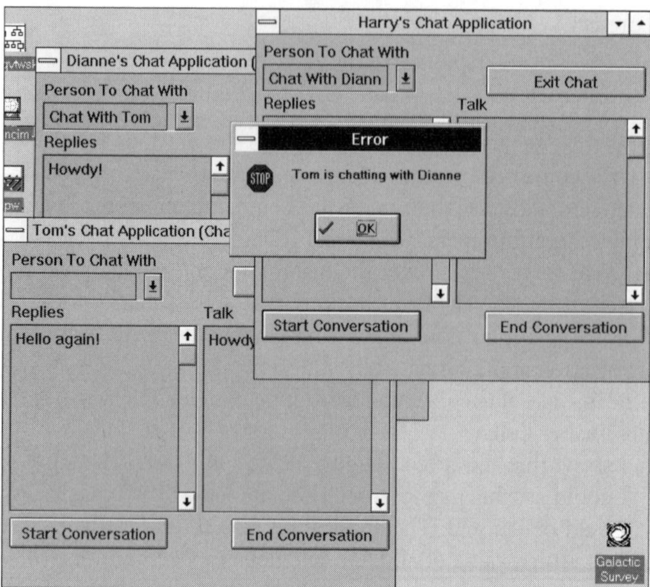

Figure 10-6 DIANNE, TOM, and HARRY at run time showing an information busy signal

Technique

Delphi permits applications to have multiple DDE servers active at once without disturbing their conversations. You can use the RequestData function over a DDE link to find out if your application is getting an information busy signal.

Steps

Run DIANNE.EXE from the CH1005 directory. It is identical to the Chat client created in the previous How-To. Select Chat with Tom and open a conversation. From File Manager, start HARRY.EXE. Select Chat with Dianne and attempt to establish a conversation. You will see an Error dialog box similar to the one pictured in Figure 10-6.

1. To save typing and time, open DIANNE.DPR from the CH1004 directory on the CD. Keep the same name for the project and its unit, but save it to a new directory.

2. Add the new components and set their properties as shown in Table 10-9.

Table 10-9 Components, properties, and settings for ChatForm in CH10/HOW TO 05/DIANNE

COMPONENT	PROPERTY	SETTING
StatusServerItem	Type	TDdeServerItem
	ServerConv	StatusServer
	Text	Free
StatusServer	Type	TDdeServerConv

3. Select the Button1 component and double-click on its OnClick event handler. This takes you to the Code Editor, where you will find the code already written for the previous unit. Compare the following code with the code in the Editor, and where there is grayed text here, change the code in the Editor to match it. These changes set up the DDE conversation routine to check for the information busy signal.

```
procedure TChatForm.Button1Click(Sender: TObject);

var OtherPChar ,
    MacroPChar : PChar;
    DDE_OK : Boolean;
    CheckString : String;

begin
  {save the old caption string}
  HoldCaption := ChatForm.Caption;
  {if the user hasn't selected a callee set default}
  if ServiceString = '' then ServiceString := 'Tom';
  {set up the PChar for our server name}
  GETMEM( MacroPChar , 80 );
  MacroPChar := 'Dianne';
  {set up the link to our callee and save the returned value}
  DDE_OK := ChatClient.SetLink ( ServiceString , 'StatusServer' );
  {if the value was false DDE couldn't locate the callee so}
  {give an error message and leave.                        }
  if not DDE_OK then
  begin
    {Give the name of our callee in the error message}
    CheckString := ServiceString + ' is not logged on!';
    MessageDlg( CheckString , mtError,
     [mbOK], 0);
    {jump out of the routine but stay in the program}
    exit;
  end;
  {ddeAutomatic means we don't need to do OpenLink}
  {set up our client field}
  ChatClientItem.DdeConv := ChatClient;
  {all our callees will have the same server name}
  ChatClientItem.DdeItem := 'StatusServerItem';
  {Now we set up to obtain the current status of our callee's}
  {application via the RequestData call.                     }
  GetMem( OtherPChar , 80 );
```

continued on next page

continued from previous page

```
  OtherPChar :=
   ChatClient.RequestData( ChatClientItem.DdeItem );
  {convert the returned PChar to a string}
  CheckString := StrPas( OtherPChar );
  {Close this link to be polite}
  ChatClient.CloseLink;
  {if we don't get the Free string (with CR and LF due to DDE)}
  if CheckString  'Free'#13#10 then
  begin
    {Send error dialog with the name the person is now talking to!}
    CheckString := ServiceString + ' is chatting with ' +
     CheckString;
    MessageDlg(  CheckString , mtError,
     [mbOK], 0);
    {and exit without leaving the program}
    exit;
  end
  else
  {if they are free we begin our conversation normally}
  begin
    {now we control our callee's application to get it}
    {to turn on its chat link to us!                   }
    ChatClient.SetLink ( ServiceString , 'ChatServer' );
    ChatClientItem.DdeConv := ChatClient;
    ChatClientItem.DdeItem := 'ChatServerItem';
    ChatClient.ExecuteMacro( MacroPChar , False );
    {Turn off the start conversation button and turn on the}
    {end conversation button                               }
    Button1.Enabled := False;
    Button2.Enabled := True;
    {change the caption of our form to indicate who we're talking with}
    ChatForm.Caption := HoldCaption + ' (Chatting with ' + ServiceString + ')';
    {and we set our status field to reflect our current conversation}
    StatusServerItem.Text := ServiceString;
  end;
end;
```

4. Now select the Button2 component and double-click on its OnClick event handler. Once again, change the code in the Editor to match the following code by adding the grayed segment, which sets up a default variable for use in determining whether or not the client is free to accept a conversation.

```
procedure TChatForm.Button2Click(Sender: TObject);

var MacroPChar : PChar;

begin
  {set up our command PChar for ending the conversation}
  GetMem( MacroPChar , 80 );
  MacroPChar := 'End Conversation';
  {call our callee's application and tell it to end our conversation}
  ChatClient.ExecuteMacro( MacroPChar , False );
  {close the link on our end}
  ChatClient.CloseLink;
```

```
  {change the buttons back to the starting state}
  Button1.Enabled := True;
  Button2.Enabled := False;
  {return the form's caption to the default state}
  ChatForm.Caption := HoldCaption;
  {reset our status item to Free so we can be called again}
  StatusServerItem.Text := 'Free';
end;
```

5. Finally, select the OnExecuteMacro event and make the changes shown here to take advantage of the new information available through the second Dde server link.

```
procedure TChatForm.ChatServerExecuteMacro(Sender: TObject; Msg: TStrings);
begin
  {check our message to see if we are being told to shut down}
  if Msg.Strings[ 0 ] = 'End Conversation' then
  begin
    {if so shut our link to the caller and reset our buttons and caption}
    ChatClient.CloseLink;
    Button1.Enabled := True;
    Button2.Enabled := False;
    ChatForm.Caption := HoldCaption;
    {reset our status to Free to if we've closed a link}
    StatusServerItem.Text := 'Free';
  end
  else
  begin
    {otherwise we assume we're being given the name of the person calling}
    {us and so set up a dde link to their server                        }
    HoldCaption := ChatForm.Caption;
    ChatClient.SetLink ( Msg.Strings[ 0 ] , 'ChatServer' );
    ChatClientItem.DdeConv := ChatClient;
    ChatClientItem.DdeItem := 'ChatServerItem';
    Button1.Enabled := False;
    Button2.Enabled := True;
    ChatForm.Caption := HoldCaption + ' (Chatting with ' + Msg.Strings[ 0 ] +
     ')';
    {set our status to the name of our current caller}
    StatusServerItem.Text := Msg.Strings[ 0 ];
  end;
end;
```

6. As in the previous How-To, you can either copy the HARRY.DPR and TOM.DPR files from the CD or copy the files over and make changes. The components and properties are identical in all three projects; the changed code is reproduced below. This is the code for the HARRY application.

```
unit Hchtclsv;
procedure TChatForm.Button1Click(Sender: TObject);

var OtherPChar ,
    MacroPChar : PChar;
    DDE_OK : Boolean;
```

continued on next page

continued from previous page

```
    CheckString : String;

begin
  {save the old caption string}
  HoldCaption := ChatForm.Caption;
  {if the user hasn't selected a callee set default}
  if ServiceString = '' then ServiceString := 'Dianne';
  {set up the PChar for our server name}
  GetMem( MacroPChar , 80 );
  MacroPChar := 'Harry';
  {set up the link to our callee and save the returned value}
  DDE_OK := ChatClient.SetLink ( ServiceString , 'StatusServer' );
  {if the value was false DDE couldn't locate the callee so}
  {give an error message and leave.                         }
  if not DDE_OK then
  begin
    {Give the name of our callee in the error message}
    CheckString := ServiceString + ' is not logged on!';
    MessageDlg( CheckString , mtError,
     [mbOK], 0);
    {jump out of the routine but stay in the program}
    exit;
  end;
  {ddeAutomatic means we don't need to do OpenLink}
  {set up our client field}
  ChatClientItem.DdeConv := ChatClient;
  {all our callees will have the same server name}
  ChatClientItem.DdeItem := 'StatusServerItem';
  {Now we set up to obtain the current status of our callee's}
  {application via the RequestData call.                      }
  GetMem( OtherPChar , 80 );
  OtherPChar :=
   ChatClient.RequestData( ChatClientItem.DdeItem );
  {convert the returned PChar to a string}
  CheckString := StrPas( OtherPChar );
  {Close this link to be polite}
  ChatClient.CloseLink;
  {if we don't get the Free string (with CR and LF due to DDE)}
  if CheckString  'Free'#13#10 then
  begin
    {Send error dialog with the name the person is now talking to!}
    CheckString := ServiceString + ' is chatting with ' +
     CheckString;
    MessageDlg(  CheckString , mtError,
     [mbOK], 0);
    {and exit without leaving the program}
    exit;
  end
  else
  {if they are free we begin our conversation normally}
  begin
    {now we control our callee's application to get it}
    {to turn on its chat link to us!                   }
    ChatClient.SetLink ( ServiceString , 'ChatServer' );
    ChatClientItem.DdeConv := ChatClient;
```

```
    ChatClientItem.DdeItem := 'ChatServerItem';
    ChatClient.ExecuteMacro( MacroPChar , False );
    {Turn off the start conversation button and turn on the}
    {end conversation button                                }
    Button1.Enabled := False;
    Button2.Enabled := True;
    {change the caption of our form to indicate who we're talking with}
    ChatForm.Caption := HoldCaption + ' (Chatting with ' + ServiceString + ')';
    {and we set our status field to reflect our current conversation}
    StatusServerItem.Text := ServiceString;
  end;
end;

procedure TChatForm.Button2Click(Sender: TObject);

var MacroPChar : PChar;

begin
  {set up our command PChar for ending the conversation}
  GetMem( MacroPChar , 80 );
  MacroPChar := 'End Conversation';
  {call our callee's application and tell it to end our conversation}
  ChatClient.ExecuteMacro( MacroPChar , False );
  {close the link on our end}
  ChatClient.CloseLink;
  {change the buttons back to the starting state}
  Button1.Enabled := True;
  Button2.Enabled := False;
  {return the form's caption to the default state}
  ChatForm.Caption := HoldCaption;
  {reset our status item to Free so we can be called again}
  StatusServerItem.Text := 'Free';
end;

procedure TChatForm.ChatServerExecuteMacro(Sender: TObject; Msg: TStrings);
begin
  {check our message to see if we are being told to shut down}
  if Msg.Strings[ 0 ] = 'End Conversation' then
  begin
    {if so shut our link to the caller and reset our buttons and caption}
    ChatClient.CloseLink;
    Button1.Enabled := True;
    Button2.Enabled := False;
    ChatForm.Caption := HoldCaption;
    {reset our status to Free to if we've closed a link}
    StatusServerItem.Text := 'Free';
  end
  else
  begin
    {otherwise we assume we're being given the name of the person calling}
    {us and so set up a dde link to their server                          }
    HoldCaption := ChatForm.Caption;
    ChatClient.SetLink ( Msg.Strings[ 0 ] , 'ChatServer' );
    ChatClientItem.DdeConv := ChatClient;
    ChatClientItem.DdeItem := 'ChatServerItem';
```

continued on next page

continued from previous page

```
    Button1.Enabled := False;
    Button2.Enabled := True;
    ChatForm.Caption := HoldCaption + ' (Chatting with ' + Msg.Strings[ 0 ] +
     ')';
    {set our status to the name of our current caller}
    StatusServerItem.Text := Msg.Strings[ 0 ];
  end;
end;
```

7. This is the code for the TOM application:

```
unit Tchtclsv;
procedure TChatForm.Button1Click(Sender: TObject);

var OtherPChar ,
    MacroPChar : PChar;
    DDE_OK : Boolean;
    CheckString : String;

begin
  {save the old caption string}
  HoldCaption := ChatForm.Caption;
  {if the user hasn't selected a callee set default}
  if ServiceString = '' then ServiceString := 'Dianne';
  {set up the PChar for our server name}
  GetMem( MacroPChar , 80 );
  MacroPChar := 'Tom';
  {set up the link to our callee and save the returned value}
  DDE_OK := ChatClient.SetLink ( ServiceString , 'StatusServer' );
  {if the value was false DDE couldn't locate the callee so}
  {give an error message and leave.                        }
  if not DDE_OK then
  begin
    {Give the name of our callee in the error message}
    CheckString := ServiceString + ' is not logged on!';
    MessageDlg( CheckString , mtError,
     [mbOK], 0);
    {jump out of the routine but stay in the program}
    exit;
  end;
  {ddeAutomatic means we don't need to do OpenLink}
  {set up our client field}
  ChatClientItem.DdeConv := ChatClient;
  {all our callees will have the same server name}
  ChatClientItem.DdeItem := 'StatusServerItem';
  {Now we set up to obtain the current status of our callee's}
  {application via the RequestData call.                     }
  GetMem( OtherPChar , 80 );
  OtherPChar :=
   ChatClient.RequestData( ChatClientItem.DdeItem );
  {convert the returned PChar to a string}
  CheckString := StrPas( OtherPChar );
  {Close this link to be polite}
  ChatClient.CloseLink;
  {if we don't get the Free string (with CR and LF due to DDE)}
```

```
if CheckString  'Free'#13#10 then
begin
  {Send error dialog with the name the person is now talking to!}
  CheckString := ServiceString + ' is chatting with ' +
   CheckString;
  MessageDlg(  CheckString , mtError,
   [mbOK], 0);
  {and exit without leaving the program}
  exit;
end
else
{if they are free we begin our conversation normally}
begin
  {now we control our callee's application to get it}
  {to turn on its chat link to us!                  }
  ChatClient.SetLink ( ServiceString , 'ChatServer' );
  ChatClientItem.DdeConv := ChatClient;
  ChatClientItem.DdeItem := 'ChatServerItem';
  ChatClient.ExecuteMacro( MacroPChar , False );
  {Turn off the start conversation button and turn on the}
  {end conversation button                               }
  Button1.Enabled := False;
  Button2.Enabled := True;
  {change the caption of our form to indicate who we're talking with}
  ChatForm.Caption := HoldCaption + ' (Chatting with ' + ServiceString + ')';
  {and we set our status field to reflect our current conversation}
  StatusServerItem.Text := ServiceString;
 end;
end;

procedure TChatForm.Button2Click(Sender: TObject);

var MacroPChar : PChar;

begin
  {set up our command PChar for ending the conversation}
  GetMem( MacroPChar , 80 );
  MacroPChar := 'End Conversation';
  {call our callee's application and tell it to end our conversation}
  ChatClient.ExecuteMacro( MacroPChar , False );
  {close the link on our end}
  ChatClient.CloseLink;
  {change the buttons back to the starting state}
  Button1.Enabled := True;
  Button2.Enabled := False;
  {return the form's caption to the default state}
  ChatForm.Caption := HoldCaption;
  {reset our status item to Free so we can be called again}
  StatusServerItem.Text := 'Free';
end;

procedure TChatForm.ChatServerExecuteMacro(Sender: TObject; Msg: TStrings);
begin
  {check our message to see if we are being told to shut down}
  if Msg.Strings[ 0 ] = 'End Conversation' then
```

continued on next page

continued from previous page

```
    begin
      {if so shut our link to the caller and reset our buttons and caption}
      ChatClient.CloseLink;
      Button1.Enabled := True;
      Button2.Enabled := False;
      ChatForm.Caption := HoldCaption;
      {reset our status to Free to if we've closed a link}
      StatusServerItem.Text := 'Free';
    end
    else
    begin
      {otherwise we assume we're being given the name of the person calling}
      {us and so set up a dde link to their server                         }
      HoldCaption := ChatForm.Caption;
      ChatClient.SetLink ( Msg.Strings[ 0 ] , 'ChatServer' );
      ChatClientItem.DdeConv := ChatClient;
      ChatClientItem.DdeItem := 'ChatServerItem';
      Button1.Enabled := False;
      Button2.Enabled := True;
      ChatForm.Caption := HoldCaption + ' (Chatting with ' + Msg.Strings[ 0 ] +
       ')';
      {set our status to the name of our current caller}
      StatusServerItem.Text := Msg.Strings[ 0 ];
    end;
  end;

  end.
```

8. Compile and test the project.

How It Works

The RequestData function is the key to finding out whether someone you wish to chat with is talking to someone else. By adding a second DdeServer to the program, a copy of the application could set its data item to a status string that held either the keyword "Free" or the name of the person it is currently chatting with. The contact procedure changes to check both for no answer (when the initial SetLink returned False) and for the second data item holding a non-Free name, which is then reported as a busy signal. The remaining changes to the other parts of the program simply make sure the program keeps track of whether it is talking to someone or not.

Comments

The only limit to the number of DDE Server items an application can have is the amount of memory available for compilation and execution. You could use this same system to create an electronic mail utility by adding file loading and saving to the memo fields and putting the names of the persons who contacted the application in the combo box.

10.6 How do I...
View the contents of an OLE 2.0 file?

COMPLEXITY: INTERMEDIATE

Problem

Object Linking and Embedding (OLE) is in its second version and continues to increase its functionality and power. A number of applications are beginning to distribute data in the OLE file format. Can I give users the ability to examine the contents of these files without extensive C language SDK programming?

Technique

Delphi's version 1.0 includes support for OLE containers, which allows you to put OLE items in your programs. You will use the OLEContainer component to open and view the data contained in an OLE 2.0 file.

Steps

Run OLEVIEW.EXE. Open the accompanying DHT1006A.OLE file and view its contents. Then run OLEVIEW twice more from File Manager, opening DHT1006B.OLE and DHT1006C.OLE.You will see a display similar to Figure 10-7.

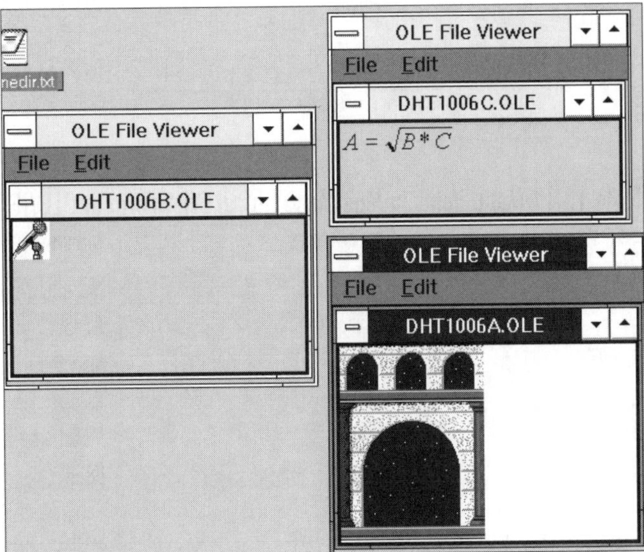

Figure 10-7 OLEVIEW at run time showing a bitmap, sound file, and rich text document

Click on the sound object, and Windows will play the sound file if you have a sound card.

1. Create a new MDI project with a blank form. Name the project OLEVIEW.DPR and the unit OLEFLOOK.PAS.
2. Add components and set properties as shown in Table 10-10.

Table 10-10 Components, properties, and settings of OLEViewForm in OLEVIEW

COMPONENT	PROPERTY	SETTING
OLEViewForm	Type	Application Main Form
	Left	43
	Top	39
	Width	435
	Height	300
	Caption	OLE File Viewer
	BorderStyle	bsSizable
MainMenu1	Type	TMainMenu
	AutoMerge	False
OpenDialog	Type	TOpenDialog
	DefaultExt	ole
	FileName	*,.ole
	Filter	OLE files(*.ole)|*.ole

3. Activate the TMainMenu component to bring up the Menu Editor. Add menu items as shown in Table 10-11.

Table 10-11 Menu items in MainMenu1 of OLEViewForm in OLEVIEW

COMPONENT	PROPERTY	SETTING
File1	Type	MenuItem (top level)
	Caption	&File
Open1	Type	MenuItem (under File1)
	Caption	&Open...
Exit1	Type	MenuItem (under File1)
	Caption	E&xit

4. Choose the Open1 item's OnClick event handler and type in the following lines to open and load an OLE file. (Don't worry about unfamiliar references, as you have another form to add in a moment.)

```
procedure TOLEViewForm.Open1Click(Sender: TObject);
var
  NewChild: TOLEFileObjectForm;
begin
  {if we don't cancel from the dialog then do OLE file open}
  if OpenDialog.Execute then
  begin
    {create the new OLE window}
    NewChild := CreateChild;
    {set the OLE container to size itself to the loaded object}
    NewChild.OLEContainer.Autosize := true;
    {load the OLE object from the file}
    NewChild.OLEContainer.LoadFromFile(OpenDialog.FileName);
    {set the window's size to correspond to the loaded object}
    NewChild.Height := NewChild.OLECOntainer.Height + 36;
    NewChild.Width := NewChild.OLEContainer.Width + 10;
    {tell Delphi to redraw itself}
    NewChild.Invalidate;
    {set caption to the name of the loaded file without path}
    Newchild.Caption := ExtractFileName( OpenDialog.Filename );
  end
end;
```

5. Select the Exit1 item's OnClick event handler and type in the following code to close the application.

```
procedure TOLEViewForm.Exit1Click(Sender: TObject);
begin
  Close
end;
```

6. Now move back to the main form and activate its OnCreate event handler. Add these lines to handle initializing the program.

```
procedure TOLEViewForm.FormCreate(Sender: TObject);
begin
  {Set up clipboard formats with OLE system}
  FEmbedClipFmt := RegisterClipboardFormat('Embedded Object');
  FLinkClipFmt := RegisterClipboardFormat('Link Source');
  Fmts[0].fmtId := FEmbedClipFmt;
  Fmts[0].fmtMedium := BOLEMediumCalc(FEmbedClipFmt);
  Fmts[0].fmtIsLinkable := False;
  StrPCopy(Fmts[0].fmtName, '%s');
  StrPCopy(Fmts[0].fmtResultName, '%s');
  Fmts[1].fmtId := FLinkClipFmt;
  Fmts[1].fmtMedium := BOLEMediumCalc(FLinkClipFmt);
  Fmts[1].fmtIsLinkable := True;
  StrPCopy(Fmts[1].fmtName, '%s');
  StrPCopy(Fmts[1].fmtResultName, '%s');
end;
```

7. Move up to just below the *private* keyword and add this code to let Delphi recognize your helper function and variables.

```
private
    FEmbedClipFmt: Word;
    FLinkClipFmt: Word;
    function CreateChild: TOLEFileObjectForm;
  public
    Fmts: array[0..1] of BOleFormat;
  end;
```

8. Continue down to just below the *implementation* keyword and add this helper function to create and display an OLEContainer object.

```
function TOLEViewForm.CreateChild: TOLEFileObjectForm;
begin
  {When we open a file create a new OLE object}
  CreateChild := TOLEFileObjectForm.Create(Self);
  {Show the newly loaded object}
  CreateChild.Show
end;
```

9. Create a new blank form. Save the unit as OLEFOBJ.PAS and add components and set properties as shown in Table 10-12.

Table 10-12 Components, properties, and settings of OLEFileObjectForm in OLEFOBJ

COMPONENT	PROPERTY	SETTING
OLEFileObjectForm	Type	Blank Form
	Left	70
	Top	83
	Width	435
	Height	300
	Caption	OLE File Object
	BorderStyle	bsSizable
OleContainer	Type	TOleContainer
	Align	alClient
	AutoActivate	aaDoubleClick
	AutoSize	True
MainMenu1	Type	TMainMenu
	AutoMerge	False
SaveAsDialog	Type	TSaveDialog
	DefaultExt	ole
	FileName	*,.ole
	Filter	OLE files(*.ole)|*.ole

10. Double-click on the TMainMenu component to bring up the Menu Editor. Add menu items as shown in Table 10-13.

Table 10-13 Menu items in MainMenu1 of OLEFileObjectForm in OLEFOBJ

COMPONENT	PROPERTY	SETTING
File1	Type	MenuItem (top level)
	Caption	&File
Edit1	Type	MenuItem (top level)
	Caption	&Edit
SaveAs1	Type	MenuItem (under File1)
	Caption	&Save As...
OLEObjectMenuItem	Type	MenuItem (under Edit1)
	Caption	&Object
Exit1	Type	MenuItem (under File1)
	Caption	E&xit

11. Select the Exit1 item's OnClick event handler and type in the following code to close the application from a child window.

```
procedure TOLEFileObjectForm.Exit1Click(Sender: TObject);
begin
  {call the parent form's exit method}
  OLEViewForm.Exit1Click(Sender)
end;
```

12. Go to the SaveAs1 item's OnClick event handler and type in these lines to save an OLE object in a child window.

```
procedure TOLEFileObjectForm.SaveAs1Click(Sender: TObject);
begin
  {if the dialog tells us to save then use the filename entered}
  if SaveAsDialog.Execute then
    OLEContainer.SaveToFile(SaveAsDialog.Filename)
end;
```

13. While still in the Code Editor type in the following helper function below the one you just entered.

```
procedure TOLEFileObjectForm.InitializeOLEObject(Info: Pointer);
begin
  OLEContainer.PInitInfo := Info;
  Height := OLECOntainer.Height + 40;
  Width := OLEContainer.Width + 40;
  Invalidate;
  ReleaseOLEInitInfo(Info)
end
```

14. Move up under the *private* keyword and add this code to let Delphi recognize the previous helper procedure.

```
private
    procedure InitializeOLEObject(Info: Pointer);
```

15. Compile and test the project.

How It Works

The OLEContainer object handles virtually all of the work for the application. The first form registers the OLE formats it will accept from the OLE system with the RegisterClipboardFormat calls. Then the OLEFOBJ unit calls its embedded OLEContainer object with the PInitInfo data it obtained from the OLE system. Delphi does everything else.

Comments

This little program gets your feet wet with OLE, but even as it is, it shows considerable versatility. You can display graphics, play sounds—even show text formatted by Microsoft Word. But there are a number of OLE functions not yet implemented in Delphi's first release. Once available in Delphi, you will be able to build much more powerful OLE capabilities for the program. In the meantime, the next How-To demonstrates a way Delphi's current OLE containers can implement a sophisticated multimedia display application.

10.7 How do I...
Create documents with text, graphics, and sound?

COMPLEXITY: ADVANCED

Problem

A cutting-edge application in the modern Windows environment should incorporate rich text, full-color graphics, sound, and music. Can I use Delphi to give my program this level of sophistication without having to write all the drivers myself?

Technique

With the OLE technology incorporated in Windows 3.1, applications can display and even edit data using other programs' functions. As in the previous How-To, you use the OLEContainer object in Delphi to take advantage of this technology.

Steps

Run MULTIAPP.EXE, then load DHT1007A.DAT. You will see a display similar to Figure 10-8, with a document in Microsoft Word rich text format, a bitmap graphic,

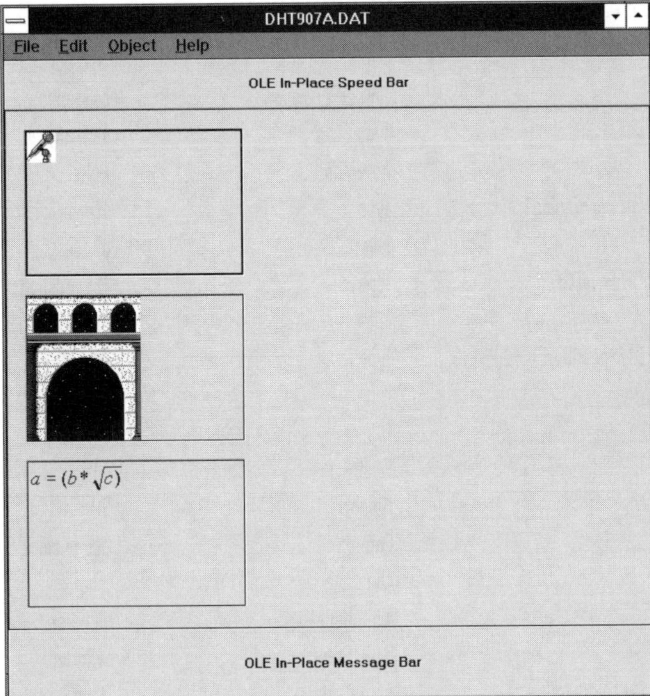

Figure 10-8 MULTIAPP at run time showing a bitmap, sound file, and rich text in one document

and a button for a sound clip. Click the sound file to play it, and edit the data in the text and graphics windows by double-clicking on them.

1. Create a new blank project with a blank form. Name the project MULTIAPP.DPR and the unit MULTIDAT.PAS.
2. Add components and set properties as shown in Table 10-14.

Table 10-14 Components, properties, and settings of OLEDocumentForm in MULTIAPP

COMPONENT	PROPERTY	SETTING
OLEDocumentForm	Type	Application Main Form
	Left	46
	Top	45
	Width	422
	Height	376

continued on next page

continued from previous page

COMPONENT	PROPERTY	SETTING
	Caption	OLE Document Editor
	BorderStyle	bsSizable
OLEMainMenu1	Type	TMainMenu
	AutoMerge	False
OLEOpenDialog1	Type	TOpenDialog
	Filter	all files(*.*)|*.*
OLESaveDialog1	Type	TSaveDialog
	Filter	all files(*.*)|*.*
OLESpeedBar	Type	TPanel
	Left	0
	Top	0
	Width	414
	Height	50
	Caption	OLE In-Place Speed Bar
	Align	alTop
	Alignment	taCenter
	BevelOuter	bvRaised
OLEMessageBar	Type	TPanel
	Left	0
	Top	244
	Width	414
	Height	70
	Caption	OLE In-Place Message Bar
	Align	alBottom
	Alignment	taCenter
	BevelOuter	bvRaised
OLEScrollBox1	Type	TScrollBox
	Left	0
	Top50	
	Width	414
	Height	194
	Align	alClient
OLEContainer1	Type	TOleContainer
	Left	0
	Top	0
	Width	100

COMPONENT	PROPERTY	SETTING
	Height	100
	Visible	False

3. Select the TMainMenu component to bring up the Menu Editor. Add menu items as shown in Table 10-15.

Table 10-15 Menu items in MainMenu1 of OLEDocumentForm in MULTIAPP

COMPONENT	PROPERTY	SETTING
File1	Type	MenuItem (top level)
	Caption	&File
Edit1	Type	MenuItem (top level)
	Caption	&Edit
	GroupIndex	1
Object2	Type	MenuItem (top level)
	Caption	&Object
New1	Type	MenuItem (under File1)
	Caption	&New
Load1	Type	MenuItem (under File1)
	Caption	&Load
N4	Type	MenuItem (under File1)
	Caption	(blank)
Open1	Type	MenuItem(under File1)
	Caption	&Open
N1	Type	MenuItem (under File1)
	Caption	(blank)
Save1	Type	MenuItem (under File1)
	Caption	&Save
N5	Type	MenuItem (under File1)
	Caption	(blank)
Exit1	Type	MenuItem (under File1)
	Caption	E&xit
Cut1	Type	MenuItem (under Edit1)
	Caption	Cut
Copy1	Type	MenuItem (under Edit1)
	Caption	Copy

continued on next page

continued from previous page

COMPONENT	PROPERTY	SETTING
Paste1	Type	MenuItem (under Edit1)
	Caption	Paste
N2	Type	MenuItem (under Edit1)
	Caption	(blank)
InsertObject1	Type	MenuItem (under Edit1)
	Caption	Insert Object...
PasteSpecial1	Type	MenuItem (under Edit1)
	Caption	Paste Special...
Links1	Type	MenuItem (under Edit1)
	Caption	Links...
N3	Type	MenuItem (under Edit1)
	Caption	(blank)
Object1	Type	MenuItem (under Edit1)
	Caption	Object
	Enabled	False
ResetObject1	Type	MenuItem (under Object2)
	Caption	Reset Object...
PasteInObject1	Type	MenuItem (under Object2)
	Caption	Paste In Object...

4. You have a lot of code to add, but when you're done you'll have a full-featured OLE application. First, activate the OnClick event handler of the New1 menu item and add the following code to load and display a new OLE container item. Don't worry if you see unfamiliar functions; you'll add some assistant procedures later.

```
procedure TOLEDocumentForm.NewOleWin1Click(Sender: TObject);
var
  OLEChild : TOLEDocumentForm;
begin
  {create the new child window}
  OLEChild := TOLEDocumentForm.Create(Self);
  {make it visible}
  OLEChild.Visible := True;
end;
```

5. Next, activate the OnClick event handler of the Load1 menu item and add the following code to load a previously saved MULTIAPP document.

```
procedure TOLEDocumentForm.Load1Click(Sender: TObject);
var
  AStream: TStream;
  Counter_1 : Integer;
```

```
  SaveName   : String;
  NameExt ,
  NameOnlyString : String;
  ExtPos : Integer;
  The_File_Record : Longint;
  The_File : File of Longint;
  OLEForm : TOLEDocumentForm;
  OLEControl : TOleContainer;
  X,Y  : Integer;

begin
  {if we accept the open dialog results}
  if OLEOpenDialog1.Execute then
  begin
    {create the new form}
    OLEForm := TOLEDocumentForm.Create(Application);
    {manipulate the file name to get it without extension}
    SaveName := OLEOpenDialog1.FileName;
    NameExt := ExtractFileExt( SaveName );
    ExtPos := Pos( NameExt , SaveName );
    NameOnlyString := SaveName;
    Delete( NameOnlyString , ExtPos , Length( NameExt ));
    {open the file and read in the number of containers}
    AssignFile( The_File , OLEOpenDialog1.FileName );
    Reset( The_File );
    Seek( The_File , 0 );
    Read( The_File , The_File_Record );
    CloseFile( The_File );
    {read in the container streams and put them in windows}
    for Counter_1 := 0 to (The_File_Record-1) do
    begin
      STR( Counter_1 , NameExt );
      NameExt := '.' + NameExt;
      SaveName := NameOnlyString + NameExt;
      AStream := TFileStream.Create( SaveName , fmOpenRead);
      try
        OLEControl := TOleContainer.Create (OLEForm);
        X := 20;
        if Counter_1 = 0 then Y := 20 else
         Y := OLEForm.OLEScrollBox1.Controls[ Counter_1 - 1 ].Top +
          OLEForm.OLEScrollBox1.Controls[ Counter_1 - 1 ].Height
           + 20;
        OLEControl.SetBounds (X, Y, 230, 150);
        OLEControl.visible := True;
        OLEControl.enabled := True;
        OLEControl.AutoSize := True;
        OLEControl.LoadFromStream(AStream);
        OLEControl.OnStatusLineEvent := StatusLineEvent;
        OLEControl.Parent := OLEForm.OLEScrollBox1;
        OLEControl.Modified := False;
      finally
        AStream.Free;
      end;
    end;
    OLEForm.Caption := ExtractFileName(OLEOpenDialog1.FileName);
```

continued on next page

continued from previous page

```
    OLEForm.Visible := True;
  end;
end;
```

6. Activate the OnClick event handler of the Open1 menu item and add the following code, which loads a new OLE object from a file and adds it to the current document.

```
procedure TOLEDocumentForm.Open1Click(Sender: TObject);
var
  OLEForm : TOLEDocumentForm;
  OLEStream: TStream;
  OLEControl : TOleContainer;
begin
  {if we accept the results of the open dialog}
  if OLEOpenDialog1.Execute then
  begin
    {create a new form}
    OLEForm := TOLEDocumentForm.Create(Application);
    {create an OLE stream}
    OLEStream := TFileStream.Create(OLEOpenDialog1.FileName, fmOpenRead);
    try
      {make a new control and load it from the stream}
      OLEControl := TOleContainer.Create (OLEForm);
      OLEControl.SetBounds ( 20, 20, 230, 150);
      OLEControl.visible := True;
      OLEControl.enabled := True;
      OLEControl.AutoSize := True;
      OLEControl.LoadFromStream(OLEStream);
      OLEControl.OnStatusLineEvent := StatusLineEvent;
      OLEControl.Parent := OLEForm.OLEScrollBox1;
      ActiveControl := OLEControl;
    finally
      OLEStream.Free;
    end;
    {set up the caption of the new form and activate the control}
    OLEForm.Caption := ExtractFileName(OLEOpenDialog1.FileName);
    OLEControl.Modified := False;
    OLEForm.Visible := True;
  end;
end;
```

7. Go to the OnClick event handler of the Save1 menu item and add this code to store the current MULTIAPP document as a stream of OLEContainer objects.

```
procedure TOLEDocumentForm.Save1Click(Sender: TObject);
var
  AStream: TStream;
  Counter_1 : Integer;
  SaveName : String;
  NameExt ,
  NameOnlyString : String;
  ExtPos : Integer;
  The_File_Record : Longint;
  The_File : File of Longint;
```

```
begin
  {if we accept the results of save dialog}
  if OLESaveDialog1.Execute then
  begin
    {get the name to save under}
    SaveName := OLESaveDialog1.FileName;
    {pull off the extension}
    NameExt := ExtractFileExt( SaveName );
    {find out where it is}
    ExtPos := Pos( NameExt , SaveName );
    {put the name in a working string}
    NameOnlyString := SaveName;
    {remove the extension from the working string}
    Delete( NameOnlyString , ExtPos , Length( NameExt ));
    {set up a file of longints to hold the total OLE containers}
    AssignFile( The_File , OLESaveDialog1.FileName );
    {open it and set it to zero}
    Rewrite( The_File );
    {set the file number to the total containers in our document}
    The_File_Record := OLEScrollBox1.ControlCount;
    {write the number to the file}
    Seek( The_File , 0 );
    Write( The_File , The_File_Record );
    {close the file}
    CloseFile( The_File );
    {now write out the containers to streams using the basic file name}
    {and adding a number extension to each container file              }
    for Counter_1 := 0 to (OLEScrollBox1.ControlCount-1) do
    begin
      STR( Counter_1 , NameExt );
      NameExt := '.' + NameExt;
      SaveName := NameOnlyString + NameExt;
      AStream := TFileStream.Create( SaveName , fmCreate);
      try
        TOleContainer(OLEScrollBox1.Controls[ Counter_1 ]).SaveToStream(AStream);
      finally
        AStream.Free;
      end;
    end;
  end;
end;
```

8. Activate the OnClick event handler of the Exit1 menu item and add the following code to close the program.

```
procedure TOLEDocumentForm.Exit1Click(Sender: TObject);
begin
  Close;
end;
```

9. Choose the OnClick event handler of the Cut1 menu item. Add this code to remove an OLE item from the current document.

```
procedure TOLEDocumentForm.Cut1Click(Sender: TObject);
begin
  {if our active control is an OLE container}
  if ActiveControl.InheritsFrom (TOleContainer) then
  begin
    {Copy its contents to the clipboard}
    TOleContainer (ActiveControl).CopyToClipboard (True);
    {then remove the active control}
    ActiveControl.Free;
  end;
end;
```

10. Bring up the OnClick event handler of the Copy1 menu item and add the following code to copy the contents of an OLE item in the current document to the Clipboard.

```
procedure TOLEDocumentForm.Copy1Click(Sender: TObject);

begin
  {if our active control is an OLE container}
  if ActiveControl.InheritsFrom (TOleContainer) then
  begin
    {copy its contents to the clipboard}
    TOleContainer (ActiveControl).CopyToClipboard (True);
  end;
end;
```

11. Select the OnClick event handler of the InsertObject1 menu item and add the following code to insert an OLE object in the current document.

```
procedure TOLEDocumentForm.InsertObject1Click(Sender: TObject);
var
   PInfo: Pointer;
begin
  {if we accept the results of the InsertObject dialog}
  if InsertOleObjectDlg (Self, 0, PInfo) then
    {create a new OLE container in our form with the dialog info}
    CreateOleObject (PInfo);
  {and tell the OLE server to release the pointer}
  ReleaseOleInitInfo (PInfo);
end;
```

12. Pick the OnClick event handler of the PasteSpecial1 menu item and add the following code to handle pasting OLE objects from the Clipboard.

```
procedure TOLEDocumentForm.PasteSpecial1Click(Sender: TObject);
var
  APointer  : PChar;
  AString  : String;
  AFormat  : Word;
  AHandle  : THandle;
  PInfo : Pointer;
begin
  {if we approve the contents of the Paste Special Dialog}
  if PasteSpecialDlg (Self,
```

```
    [OleFormat (FEmbedClipFmt, '%s', '%s', TRUE),
     OleFormat (FLinkClipFmt,  '%s', '%s', TRUE)],
    0, AFormat, AHandle, PInfo) then
  begin
    {if the clipboard doesn't have OLE objects then give errors}
    if (AFormat = CF_TEXT) then
    begin
      APointer := GlobalLock (AHandle);
      AString := StrPas (APointer);
      GlobalUnlock (AHandle);
      AString := Format('Text on the clipboard = %s', [AString]);
      MessageDlg (AString, mtInformation, [mbOK], 0);
      GlobalFree (AHandle);
    end
    else if (AFormat = CF_METAFILEPICT) then
    begin
      MessageDlg ('MetaFile on the clipboard.', mtInformation, [mbOK], 0);
      GlobalFree (AHandle);
    end
    else
      {otherwise create the new OLE container}
      CreateOleObject (PInfo);
    ReleaseOleInitInfo (PInfo);
  end;
end;
```

13. Activate the OnClick event handler of the Links1 menu item and add the following code. This activates the prepackaged links dialog for pasting OLE objects into the document as a link rather than data.

```
procedure TOLEDocumentForm.Links1Click(Sender: TObject);
begin
  {run the link dialog if the user asks}
  LinksDlg (Self, 0);
end;
```

14. Go to the OnClick event handler of the ResetObject1 menu item and add this code to place a new OLE item in an existing container within the current document.

```
procedure TOLEDocumentForm.ResetObjectClick(Sender: TObject);
var
  InitInfo : Pointer;
begin
  {check that our active control is an OLE container}
  if ActiveControl.InheritsFrom (TOleContainer) then
  begin
    {if we accept the Insert dialog selection}
    if InsertOleObjectDlg (Self, 0, InitInfo) = True then
    begin
      {reset the OLE information in the active control}
      TOleContainer(ActiveControl).PInitInfo := InitInfo;
      {and tell the OLE server to release the pointer}
      ReleaseOleInitInfo (InitInfo);
```

continued on next page

continued from previous page

```
      end;
    end;
end;
```

15. Select the OnClick event handler of the PasteInObject1 menu item and add the following code. This calls the paste special dialog and puts data from a currently open, independent, OLE-aware application into an OLE container in the current document.

```
procedure TOLEDocumentForm.PasteInObject1Click(Sender: TObject);
var
  InitInfo : Pointer;
begin
  {if our active control is an OLE container}
  if ActiveControl.InheritsFrom (TOleContainer) then
  begin
    {and we accept the results of the Paste Special dialog}
    if PasteSpecialOleDlg (Self, 0, InitInfo) = True then
    begin
      {reset the OLE information in the active control}
      TOleContainer(ActiveControl).PInitInfo := InitInfo;
      {and tell the OLE server to release the pointer}
      ReleaseOleInitInfo (InitInfo);
    end;
  end;
end;
```

16. Now you need to add an assistant function. In the Code Editor, move up to the *private* keyword and add the next lines of code. Then under the *public* keyword add the constructor declaration.

```
private
    { Private declarations }
    FLinkClipFmt   : Word;
    FEmbedClipFmt  : Word;
    procedure CreateOleObject (PInfo : Pointer);
  public
    { Public declarations }
    constructor Create(AOwner: TComponent); override;
```

17. While still in the Code Editor, move down to just below the *implementation* keyword and add the following helper function to handle the actual insertion of a new OLEContainer object into the document.

```
procedure TOLEDocumentForm.CreateOleObject (PInfo : Pointer);
var
  OLEControl : TOleContainer;
  NewLeft,NewTop   : Integer;
begin
  {Create a new OLE container}
  OLEControl := TOleContainer.Create (Self);
  {set its position based on the last control added's position}
  NewLeft := OLEScrollBox1.Controls [OLEScrollBox1.ControlCount - 1].Left;
```

```
  NewTop := OLEScrollBox1.Controls [OLEScrollBox1.ControlCount - 1].Top +
       OLEScrollBox1.Controls [OLEScrollBox1.ControlCount - 1].Height + 20;
  {set up minimum size of the control}
  OLEControl.SetBounds (NewLeft, NewTop, 50, 50);
  {make the control visible and selectable}
  OLEControl.visible := True;
  OLEControl.enabled := True;
  {tell the control to size itself to its data}
  OLEControl.AutoSize := True;
  {send its status line actions to the event manager}
  OLEControl.OnStatusLineEvent := StatusLineEvent;
  {set its information to the imported data}
  OLEControl.PInitInfo := PInfo;
  {make the control a child of the scroll box control}
  OLEControl.Parent := OLEScrollBox1;
  {make it the active control}
  ActiveControl := OLEControl;
end;
```

18. Move up in the Code Editor to just below the *implementation* keyword and add the following code statement to prevent circular unit references.

```
uses SysUtils;
```

19. Now move down and type in this assistant function to handle creation of the basic MULTIAPP document.

```
constructor TOLEDocumentForm.Create(AOwner: TComponent);
begin
  {call inherited Create method}
  inherited Create (AOwner);
  {call the OLE registration functions}
  FEmbedClipFmt := RegisterClipboardFormat ('Embedded Object');
  FLinkClipFmt  := RegisterClipboardFormat ('Link Source');
  {register the form as a draganddrop target}
  RegisterFormAsOleDropTarget (Self,
    [OleFormat (FEmbedClipFmt, '%s', '%s', TRUE),
     OleFormat (FLinkClipFmt,  '%s', '%s', TRUE)]);
  OnDragDrop := DoDrop;
end;
```

20. Return to the Object Inspector and select the OLEDocumentForm's OnDragDrop event handler. Add these lines of code to handle dropping an OLE object onto the current MULTIAPP document.

```
procedure TOLEDocumentForm.DoDrop(DragTgt, DragSource: TObject; X, Y: Integer);
var
  OLEControl: TOleContainer;
  Point: TPoint;
begin
  {if our dragged object is an OLE object}
  if DragSource.InheritsFrom (TOleDropNotify) then
  begin
    {if we get approval to drop}
```

continued on next page

continued from previous page

```
    if TOleDropNotify(DragSource).PInitInfo  Nil then
    begin
      {convert position information}
      Point.X := X;
      Point.Y := Y;
      Point := ClientToScreen(Point);
      Point := OLEScrollBox1.ScreenToClient(Point);
      {create the new OLE control and set its info to the dropped data}
      OLEControl := TOleContainer.Create (TForm(DragTgt));
      OLEControl.SetBounds (Point.X, Point.Y, 50, 50);
      OLEControl.visible := True;
      OLEControl.enabled := True;
      OLEControl.AutoSize := True;
      OLEControl.Parent := OLEScrollBox1;
      {tell the sending object we took the drop}
      OLEControl.PInitInfo := TOleDropNotify(DragSource).PInitInfo;
    end;
  end;
end;
```

21. The last code to enter is another helper function. In the Code Editor, move to just below the previous procedure and add the following code to handle updating the status bar from an OLE in-place server.

```
procedure TOLEDocumentForm.StatusLineEvent(Sender: TObject;
  Msg: String);
begin
  {set the caption of the message bar to the message from the OLE server}
  OLEMessageBar.Caption := Msg;
end;
```

22. Compile and test the project.

How It Works

At first glance the code seems generic and repetitious, but that belies the tremendous power under its hood. These functions tie the application fully into the OLE system, allowing any OLE object to be placed in the document, viewed, and edited either in place or in the server application's window. When the application is done, it can save the document and reload it intact as a set of OLE containers. While most of the comments in the code are self-explanatory, a few can use further explanation.

One important trick lies in making the scroll box component the parent of the OLE containers. This handles the positioning and display of the containers. Another useful tip is setting the Autosize flag on the OLE containers, which causes them to resize themselves to their internal data. The SetBounds function likewise puts a minimum value on the containers' size so they don't become invisible if they show a very small object or nonvisual information. Also worth noting is the use of the new OLEForm as the parent of the new containers created in the Load event manager. This makes them part of the new form rather than the current form. The creation of the StatusLineEvent handler as part of the main form allows any control which is a child of that form to call it.

Finally, notice that the program does not implement containers for data such as raw text or metafiles, but only for fully OLE-linked Clipboard information. A possible upgrade of the application could make forms that handle both of these formats.

Comments

When server and automation support is added to the OLEContainer component, Delphi will be in the lead for creating cutting-edge applications in the new Windows environment.

11

11

THE POLISHED APPLICATION

How Do I...

There are applications and there are applications. Often, the things that set high-quality, professional-looking programs apart from lesser applications turn out to be fairly minor details. What this means is that details count. Users typically expect certain things from your program, and some of these things fall into the bells-and-whistles category, such as the configurable toolbar project of How-To 11.4 in this chapter.

11.1 Customize the default exception handler

Delphi's robust exception handling ability lets you deal with exceptions that you may anticipate, such as file I/O exceptions, locally—but what if an exception you didn't anticipate happens while your program is running? The exception will be handled by a generic exception handler that is supplied in Delphi's runtime library. This generic handler will display a dialog that could be confusing or even frightening to users. This How-To shows how to override the default exception handler with something that is friendlier and more informative.

11.2 Make a professional-style About box

A popular last-minute item to polish up is the application's About box. Many programmers use the About box to show system information and a list of credits for the development team, and generally, to spruce up the program. You'll explore some of the possibilities that this potentially huge outlet for creativity offers.

11.3 Create separate help hints and status line help

With Delphi you can show pop-up "help hints" to describe the purpose of speed buttons or other elements in your program. Unfortunately, it is difficult to be very descriptive in the small amount of space that the hint window is expected to use. A popular solution to this problem is to give a brief description of the control in the hint window, then give a more detailed description on the status bar. Delphi supports this automatically—but the technique isn't obvious, so this How-To goes over it step by step.

11.4 Make a customizable toolbar like Delphi's

One really nice feature to add to programs is the ability to configure the toolbar. There are a few programs on the market that allow this, but the implementation is usually not very user-friendly. Several programs allow users to add or delete tools, but few do it in an intuitive manner. You do not have to venture very far to find an outstanding configurable toolbar—Delphi has one of the best around. Guess which one this How-To was modeled after?

11.1 How Do I...
Customize the default exception handler?

COMPLEXITY: INTERMEDIATE

Problem

If my application causes an exception that my code does not handle, the default exception handler may be called. I would like to customize this exception handler so it gives more information to the user and looks more like a part of my program. How can I do this with Delphi?

Technique

Delphi provides a hook into the exception handler called OnException that allows you to customize your application's default exception handler. You can use this hook to define an exception handler that will be called if the exception does not get handled elsewhere in your code.

Steps

Run EXCEPTOR.EXE. There are three buttons that will cause exceptions when clicked, in addition to the Close button at the bottom of the form, as shown in Figure 11-1. Try each of the exceptions and note the form that is shown following the exception.

1. Create a new project with a blank form and name it EXCEPTOR.DPR. Name the unit EXCEPT1.PAS.

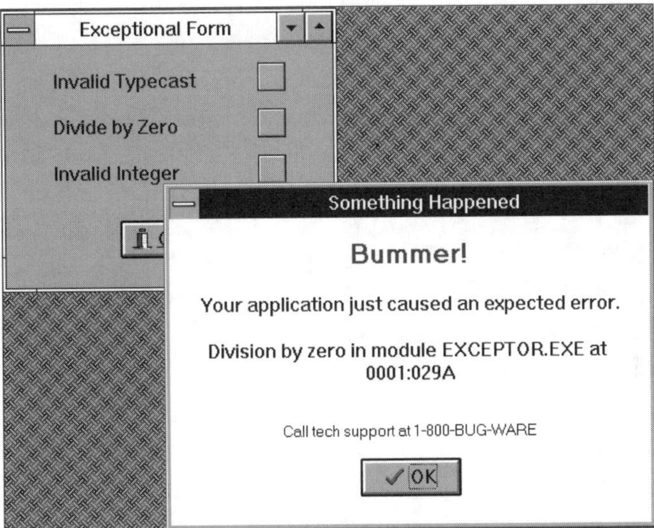

Figure 11-1 EXCEPTOR at run time

2. Add components and set their properties as shown in Table 11-1.

Table 11-1 Components, properties, and settings for Form1 in the EXCEPTOR project

COMPONENT	PROPERTY	SETTING
Form1	Left	199
	Top	118
	Width	301
	Height	245

continued on next page

continued from previous page

COMPONENT	PROPERTY	SETTING
	Caption	Exceptional Form
	+Font	
	-Color	clWindowText
	-Size	10
	-Name	System
SpeedButton1	Left	226
	Top	16
	Width	25
	Height	25
SpeedButton2	Left	226
	Top	56
	Width	25
	Height	25
SpeedButton3	Left	226
	Top	96
	Width	25
	Height	25
Label1	Left	42
	Top	21
	Width	160
	Height	20
	AutoSize	False
	Caption	Invalid Typecast
Label2	Left	42
	Top	61
	Width	160
	Height	20
	AutoSize	False
	Caption	Divide by Zero
Label3	Left	42
	Top	101
	Width	160
	Height	20
	AutoSize	False
	Caption	Invalid Integer

COMPONENT	PROPERTY	SETTING
BitBtn1	Left	102
	Top	152
	Width	89
	Height	33
	Kind	bkClose

3. Double-click on SpeedButton1 (the speed button for Invalid Typecast) and add the following code to the resulting OnClick event handler.

```
procedure TForm1.SpeedButton1Click(Sender: TObject);
begin
  with Sender as TForm do;
end;
```

4. Double-click on SpeedButton2 (the speed button for Divide by Zero) and add the following code to the resulting OnClick event handler.

```
procedure TForm1.SpeedButton2Click(Sender: TObject);
var
  A, B, C : integer;
begin
  A := 0;
  B := 1;
  C := B div A;
end;
```

5. Double-click on SpeedButton3 (the speed button for Invalid Integer) and add the following code to the resulting OnClick event handler.

```
procedure TForm1.SpeedButton3Click(Sender: TObject);
begin
  StrToInt('Doh!');
end;
```

6. Double-click on the Close button and add the following code to the resulting OnClick event handler.

```
procedure TForm1.BitBtn1Click(Sender: TObject);
begin
  Close;
end;
```

7. Double-click on Form1 and add the following code to the resulting OnCreate event handler.

```
procedure TForm1.FormCreate(Sender: TObject);
begin
  Application.OnException := MyException;
end;
```

8. While still in the Code Editor, move up to the object declaration for Form1. Add a method declaration for the MyException method as shown here:

```
type
  TForm1 = class(TForm)
    SpeedButton1: TSpeedButton;
    SpeedButton2: TSpeedButton;
    SpeedButton3: TSpeedButton;
    Label1: TLabel;
    Label2: TLabel;
    Label3: TLabel;
    BitBtn1: TBitBtn;
    procedure SpeedButton1Click(Sender: TObject);
    procedure SpeedButton2Click(Sender: TObject);
    procedure SpeedButton3Click(Sender: TObject);
    procedure FormCreate(Sender: TObject);
    procedure BitBtn1Click(Sender: TObject);
  private
    { Private declarations }
    procedure MyException(Sender: TObject; E: Exception);
  public
    { Public declarations }
  end;
```

9. Now add the MyException method itself to the *implementation* section of the unit, as shown here. You'll also need to add a *uses* clause so you have access to Form2, which you'll be adding next.

```
implementation

uses Except2;

{$R *.DFM}

procedure TForm1.MyException(Sender: TObject; E: Exception);
begin
  Form2.Label3.Caption := E.Message;
  Form2.Show;
end;
```

10. Add a new blank form to the project. Name the unit EXCEPT2.PAS.

11. Add components and set their properties as shown in Table 11-2.

Table 11-2 Components, properties, and settings for Form2 in the EXCEPTOR project

COMPONENT	PROPERTY	SETTING
Form2	Left	200
	Top	118
	BorderIcons	[biSystemMenu]
	BorderStyle	bsDialog
	Caption	Something Happened
	ClientHeight	265
	ClientWidth	427
	Color	clWhite
	+Font	
	-Color	clWindowText
	-Size	10
	-Name	System
	Position	poScreenCenter
Label1	Left	161
	Top	16
	Width	105
	Height	29
	Caption	Bummer!
	+Font	
	-Color	clRed
	-Size	14
	-Name	MS Sans Serif
	-Style	[fsBold]
	ParentFont	False
Label2	Left	27
	Top	64
	Width	374
	Height	20
	Caption	Your application just caused an expected error.
Label3	Left	25
	Top	104
	Width	377
	Height	49
	Alignment	taCenter

continued on next page

continued from previous page

COMPONENT	PROPERTY	SETTING
	AutoSize	False
	Caption	Label3
Label4	Left	100
	Top	176
	Width	226
	Height	16
	Caption	Call tech support at 1-800-BUG-WARE
	+Font	
	-Color	clBlack
	-Size	8
	-Name	MS Sans Serif
	ParentFont	False
BitBtn1	Left	169
	Top	208
	Width	89
	Height	33
	Kind	bkOK

12. Double-click the OK button on Form2 and add the following code to the resulting OnClick event handler.

```
procedure TForm2.BitBtn1Click(Sender: TObject);
begin
  Close;
end;
```

13. Compile and test the project.

How It Works

Prior to calling the default exception handler, the VCL checks to see if there is a handler assigned to the OnException event. If there is, the assigned handler is used to handle the exception.

The OnException event handler in this How-To demonstrates the basic technique in a straightforward way.

Comments

As you can imagine, it's a good idea to provide some sort of customized default exception handler for your applications. If you code carefully and test thoroughly, the code in the default exception handler should execute rarely if ever. If it ever does, you can provide users with detailed instructions and information that will help your troubleshooting efforts.

11.2 How Do I...
Make a professional-style About box?

COMPLEXITY: INTERMEDIATE

Problem

I've noticed that many commercial applications have hidden messages or credits in the About box. I think that's a nice touch and would like to add something similar to my Delphi application. How can I do this?

Technique

Sometimes it seems that developers put more time into the About box than other areas of the program. Some applications have elaborate animations, for example, of their product squashing the competition, and so on. While this How-To isn't quite that fancy, it does show some solid techniques that can be used as a starting point in a Delphi application.

Steps

Run ABOUTDEM.PAS. This project only has one form, which is modeled after a typical About box, as shown in Figure 11-2. Click on the bitmap in the upper left-hand corner of the form. The bitmap appears to press down when you click on it, but nothing else happens unless you double-click the bitmap while holding down the ALT key.

Figure 11-2 ABOUTDEM at run time

1. Create a new project based on a blank form and name it ABOUTDEM.DPR. Name the unit ABOUT1.PAS.
2. Add components and set their properties as shown in Table 11-3.

Table 11-3 Components, properties, and settings for Form1 in the ABOUTDEM project

COMPONENT	PROPERTY	SETTING
Form1	Name	AboutBox
	Left	333
	Top	130
	BorderStyle	bsDialog
	Caption	About
	ClientHeight	218
	ClientWidth	298
	+Font	
	-Color	clWindowText
	-Size	10
	-Name	System
	Position	poScreenCenter
	Scaled	False
BitBtn1	Name	OKButton
	Left	120
	Top	178
	Width	65
	Height	33
	Kind	bkOK
Panel1	Name	AboutPanel
	Left	8
	Top	8
	Width	281
	Height	161
	BevelOuter	bvLowered
Shape1	Left	96
	Top	12
	Width	4
	Height	80

COMPONENT	PROPERTY	SETTING
	Brush.Color	clGray
	Pen.Style	psClear
Label1	Name	Copyright
	Left	31
	Top	95
	Width	218
	Height	17
	Caption	Copyright © 1994 by Waite Group
	+Font	
	-Color	clBlack
	-Size	9
	-Name	Arial
	ParentFont	False
Label2	Name	Comments
	Left	18
	Top	119
	Width	249
	Height	41
	AutoSize	False
	Caption	This space can be used for licensing and other misc.
		comments or other useless stuff that shows up in the
		fine print in About boxes thanks to our lawyers.
	+Font	
	-Color	clBlack
	-Size	6
	-Name	Small Fonts
	ParentFont	False
	WordWrap	True
Image1	Name	AboutImage
	Left	16
	Top	8
	Width	80
	Height	80
	Picture	ABOUT.BMP
	Stretch	True

continued on next page

continued from previous page

COMPONENT	PROPERTY	SETTING
Shape2	Left	20
	Top	88
	Width	80
	Height	4
	Brush.Color	clGray
	Pen.Style	psClear
NoteBook1	Name	AboutNotebook
	Left	106
	Top	4
	Width	169
	Height	89

3. Select the Notebook component in Form1 and double-click in the right-hand column of the Notebook's Pages property in the Object Inspector to bring up the Notebook Editor. The Notebook Editor should have one page listed—the Default page. Add two more pages, naming them SystemStats and Credits. Close the Notebook Editor.
4. Be sure that Notebook1's ActivePage property is set to Default. Then, to the Default page of the Notebook component, add the components and set their properties as shown in Table 11-4.

Table 11-4 Components, properties, and settings for the Default page of Notebook1

COMPONENT	PROPERTY	SETTING
Label1	Name	ProgramName
	Left	16
	Top	6
	Width	136
	Height	26
	Caption	About Demo
	+Font	
	-Color	clBlack
	-Size	14
	-Name	Arial
	-Style	[fsBold]
	ParentFont	False

COMPONENT	PROPERTY	SETTING
Label2	Name	ProgramNameTwo
	Left	32
	Top	32
	Width	104
	Height	19
	Caption	for Windows
	+Font	
	-Color	clBlack
	-Size	10
	-Name	Arial
	-Style	[fsBold]
	ParentFont	False
Label3	Name	VersionLabel
	Left	42
	Top	56
	Width	84
	Height	19
	Caption	Version 1.0
	+Font	
	-Color	clBlack
	-Size	10
	-Name	Arial
	ParentFont	False

5. Set Notebook1's ActivePage property to SystemStats. Then, to the SystemStats page of the Notebook component, add components and set their properties as shown in Table 11-5.

Table 11-5 Components, properties, and settings for the SystemStats page of Notebook1

COMPONENT	PROPERTY	SETTING
Label1	Name	GDILabel
	Left	134
	Top	69
	Width	22
	Height	16

continued on next page

continued from previous page

COMPONENT	PROPERTY	SETTING
	Caption	GDI
	+Font	
	-Color	clNavy
	-Size	8
	-Name	Arial
	ParentFont	False
Label2	Name	UserLabel
	Left	67
	Top	69
	Width	27
	Height	16
	Caption	User
	+Font	
	-Color	clNavy
	-Size	8
	-Name	Arial
	ParentFont	False
Label3	Name	MemLabel
	Left	106
	Top	35
	Width	47
	Height	16
	Caption	Memory
	+Font	
	-Color	clNavy
	-Size	8
	-Name	Arial
	ParentFont	False
Label4	Name	
	Left	8
	Top	52
	Width	112
	Height	16
	Caption	Free Resources:
	+Font	

COMPONENT	PROPERTY	SETTING
	-Color	clBlack
	-Size	8
	-Name	Arial
	-Style	[fsBold]
	ParentFont	False
Label5	Name	
	Left	8
	Top	35
	Width	94
	Height	16
	Caption	Free Memory:
	+Font	
	-Color	clBlack
	-Size	8
	-Name	Arial
	-Style	[fsBold]
	ParentFont	False
Label6	Name	
	Left	8
	Top	18
	Width	88
	Height	16
	Caption	DOS Version:
	+Font	
	-Color	clBlack
	-Size	8
	-Name	Arial
	-Style	[fsBold]
	ParentFont	False
Label7	Name	
	Left	8
	Top	1
	Width	122
	Height	16
	Caption	Windows Version:

continued on next page

continued from previous page

COMPONENT	PROPERTY	SETTING
	+Font	
	-Color	clBlack
	-Size	8
	-Name	Arial
	-Style	[fsBold]
	ParentFont	False
Label8	Name	
	Left	26
	Top	69
	Width	37
	Height	16
	Caption	User:
	+Font	
	-Color	clBlack
	-Size	8
	-Name	Arial
	-Style	[fsBold]
	ParentFont	False
Label9	Name	
	Left	99
	Top	69
	Width	31
	Height	16
	Caption	GDI:
	+Font	
	-Color	clBlack
	-Size	8
	-Name	Arial
	-Style	[fsBold]
	ParentFont	False
Label10	Name	DosLabel
	Left	100
	Top	18
	Width	23
	Height	16

COMPONENT	PROPERTY	SETTING
	Caption	DOS
	+Font	
	-Color	clNavy
	-Size	8
	-Name	Arial
	ParentFont	False
Label11	Name	WinLabel
	Left	134
	Top	1
	Width	23
	Height	16
	Caption	Win
	+Font	
	-Color	clNavy
	-Size	8
	-Name	Arial
	ParentFont	False

6. Set Notebook1's ActivePage property to Credits. Then, to the Credits page of the Notebook component, add the component and set its properties as shown in Table 11-6.

Table 11-6 Component, properties, and settings for the Credits page of Notebook1

COMPONENT	PROPERTY	SETTING
Label1	Left	35
	Top	34
	Width	99
	Height	20
	Caption	Hello, World!

7. Return Notebook1's ActivePage property to Default.

8. Create an OnMouseDown event handler for AboutImage (Image1) and add the following code to the event handler.

```
procedure TAboutBox.AboutImageMouseDown(Sender: TObject;
  Button: TMouseButton; Shift: TShiftState; X, Y: Integer);
```

continued on next page

continued from previous page

```
begin
  Shape1.Visible := False;
  Shape2.Visible := False;
end;
```

9. Create an OnMouseUp event handler for AboutImage and add the following code to the event handler.

```
procedure TAboutBox.AboutImageMouseUp(Sender: TObject;
  Button: TMouseButton; Shift: TShiftState; X, Y: Integer);
begin
  Shape1.Visible := True;
  Shape2.Visible := True;
end;
```

10. Create an OnDblClick event handler for AboutImage and add the following code to the event handler. This is the code that will show the different pages of Notebook1.

```
procedure TAboutBox.AboutImageDblClick(Sender: TObject);
var
  Heap: TSysHeapInfo;
  User, GDI: string;
  DosVer, WinVer: word;
begin
  if GetKeyState(vk_Menu) and $8000 <> 0 then
    case AboutNotebook.PageIndex of
      0 : begin
            WinVer := LoWord(GetVersion);
            DosVer := HiWord(GetVersion);
            WinLabel.Caption := IntToStr(Lo(WinVer))+'.'+IntToStr(Hi(WinVer));
            DosLabel.Caption := IntToStr(Hi(DosVer))+'.'+IntToStr(Lo(DosVer));
            MemLabel.Caption := IntToStr(GetFreeSpace(0) div 1024) + 'k';
            Heap.dwSize := SizeOf(TSysHeapInfo);
            SystemHeapInfo(@Heap);
            UserLabel.Caption := IntToStr(Heap.wUserFreePercent) + '%';
            GDILabel.Caption := IntToStr(Heap.wGDIFreePercent) + '%';
            AboutNotebook.PageIndex := AboutNotebook.PageIndex + 1
          end;
      1 : AboutNotebook.PageIndex := AboutNotebook.PageIndex + 1;
      2 : AboutNotebook.PageIndex := 0;
    end;
end;
```

11. Double-click on the OK button and add the following code to the resulting OnClick event handler.

```
procedure TAboutBox.OKButtonClick(Sender: TObject);
begin
  Close;
end;
```

12. While still in the Code Editor, move to the top of the unit and add Toolhelp to the *uses* clause that follows the *interface* keyword.

13. Compile and test the project.

How It Works

This How-To makes use of the Notebook component to hide credit and information screens from the user. Access to the hidden notebook pages is controlled by checking for the ALT key when the image on the form is double-clicked.

Note: This How-To uses the Windows API function GetVersion to determine the version of Windows that the application is running on. The GetVersion API does not return the correct version in all cases. Refer to Chapter 7 for details on how to overcome this limitation.

Comments

This How-To is not necessarily designed to be the ultimate in About boxes; it is meant to give you some ideas and point you in the right direction for developing your own. If you have seen some of the hidden features or "Easter Eggs" in the About boxes of commercial-quality programs, you probably understand that the About box is an opportunity for developers to add a unique signature to the application. Be creative.

You may be wondering whether Delphi has an Easter Egg in its About box. It actually has more than one. Try holding down the ALT key and typing **version**, **team**, **developers**, or **and**. The last one shows a picture of Anders Hejlsberg, who originally developed Borland's Turbo Pascal and helped it evolve over the course of 12 years into what is now known as Delphi.

11.3 How Do I...
Create separate help hints and status line help?

COMPLEXITY: INTERMEDIATE

Problem

Delphi makes it easy to add help hints to my toolbars and other controls. I'd like to be able to add more detailed hints to the status line of my application for each control. How can I do this with Delphi?

Technique

Adding detailed status line help is easy with Delphi. The capability is actually built in, but it is not immediately obvious how to do it. This How-To demonstrates the technique and shows off a few other things you can do with hints in Delphi.

Steps

Run HINT.EXE. Move the mouse cursor over the various components on the toolbar, as shown in Figure 11-3. Notice some of the effects demonstrated with this How-To—there are separate help hints and status line help and different colors for the hints; you can move the help hints to positions other than their default positions, and have different hints for different regions of a single component.

1. Create a new project with a blank form and name it HINT.DPR. Name the unit HINT1.PAS.

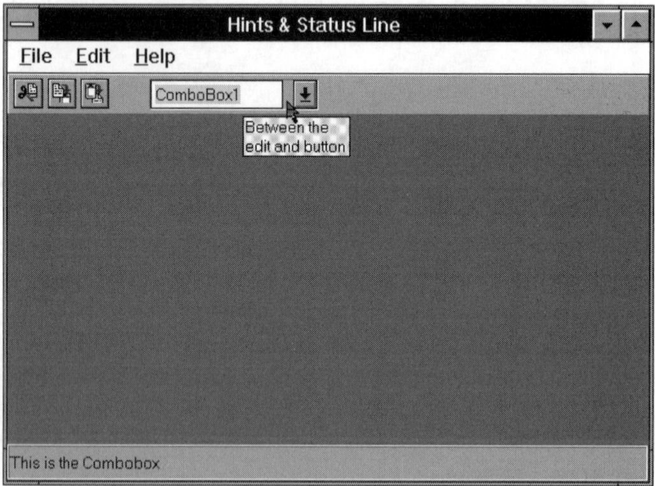

Figure 11-3 HINT at run time

2. Add components and set their properties as shown in Table 11-7.

Table 11-7 Components, properties, and settings for Form1 of the HINT project

COMPONENT	PROPERTY	SETTING
Form1	Left	199
	Top	118
	Width	435
	Height	300
	Caption	Hints & Status Line
	Color	clTeal
	+Font	
	-Color	clBlack

COMPONENT	PROPERTY	SETTING
	-Size	10
	-Name	MS Sans Serif
	Scaled	False
	ShowHint	True
Panel1	Left	0
	Top	208
	Width	427
	Height	30
	Align	alBottom
	Alignment	taLeftJustify
	BevelInner	bvLowered
	+Font	
	-Color	clBlack
	-Size	8
	-Name	MS Sans Serif
	ParentFont	False
Panel2	Left	0
	Top	0
	Width	427
	Height	34
	Align	alTop

3. Add components to Panel1 and set their properties as shown in Table 11-8.

Table 11-8 Components, settings, and properties for Panel1 in the HINT project

COMPONENT	PROPERTY	SETTING
SpeedButton1	Left	5
	Top	4
	Width	25
	Height	25
	Hint	Cut|Cut selected text to the Clipboard
	Glyph	
SpeedButton2	Left	34
	Top	4

continued on next page

continued from previous page

COMPONENT	PROPERTY	SETTING
	Width	25
	Height	25
	Hint	Copy|Copy selected text to the Clipboard
	Glyph	
SpeedButton3	Left	63
	Top	4
	Width	25
	Height	25
	Hint	Paste|Paste from the Clipboard
	Glyph	
ComboBox1	Left	123
	Top	5
	Width	145
	Height	24
	Hint	This is the ComboBox
	+Font	
	-Color	clBlack
	-Size	8
	-Name	MS Sans Serif
	ParentFont	False
	Text	ComboBox1

4. Add a MainMenu component to Form1 and create File, Edit, and Help menus.
5. Add submenus and set the Hint property for each menu item as shown in Table 11-9.

Table 11-9 Menu item captions and hints for MainMenu1 in the HINT project

MENU CAPTION	HINT
&File	|File-related functions
&New	|Create a new file
&Open	|Open a file
-	
&Print	|Print a file
Print &Setup	|Set up the printer
-	

MENU CAPTION	HINT
E&xit	|Exit the application
&Edit	|Editing functions
Cu&t	|Cut selected text to the Clipboard
&Copy	|Copy selected text to the Clipboard
&Paste	|Paste from the Clipboard
&Help	|Help-related functions
&Contents	|Display the help contents
&About	|Display the About box

6. Create an OnClick event handler for the Exit menu item in the File menu. Add the following code to the event handler.

```
procedure TForm1.Exit1Click(Sender: TObject);
begin
  Close;
end;
```

7. Double-click on Form1 and add the following code to the resulting OnCreate event handler. This code defines event handlers for the Application.OnHint and Application.OnShowHint events.

```
procedure TForm1.FormCreate(Sender: TObject);
begin
  Application.OnHint := DoHint;
  Application.OnShowHint := DoShowHint;
end;
```

8. While still in the Code Editor, move up to the class declaration for Form1 and add method declarations for the two event handlers as follows:

```
type
  TForm1 = class(TForm)
    MainMenu1: TMainMenu;
    ...
    Panel1: TPanel;
    Panel2: TPanel;
    SpeedButton1: TSpeedButton;
    SpeedButton2: TSpeedButton;
    SpeedButton3: TSpeedButton;
    ComboBox1: TComboBox;
    procedure Exit1Click(Sender: TObject);
    procedure FormCreate(Sender: TObject);
  private
```

continued on next page

continued from previous page

```
    { Private declarations }
    procedure DoHint(Sender: TObject);
    procedure DoShowHint(var HintStr: string; var CanShow: Boolean;
      var HintInfo: THintInfo);
  public
    { Public declarations }
  end;
```

9. Add the DoHint event handler following the *implementation* keyword as shown here:

```
implementation

{$R *.DFM}

procedure TForm1.DoHint(Sender: TObject);
begin
  Panel1.Caption := Application.Hint;
end;
```

10. Add the DoShowHint event handler following the DoHint event handler you just added:

```
procedure TForm1.DoHint(Sender: TObject);
begin
  Panel1.Caption := Application.Hint;
end;

procedure TForm1.DoShowHint(var HintStr: string; var CanShow: Boolean;
  var HintInfo: THintInfo);
begin
  with HintInfo do begin
    if HintControl = SpeedButton1 then
      HintColor := clAqua;
    if HintControl = SpeedButton2 then
      HintPos.Y := HintPos.Y - 55;
    if HintControl = SpeedButton3 then
      HintColor := clLime;
    if HintControl = Combobox1 then begin
      if CursorPos.X < 116 then begin
        CursorRect.Right := 116;
        HintStr := 'Edit portion of Combobox1';
      end;
      if (CursorPos.X >= 116) and (CursorPos.X < 125) then begin
        CursorRect.Left := 116;
        CursorRect.Right := 125;
        HintPos.X := HintPos.X + 80;
        HintMaxWidth := 90;
        HintStr := 'Between the edit and button';
      end;
      if CursorPos.X >= 125 then begin
        CursorRect.Left := 125;
        CursorRect.Right := 145;
```

```
        HintPos.X := HintPos.X + 70;
        HintStr := 'Button portion of Combobox1';
      end;
    end;
  end;
end;
```

11. Compile and test the project.

How It Works

Delphi has built-in support to display short and long hints. The *pipe* character (|) is used in a component's Hint property to separate the short hint from the long hint. The long hint is automatically routed to the OnHint event handler if one is assigned, and the short hint is used for the help hint windows.

The OnShowHint event handler gives you much more control over the display of the help hints. This How-To demonstrates several of the things you can do simply by manipulating the parameters in the OnShowHint event handler.

Comments

This How-To doesn't really add to Delphi's functionality; it merely demonstrates how to use some features that are hard to find in the documentation. The help hints typically make an application much easier to use—provide them wherever you think they are appropriate.

11.4 How Do I...
Make a customizable toolbar like Delphi's?

COMPLEXITY: ADVANCED

Problem

I'd like to add a professional touch to my application by having a customizable toolbar. I really like the way Delphi lets me drag tool buttons on and off the toolbar to configure it exactly the way I want it. Is there a way I can do this in my Delphi applications?

Technique

As mentioned before, an interesting (and useful) aspect of Delphi is the fact that it was used to build Delphi. This means that most anything you see in the Delphi Integrated Development Environment (IDE) can be duplicated at home. Many times, these effects aren't too difficult to reproduce—but other times the effects can be time-consuming and difficult to accomplish. This How-To brings together many of the tips and techniques covered throughout the book to mold a highly professional, customizable toolbar almost exactly like the one found in Delphi. It is based on (and can replace) the SDI Application template in Delphi's Gallery.

Steps

Run SDIAPP.EXE. Right-click on the toolbar and select the Configure option from the pop-up menu. When the Speedbar Editor dialog shows, as shown in Figure 11-4, the toolbar is put into the edit mode. Notice that you can add tool buttons to the toolbar by dragging them from the list box onto the toolbar. You can remove tool buttons from the toolbar by dragging them off of the toolbar. You can also move tool buttons on the toolbar by dragging them to the desired position.

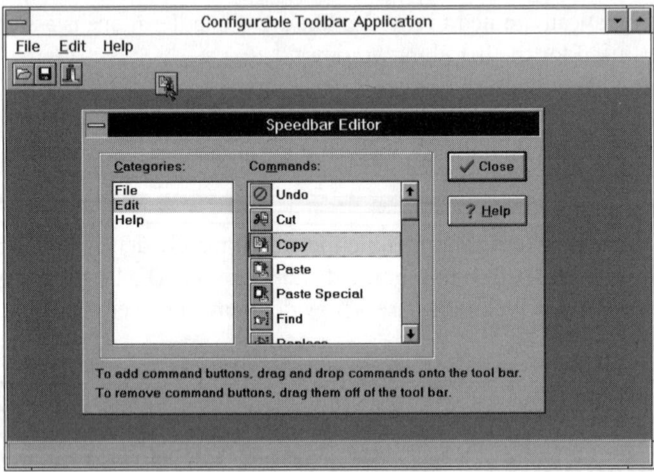

Figure 11-4 Speedbar Editor dialog

Creating the TDragSpeedButton Component

Before diving into the application itself, you need to create a SpeedButton component that can handle drag-and-drop operations. The existing SpeedButton has this capability, but the necessary properties are not published. You can create a TDragSpeedButton component as follows.

1. Select File|New Component from Delphi's main menu to run the Component Expert.
2. Enter **TDragSpeedButton** in the Class Name edit field. Choose TSpeedButton for the Ancestor Type from the drop-down list and choose Samples for the Palette Page.
3. Click the OK button. A new component unit will be shown in the Code Editor.

4. Change the name of the unit by saving it as DRAGSB.PAS and add the following code to the object declaration in the component's unit. This will allow you to get access to the drag-and-drop properties via the Object Inspector.

```
type
  TDragSpeedButton = class(TSpeedButton)
  private
    { Private declarations }
  protected
    { Protected declarations }
  public
    { Public declarations }
  published
    { Published declarations }
    property DragMode;
    property DragCursor;
    property OnDragDrop;
    property OnDragOver;
    property OnEndDrag;
  end;
```

5. Choose Options|Install Components from Delphi's main menu to add your new component to the Component Palette in the following steps.
6. Click on the Add button in the Install Components dialog and enter the path for your newly created DRAGSB.PAS file, or select it by clicking on the Browse button in the Add Module dialog.
7. Click on the OK buttons in the Add Module and Install Components dialogs. Delphi will then compile your Component Palette and add the DragSpeedButton component to the Samples page.
8. Verify that the new component is on the Samples page, and save and close the DRAGSB.PAS file.

Building the SDIAPP Application

Now that you've added DragSpeedButton to the Component Palette, you can continue building your application.

1. Select Options|Environment from Delphi's main menu. Ensure that the Use Gallery On New Project option is enabled on the first page of the Environment Options dialog, and close the dialog by clicking on the OK button.
2. Select File|New Project from Delphi's main menu. Double-click on the SDI Application template in the Browse Gallery dialog and choose an appropriate directory for your project files.
3. You now need to update the existing template to use the new TDragSpeedButton class. Open the DFM file for the main form by choosing File|Open File from

Delphi's main menu. Select DFM from the File Type combo box and open SDIMAIN.DFM.

4. Perform a Search and Replace on SDIMAIN.DFM to replace all instances of TSpeedButton with TDragSpeedButton. Save and close the file.
5. Select View|Forms from Delphi's main menu and double-click on SDIAppForm in the View Form dialog. Activate the Code Editor and perform a Search and Replace in the SDIMAIN.PAS unit to replace all instances of TSpeedButton with TDragSpeedButton.
6. Rename the project to CONFIG.DPR and rename SDIMAIN.PAS to CONFIG1.PAS to avoid any conflicts with other SDI projects.
7. Check the settings of the components and properties of the SDIAppForm as shown in Table 11-10.

Table 11-10 Components, properties, and settings for SDIAppForm in the SDIApp project

COMPONENT	PROPERTY	SETTING
SDIAppForm	Left	225
	Top	143
	Width	502
	Height	300
	Color	clTeal
	Scaled	False
SpeedPanel	Height	33
	DragCursor	crDefault
OpenBtn	Left	7
	Top	3
	Width	25
	Height	25
	Hint	Open|Open File
	DragCursor	crDefault
SaveBtn	Left	31
	Top	3
	Width	25
	Height	25
	Hint	Save|Save Current File
	DragCursor	crDefault
ExitBtn	Left	60

COMPONENT	PROPERTY	SETTING
	Top	3
	Width	25
	Height	25
	Hint	Exit|Exit Program
	DragCursor	crDefault

8. Double-click on the MainMenu component to show the Menu Editor. Highlight the Help menu item, press INS and type **&Edit** to add an Edit menu.
9. Add items to the Edit menu as shown in Table 11-11.

Table 11-11 Menu items and captions for the Edit menu in MainMenu of the SDIApp project

MENU ITEM	CAPTION
Undo1	&Undo
N2	-
Cut1	Cu&t
Copy1	&Copy
Paste1	&Paste
PasteSpecial1	Paste &Special...
N3	-
Find1	&Find
Replace1	R&eplace
Goto1	&Go To...
N4	-
Links1	Lin&ks...
Object1	&Object

10. Highlight the About item in the Help menu, press INS and type **&Contents** to add a Contents item to the Help menu.
11. Create an OnClick event handler for the Undo1 menu item. In the Object Inspector, change the name of the event handler to ItemClick and add the following code to the event handler. This code simply shows a message dialog verifying the operation of the menu item and matching speed button.

```
procedure TSDIAppForm.ItemClick(Sender: TObject);
begin
```

continued on next page

continued from previous page

```
  ShowMessage('You picked ' + TComponent(Sender).Name);
end;
```

12. Create OnClick event handlers and add similar code to the other menu items that you have added to the MainMenu component.

13. Add a PopupMenu component to SDIAppForm and add menu items as shown in Table 11-12.

Table 11-12 Menu items and captions for PopupMenu1 of the SDIApp project

MENU ITEM	CAPTION
Configure1	&Configure...
ShowHints1	&Show Hints

14. Set the Checked property of the ShowHints1 menu item to True. Create an OnClick event handler for ShowHints1 and add the following code.

```
procedure TSDIAppForm.ShowHints1Click(Sender: TObject);
begin
  ShowHints1.Checked := not(ShowHints1.Checked);
  SpeedPanel.ShowHint := ShowHints1.Checked;
end;
```

15. Create an OnClick event handler for the Configure1 menu item and add the following code to the event handler.

```
procedure TSDIAppForm.Configure1Click(Sender: TObject);
begin
  SBEditor.Show;
end;
```

16. Close the Menu Editor. Set SpeedPanel's PopupMenu property to PopupMenu1.

17. Add 12 DragSpeedButton components to the SpeedPanel. Remember to use the DragSpeedButton component that you created at the beginning of this How-To and not the regular SpeedButton component.

18. Set the DragSpeedButton component properties and event handlers as shown in Table 11-13. Add an appropriate glyph to each button.

Note: Sample glyphs can be found in the DELPHI\IMAGES\BUTTONS directory.

Table 11-13 Components, properties, and settings for SpeedPanel of the SDIApp project

COMPONENT	PROPERTY	SETTING
SpeedButton1	Tag	1
	Left	178
	Top	3
	Width	25
	Height	25
	Hint	Undo|Undo an edit operation
	Visible	False
	OnClick	ItemClick
	DragCursor	crDefault
SpeedButton2	Tag	1
	Left	204
	Top	3
	Width	25
	Height	25
	Hint	Cut|Cut selected text to the Clipboard
	Visible	False
	OnClick	ItemClick
	DragCursor	crDefault
SpeedButton3	Tag	1
	Left	230
	Top	3
	Width	25
	Height	25
	Hint	Copy|Copy the selected text to the Clipboard
	Visible	False
	OnClick	ItemClick
	DragCursor	crDefault
SpeedButton4	Tag	1
	Left	256
	Top	3
	Width	25
	Height	25
	Hint	Paste|Paste text from the Clipboard
	Visible	False

continued on next page

continued from previous page

COMPONENT	PROPERTY	SETTING
	OnClick	ItemClick
	DragCursor	crDefault
SpeedButton5	Tag	1
	Left	282
	Top	3
	Width	25
	Height	25
	Hint	Paste Special|Paste text from the Clipboard using
		special paste
	Visible	False
	OnClick	ItemClick
	DragCursor	crDefault
SpeedButton6	Tag	1
	Left	308
	Top	3
	Width	25
	Height	25
	Hint	Find|Find text
	Visible	False
	OnClick	ItemClick
	DragCursor	crDefault
SpeedButton7	Tag	1
	Left	334
	Top	3
	Width	25
	Height	25
	Hint	Replace|Find text and replace it
	Visible	False
	OnClick	ItemClick
	DragCursor	crDefault
SpeedButton8	Tag	1
	Left	360
	Top	3
	Width	25
	Height	25

COMPONENT	PROPERTY	SETTING
	Hint	Go To|Go to a line in the text
	Visible	False
	OnClick	ItemClick
	DragCursor	crDefault
SpeedButton9	Tag	1
	Left	386
	Top	3
	Width	25
	Height	25
	Hint	Links|Examine links with other programs
	Visible	False
	OnClick	ItemClick
	DragCursor	crDefault
SpeedButton10	Tag	1
	Left	412
	Top	3
	Width	25
	Height	25
	Hint	Object|Examine object
	Visible	False
	OnClick	ItemClick
	DragCursor	crDefault
SpeedButton11	Tag	2
	Left	464
	Top	3
	Width	25
	Height	25
	Hint	Help Contents|Show the help contents
	Visible	False
	OnClick	ItemClick
	DragCursor	crDefault
SpeedButton12	Tag	2
	Left	438
	Top	3
	Width	25

continued on next page

continued from previous page

COMPONENT	PROPERTY	SETTING
	Height	25
	Hint	About|Show the About box
	Visible	False
	OnClick	About1Click
	DragCursor	crDefault

19. Add a new form to the project. Name the form SBEditor and save the unit as SBEDIT.PAS.
20. Add components and set their properties as shown in Table 11-14.

Table 11-14 Components, properties, and settings for SBEditor of the SDIApp project

COMPONENT	PROPERTY	SETTING
SBEditor	Left	242
	Top	153
	BorderStyle	bsDialog
	Caption	Speedbar Editor
	+Font	
	-Color	clBlack
	-Size	8
	-Name	MS Sans Serif
	-Style	[fsBold]
	Position	poScreenCenter
Bevel1	Left	16
	Top	16
	Width	377
	Height	225
	Shape	bsFrame
Label1	Left	34
	Top	23
	Width	81
	Height	16
	Caption	&Categories:
	FocusControl	ListBox1
Label2	Left	186

COMPONENT	PROPERTY	SETTING
	Top	23
	Width	82
	Height	16
	Caption	Co&mmands:
	FocusControl	FileListBox
Label3	Left	11
	Top	248
	Width	489
	Height	17
	AutoSize	False
	Caption	To add command buttons, drag and drop commands
		onto the toolbar.
Label4	Left	11
	Top	269
	Width	489
	Height	17
	AutoSize	False
	Caption	To remove command buttons, drag them off
		of the toolbar.
ListBox1	Left	32
	Top	48
	Width	137
	Height	177
	ItemHeight	16
	Items	File
		Edit
		Help
BitBtn1	Left	408
	Top	16
	Width	89
	Height	33
	Caption	Close
	Kind	bkOK
BitBtn2	Left	408
	Top	64

continued on next page

continued from previous page

COMPONENT	PROPERTY	SETTING
	Width	89
	Height	33
	Kind	bkHelp
Notebook1	Left	180
	Top	44
	Width	201
	Height	185

21. Create three pages for the Notebook component and name them FileMenu, EditMenu, and HelpMenu.

22. Add a ListBox component to each page. Name the ListBox component on the FileMenu page FileListBox, the one on the EditMenu page EditListBox, and the one on the HelpMenu page HelpListBox.

23. Set the properties for each ListBox component as shown in Table 11-15.

Table 11-15 Component, properties, and settings for the ListBox components in Notebook1

COMPONENT	PROPERTY	SETTING
ListBox	Left	4
	Top	4
	Width	193
	Height	177
	DragCursor	crDefault
	ItemHeight	26
	Style	lbOwnerDrawFixed

24. Create an OnClick event handler for ListBox1 and add the following code to the event handler.

```
procedure TSBEditor.ListBox1Click(Sender: TObject);
begin
  { Control the synchronization of listbox and notebook }
  NoteBook1.PageIndex := ListBox1.ItemIndex;
  case Notebook1.PageIndex of
    0: Label2.FocusControl := FileListBox;
    1: Label2.FocusControl := EditListBox;
    2: Label2.FocusControl := HelpListBox;
    else ShowMessage('Label2.FocusControl is incorrectly defined');
  end;
end;
```

25. Create an OnCreate event handler for the SBEditor form and add the following code to the event handler. This code puts the speed buttons in edit mode and fills the Owner-Draw list boxes with images of the speed buttons.

```
procedure TSBEditor.FormCreate(Sender: TObject);
var
  I : Integer;
  ButtonImage: TButtonImage;
  SBHint: String;
begin
  { Initialize flag used during dragging }
  FAlreadyDragging := False;
  { Ensure listbox and notebook are synchronized }
  ListBox1.ItemIndex := 0;
  NoteBook1.PageIndex := ListBox1.ItemIndex;
  { Load listboxes with images for each speedbutton on the form }
  with Application.MainForm do
  for I := 0 to ComponentCount - 1 do
     if Components[I] is TDragSpeedButton then
     begin
        ButtonImage := TButtonImage.Create;
        ButtonImage.SpeedButton := TSpeedButton(Components[I]);
        SBHint := GetShortHint(TSpeedButton(Components[I]).Hint);
        { Sort speedbuttons according to their Tag property }
        case TSpeedButton(Components[I]).Tag of
          0: FileListBox.Items.AddObject(SBHint, ButtonImage);
          1: EditListBox.Items.AddObject(SBHint, ButtonImage);
          2: HelpListBox.Items.AddObject(SBHint, ButtonImage);
          else ShowMessage('Speedbuttons exist with incorrect Tags');
        end;
     end;
  FileListBox.ItemHeight := ButtonImage.SpeedButton.Height + 2;
  EditListBox.ItemHeight := ButtonImage.SpeedButton.Height + 2;
  HelpListBox.ItemHeight := ButtonImage.SpeedButton.Height + 2;
end;
```

26. While still in the Code Editor, move up to the form's object declaration and add the following variables to the *private* section and a CreateParams procedure declaration to the object's *public* section.

```
TSBEditor = class(TForm)
  ...
  private
    { Private declarations }
    FButtonImage: TButtonImage;
    FAlreadyDragging: Boolean;
  public
    { Public declarations }
    procedure CreateParams(var Params: TCreateParams); override;
  end;
```

27. Move down to the *implementation* section of the unit and add the CreateParams procedure as shown here. This code sets the SBEditor's window style to stay on top of the parent form even when the parent form has the focus.

```
implementation

uses SDIMain;

{$R *.DFM}

{ Form }
procedure TSBEditor.CreateParams(var Params: TCreateParams);
begin
  inherited CreateParams(Params);
  with Params do
  begin
    { Ensures form stays on top of parent form }
    Style := Style or ws_Overlapped;
    WndParent := Application.MainForm.Handle;
  end;
end;
```

28. Create an OnDestroy event handler for the SBEditor and add the following code to ensure the ButtonImages in the list boxes are cleaned up when the form is destroyed.

```
procedure TSBEditor.FormDestroy(Sender: TObject);
var
  I: integer;
begin
  for I := 0 to FileListBox.Items.Count - 1 do
    TButtonImage(FileListBox.Items.Objects[I]).Free;
  for I := 0 to EditListBox.Items.Count - 1 do
    TButtonImage(EditListBox.Items.Objects[I]).Free;
  for I := 0 to HelpListBox.Items.Count - 1 do
    TButtonImage(HelpListBox.Items.Objects[I]).Free;
end;
```

29. Create an OnShow event handler for the SBEditor form and add the following code to the event handler. This code places the toolbar in the speed button edit mode.

```
procedure TSBEditor.FormShow(Sender: TObject);
var
  I : Integer;
begin
  { Enter edit mode when form opens }
  with SDIAppForm do
  for I := 0 to ComponentCount - 1 do
    if Components[I] is TDragSpeedButton then
      TDragSpeedButton(Components[I]).DragMode := dmAutomatic;
end;
```

30. Create an OnClose event handler for the SBEditor form and add the following code to the event handler. This code exits the speed button edit mode.

```
procedure TSBEditor.FormClose(Sender: TObject; var Action: TCloseAction);
var
  I : Integer;
begin
  { Exit edit mode when form closes }
  with SDIAppForm do
  for I := 0 to ComponentCount - 1 do
    if Components[I] is TDragSpeedButton then
      TDragSpeedButton(Components[I]).DragMode := dmManual;
end;
```

31. Create an OnClick event handler for the Close button and add the following code to the event handler.

```
procedure TSBEditor.BitBtn1Click(Sender: TObject);
begin
  Close;
end;
```

32. While still in the Code Editor, add DragSB to the *interface* section's *uses* clause, as shown here:

```
unit Sbedit;

interface

uses
  SysUtils, WinTypes, WinProcs, Messages, Classes, Graphics, Controls,
  Forms, Dialogs, StdCtrls, ExtCtrls, Buttons, DragSB;

type
  TSBEditor = class(TForm)
```

33. In this step, add a *forward* declaration just before the TSBEditor class for the TButtonImage class that you will be adding shortly. This allows the TSBEditor class to reference the TButtonImage class even though the TButtonImage class is declared after the TSBEditor class.

```
uses
  SysUtils, WinTypes, WinProcs, Messages, Classes, Graphics, Controls,
  Forms, Dialogs, StdCtrls, ExtCtrls, Buttons, DragSB;

type
  TButtonImage = class;

  TSBEditor = class(TForm)
```

34. Add a class declaration for the TButtonImage class to the *interface* section of the unit following the TSBEditor class, as shown here. The TButtonImage class handles all of the drawing and moving of the speed button images.

```
TSBEditor = class(TForm)
...
private
    { Private declarations }
    FButtonImage: TButtonImage;
    FAlreadyDragging: Boolean;
  public
    { Public declarations }
    procedure CreateParams(var Params: TCreateParams); override;
  end;

  TButtonImage = class(TObject)
  private
    FSpeedButton: TSpeedButton;
    FNumGlyphs: Integer;
    FImage: TBitmap;
    FBackGround: TBitmap;
    FImagePos: TPoint;
    FOffSet: TPoint;
    procedure SetSpeedButton(Value: TSpeedbutton);
  public
    constructor Create;
    destructor Destroy; override;
    procedure Draw(Canvas: TCanvas; X, Y: Integer);
    procedure DrawToScreen(X, Y: Integer; OffSet: TPoint);
    procedure EraseScreenImage(X, Y: Integer);
    procedure DragImage(X, Y: Integer);
    property SpeedButton: TSpeedButton read FSpeedButton write SetSpeedButton;
    property NumGlyphs: Integer read FNumGlyphs write FNumGlyphs;
    property Offset: TPoint read FOffSet write FOffSet;
  end;

var
  SBEditor: TSBEditor;

implementation
```

35. In the *implementation* section of the unit, add the TButtonImage's Create and Destroy methods as shown here. While you're in the area, you can add a *uses* clause so you can also reference the main form.

```
implementation

uses SDIMain;

{$R *.DFM}

{ TButtonImage }
constructor TButtonImage.Create;
begin
  FImage := TBitmap.Create;
```

```
  FBackGround := TBitmap.Create;
  FNumGlyphs := 1;
end;

destructor TButtonImage.Destroy;
begin
  FImage.Free;
  FBackGround.Free;
  inherited Destroy;
end;
```

36. Immediately following the Create and Destroy methods, add TButtonImage's SetSpeedButton method:

```
procedure TButtonImage.SetSpeedButton(Value: TSpeedButton);
begin
  if FSpeedButton  Value then
  begin
    FSpeedButton := Value;
    FNumGlyphs := Value.NumGlyphs;
  end;
end;
```

37. Immediately following the SetSpeedButton method, add the Draw method:

```
procedure TButtonImage.Draw(Canvas: TCanvas; X, Y: Integer);
var
  BX, BY: Integer;
  Target: TRect;
  Source: TRect;
  SavePen, SaveBrush: TColor;
begin
  with Canvas do
  begin
    SavePen := Canvas.Pen.Color;
    SaveBrush := Canvas.Brush.Color;

    { Draws a blank buttonface on the target canvas }
    Target := DrawButtonFace(Canvas, Bounds(X, Y, FSpeedButton.Width,
      FSpeedButton.Height), 1, bsWin31, False, False, False);

    { Copy glyph from speedbutton to buttonface }
    BX := FSpeedButton.Glyph.Width div FSpeedButton.NumGlyphs;
    if BX > 0 then
    begin
      Target := Bounds(X, Y, BX, FSpeedButton.Glyph.Height);
      OffsetRect(Target, (FSpeedButton.Width div 2) - (BX div 2),
        (FSpeedButton.Height div 2) - (FSpeedButton.Glyph.Height div 2));
      Source := Bounds(0, 0, BX, FSpeedButton.Glyph.Height);
      BrushCopy(Target, FSpeedButton.Glyph, Source,
        FSpeedButton.Glyph.Canvas.Pixels[0, FSpeedButton.Glyph.Height - 1]);
    end;
```

continued on next page

continued from previous page

```
    Canvas.Pen.Color := SavePen;
    Canvas.Brush.Color := SaveBrush;
  end;
end;
```

38. Add TButtonImage's DrawToScreen method:

```
{Draws image of speedbutton to screen at specified coordinates }
procedure TButtonImage.DrawToScreen(X, Y: Integer; OffSet: TPoint);
var
  DC: HDC;
begin
  { Save offset for future use }
  FOffSet := OffSet;
  { Save coordinates for future use }
  FImagePos := Point(X, Y);
  { Initialize bitmaps }
  FImage.Width := FSpeedButton.Width;
  FImage.Height := FSpeedButton.Height;
  FBackGround.Width := FSpeedButton.Width;
  FBackGround.Height := FSpeedButton.Height;
  { Draw a copy of the speedbutton on the FImage bitmap }
  Draw(FImage.Canvas, 0, 0);
  { Get DC of the screen }
  DC := GetDC(0);
  try
    { Store background where the image is going to go }
    BitBlt(FBackGround.Canvas.Handle, 0, 0, FBackGround.Width,
      FBackGround.Height, DC, X - OffSet.X, Y - OffSet.Y, SRCCOPY);
    { Copy the image onto the screen }
    BitBlt(DC, X - OffSet.X, Y - OffSet.Y, FImage.Width, FImage.Height,
      FImage.Canvas.Handle, 0, 0, SRCCOPY);
  finally
    ReleaseDC(0, DC);
  end;
end;
```

39. Add TButtonImage's EraseScreenImage method:

```
{ Erases the button image }
procedure TButtonImage.EraseScreenImage(X, Y: Integer);
var
  DC: HDC;
begin
  { Get Screen DC }
  DC := GetDC(0);
  try
    { Copy background image to the screen }
    BitBlt(DC, X - FOffSet.X, Y - FOffSet.Y, FBackGround.Width,
      FBackGround.Height, FBackGround.Canvas.Handle, 0, 0, SRCCopy);
  finally
    ReleaseDC(0, DC);
  end;
  { Erase the bitmaps }
```

```
  FImage.Height := 0;
  FBackGround.Height := 0;
end;
```

40. Now add TButtonImage's DragImage method. This method manages the dragging of the bitmap image.

```
{ Update image position during drag operation }
procedure TButtonImage.DragImage(X, Y: Integer);
var
  DC: HDC;
  SourceRect, DestRect: TRect;
begin
  { Get screen DC }
  DC := GetDC(0);
  try
    { Copy stored background to screen }
    BitBlt(DC, FImagePos.X - FOffSet.X, FImagePos.Y - FOffSet.Y,
      FImage.Width, FImage.Height, FBackGround.Canvas.Handle, 0, 0, SRCCOPY);
    { Get background for new position }
    BitBlt(FBackGround.Canvas.Handle, 0, 0, FBackGround.Width,
      FBackGround.Height, DC, X - FOffSet.X, Y - FOffSet.Y, SRCCOPY);
    { Copy image to screen at new position }
    BitBlt(DC, X - FOffSet.X, Y - FOffSet.Y, FImage.Width, FImage.Height,
      FImage.Canvas.Handle, 0, 0, SRCCOPY);
  finally
    ReleaseDC(0, DC);
  end;
  { Update stored position }
  FImagePos := Point(X, Y);
end;
```

41. Create an OnDragOver event handler for the FileListBox. In the Object Inspector, delete File from the name of the event handler so it is named ListBoxDragOver. Add the following code to the event handler.

```
procedure TSBEditor.ListBoxDragOver(Sender, Source: TObject; X,
  Y: Integer; State: TDragState; var Accept: Boolean);
var
  S, OffSet: TPoint;
begin
  Accept := Source is TListBox;
  if Source is TListBox then
    if not FAlreadyDragging then
    begin
      S := TListBox(Source).ClientToScreen(Point(X, Y));
      { Calculate OffSet to center cursor in image }
      OffSet.X := FButtonImage.SpeedButton.Width div 2;
      OffSet.Y := FButtonImage.SpeedButton.Height div 2;
      { Draw button at cursor }
      FButtonImage.DrawToScreen(S.X, S.Y, OffSet);
      FAlreadyDragging := True;
    end;
end;
```

42. Create an OnDrawItem event handler for the FileListBox. In the Object Inspector, delete File from the name of the event handler so it is named ListBoxDrawItem. Add the following code to the event handler.

```
procedure TSBEditor.ListBoxDrawItem(Control: TWinControl;
  Index: Integer; Rect: TRect; State: TOwnerDrawState);
var
  ButtonImage: TButtonImage;
  R: TRect;
  C: array[0..255] of Char;
begin
  ButtonImage := TButtonImage(TListBox(Control).Items.Objects[Index]);
  { Make a space for the button }
  ExtTextOut(TListBox(Control).Canvas.Handle, R.Left, R.Top, ETO_OPAQUE,
    @Rect, nil, 0, nil);
  { Draw the button in the list box }
  ButtonImage.Draw(TListBox(Control).Canvas, Rect.Left + 2, Rect.Top + 1);

  R := Rect;
  { Move over for the text string }
  Inc(R.Left, ButtonImage.SpeedButton.Width + 2 + 4);
  { Draw the text string for the button item }
  DrawText(TListBox(Control).Canvas.Handle, StrPCopy(C,
    TListBox(Control).Items[Index]), -1, R, DT_VCENTER or DT_SINGLELINE);
end;
```

43. Create an OnMouseDown event handler for the FileListBox. In the Object Inspector, delete File from the name of the event handler so it is named ListBoxMouseDown. Add the following code to the event handler.

```
procedure TSBEditor.ListBoxMouseDown(Sender: TObject;
  Button: TMouseButton; Shift: TShiftState; X, Y: Integer);
begin
  { Make sure dragging only starts if cursor is over an item }
  if Button = mbLeft then
    with Sender as TListBox do
    begin
      FButtonImage := TButtonImage(TListBox(Sender).Items.Objects[ItemIndex]);
      if ItemAtPos(Point(X,Y), True) >= 0 then
        BeginDrag(False);
    end;
end;
```

44. Create an OnMouseMove event handler for the FileListBox. In the Object Inspector, delete File from the name of the event handler so it is named ListBoxMouseMove. Add the following code to the event handler.

```
procedure TSBEditor.ListBoxMouseMove(Sender: TObject;
  Shift: TShiftState; X, Y: Integer);
var
  S, OffSet: TPoint;
begin
```

```
  if FAlreadyDragging then
  begin
    S := TListBox(Sender).ClientToScreen(Point(X,Y));
    { Move image with cursor }
    FButtonImage.DragImage(S.X, S.Y);
  end
end;
```

45. Create an OnMouseUp event handler for the FileListBox. In the Object Inspector, delete File from the name of the event handler so it is named ListBoxMouseUp. Add the following code to the event handler.

```
procedure TSBEditor.ListBoxMouseUp(Sender: TObject;
  Button: TMouseButton; Shift: TShiftState; X, Y: Integer);
var
  S: TPoint;
begin
  S := TListBox(Sender).ClientToScreen(Point(X, Y));
  if FAlreadyDragging then
  begin
    { Erases image if MouseUp was a result of ending a drag }
    FButtonImage.EraseScreenImage(S.X, S.Y);
    FAlreadyDragging := False;
  end;
end;
```

46. Select EditListBox in the Object Inspector. On the Events page, connect the EditListBox's events to the OnDragOver, OnDrawItem, OnMouseDown, OnMouseMove, and OnMouseUp event handlers that you just created by dropping down the list box for each event and selecting the appropriate item. Do the same for the HelpListBox.

47. Connect Notebook1's OnDragOver event to the ListBoxDragOver event handler.

48. Switching back to the main form (SDIAppForm), create an OnCreate event handler and add the following code to the event handler.

```
procedure TSDIAppForm.FormCreate(Sender: TObject);
begin
  Application.OnHint := ShowHint;
  FSBImage := TButtonImage.Create;
end;
```

49. While still in the Code Editor, move up to the SDIAppForm object declaration and add the following variables to the object's *private* section.

```
type
  TSDIAppForm = class(TForm)
  ...
  private
```

continued on next page

continued from previous page

```
    { Private declarations }
    FSBImage: TButtonImage;
    FAlreadyDragging: Boolean;
  public
    { Public declarations }
  end;

var
  SDIAppForm: TSDIAppForm;

implementation
```

50. Create an OnDestroy event handler for SDIAppForm and add the following code to the event handler.

```
procedure TSDIAppForm.FormDestroy(Sender: TObject);
begin
  FSBImage.Free;
end;
```

51. Create an OnDragDrop event handler for the SpeedPanel and add the following code to the event handler.

```
procedure TSDIAppForm.SpeedPanelDragDrop(Sender, Source: TObject; X,
  Y: Integer);
var
  ButtonImage: TButtonImage;
  S, P: TPoint;
begin
  if Sender is TDragSpeedButton then
  begin
    { Convert the speedbutton client coordinates to panel client coordinates }
    S := TDragSpeedButton(Sender).ClientToScreen(Point(X, Y));
    P := SpeedPanel.ScreenToClient(S);
  end
  else P.X := X;
  if Source is TListBox then
    with TListBox(Source) do
      with TButtonImage(Items.Objects[ItemIndex]) do
      begin
        { Ensure speedbutton will drop on top of others }
        SpeedButton.Parent := Nil;
        SpeedButton.Parent := SpeedPanel;
        { Set position and make visible }
        SpeedButton.Left := P.X - OffSet.X;
        SpeedButton.Top := 3;
        SpeedButton.Visible := True;
      end
  else if Source is TDragSpeedButton then
    with TDragSpeedButton(Source) do
    begin
      { Ensure speedbutton will drop on top of others }
```

```
      Parent := Nil;
      Parent := SpeedPanel;
      { Set position and make visible }
      Left := P.X - FSBImage.OffSet.X;
      Top := 3;
      Visible := True;
  end;
end;
```

52. Create an OnDragOver event handler for the SpeedPanel and add the following code to the event handler.

```
procedure TSDIAppForm.SpeedPanelDragOver(Sender, Source: TObject; X,
  Y: Integer; State: TDragState; var Accept: Boolean);
begin
  Accept := (Source is TListBox) or (Source is TDragSpeedButton);
end;
```

53. Connect the OnDragDrop and OnDragOver events of each speed button to the OnDragDrop and OnDragOver event handlers you just created.

54. Create an OnMouseMove event handler for the OpenBtn speed button. Using the Object Inspector, rename the event handler to SpeedBtnMouseMove. Add the following code to the event handler.

```
procedure TSDIAppForm.SpeedBtnMouseMove(Sender: TObject; Shift: TShiftState;
  X, Y: Integer);
var
  C, S, P, OffSet: TPoint;
begin
  GetCursorPos(S);
  if Sender is TDragSpeedButton then
    if TDragSpeedButton(Sender).Dragging then
    begin
      if FAlreadyDragging then
        FSBImage.DragImage(S.X, S.Y)
      else
      begin
        { Hide speedbutton }
        TDragSpeedButton(Sender).Visible := False;
        { Calculate OffSet based on cursor position }
        P.X := TDragSpeedButton(Sender).Left;
        P.Y := TDragSpeedButton(Sender).Top;
        C := SpeedPanel.ClientToScreen(P);
        OffSet.X := S.X - C.X;
        OffSet.Y := S.Y - C.Y;
        { Set the image to the correct speedbutton }
        FSBImage.SpeedButton := TDragSpeedButton(Sender);
        { Allow the application to paint the speedbutton hidden }
        Application.ProcessMessages;
        { Draw the image }
        FSBImage.DrawToScreen(S.X, S.Y, OffSet);
```

continued on next page

continued from previous page

```
        FAlreadyDragging := True;
      end;
    end;
end;
```

55. Create an OnMouseUp event handler for the OpenBtn speed button. Using the Object Inspector, rename the event handler to SpeedBtnMouseUp. Add the following code to the event handler.

```
procedure TSDIAppForm.SpeedBtnMouseUp(Sender: TObject; Button: TMouseButton;
  Shift: TShiftState; X, Y: Integer);
var
  C, S, P: TPoint;
begin
  GetCursorPos(S);
  P.X := X + TDragSpeedButton(Sender).Left;
  P.Y := Y + TDragSpeedButton(Sender).Top;
  WinProcs.ClientToScreen(SpeedPanel.Handle, P);
  if FAlreadyDragging then
  begin
    { Finish dragging }
    FSBImage.EraseScreenImage(S.X, S.Y);
    FAlreadyDragging := False;
  end;
end;
```

56. Connect the OnMouseMove and OnMouseUp events of each speed button to the OnMouseMove and OnMouseUp event handlers you just created.

57. Compile and test the project.

How It Works

This How-To demonstrates several advanced concepts—most notably drag-and-drop processing and Owner-Draw list boxes. Instead of dragging the actual tool buttons from the list box to the toolbar, bitmap representations of the tool buttons are used. When a drop is detected on the toolbar, the appropriate tool button is moved into place and made visible.

There are a few key areas in the code that you should be aware of. First of all, notice the code in the CreateParams method of TSBEditor. This code sets the style of the SBEditor form so that it will stay on top of the parent form, even if the parent form has focus. This is a very useful technique that you can use in other areas in your Delphi applications.

Another important point worth noting is the control of the Accept variable in an OnDragOver event. This variable must be explicitly set to False for all objects you don't want to accept a drop operation from. This is not clearly shown in the Delphi manuals, but can be proven by experimentation. If you merely set Accept to True for objects you want to accept by using a statement like this:

```
if Source is TListBox then Accept := True;
```

your component will actually accept anything. In fact, if you want to set a component to accept anything, all you have to do is create an empty OnDragOver event handler and put a comment in it so the Delphi scanner doesn't delete the handler. Keep this is mind—because if you don't properly control the Accept parameter, someone may drop something on your component that you aren't prepared to handle.

The majority of this project makes standard use of Delphi's Drag and Drop support. Showing the speed button image during the drag operation is accomplished by using the TButtonImage class. This class paints to the screen DC and therefore has the ability to draw itself anywhere on the screen. It gives the appearance of dragging by erasing its image and repainting it in a new location. Due to the small size of the button image, a fairly simple technique of erasing and redrawing the image can be used without producing unacceptable flicker.

Comments

The current form of this project lends itself well for use as a template. In order to provide additional tool buttons for users, simply place them on the toolbar. If you want a tool button to be available in the configuration dialog but not visible on the form, simply set the tool button's Visible property to False. Be sure to set the Tag property so it identifies the proper list box to show the tool button in. Of course, if you add more menus — you will need to add a ListBox component for each menu added, and adjust the rest of the code as necessary to support the additions.

This How-To is a potential starting point for a self-contained toolbar component, if you wish to build one. The majority of techniques used would still apply, though you may want to improve the programmer interface for building the toolbar, defining the available tools and so on.

Another thing that is lacking from this project is a way to store the user's toolbar after it has been modified. This would likely be done by saving the appropriate values to an INI file.

12

12

TIPS AND TRICKS

How do I...

Perhaps the most important feature of Delphi is its extendibility. You will find it easier to add functionality to Delphi than to any other development environment because of the extensive use of object-oriented programming (OOP) features within its own design. You can augment the capabilities of Delphi's off-the-shelf components—both Borland VCL and Visual Basic VBX—with new variables and methods, and you can register these modified components with the Delphi environment and use them directly from the Object Inspector. Even new property editor dialog boxes can be defined and used directly in the Delphi design environment.

The exception handling system is also defined via the OOP interface and can be accessed at run time to create and raise your own exception classes. In addition, the exception handling system makes it possible to avoid one of the more crippling Windows problems, namely, losing memory and vital resources when a program crashes.

Finally, Delphi components can be placed in a DLL and called via a (relatively) language-independent interface from non-Delphi programming environments. The How-To's in this chapter explore all of these exciting areas.

12.1 Use OOP to customize existing VCL components

OOP has been touted for some time as the wave of the future for programming. This How-To demonstrates the use of object-oriented programming to enhance the range of colors available in the Delphi TPanel control.

12.2 Create a custom VCL component and make it available at design time

If the only way to use OOP-customized VCL components was at run time, the power of Delphi would be seriously compromised. Fortunately, Delphi provides a way to include customized components in the component palette, and this How-To demonstrates the process by adding the custom TPanel control to the system.

12.3 Make a custom property editor available via the Object Inspector

Due to the power of OOP, some Delphi component properties are too complex for simple values. To allow setting these values at design time, property editor dialog boxes are provided for the built-in VCL components that need them. This How-To shows the procedure to create and add a custom property editor for the color properties of the custom TPanel component added in How-To 12.2.

12.4 Override the VCL object method properties default procedures

Method is the Delphi term for a procedure or function that is a property of a VCL object. This How-To lays out the procedure to override the default function for a given component at run time by creating a generic Verification dialog box that calls user-defined methods for its button clicks.

12.5 Put components in a DLL for use by non-Delphi programs

DLLs (Dynamic Link Libraries) are a method used to share program code under Windows 3.1. Normally written in C, C++, or Pascal, these reusable libraries can also be created by Delphi and include VCL components. This How-To demonstrates the use of the Verification dialog box from How-To 12.4 via a DLL.

12.6 Use OOP to extend the capabilities of an imported VBX control

Delphi can import Level One Visual Basic VBX controls. The VBXs are imported in such a way that OOP techniques can be used to enhance their functionality. This How-To demonstrates adding custom colors to the VBX progress meter control distributed with Delphi.

12.7 Manipulate VCL components like a Visual Basic controls array

Visual Basic offers the powerful technique of creating arrays of its controls and manipulating them at run time. You can manipulate Delphi VCL components in exactly the same way. This How-To outlines the method by creating dynamic arrays of text buttons at run time in a personal memo notebook application.

12.8 Override a default Delphi exception handler

Delphi's exception mechanism is one of the most powerful new features of the system. This How-To shows a way to deal with mathematical errors in a simple calculator application.

12.9 Create and raise a customized Delphi exception

Delphi's exception mechanism is part of Object Pascal, and like the other elements of OOP, exceptions can be modified via OOP techniques. This How-To uses programmer-defined exceptions to create a customizable data entry dialog that validates user inputs as part of a simple address book application.

12.10 Use exception handling to avoid memory and resource leaks

Due to the limited resources of its underlying system, Windows can be severely compromised if a program terminates in an ill-behaved way. This loss of resources is called a *leak*. This How-To demonstrates a method to avoid resource and memory leaks in a simple slide show application.

12.1 How do I...
Use OOP to customize existing VCL components?

COMPLEXITY: ADVANCED

Problem

Delphi's off-the-shelf components are great, but there are some features I'd like to change. Can I do this without rewriting the component from scratch?

Technique

Delphi's use of object-oriented programming (OOP) techniques in its design means you can customize any of the installed VCL components at run time without rewriting their core functionality. This How-To shows you how to change the default highlight and shadow colors of the TPanel component to something other than system defaults.

Steps

Run CUSTPANL.EXE. Notice that, unlike a standard VCL panel, the colors of the beveled edges match the interior color, instead of being dark and light gray or similar inappropriate system-default colors..

1. Create a new blank project and name it CUSTPANL.DPR. Name the unit CPANLFRM.PAS.

2. Add the components to Form1 and set their properties as shown in Table 12-1.

Table 12-1 Components, properties, and settings for Form1 of CUSTPANL

COMPONENT	PROPERTY	SETTING
Form1	Type	Application Main Form
	Width	435
	Height	300
	Left	81
	Top	66
	Caption	Custom Bevel Colors Component Test

3. Create a new unit and name it CUSTCOLP.PAS. Type in the following code to inform Delphi about the changes being made to the TPanel component in the new version.

```
Unit CustColp;

interface

uses
  SysUtils, WinTypes, WinProcs, Messages, Classes, Graphics, Controls,Forms,
 Dialogs, ExtCtrls;
type
  TCustomColorPanel = class(TPanel)
  private
    { Private declarations }
    FHighLightColor : TColor;
    FShadowColor : TColor;
  protected
    { Protected declarations }
    procedure Paint; override;
  public
    { Public declarations }
    constructor Create(AOwner : TComponent); override;
  published
    { Published declarations }
    property HighLightColor : TColor read FHighLightColor
     write FHighLightColor default clBtnHighLight;
    property ShadowColor : TColor read FShadowColor
     write FShadowColor default clBtnShadow;
  end;

implementation
```

4. Now type in the following Create method to allow altering the default behavior of a TPanel component at startup.

```
constructor TCustomColorPanel.Create(AOwner : TComponent);
begin
  { Call inherited method to make sure all default behavior occurs }
  inherited Create(AOwner);
  { Set the default values for the highlight and shadow colors }
  FHighLightColor := clBtnHighLight;
  FShadowColor := clBtnShadow;
end;
```

5. To complete the unit, add the following Paint method to handle painting the customized TPanel component.

Note: This code is modified from the VCL source code, which is copyright 1995 by Borland International, and used here with permission.

```
{ This is copied from the VCL Source library }
procedure TCustomColorPanel.Paint;
var
  Rect: TRect;
  TopColor, BottomColor: TColor;
  Text: array[0..255] of Char;
  FontHeight: Integer;
```

continued on next page

continued from previous page

```
const
  Alignments: array[TAlignment] of Word = (DT_LEFT, DT_RIGHT, DT_CENTER);

  { This is the procedure which needs modification }
  procedure AdjustColors(Bevel: TPanelBevel);
  begin
    { Rather than 'hardwiring' the default color, make it a property }
    TopColor := FHighLightColor;
    { Invert the color if lowered rather than raised }
    if Bevel = bvLowered then TopColor := FShadowColor;
    { Rather than 'hardwiring' the default color, make it a property }
    BottomColor := FShadowColor;
    { Invert the color if lowered rather than raised }
    if Bevel = bvLowered then BottomColor := FHighLightColor;
  end;

begin
  { Find out how big the panel is }
  Rect := GetClientRect;
  { If there is an outer bevel draw it }
  if BevelOuter  bvNone then
  begin
    { Get the raised/lowered highlight/shadow colors }
    AdjustColors(BevelOuter);
    { Call the internal procedure to draw the bevels }
    { Note that rect comes back modified for next op }
    Frame3D(Canvas, Rect, TopColor, BottomColor, BevelWidth);
  end;
  { Draw the border between bevels }
  { Rect comes back modified again }
  Frame3D(Canvas, Rect, Color, Color, BorderWidth);
  { If there is an inner bevel draw it }
  if BevelInner  bvNone then
  begin
    { Get highlight/shadow colors for raised/lowered }
    AdjustColors(BevelInner);
    { Draw using the private procedure    }
    { Rect is now the center of the panel }
    Frame3D(Canvas, Rect, TopColor, BottomColor, BevelWidth);
  end;
  { Use the canvas property to draw the center of the panel }
  with Canvas do
  begin
    { Set up the brush color }
    Brush.Color := Color;
    { Fill up the interior }
    FillRect(Rect);
    { Set the brush to empty }
    Brush.Style := bsClear;
    { Get the current font }
    Font := Self.Font;
    { Find out how high letters are }
    FontHeight := TextHeight('W');
    { Use the rect to draw in }
    with Rect do
```

```
    begin
      { Find the middle and set rect's top to it}
      Top := ((Bottom + Top) - FontHeight) shr 1;
      { Set the bottom of rect to the height of the font }
      Bottom := Top + FontHeight;
    end;
    { Set up an ASCIIZ String }
    StrPCopy(Text, Caption);
    { Draw caption in the rect with alignment styles }
    DrawText(Handle, Text, StrLen(Text), Rect, (DT_EXPANDTABS or
      DT_VCENTER) or Alignments[Alignment]);
  end;
end;
```

6. Select the OnCreate event of Form1 and enter the following code to initialize the application and set up an instance of the custom TPanel component.

Note: This code, and the code in step 7, is entered in the CPanlFm unit, not the CustColP unit above.

```
procedure TForm1.FormCreate(Sender: TObject);
begin
  { Create the new component }
  TheNewPanel := TCustomColorPanel.Create(Self);
  { Set its parent property to the owning form }
  TheNewPanel.Parent := Self;
  { Set the align property to fill the form }
  TheNewPanel.Align := alClient;
  { Set the base color to blue }
  TheNewPanel.Color := clBlue;
  { Set the Highlight color to aqua; this is due to OOP }
  TheNewPanel.HighLightColor := clAqua;
  { Set the Shadow color to black; this is also due to OOP }
  TheNewPanel.ShadowColor := clBlack;
  { Set the remaining display properties as desired }
  TheNewPanel.BevelWidth := 4;
  TheNewPanel.Visible := true;
  TheNewPanel.BevelInner := bvLowered;
  TheNewPanel.BorderWidth := 20;
end;
```

7. While still in the Code Editor, move up to the *type* keyword and type in the following helper variable to hold the custom TPanel component.

```
type
  TForm1 = class(TForm)
    procedure FormCreate(Sender: TObject);
  private
    { Private declarations }
  public
    { Public declarations }
    TheNewPanel : TCustomColorPanel;
  end;
```

8. Move up to the *uses* keyword and add the CustColP unit, which allows Delphi to compile the references to the custom TPanel component in the main form.

```
uses
  SysUtils, WinTypes, WinProcs, Messages, Classes, Graphics, Controls,
  Forms, Dialogs , CustColP, ExtCtrls;
```

9. Compile and test the project.

How It Works

In order to understand the way this How To does its job, a bit of explanation about 3D effects in Windows is useful. All images on a computer screen are flat—two-dimensional. In order to simulate a sculptured, three-dimensional look, extra areas of color are added to the inner and outer edges of flat portions of the display. These colored areas are called bevels, after a term from woodworking. Figure 12-1 illustrates the layout of the standard TPanel component in terms of bevels.

As shown in the figure, the key to creating the sculptured appearance is the use of lighter and darker colors for the bevels. Outer bevels are colored more brightly to simulate more exposure to light, while inner bevels have a darker color, to simulate being in shadow. The How-To changes the colors used to draw the highlighted and shadowed bevels, using OOP techniques.

OOP is based on the concept of *inheritance*. In order for the TCustomColorPanel not to require rewriting all the code for its parent TPanel component, the following line is used in its initial declaration:

```
TCustomColorPanel = class(TPanel)
```

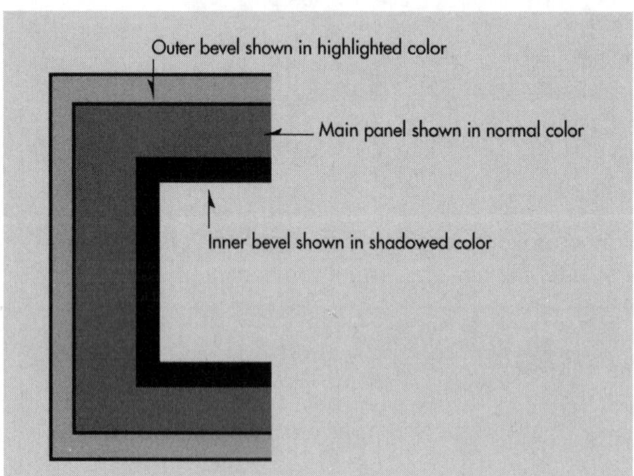

Figure 12-1 Diagram of the bevels on a standard TPanel component and their color types

By placing the *class* keyword in front of TPanel, the application informs Delphi that TCustomColorPanel inherits all the methods, properties, and events of TPanel, except for those items defined later. By this mechanism, all of the already compiled code for TPanel is made available to TCustomColorPanel without any other code being written.

This would not be terribly useful if there were not some way to modify the behavior of the base object. This is done by the following lines of code:

```
private
  FHighLightColor : Tcolor;
  FShadowColor : TColor;
```

Placing the new variables, FHighLightColor and FShadowColor, under the *private* keyword informs Delphi that these are new data elements of the customized object, different from TPanel. Since it is under *private*, only the owning data object and other objects in its unit can access the variables. In this way they are protected from accidental changes by end users, which might introduce unstable behavior at run time.

For the new component to work properly, however, an inherited method must be changed, namely, the one used to draw the panel. This is done with these lines of code:

```
protected
  procedure Paint; override;
```

Note that this procedure is under the *protected* keyword. This is almost identical to *private*, making the method inaccessible by other units or at run time. However, it does allow objects that have been defined as descendants from its base class (TCustomColorPanel is a descendant of TPanel) to access it at run time.

Pay particular attention to the keyword *override*. This is what tells Delphi that a new method is being used here, and when TCustomColorPanel is drawn, the new procedure should be invoked rather than the old one. In this particular case, the entire old method is replaced; there are alternative ways to handle this replacement, such as virtual methods, which are discussed more fully in the *Component Writer's Guide*.

A similar declaration is made for the Create method:

```
public
constructor Create(AOwner : TComponent); override;
```

Create is placed under the *public* section of the object definition, which allows a programmer to modify the method at run time. However, because it is not marked as *published*, the method is only available via typing in code in the Code Editor; it will not show up in the Events page of the Object Inspector. Again, the *override* directive tells Delphi to use this method rather than the inherited one when TCustomColorPanel is created.

The final entries in the new object's definition are properties, as follows:

```
published
  property HighLightColor : TColor read FHighLightColor
    write FHighLightColor default clBtnHighLight;
  property ShadowColor : TColor read FShadowColor
    write FShadowColor default clBtnShadow;
```

Because these definitions appear under the *published* keyword and are properties, they will appear on the properties list in the Object Inspector when the component is registered, which will be demonstrated in the next How-To. For now, they simply are available for runtime use. Also note the *read, write,* and *default* keywords. These tell Delphi which procedure, function, or variable to use to get and set the values for each property (in this case both properties simply read and write the private storage variables defined earlier), and they tell the compiler what value is the default for the property in case it is not set at run time or design time.

Having created a definition for the component, you must write code for the two overridden methods. This code is reproduced in steps 4 and 5, with explanatory comments. Two important points can be raised here, however. First, note this line of code in the new Create procedure:

```
inherited Create(AOwner);
```

This tells Delphi to call the Create method of the previous class, with the owner variable passed to the new method. This is critical, because it guarantees that the new TCustomColorPanel will reproduce all the expected behaviors of TPanel. Had this not been included, all the code from the TPanel unit's Create method would have to be included in the new method.

The other important point is contained in these lines of code in the new Paint method:

```
TopColor := FHighLightColor;
if Bevel = bvLowered then TopColor := FShadowColor;
```

Notice that these two lines of code access the private FHighLightColor and FShadowColor variables. This is done for two reasons: first, to avoid the overhead of procedure calls every time the bevels are drawn, and second, because in this case it is certain that the data in the two private variables is not going to change. If the way in which the shadow and highlight colors are calculated might change, then it would be better to use the property variables here (HighLightColor and ShadowColor).

Comments

In order to display the new custom TPanel component, it has to be created at run time within the OnCreate event handler of Form1. The reason is that, as yet, Delphi's design-time system knows nothing about TCustomColorPanel. The next How-To will demonstrate how to overcome that limitation.

Object orientation is by far the most powerful concept in programming since the advent of the subroutine. While various pundits laud its potential for code reuse, in truth it is an entirely new and different way to program, requiring a considerable shift in thinking about the whole development process. At first it may seem like a waste of time, not enough bang for the buck, and so forth. But once the mental shift (the *aha* experience as an early Borland reference called it) occurs, OOP comes to life and programming is never the same again.

12.2 How do I...
Create a custom VCL component and make it available at design time?

COMPLEXITY: EASY

Problem

It's all well and good to be able to create code that modifies existing Delphi components, but what I really need is to be able to give users access to the custom component at design time. Can I do this in Delphi without complex programming?

Technique

The Object Pascal language includes functions specifically designed to interact with the design-time Delphi environment. You can use the RegisterComponents procedure to add the custom TPanel component created in the previous How-To to the VCL palette of Delphi.

Steps

Run CUSTPNL2.EXE. Look on your screen to see the new colors on the custom bevel colors panel. When you have finished creating the application, you will see a display similar to Figure 12-2, with the CustomColorPanel component installed on a new Waite Group component tab in the components palette.

Figure 12-2 DELPHI at design time with the CustomColorPanel component on the Waite Group palette tab entry

1. Copy the project and unit files from How-To 12.1 into a new directory. Rename the project file CUSTPNL2.DPR, but leave the other files the same.
2. Go into the Code Editor in the CUSTCOLP.PAS unit and just above the *implementation* keyword add the following code, which allows Delphi to recognize the unit as containing VCL component code.

```
{ This is required to add the component to the VCL palette }
procedure Register;
```

3. Staying in the unit, move to just below the *implementation* keyword and type in the following code to actually place the component in the Delphi design-time environment.

```
procedure Register;
begin
  { Put the component in a waite group tab with their name }
  RegisterComponents('waite group', [TCustomColorPanel]);
end;
```

4. From the CD, copy CUSTCOLP.DCR into the current working directory, or into the directory where you wish to place the custom component. This file is essential for Delphi to be able to display a custom bitmap on the VCL palette after the next step.
5. In the Delphi environment, choose the Options|Install Components menu item. Choose the Add button and type in **CUSTCOLP** (with any pertinent directory path information). Select OK in the Add dialog box, then select OK in the Installation dialog box. Delphi will rebuild its component library, and a new Waite Group tab should appear on the component palette with the CustomColorPanel component on it.

Note: If you encounter errors in this step, select Revert to return the Component Library to its previous state. Then make sure that (a) your copy of CustColP has no syntax errors and (b) the path information in the Add dialog box edit field is accurate. (See page 69 in the *User's Guide* for more information on the installation process.)

6. Now add the components to Form1 of the project and set their properties as shown in Table 12-2.

Table 12-2 Components, properties, and settings for Form1 of CUSTPNL2

COMPONENT	PROPERTY	SETTING
Form1	Type	Application Main Form
	Width	435
	Height	300

COMPONENT	PROPERTY	SETTING
	Left	95
	Top	70
	Caption	Custom Bevel Colors Component Test 2
CustomColorPanel1	Type	TCustomColorPanel
	Left	0
	Top	0
	Width	427
	Height	265
	Caption	CustomColorPanel1
	Align	alClient
	Color	clMaroon
	HighLightColor	clRed
	ShadowColor	clBlack
	BevelOuter	bvRaised
	BevelInner	bvLowered
	BevelWidth	4
	BorderWidth	20

7. Compile and test the project.

How It Works

Because Delphi's design-time environment and Object Pascal are interlocking, what might have been an intricate and/or involved process to register new components with the system is reduced to a few elegantly simple lines of code.

This top line

```
procedure Register;
```

simply tells Delphi to expect a procedure named Register later in the code. The actual code contains the key line:

```
RegisterComponents('Waite Group', [TCustomColorPanel]);
```

RegisterComponents is a defined procedure within the Object Pascal language that handles actually modifying the VCL system. Its two parameters contain the name of the new tab to be created, or the name of an existing one to have component(s) added, and the names of the type definitions of the components inside the brackets, separated by commas if multiple entries are desired. Delphi allows putting multiple components onto the palette at once, but all must be in the same unit. Also, multiple calls are allowed within the Register procedure to RegisterComponents, to add multiple pages or place new components on several new or existing pages of the palette; but only one palette page can be named in any single call to the procedure.

However, the code is only half the story. Notice that when the menu item/dialog boxes are brought up and chosen, Delphi shuts down all existing code units and then recompiles the new component unit before adding its functionality to the VCL system. This type of self-modifying capability is another example of just how unique and groundbreaking Delphi is.

Once the component is available on the palette, creating the second project is quite simple. Note that the highlight and shadow colors become available directly from the Object Inspector, with the same color list as the basic Color property. Each component's properties have type information; in the case of HighLightColor and ShadowColor, this is TColor. Delphi uses a type of object for each known type called TPropertyEditor. This object defines how to obtain values for a property in the Object Inspector. In the case of TColor, it defines an enumerated type, which is shown in a drop-list format. Other property editors exist, and new ones can be created, which is the focus of the next How-To.

There is one very interesting point shown by this How To that might go unnoticed. Once the new component is installed on the palette and thus available to the Delphi IDE, you might be surprised that when a custom panel is created and its colors chosen, the custom panels paint themselves with the new colors at design time. This is because Delphi uses Object Pascal compiled code as part of its design-time environment. Figure 12-3 below illustrates the interlocking relationship between the design-time environment and the Object Pascal code used to create and define components.

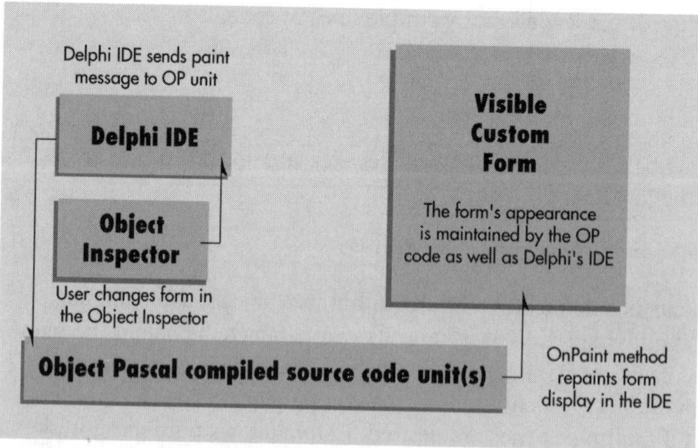

Figure 12-3 Relationships between Delphi's Design IDE and the compiled component Object Pascal code

Pay particular attention to the link between the IDE and the OnPaint method call used to display the custom component. This is important, because if the new component's OnPaint method requires runtime information not available in the IDE, the Delphi design environment may behave unpredictably.

Comments

Two points of interest are noteworthy for this How-To. First, at the time of writing there is a bit of incorrect information in the Delphi manual involving DCR files. It states on page 77 of the *Component Writer's Guide* under "Adding Palette Bitmaps" that name entries in the DCR file for the bitmap must match the component type definition, but are *not* case sensitive. This is incorrect as of the first release of Delphi. The name in the DCR file *must be all uppercase* for the system to recognize it and place the bitmap on the palette. The name in the unit, however, can be any combination of upper and lowercase desired.

The other point is that, to keep the component available over the long haul, the PAS and DCR files should be placed in the LIB subdirectory of the DELPHI directory and reinstalled.

12.3 How do I...
Make a custom property editor available via the Object Inspector?

COMPLEXITY: INTERMEDIATE

Problem

The number of colors with defined constants is rather small. Is there a way to make the entire range of colors available to my components?

Technique

Delphi accepts user-created property editors. This How-To will demonstrate the creation of an RGB property editor for the custom panel control created in How-To 12.2.

Steps

Run CUSTPNL3.EXE, and you will see a custom panel component that has nonstandard colors for its bevels and central area. Once you have finished this How-To, you will be able to bring up a property editor similar to that shown in Figure 12-4 to set these special colors.

1. Create a new blank project and name it CUSTPNL3.DPR. Once again, use CPANLFM.PAS from How-To's 12.1 and 12.2 as the base unit of the project.

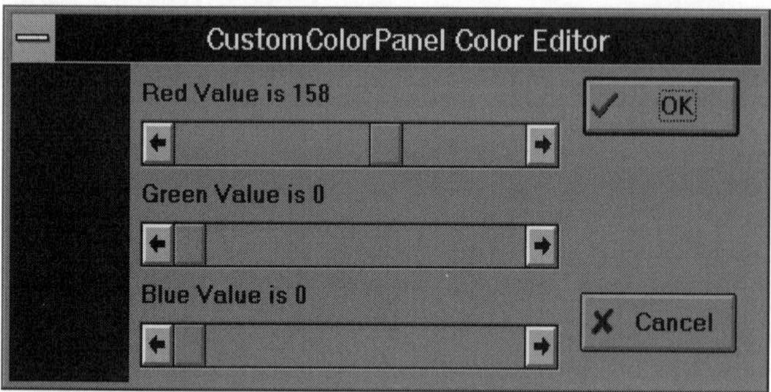

Figure 12-4 Using the RGB property editor in Delphi

Steps

Run CUSTPNL3.EXE, and you will see a custom panel component that has nonstandard colors for its bevels and central area. Once you have finished this How-To, you will be able to bring up a property editor similar to that shown in Figure 12-4 to set these special colors.

1. Create a new blank project and name it CUSTPNL3.DPR. Once again, use CPANLFM.PAS from How-To's 12.1 and 12.2 as the base unit of the project.
2. Open the CUSTCOLP.PAS file, which you created in How-To 12.2; you will make changes to it shortly.
3. Create a new blank form; name the unit CCPPEDIT.PAS. It will hold the form used by the RGB property editor dialog box.
4. Add the components to RGBEditDialog and set their properties as shown in Table 12-3.

Table 12-3 Components, properties, and settings for RGBEditDialog of CCPPEDIT

COMPONENT	PROPERTY	SETTING
RGBEditDialog	Type	Application Main Form
	Width	468
	Height	212
	Left	46
	Top	41
	Caption	CustomColorPanel Color Editor
Shape1	Type	TShape

COMPONENT	PROPERTY	SETTING
	Width	94
	Height	16
	Caption	Red Value is
Label2	Type	TLabel
	Left	80
	Top	64
	Width	103
	Height	16
	Caption	Green Value is
Label3	Type	TLabel
	Left	80
	Top	120
	Width	92
	Height	16
	Caption	Blue Value is
Scrollbar1	Type	TScrollbar
	Left	80
	Top	32
	Width	257
	Height	25
	Min	0
	Max	255
	Kind	sbHorizontal
Scrollbar2	Type	TScrollbar
	Left	80
	Top	88
	Width	257
	Height	25
	Min	0
	Max	255
	Kind	sbHorizontal
Scrollbar3	Type	TScrollbar
	Left	80
	Top	144
	Width	257
	Height	25

continued on next page

continued from previous page

COMPONENT	PROPERTY	SETTING
	Min	0
	Max	255
	Kind	sbHorizontal
OKBtn	Type	TBitBtn
	Left	351
	Top	6
	Width	95
	Height	33
	Kind	bkOK
CancelBtn	Type	TBitBtn
	Left	350
	Top	126
	Width	95
	Height	33
	Kind	bkCancel

5. In the Code Editor, move up in the type declaration of the TRGBEditDialog object. Enter the code shown under the *private* keyword. Then move down under the *public* keyword and enter the two lines of code shown here. These values are used to customize the object's behavior.

```
private
    { Private declarations }
    procedure SetInitialRGBValue( The_Value : Longint );
  public
    { Public declarations }
    StartingRGBValue ,
    FinalRGBValue : Longint;
```

6. Move down to the *var* keyword and enter the following code as helper variables.

```
var
  RGBEditDialog: TRGBEditDialog;
  CurrentRedValue ,
  CurrentBlueValue ,
  CurrentGreenValue   : Byte;
```

7. Move down below the *implementation* keyword and enter the following helper procedure.

```
procedure TRGBEditDialog.SetInitialRGBValue( The_Value : Longint );
var TheString : String;
begin
  { Get the three components of the property value using API call }
  CurrentRedValue := GetRValue( The_Value );
```

```
  CurrentGreenValue := GetGValue( The_Value );
  CurrentBlueValue := GetBValue( The_Value );
  { Set the scrollbars based on the imported values }
  Scrollbar1.Position := CurrentRedValue;
  Scrollbar2.Position := CurrentGreenValue;
  Scrollbar3.Position := CurrentBlueValue;
  { Set up the default return value and default starting value }
  FinalRGBValue := The_Value;
  StartingRGBValue := The_Value;
  { Set up the label captions }
  Str( CurrentRedValue , TheString );
  Label1.Caption := 'Red Value is ' + TheString;
  Str( CurrentGreenValue , TheString );
  Label2.Caption := 'Green Value is ' + TheString;
  Str( CurrentBlueValue , TheString );
  Label3.Caption := 'Blue Value is ' + TheString;
  { Make the shape's brush color that of the starting color to see it }
  Shape1.Brush.Color := StartingRGBValue;
end;
```

8. Select the OnCreate event handler and enter this code to initialize the helper variables:

```
procedure TRGBEditDialog.FormCreate(Sender: TObject);
begin
  { Initialize everything to zero }
  CurrentRedValue := 0;
  CurrentBlueValue := 0;
  CurrentGreenValue := 0;
  FinalRGBValue := RGB(  0 , 0 , 0 );
  Label1.Caption := 'Red Value is 0';
  Label2.Caption := 'Green Value is 0';
  Label3.Caption := 'Blue Value is 0';
end;
```

9. Select the OnChange event handler for each scrollbar and enter this code to handle altering the current RGB value via scrollbar input:

```
procedure TRGBEditDialog.ScrollBar1Change(Sender: TObject);
var ValueString : String;
begin
  { Set up the string for scrollbar position }
  ValueString := IntToStr( ScrollBar1.Position );
  { Typecast the value to a byte for the holders }
  CurrentRedValue := Byte( ScrollBar1.Position );
  { Set up the caption }
  Label1.Caption := 'Red Value is ' + ValueString;
  { Create the final RGB value again }
  FinalRGBValue := RGB( CurrentRedValue ,
   CurrentBlueValue , CurrentGreenValue );
  { And make the shape show it }
  Shape1.Brush.Color := FinalRGBValue;
end;

procedure TRGBEditDialog.ScrollBar2Change(Sender: TObject);
```

continued on next page

continued from previous page

```
var ValueString : String;
begin
  { Set up the string for scrollbar position }
  ValueString := IntToStr( ScrollBar1.Position );
  { Typecast the value to a byte for the holders }
  CurrentGreenValue := Byte( ScrollBar2.Position );
  { Set up the caption }
  Label2.Caption := 'Green Value is ' + ValueString;
  { Create the final RGB value again }
  FinalRGBValue := RGB( CurrentRedValue ,
   CurrentBlueValue , CurrentGreenValue );
  { And make the shape show it }
  Shape1.Brush.Color := FinalRGBValue;
end;

procedure TRGBEditDialog.ScrollBar3Change(Sender: TObject);
var ValueString : String;
begin
  { Set up the string for scrollbar position }
  ValueString := IntToStr( ScrollBar1.Position );
  { Typecast the value to a byte for the holders }
  CurrentBlueValue := Byte( ScrollBar3.Position );
  { Set up the caption }
  Label3.Caption := 'Blue Value is ' + ValueString;
  { Create the final RGB value again }
  FinalRGBValue := RGB( CurrentRedValue ,
   CurrentBlueValue , CurrentGreenValue );
  { And make the shape show it }
  Shape1.Brush.Color := FinalRGBValue;
end;
```

10. Select the OnClick event handlers for the two buttons and enter this code to exit the editor.

```
procedure TRGBEditDialog.OKBtnClick(Sender: TObject);
begin
  { Return an OK result }
  ModalResult := mrOK;
end;

procedure TRGBEditDialog.CancelBtnClick(Sender: TObject);
begin
  { Return a cancel result }
  ModalResult := mrCancel;
```

11. Go into the code of the CUSTCOLP.PAS unit, move down to the *uses* keyword, and enter the unit of the property editor.

```
interface

uses
  SysUtils, WinTypes, WinProcs, Messages, Classes, Graphics, Controls,
  Forms, Dialogs, ExtCtrls , CcPpEdit , DsgnIntf;
```

12. Move down to the *type* keyword and enter this definition of the new property editor object.

```
TRGBPropertyEditor = class(TPropertyEditor)
  public
    procedure Edit; override;
    function GetAttributes: TPropertyAttributes; override;
    function GetValue : String; override;
    procedure SetValue( const value : String ); override;
  end;
```

13. Move down to the Register procedure and add the following code to register the new property editor as part of the TCustomColorPanel object.

```
procedure Register;
begin
  { Put the component in a Waite Group tab with their name }
  RegisterComponents('Waite Group', [TCustomColorPanel]);
  { Register the property editor for the TColor properties }
  RegisterPropertyEditor( TypeInfo( TColor ) ,
                          TCustomColorPanel   ,
                          ''         ,
                          TRGBPropertyEditor    );
end;
```

14. Move below the Register procedure and enter this helper function to call the RGBEditDialog when the linked property is activated in the Object Inspector.

```
procedure TRGBPropertyEditor.Edit;
var TheEditForm : TRGBEditDialog;
    TheResult : Integer;
begin
  { Create the color edit dialog }
  TheEditForm := TRGBEditDialog.Create( Application );
  { Set the initial RGB value from existing color }
  TheEditForm.SetInitialRGBValue( GetOrdValue );
  try
    { Show the dialog box modally and get result }
    TheResult := TheEditForm.ShowModal;
    if TheResult = mrOK then
    begin
      { Set the value if an OK is entered }
      SetOrdValue( TheEditForm.FinalRGBValue );
    end;
  finally
    { Get rid of the dialog box }
    TheEditForm.Free;
  end;
end;
```

15. Below the Edit procedure, add this helper procedure to tell the Object Inspector to use the dialog box for data only.

```
function TRGBPropertyEditor.GetAttributes: TPropertyAttributes;
begin
  { allow only dialog box editing of this property type }
  Result :=  [paDialog];
end;
```

16. Under the GetAttributes function, enter this assistant function to format the display of RGB values in the Object Inspector.

```
function TRGBPropertyEditor.GetValue : String;
var The_String : String;
begin
  { Create an RGB triplet string }
  The_String := IntToStr( GetRValue( GetOrdValue ) );
  The_String := The_String + ',';
  The_String := The_String + IntToStr( GetGValue( GetOrdValue ) );
  The_String := The_String + ',';
  The_String := The_String + IntToStr( GetBValue( GetOrdValue ) );
  Result := The_String;
end;
```

17. Finally, enter this helper function to convert the string representation of the RGB value to a number for export to other functions.

```
Procedure TRGBPropertyEditor.SetValue( const Value : String );
begin
  { convert the string to an integer for setting the value }
  SetOrdValue( StrToInt( Value ) );
end;
```

18. Select the Options|Install Components menu item; then select the CustColP component and click Remove. Choose Add and select it again as in step 5 of How-To 12.2. This will reinstall the component with the new property editor available.

Note: If you do not remove the CustColP component first, the installation process will hang on an error message of "component already installed" and Delphi will have no available components. Should this happen, immediately select the Revert option from the Installation dialog box; otherwise you will have to reinstall the COMPLIB.DCR file (the run time VCL file) from the Delphi CD. If you reinstall this, remember to use a file utility to reset the read-only flag on the COMPLIB.DCR file.

19. Select the color values for the CustomColorPanel1 component of CUSTPNL3.DPR and select interesting values for the main panel and its highlight and shadow bevel colors. The values for the provided project are [158,0,0] for the main panel, [255,0,0] for the highlight, and [125,18,29] for the shadow (in red/green/blue order).

20. Compile and test the project.

How It Works

A bit of discussion about how computers display color is useful at this point. Since the discovery of the prism, scientists have known that light is composed of many color shades that blend together to produce white. The development of artificial chemical pigments reversed this process: Combining all pigments in ink or paint produces black instead of white. Color television (the technology that underlies computer displays) combines these approaches. Each pixel on a television screen or computer monitor is a group of three phosphor dots in the so-called primary colors: red, green, and blue (RGB). This system allows up to 256 values for each of the three colors, with 255 for all being seen as white, and 0 for all being seen as black (the coating surrounding the phosphors). Varying the intensities produces up to 16 million colors, the range of human color vision and color TV. Table 12-4 lists some sample colors as examples of how RGB values relate to perceived colors.

Table 12-4 The sixteen basic VGA colors and their RGB equivalents

COLOR	RED	GREEN	BLUE
Black	0	0	0
Blue	0	0	127
Green	0	127	0
Cyan	0	127	127
Red	127	0	127
Magenta	127	0	127
Brown	127	127	0
Light gray	127	127	127
Dark gray	192	192	192
Light blue	0	0	255
Light green	0	255	255
Light cyan	0	255	255
Light red	255	0	0
Light magenta	255	0	255
Yellow	255	0	255
White	255	255	255

This How-To is based on the built-in capabilities of Delphi to redefine itself using end-user program functionality. You can use the RegisterPropertyEditor procedure to completely replace or modify the behavior of any element on the Object Inspector. Properties can have enumerated lists, be objects themselves, or they can open dialog boxes.

The RegisterPropertyEditor procedure takes four arguments. The first is the data type of the property being edited (obtained as an internal value by the TypeInfo function call), which in this case is TColor. The second is the name of the component that will use the property editor for values of the given type; if the value here is the empty string, then all values of the given type will use the property editor. In this case, only the TCustomColorPanel component will use the editor. The next argument is the specific property name to which the editor applies; this is only valid if a specific component is listed in the previous parameter. If an empty string is used here, all properties of the given type in the named component will use the editor, which is done here. Finally, the name of the descendant object (from TPropertyEditor) is given so that the Object Inspector knows which editor object to call. It is important to notice that the name given here is the editor object itself, not the form name used by the editor object.

The property editor itself has several key procedures that must be written. First, and most important, is the Edit procedure. Delphi will call this procedure if the paDialog style is used in the GetAttributes function (as shown below), so in order to actually obtain user input, this procedure must somehow get the needed information. In this case the Edit procedure invokes the RGBEditDialog. Notice the calls to GetOrdValue and SetOrdValue; these are built-in functions of the base TPropertyEditor object and should not be overridden. They handle moving the values for the property in and out of the Object Inspector and the compiler. Instead of overriding these methods, the GetValue and SetValue methods are redefined, as shown above.

Next most important in the new Editor object is the GetAttributes function. This defines the type of displays the Object Inspector can use for the property type. By setting it to only paDialog, the editor does not have to deal with constructing lists of strings for display as enumerated types or list box elements.

Finally, there are the GetValue and SetValue methods. They need to be defined for the new type, but do not have to change previous behavior. In the case of SetValue, the original functionality is maintained by calling the built-in SetOrdValue on the number-converted property. (Notice that internal values are stored as strings, apparently for consistency.) GetValue, however, uses string techniques to represent the long integer as three separate numbers for the red, green, and blue components separated by commas.

Comments

As mentioned before, Delphi is written primarily in Object Pascal; many of its displays, such as the Object Inspector, are actually components written in Delphi itself. As long as third party developers adhere to the provided system, they can build very complex add-on capabilities directly into the Delphi IDE.

12.4 How do I...
Override the default procedures used by VCL object method properties?

COMPLEXITY: INTERMEDIATE

Problem

Delphi provides built-in methods for many of its components and allows me to define a single method for those I create, but sometimes I need to change the behavior of one of my components while my program is running. Does Delphi allow me to redefine the methods attached to components at run time?

Technique

In Delphi, methods are simply procedures attached to objects. Since a procedure is, when all is said and done, simply a pointer in the compiled code, Delphi allows you to reassign procedure pointers at run time. In this How-To you will create a Verification dialog box with methods attached to button clicks that change depending on the nature of the input.

Steps

Run GENVFORM.EXE. A file list box will appear showing the files in the directory where the program resides. Select a file and choose the Rename button, then click the Help button on the Verification dialog box that appears. You will see a display similar to Figure 12-5. Close the Help message dialog and either rename the file or cancel the operation.

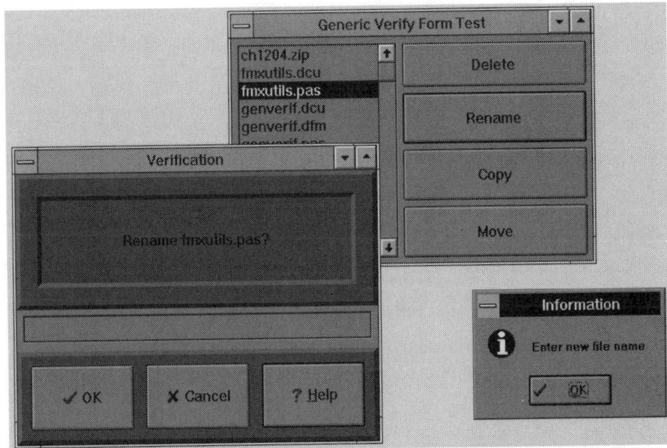

Figure 12-5 GENVFORM at run time, showing the generic Verification dialog and a specific help method message dialog

Now select Delete on the same file and notice that the same dialog appears with a different message. Click Help again and you will see a different help message. If you select OK, the file will be deleted, instead of renamed as it was if you selected OK the first time. The Verification dialog's buttons have had their methods redefined during program execution.

1. Create a new blank project and name it GENVFORM.DPR. Name the unit GENVERIF.PAS.
2. Add the components to Form1 and set their properties as shown in Table 12-5.

Table 12-5 Components, properties, and settings for Form1 of GENVERIF

COMPONENT	PROPERTY	SETTING
Form1	Type	Application Main Form
	Width	431
	Height	290
	Left	50
	Top	50
	Caption	Generic Verify Form Test
FileListBox1	Type	TFileListBox
	Left	8
	Top	8
	Width	185
	Height	241
Button1	Type	TButton
	Left	200
	Top	8
	Width	217
	Height	49
	Caption	Delete
Button2	Type	TButton
	Left	200
	Top64	
	Width	217
	Height	57
	Caption	Rename
Button3	Type	TButton

COMPONENT	PROPERTY	SETTING
	Left	200
	Top	128
	Width	217
	Height	57
	Caption	Copy
Button4	Type	TButton
	Left	200
	Top	192
	Width	217
	Height	49
	Caption	Move

3. Add a new blank form; name its unit VFORM.PAS.
4. Add the components to Form2 and set their properties as shown in Table 12-6.

Note: This form assumes that you have installed the TCustomColorPanel component from How-To 12.2. If not, use a standard TPanel component instead and use default color settings. Also, be sure to place the three BitBtn components inside the lower panel component for proper display.

Table 12-6 Components, properties, and settings for Form2 of VFORM

COMPONENT	PROPERTY	SETTING
Form2	Type	Application Main Form
	Width	433
	Height	340
	Left	49
	Top	40
	Caption	Verification
BitBtn1	Type	TBitBtn
	Left	16
	Top	16
	Width	121
	Height	73
	Kind	bkOK
BitBtn2	Type	TBitBtn

continued on next page

continued from previous page

COMPONENT	PROPERTY	SETTING
	Left	152
	Top	16
	Width	121
	Height	73
	Kind	bkCancel
BitBtn3	Type	TBitBtn
	Left	288
	Top	16
	Width	121
	Height	73
	Kind	bkHelp
Edit1	Type	TEdit
	Left	8
	Top	160
	Width	409
	Height	29
	Text	(blank)
CustomColorPanel1	Type	TCustomColorPanel
	Left	0
	Top	0
	Width	425
	Height	153
	Color	0,177,0
	HighLightColor	0,255,0
	ShadowColor	0,104,0
CustomColorPanel2	Type	TCustomColorPanel
	Left	0
	Top	200
	Width	425
	Height	105
	Color	0,177,0
	HighLightColor	0,255,0
	ShadowColor	0,104,0

5. Go into the Code Editor for the GENVERIF.PAS unit and add the FMXUtils unit to the *uses* clause to enable using Copy and Move functions.

```
uses
  SysUtils, WinTypes, WinProcs, Messages, Classes, Graphics, Controls,
  Forms, Dialogs, StdCtrls, FileCtrl, FMXUtils , Vform;
```

Note: At the time of writing, the FMXUtils shipped with Delphi has a bug in the Copy and Move functions. The CD shipped with this book contains a fixed version of the unit; it should be used in place of the defective file.

6. Move down to the *public* section of the TForm1 type declaration and add these helper procedures to allow the generic Verification form to perform multiple actions.

```
public
    { Public declarations }
    procedure DelProc(Sender: TObject );
    procedure RenProc(Sender: TObject );
    procedure CopyProc(Sender: TObject );
    procedure MoveProc(Sender: TObject );
    procedure DelHelpProc(Sender: TObject );
    procedure RenHelpProc(Sender: TObject );
    procedure CopyHelpProc(Sender: TObject );
    procedure MoveHelpProc(Sender: TObject );
    procedure CloseProc(Sender: TObject );
```

7. Continue down in the code to the *implementation* keyword and enter the following assistant procedures. They encompass the functions desired from the three buttons on the generic Verification form, depending on which button calls the form.

```
implementation
procedure TForm1.CloseProc(Sender: TObject );
begin
  TheForm.Close;
end;

procedure TForm1.DelProc(Sender: TObject );
begin
  { Delete the selected file }
  DeleteFile( FileListBox1.Items[ FileListBox1.ItemIndex ] );
  TheForm.Close;
end;

procedure TForm1.RenProc(Sender: TObject );
begin
  { Rename the file to the name in the edit box }
  RenameFile( FileListBox1.Items[ FileListBox1.ItemIndex ] ,
              TheForm.Edit1.Text );
  TheForm.Close;
end;

procedure TForm1.CopyProc(Sender: TObject );
begin
```

continued on next page

continued from previous page

```
  { copy the file to the name or directory in the edit box }
  CopyFile( FileListBox1.Items[ FileListBox1.ItemIndex ] ,
            FileListBox1.Directory + '\' + TheForm.Edit1.Text );
  TheForm.Close;
end;

procedure TForm1.MoveProc(Sender: TObject );
begin
  { Move the file to the name/directory in the edit box }
  MoveFile( FileListBox1.Items[ FileListBox1.ItemIndex ] ,
            FileListBox1.Directory + '\' + TheForm.Edit1.Text );
  TheForm.Close;
end;

procedure TForm1.DelHelpProc(Sender: TObject );
begin
  { Help for the delete command }
  MessageDlg( 'Ok confirms delete; cancel aborts' , mtInformation , [mbOK] , 0 ) ;
end;

procedure TForm1.RenHelpProc(Sender: TObject );
begin
  { Help for the rename command }
  MessageDlg( 'Enter new file name' , mtInformation , [mbOK] , 0 ) ;
end;

procedure TForm1.CopyHelpProc(Sender: TObject );
begin
  { Help for the copy command }
  MessageDlg( 'Enter full path and name to copy to' , mtInformation , [mbOK] , 0 ) ;
end;

procedure TForm1.MoveHelpProc(Sender: TObject );
begin
  { Help for the move command }
  MessageDlg( 'Enter full path and name to move to' , mtInformation , [mbOK] , 0 ) ;
end;
```

8. Select the OnClick event of Button1 and enter this code to call the generic Verification dialog box to delete a selected file:

```
procedure TForm1.Button1Click(Sender: TObject);
begin
  { if no item selected exit }
  if FileListBox1.ItemIndex < 0 then exit;
  try
    { attempt to create the generic verifcation form }
    TheForm := TForm2.Create( Self );
    { put in the delete caption and file name }
    TheForm.CustomColorPanel1.Caption := 'Delete ' +
     FileListBox1.Items[ FileListBox1.ItemIndex ] + '?';
    { Set the four methods to ones for delete }
    TheForm.BitBtn1.OnClick := DelProc;
    TheForm.BitBtn2.OnClick := CloseProc;
```

```
    TheForm.BitBtn3.OnClick := DelHelpProc;
    { Invoke the form modally }
    TheForm.ShowModal;
    { Update the file listbox regardless of results }
    FileListBox1.Update;
  finally
    { Free the resources regardless of success }
    TheForm.Free;
  end;
end;
```

9. Select the OnClick event of Button2 and enter this code to call the generic Verification dialog box to rename a selected file.

```
procedure TForm1.Button2Click(Sender: TObject);
begin
  { if no item selected exit }
  if FileListBox1.ItemIndex < 0 then exit;
  try
    { attempt to create the generic verifcation form }
    TheForm := TForm2.Create( Self );
    { put in the rename caption and file name }
    TheForm.CustomColorPanel1.Caption := 'Rename ' +
     FileListBox1.Items[  FileListBox1.ItemIndex ] + '?';
    { Set the four methods to ones for rename }
    TheForm.BitBtn1.OnClick := RenProc;
    TheForm.BitBtn2.OnClick := CloseProc;
    TheForm.BitBtn3.OnClick := RenHelpProc;
    { Invoke the form modally }
    TheForm.ShowModal;
    { Update the file listbox regardless of results }
    FileListBox1.Update;
  finally
    { Free the resources regardless of success }
    TheForm.Free;
  end;
end;
```

10. Select the OnClick event of Button1 and enter this code to call the generic Verification dialog box to copy a selected file.

```
procedure TForm1.Button3Click(Sender: TObject);
begin
  { if no item selected exit }
  if FileListBox1.ItemIndex < 0 then exit;
  try
    { attempt to create the generic verifcation form }
    TheForm := TForm2.Create( Self );
    { put in the copy caption and file name }
    TheForm.CustomColorPanel1.Caption := 'Copy ' +
     FileListBox1.Items[  FileListBox1.ItemIndex ] + '?';
    { Set the four methods to ones for copy }
    TheForm.BitBtn1.OnClick := CopyProc;
    TheForm.BitBtn2.OnClick := CloseProc;
    TheForm.BitBtn3.OnClick := CopyHelpProc;
```

continued on next page

continued from previous page

```
    { Invoke the form modally }
    TheForm.ShowModal;
    { Update the file listbox regardless of results }
    FileListBox1.Update;
  finally
    { Free the resources regardless of success }
    TheForm.Free;
  end;
end;
```

11. Select the OnClick event of Button4 and enter this code to call the generic Verification dialog box to move a selected file.

```
procedure TForm1.Button4Click(Sender: TObject);
begin
  { if no item selected exit }
  if FileListBox1.ItemIndex < 0 then exit;
  try
    { attempt to create the generic verifcation form }
    TheForm := TForm2.Create( Self );
    { put in the move caption and file name }
    TheForm.CustomColorPanel1.Caption := 'Move ' +
     FileListBox1.Items[  FileListBox1.ItemIndex ] + '?';
    { Set the four methods to ones for move }
    TheForm.BitBtn1.OnClick := MoveProc;
    TheForm.BitBtn2.OnClick := CloseProc;
    TheForm.BitBtn3.OnClick := MoveHelpProc;
    { Invoke the form modally }
    TheForm.ShowModal;
    { Update the file listbox regardless of results }
    FileListBox1.Update;
  finally
    { Free the resources regardless of success }
    TheForm.Free;
  end;
```

12. Finally, go into the code for GENVERIF.PAS and find the *var* keyword near the top of the file. Enter the variable used to hold the generic Verification dialog.

```
var
  Form1: TForm1;
  TheForm : TForm2;
```

13. Go into the code of the VFORM.PAS unit and move down to the type declaration of Form2 just under the *public* keyword. Enter these assistant procedures, which are stubs that will be replaced by the calling procedures in GENVERIF.PAS.

```
public
    { Public declarations }
    procedure AcceptProc;
    procedure CancelProc;
    procedure HelpProc;
```

14. Select the OnClick event for each of the three BitBtn controls and enter the appropriate code from each of the following listings. This calls the dummy assistant functions when the buttons are selected.

```
procedure TForm2.BitBtn1Click(Sender: TObject);
begin
  { Default accept procedure call }
  AcceptProc;
end;

procedure TForm2.BitBtn2Click(Sender: TObject);
begin
  { Default cancel procedure call }
  CancelProc;
end;

procedure TForm2.BitBtn3Click(Sender: TObject);
begin
  { Default Help procedure call }
  HelpProc;
end;
```

15. In the Code Editor, move down to below the *implementation* keyword and enter these three stub assistant procedures. They are never called, but are here to allow the compiler to create the base object.

```
procedure TForm2.AcceptProc;
begin
  { Default acceptance puts up dialog box with accept }
  MessageDlg( ' Accept ' , mtInformation , [mbOK] , 0 ) ;
end;

procedure TForm2.CancelProc;
begin
  { Default cancelation puts up dialog box with cancel }
  MessageDlg( ' Cancel ' , mtInformation , [mbOK] , 0 ) ;
end;

procedure TForm2.HelpProc;
begin
  { Default help puts up dialog box with help }
  MessageDlg( ' Help ' , mtInformation , [mbOK] , 0 ) ;
end;
```

16. Compile and test the project.

How It Works

Delphi is based on the Borland dialect of Pascal, now called Object Pascal. This has been in release since 1990, starting in Turbo Pascal 5.5. One of the major features of Pascal is a Pointer data type, used similarly but not identically with pointer types in the C language. Because Pascal is a “strongly typed” language, the compiler requires that any conversion of one data type to another be done at compilation time, and it is very strict about making sure every such change is valid. (By way of contrast, C is a "weakly typed" language, which allows almost unlimited run-type pointer conversions. As a result, programs written in C are much more powerful, but much harder to correct when they develop bugs.)

Why is all this important? Because up until Delphi, pointers in Pascal were strictly enforced as data types and had to be used with careful syntax (the ^ or dereference operator). Delphi points out in the *Component Writer's Guide*, on page 30, that since almost all Delphi components and data objects are pointers anyway, the language abstracts out the whole pointer concept and handles it behind the scenes. This makes it appear that variables of seemingly different types, or of no types at all, can be freely assigned to one another.

In fact, this is not the case. Delphi still does strong type-checking at compilation, but it is using somewhat different rules than before. The key passages are on pages 141 to 142 of the *Component Writer's Guide*, where the syntax for method pointers is explained. The upshot of the description is that if an object's method is declared as being of type MyType *of object,* then any other method or procedure with the same number, order, and types of input parameters (and optionally, return value for functions) are assignment-compatible at run time.

For confirmation, look at the declarations of the replacement procedures for the OnClick methods of Form2:

```
procedure TForm2.BitBtn1Click(Sender: TObject);
procedure DelProc(Sender: TObject );
```

The first method is Delphi-written, and is of type TNotifyEvent. The second method is user-written, but has no type declaration. What is not shown is that the method declaration for the first has an internal of object attached to it, and so is available for runtime assignment. Given that, the two methods are clearly type-compatible, since they both take the single TObject parameter and return no value. All event methods in Delphi have this capability of being reassigned at run time.

Comments

There are three interesting points here. First, the ability to assign functions and procedures to variables has been fully available since Borland Pascal 6.0, and forms of it were available even earlier. Delphi is continuing a Borland tradition of improving performance without sacrificing safety for the programmer.

Second, the *of object* declaration does not just apply to Delphi-written methods. User-defined objects can use this language extension as well, allowing a program to virtually redefine itself on the fly as needed during execution. Previously, such mutability required clever programming in C or assembly language; Delphi makes it available in an environment with a good safety net for the developer.

Finally, Delphi's implicit pointer conversions do not take away the ability of programmers to use older Pascal-style pointers directly if they choose. Several of the next How-To's contain explicit pointers and demonstrate their utility.

12.5 How do I...
Put components in a DLL so that non-Delphi programs can use them?

COMPLEXITY: EASY

Problem

Some of my programs are written in C or C++. Is there a way to use some of the forms I've created in Delphi in the non-Delphi code?

Technique

A major advance in program development first made available in Windows 3.0 is the Dynamic Link Library, or DLL. These files are specialized repositories of compiled code, much like an executable file, but they are designed to be accessed by outside programs. Delphi can place almost any of its forms in a DLL; the DLL can then be called by non-Delphi programs, just as Delphi calls the Windows API via DLLs written in C. In this How-To you will place the generic Verification dialog and calling file list box forms from How-To 12.4 in a DLL and invoke them with one procedure call.

Steps

Run DLLTEST.EXE. Click the button, and the list box from How-To 12.4 will appear. Select a file for deletion, click the Delete button, then select Help on the Verification dialog. You should see a display similar to Figure 12-6, reproducing the same behavior as before.

1. Copy the file from How-To 12.4 to a new directory. Rename the project DLLFORM.DPR; rename the GENVERIF.PAS unit to GENVER2.PAS; rename the VFORM.PAS unit to DLLVFORM.PAS.

2. In the Code Editor for GENVER2.PAS, change the name of the Vform unit to DLLVFORM as shown here.

```
uses
  SysUtils, WinTypes, WinProcs, Messages, Classes, Graphics, Controls,
  Forms, Dialogs, StdCtrls, FileCtrl, FMXUtils , dllVform;
```

3. Move down to just above the *implementation* keyword and enter this line of code to allow Delphi to convert the unit into a DLL.

```
{ This is the procedue exported by the dll }
procedure DoTheForm; export;
implementation
```

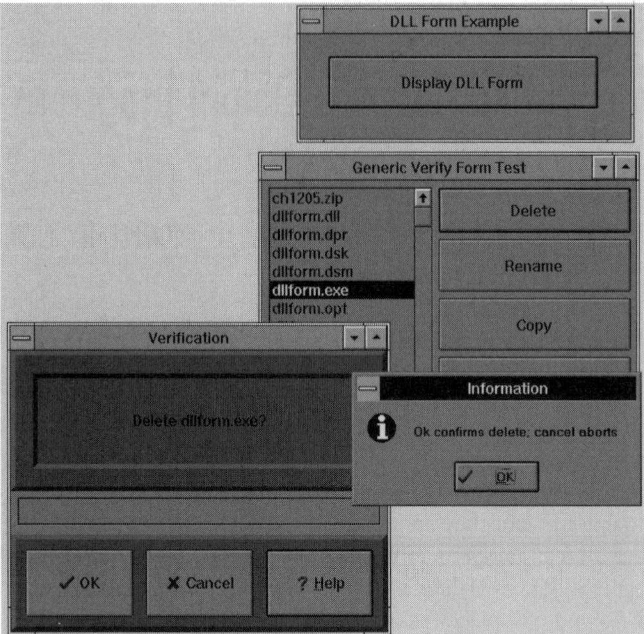

Figure 12-6 DLLTEST at run time, showing the list box, generic Verification dialog, and custom help message dialog

4. Just below the *implementation* keyword, enter the following procedure, which will be called by the Windows operating system once the unit has been converted into a DLL.

```
procedure DoTheForm;
begin
  try
    { Create the basic viewer form }
    Form1 := TForm1.Create(Application);
    { Show it modally to get focus }
    Form1.ShowModal;
  finally
    { regardless of success, destroy form }
    { to release resources              }
    Form1.Free;
  end;
end;
```

5. Bring up the DLLFORM.DPR file in the Code Editor. Make the changes indicated in the following code so that Delphi can produce a DLL instead of an executable file from the project. (For more details, see pages 129 to 135 of the *Component Writer's Guide*.)

```
library Dllform;

uses
  Dllvform in 'DLLVFORM.PAS' {Form2},
  Genver2 in 'GENVER2.PAS' {Form1};

exports
  DoTheForm;

{$R *.RES}

begin
end.
```

6. Compile the project to create the DLL. If you encounter errors, make sure all syntax problems have been corrected and that the DPR file meets the requirements in the *Component Writer's Guide* listings in step 5.

7. Create a new blank project. Name it DLLTEST.DPR and name the unit DLLFTEST.PAS

8. Add the components to Form1 and set their properties as shown in Table 12-7.

Table 12-7 Components, properties, and settings for Form1 of DLLFTEST

COMPONENT	PROPERTY	SETTING
Form1	Type	Application Main Form
	Width	382
	Height	149
	Left	57
	Top	83
	Caption	DLL Form Example
Button1	Type	TButton
	Left	32
	Top	24
	Width	305
	Height	57
	Caption	Display DLL Form

9. Go into the Code Editor in DLLFTEST.PAS and enter the following line just under the *implementation* keyword. This allows the unit to invoke the forms stored in the DLL.

```
procedure DoTheForm; far;
external 'DLLFORM';
```

10. Select the OnClick event of the Button1 component and enter this line of code to call the dialog box from the DLL.

```
procedure TForm1.Button1Click(Sender: TObject);
begin
  DoTheForm;
end;
```

11. Compile and test the project.

How It Works

What this application does may seem trivial at first, but in fact it is little short of astounding. In order to understand why this is so, and how it relates to the future of Delphi, some background is required.

Since the release of the Object Windows Library with Turbo Pascal for Windows 1.0, and its C++ counterpart Application Frameworks, Borland compilers have been able to produce DLLs for the Windows 3.x operating system. This is relatively straightforward, since all that is involved are direct calls into the Windows API and normal PC data manipulation. Then Visual Basic 1.0 arrived, allowing creation of DLLs that included VBX controls and other sophisticated elements that were definitely not part of the standard Windows 3.x API. How is this wizardry accomplished?

The answer lies in the VBRUNxxx.DLL files, which all Visual Basic applications must either distribute or have access to, and in a version as good as or better than the one under which they were created. Many a frustrated user acquires a Visual Basic program only to receive the dreaded "VBRUN version incompatible" error dialog, and then spends hours searching local BBSs or the Internet for the later version. Even more delightful is the occasional tendency of a new VB application to overwrite existing VB DLLs with its own version, which may be incompatible with those used by existing programs, making them suddenly nonfunctional.

Delphi, however, is a natively compiled environment. Each Delphi application is a stand-alone executable that runs with complete functionality, even without Delphi-based files. It does this by placing the entire functionality of the Delphi VCL in each and every Delphi application, whether it is an EXE or a DLL. In the end, it's a trade-off: Delphi executables will occupy fractionally more disk space than their VB cousins, but they will never suffer the incompatibility or missing file problems of the runtime-module-based applications.

The actual code needed to make the units created in How-To 12.4 into a DLL is quite simple, and is contained in the DoTheForm procedure. The following line of code contains the critical instructions for Delphi:

```
procedure DoTheForm; export;
```

The *export* keyword tells Delphi that this procedure is to be made available via the DLL function exposure methods defined by Microsoft in the Windows SDK.

Since the procedure takes no parameters, an important point must be raised: DLLs tend to be called by C-based programs, which do not use types like Boolean or String. In order to make your DLL safely usable by non-Delphi programs, it is a good idea to have as few passed parameters as possible in the exported function, and make those that you do have of C/Pascal equivalent types. (There are several excellent books on C-to-Pascal conversions that cover this topic.)

The exported procedure itself is standard Delphi, and can have local variables and all the other capabilities of a normal Delphi procedure. Two important factors do arise, however. First, notice that the form is invoked in the ShowModal format. This is required because if the form is called using the standard Show method, it immediately terminates without remaining visible. This may be a bug, or it may be a result of interactions between the VCL and Windows. Second, any Delphi-based cleanup, such as calling the Free method to release resources, is needed inside the exported procedure. This is necessary because the DLL system does not use Delphi method passing and so may not correctly invoke a normal Delphi cleanup.

The complementary code inside DLLFTEST.PAS, which calls the DLL procedures, is:

```
procedure DoTheForm; far;
external 'DLLFORM';
```

The three items after the normal Delphi procedure declaration are the critical ones. You need the *far* keyword due to the segmented memory architecture of the 16-bit Intel processors (this need evaporates in 32-bit environments). Those interested in exactly why it is needed should peruse books on Windows programming in assembly language. The *external* keyword tells Delphi that this procedure doesn't live in a Delphi unit but is imported via the DLL mechanism. The final parameter, DLLFORM, tells Delphi which DLL to look in for the procedure. Notice that unless the DLL resides in the unit where the Delphi executable lives, or is on the path, the call will fail.

A final area of interest is the way in which the DPR file needs to be modified to allow turning the previous executable project into a DLL. Normally Borland warns against hand-modifying the DPR file, and experience suggests they mean what they say. Inside the DPR, normal Object Pascal rules are somewhat suspended; directives that apply faithfully in normal units are ignored, and code that is placed in seemingly proper places either is removed, or gives strange error messages. The bottom line is, don't mess with the DPR file!

However, in this case Borland gives very clear directions on what is allowed in the *Component Writer's Guide*, as referenced in the steps in the How-To. As long as these guidelines are strictly adhered to, no problems should result.

Comments

Developers who are concerned about the high overhead of including the entire VCL with each executable can use the DLL mechanism to avoid much of the problem by placing often-used forms in a DLL rather than in the main application. This way, if several applications are being run on the same machine, only one copy of the form's code is needed, taking up less space.

12.6 How do I...
Use OOP to extend the capabilities of an imported VBX control?

COMPLEXITY: INTERMEDIATE

Problem

A lot of good controls are currently available only in VBX format. Can I import these controls into Delphi and then modify them?

Technique

Delphi can import any licensed Level One VBX control. In the process it creates a component wrapper around the VBX, which allows you to modify it using Delphi's Object Pascal OOP techniques. This How-To demonstrates how to modify the progress gauge VBX distributed with Delphi.

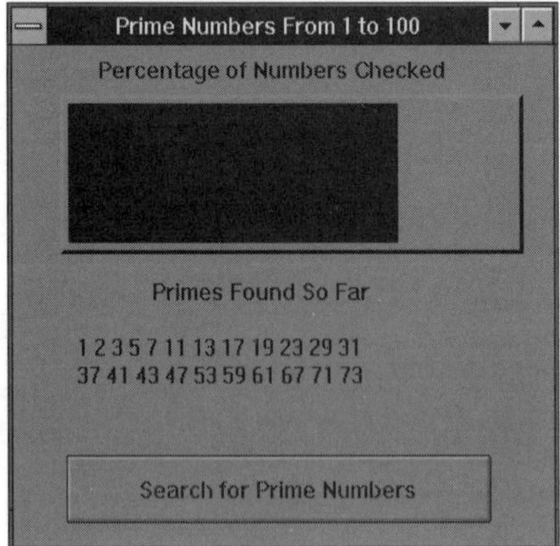

Figure 12-7 PRIMES at run time, showing the progress indicator VBX; the screen displays custom colors

Steps

Run PRIMES.EXE. Click the button, and a list of prime numbers (those evenly divisible only by themselves and 1) will appear in the label field. As they appear, the progress gauge displays the total numbers checked as a percentage. The form will look something like Figure 12-7. Unlike the normal VBX, which can only use default colors for its 3D look, this progress indicator has custom beveling colors.

1. Create a new blank project and name it PRIMES.DPR. Name the unit PRIMEPRG.PAS.
2. Add the components to Form1 and set their properties as shown in Table 12-8.

Table 12-8 Components, properties, and settings for Form1 of PRIMEPRG

COMPONENT	PROPERTY	SETTING
Form1	Type	Application Main Form
	Width	417
	Height	397
	Left	47
	Top	21
	Caption	Prime Numbers From 1 to 100
Button1	Type	TButton
	Left	40
	Top	296
	Width	321
	Height	49
	Caption	Search for Prime Numbers
Label1	Type	TLabel
	Left	64
	Top	8
	Width	263
	Height	20
	Caption	Percentage of Numbers Checked
Label2	Type	TLabel
	Left	104
	Top	1688
	Width	165
	Height	20
	Caption	Primes Found So Far

continued on next page

continued from previous page

COMPONENT	PROPERTY	SETTING
Label3	Type	TLabel
	Left	48
	Top	208
	Width	313
	Height	81
	Caption	(blank)

3. Go into the Code Editor and move up to the *uses* keyword, then enter the keyword *VBXCtrl* in the clause to enable use of VBX controls.

```
unit Primeprg;
uses
  SysUtils, WinTypes, WinProcs, Messages, Classes, Graphics, Controls,
  Forms, Dialogs, StdCtrls, ExtCtrls, Gauges, VBXCtrl, Gauge;
```

4. Drop down to the *type* keyword and enter the following code to define a new class object that adds to the functionality of a VBX control.

```
type
  { Start the OOP modification by creating new object class }
  TMyGauge = class( TBiGauge )
    private
      { Add two private color variables }
      FHighLightColor : TColor;
      FShadowColor : TColor;
    public
      { Then make them into properties }
      property HighLightColor: TColor Read FHighLightColor
       Write FHighLightColor Default clBtnHighlight;
      property ShadowColor: TColor Read FShadowColor
       Write FShadowColor Default clBtnShadow;
      { Add a paint procedure to draw the new outline }
      procedure Paint;
  end;
```

5. Continue down to the *var* keyword and enter the following code to allocate a storage variable for the new VBX class.

```
var
  Form1: TForm1;
  TheGauge : TMyGauge;
```

6. Select the OnCreate event handler for Form1 and type in this code to create the enhanced progress gauge VBX at run time.

```
procedure TForm1.FormCreate(Sender: TObject);
begin
  { Create the new VBX at run time }
  TheGauge := TMyGauge.Create( Self );
```

```
  TheGauge.Parent := Self;
  TheGauge.Top := 40;
  TheGauge.Left := 40;
  TheGauge.Height := 105;
  TheGauge.Width := 340;
  TheGauge.Orientation := 0;
  TheGauge.BarColor := clBlue;
  TheGauge.Max := 100;
  { Turn off its normal beveling so we can override it }
  TheGauge.BevelSize := 0;
  TheGauge.Value := 0;
  TheGauge.Visible := true;
  { Set the values of the new color variables }
  TheGauge.HighLightColor := clAqua;
  TheGauge.ShadowColor := clBlack;
end;
```

7. Return to the Code Editor, move down below the *implementation* keyword, and type in this helper function to handle drawing the enhanced border around the control.

```
{ This is the new paint procedure for the derived class }
procedure TMyGauge.Paint;
var TheRect : TRect;
begin
  { Create a rectangle outside the VBX object }
  TheRect.Left := TheGauge.Left - 4;
  TheRect.Top := TheGauge.Top - 4;
  TheRect.Right := TheGauge.Left + TheGauge.Width + 6;
  TheRect.Bottom := TheGauge.Top + TheGauge.Height + 6;
  { Draw the beveled rectangle using ExtCtrls routine }
  Frame3D( Form1.Canvas , TheRect , TheGauge.HighLightColor ,
          TheGauge.ShadowColor , 3 );
end;
```

8. Choose the OnClick event for Button1 and enter the following code. This is what actually determines the primes and displays them, along with increasing the length of the enhanced progress gauge VBX.

```
procedure TForm1.Button1Click(Sender: TObject);
var LengthAdded ,
    TheTest ,
    Counter_2 ,
    Counter_1 : Integer;
    PrimeFound : Boolean;
begin
  { Make the call to paint the outer rectangle around the VBX }
  TheGauge.Paint;
  { Prevent restarting the process }
  Button1.Enabled := false;
  LengthAdded := 0;
  { Run through the candidate numbers }
  for Counter_1 := 1 to 100 do
  begin
```

continued on next page

continued from previous page

```
    { Move up the gauge one for every number tried }
    TheGauge.Value := TheGauge.Value + 1;
    { Assume the number is prime }
    PrimeFound := true;
    { Check from 2 to 1 less than target (this gets 1 & 2) }
    for Counter_2 := 2 to Counter_1 - 1 do
    begin
      { Do a div test }
      TheTest := ( Counter_1 div Counter_2 );
      { If the div was exact number isn't prime }
      if TheTest * Counter_2 = Counter_1 then
       PrimeFound := false;
      { Be nice and let other people go }
      Application.ProcessMessages;
    end;
    { Add the new prime to the list }
    if PrimeFound then
    begin
      Label3.Caption := Label3.Caption + IntToStr( Counter_1 ) + ' ';
      { If the list is too long wrap it by adding LF and CR }
      LengthAdded := LengthAdded +
       Length( IntToStr( Counter_1 )) + 1;
      if LengthAdded > 30 then
      begin
        Label3.Caption := Label3.Caption + #10#13;
        LengthAdded := 0;
      end;
    end;
  end;
end;
```

9. Select the OnDestroy event for Form1 and enter this code to free the resources of the VBX when the program ends.

```
procedure TForm1.FormDestroy(Sender: TObject);
begin
  { Be sure and free up the VBX when done }
  TheGauge.Free;
end;
```

10. Compile and test the project.

How It Works

VBX controls are an unusual hybrid; although created in a dialect of Visual Basic, much of their behavior is based on using the DLL functionality of Windows. The reason this is important is that although Delphi allows importing Level One VBX controls, the resulting objects do not fit perfectly into the Object Pascal/Delphi system. There are three major areas of concern: extensibility, compatibility, and portability.

An imported VBX lives as a standard Delphi Object Pascal class. What this means in practical terms is that the OOP techniques for extending the functionality of a Delphi object type, which have been discussed in previous How-Tos and the various Delphi manuals, work normally on an imported VBX, *up to a point!* As an example, consider the following code:

```
TMyGauge = class( TBiGauge )
   private
     FHighLightColor : TColor;
   public
     property HighLightColor: TColor Read FHighLightColor
      Write FHighLightColor Default clBtnHighlight;
```

TBiGauge is the imported VBX control. The FHighLightColor and HighLightColor entries are normal Delphi syntax, and they behave just as you would expect. However, in the following code entry,

```
procedure Paint;
```

notice that there is no *override* declaration at the end of the line. This is not an oversight or design decision. If you attempt to place the *override* directive and access the built-in Paint method of the imported control, a compiler error occurs, saying that the declared method does not exist in the base class.

Investigation will show that, in fact, there is no consistency in the way methods are exposed to Delphi by the VBX importation mechanism. In the case of the TBiGauge VBX, only mouse-message methods are made available; all other internal functionality is completely hidden. Borland states that the technique used to import the VBX controls uses calls into the underlying VBRUNxxx.DLL code and cannot be divulged because it is proprietary to Microsoft. This is a very serious limitation to using VBX controls in Delphi.

To prove the point, notice that the Paint method is not called within any method used by the TBiGauge object. Instead it is called by an external method, the Button1 OnClick procedure. It could also be called by the OnPaint method of the parent form for consistency. In neither case does the actual VBX know anything about the extra detail being drawn around it; in fact, it is necessary to shut down its built-in sculpturing to allow the grafted-on method to work properly.

Imported VBX controls are, however, perfectly compatible with the Delphi system, *provided they are not data aware and are Level One*. Level Two or Three VBX controls, and those that need a data import via the OLE/DDE mechanism, are not supported. Beyond this limitation, though, a VBX is just like a Delphi control for runtime and design-time functionality.

The portability of VBX controls is another thorny issue. As a test, locate a VBX control on your PC other than those provided with Delphi and attempt to add it to the component palette using the VBX button on the Import Component dialog. Unless you have bought the rights to use the control from its author, you will receive an error dialog telling you, in one form or another, that you are not authorized to access the VBX in design mode. Why is this important? Imagine that you develop a component based on an underlying VBX, and then attempt to distribute the Delphi control for use on the component palette by other users. When users try to import the new component, the underlying VBX will be required, along with its registration key, or the Delphi control will fail to install correctly.

Comments

This is an unusual How-To; it might almost be called a How Not To! Although VBX controls can be minimally utilized as design-time components in Delphi, using them in a more sophisticated runtime environment, or in distributed libraries, is problematical to say the least. Let's hope that either VBX controls will be superseded by native Delphi controls, or Microsoft will allow access to the underlying mechanisms of the VBX DLL calls to permit efficient runtime interactions. In any case, due to the registration limitations, use of VBXs ought to be limited to application distribution rather than as part of component libraries.

12.7 How do I...
Manipulate VCL components in the same way as a Visual Basic controls array?

COMPLEXITY: INTERMEDIATE

Problem

A very powerful technique available in Visual Basic is an array of controls, created and manipulated at run time rather than design time. Does Delphi have equivalent capabilities?

Technique

Delphi has component and control arrays built in, as part of the system used at run time to maintain forms. This How-To demonstrates Visual Basic style manipulation of these arrays in a memo application.

Steps

Run NOTEBOOK.EXE. Press the first text button and you will see a display similar to Figure 12-8. Type some text in the edit control and then choose New Memo from the menus. A new text button is created and placed in the scroll box. Type some text in the memo control and then press the first button again. You will be prompted to save the new text, and then the original memo returns. The program has other features that you can experiment with also.

1. Create a new blank project and name it NOTEPAD.DPR. Name the unit CTRLARRY.PAS.

2. Add the components to Form1 and set their properties as shown in Table 12-9.

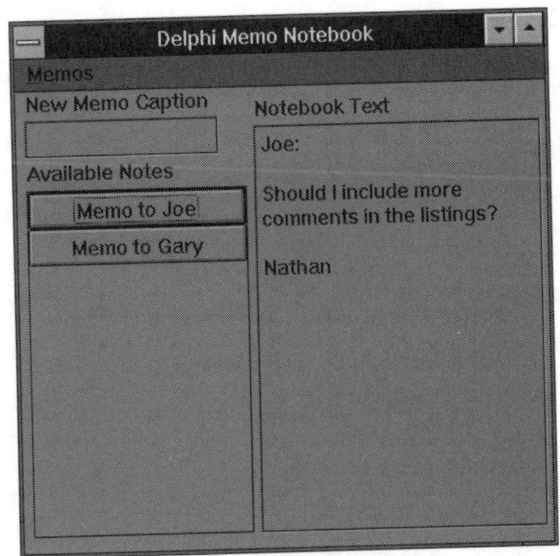

Figure 12-8 NOTEPAD at run time, showing the first memo's text

Table 12-9 Components, properties, and settings for Form1 of CTRLARRY

COMPONENT	PROPERTY	SETTING
Form1	Type	Application Main Form
	Width	454
	Height	436
	Left	37
	Top	9
	Caption	Delphi Memo Notebook
Edit1	Type	TEdit
	Left	8
	Top	24
	Width	161
	Height	29
	Text	(blank)
ScrollBox1	Type	TScrollBox
	Left	8
	Top	80
	Width	185
	Height	281
Memo1	Type	TMemo

continued on next page

continued from previous page

COMPONENT	PROPERTY	SETTING
	Left	200
	Top	32
	Width	241
	Height	329
	Lines	(blank)
SaveDialog1	Type	TSaveDialog
MainMenu1	Type	TMainMenu
Memos1	Type	TMenuItem (Top Level)
	Caption	&Memos
New1	Type	TMenuItem (Under Memos1)
	Caption	&New
Save1	Type	TMenuItem (Under Memos1)
	Caption	&Save
Rename1	Type	TMenuItem (Under Memos1)
	Caption	&Rename
Delete1	Type	TMenuItem (Under Memos1)
	Caption	&Delete
Exit1	Type	TMenuItem (Under Memos1)
	Caption	&Exit
Label1	Type	TLabel
	Width	115
	Height	20
	Left	200
	Top	8
	Caption	Notebook Text
Label2	Type	TLabel
	Width	124
	Height	20
	Left	8
	Top	56
	Caption	Available Notes
Label3	Type	TLabel
	Width	154
	Height	20
	Left	8
	Top	0
	Caption	New Memo Caption

3. Go into the Code Editor, move up to the *type* keyword, and type in the following code to define the basic helper record used to store information about the memos.

```
type
  TDNBRecord = record
    MemoName : String;
    FileName : String;
  end;
```

4. Continue down to the type definition for Form1 and enter this code to set up helper functions for saving memos and responding to mouse clicks on new buttons.

```
  TForm1 = class(TForm)
  public
    { Public declarations }
    function SaveActiveMemo : Boolean;
    procedure DefaultClick(Sender: TObject );
  end;
```

5. Move down to the *var* keyword and put in these assistant variables.

```
var
  Form1: TForm1;
  TheDataFile : File of TDNBRecord;
  ActiveMemo ,
  Counter_Top : Integer;
  TheWorkingDataRecord : TDNBRecord;
  DirtyFlag : Boolean;
```

6. Drop down below the *implementation* keyword and type in this helper function to save a memo to a text file.

```
function TForm1.SaveActiveMemo : Boolean;
begin
  { Assume no save }
  SaveActiveMemo := false;
  { Set working filename }
  SaveDialog1.Filename := TheWorkingDataRecord.Filename;
  SaveDialog1.Filter := '*.txt'
  { If ok save then do it }
  if SaveDialog1.Execute then
  begin
    try
      { Get the filename and save to it }
      TheWorkingDataRecord.Filename := SaveDialog1.Filename;
      Memo1.Lines.SaveToFile( TheWorkingDataRecord.Filename );
      { Then put the data in the memo file }
      Seek( TheDataFile , ActiveMemo );
      Write( TheDataFile , TheWorkingDataRecord );
    except
      { Report any error and exit unsaved}
      on EInOutError do
```

continued on next page

continued from previous page

```
        begin
          MessageDlg('Unable to Save Memo!', mtError,
               [mbOk], 0);
          exit;
        end;
      end;
      { Set valid save and clear mod flag }
      SaveActiveMemo := true;
      DirtyFlag := false;
    end;
end;
```

7. Below it, enter the following assistant function. This will determine which button has been pressed and activate the appropriate memo file.

```
procedure TForm1.DefaultClick(Sender: TObject);
var Counter_1 : Integer;
    TheWorkingRecord : TDNBRecord;
begin
  { If modifications made then try to save and exit if no }
  if DirtyFlag then if not SaveActiveMemo then exit;
  { Check through the component array for the one that }
  { matches the sending button object                   }
  for Counter_1 := 0 to ScrollBox1.ComponentCount -1 do
  begin
    { Once match is found use its data }
    if ScrollBox1.Components[ Counter_1 ] = Sender then
    begin
      { Set the active memo to the current number }
      ActiveMemo := Counter_1;
      { Clear previous data }
      Memo1.Clear;
      { Use try to avoid data corruption }
      try
        { Move to file position and read in new data  }
        Seek( TheDataFile , Counter_1 );
        Read( TheDataFile , TheWorkingRecord );
        { Read in the data from the memo file }
        Memo1.Lines.LoadFromFile( TheWorkingRecord.Filename );
      except
        on EInOutError do
        begin
          { If can't access file abort program }
          MessageDlg( 'Unable to read file! Exiting!' , mtError , [mbOK] , 0 );
          Close;
        end;
      end;
      { Set up the working record and clear mods flag }
      TheWorkingDataRecord := TheWorkingRecord;
      DirtyFlag := false;
    end;
  end;
end;
```

8. Select the OnCreate event handler for Form1 and type in these program lines to handle either loading in an existing memo database or creating a new one.

```
procedure TForm1.FormCreate(Sender: TObject);
var Counter_1 : Integer;
    TheWorkingRecord : TDNBRecord;
    TheNewButton : TButton;
begin
  { Use try accept to deal with no existing file }
  try
    { Attempt to open an existing data file }
    AssignFile( TheDataFile , 'DLMEMONB.INF' );
    Reset( TheDataFile );
    { If succeed, read in the data records }
    for Counter_1 := 1 to FileSize( TheDataFile ) do
    begin
      { Move to the current data position and read in the data }
      Seek( TheDataFile , Counter_1 - 1 );
      Read( TheDataFile , TheWorkingRecord );
      { Create a new text button, making its parent the scrollbox }
      TheNewButton := TButton.Create( ScrollBox1 );
      { Make its parent the scrollbox }
      TheNewButton.Parent := ScrollBox1;
      { Set the position using the incremented top variable }
      TheNewButton.Left := 0;
      TheNewButton.Top := Counter_Top;
      TheNewButton.Height := 30;
      Counter_Top := Counter_Top + 30;
      { Put the loaded memo name in the button }
      TheNewButton.Caption := TheWorkingRecord.MemoName;
      { Set the width }
      TheNewButton.Width := 183;
{ Set the default click method }
      TheNewButton.OnClick := DefaultClick;
    end;
  except
    { If file not found then create it }
    on EInOutError do
    begin
      ReWrite( TheDataFile );
    end;
  end;
  { Regardless, set no active memo and no modifications }
  ActiveMemo := -1;
  DirtyFlag := false;
end;
```

9. Activate the OnClick event of the New1 menu item and type in this code to handle creating a new text button and using VB-like control array techniques to access it.

```
procedure TForm1.New1Click(Sender: TObject);
var TheNewButton : TButton;
begin
  { If modifications to current memo save or exit }
```

continued on next page

continued from previous page

```
    if DirtyFlag then if not SaveActiveMemo then exit;
    { Reset modifications flag since new data added after save }
    DirtyFlag := true;
    { Set the name to the edit control data }
    TheWorkingDataRecord.MemoName := Edit1.Text;
    { Set no current save filename }
    TheWorkingDataRecord.Filename := '';
    { Create the new button, making its parent the scrollbox }
    TheNewButton := TButton.Create( ScrollBox1 );
    { Make the scrollbox the parent of the button }
    TheNewButton.Parent := ScrollBox1;
    { Set the position values, using incremented top counter}
    TheNewButton.Left := 0;
    TheNewButton.Top := Counter_Top;
    TheNewButton.Height := 30;
    { Move the counter down one level }
    Counter_Top := Counter_Top + 30;
    { Put the name of the memo in the button }
    TheNewButton.Caption := TheWorkingDataRecord.MemoName;
    { Set a fixed width to the button }
    TheNewButton.Width := 183;
    { Set a default click procedure for all buttons }
    TheNewButton.OnClick := DefaultClick;
    try
      { Move to the end of the data file and write the new record }
      Seek( TheDatafile , FileSize( TheDataFile ));
      Write( TheDatafile , TheWorkingDataRecord );
      { Make the new memo the active memo }
      ActiveMemo := FileSize( TheDataFile ) - 1;
      { Clear the memo component }
      Memo1.Clear;
    except
      { If cannot access data file exit at once to avoid corruption! }
      on EInOutError do
      begin
        { Warn the user }
        MessageDlg( 'Error using data file! Closing!' , mtError , [mbOK] , 0 );
        { Shut down }
        Close;
      end;
    end;
end;
```

10. Choose the Save1 menu item's OnClick handler and enter this line to save the active memo.

```
procedure TForm1.Save1Click(Sender: TObject);
begin
  { Call internal save procedure }
  SaveActiveMemo;
end;
```

11. Activate the Rename1 menu item's OnClick event and type in these lines to rename a text button from the data in the edit control.

```
procedure TForm1.Rename1Click(Sender: TObject);
begin
  { if no active memo leave }
  if ActiveMemo < 0 then exit;
  { Reset the caption of the memo button }
  TButton( ScrollBox1.Components[ ActiveMemo ]).Caption := Edit1.Text;
  { Also reset the working record and the internal mod flag }
  TheWorkingDataRecord.MemoName := Edit1.Text;
  DirtyFlag := True;
end;
```

12. Select the Delete1 menu item's OnClick event handler and put in the following code to delete a memo by removing its data file and making the corresponding text button disabled. (Actually removing the record from the database is done at program exit.)

```
procedure TForm1.Delete1Click(Sender: TObject);
begin
  { Prompt for deletion approval }
  if MessageDlg( 'Delete Memo ' + TheWorkingDataRecord.MemoName + '?' ,
                 MtWarning , [mbYes,mbNo] , 0 )= mrNo then exit;
  try
    { Delete the data file for the memo }
    DeleteFile( TheWorkingDataRecord.Filename );
  finally
    { Regardless of success of deletion clear the memo }
    Memo1.Clear;
    { Set enabled property to false to make unusable }
    TButton(ScrollBox1.Components[ ActiveMemo ]).Enabled := false;
    { Clear the data record }
    TheWorkingDataRecord.MemoName := '';
    TheWorkingDataRecord.Filename := '';
    { Set no active memo and no modifications }
    ActiveMemo := -1;
    DirtyFlag := false;
  end;
end;
```

13. Activate the Exit1 menu item's OnClick event and type in this code to rebuild the data file and remove deleted items on exit.

```
procedure TForm1.Exit1Click(Sender: TObject);
var TheOtherFile : File of TDNBRecord;
    Counter_1 : Integer;
begin
  { Prompt for exit approval and exit if no }
  if MessageDlg( 'Are you sure you want to Exit?' , mtWarning ,
                 [ mbYes,mbNo] , 0 ) = mrNo then exit;
  try
    { Set delay cursor }
    Screen.Cursor := crHourGlass;
    { Create a temporary file and open it }
    AssignFile ( TheOtherFile , 'Temp.Dat' );
    Rewrite( TheOtherFile );
```

continued on next page

continued from previous page

```
      { read in all non-diabled components and write them to temp file }
      for Counter_1 := 0 to ScrollBox1.ComponentCount - 1 do
      begin
        if TButton(ScrollBox1.Components[ Counter_1 ]).Enabled then
        begin
          Seek( TheDataFile , Counter_1 );
          Read( TheDataFile , TheWorkingDataRecord );
          Seek( TheOtherFile , FileSize( TheOtherFile ));
          Write( TheOtherFile , TheWorkingDataRecord );
        end;
      end;
      { Close the files }
      CloseFile( TheDataFile );
      CloseFile( TheOtherFile );
      { Delete the old data file and rename the temp file to it }
      DeleteFile( 'DLMEMONB.INF' );
      RenameFile( 'Temp.Dat' , 'DLMEMONB.INF' );
    except
      { If there's any IO error then warn and allow abort }
      on EInOutError do
      begin
        { Reset the cursor }
        Screen.Cursor := crDefault;
        if MessageDlg( 'Unable to save file! Continue Exit?' ,
         mtError , [mbYes,mbNo] , 0 ) = mrNo then exit;
      end;
    end;
    { Reset the cursor }
    Screen.Cursor := crDefault;
    { Close if no error or allowed to continue }
    Close;
end;
```

14. Select the OnChange event of the Memo1 component and put in these lines to maintain an internal consistency flag so that changes to the memo are always saved.

```
procedure TForm1.Memo1Change(Sender: TObject);
begin
  { If a memo has been created and the internal flag is not }
  { set, set it to indicate modifications have been made     }
  if (( ActiveMemo <> -1 ) and ( not DirtyFlag )) then
   DirtyFlag := true;
end;
```

15. Compile and test the project.

How It Works

Visual Basic's control arrays are a powerful aid to runtime programming in that environment. Designed as a way to give programmers access to design-time controls during program execution, they often become conduits for clever tricks, such as creating custom check boxes or compressing a large number of control events into one. (For many more such examples, see *Visual Basic How-To, Second Edition*, by Thomas, Arnson, and Waite, from Waite Group Press.)

However, VB's control arrays have some interesting limitations. They are all lumped together by type, and you have to assign a distinct index property to differentiate them at run time. Accessing the various data fields of the controls is sometimes syntactically clumsy, simply because Visual Basic is not in any sense object-oriented, and by nature a form/controls design environment is strongly object-oriented. Since it is based on Object Pascal, Delphi avoids these limits while adding considerable extra functionality at the same time.

To start, consider these two lines of code in the FormCreate and New1Click methods:

```
TheNewButton := TButton.Create( ScrollBox1 );
TheNewButton.Parent := ScrollBox1;
```

The Create method call takes an object parameter called Owner. This object is responsible for destroying (and freeing the resources allocated to) the new component when the application closes. The Parent property also takes an object, and normally this is the same as the Owner, but its purpose is to allocate responsibility for drawing and handling messages to and from the component. The documentation mentions that Parent should always be the first property set after creating a component at run time to avoid inconsistent behavior.

The reason these two objects need to be synchronized lies in the two built-in arrays in each component in Delphi, called Components and Controls. Components are all those components *owned* by a given control (not *parented* by!). This includes nonwindowed components such as Timers and Dialogs, as well as components like Images, which cannot receive input focus. Controls, on the other hand, are components that can receive input focus and thus have additional Windows capabilities. They too, like components, must be owned by a component to get listed in its Controls array.

Why is this important? If the normal procedure is followed in the New and Create methods, namely, assigning Self as the parameter for Create and then ScrollBox1 as the parameter for Parent (since the scroll box will draw the buttons), then attempting to use VB-like control array addressing will fail, because the buttons are in the Form1 Components list (since Self will be set to Form1 in its OnCreate method), not ScrollBox1's. Since the scroll box can just as easily destroy the text buttons as Form1, they are all assigned to it and the technique works fine.

Now that the text buttons are available in the ScrollBox1.Components array, here is an example of how they are accessed:

```
TButton( ScrollBox1.Components[ ActiveMemo ]).Caption :=    Edit1.Text;
```

The first point to notice is that an outside variable keeps track of which element of the Components array is currently being used. Although in this example all the elements of the array are of the same type, in a more general sense this is not necessarily the case. However, as you will see in a moment, using the exact object equivalence of Delphi overcomes this difference from Visual Basic.

Next, pay attention to the fact that a *typecast* is needed to access the fields of the component. A typecast means that a raw set of bits in memory is *coerced*, or treated as a specific type of pointer by the computer during execution of the program. This is one of the most powerful capabilities of modern computers, and unfortunately it is also the most common reason that modern computer programs cover the screen with random garbage, or lock the keyboard! In C, typecasting is done on faith, often with unfortunate results. In Object Pascal, due to the strongly typed nature of the language, the running Delphi application knows whether a typecast is correct and will halt execution safely if it isn't. In practical terms, the Components array reference is enclosed in parentheses and prefixed by the type name of the desired component, in this case TButton. Alternatively, the *as* keyword could have been used to do an implicit typecast.

Finally, notice that once these two criteria are met, the element of the array has all the abilities of the original variable, and changing its properties changes the correct button's appearance and behavior.

Next, examine this line of code used in the initial creation of each new text button:

```
TheNewButton.OnClick := DefaultClick;
```

DefaultClick is a generic procedure defined earlier to be compatible with the OnClick method (see How-To 12.4 for more information on this area). In practical terms, it means that every button has the same procedure called when any of them is clicked, so how does the application determine which one has been pressed?

The answer lies in Delphi's absolute object equality. Check this line of code from the DefaultClick procedure:

```
if ScrollBox1.Components[ Counter_1 ] = Sender then
```

Remember that Sender is a parameter sent to every message method call by the Delphi message handling system. Because in the end every Delphi object is an exact address in memory (perhaps with some internal thunking), the computer can, at run time, determine whether two objects have the same address, and are thus the same object. This is the method that allows accessing an exact component without needing a numerical index such as the one used in Visual Basic. Once a given component's identity is established, a counter can be set and the object referenced throughout the entire program from that point.

Comments

One capability which Delphi's Components array system allows that Visual Basic doesn't is to loop through all the components that are owned by another component without knowing in advance what type of components they are. This is possible using the *is* keyword to check for the desired types and then the *as* keyword or an explicit typecast to access them. A similar system is undoubtedly used in Delphi IDE, since the program is largely written in Delphi itself.

Another point to note is that for the EInOutError exception to become available, the {$I+} (I/O checking) compiler directive must be set in the OptionsCompiler dialog box or explicitly in the code.

12.8 How do I...
Override a default Delphi exception handler?

COMPLEXITY: EASY

Problem

Delphi provides default error messages for its exceptions but not for any other behavior. Is there a way I can take care of error conditions myself while still using Delphi's exception system?

Technique

Delphi provides the *On Exception Do* construct inside a *try except* or *try finally* block to allow custom handling of standard exceptions. This How-To demonstrates use of this technique in a simple calculator application.

Steps

Run CALCULATE.EXE. Enter 1000 in the upper-left edit control and 0 in the upper-right edit control. Select the / button, and you will receive an error dialog, as shown in Figure 12-9. Similar error messages will appear for non-number inputs as well as overflow and underflow conditions.

1. Create a new blank project and name it CALCULAT.DPR. Name the unit DELCALC.PAS.

2. Add the components to Form1 and set their properties as shown in Table 12-10.

Table 12-10 Components, properties, and settings for Form1 of DELCALC

COMPONENT	PROPERTY	SETTING
Form1	Type	Application Main Form
	Width	10
	Height	253
	Left	27
	Top	116
	Caption	Delphi Calculator
Button1	Type	Button
	Left	8
	Top	136

continued on next page

continued from previous page

COMPONENT	PROPERTY	SETTING
	Width	89
	Height	33
	Caption	+
Button2	Type	Button
	Left	104
	Top	136
	Width	89
	Height	33
	Caption	-
Button3	Type	Button
	Left	8
	Top	176
	Width	89
	Height	33
	Caption	*

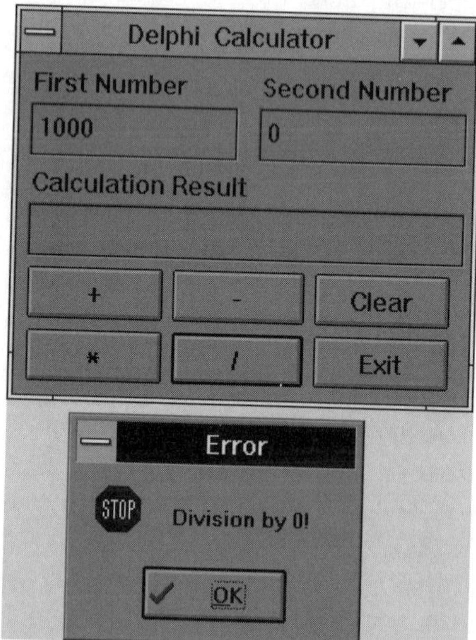

Figure 12-9 CALCULAT at run time, showing a Divide By Zero exception message dialog

COMPONENT	PROPERTY	SETTING
Button4	Type	Button
	Left	104
	Top	176
	Width	89
	Height	33
	Caption	/
Button5	Type	Button
	Left	200
	Top	136
	Width	89
	Height	33
	Caption	Clear
Button6	Type	Button
	Left	200
	Top	176
	Width	89
	Height	33
	Caption	Exit
Label1	Type	TLabel
	Left	8
	Top	8
	Width	103
	Height	20
	Caption	First Number
Label2	Type	TLabel
	Left	160
	Top	8
	Width	127
	Height	20
	Caption	Second Number
Label3	Type	TLabel
	Left	8
	Top	72
	Width	144
	Height	20
	Caption	Calculation Result

continued on next page

continued from previous page

COMPONENT	PROPERTY	SETTING
Edit1	Type	TEdit
	Left	8
	Top	32
	Width	137
	Height	33
	Text	(blank)
Edit2	Type	TEdit
	Left	160
	Top	32
	Width	137
	Height	33
	Text	(blank)
Edit3	Type	TEdit
	Left	8
	Top	96
	Width	289
	Height	33
	Text	(blank)

3. Activate the Code Editor and move up to the type declaration of Form1. Just below the *private* keyword, enter this helper function declaration to validate user input safely.

```
private
    { Private declarations }
    function GetValidResults : Boolean;
```

4. Move down to the *var* keyword and type in these three assistant variables to store the input and output data.

```
var
  Form1: TForm1;
  Operand1, Operand2, Operand3 : Real;
```

5. Drop to just below the *implementation* keyword and put in this code for the helper function to validate user input with exception handling.

```
function TForm1.GetValidResults : Boolean;
begin
  { Assume invalid data }
  GetValidResults := false;
  try
    { Attempt to convert first number to a float }
```

```
    Operand1 := StrToFloat( Edit1.Text );
  except
    { Message on conversion error; not a number; exit invalid }
    on EConvertError do
    begin
      MessageDlg( 'Operand 1 is not a valid Number!' , mtError ,
            [mbOK] , 0 );
      exit;
    end;
    { Message on too large number; exit invalid}
    on EOverFlow do
    begin
      MessageDlg( 'Operand 1 Overflow!' , mtError ,
            [mbOK] , 0 );
      exit;
    end;
    { Message on too small number; exit invalid }
    on EUnderFlow do
    begin
      MessageDlg( 'Operand 1 Underflow!' , mtError ,
            [mbOK] , 0 );
      exit;
    end;
  end;
  try
    { Attempt to convert second operand to float }
    Operand2 := StrToFloat( Edit2.Text );
  except
    { Message on not a number error; exit invalid }
    on EConvertError do
    begin
      MessageDlg( 'Operand 2 is not a valid Number!' , mtError ,
            [mbOK] , 0 );
      exit;
    end;
    { Message on too large error; exit invalid }
    on EOverFlow do
    begin
      MessageDlg( 'Operand 2 Overflow!' , mtError ,
            [mbOK] , 0 );
      exit;
    end;
    { Message on too small error; exit invalid }
    on EUnderFlow do
    begin
      MessageDlg( 'Operand 2 Underflow!' , mtError ,
            [mbOK] , 0 );
      exit;
    end;
  end;
  { if no exception set ok inputs and return }
  GetValidResults := true;
end;
```

6. Choose the OnClick event handler of Button1 and enter this code to handle an addition operation request.

```
procedure TForm1.Button1Click(Sender: TObject);
var TheString : String;
begin
  { If not valid data abort }
  if not GetValidResults then exit;
  try
    { Perform the addition }
    Operand3 := Operand1 + Operand2;
    { If successful put in the control }
    Str( Operand3 : 5 : 5, TheString );
    Edit3.Text := TheString;
  except
    { Overflow message }
    on EOverFlow do
    begin
      MessageDlg( 'Addition Overflow!' , mtError ,
            [mbOK] , 0 );
      { Clear inputs }
      Button5Click( Sender );
    end;
    { Underflow message }
    on EUnderFlow do
    begin
      MessageDlg( 'Addition Underflow!' , mtError ,
            [mbOK] , 0 );
      { Clear inputs }
      Button5Click( Sender );
    end;
  end;
end;
```

7. Choose the OnClick event handler of Button3 and enter this code to handle a multiplication operation request.

```
procedure TForm1.Button3Click(Sender: TObject);
var TheString : String;
begin
  { If invalid data then exit }
  if not GetValidResults then exit;
  try
    { Do the multiplication }
    Operand3 := Operand1 * Operand2;
    { If successful put result in the control }
    Str( Operand3 : 5 : 5 , TheString );
    Edit3.Text := TheString;
  except
    { Overflow message }
    on EOverFlow do
    begin
      MessageDlg( 'Multiplication Overflow!' , mtError ,
            [mbOK] , 0 );
      { Clear inputs }
```

```
      Button5Click( Sender );
    end;
    { Underflow message }
    on EUnderFlow do
    begin
      MessageDlg( 'Multiplication Underflow!' , mtError ,
            [mbOK] , 0 );
      { Clear inputs }
      Button5Click( Sender );
    end;
  end;
end;
```

8. Choose the OnClick event handler of Button2 and enter this code to handle a subtraction operation request.

```
procedure TForm1.Button2Click(Sender: TObject);
var TheString : String;
begin
  { Exit if invalid data }
  if not GetValidResults then exit;
  try
    { Do subtraction }
    Operand3 := Operand1 - Operand2;
    { If successful then put result in edit control }
    Str( Operand3 : 5 : 5, TheString );
    Edit3.Text := TheString;
  except
    { Message on overflow }
    on EOverFlow do
    begin
      MessageDlg( 'Subtraction Overflow!' , mtError ,
            [mbOK] , 0 );
      { Clear all inputs }
      Button5Click( Sender );
    end;
    { Message on underflow }
    on EUnderFlow do
    begin
      MessageDlg( 'Subtraction Underflow!' , mtError ,
            [mbOK] , 0 );
      { Clear all inputs }
      Button5Click( Sender );
    end;
  end;
end;
```

9. Choose the OnClick event handler of Button4 and enter this code to handle a division operation request.

```
procedure TForm1.Button4Click(Sender: TObject);
var TheString : String;
begin
  { Abort if not valid data }
  if not GetValidResults then exit;
```

continued on next page

continued from previous page

```
  { Use exception handling }
  try
    { Do the division calculation }
    Operand3 := Operand1 / Operand2;
    { If succeed, put in third edit control }
    Str( Operand3 : 5 : 5, TheString );
    Edit3.Text := TheString;
  except
    { Message for division by zero error }
    on EZeroDivide do
    begin
      MessageDlg( 'Division by 0!' , mtError ,
            [mbOK] , 0 );
      { Clear offending data field }
      Edit2.Text := '';
    end;
    { Message for overflow error }
    on EOverFlow do
    begin
      MessageDlg( 'Division Overflow!' , mtError ,
            [mbOK] , 0 );
      { Clear all fields }
      Button5Click( Sender );
    end;
    { Message for underflow error }
    on EUnderFlow do
    begin
      MessageDlg( 'Division Underflow!' , mtError ,
            [mbOK] , 0 );
      { Clear all fields }
      Button5Click( Sender );
    end;
  end;
end;
```

10. Choose the OnClick event handler of Button5 and enter this code to handle a clear operation request.

```
procedure TForm1.Button5Click(Sender: TObject);
begin
  { Clear all the input fields }
  Edit1.Text := '';
  Edit2.Text := '';
  Edit3.Text := '';
end;
```

11. Choose the OnClick event handler of Button6 and enter this code to handle an exit request.

```
procedure TForm1.Button6Click(Sender: TObject);
begin
  Close;
end;
```

12. Compile and test the project.

How It Works

There is a truism in program development that runs something like this: It is impossible to make a program foolproof, because fools are so ingenious. Well over half of the code in most commercial applications is estimated to be for error trapping and handling. Delphi provides an exciting new mechanism called Exceptions to assist with this arduous work. There are two issues to consider in this area: Delphi's default error handling and the ability to override it.

Whenever a runtime error occurs, whether it is due to a hardware problem, a Windows General Protection Fault, invalid data in a user-input variable, or some problem within the Delphi system, an exception occurs. Delphi provides a default exception handling object called Exception, which deals with all the basic types of runtime errors. There are two major classes of exceptions: those that generate some sort of message to the user, and those that do not, and thus are called silent exceptions.

In the first case, Delphi puts up a dialog or message box to warn the user of the problem. In some cases execution can continue; in others the program is terminated. In either case Delphi does not deal with any programmer-caused issues—that is to say, the default exception handling mechanism is little more than a message generator coupled with some code to drop out of offending procedure calls.

Fortunately, Delphi provides a mechanism for letting programmers override the default non-behavior. This capability is encapsulated in the *try except* or the *try finally* blocks used in this How-To. Here is the one for the division by zero error:

```
try
  { Do the division calculation }
  Operand3 := Operand1 / Operand2;
  { If succeed, put in third edit control }
  Str( Operand3 : 5 : 5, TheString );
  Edit3.Text := TheString;
except
  { Message for division by zero error }
  on EZeroDivide do
  begin
    MessageDlg( 'Division by 0!' , mtError ,
     [mbOK] , 0 );
    { Clear offending data field }
    Edit2.Text := '';
  end;
end;
```

Notice that inside the *try* portion of the block are all the statements desired by normal execution of the procedure. Starting in the *except* portion of the block are a series of *on ErrorType do* constructions, such as *on EZeroDivide do* in the preceding code. This construct tells the compiler that if an exception has been raised, do a type equivalence check between the Exception object and the listed type; if they are the same, then execute the *do* loop code. (This is similar to the *as/is* constructs used in previous How-Tos.) If the typecast fails, execution drops immediately to the next *on ErrorType* block. Putting any other constructs inside the *except* portion will generate a syntax error at compile time.

Inside the do loop of the *on ErrorType* block, almost any statements are legal, although in the case of a hardware runtime error, consistent behavior is not guaranteed for obvious reasons. Unless the error causes a hard shutdown of the program or Windows, the application can clean up the mess and continue, at least long enough to save critical data and release Windows resources.

The important point to note about this overriding of the default exception behavior is that it is complete; if a programmer does not put up a message box or dialog to warn the user, Delphi will not do so either unless specifically invoked. Therefore, if you override the default exception handlers, it is your responsibility to keep the user informed about the current state of the application.

Comments

Another important and relatively undocumented aspect of exception handling is that when using the IDE debugger, exception dialogs are not necessarily displayed, particularly if they are created using the default mechanisms, as shown in the next How-To. Running outside the debugger, however, the messages display normally.

12.9 How do I...
Create and raise a customized Delphi exception?

COMPLEXITY: INTERMEDIATE

Problem

Delphi's exception handling system is so sophisticated, I'd like to be able to use it to trap some specific errors in my code. Is there a way to customize Delphi's exceptions?

Technique

Since Exception is an object, you can use OOP techniques to redefine and enhance its functionality. This How-To demonstrates this capability in a simple but powerful address book application.

Steps

Run ADDRBOOK.EXE. Choose the first entry in the combo box, then click on the State field. A dialog box will appear prompting you to enter a state; type in COLORADO and click OK. An error message dialog will appear, as shown in Figure 12-10. Cancel the operations, and then if you wish, experiment with adding new entries in the address book. You will find that invalid zip codes, area codes, and

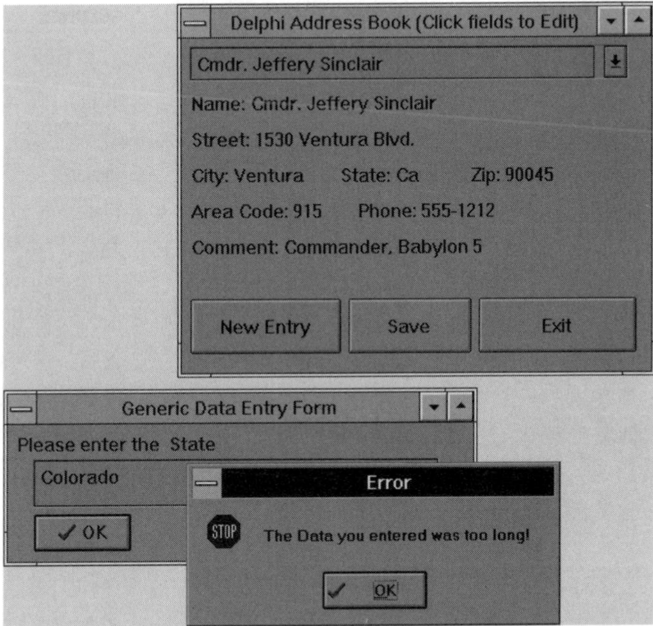

Figure 12-10 ADDRBOOK at run time, showing an error message dialog due to incorrect state entry

phone numbers all have specific message dialogs along with the generic "data too long" message.

1. Create a new blank project and name it ADDRBOOK.DPR. Name the unit ADRBK.PAS.
2. Add the components to Form2 and set their properties as shown in Table 12-11.

Table 12-11 Components, properties, and settings for Form2 of ADRBK

COMPONENT	PROPERTY	SETTING
Form1	Type	Application Main Form
	Width	439
	Height	333
	Left	41
	Top	101
	Caption	Delphi Address Book (Click Fields to Edit)
ComboBox1	Type	TComboBox
	Left	8

continued on next page

continued from previous page

COMPONENT	PROPERTY	SETTING
	Top	8
	Width	401
	Height	29
	Items	(none)
Button1	Type	TButton
	Width	137
	Height	49
	Left	8
	Top	232
	Caption	New Entry
Button2	Type	TButton
	Width	113
	Height	49
	Left	152
	Top	232
	Caption	Save
Button3	Type	TButton
	Width	145
	Height	49
	Left	272
	Top	232
	Caption	Exit
Label1	Type	TLabel
	Width	401
	Height	25
	Left	8
	Top	48
	Caption	Name:
Label2	Type	TLabel
	Width	409
	Height	33
	Left	8
	Top	80
	Caption	Street:
Label3	Type	TLabel
	Width	129
	Height	33

COMPONENT	PROPERTY	SETTING
	Left	8
	Top	112
	Caption	City:
Label4	Type	TLabel
	Width	121
	Height	33
	Left	144
	Top	112
	Caption	State:
Label5	Type	TLabel
	Width	153
	Height	25
	Left	264
	Top	112
	Caption	Zip:
Label6	Type	TLabel
	Width	153
	Height	33
	Left	8
	Top	144
	Caption	Area Code:
Label7	Type	TLabel
	Width	257
	Height	33
	Left	160
	Top	144
	Caption	Phone:
Label8	Type	TLabel
	Width	417
	Height	57
	Left	8
	Top	176
	Caption	Comment:

3. Go into the Code Editor and move up to the *uses* keyword. Enter the GENDEFRM unit declaration, which allows the ADRBK unit to use the generic data entry form created later.

```
uses
  SysUtils, WinTypes, WinProcs, Messages, Classes, Graphics, Controls,
  Forms, Dialogs, StdCtrls, GenDeFrm;
```

4. Move down to the *type* keyword and add these declarations to allow the application to store and save the address information.

```
type
  PAddressRecord = ^TAddressRecord;
  TAddressRecord = Record
    TheName : String;
    TheStreet : String;
    TheCity : String;
    TheState : String;
    TheZip : Longint;
    TheAreaCode : Integer;
    ThePhoneNumber : String;
    TheNote : String;
  end;
```

5. Continue down to the *var* keyword and add these helper variables to store the address book data on disk and in memory as an array of pointers.

```
var
  Form2: TForm2;
  TheAddressFile : File of TAddressRecord;
  TheWorkingRecord : PAddressRecord;
  Total_Records ,
  Current_Selection : Integer;
  TheAddressArray : Array[ 0 .. 256 ] of PAddressRecord;
  DirtyFlag : Boolean;
```

6. Activate the OnCreate event handler for Form2 and enter this code to initialize the form by either loading an existing address book database or creating a new one.

```
procedure TForm2.FormCreate(Sender: TObject);
var Counter_1 : Integer;
begin
  { Use exception handling for first try FNF error override }
  try
    { Use default filename and path }
    AssignFile( TheAddressFile , 'DADRBOOK.INF' );
    { Attempt to use existing file }
    Reset( TheAddressFile );
    { If the file exists, get total records }
    Total_Records := Filesize( TheAddressFile ) - 1;
    { And create array entries and read them in }
    for Counter_1 := 0 to FileSize( TheAddressFile) - 1 do
    begin
      { Move to the record position }
      Seek( TheAddressFile , Counter_1 );
      { Create a place to hold the data }
      New( TheAddressArray[ Counter_1 ] );
```

```
      { Set up a temporary variable }
      TheWorkingRecord := TheAddressArray[ Counter_1 ];
      { Read the data into it }
      Read( TheAddressFile , TheWorkingRecord^ );
      { Then set the combobox to add the new item }
      ComboBox1.Items.Add( TheAddressArray[ Counter_1 ]^.TheName );
    end;
  except
    { Assume any error means a new file and rewrite it }
    on EInOutError do
    begin
      Rewrite( TheAddressFile );
      { Set no records available }
      Total_Records := -1;
    end;
  end;
  { Close file regardless }
  CloseFile( TheAddressFile );
  { Set no current selection }
  Current_Selection := -1;
  { And no internal modifications }
  DirtyFlag := false;
end;
```

7. Select the OnChange event of ComboBox1 and add this code to handle selecting an entry in the address database.

```
procedure TForm2.ComboBox1Change(Sender: TObject);
begin
  { Set current selection to the itemindex of the combobox }
  { Note that in an internal call this value is preset      }
  Current_Selection := ComboBox1.ItemIndex;
  { Abort if no selection }
  if Current_Selection <> -1 then
  begin
    { Otherwise get current record in dummy and set values }
    TheWorkingRecord := TheAddressArray[ Current_Selection ];
    with TheWorkingRecord^ do
    begin
      Label1.Caption := 'Name: ' + TheName;
      Label2.Caption := 'Street: ' + TheStreet;
      Label3.Caption := 'City: ' + TheCity;
      Label4.Caption := 'State: ' + TheState;
      Label5.Caption := 'Zip: ' + IntToStr( TheZip );
      Label6.Caption := 'Area Code: ' + IntToStr( TheAreaCode );
      Label7.Caption := 'Phone: ' + ThePhoneNumber;
      Label8.Caption := 'Comment: ' + TheNote;
    end;
  end;
end;
```

8. Select the OnClick event of Button1 and add this code to handle adding a new entry in the address database.

```
procedure TForm2.Button1Click(Sender: TObject);
var TheResult : Integer;
    HoldingString : String;
begin
  { Don't overrun available record space in this demo version }
  if Total_Records = 256 then
  begin
    MessageDlg( 'Addressbook data limit reached!' , mtWarning ,
         [mbOK], 0 );
    exit;
  end;
  { Reset basic captions }
  Label1.Caption := 'Name: ';
  Label2.Caption := 'Street: ';
  Label3.Caption := 'City: ';
  Label4.Caption := 'State: ';
  Label5.Caption := 'Zip: ';
  Label6.Caption := 'Area Code: ';
  Label7.Caption := 'Phone: ';
  Label8.Caption := 'Comment: ';
  { Use exceptions in case fail to get new item }
  try
    { Create a dummy record for ease of dialog use }
    New( TheWorkingRecord );
    { Clear the name field, only one used }
    TheWorkingRecord^.TheName := '';
    { Now make the input form }
    Form1 := TForm1.Create(self);
    { Set it to name data }
    Form1.DataInputType := 1;
    { Show it modally and get result }
    TheResult := Form1.ShowModal;
    { Either way, kill off temporary data record }
    Dispose( TheWorkingRecord );
    { If okayed new entry }
    if TheResult = mrOK then
    begin
      { Store the input data }
      HoldingString := Form1.Edit1.Text;
      { Close the input form }
      Form1.Close;
      { Set up display caption }
      Label1.Caption := Label1.Caption + HoldingString;
      { Create new record }
      Total_Records := Total_Records + 1;
      { Set new item as current selection }
      Current_Selection := Total_Records;
      { Create new address book record in the array }
      New( TheAddressArray[ Total_Records ] );
      { Put it in the working record }
      TheWorkingRecord := TheAddressArray[ Total_Records ];
      { Set up new name and default data }
      with TheWorkingRecord^ do
      begin
        TheName := HoldingString;
```

```
        TheStreet := '158 MyStreet';
        TheCity := 'MyCity';
        TheState := 'CO';
        TheZip := 80000;
        TheAreaCode := 303;
        ThePhoneNumber := '555-1212';
        TheNote := 'This is a dummy address entry';
      end;
      { Add the new item to the combobox }
      ComboBox1.ItemIndex := ComboBox1.Items.Add( HoldingString );
      { Call the update method via onclick call }
      ComboBox1Change( Self );
      { And set internal modification flag }
      DirtyFlag := true;
    end
    { Close the input form regardless }
    else Form1.Close;
  finally
    { Regardless of what happened, free resources }
    Form1.Free;
  end;
end;
```

9. Select the OnClick event of Button2 and add this code to handle saving the address database.

```
procedure TForm2.Button2Click(Sender: TObject);
var Counter_1 : Integer;
    TheOtherWorkingRecord : PAddressRecord;
begin
  { Abort if no data with message box warning }
  if Total_Records = -1 then
  begin
    MessageDlg( 'No records to save!' , mtWarning ,
           [mbOK],0);
    exit;
  end;
  { Use exception code to attempt saving file }
  try
    { use default filename and path }
    AssignFile( TheAddressFile , 'DADRBOOK.INF' );
    { Use Rewrite to zero out the file }
    ReWrite( TheAddressFile );
    { Save all the current records }
    for Counter_1 := 0 to Total_Records do
    begin
      { Seek to next position }
      Seek( TheAddressFile , Counter_1 );
      { Get a record from the array }
      TheOtherWorkingRecord := TheAddressArray[ Counter_1 ];
      { Write it out to the disk }
      Write( TheAddressFile , TheOtherWorkingRecord^ );
    end;
  except
    { If any sort of IO error, assume failure and abort }
```

continued on next page

continued from previous page

```
    on EInOutError do
    begin
      MessageDlg( 'Unable to save addressbook!' , mtError ,
                  [mbOK] , 0 );
      { Close the file on general principles }
      CloseFile( TheAddressFile );
      { Abort to avoid resetting dirty flag }
      exit;
    end;
  end;
  { Assume good save at this point so close and reset flag }
  CloseFile( TheAddressFile );
  DirtyFlag := false;
end;
```

10. Select the OnClick event of Button3 and add the following code to handle closing the form. This saves the address database if it has been changed since the last save operation.

```
procedure TForm2.Button3Click(Sender: TObject);
var TheResult : Integer;
begin
  { If data changed, confirm saving }
  if DirtyFlag then
  begin
    TheResult := MessageDlg( 'Address Book Changed! Save?', mtWarning ,
                 mbYesNoCancel,0);
    { Don't exit on a cancel result! }
    if TheResult = mrCancel then Exit;
    { Call the save procedure via its onclick method }
    if TheResult = mrYes then Button2Click( Self );
  end;
  { Shut down unless cancelled }
  Close;
end;
```

11. Select the OnClick event of Label1 and add this code to edit the Name field of the address book record, bringing up the generic data entry form.

```
{ Procedure to enter/change Name field }
procedure TForm2.Label1Click(Sender: TObject);
var TheResult : Integer;
begin
  { Use the try format in case can't create modal form }
  try
    { Create input form }
    Form1 := TForm1.Create( Self );
    { Set the data type to name }
    Form1.DataInputType := 1;
    { Display in modal format and get result }
    TheResult := Form1.ShowModal;
    { Only update address book if accepted result }
    if TheResult = mrOK then
    begin
```

```
      { Reset the data field on the form }
      Label1.Caption := 'Name: ' + Form1.Edit1.Text;
      { And in the data record }
      TheWorkingRecord^.TheName := Form1.Edit1.Text;
      { Set internal modification flag }
      DirtyFlag := true;
    end;
  finally
    { Regardless of results close and free modal form }
    Form1.Close;
    Form1.Free;
  end;
end;
```

12. Select the OnClick event of Label2 and add this code to edit the Street field of the address book record, bringing up the generic data entry form.

```
{ Procedure to enter/change Address field }
procedure TForm2.Label2Click(Sender: TObject);
var TheResult : Integer;
begin
  { Use the try format in case can't create modal form }
  try
    { Create input form }
    Form1 := TForm1.Create( Application );
    { Set the data type to address }
    Form1.DataInputType := 2;
    { Display in modal format and get result }
    TheResult := Form1.ShowModal;
    { Only update address book if accepted result }
    if TheResult = mrOK then
    begin
      { Reset the data field on the form }
      Label2.Caption := 'Street: ' + Form1.Edit1.Text;
      { And in the data record }
      TheWorkingRecord^.TheStreet := Form1.Edit1.Text;
      { Set internal modification flag }
      DirtyFlag := true;
    end;
  finally
    { Regardless of results close and free modal form }
    Form1.Close;
    Form1.Free;
  end;
end;
```

13. Select the OnClick event of Label3 and add this code to edit the City field of the address book record, bringing up the generic data entry form.

```
{ Procedure to enter/change City field }
procedure TForm2.Label3Click(Sender: TObject);
var TheResult : Integer;
begin
  { Use the try format in case can't create modal form }
  try
```

continued on next page

continued from previous page

```
    { Create input form }
    Form1 := TForm1.Create( Self );
    { Set the data type to city }
    Form1.DataInputType := 3;
    { Display in modal format and get result }
    TheResult := Form1.ShowModal;
    { Only update address book if accepted result }
    if TheResult = mrOK then
    begin
      { Reset the data field on the form }
      Label3.Caption := 'City: ' + Form1.Edit1.Text;
      { And in the data record }
      TheWorkingRecord^.TheCity := Form1.Edit1.Text;
      { Set internal modification flag }
      DirtyFlag := true;
  end;
  finally
    { Regardless of results close and free modal form }
    Form1.Close;
    Form1.Free;
  end;
end;
```

14. Select the OnClick event of Label4 and add this code to edit the State field of the address book record, bringing up the generic data entry form.

```
{ Procedure to enter/change State field }
procedure TForm2.Label4Click(Sender: TObject);
var TheResult : Integer;
begin
  { Use the try format in case can't create modal form }
  try
    { Create input form }
    Form1 := TForm1.Create( Self );
    { Set the data type to state }
    Form1.DataInputType := 4;
    { Display in modal format and get result }
    TheResult := Form1.ShowModal;
    { Only update address book if accepted result }
    if TheResult <> mrOK then
    begin
      { Reset the data field on the form }
      Label4.Caption := 'State: ' + Form1.Edit1.Text;
      { And in the data record }
      TheWorkingRecord^.TheState := Form1.Edit1.Text;
      { Set internal modification flag }
      DirtyFlag := true;
  end;
  finally
    { Regardless of results close and free modal form }
    Form1.Close;
    Form1.Free;
  end;
end;
```

15. Select the OnClick event of Label5 and add this code to edit the Zip field of the address book record, bringing up the generic data entry form.

```
{ Procedure to enter/change Zip Code field }
procedure TForm2.Label5Click(Sender: TObject);
var TheResult : Integer;
begin
  { Use the try format in case can't create modal form }
  try
    { Create input form }
    Form1 := TForm1.Create( Self );
    { Set the data type to zip }
    Form1.DataInputType := 5;
    { Display in modal format and get result }
    TheResult := Form1.ShowModal;
    { Only update address book if accepted result }
    if TheResult = mrOK then
    begin
      { Reset the data field on the form }
      Label5.Caption := 'Zip: ' + Form1.Edit1.Text;
      { And in the data record }
      TheWorkingRecord^.TheZip := StrToInt( Form1.Edit1.Text );
      { Set internal modification flag }
      DirtyFlag := true;
  end;
  finally
    { Regardless of results close and free modal form }
    Form1.Close;
    Form1.Free;
  end;
end;
```

16. Select the OnClick event of Label6 and add this code to edit the Area Code field of the address book record, bringing up the generic data entry form.

```
{ Procedure to enter/change Area Code field }
procedure TForm2.Label6Click(Sender: TObject);
var TheResult : Integer;
begin
  { Use the try format in case can't create modal form }
  try
    { Create input form }
    Form1 := TForm1.Create( Self );
    { Set the data type to area code }
    Form1.DataInputType := 6;
    { Display in modal format and get result }
    TheResult := Form1.ShowModal;
    { Only update address book if accepted result }
    if TheResult = mrOK then
    begin
      { Reset the data field on the form }
      Label6.Caption := 'Area Code: ' + Form1.Edit1.Text;
      { And in the data record }
      TheWorkingRecord^.TheAreaCode := StrToInt( Form1.Edit1.Text );
      { Set internal modification flag }
```

continued on next page

continued from previous page

```
      DirtyFlag := true;
    end;
  finally
    { Regardless of results close and free modal form }
    Form1.Close;
    Form1.Free;
  end;
end;
```

17. Select the OnClick event of Label7 and add this code to edit the Phone field of the address book record, bringing up the generic data entry form.

```
{ Procedure to enter/change Phone Number field }
procedure TForm2.Label7Click(Sender: TObject);
var TheResult : Integer;
begin
  { Use the try format in case can't create modal form }
  try
    { Create input form }
    Form1 := TForm1.Create( Self );
    { Set the data type to phone number }
    Form1.DataInputType := 7;
    { Display in modal format and get result }
    TheResult := Form1.ShowModal;
    { Only update address book if accepted result }
    if TheResult = mrOK then
    begin
      { Reset the data field on the form }
      Label7.Caption := 'Phone: ' + Form1.Edit1.Text;
      { And in the data record }
      TheWorkingRecord^.ThePhoneNumber := Form1.Edit1.Text;
      { Set internal modification flag }
      DirtyFlag := true;
  end;
  finally
    { Regardless of results close and free modal form }
    Form1.Close;
    Form1.Free;
  end;
end;
```

18. Select the OnClick event of Label8 and add this code to edit the Comment field of the address book record, bringing up the generic data entry form.

```
{ Procedure to enter/change Comment field }
procedure TForm2.Label8Click(Sender: TObject);
var TheResult : Integer;
begin
  { Use the try format in case can't create modal form }
  try
    { Create input form }
    Form1 := TForm1.Create( Self );
    { Set the data type to comments }
    Form1.DataInputType := 8;
    { Display in modal format and get result }
```

```
    TheResult := Form1.ShowModal;
    { Only update address book if accepted result }
    if TheResult = mrOK then
    begin
      { Reset the data field on the form }
      Label8.Caption := 'Comment: ' + Form1.Edit1.Text;
      { And in the data record }
      TheWorkingRecord^.TheNote := Form1.Edit1.Text;
      { Set internal modification flag }
      DirtyFlag := true;
    end;
  finally
    { Regardless of results close and free modal form }
    Form1.Close;
    Form1.Free;
  end;
end;
```

19. Create a new blank form and name the unit GENDEFRM.PAS.

20. Add the components to Form1 and set their properties as shown in Table 12-12.

Table 12-12 Components, properties, and settings for Form1 of GENDEFRM

COMPONENT	PROPERTY	SETTING
Form1	Type	Application Main Form
	Width	434
	Height	157
	Left	48
	Top	140
	Caption	Generic Data Entry Form
Edit1	Type	TEdit
	Left	24
	Top	32
	Width	369
	Height	41
	Text	(blank)
Label1	Type	TLabel
	Left	8
	Top	0
	Width	417
	Height	25
	Caption	Please Enter The
BitBtn1	Type	TBitBtn

continued on next page

continued from previous page

COMPONENT	PROPERTY	SETTING
	Left	24
	Top	80
	Width	89
	Height	33
	Kind	bkOK
BitBtn2	Type	TBitBtn
	Left	304
	Top	80
	Width	89
	Height	33
	Kind	bkCancel

21. Go into the Code Editor and add this program code to define the new exception types for errors in data entry.

```
type
  EDataTooLong = class( Exception )
  end;
  EInvalidZipCode = class( Exception )
  end;
  EInvalidAreaCode = class( Exception )
  end;
  EInvalidPhoneNumber = class( Exception )
  end;
```

22. Move down to the *public* keyword in the Form1 type declaration. Add three helper functions to determine whether input data is valid and one assistant variable to determine type of input.

```
  TForm1 = class(TForm)
  public
{ Public declarations }
    DataInputType : Integer;
    function ValidZipCode : Boolean;
    function ValidAreaCode : Boolean;
    function ValidPhoneNumber : Boolean;
```

23. Continue down to below the *implementation* keyword and add a *uses* clause for the ADRBK unit, placed here to avoid circular unit references.

```
implementation
uses Adrbk;
```

24. Below the declaration in step 23, add the following helper function to validate zip code entry using the newly defined exception classes.

```
{ Function to return valid US zip code }
```

```
function TForm1.ValidZipCode : Boolean;
var Holder : Integer;
begin
  { Assume bad }
  ValidZipCode := false;
  { Abort if too short }
  if Length( Edit1.Text ) < 5 then exit;
  try
    Holder := StrToInt( Edit1.Text );
  except
    { Abort if not a number }
    exit;
  end;
  { Only here is it decided valid }
  ValidZipCode := true;
end;
```

25. Below the function in step 24, add the following assistant function to validate area code entry using the newly defined exception classes.

```
{ This function checks for a valid US area code }
function TForm1.ValidAreaCode : Boolean;
var Holder : Integer;
begin
  { Assume invalid }
  ValidAreaCode := false;
  { Abort if too short }
  if Length( Edit1.Text ) < 3 then exit;
  try
    Holder := StrToInt( Edit1.Text );
  except
    { Abort if not a valid number; don't display exception }
    exit;
  end;
  { Only if we get here is it valid area code }
  ValidAreaCode := true;
end;
```

26. Below the function in step 25, add the following secondary function to validate phone number entry using the newly defined exception classes.

```
{ This function checks for a valid US phone number }
function TForm1.ValidPhoneNumber : Boolean;
var Holder : Integer;
    TheString : String;
begin
  { Assume false }
  ValidPhoneNumber := false;
  { Abort if too short }
  if Length( Edit1.Text ) < 7 then exit;
  try
    { Check for a hypenated number }
    TheString := Edit1.Text;
    if TheString[ 4 ] = '-' then
    begin
```

continued on next page

continued from previous page

```
      { replace it if so }
      TheString[ 4 ] := '0';
      Holder := StrToInt( TheString );
    end
    else
    begin
      Holder := StrtoInt( Edit1.Text );
    end;
  except
    { if no valid phone number exit; dont display Exception here }
    exit;
  end;
  { Only if we get to here was it a valid US phone number }
  ValidPhoneNumber := true;
end;
```

27. Choose the OnShow event handler and enter this code to reset the data type displayed whenever the form is shown.

```
{ Do this each time form is shown to allow reuse }
procedure TForm1.FormShow(Sender: TObject);
begin
  { Set up the label caption and edit string by input type }
  case DataInputType of
    1 : begin
          Label1.Caption := Label1.Caption + ' Name';
          Edit1.Text := TheWorkingRecord^.TheName;
        end;
    2 : begin
          Label1.Caption := Label1.Caption + ' Street Address';
          Edit1.Text := TheWorkingRecord^.TheStreet;
        end;
    3 : begin
          Label1.Caption := Label1.Caption + ' City';
          Edit1.Text := TheWorkingRecord^.TheCity;
        end;
    4 : begin
          Label1.Caption := Label1.Caption + ' State';
          Edit1.Text := TheWorkingRecord^.TheState;
        end;
    5 : begin
          Label1.Caption := Label1.Caption + ' Zip Code';
          Edit1.Text := IntToStr( TheWorkingRecord^.TheZip );
        end;
    6 : begin
          Label1.Caption := Label1.Caption + ' Area Code';
          Edit1.Text := IntToStr( TheWorkingRecord^.TheAreaCode );
        end;
    7 : begin
          Label1.Caption := Label1.Caption + ' Phone Number';
          Edit1.Text := TheWorkingRecord^.ThePhoneNumber;
        end;
    8 : begin
          Label1.Caption := Label1.Caption + ' Comment';
```

```
      Edit1.Text := TheWorkingRecord^.TheNote;
    end;
  end;
end;
```

28. Activate the OnClick event handler for BitBtn1 and enter the following code to validate user entry when acceptance is indicated, using the new exception data types in the normal Delphi exception handling mechanism.

```
procedure TForm1.BitBtn1Click(Sender: TObject);
begin
  { Override button settings to avoid automatic closing }
  ModalResult := 0;
  try
    { Determine valid data input }
    case DataInputType of
      1 : begin
           { If the data is too long raise special exception }
           { otherwise signal accepted data input             }
           if Length( Edit1.Text ) > 40 then
            raise EDataTooLong.Create('')
            else ModalResult := mrOK;
         end;
      2 : begin
           { If the data is too long raise special exception }
           { otherwise signal accepted data input             }
           if Length( Edit1.Text ) > 40 then
            raise EDataTooLong.Create('')
             else ModalResult := mrOK;
         end;
      3 : begin
           { If the data is too long raise special exception }
           { otherwise signal accepted data input             }
           if Length( Edit1.Text ) > 20 then
            raise EDataTooLong.Create('')
             else ModalResult := mrOK;
         end;
      4 : begin
           { If the data is too long raise special exception }
           { otherwise signal accepted data input             }
           if Length( Edit1.Text ) > 2 then
            raise EDataTooLong.Create('')
             else ModalResult := mrOK;
         end;
      5 : begin
           { If the data is too long raise special exception }
           if Length( Edit1.Text ) > 5 then
            raise EDataTooLong.Create('');
           { otherwise check for a valid item and signal if not }
           { else let data flow through to calling form          }
           if not ValidZipCode then
            raise EInvalidZipCode.Create('')
             else ModalResult := mrOK;
         end;
```

continued on next page

continued from previous page

```
    6 : begin
          { If the data is too long raise special exception }
          if Length( Edit1.Text ) > 3 then
           raise EDataTooLong.Create('');
          { otherwise check for a valid item and signal if not }
          { else let data flow through to calling form         }
          if not ValidAreaCode then raise
           EInvalidAreaCode.Create( '' )
           else ModalResult := mrOK;
        end;
    7 : begin
          { If the data is too long raise special exception }
          if Length( Edit1.Text ) > 8 then
           raise EDataTooLong.Create('');
          { otherwise check for a valid item and signal if not }
          { else let data flow through to calling form         }
          if not ValidPhoneNumber then raise
           EInvalidPhoneNumber.Create( '' )
            else ModalResult := mrOK;
        end;
    8 : begin
          { If the data is too long raise special exception }
          { otherwise signal accepted data input            }
          if Length( Edit1.Text ) > 40 then
           raise EDataTooLong.Create('')
            else ModalResult := mrOK;
        end;
  end;
except
  { Handle custom overlong data error }
  on EDataTooLong do
  begin
    { Display warning dialog }
    MessageDlg( 'The Data you entered was too long!' , mtError , [mbOK] , 0);
    { Reset the data back to the original input }
    case DataInputType of
      1 : Edit1.Text := TheWorkingRecord^.TheName;
      2 : Edit1.Text := TheWorkingRecord^.TheStreet;
      3 : Edit1.Text := TheWorkingRecord^.TheCity;
      4 : Edit1.Text := TheWorkingRecord^.TheState;
      5 : Edit1.Text := IntToStr( TheWorkingRecord^.TheZip );
      6 : Edit1.Text := IntToStr( TheWorkingRecord^.TheAreaCode );
      7 : Edit1.Text := TheWorkingRecord^.ThePhoneNumber;
      8 : Edit1.Text := TheWorkingRecord^.TheNote;
    end;
  end;
  { Handle invalid zip code entry }
  on EInvalidZipCode do
  begin
    { Display warning dialog }
    MessageDlg( 'The Zip Code is not valid!' , mtError , [mbOK] , 0);
    { Reset data }
    Edit1.Text := IntToStr( TheWorkingRecord^.TheZip );
  end;
```

```
    { Deal with unusable area code input }
    on EInvalidAreaCode do
    begin
      { Warning dialog }
      MessageDlg( 'The Area Code is not valid!' , mtError , [mbOK] , 0);
      { Original data }
      Edit1.Text := IntToStr( TheWorkingRecord^.TheAreaCode );
    end;
    { Take care of bad phone number }
    on EInvalidPhoneNumber do
    begin
      { Show message }
      MessageDlg( 'The Phone Number is not valid!' , mtError , [mbOK] , 0);
      { Reset information }
      Edit1.Text := TheWorkingRecord^.ThePhoneNumber;
    end;
  end;
end;
```

29. Activate the OnClick event handler for BitBtn2 and enter this code, which simply closes the data entry form, discarding any input.

```
procedure TForm1.BitBtn2Click(Sender: TObject);
begin
  { End modal state as cancelled }
  ModalResult := mrCancel;
end;
```

30. Compile and test the project.

How It Works

This How-To illustrates the use of programmer-defined Exception objects in a meaningful way, namely, handling error trapping for finely detailed user input. Two major issues are normally associated with this level of code design: completeness and code reuse. Delphi exceptions give programmers the best of both worlds.

Completeness in error trapping means what it says: All possible errors are anticipated and handled. The cost for such completeness is normally a trade-off with code reuse, because in order to catch each possible error, many error conditions have to be tested, each in its own little block of code. In the days of BASIC, GOTO statements could alleviate some of this, but at the cost of spaghetti-code unreadability later. Procedural languages like Pascal and C normally discourage use of GOTO statements, and so the trade-off returns.

Delphi's exception system helps considerably in this area. By defining the new exceptions as derivatives of the base Exception object, programmers can tap into all the compiler support available for runtime exceptions with almost no effort. Notice the simplicity of the required code:

```
EDataTooLong = class( Exception )
end;
```

In this declaration, there are no code statements, just a declaration that this is a new object with the given name derived from type Exception. Now look at how the object is invoked:

```
if Length( Edit1.Text ) > 40 then
 raise EDataTooLong.Create('')
```

The *raise* keyword tells the compiler to insert code to simulate a runtime exception, setting the internal variable to the type of EDataTooLong, and to use the Create call to instantiate the stored Exception object as that type. Since this program has no interest in using the stored Exception object, no message string is defined for the Exception object and the derived class adds no special behavior. Had it been preferable to allow the Exception object to deal with runtime error handling, the code found in the *except* portion of the Button1 procedure could have been placed there instead.

Finally, notice how the new exception is handled inside the *except* portion of the code:

```
on EDataTooLong do
  begin
  MessageDlg( 'The Data you entered was too long!' , mtError ,
  [mbOK] , 0);
  end;
end;
```

If you examine the code from How-To 12.8, you can see how this invocation of the new exception class is done exactly as a predefined runtime exception type, and is handled by the compiler in the same way. The application can display a message dialog and then clean up after the mistake.

Comments

An even more interesting aspect of the exception mechanism is the ability to re-raise the same exception inside an exception handler, to do custom cleanup, and then force the standard Delphi exception mechanism to take over. This allows even fatal errors to be trapped and dealt with while still ensuring program shutdown.

12.10 How do I...

Use Delphi's exception handling system to avoid memory and resource leaks?

COMPLEXITY: EASY

Problem

Some of my programs are user driven, but resource intensive. Despite my best efforts, sometimes the programs crash and don't recover the Windows resources, and users must restart the computer. Is there a way in Delphi to make my programs more leakproof?

Technique

Resource leaks, causing Windows to lose access to resources due to a program crash or other unfriendly behavior, is indeed a major problem in current PC programming. Delphi's exception system can make such leaks very rare. This How-To uses a simple slide show application to demonstrate how to control behavior that would normally cause GPFs.

Steps

Run SLIDSHOW.EXE. Select the menu option Images|Add Image to Slide Show, then select the BADBMP.BMP file to load. You should see an error dialog similar to the one shown in Figure 12-11. You can experiment with the functionality of the program,

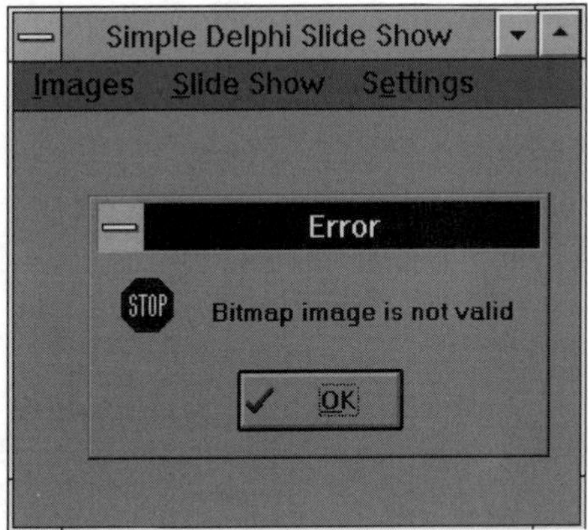

Figure 12-11 SLIDSHOW at run time, showing the invalid bitmap exception error dialog

which will load bitmaps, icons, and metafiles and display them either automatically or manually. No matter what files the user attempts to load, the program will not crash and leak resources.

1. Create a new blank project and name it SLIDSHOW.DPR. Name the unit SIMPSLID.PAS.
2. Add the components to Form1 and set their properties as shown in Table 12-13.

Table 12-13 Components, properties, and settings for Form1 of SIMPSLID

COMPONENT	PROPERTY	SETTING
Form1	Type	Application Main Form
	Width	331
	Height	291
	Left	72
	Top	22
	Caption	Simple Delphi Slide Show
OpenDialog1	Type	TOpenDialog
	DefaultExt	bmp
	FileName	*.bmp
	Filter	*.*
Timer2	Type	TTimer
	Enabled	False
	Interval	1000
MainMenu1	Type	TMainMenu
Images1	Type	TMenuItem (Top Level)
	Caption	&Images
SlideShow1	Type	TMenuItem (Top Level)
	Caption	&Slide Show
Settings1	Type	TMenuItem (Top Level)
	Caption	S&ettings
AddImageToShow1	Type	TMenuItem (Under Images)
	Caption	&Add Image to Slide Show
Exit1	Type	TMenuItem (Under Images)
	Caption	E&xit
BeginShow1	Type	TMenuItem (Under Slide Show)
	Caption	&Begin Show
	Enabled	False

COMPONENT	PROPERTY	SETTING
PauseShow1	Type	TMenuItem (Under Slide Show)
	Caption	&Pause Show
	Enabled	False
CancelShow1	Type	TMenuItem (Under Slide Show)
	Caption	&Cancel Show
	Enabled	False
NextSlide1	Type	TMenuItem (Under Slide Show)
	Caption	&Next Slide
	Enabled	False
Timer1	Type	TMenuItem (Under Settings)
	Caption	&Up Timer 30 Seconds
DownTimer30Seconds1	Type	TMenuItem (Under Settings)
	Caption	&Down Timer 30 Seconds
Automatic1	Type	TMenuItem (Under Settings)
	Caption	&Automatic
	Checked	True
Manual1	Type	TMenuItem (Under Settings)
	Caption	&Manual

3. Go into the Code Editor and move to the *var* keyword. Enter these assistant variables to store images and handle control variables.

```
var
  Form1: TForm1;
  TheImageArray : Array[0 .. 24] of TImage;
  ShowPaused ,
  AutomaticShow : Boolean;
  Total_Images : Integer;
  Timer_Interval : Longint;
  TimeElapsed : Longint;
  Current_Image : Integer;
```

4. Activate the OnCreate event handler for Form1 and enter the following code to initialize this application.

```
procedure TForm1.FormCreate(Sender: TObject);
begin
  { Set up default conditions }
  AutomaticShow := true;
  ShowPaused := false;
  Total_Images := 0;
  Timer_Interval := 60000;
  Current_Image := 1;
end;
```

5. Activate the OnDestroy event handler for Form1 and enter this code to free resources when the program closes.

```
procedure TForm1.FormDestroy(Sender: TObject);
var Counter_1 : Integer;
begin
  { Do a cleanup look to free all resources }
  for Counter_1 := 1 to Total_Images do
  begin
    TheImageArray[ Counter_1 - 1 ].Free;
  end;
end;
```

6. Choose the OnClick event handler for the Manual1 menu item and enter this code to handle switching from an automatic show to a manual one.

```
procedure TForm1.Manual1Click(Sender: TObject);
begin
  { Deal with menu consistency }
  Manual1.Checked := true;
  Automatic1.Checked := false;
  Timer1.Enabled := false;
  { Turn off internal flag }
  AutomaticShow := false;
end;
```

7. Choose the OnClick event handler for the Automatic1 menu item and enter this code to handle switching from a manual show to an automatic one.

```
procedure TForm1.Automatic1Click(Sender: TObject);
begin
  { Take care of menu items }
  Manual1.Checked := false;
  Automatic1.Checked := true;
  Timer1.Enabled := true;
  { Set internal flag }
  AutomaticShow := true;
end;
```

8. Choose the OnClick event handler for the Timer1 menu item and enter this code to add 30 seconds to the time of the wait between slides.

```
procedure TForm1.Timer1Click(Sender: TObject);
begin
  { If below maximum then increase by 30 seconds }
  if Timer_Interval < 180000 then
   Timer_Interval := Timer_Interval + 30000;
  { Deal with menus }
  if Timer_Interval > 30000 then
    DownTimer30Seconds1.Enabled := True;
  if Timer_Interval > 150000 then
    Timer1.Enabled := False;
end;
```

9. Choose the OnClick event handler for the DownTimer30Seconds1 menu item and enter this code to subtract 30 seconds from the time of the wait between slides.

```
procedure TForm1.DownTimer30Seconds1Click(Sender: TObject);
begin
  { If above minimum amount reduce by 30 seconds }
  if Timer_Interval > 30000 then Timer_Interval :=
   Timer_Interval - 30000;
  { Handle Menu consistency }
  if Timer_Interval < 60000 then
   DownTimer30Seconds1.Enabled := False;
  if Timer_Interval < 180000 then
   Timer1.Enabled := true;
end;
```

10. Choose the OnClick event handler for the BeginShow1 menu item and enter this code to start showing the slide bitmaps in memory.

```
procedure TForm1.BeginShow1Click(Sender: TObject);
begin
  { Reset to start at beginning }
  Current_Image := 1;
  { Show image on form's canvas using StretchDraw }
  Form1.Canvas.StretchDraw( Form1.ClientRect ,
   TheImageArray[ Current_Image - 1 ].Picture.Graphic );
  if AutomaticShow then
  { automatic show, turn on timer and do menus }
  begin
    Timer2.Enabled := true;
    TimeElapsed := 0;
    BeginShow1.Enabled := false;
    PauseShow1.Enabled := true;
    CancelShow1.Enabled := true;
  end
  else
  { Manual show, do menu consistency only }
  begin
    BeginShow1.Enabled := false;
    CancelShow1.Enabled := true;
    NextSlide1.Enabled := true;
  end;
end;
```

11. Choose the OnClick event handler for the PauseShow1 menu item and enter this code to handle pausing a running slide show.

```
procedure TForm1.PauseShow1Click(Sender: TObject);
begin
  { If currently paused }
  if ShowPaused then
  begin
    { Turn the timer back on }
    Timer2.Enabled := true;
    { Take care of menu consistency }
```

continued on next page

continued from previous page

```
      ShowPaused := false;
      PauseShow1.Checked := false;
    end
    else
    { Starting pause }
    begin
      { Turn off the timer }
      Timer2.Enabled := false;
      { Take care of menu consistency }
      ShowPaused := true;
      PauseShow1.Checked := true;
    end;
end;
```

12. Choose the OnClick event handler for the CancelShow1 menu item and enter this code to handle stopping a running slide show.

```
procedure TForm1.CancelShow1Click(Sender: TObject);
begin
  { Turn off the timer }
  Timer2.Enabled := false;
  { Take care of menu consistency }
  BeginShow1.Enabled := true;
  PauseShow1.Enabled := false;
  CancelShow1.Enabled := false;
  NextSlide1.Enabled := false;
  { Reset the form caption }
  Form1.Caption := 'Simple Delphi Slide Show';
end;
```

13. Choose the OnClick event handler for the NextSlide1 menu item and enter this code to move to the next bitmap slide in a manual slide show.

```
{ This function is called during manual showing }
procedure TForm1.NextSlide1Click(Sender: TObject);
begin
  { Move to next image and wrap if at end }
  Current_Image := Current_Image + 1;
  if Current_Image > Total_Images then
   Current_Image := 1;
  { Place image on form's canvas using StretchDraw }
  Form1.Canvas.StretchDraw( Form1.ClientRect ,
   TheImageArray[ Current_Image - 1 ].Picture.Graphic );
end;
```

14. Choose the OnTimer event handler for the Timer2 component and enter this code to show the next bitmap slide during an automatic slide show.

```
{ This procedure isn't called during manual showing }
procedure TForm1.Timer2Timer(Sender: TObject);
begin
  { Increase the elapsed time by 1000, equal to 1 second }
  TimeElapsed := TimeElapsed + 1000;
  { Update the form caption as progress indicator }
```

```
  Form1.Caption := 'Next Slide In ' +
   IntToStr(( Timer_Interval - TimeElapsed ) div 1000 ) + ' Seconds';
  { If need to do next slide }
  if TimeElapsed = Timer_Interval then
  begin
    { Reset the elapsed time }
    TimeElapsed := 0;
    { Move to the next image and wrap to start if at end }
    Current_Image := Current_Image + 1;
    if Current_Image > Total_Images then
     Current_Image := 1;
    { Draw the image on the form's canvas using StretchDraw }
    Form1.Canvas.StretchDraw( Form1.ClientRect ,
     TheImageArray[ Current_Image - 1 ].Picture.Graphic );
    { Reset the progress caption }
    Form1.Caption := 'Next Slide In ' +
     IntToStr(( Timer_Interval - TimeElapsed ) div 1000 )+ ' Seconds';
  end;
end;
```

15. Choose the OnClick event handler for the Exit1 component and enter this code to exit the application.

```
procedure TForm1.Exit1Click(Sender: TObject);
begin
  Close;
end;
```

16. Choose the OnClick event handler for the AddImageToShow1 menu item. Enter the following code, which loads a new bitmap slide and uses exception handlers to avoid resource leaks when an invalid file is opened.

```
procedure TForm1.AddImageToshow1Click(Sender: TObject);
begin
  { Set the dialog filename to a wildcard again }
  OpenDialog1.Filename := '*.bmp';
  { If cancel drop through; otherwise do stuff }
  if OpenDialog1.Execute then
  begin
    try
      { Increase total image count and create new }
      { component on faith image is valid          }
      Total_Images := Total_Images + 1;
      TheImageArray[ Total_Images - 1 ] :=
       TImage.Create(self);
      { Use LoadFromFile method assuming ok image }
      TheImageArray[ Total_Images - 1 ].Picture.
       LoadFromFile( OpenDialog1.Filename );
      { Take care of menu consistency }
      if Total_Images = 25 then
       AddImageToShow1.Enabled := false;
      BeginShow1.Enabled := true;
    except
      { Handle problem with loading invalid picture     }
```

continued on next page

continued from previous page

```
      { Use the E: notation to get a copy of exception }
      on E:EInvalidGraphic do
      begin
        { Reuse the error message in our dialog }
        MessageDlg( E.Message , mtError , [mbOK], 0 );
        { Prevent resource leak by cleaning up the }
        { invalid image component and our pointers }
        TheImageArray[ Total_Images - 1 ].Free;
        Total_Images := Total_Images - 1;
        { Take care of menu consistency }
        if Total_Images < 25 then
         AddImageToShow1.Enabled := true;
        if total_Images < 1 then
        BeginShow1.Enabled := false;
      end;
    end;
  end;
end;
```

17. Compile and test the project.

How It Works

In normal programming for Windows, one of the more deadly errors is the General Protection Fault, or GPF. It is usually caused by an attempt to address invalid memory locations, normally due to a bad pointer conversion or incorrect data. Once this event has happened, there is little an application can do, since Windows shuts the program down virtually instantly. If the program uses a considerable amount of resources (handles to device contexts, memory blocks, GDI elements), these items are normally permanently unavailable until Windows is shut down. This problem is called a *resource leak*.

Delphi's exception system allows considerable control over behavior that would normally cause GPFs. One place where this occurs is in the LoadFromFile methods of the graphics elements, such as TImage. The slide show application in this How-To takes advantage of Delphi's error handling to prevent losing resources due to a GPF when an invalid bitmap file is loaded.

Notice this line of code:

```
on E:EInvalidGraphic do
```

This line is placed after the *except* statement in a *try except* construct during addition of bitmaps to the slide show. What is important about the line is the use of the E: syntax, as opposed to simply using *on EInvalidGraphic do*. The E: notation tells Delphi's compiler that the application wishes to use information placed in the Exception object created by the VCL runtime library when the exception was raised, and this object is made available in the generic exception variable E.

This line of code shows the access to this variable:

```
MessageDlg( E.Message , mtError , [mbOK], 0 );
```

The E.Message reference obtains the text string that the TImage component's LoadFromFile method placed in the Exception object to explain which problem occurred. This is important because there are two possible types of EInvalidGraphic errors: an unknown file extension, such as .GIF or .JPG, or a properly named file that is internally either corrupted or not a valid bitmap image (this is the case in the BADBMP.BMP file, which is actually a renamed GIF file). By simply passing this explanation on to the user, the application doesn't need to worry about finding it out for itself in order to display the proper message.

The beauty of the exception system is that what normally would have been a GPF due to invalid data or bad pointer manipulation has been converted into a safe, graceful exit from the situation. This code in the *except* portion

```
TheImageArray[ Total_Images - 1 ].Free;
```

makes sure that all the Windows resources allocated by Delphi to the TImage component for the invalid bitmap are released safely.

Likewise, this code in the OnDestroy method,

```
for Counter_1 := 1 to Total_Images do
  TheImageArray[ Counter_1 - 1 ].Free;
```

ensures that resources allocated to valid bitmaps are released when the application closes. Had an unhandled GPF occurred, these resources might not have been freed either.

One point is noteworthy: In many cases rather than a *try except* block, you'll use a *try finally* block, because regardless of the success or failure of a process, resources need to be cleaned up. The *try finally* construct ensures that whether or not an exception occurs, the cleanup is done.

Comments

You've only scratched the surface of Delphi's exception handling system in this and the two previous How-Tos. It has the ability to handle range errors, component creation and usage errors, and a host of other minor bugs that often creep into finished applications, only to bedevil users and maintainers, since their effects may be felt far from the actual place where an error occurs.

A common example is writing a value one past the end of an array. As long as the memory location used is inside the area allocated for the running application (and it often is), no GPF will occur. But if other data resides in the affected memory address, it will mysteriously be corrupted. Worse, if code resides there, random program behavior may occur, making it appear that bugs exist in code that is perfectly fine when compiled.

Delphi's exception system has a range-error exception object, which can be enabled via the Options|Compiler menu. Turning on this option while creating an application is equivalent to turning on range-checking in Pascal or C, but it is more user-friendly and, in combination with the Delphi debugger, far easier to correct.

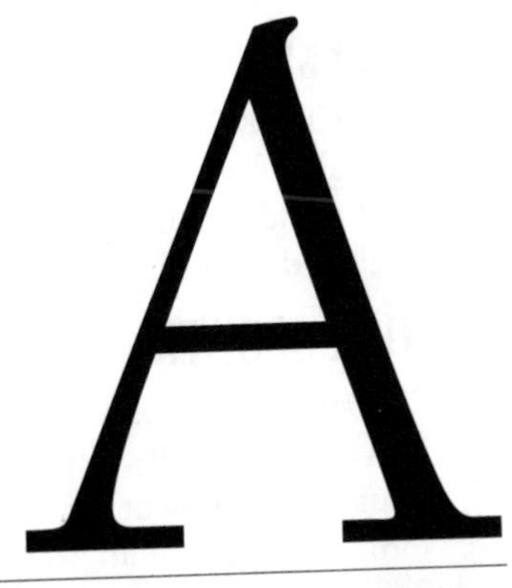

ABOUT THE CD

Aside from the source code and EXEs for the How-To's developed in this book, you'll find additional software on the CD to help you with your Delphi programming.

Goodies

There are three extra programs, complete with source code

DEVCAPAD

This program gives a complete display of all the output capabilities of the monitor and default printer for a system under Windows 3.x. It can also be modified to give information about any display device in the system, such as a plotter.

HTMLEDIT

HTMLEDIT is an application that simplifies putting HTML tags into text for use with WWW browsers or the DHTMLVWR application How-To's. It can be modified to include any HTML syntax desired.

SPRITEDIT

The DHTMLVWR application uses a sprite file, but doesn't give the code to create one. This utility takes in bitmap images and makes a sprite file from them which can be used in the DHTMLVWR application or custom viewers as desired.

Commercial Demos

There are two commercial demos available on the CD, from CIUPKC software and TurboPower software.

CIUPKC

The CIUPKC software demo is an executable that showcases the first component set available from CIUPKC, the "User-Friendly VCL" set. By invoking the various buttons and menus, all the power of the system is displayed. Ordering information is included with the program.

TURBOPOWER

TurboPower software has been associated with Borland since virtually day one, and it has outdone itself with two excellent offerings for Delphi: Orpheus and the Asynch Professional Toolkit. Both are installed into separate directories by the Installation program and contain excellent documentation for their use.

Shareware

There are three very nice shareware/freeware component sets and applications on the CD also.

CCCLOCK

This is a simple digital clock application which is freeware from Nathan Wallace.

EZDSL

EZDSL is a group of components and data structure elements from Julian Bucknall.

TCGI

TCGI are a group of CGI components for the WWW from Amy Lynnworth.

INDEX

D

E

F

G

H

W

ENVIRONMENTAL AWARENESS

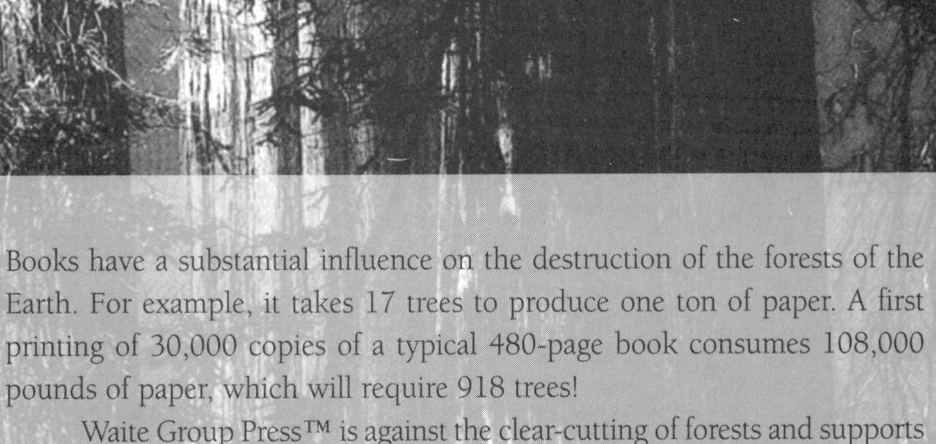

Books have a substantial influence on the destruction of the forests of the Earth. For example, it takes 17 trees to produce one ton of paper. A first printing of 30,000 copies of a typical 480-page book consumes 108,000 pounds of paper, which will require 918 trees!

Waite Group Press™ is against the clear-cutting of forests and supports reforestation of the Pacific Northwest of the United States and Canada, where most of this paper comes from. As a publisher with several hundred thousand books sold each year, we feel an obligation to give back to the planet. We will therefore support organizations which seek to preserve the forests of planet Earth.